A HISTORY OF
BRITISH
TRADE UNIONS
SINCE 1889

A HISTORY OF
BRITISH
TRADE UNIONS
SINCE 1889

VOLUME I · 1889–1910

BY

H. A. CLEGG
Fellow of Nuffield College, Oxford

ALAN FOX
Research Fellow of Nuffield College, Oxford

AND

A. F. THOMPSON
Fellow of Wadham College, Oxford

OXFORD
AT THE CLARENDON PRESS
1964

Oxford University Press, Amen House, London E.C.4

GLASGOW NEW YORK TORONTO MELBOURNE WELLINGTON
BOMBAY CALCUTTA MADRAS KARACHI LAHORE DACCA
CAPE TOWN SALISBURY NAIROBI IBADAN ACCRA
KUALA LUMPUR HONG KONG

© *Oxford University Press 1964*

Preface

IN 1956 the Leverhulme Trustees made a grant to Nuffield College for 'research into industrial relations and trade union studies'. It was understood from the first that one of the major projects was to be a history of British trade unions, and work began during the following year.

The Webbs published the first edition of their *History of Trade Unionism* in 1894, but the three additional chapters which they included in their 1920 edition to cover the intervening period are of little value. There would be little justification, however, for beginning our first volume in 1894, a year of no special significance in the history of British unions, whereas many new developments can be traced to 1889. Even so, we have had to include a substantial introductory chapter describing the main outlines of the movement before 1889, both to provide a background and because much of what the Webbs wrote, even in their first edition, now requires revision.

Our first volume runs to 1910 because some of the strands in the story come to an end in that year, and a number of developments which had their origin about that time continued to affect the whole trade union movement until well after the First World War. A break at any point in time, however, must be untidy, and we have covered only briefly or entirely omitted those events of 1910 which we felt belonged to the next volume.

We should like to record our thanks to Nuffield College and the Leverhulme Trustees for giving us the opportunity to carry out the work; to the officers of the Trades Union Congress and the many unions which have opened their records; and to several individuals who have helped us: Miss Barbara Jervis and Miss Penelope Harmsworth, both of whom worked as research assistants for a year; R. M. Hartwell, Reader in Recent Social and Economic History in the University of Oxford, who read the whole volume in draft and made valuable suggestions; and Mrs. Yates who typed draft after draft with speed, skill, and good humour.

H. A. CLEGG
ALAN FOX
A. F. THOMPSON

November 1962

Contents

List of Tables

1

The Trade Union Movement before 1889

Size and Distribution

IT is impossible to give an exact picture of the size and distribution of
trade unions at the beginning of 1889. Government returns can be supplemented from union records, and earlier figures exist for most of the major
craft societies as well as many others; but 1892 is the first year adequately
covered by official statistics of trade union membership. Though the
Labour Department of the Board of Trade was set up in 1886, its *First
Report on Trade Unions* in the following year dealt with only a small selection. Succeeding reports improved in accuracy, and their coverage was
widened until, with the *Sixth Report*,[1] it included 'nearly the whole of
what may be termed the solid and active Trade Unionism of the Kingdom'.[2] The Department classified the unions into 'industrial groups'; and
on the assumption that within each of these categories all unions grew
between 1888 and 1892 at the same rate as those for which there are
figures, and after making due allowance for new unions, Table 1 shows
their estimated strength in 1888.

TABLE 1

Trade union membership, 1888

Industrial Group	Membership
Metals, Engineering, and Shipbuilding	190,000
Mining and Quarrying	150,000
Textiles	120,000
Building	90,000
Transport	60,000
Clothing	40,000
Printing and Paper	30,000
Woodworking and Furnishing	20,000
Agriculture and Fishing	10,000
Other Trades	40,000
TOTAL	750,000

Since the 'occupied population' returned by the Census of 1891 was
16,545,000, this total suggests that about 5 per cent. were organized in

[1] C-7436, 1894, which gives the figures for trade union membership in 1892.
[2] Ibid., p. 2.

unions in 1888. The occupied population, however, included both men and women, as well as the self-employed, employers and managers, white-collar employees, and young workers. If account is taken only of those who might reasonably be expected to have come within the range of potential membership in 1888—adult male manual workers—the proportion rises to about 10 per cent.[1] The distribution of these trade unionists was closely related to the distribution of industry; and their geographical concentration was probably much the same as that discovered by the Webbs in their survey of 1892. Nearly half the entire union membership of the United Kingdom was then to be found in the six counties of England north of the Humber and the Mersey. The industrial Midlands, Greater London, South Wales and Monmouthshire, and the narrow belt between the Forth and the Clyde, contained almost all the remainder.[2]

Because of the difficulty of determining the number of adult manual workers in each industrial group, figures for trade union 'density' (or the degree of organization) can only be rough estimates. Metals, Engineering and Shipbuilding and Mining and Quarrying may have had densities of over 20 per cent., Building and Printing perhaps 15 per cent., Textiles and Woodworking about 10 per cent., and Transport rather more than 5 per cent. Elsewhere, the proportion was negligible. There were also wide variations within the groups. Craftsmen in engineering, shipbuilding, building, printing, woodworking, and clothing were better organized than the less-skilled workers. Among shipbuilding craftsmen density may not have been far from 50 per cent., and among Northumberland and Durham miners it was over 50 per cent., though no other coalfield approached this level. In cotton the overall density was nearly 25 per cent., ranging from about 90 per cent. among male spinners to less than 20 per cent. among female operatives in the cardroom. In weaving, however, women were almost as well organized as men. The other major textile industry, wool, was virtually without organization.

Estimates of trade union membership during the first half of the nineteenth century are rarely reliable;[3] but from 1850 it is possible to trace the steady growth of the major craft societies with some precision. The largest, the Amalgamated Society of Engineers, grew from 5,000 at its foundation in 1851 to 21,000 in 1860, 35,000 in 1870, 45,000 in 1880, and 54,000 in 1888. Comparable patterns of growth were achieved by the Friendly

---

[1] Estimates of the numbers of adult manual wage-earners are discussed more fully on p. 466.

[2] Sidney and Beatrice Webb, *The History of Trade Unionism*, 1920 edition, appendix v.

[3] For example the Webbs suggested a figure of 'at least half a million' for the Grand National Consolidated Trades Union in 1834 (op. cit., p. 135); but the union may not have had 20,000 paying members at its peak. W. H. Oliver has shown that the income of the Grand National up to 26 Apr. 1834 was £1005. The total of the registration fee and the levy to support the Derby 'turn-outs' was 1s. 3d. a head, giving a paying membership of just over 16,000 (*Organizations and Ideas Behind the Efforts to Achieve a General Union of Working Classes in England in the Early 1830s*, D.Phil. thesis, Oxford, 1954).

Society of Ironfounders, the United Society of Boilermakers and Iron and Steel Shipbuilders, the Amalgamated Society of Carpenters and Joiners, the London Society of Compositors, and the Typographical Association. Excluding the Carpenters and Joiners, their aggregate membership rose from 8,000 in 1850 to 16,000 in 1860, 22,000 in 1870, 40,000 in 1880, and 54,000 in 1888. The Carpenters and Joiners were founded in 1860 with 600 members. They had 10,000 in 1870, 18,000 in 1880, and 25,000 in 1888. One important society, the Friendly Society of Operative Stonemasons, certainly followed a more uneven path, but generally its course was upwards. 5,000 in 1850 and 10,000 in 1888, they had touched 27,000 in 1874.

Over the same period the cotton unions present a similar picture. The Amalgamated Association of Operative Cotton Spinners, originally founded in 1853, was reorganized with 11,000 members in 1870, and rose to 12,000 members in 1880 and 17,000 in 1888. The North-east Lancashire Amalgamated Weavers' Association, founded in 1858, had 5,000 members in 1863, 13,000 in 1871, and 16,000 in 1878. At no time, however, did this Association represent a majority of organized weavers, and it was replaced by the more inclusive Northern Counties Amalgamated Weavers' Association, which began with 38,000 members in 1884 and rose to 46,000 by 1890.

The development of trade unionism in coal was much more erratic. The Miners' Association of Great Britain and Ireland may perhaps have possessed a very considerable membership in 1844, but it had disappeared by 1848.[1] Two national organizations competed for the support of the miners in the boom period from 1871 to 1874. The affiliated membership of the National Miners' Association in Northumberland, Durham, Yorkshire, Scotland, and parts of the Midlands totalled 123,406 at its Leeds Conference in 1873, and that of the Amalgamated Association of Miners in Lancashire, the West Midlands, and South Wales 99,145 at its Bristol Conference of the same year.[2] If these figures can be accepted, there were then over 200,000 organized miners in Britain, but by the end of the decade few unions of any importance survived outside the North-east. The Northumberland Miners' Mutual Confident Association had been founded in 1864, the Durham Miners' Association in 1869. By 1875 their combined membership was above 50,000, and subsequently it did not drop below 40,000.

The membership of the Trades Union Congress shows that such fluctuations were not confined to the mining unions. From just short of a million in 1874, the total membership affiliated through trade unions fell to 379,000 in 1884 before rising again to 568,000 in 1888. Much of the explanation lies in the trade cycle, since unions tend to flourish in prosperity

---

[1] 'The membership rose, it is said, to at least 100,000' (Webbs, op. cit., p. 182).

[2] G. D. H. Cole, 'Some Notes on British Trade Unionism in the Third Quarter of the Nineteenth Century', *International Review of Social History*, 1937.

and wither in depression. But the effects of the cycle varied from industry to industry, and other influences were also at work. Industrial expansion often helped. In the two best-organized groups, Mining and Quarrying and Metals, Engineering and Shipbuilding, the numbers occupied rose by about 180 per cent. and 80 per cent. respectively between 1851 and 1891. In Building the labour force almost doubled, and in Printing it more than trebled. At the other extreme, two of the worst-organized industries, wool and agriculture, both suffered a decline.

But this correlation between industrial expansion and union growth was not universal. In rail and road transport, for example, where the labour force increased by over 600 per cent. and nearly 300 per cent. respectively, trade unionism on the railways was weak, and road transport workers were virtually unorganized. By contrast the cotton labour force of the United Kingdom remained almost stationary between 1851 and 1891, yet the cotton unions were strong and growing stronger. It is therefore clear that the varied fortunes of the unions in different industries can only be explained by a closer look at the circumstances of each of them.

The Craft Societies

A craft society may be defined as a trade union of skilled workers who have attained their status through a prescribed apprenticeship. It is true that many societies have had to recognize alternative methods of acquiring skill. The Engineers, for example, always admitted that the man who had worked for five years at the trade had the right to a craftsman's privileges whether he had 'served his time' or not. But so long as the basis of a society's membership was a sharp distinction between qualified and unqualified workers, with qualification defined primarily in terms of a formal apprenticeship, it could claim to be a craft society.

Craft attitudes and policies were rooted in the doctrine that by serving an apprenticeship a man secured the right to exercise his skill and receive the 'customary' wage. 'We take an account book, and we claim that book as our craft', said a member of the Vellum Account Book Binders' executive council as late as 1908. 'We have served our time to it. . . . When I am out of my time I expect to have what rightly belongs to me—a journeyman's wage.'[1] In the same spirit, the Engineers declared in the preface to their Rules that

if constrained to make restrictions against the admission into our trade of those who have not earned a right by a probationary servitude, we do so knowing that such encroachments are productive of evil, and when persevered in unchecked, result in reducing the condition of the artisan to that of the unskilled labourer, and confer no permanent advantage on those admitted.

[1] *Departmental Committee on Fair Wages; Minutes of Evidence*, Cd. 4423, 1908, Q. 1130.

Consequently, it was a craftsman's duty 'to exercise the same care and watchfulness over that in which we have a vested interest, as the physician does who holds a diploma, or the author who is protected by a copyright'.[1]

The traditions of apprenticeship were inherited from guild regulation and statutory enforcement, but by the middle of the nineteenth century these supports had long been withdrawn, and the system survived through custom maintained by the craftsmen and acquiesced in by the employers. It was the first objective of the societies to turn this custom into a universal and uniform rule so as to exert a firm control over the size of the labour force. There was, however, little to be gained by insistence on qualification unless certain types of work were reserved for the qualified worker. Here again the societies built on custom to delimit a preserve of craftsman's work, defined sometimes by the material, sometimes by the tools and machinery, and sometimes by the product; and this preserve was then defended against the unqualified, against changes in the techniques or organization of production, and against encroachments by other crafts.

On the basis of these fundamental rules the craft society could erect others; and from time to time this led to major clashes with the employers. Employers in London and Manchester combined to challenge the Engineers in 1852; and the Midland Association of Flint Glass Manufacturers was formed in 1858 to defend its members against a series of strikes aimed at controlling the number of apprentices. In the following year the London building contractors together defeated a demand for the nine-hour day, and in 1866 master tailors in London, Manchester, Birmingham and other major cities combined to oppose the demands of their craftsmen.[2] In some cases, as with the glassmakers and the tailors, these conflicts led to joint conferences of the unions and representatives of the employers.

However, such widespread conflict and collective bargaining with organized employers were both untypical. Indeed, it was commonly held that craftsmen should regulate 'what we alone have a right to regulate, the value of our labour', as the London Union of Compositors put it in 1834; and a year later their executive told the members that 'those . . . who argue that our employers ought to have been consulted, do not see the extent to which the argument may be applied, for . . . it will ultimately lead us into the argument that the masters have the right to regulate [piece] prices'.[3] The enforcement of craft rules usually involved contacts with the

[1] *Royal Commission on the Organization and Rules of Trade Unions and Other Associations, 1867–1869. Eleventh and Final Report*, 1869, appendix, p. 246.

[2] Some of these employers' associations availed themselves of the Free Labour Registration Society, an organization based on London which was operating in the sixties. A benefit club was attached. Moulders, joiners, and shipbuilding labourers were sent to places as far distant as Glasgow and Hull (ibid., *Fifth Report*, 1868, Qs. 11077, 11085; *Ninth Report*, 1868, Qs. 18063–5).

[3] John Child, *A History of Industrial Relations in the British Printing Industry*, D.Phil. thesis, Oxford, 1953.

individual employer through letters, memorials, or deputations, and occasionally strikes; but in some instances none of these was necessary. 'Formerly I, as the master, used to fix the price', reported a London shipbuilder in 1868, but 'lately . . . I was obliged to submit to a way of engaging men at the price they themselves in their own unions regulated that they would take. I must take those men or leave them alone, because if I did not take those men no other men were allowed to come to my yard to take those places.'[1]

A crucial element in control of working conditions was the system of friendly benefits which every craft union provided. Friendly societies were already well established before the century began and had received statutory protection. Such societies of men working at the same craft inevitably turned their attention to trade matters from time to time; and this might become a permanent and organized interest, as when the London compositors' clubs transformed themselves into the London Union of Compositors in 1834. In addition, trade union leaders had realized, at least since the days of Francis Place,[2] the advantages of disguising a trade society as a friendly club acceptable to employers and protected by the law. In either case, benefits came to act as a support for the rules of the craft.

Accident, sickness, and superannuation benefits all helped to keep off the labour market men whose quality of work had suffered some temporary or permanent decline which might tempt them to undermine customary wage rates or working conditions; but it was the 'out-of-work' (or 'donation') benefit which offered most protection for the rules. In many unions this began as a 'tramping' grant paid by each branch to the unemployed journeyman as he travelled from town to town in search of work. Experience, however, taught the unions that tramping, especially in times of bad trade, drove men to seek employment in 'illegal'[3] or non-union shops, thus reducing the area of control, and that the system tended to attract the feckless and the footloose, ever ready to break a strike or undermine local conditions. Moreover, as markets became increasingly 'national', it became more likely that all areas would experience unemployment at the same time. Accordingly the 'tramping' began to give way to the 'stationary' allowance. In 1844, for example, the compositors' societies came together in the short-lived National Typographical Association mainly in order to finance an 'out-of-work' benefit, so that 'those men who quit their situations to uphold the principles of the profession, are no longer to be exposed

---

[1] *Royal Commission on the Organization and Rules of Trade Unions, Ninth Report,* 1868, Q. 16786.　　　　　　　　　　　　　[2] Graham Wallas, *Francis Place,* 1898, p. 19.

[3] The term 'illegal' was a survival from the days of statutory prescription of apprenticeship. A man who practised a craft without having served his time, or who violated any other of its rules, was an 'illegal' man. Sometimes the term was applied simply to non-unionists. It lingered in use until the end of the century.

to the demoralising and debasing tramping system, but are henceforth to be provided for as long as they ought to be'.[1]

Similarly, the emigration grant was designed to strengthen bargaining power by reducing the available labour force. The commonest benefit of all, the funeral allowance,[2] afforded no direct support for trade objectives, but, along with the other benefits, it provided a cohesive force in bad times. Benefits which might be needed any day held more attraction for a society's members than the distant possibility of campaigns against the employers over wages or conditions when times should improve. Benefits were also a disciplinary weapon. The member expelled for behaviour 'contrary to the interests of the trade' had no claim on the money he had contributed; and any member who had been paying in for some years was likely to feel that he had an investment not lightly to be sacrificed.

The rules upheld by this 'Method of Mutual Insurance'[3] varied, but all societies enforced apprenticeship and defended the boundaries of the craft. Most imposed, or tried to impose, a limit on the number of apprentices, usually in terms of a ratio of apprentices to journeymen; and most prohibited working with 'illegal' men. Craftsmen on time-work, those paid by the hour, the day, or the week, like the engineers and the builders, normally rejected payment by the piece, whereas others, like the London compositors and the tailors, worked to piece-price lists. Since the societies built on traditions, many of their rules were unwritten or might enjoin no more than observance of the 'customs of the trade' on the assumption that members knew well enough what these were. Indeed, rules prescribing the 'closed shop'[4] or restrictive practices proper, which limited the amount of work a man should be expected to do during the day, were best left out of the constitution altogether. These could obviously be used by opponents, and unions registered as friendly societies feared that their inclusion might lead to trouble in the courts.

During the third quarter of the century many local or regional societies were amalgamated into 'new model unions' aiming at national coverage; but the novelty of this achievement can be exaggerated.[5] Even before the foundation in 1851 of the original 'new model', the Amalgamated Society of Engineers, its main constituent, the Journeymen Steam Engine and

---

[1] *The Printer*, 1844, p. 116, quoted in Child, op. cit. See also George Howell, *Trade Unionism, New and Old*, 1892, pp. 112–13, for the general decay of the practice by 1889.

[2] 'In the industrial life of England there is perhaps no point so tender as the idea of being buried by the parish. A pauper's grave and funeral are more repugnant to the sensibilities of the working-class than any other social degradation' (Howell, op. cit., p. 100).

[3] Sidney and Beatrice Webb, *Industrial Democracy*, 1920 edition, pp. 152–72.

[4] A shop in which a worker could not secure or retain employment unless he was a union member or agreed to become one.

[5] The Preface to the *Rules of the Amalgamated Society of Engineers* (1851; revised in 1864) declared that 'there is nothing novel in its constitution. . . . By it we hope to protect our interests more effectually . . . than is possible by any partial union.'

Machine Makers' Friendly Society, had achieved more than local organization. So had the Ironfounders and the Boilermakers. The Stonemasons had been operating nationally for twenty years and theirs was the largest of the craft societies at this time. But the most characteristic of the 'new models', the Engineers and the Carpenters and Joiners, soon outdistanced all other craft organizations both in numbers and resources; and they did so by perfecting a system of national benefit insurance combined with the local control of wages and conditions which had been only imperfectly realized before.

Trade unionists had already appreciated the advantages of a wide coverage for insurance purposes. The main motive behind all early attempts at national organization[1] was to spread the risks of striking by establishing a central fund, but each of them in turn had been destroyed by encouraging expenditure beyond its resources and by the failure to discover any means of controlling its constituents. The amalgamated societies, on the other hand, were able to use centralized finance for the central control of strikes. Their success depended on strict and uniform rules regulating the payment of benefits by branch secretaries and the disposal of their surpluses. Such rules were interpreted by the executive, which alone had the power to sanction strikes and strike pay.

The apparent reduction of local autonomy was mitigated by the absence of any attempt to dictate 'custom and practice'. Standard rates and hours, bans on illegal men, limitation of apprentices, and monopolies of materials and machines were left to the branches, to be imposed by withdrawing men from illegal shops and supporting them by an unemployment benefit rendered all the more secure by centralized finance. This decentralization of authority made it possible for the leaders of the amalgamated societies, anxious to win parliamentary and public approval, to deny that their unions enforced restrictive practices or the closed shop,[2] and to speak the truth—at least so far as the head office and the national rules were concerned. Even if they were well aware of them, they had no direct responsibility for such practices; for that was the job of the branches.

Similarly, the national leaders also made much of their societies' relative freedom from strikes.[3] This freedom is not to be explained by their alleged pacifism, or that of their members; it arose rather from the role of the

---

[1] For example, the National Association for the Protection of Labour in 1831, the Grand National Consolidated Trades Union of 1834, and the National Association of United Trades for the Protection of Labour of 1845.

[2] See the evidence of William Allan, secretary of the Amalgamated Society of Engineers, to the *Royal Commission on the Organization and Rules of Trade Unions, First Report*, 1867, Qs. 627–45, 905–8.

[3] Allan told the Royal Commission that 'we believe that all strikes are a complete waste of money' (*First Report*, 1867, Q. 827). Such statements have been accepted at their face value by many historians including even the Webbs (*History*, pp. 320–1), though theirs is by far the best account of craft methods at this time (*Industrial Democracy*, Part II).

strike in craft methods. The strike was then used mainly to fight infringe-
ments of the rules in particular shops, and to extend a society's control to
shops not previously covered. The technique of withdrawing small groups
of men, or even individuals, was sometimes known as the 'strike-in-detail',
but the 'strikers' were supported by unemployment benefit, not strike pay.
Craft rules were thus enforced for the most part without large-scale
collisions with the employers as a body.

The façade of 'pacifism' was often thin. In 1860, for instance, the Blacksmiths prefaced the rules of their society with the statement that

in the year 1845 . . . it was unanimously considered and determined, that strikes
of all kinds, however seemingly just in their nature, were . . . an unpremeditated
evil on the part of the operatives, and an unmitigated one to all concerned—in
fact an infliction upon society at large . . . it was most wisely determined for the
future, to avoid all such contests . . . and thus this Society became incorporated,
in point of fact, as the original anti-strike society. . . . Disputes . . . can only be
settled by friendly consultations between both master and man, imbued with
the spirit of mutually imparting facts, with a view to render assistance to each
other; if this, in connection with the efforts of mutual and disinterested friends,
cannot be accomplished, we say then let men and masters part; offer no opposition; the men, however great or small their number, to be supplied with means
of existence until they obtain other situations of work, from the funds of the
Society; and the employers to obtain other men as best they may.[1]

The Blacksmiths left no doubt of their terms, however, by insisting that
'no member [is] to be allowed to enter into any employment except he
receive the average wages of such employment'.[2] Others were equally
polite—and equally firm. 'They are very nice people if they have their own
way', said a Manchester foundry owner of the Engineers in 1868, 'but if
they have not they will fight, and they can fight anything and anybody,
they are so strong.'[3]

Another aspect of the front presented by the amalgamated societies
was an apparent addiction to arbitration. When the London Trades
Council, which their leaders dominated, condemned the Staffordshire
puddlers for refusing arbitration in 1865,[4] this impression seemed to be
confirmed. Craft methods, however, by allowing the unions to avoid major
clashes except on rare occasions, reduced the number of instances in which
arbitration could be relevant. Perhaps as a tactical move, the Engineers
had proposed arbitration in the national lock-out of 1852; but it did not
follow that the branches were ready to submit their local rules to arbitration. Indeed, even in major disputes few societies shared the whole-hearted

[1] G. Shaw Lefevre, 'Report on Trades' Societies Rules', in *Trades' Societies and Strikes*,
Report of the Committee on Trades' Societies appointed by the National Association for the
Promotion of Social Science, 1860, pp. 119–20.   [2] Ibid., p. 121.
[3] *Royal Commission on the Organization and Rules of Trade Unions, Tenth Report*, 1868,
Q. 18887.   [4] Webbs, *History*, p. 254.

approval for arbitration displayed by Robert Applegarth and his Carpenters and Joiners. More typical was the attitude of the London Compositors who toyed half-heartedly with arbitration in 1853 but refused to submit to the one award which went against them. The Stonemasons' branches also generally refused to commit themselves to arbitration, Wolverhampton declaring that, though other trades might submit 'to that most detested of all things arbitration . . . we shall uphold our own principle and honour'.[1]

Moreover, as the Webbs pointed out in 1897, 'there has been, until quite recently, no clear distinction drawn between Collective Bargaining, Conciliation and Arbitration. Much of what is called Arbitration or Conciliation in the early writings on the subject amounts to nothing more than organised Collective Bargaining.'[2] Favourable references to 'arbitration' by union leaders in the nineteenth century do not, therefore, mean that they had necessarily embraced the principle of arbitration as it is understood today.

In the early years of the 'new model' unions, there appeared to be a wide gulf between them and two other types of craft organization: the independent local clubs and those national societies which, like the Stonemasons, allowed wide branch autonomy in relation to benefits and strikes. The clubs, however, were gradually absorbed, and the differences between the amalgamated societies and the others soon diminished. In addition, all the major crafts began to be affected during the last quarter of the century by forces making for changes in their methods. The boom years of 1871–4, with a lower rate of unemployment than any other period before the First World War, produced problems which the traditional techniques of piecemeal action could not easily solve. Rapidly rising prices created widespread demands within the societies for general improvements in wages and conditions, and full employment provided the bargaining power to secure them.

By this time the printers had developed their methods of control beyond the capacity of most other crafts. The societies were able to take as a firm foundation the ancient institution of the 'chapel', or self-governing workshop group, headed by the 'Father of the Chapel', which preserved custom, protected the status of the trade by prohibiting fighting, drunkenness, and swearing, and maintained various rites and rituals. The chapel thus mobilized shop solidarity, and its decisions were enforced by fines or even by physical violence.[3] The local union had emerged as a grouping of chapels, which in practice retained considerable autonomy; and neither the provincial Typographical Association of 1849, nor the Scottish

---

[1] *Royal Commission on the Organization and Rules of Trade Unions, Third Report*, 1867, Q. 4165.   [2] *Industrial Democracy*, p. 223, footnote.
[3] A. E. Musson, *The Typographical Association*, 1954 (unabridged edition), pp. 12–13; A. J. M. Sykes, 'Trade-union Workshop Organization in the Printing Industry—The Chapel', in *Human Relations*, 1960, vol. 13, no. 1.

Typographical Association of 1853, had interfered with the powers of the chapel when they brought the unions together.

However, when a general agitation for higher wages after 1866 led employers to combine locally in self-defence, the executive of the Typographical Association welcomed this development and recommended joint conferences between its branches and the employers.[1] For both national and branch leaders, collective settlement with representatives of the employers promised to be more convenient and effective than the old methods of regulation shop by shop; and, in addition, might well heighten their own prestige and power within the union. But the reception of this policy by the chapels was mixed. Some members regarded branch negotiation with the employers as an unnecessary and undignified abdication of the society's right to determine unilaterally the rules of the craft.[2] It also threatened chapel autonomy in that it by-passed them and put more power into the hands of branch officers. Nevertheless, conferences were held during the early seventies in Sheffield, Manchester, and other towns to settle wages, working conditions, and other issues.[3] In some centres, as in Manchester, the employers' association survived, but others broke up when returning unemployment eased the pressure upon their members.

A similar trend also appeared in engineering. In 1871 a rank-and-file movement for a nine-hour day on Tyneside began with a strike in Sunderland, and in due course the local employers' association let the unions know that they would welcome a conference. The Newcastle Central District Committee of the Engineers responded doubtfully to this approach. However, after 'a lengthened discussion' on 'the propriety of soliciting an interview with the Employers' Association', the convenience of a central settlement carried the day. Delegates were appointed, and the nine-hour day agreed.[4] Thereafter the practice of local or district joint conferences gradually spread. In the Manchester area, for example, efforts to improve conditions in lower-paid shops led to meetings in 1875 between the Manchester Employers' Association and the Amalgamated Engineers' District Committee;[5] and there were even occasions when the national leadership persuaded members to accept *ad hoc* arbitration on straightforward local wage issues.[6]

The union had already developed the notion of a 'standard district rate'. Each district had long had its customary rate for the skilled man, and the middle sixties saw the beginning of local campaigns to tighten up enforcement.[7] In the process the idea of minimum district standards became more explicit. But employers refused to give formal recognition to these district

[1] Musson, op. cit., pp. 157–8; *Royal Commission on Labour*, C–6894–IX, 1893, Q. 22824.
[2] Child, op. cit.　　　　　　　　　　　　　　　[3] Musson, op. cit., p. 158.
[4] Amalgamated Society of Engineers, *Monthly Report*, June 1871.
[5] Ibid., Sept., Oct., and Nov. 1875.
[6] Ibid., Sept. 1873.　　　　　　　　　　　　　[7] Ibid., Apr. 1866.

standards, and such collective bargaining as took place dealt simply with uniform advances or reductions in the existing spread of rates for the district. Thus it was on the assumption of unilateral regulation of the old type that the Bradford Central District Committee recommended in 1875 'that the local district committees . . . establish a minimum rate in their respective towns or districts', and that the union assist them by pooling information from all its branches on wage rates, overtime payments, working hours, and other conditions of employment.[1]

However, whether it was a question of formulating aspirations or of negotiating with employers' associations, the Engineers' district committees were gaining power at the expense of the branches, just as in printing the branches were gaining power at the expense of the chapels. Meanwhile, the employers' associations were growing in number. The Clyde shipbuilding and engineering employers had formed an association in 1866, and from the early seventies similar bodies appeared in many other centres, including Liverpool, Sheffield, Bolton, Bristol, and Derby.[2] Some of them were linked in the 'General Association of Master Engineers, Shipbuilders, Machinists, Founders and other Kindred Trades', usually known as the Iron Trades Employers' Association, which was set up in the North-east during the nine-hours struggle in 1871 to provide 'mutual protection against the action of trade unions',[3] and soon developed into perhaps the most vigorous of all such associations.

In shipbuilding the revolutionary changes from wood to iron and from sail to steam had established the United Society of Boilermakers and Iron Shipbuilders as the predominant union. The old shipwrights' societies were forced into second place, and in 1882 most of them federated into the Associated Shipwrights' Society. The Boilermakers' secretary, Robert Knight,[4] had to deal with greater difficulties than either the engineers or the printers, for shipbuilding was subject to unusually violent fluctuations, which led to frequent wage changes and could produce heavy unemployment—28 per cent. in 1886, for example. In the fourteen years from 1879 to 1892 there were as many general adjustments of wages,[5] and the shipbuilding unions suffered a higher rate of disputes than other craft societies. Moreover, a strike of 25,000 workers on the Clyde in 1877 lasting twenty-three weeks dwarfed any previous stoppage, including the more famous Engineers' lock-out of 1852 and the London builders' lock-out of 1859–60.[6]

---

[1] Amalgamated Society of Engineers, *Monthly Report*, June 1875. In 1876 the national executive duly drew up and distributed an appropriate questionnaire.

[2] J. B. Jefferys, *The Story of the Engineers*, 1945, p. 94.

[3] *Royal Commission on Labour*, C–6894–VII, 1893, Qs. 25462–73.

[4] Knight, Robert (1833–1911), General secretary, United Society of Boilermakers and Iron and Steel Shipbuilders, 1871–1900. Parliamentary Committee, Trades Union Congress, 1875–83, 1896–1901.   [5] *Royal Commission on Labour*, C–6894–VII, 1893, Q. 21176.

[6] The first of the Labour Department's *Reports on Strikes and Lockouts* is for the year 1888, so that there is no reliable source of information on the size and duration of strikes and lock-outs

General wage changes of this frequency could only be accomplished without widespread stoppages if there was some form of joint regulation. Consequently during the eighties Knight began to foster systematic collective bargaining as a substitute for craft regulation supplemented by occasional *ad hoc* conferences. He did not do this through new institutions, but by showing that the employers could have local conferences when they wished, and by insisting that his branches should deal with their problems by seeking such conferences.[1]

Within the Society Knight met considerable resistance to his discouragement of unofficial strikes and the submission of claims without head-office permission. He therefore built up a 'virtual cabinet'[2] of the full-time district officers, who could deal with local disaffection by acting together. His success can be measured by the statement of a Belfast shipbuilder in 1893 that wage disputes had been less bitter since the early eighties. 'It has now become thoroughly recognised by both parties that wages must fluctuate.'[3]

Building presented the unions with problems of a different sort. The industry's many small employers made it difficult enough to regulate; but, in addition, the workers were usually employed on a casual basis and moved from site to site. Because of these factors the societies of building craftsmen had a stronger interest in joint regulation than most others. Once a printing or engineering shop had been organized the union had only to keep it organized; but in building each site had to be organized anew, and this might also involve dealing with a new employer. Joint regulation was thus only made possible by the relatively advanced state of organization among the contractors or master builders.

Many local employers' associations had come into being primarily to withstand the intermittent pressure for the nine-hour day which the unions had maintained since the fifties. The first National Master Builders' Association was formed in 1857, re-formed in 1865 as the General Builders' Association, and succeeded in 1878 by the National Association of Master Builders, an organization which still survives as the National Federation of Building Trade Employers. Its objects were to secure common action by local associations on such questions as working hours, sub-contracting, overtime, apprentices, the use of machinery, and the employment of non-unionists; and to arrange mutual defence against unions seeking 'to impose restrictive conditions on the building trades'.[4]

before that date. The first *Report* does, however, attempt to put together the material available on earlier disputes, and describes the Engineers' lock-out as affecting 13,000 workers for three months and the builders' lock-out 2,500 for seven months.

[1] D. C. Cummings, *A Historical Survey of the Boiler Makers' and Iron and Steel Ship Builders' Society*, 1905, p. 117.

[2] Webbs, *Industrial Democracy*, p. 30.

[3] *Royal Commission on Labour*, C–6894–VII, 1893, Q. 26473.

[4] National Association of Master Builders, *Minutes*, 9 and 23 Jan. 1878. The employers' associations did not include speculative builders, but some of them admitted master craftsmen

The following years of depression, however, brought forth no serious challenge from the societies. The National Association concerned itself with commercial matters and gave little attention to labour problems until the nineties. Its constituent associations, on the other hand, had almost as strong an interest in joint regulation as the unions.[1] Standard wage rates obviously facilitated tendering, and the employers were particularly anxious that wages should not be pushed up half-way through a contract.[2] From the sixties onwards, therefore, the craftsmen and their employers in the principal towns had begun to negotiate local agreements called 'working rules'.

These agreements usually fixed terms and conditions for a period of twelve months, and required three or six months' notice of any proposal for change. Sometimes all the crafts—carpenters, bricklayers, stonemasons, plasterers, and plumbers prominent among them—and even the labourers were included under one agreement. Elsewhere, different crafts had their own rules, negotiated either with the master builders or with the appropriate associations of master craftsmen. Besides wage rates and hours, these rules might cover such questions as overtime, the regulation of apprenticeship, and allowances for travelling or lodging.[3] The employers usually urged the inclusion of a rule committing the unions to peaceful negotiation of disputes and, if necessary, arbitration. Some societies, especially the Carpenters and Joiners, often consented; but the characteristic response of the Stonemasons was bitter opposition.[4]

The 1886 wage census convinced the Board of Trade 'that rates of wages and hours in this industry were almost universally the subject of district collective agreements, and that the vast majority of workers in any grade were actually paid the agreed rates, and worked the standard hours in a full normal week'.[5] This was probably an exaggeration; and a more realistic assessment would suggest that collective bargaining was 'extremely effective' in all towns down to those 'of quite moderate size', but that elsewhere and especially in the country districts 'there was still much individual bargaining'.[6]

(e.g. master bricklayers or master plasterers), who were specialist sub-contractors. These might also have their own local associations.

[1] 'The employers in the Leicester building trades have formed a Builders' Association. . . . One of the rules is that every member should strictly conform to the trade rules and rates of wages agreed to by the association and the representatives of the workmen. . . . The chairman explained that the object of the rule was to secure uniformity of action and wages paid' (*Workman's Times*, 6 Mar. 1891).

[2] 'We . . . enter into a contract to do all our work for a specific price, and if we are to be subject to continual alterations of the great basis upon which our contract is founded, it must tell injuriously upon the trade . . . ' (*Royal Commission on the Organization and Rules of Trade Unions, Third Report*, 1867, Q. 4257. Evidence of A. Mault, secretary of the General Builders' Association).   [3] Webbs, *Industrial Democracy*, p. 175.   [4] See p. 10.

[5] J. W. F. Rowe, *Wages in Practice and Theory*, 1928, appendix ii.

[6] Ibid., p. 126.

Coal and Iron

Trade unionism in the craft industries was built on apprenticeship and on customs inherited from the days before the industrial revolution. This was true not only of printing and building, which were little affected by that revolution, but also of the large number of metal-working crafts brought into being by the subdivision of earlier and more comprehensive trades, such as that of the millwright, into new and narrower categories. In industries created by the industrial revolution, like the railways, there could be no hallowed customs and no traditional basis for apprenticeship; while others, notably coal, iron, cotton, and wool, were so profoundly altered that any protective customs which existed were swept away. The new skills were acquired by experience and by promotion from less-skilled to more-skilled jobs without a prescribed period of formal apprenticeship. Thus in cotton the 'little piecer' was promoted to 'big piecer', and the latter to spinner as vacancies occurred. In iron the 'underhand' became a puddler or a furnace-man; and in the mines the haulage worker was promoted to the coalface.

Another characteristic of several of these industries was subcontracting with the leading man in the working group virtually a small master employing subordinate labour. Many nineteenth-century unions were thus primarily associations of contractors. The piecers could join the spinners' unions (and were sometimes forced to do so) and the underhands the ironworkers' unions; but their wages were paid by the spinner or the puddler or the furnaceman who employed them, and they were debarred from office and any part in union government. Similarly, in some Midlands coalfields a 'butty' employed a group of colliers at the coalface, and in the North-east the hewers employed their own 'putters', or haulage workers.

Up to the sixties the development of trade unionism in the mines was marked by violent upheavals. Within two or three years unions could leap into prominence, win tens of thousands of members, and disappear. There were three reasons for this pattern: a persistent rudimentary organization among the miners which provided the basis for rapid union growth; wide and recurrent fluctuations in the selling price of coal; and strong district organization among the employers.

The calling of colliery meetings, the election of colliery delegates, and the holding either of county delegate meetings or of mass meetings of men from a county's collieries all preceded trade unionism proper. More-over, when the unions were formed, they were associations of *collieries*.[1] One was already in existence at the time of the North-east strike of 1831, but a mass meeting nevertheless decided that 'the men of every colliery should meet twice a week', and 'that each pit should send a delegate to form a general committee for carrying the resolutions into effect'.[2]

[1] Shaw Lefevre, loc. cit., p. 143.
[2] R. Fynes, *The Miners of Northumberland and Durham*, 1873, pp. 17–18.

The role of the 'pit lodge' as the nucleus of mining unionism was much strengthened by legislation providing for a 'checkweighman' to be elected and paid by the men of each pit to protect their interests in the measurement of output. With the first Act of 1860, 'the lodge was provided with a permanent official, whose mere willingness to stand for election in those early days of frequent victimisation was itself a test of character and ability'.[1] Subsequent court cases and legislation gave him increasing protection against victimization. This development, however, did not always strengthen the county unions. Many miners considered their compulsory contributions to the checkweighman's wages as alternatives to union dues.

Price movements were frequent and sharp. In West Yorkshire, for instance, the average pithead price rose by about 60 per cent. between 1850 and 1854 and then fell by over 20 per cent. in less than two years.[2] Prices dragged wages with them, since the latter were the most important item in costs. A government inquiry of 1891 concluded that 'of the cost of production of coal of average hardness, about 55 per cent was chargeable to wages', but added that this might be an underestimate.[3]

Collieries were unusually large establishments by nineteenth-century standards. The employers were therefore relatively few in number and thus easy to organize, especially in the North-east, where 'pits were great and deep with large average outputs and large working staffs'[4] and the owners had long worked together to monopolize the London market. They agreed among themselves upon the terms for the renewal of the miners' annual bond,[5] and in 1844 their workers could claim that 'the masters set us the example, for the masters formed a union for the protection of their interest'.[6] However, because of the district regulation of wages and conditions by the owners, the miners had no opportunity to imitate the craftsmen by gradually extending control from colliery to colliery. If they were to have any effective influence, they must exert pressure directly upon the county-wide associations of the employers.

In good times a union could come into existence and obtain some concession, as Tommy Hepburn's did in the North-east in 1831. During the following year the masters retaliated with the 'document', by signing which the men pledged themselves to have no further connexion with the union as a condition of the renewal of their bond. Nevertheless, even if

---

[1] R. Page Arnot, *The Miners*, vol. i, 1949, p. 46.

[2] J. M. Ludlow, 'Account of the West Yorkshire Coal Strike and Lock-out', in *Trades' Societies and Strikes*, pp. 19, 25.

[3] *Report on the Relation of Wages in Certain Industries to the Cost of Production*, C–6535, 1891, pp. 13–26. In shipbuilding, labour costs were estimated at between one-third and two-fifths of total outlay, and in cotton at between 21 and 38 per cent.

[4] J. H. Clapham, *An Economic History of Modern Britain*, vol. i, 1926, p. 186.

[5] The bond was a twelve-month contract of service without provision for change of terms or for notice during the year.   [6] Fynes, op. cit., p. 64.

Hepburn's union had survived it would inevitably have faced wage reductions when coal prices fell.

The Scottish miners fought three mass strikes against wage reductions in 1837, 1842, and 1856.[1] All were unsuccessful. In 1855 they had formed the Scottish Coal and Iron Miners' Association, which by the end of the year 'appeared to have struck deep roots'. Next March 30,000 men tried to fight a 20 per cent. reduction, but after 'a most painful struggle' lasting two months they were forced to submit, and next year victimization virtually destroyed what was left of the union's strength. By 1859 it was 'little more . . . than an empty shell'.[2]

For the most part, however, prices were rising between the late fifties and 1873, and this provided a basis for more permanent unions. South Yorkshire claims continuous organization from 1858, though 1864, when John Normansell became secretary, is probably a more realistic date. The Northumberland Miners' Mutual Confident Association also dates from 1864 and the Durham Miners' Association from 1869. Trade unionism in South Staffordshire goes back to 1863, and during the sixties Thomas Halliday formed a federation of colliery organizations in Lancashire.

Scotland and South Wales faced special problems. The collieries were scattered, and in South Wales communication between the valleys was difficult. Both coalfields were expanding rapidly from the middle of the century and had to find a labour force mainly by immigration—in Scotland from Ireland[3] and in South Wales from the agricultural counties of the West of England.[4] Consequently racial and religious differences, aggravated in South Wales by a language barrier, presented unusual obstacles to the union organizer. By 1873, however, several county unions had emerged in Scotland, and Halliday had brought the South Wales miners into his Amalgamated Association of Miners, set up in 1869 as a rival to the National Miners' Association founded by Alexander Macdonald in 1863. Halliday's purpose was to build a militant organization by means of central control of strike decisions and a national strike benefit, neither of which was to be found in the National Association, which preferred district autonomy and voluntary levies.

With growth came recognition by the employers and collective agreements. From 1866 Normansell, who exercised a remarkable authority over his members, was bargaining with the South Yorkshire employers, and *ad hoc* joint committees dealt with disputes in individual collieries.[5] In

---

[1] *Royal Commission on the Organization and Rules of Trade Unions, Seventh Report*, 1868, Qs. 15601-3.   [2] R. Page Arnot, *A History of the Scottish Miners*, 1955, pp. 41-45.

[3] A. J. Youngson-Brown, 'Trade Union Policy in the Scots Coalfields, 1855–1885', *Economic History Review*, Aug. 1953.

[4] Brinley Thomas, 'The Migration of Labour into the Glamorganshire Coalfield, 1861–1911' *Economica*, Nov. 1930.

[5] F. Machin, *The Yorkshire Miners*, 1958, pp. 340, 349–50.

1871 Northumberland, led by Thomas Burt,[1] and in 1872 Durham, under William Crawford,[2] both developed similar machinery, with the additional provision of independent arbitration.[3] In West Yorkshire a conciliation board was set up in 1873,[4] and in the same year the Scottish miners met the coal-owners to settle wages for the whole of the West of Scotland.[5] Meanwhile, Halliday was making gains in Lancashire and South Wales, though without the same development of collective institutions. In South Wales, for example, he was able to bring 70,000 miners out on strike in 1873.

In 1874, when prices began to fall rapidly, most of the miners decided to resist wage cuts. The results were disastrous. In the West of Scotland Macdonald tried to lead an ordered retreat which would minimize reductions and bring the district unions into a single federation, but he went unheeded. The men fought blindly and were beaten, and their unions virtually disappeared. Similarly, South Yorkshire refused a reduction in 1874 against Normansell's advice. After a costly lock-out had drained union funds the men were forced back on the employers' terms. Normansell's death in 1875 was followed by internal quarrels, another lock-out, and another failure. West Yorkshire avoided a stoppage, but a series of reductions through negotiation and arbitration had an equally disastrous effect on membership. After a five months' lock-out the South Wales miners accepted a 12½ per cent. cut in May 1875. The Amalgamated Association, broken and bankrupt, was dissolved a few months later, and its remaining members were advised to join the National Association, now renamed the Miners' National Union.

The South Wales coal-owners now evolved the combination of selling-price sliding scales and company unionism which was to control industrial relations in their coalfield until the end of the century.[6] The miners were permitted to elect representatives to a joint Sliding Scale Committee which 'negotiated' the basis of the scale. Half the costs were met by levies deducted from the workers' wages by the colliery management. This

[1] Burt, Thomas, P.C. (1837–1922). General secretary, Northumberland Miners' Association, 1865–1913. Liberal M.P., 1874–1918. Parliamentary Secretary to Board of Trade, 1892–5. Member of Royal Commission on Labour, 1891–4.

[2] Crawford, William (1833–90). General secretary, Northumberland Miners' Association, 1863–5. Agent, Durham Miners' Association, 1870; president, 1870; general secretary, 1871–90. Parliamentary Committee, Trades Union Congress, 1878–81, 1882–90. M.P., 1885–90.

[3] E. Welbourne, *The Miners' Unions of Northumberland and Durham*, 1923, pp. 134, 151, 157, 158.

[4] Machin, op. cit., pp. 177–9.   [5] Page Arnot, op. cit., p. 54.

[6] A selling-price sliding scale is an arrangement whereby adjustments to wage rates are directly governed by upward or downward movements in prices. Strictly speaking a 'company union' is a union existing within a single company and controlled by that company. The South Wales 'sliding-scale associations' covered a number of collieries, but they had no independent authority or financial strength, and could not have challenged the owners even if they had wished to.

system offered some protection against arbitrary action by the owners,[1] and the miners were encouraged to accept it by their new leaders. Chief among these was William Abraham,[2] or 'Mabon', a spell-binder in 'the old Nonconformist preaching style in Welsh', who could often 'split the conference delegates clean along the language line'.[3] In Monmouthshire alone there remained some shreds of independent unionism among English-speaking miners who were impervious to Mabon's persuasive powers.

After failing to avert a wage cut by a strike in 1874, South Staffordshire signed a sliding-scale agreement in which the role of the leaders was very much the same as that of Mabon and his colleagues in South Wales. Even in Yorkshire, after the unions had lost the bulk of their members, the leaders turned to sliding scales as a device which might save their organizations from extinction by maintaining some degree of joint regulation. West Yorkshire had asked for a scale in 1874, but could not persuade the owners before 1880. By that time South Yorkshire owners were also ready to operate a scale until disagreement among the union leaders about its terms led the employers to break off negotiations. Scales were set up at some pits but no general system emerged. In 1881 the remnants of the two unions came together in the Yorkshire Miners' Association, with Ben Pickard[4] as secretary and Ned Cowey[5] as president. In an area employing 60,000 miners they had 3,000 members.

Northumberland and Durham survived the disaster, and between 1875 and 1880 their combined membership fell only from 56,000 to 41,000, recovering to 48,000 by 1885. Burt and Crawford were convinced that their unions must be ready to accept wage cuts when prices fell. They therefore used friendly benefits to encourage stability and discipline amongst their members. Usually opposed to strikes, they were always hostile to output restriction—the traditional device by which miners in a falling market hoped to stabilize prices and therefore wages. The key to their attitude was the importance they attached to the position of the North-east coalfield as a major exporting area. Here orders did not accumulate during a strike or period of output restriction; they went elsewhere, perhaps for good.[6] Moreover, export prices were even more volatile

---

[1] J. H. Morris and L. J. Williams, *The South Wales Coal Industry 1841–1875*, 1958, p. 284.

[2] Abraham, William, P.C. (1842–1922). South Wales miners' agent, 1871–98. President, South Wales Miners' Federation, 1898–1911. Treasurer, Miners' Federation of Great Britain, 1904–18. M.P., 1885–1920. Member of Royal Commission on Labour, 1891–4.

[3] Ness Edwards, *History of the South Wales Miners*, 1926, p. 81.

[4] Pickard, Ben (1842–1904). Assistant secretary, West Yorkshire Miners' Association, 1873–6; secretary, 1876–81. General secretary, Yorkshire Miners' Association, 1881–1904. President, Miners' Federation of Great Britain, 1889–1904. Parliamentary Committee, Trades Union Congress, 1890–1. M.P., 1885–1904.

[5] Cowey, Edward (1839–1903). President, West Yorkshire Miners' Association, 1873–81. President, Yorkshire Miners' Association, 1881–1903. Parliamentary Committee, Trades Union Congress, 1893–1903.

[6] W. J. Ashley, *The Adjustment of Wages*, 1903, p. 41.

than prices on the home market, and this increased the eagerness of the owners for rapid adjustments in wages.

When prices began to fall, both county boards had turned to arbitration by their independent chairmen, who awarded a series of reductions. Discontent inevitably mounted among the miners; and their leaders sought for some device which might enable them to accept inescapable reductions with less danger to discipline. The automatic, impersonal mechanism of the sliding scale seemed to be the answer. Durham therefore adopted a scale in 1877; Northumberland, after striking against a proposed cut which the employers refused to put to arbitration, followed a year later. Durham's scale included a minimum below which wages should not fall. But, as prices continued to drop, some colliery managers made local arrangements for further reductions which threatened the whole structure of agreements.[1] In 1879 the owners gave notice to terminate the scale and substitute another without a minimum. Crawford was unable to avert a strike, but when it was over he relinquished the minimum and never tried to negotiate another.

The Fife coalfield was also an exporting area, and the Fife and Kinross Miners' was a third union which survived. Its members were helped to maintain stable trade unionism by being set apart from the main stream of restless immigrants which unsettled the West of Scotland. In 1870 the Fife miners had been the first in Europe to win the eight-hour day. When the depression came, theirs were the only leaders in Scotland to follow Macdonald's advice to accept small reductions but resist big ones; after accepting one reduction in 1876, they successfully resisted a lock-out to enforce another in 1877. By 1880, with some 5,000 members, they were the only miners' union left in Scotland.

The economic revival of the early eighties led many English miners towards new and wider alliances. In 1881 a strike in Lancashire brought together a federation of a dozen or so tiny organizations with Thomas Ashton[2] as secretary. Thereafter, under the leadership of Pickard and Ashton, Yorkshire, Lancashire and the Midlands (where new unions were being formed in Nottingham and Derby) began to move towards common action for a minimum wage and an eight-hour day. This informal collaboration promised a better chance of unity than either the Amalgamated Association or the National Association, both of which had included exporting areas, with their widely fluctuating prices, as well as coalfields serving the home market, where fluctuations were relatively limited. Pickard and Ashton's following, however, produced almost entirely for

[1] Welbourne, op. cit., p. 191.

[2] Ashton, Thomas, P.C. (1844–1927). Secretary, Ashton and Oldham Miners' Association, 1879–81. General secretary, Lancashire and Cheshire Miners' Federation, 1881–1919. General secretary, Miners' Federation of Great Britain, 1889–1919. Executive Committee, Labour Party, 1910–11.

domestic consumption. In the depression of 1885–7 they lost most of their slender gains; but by 1889, with prices rising rapidly, the unions were growing apace and negotiating for a formal alliance to achieve their new objectives.

In iron, relationships during the sixties were as turbulent as those in any other industry.[1] In 1863 Staffordshire was struck, a few works at a time, over a period of fourteen weeks, and the following year saw a twenty-seven weeks' lock-out by the ironmasters of the Leeds district. In 1864–5, when 30,000 North Staffordshire men struck for twenty-one weeks against a reduction, the masters of the North-east, South Staffordshire, Sheffield, and Derbyshire locked out in sympathy until the men capitulated. The North-east saw a constant series of stoppages, the largest of which, another unsuccessful attempt to resist a reduction, was a strike by 12,000 workers for twenty weeks in 1866.[2] As in coal, rapid expansion, fluctuating prices, an influx of Irish labour, and the unions' determination to 'take a decided stand against all reductions',[3] provided the main elements of conflict.

After yet another unsuccessful strike against a reduction in 1868, two ironworkers' unions based on Staffordshire finally collapsed.[4] This left only the severely weakened National Amalgamated Association of Ironworkers, led by John Kane, in the North-east. By now employers and workmen were equally anxious to find some escape from recurrent conflict. 'I think they would adopt any consistent system in order to put an end to strikes and lock-outs', said one union leader.[5] In 1869, therefore, both sides were ready to establish the Board of Conciliation and Arbitration for the Manufactured Iron Trade of the North of England, the most famous and successful of the nineteenth-century boards; and in the major centre of the industry there began an era of peace which has hardly been broken since.

Much of the credit must go to Kane, but the chief author of this transformation was an employer, David Dale.[6] He and his fellow ironmasters had two prime interests in the field of industrial relations: first, freedom from stoppages so that heavily capitalized plant could be kept going, unit overheads minimized, and waste (especially of fuel) reduced;[7] and, second, the need, which they shared with the coal-owners, for reductions in wages

[1] An ironworkers' leader said of the 'puddlers' of the sixties that 'when . . . it became known that there were 3,000 members [in the union] every puddler thought he was a gentleman, and had only to lose his hand-rag to demand a strike' (*Birmingham Weekly Post*, 26 Oct. 1872).

[2] *Royal Commission on the Organization and Rules of Trade Unions, Fifth Report*, 1868, pp. 55–56.   [3] Ibid., p. 54.

[4] This was the third set of local unions in current memory, the earlier ones also having perished (ibid., Q. 9839).

[5] W. Hobson, secretary of the Associated Ironworkers (Staffordshire), one of the unions which collapsed in 1868 (ibid., Q. 8987).

[6] Dale, Sir David (1829–1906). Managing director and chairman, Consett Iron Company; director, North Eastern Railway; chairman, Dunderhand Iron Ore Company, &c. Member of Royal Commission on Labour, 1891–4. Dale was a Quaker and a great-nephew of the David Dale whose daughter married Robert Owen.

[7] Daniel Jones, in *British Industries*, edited by W. J. Ashley, 1903, p. 48.

when prices fell.[1] Moreover, as in coal, district associations had long existed for the purpose of regulating prices and wages. 'Those in the Midlands and South Wales had a continuous tradition . . . going back at least to the 1780's'[2] and by 1867 the North of England Ironmasters' Association had been in existence 'for a considerable length of time'.[3]

In 1864 these associations and the ironmasters of North Staffordshire, Sheffield, and Derbyshire had achieved something approaching industry-wide co-operation, rare among employers at this time, in agreeing to give simultaneous notice of a 10 per cent. reduction which led to the general lock-out of that year.[4] Dale now persuaded his colleagues that their interests could best be served by a conciliation board, and he himself became its chairman.[5] Major changes on wages were settled either on the basis of a selling-price sliding scale or by negotiation, with arbitration as the last resort, prices remaining the chief criterion. In addition, a joint subcommittee dealt with works disputes.

The structure of the board appeared more like that of the South Wales miners than of the miners in the North-east. The board was partly financed by a levy on wages, and there was no formal recognition of the union, the operatives' representatives being in theory elected from the various works regardless of union membership. Before long the board even paid the salary of the secretary of the operatives' side, who was also the union's secretary, out of its joint funds. Previously he had been paid by the union, and 'had to maintain his popularity and situation by appearing to be *fighting* in the interests of the workmen—not by conciliating'.[6] But there was one important difference from the South Wales system. The union was an independent union which dominated the elections and controlled the operatives' side of the board, where its chief officer was their spokesman. Through the board the employers had in practice to negotiate with Kane's Association, which was no more in their pocket than Burt's or Crawford's unions were controlled by the coal-owners.

From the point of view of the masters, however, the Association had one big advantage over any miners' organization, for it could exert a powerful and reliable discipline over its members. These were very largely contractors, such as the puddlers, shinglers, furnacemen, rollers, and other millmen, who were paid by tonnage rates and employed their own under-hands to whom they paid day rates.[7] The contractors were very comfort-

---

[1] Wages were estimated at nearly 50 per cent. of the total production costs involved, from the mining of the ore to the finished iron or steel. See also p. 16.

[2] J. C. Carr and W. Taplin, *History of the British Steel Industry*, 1962, p. 62.

[3] *Royal Commission on the Organization and Rules of Trade Unions*, *Fifth Report*, 1868, Qs. 9393, 9829.   [4] Ibid., p. 55.

[5] A. J. Odber, 'The Manufactured Iron Trade of the North of England', *Oxford Economic Papers*, June 1951.

[6] Daniel Jones, loc. cit., p. 45.

[7] Though the underhands might join the union at half rates, they could expect no protection

ably off and there was keen competition amongst the underhands to replace them. Consequently, a contractor who disregarded a joint decision of the employers and the union would be in danger of losing his privileged position, and the union officers were not slow to remind him of it.

The ironmaking district of Staffordshire and Worcestershire followed the example of the North-east in 1871, but with less success. Firms were more numerous and agreement among employers more difficult to secure. The board had to be reformed from time to time and the Midland Iron and Steel Wages Board of 1887 was the third of its kind. There was no employer of Dale's stature, and the union faced competition from other organizations with a different approach.[1] The predominance of the North-east, however, and the power of the Association in both districts, forced the Midlands to follow the same principles of wage settlement through similar institutions.

Meanwhile, change was overtaking the industry, for 'steel was quickly displacing malleable iron'.[2] Steel production by the Siemens process began to gain ground rapidly, with the West of Scotland in the vanguard. Because the writ of the Association, in 1887 renamed the Associated Iron and Steel Workers, did not run north of the border, the British Steel Smelters' Amalgamated Association was founded by the Scots in 1886, with John Hodge[3] as its first secretary. The new union soon moved south into the North-east, the North-west, and Sheffield, taking in the small handfuls of Siemens workers which the Associated had not bothered to organize; and before long branches were also formed in South Wales.

In iron, as in coal, stable trade unionism was clearly associated with an acceptance of the principle that wage rates must fluctuate with the selling price of the product. The Webbs attributed this acceptance to the 'conversion' of the union leaders to 'capitalist' economic principles; and they gave almost uncritical approval to the opponents of sliding scales who were emerging in the late eighties.[4] But had Burt, Crawford, and Kane not accepted the wage-price link during the seventies there would have been no unions of any strength in either industry a decade later. A recognition of the need for wage reductions was a condition of union survival at that time; and their sliding-scale agreements show a realization that automatic adjustments through the formal machinery of the boards were to be preferred to the frontal clashes which had destroyed so many unions in the two industries.

against the contractors. In 1888 the union claimed only 3,725 members, so that relatively few underhands can have taken advantage of the offer.

[1] *Royal Commission on Labour*, C–6795–IV, 1892, Qs. 14790–5.

[2] D. L. Burn, *The Economic History of Steelmaking, 1867–1939*, 1940, p. 82.

[3] Hodge, John, P.C. (1855–1937). General secretary, British Steel Smelters' Amalgamated Association, 1886–1918. President, Iron and Steel Trades Confederation, 1918–31. Parliamentary Committee, Trades Union Congress, 1892–4, 1895–6. Executive Committee, Labour Party, 1900–15. M.P., 1906–23. Minister of Labour, 1916–17. Minister of Pensions, 1917–19.

[4] Webbs, *History*, pp. 338–41.

Hosiery and Footwear

Professor Phelps Brown has described the board of conciliation and arbitration as 'the characteristic form of organised British industrial relations for the thirty years from 1860 to 1890'.[1] This is an exaggeration. An institution which was then almost unknown among the major crafts and in cotton, and rare in coal-mining, cannot have been typical of 'organised industrial relations', however important its role in iron. But it was typical of other sections of industry where some of the employers saw that the unions might prove useful partners in mitigating competition. Most of these employers were to be found in the lesser textile trades, but the boot and shoe industry, and later some of the minor metal trades, also provided examples. Virtually all were industries in which piece-work was prevalent.

Established by A. J. Mundella[2] in 1860, the Nottingham Hosiery Board claimed to be the first of its kind, and regulated the many piece-prices of the industry as well as settling works disputes. The union was able to build up strength through the board's system of regulation, and then helped to enforce its decisions. Before long, a similar board was created to cover Leicester and Derby. In setting up these boards, the employers had two main motives. The industry was highly competitive, and an institution which could prevent wage-cutting might eliminate at least one of their problems.[3] Secondly, like all employers, the master hosiers wanted industrial peace. Both motives were reinforced because theirs was an industry of piece-work in which the opportunities for competitive wage-cutting and the frequency of minor disputes are usually greater than in a time-work industry.

After the mid-seventies, however, the boards fell gradually into disuse and were finally disbanded in 1884, destroyed by the competition they set out to control. When the Nottingham Board was founded, there existed a mere three to four thousand factory machine-workers but over 50,000 domestic hand-frame workers;[4] and it was principally for the latter that piece rates were laid down. In 1885 there were almost 20,000 machine workers, and by 1892 only 5,000 hand-frames were said to be left in the whole of the Midlands.[5] As their output increased, the boards had tried to bring the factories under control by including factory representatives;[6] but machines continued to take work away from the hand-knitters, some of whom were thus forced to undercut the boards' prices.[7] The machine workers might then volunteer additional cuts to get their work back,[8] and

---

[1] E. H. Phelps Brown, *The Growth of British Industrial Relations*, 1959, p. 126.

[2] Mundella, A. J., P.C. (1825–97). Liberal M.P., 1868–95. Vice-president of Committee of Council for Education, 1880–5. President of Board of Trade, 1886 and 1892–4, when he resigned.   [3] F. A. Wells, *The British Hosiery Trade*, 1935, chapter ix.

[4] Clapham, op. cit., vol. ii, 1932, p. 85.   [5] Ibid., p. 86.

[6] *Royal Commission on Labour*, C–6795–VI, 1893, Qs. 13173–7.

[7] Ibid., Qs. 12637–40.   [8] Ibid., Q. 12726.

the conflict was further exacerbated by differences between town and country, factory and hand-frame.

These stresses not only destroyed the boards but also produced weakness and fragmentation among the unions. Nevertheless, they managed to survive, and in 1889 there were about a dozen unions in the various centres of the trade. The hand-knitters among them were now largely dependent on government contracts, the competition for which was savage; and here they owed their survival to the War Office's 'antiquated specification for military pants'.[1]

The Amalgamated Cordwainers' Association of the bespoke hand-sewing boot and shoe makers had once been a powerful craft society, but in the second half of the century its members began to meet serious competition from a rapidly growing, increasingly mechanized wholesale industry. Their leaders took a far-sighted view of this development, and thus made a deep impression on the Webbs.[2] They urged the branches to organize the new classes of workers, such as riveters, lasters, and finishers, and then to negotiate piece-price lists on their behalf. However, as has so often happened when the national leaders have tried to open the ranks of a craft union, many branches quietly ignored this advice, convinced that they should fight change rather than accept it. The Association's recent recruits, some of whom were apprentice cordwainers who had switched to the new methods,[3] grew restive at continued domination by the craftsmen; and in 1874 they broke away to form the National Union of Operative Boot and Shoe Rivetters and Finishers, later the National Union of Boot and Shoe Operatives.

Only certain sections of the wholesale trade were organized by the National Union. The skilled 'clickers', who cut out the uppers, held aloof; membership was opened to women in 1884, but few of them joined; and even among riveters and finishers organization was weak for some years. Had they wished, it would have been easy for the manufacturers to smash the new union. However, apart from an early lock-out in Stafford, they showed no inclination to do so, and were ready to co-operate in setting up boards of conciliation and arbitration in the major centres. The problem of settling piece rates was at least as complex as in hosiery, but the boards were able to draw up price lists, adjudicate minor disputes, and maintain agreed labour standards.

Membership of the union rose from 4,000 in the seventies to 19,000 in 1888; and a year later the leading trade paper observed that

never in the history of the trade has [trade unionism] been so powerful, and never, on the whole, has it exerted so much influence for the good. . . . It is to

---

[1] Clapham, op. cit., vol. ii, p. 86.   [2] *Industrial Democracy*, pp. 417–20.
[3] Amalgamated Cordwainers' Association, *Quarterly Report*, Aug. 1870. In 1873 the society was re-named the Amalgamated Boot and Shoe Makers' Association.

the advantage of all concerned that chaos should be reduced to order, and that, as far as possible, uniformity of wage and practice should be attained. . . . Every manufacturer today feels that he has an interest in the wages paid by his competitors, and although the workmen were the first to point this out, yet now the principle has been acceded, employers are eager to carry it to its logical issue whenever a dispute arises.[1]

Despite this idyllic picture, however, there were already signs of difficulties that were soon to cause bitter conflict. New machinery had begun to invade the territory of the lasters and finishers, and a novel subdivision of labour, the 'team system', was transferring work to less skilled operatives on time rates, thus undercutting the agreed piece-prices not only in factories which adopted the system but also among their competitors. Both these changes led to a rapid increase in the employment of boys, and the sending of work out into the lower-cost, non-union countryside was another source of complaint. The union therefore prepared to do battle. To protect their piece-prices, some branches set up rules against time-work; and the union itself began to grope towards a restriction on the number of boys.

Thus the Boot and Shoe Rivetters were reversing the stages of development found in most craft societies during this period. Originally, the societies built up their strength by imposing craft rules supported by an elaborate system of benefits, but recently they had begun to meet new problems (and new opportunities) by making more use of the methods of collective bargaining. The Boot and Shoe Rivetters, on the other hand, first acquired such strength as they possessed through their recognition by the employers as useful partners in collective wage regulation. Industrial change now drove them to defend their gains by attempting to impose rules where the employers wanted a free hand.

Cotton

The growth of trade unionism in cotton provided a further illustration of these contrasting types of development. By 1889 the Amalgamated Association of Operative Cotton Spinners and the Northern Counties Amalgamated Weavers' Association had both achieved considerable success. But whereas from the start the Weavers relied almost exclusively upon collective bargaining, the Spinners had turned to it only after securing their own controls over the working group employed in their branch of the industry.

Powerful unions of hand mule spinners had existed early in the century, but they were much weakened by the coming of the 'self-acting' mule during the thirties and forties. In trying to resist this innovation, they suffered a series of defeats; and their organization had to be revitalized or

[1] *Shoe and Leather Record*, 7 Sept. 1889.

reconstituted as unions of self-acting mule spinners. However, while forced to accept the new machinery, the spinners of the fifties and sixties preserved the tradition of determining and controlling the working group. Despite attempts by the employers to introduce women under male supervisors, to promote 'piecers' to 'apprentice spinners' at lower rates and to impose 'joining', by which two spinners did the work and shared the earnings, the unions successfully enforced their own system—a team of one spinner and two male assistants, the 'big' and the 'little' piecers.[1]

This was not a system based on apprenticeship. The employers could always increase the number of spinners by promoting experienced piecers, whereas in the craft trades a substantial increase in skilled men required a prior increase in apprentices. This might be opposed by the unions, and could not produce results until after the prescribed period of apprenticeship. The surreptitious promotion of competent labourers offered a loophole where the societies were weak, but not an accepted or generally available method of recruitment. Consequently, control over the working group did not enable the spinners to use the normal range of craft controls. But it did permit them to protect their own high earnings both by imposing low earnings, late promotion, and heavy wastage on the piecers,[2] and at the expense of the ageing spinner, whom employers would naturally tend to replace by promoting a younger and more vigorous piecer.

The amalgamation and its constituent local associations could therefore afford to combine in providing the most comprehensive and expensive system of benefits in the country. In 1892, for example, the average contribution of the Spinners was £4. 11s. 7d., as against £3. 6s. 1½d. for the Engineers, £2. 12s. 5½d. for the Boilermakers, and £2. 9s. 11½d. for the Carpenters and Joiners.[3] The amalgamation paid strike benefit at 10s. a week and lock-out benefit at 6s., but many local associations doubled these figures. There was also out-of-work benefit and a number of other allowances.

The battle for control of the spinning team had been fought out before the amalgamation was given its final shape in 1870; but the spinners' victory explains the extraordinary strength which it rapidly attained. And until the seventies at least, the negotiation of wage rates, though important, appears to have taken second place. Payment to the spinners was by the piece, and Lancashire had developed its own elaborate formulas which

---

[1] S. J. Chapman, 'Some Policies of the Cotton Spinners' Trade Unions', *Economic Journal*, Dec. 1900.

[2] During the nineties the earnings of the spinners seem to have varied between 30s. and 45s. The total earnings of the two piecers rarely exceeded 25s. and never amounted to 30s. (G. H. Wood, *The History of Wages in the Cotton Trade during the Past 100 Years*, 1910, p. 74). Oldham piecers were paid according to a scale specified in the piece-price lists, but elsewhere it might depend on individual bargaining between the spinner and his assistants.

[3] *Report on Trade Unions in 1896*, C-8644, 1897, pp. 174-5.

permitted prices for different types of yarn to be determined within a single standard list.[1] Prices were not, as in hosiery or footwear, separately negotiated for each type of product. While payment on such lists was the common practice, it was not until 1876 that a generally supported list was negotiated in Oldham, and not until 1887 in Bolton, where as late as 1880 'the system of wage payment appears to have fallen into chaos'.[2]

By this time, these two towns were recognized as the main centres of spinning. In Scotland the whole industry had declined dramatically, the 114,000 employees of 1851 falling to 16,000 in 1891;[3] and with its separation from weaving, spinning had become concentrated in South-east Lancashire, where Bolton specialized in fine and Oldham in coarse spinning.[4] The negotiation of the Oldham and Bolton lists thus gave the amalgamation control over the wages of a large proportion of its members. Both centres, and Oldham in particular, became 'wage-leaders'.

It used to be customary for agreements to be made in several districts that wages should rise and fall with advances and reductions in some other district. Wages at Oldham in this way came to be the standard for many places. But both masters and men at Oldham finally awoke to the fact that they were fighting the battles of the trade.[5]

For the weavers interest in wages had come first. By the middle of the century weaving was already concentrated in North and North-east Lancashire, with Blackburn as the chief centre. The power-loom was firmly established, and hand-loom weavers had almost disappeared. Employers in Blackburn took the initiative in negotiating a standard list for power-loom weaving in 1853. They dealt with an *ad hoc* committee of workers on this occasion, but in the following year the Blackburn Power-loom Weavers' Association was founded. Encouraged by the results of collective regulation, a meeting of the Preston and Blackburn employers in 1866 resolved that they should form a 'United Association', and 'that a joint committee immediately be appointed to take into consideration the propriety of adopting one Uniform Standard List as a basis for the rate of Wages within the district'.[6]

This meeting led to the foundation of the North and North-east

---

[1] In weaving, similar standard formulas were constructed for the different types of cloth.

[2] J. Jewkes and E. Gray, *Wages and Labour in Cotton Spinning*, 1935, pp. 69, 82.

[3] The labour force in England rose from 389,000 in 1851 to 546,000 in 1891. Thus there was very little change in the total for the United Kingdom.

[4] Unlike the rest of the industry, Oldham during the sixties and seventies experienced a rapid switch from family firms to public companies—the 'Oldham limiteds'—as larger and more rapid mules were introduced and the size of firms increased.

[5] S. J. Chapman, *The Lancashire Cotton Industry*, 1904, p. 276.

[6] Roland Smith, *A History of the Lancashire Cotton Industry Between the Years 1873 and 1896*, Ph.D. thesis, Birmingham, 1954. This is the best source for the industrial relations of the industry at this period, and we have relied heavily upon it.

Lancashire Cotton Spinners' and Manufacturers' Association,[1] but the task of devising a uniform list proved to be impossible. A compromise which would satisfy the employers meant too many wage reductions to be acceptable to the unions and vice versa. The chief stumbling block was the Burnley list, which was below the other lists over most of its range. Burnley was the most rapidly growing centre in weaving at this time and also the weakest point in union organization, so that undercutting even of its existing list was common. In 1873 the unions made a further attempt to force Burnley into line, but without success.

Thereafter, the coming of the depression concentrated attention on general wage problems, and in 1878 came a protracted, county-wide strike in which the weavers failed to avoid a 10 per cent. reduction. This experience led to the establishment in 1881 of a joint committee to provide a means of settling disputes over the whole weaving trade. The North-east Lancashire Weavers' Association, founded in 1858 in an attempt to bring all the weavers' organizations together, had met with only limited success, but out of the broader collaboration which was needed to form the workers' side of the joint committee there developed the Amalgamated Weavers' Association in 1884.

Thus in weaving the employers made most of the running. Their motives were similar to those of the master hosiers under Mundella, or the boot and shoe manufacturers, for they laid stress on the preservation of industrial peace, and on the excellence of the Blackburn list in minimizing disputes. The proposed uniform list was expected to serve the same purpose, but it is unlikely that this was the sole explanation for the eagerness of Blackburn and Preston employers to resolve disputes in Burnley by raising Burnley's prices to the level of their own. In the opinion of two trade unionists in 1891, 'one great reason why Burnley has made such rapid strides in manufacturing over other districts is the facilities which have been offered there for small capitalists making a start'.[2] The heightened competition resulting from this ease of entry may well have given employers elsewhere a strong commercial interest in obtaining a uniform list.

In contrast to the Spinners, whose 17,000 members in 1888 represented a density in the region of 90 per cent., the Weavers' 40,000 members formed only about a quarter of the weaving labour force. But in one respect they led the country, for over half their members were women and no other union had attracted nearly so many.[3] Cotton provided

---

[1] From the first this organization represented the bulk of the weaving trade. It also covered most of the spindles within its area, particularly in Preston which had a number of vertically organized firms; but did not try to challenge the leadership of the Oldham Master Cotton Spinners' Association. In 1892 the Spinners' and Manufacturers' Association represented six million spindles compared with almost ten millions represented by the Oldham Association.

[2] *Royal Commission on Labour*, C-6708-VI, 1892, Q. 1078.

[3] In 1891 40,300, or 62 per cent., of the amalgamation's 65,000 members were women (ibid., C-7421-I, 1894, p. 252).

employment for the husband, wife, and older children of many Lancashire families, and the women might therefore be recruited through family pressure. Some unions and trades councils, indeed, debarred from office those whose families included persons eligible for membership but still outside it. Moreover, since the weavers' standard lists governed the work of both sexes, the men could only raise their own earnings by raising those of the women at the same time and thus needed their organized support. Consequently, cotton manufacture was the highest paid industry for women,[1] and high-paid workers are more readily organized than low-paid.

Some of these considerations also applied to women employed in the preparatory stages of spinning, the card and blowing room operatives. Here a relatively small number of men performed the skilled tasks while women did the less skilled work, earning much less than the men. They were also paid less than female weavers, though still considerably more than the national average for women. The local organizations of card-room operatives had a long history but were far weaker than those of the spinners and weavers. The Amalgamated Association of Card and Blowing Room Operatives was not founded until 1886. Initially it brought together about 9,000 workers, and two years later the total membership had risen to 15,000, almost three-quarters of them women.[2]

The amalgamation arose directly from a prolonged stoppage in Oldham in 1885. When the spinners struck, they automatically put out of work twice their number of piecers, and more than three times their number of card and blowing room operatives.[3] Many piecers belonged to the Oldham Spinners' Association and received an allowance from its funds; but the equally dependent cardroom workers were left to fend for themselves. They therefore decided that they would be better off with an organization of their own. The cause of the dispute had been a projected wage reduction of 10 per cent. After three months agreement was reached on 5 per cent., with a further 5 per cent. to follow in January 1886 if margins fell below certain limits. These limits were clearly passed, but the spinners refused to honour their pledge and the employers shrank from renewing the conflict. Instead they turned to planning a county-wide alliance of master spinners' associations strong enough to stand up to the spinners' amalgamation.

Meanwhile, the weaving side of the industry had at last begun to make some progress towards a uniform list. In 1885 a strike in Burnley was settled on the basis of a temporary 5 per cent. reduction on condition that a joint committee should be set up to negotiate such a list for 'plain' cloth

[1] See p. 482.

[2] In 1891 18,500, or 74 per cent., of its 25,000 members were women (*Royal Commission on Labour*, C-7421-I, 1894, p. 252).

[3] When the 4,000 or so Oldham spinners struck in 1885, the total number out was said to be 24,000.

weaving. The committee was given some encouragement in 1887 by the success of central negotiations leading up to the first uniform list for a specialist branch of the trade—the North and North-east Lancashire Fancy Goods List. Even so, the joint committee had failed to reach agreement on the uniform list for plain cloth by the beginning of 1889.

Other Industries

In addition to the major industries, there were a few minor trades and occupations in which the unions had attained some power before 1889, as well as several major industries where trade unionism was unusually weak or even non-existent. Craft societies were to be found outside engineering, shipbuilding, printing, and building: in tailoring, for example, in hat-making, in glass and in furniture. White-collar unionism had also made its appearance. The Post Office telegraphists startled the country with a strike among civil servants shortly after being taken over by the state in 1870, and in 1881 they formed the first permanent association within the Civil Service. The provincial Postal Clerks' Association was founded to present the case of its members to the Royal Commission on Civil Establishments of 1886–7, and the London sorters began to organize at the same time. A postmen's union had flourished for a time in 1873, and another appeared towards the end of the eighties.

By far the most successful of white-collar organizations, however, was the National Union of Elementary Teachers, whose members were employed by local school managers but paid partly from government grants. Robert Lowe's Revised Code of 1862 had established a system of 'payment by results', based largely on the proficiency of the children, which worsened conditions in several respects. Salaries fell;[1] teachers already lacked security and now became more subject to the whim of the managers; they had no hope of promotion to the inspectorate; and they wanted a pension scheme.[2] The parliamentary debates on the Education Act of 1870 provided an occasion when such grievances could be aired. Moreover, despite continued controversy over the vexed question of religious instruction in the schools, the Act held out some hope of a solution, and thus encouraged the existing denominational societies of teachers to come together. As a result the first conference of the National Union was held in September 1870.

The new organization concentrated on parliamentary activity. Every year its representatives sought alterations in the Code, which was reviewed annually by the Education Committee of the Privy Council, and several concessions were won. In one campaign, 'no fewer than 435 members of

[1] Donna F. Thompson, *Professional Solidarity Among the Teachers of England*, 1927, appendix I; A. Tropp, *The School Teachers*, 1957, appendix B.
[2] Thompson, op. cit., chapter ii.

the House [were] interviewed by the officers of the Executive of the Union or by representatives of local associations'.[1] From 1870 to 1884 the union was also assisted by the sympathetic attitude of Sir Francis Sandford, who as Secretary of the Committee of Council frequently consulted its officers.[2] Meanwhile, the demand for teachers was rising rapidly. Most of the new entrants remained unqualified; but in these circumstances the teachers were able to win gradual improvements in their salaries, and among more than 14,000 members in 1888 the union included over one-third of the certificated teachers.

In 1871, a year after the foundation of the National Union of Elementary Teachers, the Amalgamated Society of Railway Servants came into being with considerable encouragement from middle-class patrons, notably Michael Bass, a Member of Parliament, a major railway shareholder, and a millionaire. The Society's main objectives were to bring pressure upon Parliament to remedy the long working hours and high accident rate on the railways; and to provide the usual benefits, though its first rules made no mention of strike pay.

The railway companies were particularly hostile to trade unionism, and used a variety of devices in trying to resist its growth. They subsidized compulsory friendly societies; they operated a severe disciplinary system; and they divided their servants into a large number of grades which were played off against one another. Men from one grade or company might be used to break the strikes of other grades or of other railwaymen, and gratuities were paid to 'loyal' employees.[3] Moreover, the companies were assisted by the petty snobbery of the higher grades, especially the footplate staff, 'the silk-hatted aristocracy of the line'.[4] Few of these distinctions had much basis in skill, for even the drivers could be replaced. And porters, shunters, and labourers could be 'had practically in any number at any price'.[5]

Though the Society began with 17,000 members, more than half had been lost by the end of the first decade, for incompetent leadership, constant intrigue, and defection all added to its basic difficulties. By this time, however, the union had acquired a 'protection' benefit, which was used mainly for compensation in cases of victimization but could also provide strike pay. This innovation represented a step away from middle-class patronage; and Edward Harford, who became secretary in 1883, soon showed more ability than his predecessors. Meanwhile, the Society had developed its parliamentary campaign on railway accidents with the help of several Liberal Members, and managed to insert some special provisions

[1] Thompson, op. cit., p. 87.   [2] Tropp, op. cit., pp. 122–3.

[3] P. W. Kingsford, 'Labour Relations on the Railways, 1835–1875', *Journal of Transport History*, Nov. 1953.

[4] J. R. Raynes, *Engines and Men*, 1921, p. 1; Rowland Kenney, *Men and Rails*, 1913, pp. 149–50.   [5] Webbs, *Industrial Democracy*, p. 691.

in the Employers' Liability Act of 1880. Since these provisions were not wholly satisfactory, the agitation continued throughout the eighties.[1]

Refused recognition by the companies, the union pursued its industrial objectives by organizing petitions among the railwaymen which were presented to their company management and supported if possible by deputations. Originally members of such deputations risked victimization; but by the eighties some companies had come to accept them as a regular means of representation, though insistent that they must include none but their own employees. By these means Harford was able to restore his membership to some 15,000 out of nearly 200,000 in the operating staff by the end of 1888. In 1880, however, the footplate staff had broken away to form the Associated Society of Locomotive Engineers and Firemen, which now had 3,000 members, while another 4,000 railwaymen were organized in the Scottish Railway Servants' Society.

Weak though the railway unions were, some major industries had far less to show. For example, wholesale clothing, employing over a million people at the time of the 1891 Census, had almost no trade unionism.[2] The majority of workers were women working at home or in small workshops, and the efforts of Emma Paterson[3] did not lead to any permanent organization among them. Most attempts to set up stable unions in the rapidly growing Jewish workshops in London, Manchester, Leeds, and elsewhere had proved equally fruitless.[4] Factory production was also rising steeply, but again its employees were virtually unorganized except for a few local societies of skilled male cutters and pressers.

In the Yorkshire woollen and worsted industry the weakness of trade unionism presented a remarkable contrast to the strength of the amalgamations on the other side of the Pennines. Despite a combined labour force of about 275,000 in 1888, the two sections of the industry could boast no union with as many as 1,000 members.[5] Most of the tiny societies which did exist catered solely for specialists and supervisors. Otherwise, there was little or no organization among sorters, combers, and spinners, and only two feeble unions among the weavers. The more important of these, the West Yorkshire Power-loom Weavers, later the General Union of

---

[1] P. S. Gupta, *A History of the Amalgamated Society of Railway Servants*, D.Phil. thesis, Oxford, 1960.

[2] In bespoke tailoring, however, the Amalgamated Society of Tailors, a powerful society with 14,000 members in 1888, used all the devices of craft unionism to maintain its control over the manufacture of the higher quality products.

[3] Paterson, Mrs. Emma (1848–86). Secretary, Women's Provident and Protective League (later Women's Trade Union League), 1874–86. Promoted unions for women in clothing and garment trades, bookbinding, upholstering, &c.

[4] See p. 182.

[5] The industry had been slowly shrinking since 1851, when it employed 300,000. The worsted section was almost entirely confined to Yorkshire, but the woollen was spread over a number of other centres. In 1901 only half the woollen spindles in the kingdom were in Yorkshire (Clapham, op. cit., vol. ii, p. 27). Trade unionism was equally weak elsewhere.

Weavers and Textile Workers, emerged during a stoppage at Huddersfield in 1883; but by 1888 it had dwindled to a mere 700 members.

In cotton, spinning was a job for men; in the worsted trade it had always been a woman's occupation. The jenny was not replaced by the heavy mule, as in Lancashire, but by the relatively light throstle frame. Like the later ring frame, these were commonly operated by female labour and the majority of worsted spinners were young girls. Worsted weaving was similarly dominated by women, working on the lighter types of loom. Both men and women wove worsted coatings, but Bradford itself was the 'home of the girl weaver',[1] and the men had been gradually forced out. Under these conditions it would have been remarkable if the worsted trade had produced a strong union, either among spinners or among weavers.

In the woollen trade the male-operated mule did not appear until the thirties, and then the self-acting mule was brought in at once. Thus male spinners in Yorkshire lacked the traditions of trade unionism which their Lancashire colleagues inherited from the hand-mule period. Moreover, with small scattered units and little specialization, the average spinning department numbered only twenty-two operatives, whereas in cotton the average spinning mill employed 145,[2] which gave solidarity a better chance to develop. Such union traditions as had existed in Yorkshire were almost wiped out by the repression which followed the upsurge of 1831–4; and in any case these had been based upon the dying crafts of the cropper or shearer, the hand-comber, and the hand-loom weaver.

The power-loom only came into use in wool from the thirties, and spread much more gradually than in cotton.[3] Organization among power-loom weavers therefore appeared later in Yorkshire; and in the eighties, when it did, the woollen labour force had ceased to expand and there was a surplus of workers. The men were thus unable to build up the strength which was necessary to bring the women in. This was a crucial failure, for whereas in cotton the male weavers organized the women and brought them up towards men's standards of wages, in wool the women dragged the men down to theirs.[4] The growing substitution of women weavers for men, and changes in fashion away from wool and towards worsted, already dominated by women, only made matters worse. And this second development affected spinning as well as weaving. 'The woollen spinning trade', said a Huddersfield manufacturer in 1891, 'is . . . a changing trade— changed from the woollen yarn to the worsted yarn, which has brought about a revolution . . . the men did not quite make a living.'[5]

[1] J. H. Clapham, *The Woollen and Worsted Industries*, 1907, p. 178.
[2] Ibid., pp. 132, 139.
[3] As late as the eighties hand-loom weavers were still an important body of men in the small towns and villages about Leeds, Huddersfield, and Dewsbury (ibid., p. 128).
[4] Wage levels in both wool and worsted were well below those in cotton, both for men and women (see p. 186).   [5] *Royal Commission on Labour*, C–6708–VI, 1892, Q. 7080.

Agriculture was as poorly served as wool. In 1873 Joseph Arch's[1] National Agricultural Labourers' Union claimed to be 100,000 strong; but by 1889 it had been reduced to 4,000 members 'scattered up and down the Midland and Eastern counties, in what were virtually Sick and Funeral Clubs'.[2] Practically all the other organizations which flourished briefly at the beginning of the seventies had entirely disappeared. Indeed, in the circumstances of British agriculture in the nineteenth century it is easier to account for the virtual absence of trade unionism during the rest of the century than to explain its brief upsurge at the end of the third quarter. For in the countryside there was no mass labour force, impersonally managed, to facilitate combination; the workers were dispersed and isolated; and most of them lived in close personal contact with their employers.

The nearest approach to the conditions of urban industry was to be found in the corn-growing counties, for one acre of arable land required as much manual labour as three or more acres of grass, and corn needed more than other arable crops.[3] Consequently, the large farms of East Anglia had provided the focus of Arch's union in its moment of greatness, and here it still lingered on after the collapse of agricultural prosperity in the seventies, despite the fact that the expansion in imports of cheap corn naturally hit East Anglia hard. From 1·7 millions in 1871 the total labour force fell to 1·2 millions in 1891, and the proportion of cultivated land under permanent pasture rose from 42·1 per cent. in 1874 to 52·9 per cent. in 1904.[4] Meanwhile, earnings, after a rapid rise from the level of the middle sixties in the last phase of the mid-century boom, had fallen back to their starting-point by 1886-7.[5]

Quite as important as the structure and economics of agriculture in inhibiting rural trade unionism was a social system based on the trinity of squire, parson, and tenant farmer. The Church was the greatest of all landlords, and many clergymen were dependent on the squire for their livings. Even more obviously dependent were the squire's tenants. Between the three of them, they dominated the magistracy and owned most rural housing. Local publicans might fear the loss of their licences if they let rooms for union meetings; and since the parson normally ruled the school managers, and often the schoolmaster, the village schoolroom was also seldom available. In addition, in the tight fabric of village life, work, and charity, there were a hundred small ways of putting pressure on those who forgot their proper station.

[1] Arch, Joseph (1826-1919). President, National Agricultural Labourers' Union, 1872-95. Parliamentary Committee, Trades Union Congress, 1874-5, 1876-7. M.P., 1885-6, 1892-1900.
[2] E. Selley, *Village Trade Unions in Two Centuries*, 1919, p. 76.
[3] *Royal Commission on Labour*, C-6894-XXV, 1894, pp. 11-12.
[4] Clapham, *Economic History of Modern Britain*, vol. iii, 1938, p. 87; J. R. Bellerby, *Agriculture and Industry: Relative Income*, 1956, p. 58.   [5] Clapham, op. cit., vol. ii, p. 286.

The 'almost indescribable bitterness of feeling on the part of the squirearchy and their connections'[1] which agricultural unionism provoked in the early seventies is to be explained largely as the reaction to an attack on this social order. From the first Arch's union had campaigned for the extension of the franchise to the rural labourer, for elective councils in place of the administration of the magistrates, for the abolition of the tied cottage, and for the disestablishment of the Church. Arch was himself a Primitive Methodist lay preacher, and many of his colleagues were also Dissenters. Moreover, since trade unionism carried into the villages the Liberal Nonconformist attack on the structure of Anglican Tory prestige and power which dominated rural life, the surviving unions could rely on urban Radicals for the sympathy and encouragement which helped to keep them alive.

Trade Unionism and Social Status

There remains a further reason for the varying fortunes of unions in different occupations besides the differences in methods of work, traditions, and economic prosperity which have so far been stressed; and that is the difference in social status which existed between different groups within the working class. The organization of industries on a craft basis, for instance, did not simply provide the opportunity for craft unionism: first and foremost, it determined the high standing of the craftsmen on the shop floor and outside. But this enhanced status gave powerful reinforcement to their societies, for the members had not only rules to defend but also a respected station in life. Conversely, the lowly status of most labourers (and all women) was yet another obstacle to their effective organization.

The 'working class' was never a homogeneous body, and

a century ago [according to Cole] the social gulf between skilled craftsmen and labourers was considerably wider than it is today. It was greater in incomes, and greater in ways of living and in standards of education and culture. . . . Many labourers had hardly been to school at all, whereas most skilled workers had received some form of formal education and many had supplemented this by attendance at some sort of adult class or Sunday or evening school. . . . There was less in common between skilled and unskilled manual workers—I mean in manners and ways of life—than between the former and the small masters and tradesmen for whom many of them worked.[2]

However, as the foregoing sections have shown, a division into craftsmen and labourers is itself too crude to cover many of the important distinctions which existed within the working class. After his survey of London at the end of the eighties, Charles Booth constructed a sixfold classification for the metropolis: 'high-paid labour'; 'regular standard

---

[1] Webbs, *History*, p. 331.   [2] *Studies in Class Structure*, 1955, pp. 51–52.

earnings'; 'small regular earnings'; 'intermittent earnings'; 'casual earnings'; and the 'lowest class'. The second class was the largest, including, in Booth's opinion, almost as many people as the other five put together. Its members led 'independent lives' and possessed 'fairly comfortable homes. . . . Against anything which could be called charity their pride rises stiffly. This class is the recognised field of all forms of co-operation and combination.'[1] And it also contained 'those whose lot today is most aggravated by a raised ideal. . . . Here, rather than in the ruffianism of Class A, or the starvation of Class B, or the wasted energy of Class C, or the bitter anxieties of Class D, do we find the springs of Socialism and Revolution.'[2]

In the provinces the proportions in Booth's six categories may have differed from those in London; and members of some of the major unions, notably the cotton spinners and ironworkers, could have claimed to belong to his highest class, for the 'labour aristocracy' was not confined to craftsmen alone. But in 1889 it remained true here also that trade unionism had hitherto rarely achieved much success among workers who had failed to attain the status of his second class, and to share its attributes.

Union Government and Policy

The differences in the aims and methods of the major unions exerted a powerful influence on their forms of government. This is best illustrated by the contrast between the constitutions of the craft societies and those of the cotton amalgamations and the national miners' unions.

When craft societies became too large for 'primitive democracy',[3] the great majority entrusted day-to-day management to executive committees of members working at the trade and drawn, for reasons of economy, from a single branch or district. The chief officer was a general secretary elected by the whole society, and sooner or later paid a salary to give his full attention to union business. Some societies also arranged for a periodic change in the seat of government, which meant repeated moves for the head office. Whether temporary or not, a 'local' lay executive of this type was usually too weak to control a full-time officer elected by the membership as a whole, and most secretaries dominated their executives. For the making of rules and the determination of policy the societies generally relied upon a referendum of all qualified members, but this was sometimes supplemented by an *ad hoc* delegate conference. Neither of these devices constituted an effective check on a self-willed secretary. He could often choose the wording of a referendum to influence the result, and might prevent (or at least delay) the holding of a delegate conference if it seemed likely to disagree with him.

[1] *Life and Labour of the People in London*, vol. i, 1892, pp. 32–53.　　[2] Ibid., p. 177.
[3] Webbs, *Industrial Democracy*, chapter 1. In the early trade clubs its chief features had been rotation of office and government by the members 'in general meeting assembled'.

The new amalgamated societies of the fifties and sixties made few constitutional innovations. They centralized the control of financial business and the authority to approve strikes, but left both in the hands of 'local' executives served by full-time secretaries. In 1889, for example, the Engineers were still governed by an executive composed of delegates from the London branches.[1] The Boilermakers' executive was elected from the Tyneside district, and that of the Typographical Association from Manchester. The Engineers had a representative General Executive Council which met every two years up to 1885, when the interval was extended to three years. The final authority, the Delegate Meeting, had met only once since 1875; and the last such conference of the Typographical Association had been in 1877.

This lack of interest in securing a fully representative executive and an annual policy-determining conference is not to be explained by the readiness of craftsmen to subordinate themselves to others. They tolerated the centralization of financial business because trade policy remained a local matter, firmly in the hands of the men whom it would directly affect. Indeed, centralized finance provided greater security for the benefits on which the branches relied for the enforcement of their rules; and this security, together with uniform benefits, helped the societies to extend their geographical coverage and thus their grip on the supply of skilled labour. So long as the union's headquarters followed the prescribed procedure in dealing with contributions and benefits, the branches had no need of representative institutions to control them. Their one clear loss was the right to strike when they wished, but they had learned to use craft rules as an effective substitute, and there always remained the possibility of an unofficial strike.

National organizations in coal and cotton had to pursue their objectives by very different means. Like the miners, cotton operatives were concerned with the negotiation of wage rates on a county-wide basis; and by 1889 the miners had begun to think in terms of settlements covering a majority of the English coalfields. Their main weapon was the strike, and therefore the benefits in which the federal bodies were interested were strike and lock-out pay. This was the case with the cotton amalgamations, with Halliday's Amalgamated Association of Miners, and subsequently with the Miners' Federation of Great Britain. The Miners' National Association or Union did not provide even these benefits; but then it was never much more than the forum for annual discussions between miners' leaders from several counties. None of the organizations needed to provide

[1] 'The Society was controlled . . . by an Executive Council of eight members working at the trade during the day and meeting nightly at the office in Stamford Street. The fee was one shilling and sixpence per night. It was considered a cushy job to be won only by the worthy. During my spell on the Executive I had to leave home every night at seven and I got back about eleven' (G. N. Barnes, *From Workshop to War Cabinet*, 1924, p. 36).

uniform payment or national coverage for friendly benefits. These were parochial matters which could be left to local decisions so long as uniformity in collective bargaining was achieved.

Because they covered relatively small areas, the local associations of miners and cotton operatives had been able to establish representative executives from the start. When the federal bodies considered such vital issues as wage movements and strikes, all the associations wanted to share in their deliberations and to influence any collective bargaining which might result. Consequently they developed representative institutions at this level also. These took the form of regular conferences of delegates to make rules and decide policy, and an executive committee elected from and by the membership of the constituent associations.

Compared with their counterparts in the craft societies, these executives had another source of strength. Not only were they fully representative, they also consisted mainly of full-time officers of the local associations in cotton and of full-time 'agents' of the county unions in coal. In Lancashire all but the smallest associations had full-time secretaries to manage their affairs, and candidates for these posts were selected by written examination. Ned Whittle, the first secretary of the Blackburn Weavers, and Thomas Birtwistle, secretary of the first weavers' amalgamation, were both famous for their mathematical proficiency and their mastery of the intricate price list.[1] Each county union of miners had at least a full-time secretary, and the larger unions elected several full-time agents as well.

Thus the coal and cotton unions were far better supplied with full-time officers than the craft societies. Since it was natural for the local associations to appoint such officers as delegates to the federal body, the federal executive was likely to be better informed and endowed with greater authority than the 'local' lay executives of the societies. This did not mean that the national leaders were necessarily overshadowed by these committees of officials. Indeed, Pickard and James Mawdsley of the Spinners were to prove just the opposite. Nevertheless they had to carry their executives with them, and could not behave as autocratically as some of the secretaries of the craft societies.

Most of the smaller unions in other industries imitated the craft societies' structure of government, probably in the interests of economy; but this was not true of all, and others soon changed their minds. Almost from the first the Railway Servants adopted representative institutions. The Steel Smelters began in 1886 with an executive drawn from the West of Scotland, but before long other districts demanded a share in negotiating the agreements which would determine their wages. Similarly, in 1888 the Boot and Shoe Operatives had to change from a 'local' to a representative executive when the other branches pressed for a share in policy-making.

[1] Webbs, *History*, p. 309.

Such developments help to confirm the close connexion between the growth of collective bargaining and the demand for representation. By 1889, moreover, when most of the major craft societies had started to move towards collective bargaining, they, too, were finding traditional patterns of government increasingly criticized by some of their more militant members.

Both local and national institutions for formal co-operation between the unions appeared during the second half of the century. First came the trades councils. Several were established in provincial cities during the late fifties and London followed suit in 1860. Previously there had existed from time to time temporary and looser arrangements for local co-operation, such as the Glasgow United Trades of 1833 or the London Committee of Trade Delegates in 1845. The new councils did little more than embody these arrangements in a permanent form. Now that the unions which composed them had acquired their own stability, it was natural that their officers should meet together regularly in the centres where they worked. They had many matters of common interest to discuss—the provision of mutual support in local disputes, for example, or the selection of deserving cases for assistance elsewhere.

This did not present any serious obstacle to the centralization of power in the unions, for their representatives could commit themselves no further to the trades councils than was already within their authority as union officers. Besides, the councils made negligible demands upon the funds of the unions except when they collected voluntary subscriptions for strikers and these were seldom lavish. When trade unionists began to compete for places on school boards and similar bodies, the councils also provided a useful means of common action in local politics, approving candidatures and organizing campaigns. Before this occurred, however, co-operation on a national level through the Trades Union Congress had already been secured, partly on the initiative of some of the trades councils.

The general secretaries of the major unions with headquarters in London—William Allan of the Engineers, Robert Applegarth of the Carpenters and Joiners, Edwin Coulson of the Bricklayers, and Daniel Guile of the Ironfounders, together with George Odger, secretary of the London Trades Council from 1862 to 1872 and the most prominent of working-class Radicals—attempted to use their control of the Council to give a lead to the movement as a whole, by acting from the early sixties as 'an informal cabinet of the Trade Union world'.[1] Because of the Council's power to grant or withhold approval of fund-raising in London for disputes all over the country, the 'Junta' (as the Webbs called them) could hope to exercise a measure of discipline elsewhere in support of a cautious trade policy, not least within their own unions.

---

[1] Webbs, *History*, p. 245.

This was not to the liking of the militants, who found an effective spokesman in George Potter, a member of a minor London carpenters' club whose reputation had been made during the builders' lock-out of 1859–60. Potter directly challenged the authority of the Junta in the strikes of the Birmingham carpenters in 1864 and the Staffordshire ironworkers in 1865. He was therefore excluded from the Council, and immediately threatened 'the establishment of a counter-association'.[1] This body, the London Working Men's Association, proved to be of little importance; but Potter had been able to make good use of his lively paper, the *Beehive*, in his rivalry with the Junta, whose assumption of control was not entirely welcome to the leaders of some provincial unions. Even where the latter accepted the general outlook of Allan and Applegarth, they tended to regard the clique of Londoners as exclusive and unenterprising.

In 1861, for example, the Glasgow Trades Council was rebuffed when it attempted to launch a general agitation for the reform of trade union law; and three years later the Junta left Glasgow to take the initiative in the campaign to amend the law of Master and Servant. Potter was thus able to win the support of men like Alexander Macdonald and John Kane when in 1867 he summoned a conference at the St. Martin's Hall in London, 'the largest and most representative gathering of trade union leaders ever held', in order to consider tactics before the recently appointed Royal Commission on Trade Unions.[2] Despite the pleas of Macdonald and Kane, the Junta refused to co-operate in anything which originated with Potter, and constituted themselves as the Conference of Amalgamated Trades to deal with the Commission.[3]

With the help of their middle-class advisers, the Junta were so successful in representing the unions' case before the Royal Commission that they had established clear leadership of the movement and outmanœuvred Potter before the reports appeared in 1869. Meanwhile, provincial trades councils, expressing 'the growing desire for some representative body to voice general trade union opinion',[4] and taking 'into their serious consideration the present aspect of Trades Unions, and the profound ignorance which prevails in the public mind with reference to their operations and principles',[5] had organized Trades Union Congresses at Manchester in 1868 and Birmingham in 1869. At Birmingham the first Parliamentary Committee to be elected by Congress included not only Odger and George

---

[1] Quoted by A. E. Musson, *The Congress of 1868*, 1955, p. 16.
[2] With some justice, W. J. Davis described the meeting as 'the immediate forerunner of the existing Trades Union Congress' (*The British Trades Union Congress: History and Recollections*, vol. i, 1910, p. 138).
[3] B. C. Roberts, *The Trades Union Congress, 1868–1921*, 1958, p. 36.
[4] Musson, op. cit., p. 25.
[5] From the circular of the Manchester and Salford Trades Council summoning the first Congress, ibid., p. 38.

Howell[1] but also Potter, and was assigned the duty of watching legislation based on the Commission's reports. This task brought the two factions together, and from 1871 Congress became an annual fixture, formulating its first legislative programme in 1872 and laying down standing orders in 1873.

The Trades Union Congress did not emulate previous attempts to construct a national federation of trade unions. All had included among their aims the provision of common aid in strikes and lock-outs, and all had foundered on the difficulties of such a project. So long as the method of sustaining a strike was through voluntary levies on other trades there was little cohesive force in these ventures. Temporary committees could raise contributions almost as readily as a permanent body, especially when that body had no authority to enforce its levies. Only patient accumulation of funds and wide coverage could make strike insurance an attractive proposition. Moreover, an *ad hoc* committee need not be involved in the conduct of the dispute. Any federation had to face the almost insoluble problem of deciding which disputes should receive approval and assistance, and whether the strikers themselves, or the central body, should lay down the terms on which a dispute might be settled.

Thus the survival of Congress was primarily due to its avoiding any 'form of amalgamation or federation'.

The promoters and founders of Trade [*sic*] Union Congresses had no such ambition [wrote George Howell, the first effective secretary of the Parliamentary Committee]. Their object was to confer annually, upon urgent questions affecting workmen and labour associations, whether the result of legislation or otherwise. It was not proposed to interfere in the legitimate work of trade unions, their organisation, mode of management, constitution, rules, or other matters of internal economy, but to promote co-operation in respect of general questions affecting labour, and to watch over its interests in Parliament.[2]

The main duty of the Parliamentary Committee was, therefore, to arrange for the lobbying of Ministers and Members of Parliament to obtain the concessions which Congress demanded. By a process of logical extension, the Committee also gave what assistance it could to individual unions, like those of the miners and cotton operatives, pursuing acceptable political objectives. With such limited aims, the calls of Congress on union funds were almost as modest as those of the trades councils.

Anything more ambitious would have created great difficulties; but Congress avoided not only any attempt at strike insurance but also any interference in the trade policy of its constituent unions. Trade policy had

---

[1] Howell, George (1833–1910). Member, Operative Bricklayers. Secretary, London Trades Council, 1861–2. Secretary, Reform League, 1864–9. Parliamentary Committee, Trades Union Congress, 1869–75; secretary, 1871–5. M.P., 1885–95.

[2] *Labour Legislation, Labour Movements and Labour Leaders*, vol. i, 1905, p. 177.

been one of the issues in the conflict between Potter and the Junta, who regarded him as a 'strike jobber'. However, this was largely a clash of personalities, the only difference of principle being that Potter stood for the local autonomy of the declining trade clubs against the centralizing tendencies of the amalgamated societies represented by the Junta. This was a difference of some significance, but it was dwarfed in importance by the fundamental divergence between the craft societies and coal, cotton, and iron.

Once they were firmly established, the amalgamated societies could enforce their trade policies with very few large strikes. Unions in coal, cotton, and iron, however, had to face organized groups of employers, some of which were already settling wages and conditions over wide sections of their industries. These unions were therefore almost inevitably driven into extensive strikes. According to the imperfect records at our disposal[1] there were eighteen stoppages between 1817 and 1889 in which more than one million 'working days'[2] were lost. Nine of these were in mining, four in cotton, three in iron, and one in chain-making. Only one, among shipbuilding trades on the Clyde, affected any of the major craft societies; but the rapid fluctuations of activity in the shipyards posed problems for the Boilermakers which other societies did not share. This contrast in trade policy was rooted in the varied conditions of different industries, and cannot be seen in such simple terms as a clash between provincial militants and the 'servile generation' of leaders of the amalgamated societies.[3]

The Law, Parliament, and Public Opinion

The development of trade union law during the nineteenth century passed through three distinct phases. From 1800 to 1824 trade unions were undoubtedly illegal; from 1825 to 1875 the legality of many of their activities was at least doubtful and precarious; but from 1875 until the nineties the unions appeared to have won the legal status and rights that they desired.

In the first quarter of the century trade unions were doubly and trebly illegal. They were held by the courts to be criminal conspiracies 'in restraint of trade' at common law, and they were made expressly illegal by the Combination Acts of 1799 and 1800. There were also statutory prohibitions of combinations in particular trades. In addition, regional or national

[1] See p. 55, footnote 1.
[2] A total reached by multiplying the number of strikers by the number of working days they were on strike.
[3] The description is R. W. Postgate's (*The Builders' History*, 1923, pp. 181–2). G. D. H. Cole, on the other hand, argues that the pacifism of the craft unions has been exaggerated. 'The late 1860's and the early 1870's were in fact a period of very considerable Trade Union militancy, which extended even to the industries covered by the Amalgamated Societies' (loc. cit.).

unions might well have been held to be illegal under the Unlawful Societies Act of 1799. Finally, many actions of trade unionists taken in compliance with union decisions might be held to be punishable offences under the law of Master and Servant—for example, going on strike without completing commissioned piecework.

The Combination Acts were repealed in 1824, and the repealing Act was itself amended during the following year. Trade unions were now protected from actions for criminal conspiracy so long as they limited themselves to the determination of wages and hours, and in particular so long as they and their members avoided certain specified offences, namely violence, threats, intimidation, molestation, and obstruction. This new-found legality was shaken but not seriously affected by the conviction of the Tolpuddle labourers in 1834 under statutes of 1797 and 1819 prohibiting the administration of illegal oaths. More serious was the continued use by employers of the law of Master and Servant to hinder trade union activities, and during the forties and fifties this became the main complaint of unions against the law. In 1867, however, the Master and Servant Act removed some of the disparities between employers and workers in proceedings for breach of contract.

As the unions grew in size and their benefit funds increased, the need for those funds to be protected against embezzlement by their own officers also increased. In other words, the unions now wanted not only freedom from legal restraint but legal protection as well. For a time they thought that registration under successive Friendly Societies Acts might give them what they required. In the case of *Hornby* v. *Close* in 1867, however, it was held that since the unions, despite express legalization of certain limited trade functions in 1825, were still 'in restraint of trade', they were unlawful associations which could not claim protection for their funds.

An opportunity to revise the law came almost at once with the appointment of a Royal Commission to inquire into 'the Organization and Rules of Trade Unions and Other Associations'. The occasion of its appointment in 1867 was a public outcry over criminal offences committed by Sheffield trade unionists in their efforts to enforce union decisions, and initially it appeared that the outcome might well be stricter control over the unions. The leaders of the amalgamated societies, however, were able to monopolize the submission of trade union evidence to the Commission; and, with Applegarth as their main witness, they skilfully presented the societies as responsible bodies, reluctant to strike and free from restrictive practices.

In depicting trade unions as valuable institutions, the Junta received powerful and intelligent support from a group of middle-class allies, notably their legal advisers, Frederic Harrison and Thomas Hughes, both of whom were members of the Commission. Two reports were issued. The Majority Report was 'an inconclusive and somewhat inconsistent document',[1] which saw little value in trade unions for society in general, or even for the workers themselves, but argued for some legal protection of organizations whose rules were free from such restrictive clauses as those limiting the number of apprentices and the use of machinery, or prohibiting piecework and subcontracting. It was, however, the Minority Report, signed by Harrison, Hughes, and the chairman, the Earl of Lichfield, which formed the basis of the Trade Union Act introduced by Gladstone's government in 1871.

Since some judges held that the unions, outside the narrow range of activity permitted by the 1825 Act, were still liable to prosecution as criminal conspiracies at common law, the 1871 Act laid down that union members were not liable to such prosecution on the ground of being 'in restraint of trade'. Secondly, to dispose of the precedent in *Hornby* v. *Close*, the Act provided that the agreements and trusts of a trade union were not to be considered void or voidable on that ground. Thirdly, and it was here that Harrison's advice proved particularly useful, the Act prohibited legal action to enforce internal agreements, such as those concerning the payment of subscriptions and benefits, or agreements between unions. Trade unions, in fact, were to have the protection of the law, but to be free from its interference in their internal affairs. Fourthly, the Act provided that unions might register with the Registrar of Friendly Societies. Any union doing so would be subject to supervision by the Registrar on such points as the conformity of its rules with the law; but in return it would obtain certain advantages in the management of its property and in taking legal proceedings.

Unfortunately for the unions, this statute was coupled with the Criminal Law Amendment Act, which codified the provisions of previous legislation against the coercing of employers and workers by violence, threats, intimidation, molestation, or obstruction. The courts soon showed that they were willing to put a wide interpretation on these words, and to continue to apply the doctrine of criminal conspiracy to almost any concerted action to which such terms could be held to apply, even discerning a conspiracy to intimidate an employer in a threat to strike.

The unions reacted with a vigorous agitation, led by the new Parliamentary Committee of the Trades Union Congress, and Disraeli's government met their demands in the Conspiracy and Protection of Property Act, 1875. This Act laid down that acts done 'by two or more persons . . . in contemplation or furtherance of a trade dispute' were not liable to prosecution as criminal conspiracies. Henceforth such actions were criminal only if they would have been crimes had they been committed by individuals.[2] Omitting some of the vague language of the Criminal Law

---

[1] Webbs, *History*, p. 269.
[2] The Act did, however, make it a criminal offence for a worker employed in the public

Amendment Act, it tried to define more clearly what was permissible in a trade dispute, and what prohibited—particularly in relation to picketing. While penalizing violence, intimidation, hiding a man's tools, 'persistently following', and 'watching and besetting', it expressly declared that 'attending at or near' a house or place of work 'in order merely to obtain or communicate information', should not be deemed as 'watching or besetting'.

As a consequence of this legislation and the Trade Union Act Amendment Act of 1876,[1] the unions seemed to have secured a satisfactory legal status by obtaining protection where they most needed it. At the same time this status fell far short of the full legal personality which is possessed by corporate bodies. In part, this was because of the express exclusion of the courts from some aspects of union affairs, which was the result of Harrison's advice and the unions' desire 'to have as little to do with the Law Courts as possible'.[2] But equally important was the fact that the question of the power of the unions to sue and be sued had never arisen.

This power is possessed by corporate bodies and was to become a matter of prime importance to the unions twenty-five years later. But it had not 'engaged the attention of the Commissioners [of 1867]', and 'as the [1871] Bill passed through Parliament the question of liability for tort was not raised'.[2] Thus the object of the 1871 Act

appears to have been, while freeing Trade Unions from the last remains of their former character of criminal conspiracies, and giving full protection to their property, (1) to prevent them from having any legal rights against their members, or their members against them; and next (2) to prevent their entering into any legally enforceable contracts as bodies with each other or with outside individuals, except with regard to the management of their own funds and real estate.[3]

'These', commented the Webbs, 'were assumed to be all the cases that could arise.'[4]

This story of legal emancipation is sometimes written as if the unions depended on the law for their existence, and had wrested every element of their legalization from an unwilling and hostile legislature, dominated by a class implacably opposed to trade unionism. Both these suppositions are incorrect.

Trade unions continued to exist while the Combination Acts remained in force. It was usually left to employers to instigate proceedings, and they

supply of gas or water to break his contract in circumstances which made it probable that the public would be deprived of their supply.

[1] The object of this Act 'was to tidy up the loose ends left by the 1871 Act, which five years of experience had brought to light'. Apart from amending the legal definition of a trade union, it made no fundamental changes (N. A. Citrine, *Trade Union Law*, 1950, p. 238).

[2] *Report of the Royal Commission on Trade Disputes and Trade Combinations*, Cd. 2825, 1906, p. 5.

[3] *Royal Commission on Labour*, C–7421, 1894, p. 116.   [4] *History*, p. 602, footnote.

were often unwilling to do so. More than one of the great societies of later years—the Ironfounders, and some of the societies which afterwards joined in the Amalgamated Society of Engineers—were established during the period. The upsurge in trade union membership of the fifties and sixties was not prevented by the many legal disabilities under which the unions then suffered. This phase of growth reached its peak in 1874 when the Criminal Law Amendment Act was still in force, whereas complete emancipation (as it appeared) in 1875 was followed by many years of decline in trade union membership and power.

After the repeal of the Combination Acts hostile employers relied mainly on the 'document',[1] which was widely and successfully used against trade unionists during the thirties. Even at this time, however, there remained employers who thought they had more to gain from dealing with unions than from trying to suppress them. As the number of such men grew during the third quarter of the century, embracing not only master craftsmen and cotton manufacturers, who had generally come together to resist union pressure, but also ironmasters and some coal-owners, whose organizations often preceded the unions and at first tried to prevent their establishment, along with employers in a number of lesser industries, the basis of trade unionism was assured.

Employers' attitudes were, of course, affected by the views of Parliament and by public opinion, and in turn reacted upon them. After 1824 Parliament did not seriously entertain the possibility of further attempts to suppress the unions. During and immediately after the Napoleonic Wars, it had been widely held that all but the most obviously innocent working-class organizations were necessarily Jacobin and subversive in tendency, and Parliament had enacted accordingly. The subsequent change in outlook was clearly demonstrated by the failure to revive such repressive legislation at the time of the trade union upheaval of 1831–4, though it is true that a surviving statute was turned to useful account in the Tolpuddle case.

Parliamentary reform gradually added to the strength of business interests in the House; and many business men were influenced by the economic doctrines of the day which taught that combination could have no effect on wages, or that whatever effect it had must be harmful. The passing of successive Factory Acts shows, however, that business men in politics were not united in their acceptance of the teachings of the dismal science, or in opposition to trade union demands. But to admit in practice a right to combine did not remove all the difficulties either of Parliament or of the thoughtful layman. Freedom of association might be good; yet restraint of trade was certainly bad, both in economic theory and at law. Workers should be free to organize, but their organizations might come to

[1] See p. 16.

tyrannize over them; by strikes and restrictive practices they might injure the industries which provided their livelihood, and that of their employers, and inflict harm upon the public.[1]

Could freedom of association, therefore, be reconciled with restraints on the possibly evil consequences of combination; and how could any reconciliation be embodied in the law? Given the difficulty of answering these questions it is understandable that the extension of freedom was slow and grudging; that Parliament was content not to try to unravel complex legal problems until it was forced to do so; and that when, in 1871, they made large concessions, their first thought was to accompany them by a strengthening of what appeared to be necessary restraints against their misuse.

Trade Unions and Politics

While the unions were pressing for these reforms of their legal status they employed political tactics and developed political values which were to last them for some time to come. The successful campaign from 1867 to 1875 gave the movement a new unity, expressed in the establishment of the Trades Union Congress, and revealed the possibilities of political action provided that the unions accepted the limits within which they had to work. Despite the extension of the franchise in 1867 it was still largely true that since they were 'powerless to coerce or even to intimidate the governing class, they could win only by persuasion'.[2] In a generation which set a high price on respectability and was much influenced by the doctrines of *laissez-faire*, it was important that the Royal Commission should be induced to regard the unions as reputable institutions, and that their leading adviser should emphasize that what they wanted was 'the removal of the mischievous meddling of the past',[3] and not special privileges or protection.

Early in the century, many of the unions had strict rules against any form of political action, partly at least because they feared that such activities might make them liable to prosecution;[4] and some union leaders were

---

[1] When the National Federation of Associated Employers of Labour was founded in 1873, as the employers' response to the campaign of the unions for the repeal of the Criminal Law Amendment Act, its prime purpose, in view of 'the far-reaching, but openly avowed designs' of the unions, was announced as being 'to resist the designs so far as they are hostile to the interests of the employers, the freedom of the non-unionist operatives, and the well-being of the community' (Howell, *Labour Legislation*, vol. ii, p. 312).

[2] Webbs, *History*, p. 293.   [3] Frederic Harrison, quoted ibid., p. 295.

[4] James Ridgway, *The Character, Object, and Effects of Trades' Unions, with some remarks on the Law concerning them*, 1834, pp. 90–91. The rules of 'one of the most extensive Unions in Yorkshire' enjoined its members to 'pay a due obedience to the laws, and respect to the Government of our country, and to live as peaceable subjects, but never to disturb or embroil the Lodge with your particular opinion of state affairs'. The author of the pamphlet thought it unlikely that the unions 'would ever assume any strong political character, so long as the law on this subject remains in its present state, since such a change would instantly render them liable to the severe penalties of the 57 Geo. III c. 19'—the Seditious Meetings Act of 1817.

attracted by the essentially anti-political doctrines of Robert Owen. Nevertheless, there were men like Hepburn of the miners and Doherty of the spinners who took part in the campaign for parliamentary reform in 1832; and the cotton unions were always active in agitating for a Ten Hours bill.[1] Most unions as such stood apart from Chartism, however. For a moment during the Plug Riots of 1842 it looked as though some might be drawn into striking for the Charter;[2] but the peak years of the movement between 1837 and 1842 were a period of depression which saw the nadir of union fortunes as 'the document' did its work in so many industries.

By 1845 there had been a slight recovery, and a representative group of trade unionists defined their attitude to politics. In a report to the conference of the National Association of United Trades, the London Committee of Trade Delegates insisted that there should be a clear separation between trade matters and politics, and 'earnestly recommended . . . that no proposition of a political nature, beyond what has been already alluded to, should be introduced'. The exception was 'to vindicate the rights of labour' by opposing 'the tyranny of any legislative enactments to coerce trade societies'.[3] The Association soon passed into obscurity; and, apart from the continued interest of the coal and cotton unions in the improvement of their conditions by legislation, little was done to fulfil the promise of pressure-group activity until the sixties.

By this time the unions were beginning to venture outside the narrow limits laid down in 1845. The London leaders were the principal participants in the Reform League, whose strength in the provinces also came from the unions; and the League's campaign contributed to the passing of the second Reform Act in 1867. At the same time, several of them took part in the formation of the first International Working Men's Association in 1864, despite the domination of the organization by Marx and other continental revolutionaries. In both cases, self-interest provides only a partial explanation of their actions.

It is true that votes for working men would increase the influence of the unions, and that the International might help to prevent foreign workers from being brought over to intervene in disputes.[4] But the unions not only relied on the Radicals to supply parliamentary spokesmen for their grievances, they also shared their political creed; and the two main Radical preoccupations of the time were the democratization of the machinery of government and sympathy with European nationalism. The attitude of the London workers to continental autocracy was demonstrated by the enthusiastic reception given to men like Garibaldi. Similarly, the

---

[1] Ibid., p. 28. The Lancashire spinners included a levy for the 'Time Bill' in their union contributions (ibid., p. 25).   [2] Jefferys, op. cit., p. 22.   [3] Webbs, *History*, pp. 188–9.
[4] Henry Collins, *England and the First International, 1864–1872*, D.Phil. thesis, Oxford, 1959. The International was permitted in return to raise funds in Britain for continental strikers.

agitation for the franchise was a matter of asserting the rights of working men against class rule, on which union leaders could properly spend time and energy.

Except for the isolated instance of William Newton of the Engineers, who had stood for Tower Hamlets in 1852, the first trade union candidates appeared at the election of 1868. In addition to Newton, these were William Cremer of the Carpenters and Joiners and George Howell of the Bricklayers, who had also been secretary of the Reform League. Lacking adequate preparation, all three were defeated, though they received some Liberal support, notably (if secretly) from party headquarters. In the following year an attempt was made to create a more effective and representative organization, and the Labour Representation League was launched with the support of most sections of the trade union movement.

Stating that 'its principal duty will be to secure the return to Parliament of qualified working men', the League at first proposed to organize 'working-men's votes without reference to their opinions or party bias; its aim being to organize fully the strength of the operative classes as an electoral power, so that, when necessary, it may be brought to bear, with effect, on any important political, social or industrial question in the issue of which their interests are involved'.[1] Before long, however, its party affiliation was apparent, and by 1875 the League was declaring that 'we have ever sought to be allied to the great Liberal Party, to which we, by conviction, belong'.[2]

Up to 1874 the refusal of Gladstone's government to repeal the Criminal Law Amendment Act had prevented the full alliance with the Liberals towards which most of the union leaders were impelled by their Radical predilections and connexions. Thereafter, despite Disraeli's satisfaction of their immediate demands and the continued blandishments of the Conservatives, they took their place among the groups that made up the Liberal Party; but in 'forming, as it were, the tail of the "Great Liberal Party"',[3] the Lib-Labs retained some independence and continued to work for trade union representation. When John Bright accused the League of 'disorganising the party' in 1874 by encouraging working-class candidates, Henry Broadhurst[4] retorted that in view of the attitude of many Liberals 'we are the aggrieved party';[5] and in Bright's own constituency of Birming-

---

[1] Prospectus of the League, quoted in G. D. H. Cole, *British Working Class Politics, 1832–1914*, 1941, p. 50.

[2] Ibid., p. 72.

[3] Engels in the *Labour Standard*, 23 July 1881, reprinted in F. Engels, *The British Labour Movement*, 1934, p. 33.

[4] Broadhurst, Henry, P.C. (1840–1911). Member, Operative Stonemasons' Society. Parliamentary Committee, Trades Union Congress, 1874–90, 1893–5; secretary, 1875–86, 1886–90. M.P., 1880–92, 1894–1906. Under-Secretary to the Home Office, 1886. Member of Royal Commission on the Aged Poor, 1892–5.

[5] Henry Pelling, *Origins of the Labour Party, 1880–1900*, 1954, pp. 3–4. Broadhurst had

ham so staunch a Lib-Lab as W. J. Davis[1] of the Brassworkers insisted upon running in local elections as 'the Labour candidate, pure and simple', and managed to maintain his 'Labour Association' as 'an independent political force'.[2]

From Birmingham came Joseph Chamberlain's National Liberal Federation in 1877. For all its progressive policy and democratic organization, the Federation was under the control of provincial business men, who were anxious to secure working-class votes but reluctant to accept working-class representation. Its advent, therefore, did little to further the parliamentary ambitions of the unions. Indeed, both George Howell and Lloyd Jones regarded the Federation as a potential menace, since, in Jones's words, the 'borough caucuses would work admirably as traps in which to shut up the working men of the country, allowing them only such political action as their masters and managers may permit'.[3]

The return of trade unionists to Parliament required three things: a constituency with a considerable working-class vote; finance both for the election campaign and to maintain a successful candidate; and, at least until they decided to form their own party, arrangements with the existing parties to adopt a trade union candidate or to withdraw their candidates in his favour. After the Reform Act of 1884 the first condition was best fulfilled in some London constituencies and in the mining communities, especially in the North-east. The second could be provided only by the larger unions, who were no more willing to contribute to a common electoral effort than to be generous in their subscriptions to the Trades Union Congress. The Labour Representation League could offer them no financial inducement and had scant resources to assist the smaller unions. Finally, until the twentieth century, the state of party organization required that negotiations to find trade union candidates a constituency had to be conducted primarily on a local basis, and this was never easy.

The League was virtually dead when its secretary, Henry Broadhurst, was elected to Parliament in 1880; and the return in 1874 of two miners' candidates, Alexander Macdonald and Thomas Burt, both without Liberal opposition, had already shown that individual unions could be more effective in achieving parliamentary representation than a federal body. Meanwhile the organization of trade union opinion was taken over by the new Trades Union Congress and its Parliamentary Committee, of which

some grounds for complaint. In 1874 at least eight of the twelve trade union candidates were opposed by official Liberals.

[1] Davis, W. J. (1848–1923). General secretary, National Society of Amalgamated Brassworkers, later National Society of Metal Mechanics, 1872–83, 1889–1920. Factory Inspector, 1883–9. Parliamentary Committee, Trades Union Congress, 1881–3, 1896–1902, 1903–20. Author, *The British Trades Union Congress: History and Recollections*, 1910 (vol. i) and 1916 (vol. ii).

[2] W. A. Dalley, *The Life Story of W. J. Davis*, 1914, pp. 47–54.

[3] Henry Pelling, *America and the British Left*, 1956, p. 46.

Broadhurst had been secretary since 1875. Both Congress and the Committee could speak with far greater authority for the unions than could the League.[1]

During the years from 1871 to 1880 the political activity of the unions was rewarded by a series of important measures, despite their very limited parliamentary representation. Besides the Acts defining the legal status of trade unions, there was an Employers and Workmen Act which at last provided reasonable equality of treatment in cases of breach of contract; two Factory Acts, a Mines Act and two Merchant Shipping Acts; and in 1880 an Employers' Liability Act which was the first attempt to give the worker a fair claim against his employer for damages arising out of accidents at work. Thereafter, for a period of almost ten years, the unions could claim few legislative gains in the industrial field, though the democratization of the machinery of government went on apace, through the Corrupt Practices Act of 1883, the extension of the franchise to the rural householder in 1884, the great redistribution of seats a year later, and the County Councils Act of 1888.

Indeed, the most obvious parliamentary gain of the eighties was an increase in trade union representation. It is not easy to produce a satisfactory definition of a trade union Member of Parliament, but the increase was at least from three in 1880 (or two in 1881) to nine in 1885 and six in 1886. By more generous standards the totals were eleven in 1885 and eight in 1886.[2] These results were again achieved mainly by individual unions, but by 1886 the Trades Union Congress was ready to call into being a new organization, the Labour Electoral Committee (subsequently the Labour Electoral Association). Though attempts were made at later congresses to convert it into something like a political party, it was endowed with much the same powers and functions as the defunct Labour Representation League, and there was no reason to suppose that it could achieve much more than the League.

Meanwhile the socialist revival had begun with the formation of the Social Democratic Federation in 1884, which also saw the foundation of the Fabian Society. The middle-class leaders of these diminutive bodies were highly critical of the apparent limitations placed upon working-class political activity by the beliefs and affiliations of trade union leaders. Historians have generally followed the Webbs in accepting the socialist criticisms. The Webbs (who were, of course, interested participants) made

[1] In their Report of 1875, however, the Parliamentary Committee had claimed that after the repeal of the Criminal Law Amendment Act 'the work of emancipation is full and complete'; and, according to W. J. Davis, their secretary 'Mr. Howell thought the legislation with respect to Trade Unions was then so perfect that the natural time had run for the existence of Trade Union Congresses so far as Parliamentary action was concerned . . . but the perspicacity of other leaders knew that there was great work yet to be done' (op. cit., vol. i, p. 52).

[2] See p. 285.

two main complaints against the men whom they called the 'Front Bench' of the Trades Union Congress. The first was that they were tied to the Liberal Party, and the second that their political programme fell short even of the demands of the more extreme bourgeois Radicals of the day, Joseph Chamberlain (until 1886) and Sir Charles Dilke.[1]

The first charge is largely correct. The trade union Members shared the outlook of the Radical wing of the Liberal Party, and during the eighties they were increasingly drawn into the organization of the party. But this is a criticism of the Lib-Labs only if their allegiance prevented them from following policies which would have yielded greater benefits to the working class in general, and to their own members in particular. The measures supported by Congress during the eighties admittedly did not add up to an imposing programme of social reform, and there was nothing to equal the stir caused by Chamberlain's Unauthorized Programme of 1885 which, said the Webbs, 'found no echo in the official programme of the Trade Union world'.[2]

But except where it overlapped with their demands for political reform this Programme was largely irrelevant to the problems of the unions. Much was said about the 'ransom' that property should pay, about the acquisition of land by local authorities, about small-holdings, and about housing. Yet its proposals were only precise when concerned with rural problems,[3] and the unions represented industrial workers almost exclusively. The agricultural worker was promised 'three acres and a cow'; but, as Labouchere told Chamberlain, there was no 'urban cow'.[4] And there was certainly nothing in the Programme which seemed to have much bearing on the problem of unemployment, though in the decade from 1878 to 1887 the proportion of union members unemployed exceeded 5 per cent. in seven years and 7 per cent. in five.

The socialists, of course, did offer remedies for unemployment—municipal enterprise and nationalization. To the Webbs it seemed that the union leaders were blind not to appreciate the virtues of these suggestions; but to the latter they appeared not only contrary to the philosophy which they had embraced but also empty and impractical. For how could municipal ownership and nationalization raise wages and put men to work?

The socialists had another proposal as a palliative for unemployment—the limitation of the working day to eight hours by statute. The principle

---

[1] Webbs, *History*, chapter 7.

[2] Ibid., pp. 373–4. The Webbs apparently ignored the fact that Broadhurst, the leader of 'the old gang', was sufficiently well disposed towards Chamberlainite Radicalism to be welcomed as a candidate for a Birmingham constituency, Bordesley, in 1885, and to be a frequent speaker for the National Liberal Federation.

[3] 'The Radical today was the "Artful Dodger" who went up and down this country telling the people to take hold of the landlord thief, but to let the greater thief, the capitalist, go scot-free' (J. E. Williams, of the Social Democratic Federation, speaking at the Industrial Remuneration Conference, 1885, *Report*, p. 398).

[4] A. Thorold, *Henry Labouchere*, 1913, p. 245.

of work-sharing, however, was by no means novel. Robert Owen had put it forward; short-time working was well known in Lancashire; and limitation of output had long been debated and frequently attempted in the coalfields. These methods did not prevent heavy unemployment in coal and cotton. Burt and Crawford, moreover, had consistently opposed restriction of output as likely to lead to a loss of markets and to embitter relations with the owners. Many craftsmen feared that the statutory control of conditions of labour would undermine craft controls, weaken their societies, and thus lead to a worsening of the craftsman's lot. In good years a reduction in hours seemed more likely to cut earnings than to spread employment.

Proceedings in Congress during the depression reveal no clear-cut division between the new socialists and an 'old gang' hopelessly bound to doctrines of non-interference. From 1885 to 1887 three presidential addresses in succession stressed the shortcomings of capitalism, the need for state intervention to mitigate unemployment, and the importance of both skilled and unskilled workers combining to obtain more trade union representation in order to promote such intervention. The third speaker, Bevan of the Carpenters and Joiners, may have been a socialist; but T. R. Threlfall, secretary of the Labour Electoral Association, and Fred Maddison were undoubtedly Lib-Labs.[1] All three speeches were well received; for, as among the Boot and Shoe Operatives, there were emerging men 'who, less violently opposed to the existing social and economic structure than [the socialists], nevertheless wanted government action taken to maintain full employment, eliminate the trade cycle, and reduce inequalities of wealth'.[2]

Even leaders of the establishment shared the mood. In his *Annual Report* for 1886 Robert Knight of the Boilermakers presented a harrowing picture of the sufferings of the unemployed, concluding that 'there must be something wrong in a system which effects such unequal distribution of the wealth created by labour'. And the same year James Mawdsley of the Cotton Spinners, speaking as chairman of the Parliamentary Committee at the International Congress in Paris, admitted that 'he did not understand their Socialism; he had not studied it as perhaps he ought to have done'; but, 'seeing that there was a much larger number of unemployed, the question naturally presented itself as to whether there was any chance of improvement. He considered there was no chance of improvement so long as the present state of society continued to exist'.[3]

[1] In Threlfall's view 'there is a stronger moral activity amongst the masses, a greater restlessness under social wrongs, a more searching desire to get to the primary causes of our troubles and a louder cry for domestic reforms than has ever been heard before'. For Bevan 'state interference has assisted wealth, monopoly, and privilege long enough. Let it now be used to help the poor, the down-trodden, and the ill-paid and overworked toilers. . . . Socialism has lost its terrors for us. We recognise our most serious evils in the unrestrained, unscrupulous and remorseless forces of capitalism' (Trades Union Congress, *Annual Reports*, 1885 and 1887).

[2] Alan Fox, *A History of the National Union of Boot and Shoe Operatives, 1874–1957*, 1958, pp. 197–8.   [3] Webbs, *History*, pp. 378–9.

2

The New Unionism and the First Counter-attack

1889

THE 'new unionism' stands out as one of the most colourful and baffling phenomena in British trade union history; and a detailed account of the origins and development of the so-called 'new unions' is a necessary prelude to any explanation of its nature. The symbol of the new unionism was the 'Great Dock Strike' of 1889, and as a symbol the strike of the London dockers has won renown out of proportion to its size. Almost 700,000 working days were lost, and in these terms the dispute was the biggest of the year; but this was because in 1889, as in most other years of expanding trade, there were no really large and protracted strikes. The next nine years were to see eleven more substantial stoppages, the greatest of which, the miners' lock-out of 1893, lasted nearly four times as long as the 'Great Dock Strike', and cost thirty times as many working days. Moreover, according to the Labour Correspondent of the Board of Trade, two other disputes of 1889, both in the shipping industry, may have surpassed the dock strike in terms of the number of workers directly involved.[1]

In January and again in June a series of strikes by seamen of the National Amalgamated Union of Sailors and Firemen closed most of the ports, except for London and the South Coast. Their secretary, Havelock Wilson,[2] had previously been an active member of the North of England Sailors' and Seagoing Firemen's Union, a local body founded in 1879 which remained confined to the North-east. Having decided that a wider association was needed, Wilson tried unsuccessfully to persuade his colleagues to undertake the task.[3] Then, with the advice of the miners'

[1] *Report on the Strikes and Lockouts of 1889*, C–6176, 1890. This was only the second of such annual reports, however, and it falls below the standard of accuracy later attained through fuller coverage by a network of local correspondents, many of them trade union officers. The total of those involved in the dock strike is stated to have been 28,160, as compared with 40,000 in each of the shipping disputes. Both these figures are suspect, and the second is almost certainly too high. Seamen's strikes rarely affect large numbers unless they are prolonged, for at any one time the majority of sailors are at sea and thus unable to take part.

[2] Wilson, Joseph Havelock (1858–1929). General secretary, National Amalgamated Union of Sailors and Firemen, 1887–94; president, 1895–1929 (union later becoming the National Union of Seamen). Parliamentary Committee, Trades Union Congress, 1889–98, 1918–19. M.P. 1892–1900, 1906–10, 1918–22.

[3] J. Havelock Wilson, *My Stormy Voyage Through Life*, vol. i, 1925, chapter xiv.

leaders and the officers of other established societies on Tyneside, he drew up a constitution for a national seamen's union and set up his own in 1887. Twelve months later Wilson was venturing beyond the North-east into Glasgow and Liverpool, and within a matter of weeks his organization had leapt into prominence.

'So strong had the new union become at the beginning of 1889', wrote the Labour Correspondent, 'that in January and February extensive strikes for an advance of wages were entered upon in most of the chief ports of the kingdom.'[1] Further strikes by members of the union in June and July, all of them brief, were of the same magnitude and extent. The Seamen claimed success 'in all ports except Liverpool, but even there wages in cargo boats have been raised 30 per cent., although in the case of the Atlantic liners the union was defeated by a combination of 16 of the largest companies.' For many owners, however, mounting prosperity provided an incentive to make concessions, since 'as regards both outward and homeward freights, 1889 was the record year'.[2]

Wilson afterwards asserted that he had tried to prevent the stoppage at Liverpool,[3] where the union's difficulties were due to the employers' introduction of substitute or 'blackleg' labour.[4] In May there had already been a strike in Liverpool when firemen refused to sail with non-unionists, and contemporary accounts record frequent battles, here and elsewhere, between strikers and the 'rats', or blacklegs. 'At Liverpool', for example, 'the sailors and firemen stormed the Sailors' Home, where the masters were enlisting rats, and drove them from their holes'; and, 'despite the extra force of police, they have charged and routed a large number of rats'.[5]

When sailors strike, dock workers are out of a job; and strikes in the docks can make it impossible for ships to sail. If they carry substitute crews, this is clearly to the advantage of a seamen's union. It is therefore hardly surprising that the dramatic advent of the Seamen led not only to widespread organization among the dockers, but also to contact between the leaders of both groups. On a visit to Glasgow Wilson met two Irishmen, Edward McHugh and Richard McGhee,[6] who had established the National Union of Dock Labourers there in February 1889, six months before the London dock strike.[7] From Scotland the union spread to

---

[1] *Report on the Strikes and Lockouts of 1889*, C–6176, 1890, p. 4.

[2] A. W. Kirkaldy, *British Shipping, Its History, Organisation and Importance*, 1919, appendix xvi. Average homeward freight rates had risen from 94 in 1887 to 124 in 1889 (1900 = 100).

[3] *Royal Commission on Labour*, C–6708–V, 1892, Q. 9266.

[4] Ibid., C–6795–V, 1892, Qs. 13256–7.

[5] *Commonweal*, 22 June 1889.

[6] McHugh was a compositor by trade who had spent some time in America. He helped to found the American Longshoremen's Union, a forerunner of the present International Longshoremen's Association. McGhee, the son of an Ulster Protestant, was a member of the Amalgamated Society of Engineers before becoming a commercial traveller. Both were Henry Georgeites.   [7] *Report of Executive for Year Ending 30 June 1891.*

Liverpool and other ports in the North-west, winning a number of concessions; and during the seamen's strike of June 1889 the Glasgow dockers stopped work partly for their own demands and partly in support of the seamen.[1]

On Tyneside there already existed a National Labour Federation which was in some ways a precursor of the 'new unionism';[2] but Wilson found the dockers eager to join his sailors and firemen. He had to tell them 'that whilst I understood the seamen's question I did not understand the dockers' affairs, and it would involve so much work that I could not make a success either for one or the other. Nevertheless, I helped to establish the National Union of Labour.'[3] This was probably the Tyneside and National Labour Union, subsequently the National Amalgamated Union of Labour. Other sponsors were Thomas Burt, the Liberal leader of the Northumberland miners who had been one of Wilson's own advisers, and Dr. Robert Spence Watson, a well-known local philanthropist, historian of the National Liberal Federation, and its president from 1890 to 1901.[4]

By August 1889, however, the Seamen were still not established in London, and there is no record of any connexion between the union and the dock strike. Here the inspiration came from another source, the gas-workers, led by Will Thorne,[5] a stoker at the Beckton works. A member of the Social Democratic Federation and of Ben Tillett's[6] Tea Operatives' and General Labourers' Association, founded in 1887, Thorne had already taken part in abortive attempts to organize the London gasworkers. Early in 1889 improving trade and the introduction of a mechanical device, the 'iron man', gave him a fresh opportunity. In March he launched the National Union of Gasworkers and General Labourers at a public meeting in Canning Town. The provisional committee based on Beckton made the eight-hour day their prime objective, and received the support of a number of trade union members of the Social Democratic Federation

[1] *Commonweal*, 15 June 1889.   [2] See p. 65.

[3] J. H. Wilson, op. cit., p. 139.

[4] Watson, an arbitrator much in demand in coal, iron and steel, and on the railways, was an advocate of the general adoption of the conciliation procedures which 'had worked so well' in the North-east (Percy Corder, *Robert Spence Watson*, 1914, p. 169). His advice to new unions was to avoid 'the professional agitator, who must keep his position by promoting discord rather than peace'. He also warned them that 'the system of keeping accounts must be thoroughly thought out . . . and the scale of benefits submitted to very careful actuarial calculation' (ibid., p. 181).

[5] Thorne, Will, P.C. (1857–1946). General secretary, National Union of Gasworkers and General Labourers, later National Union of General Workers, later National Union of General and Municipal Workers, 1889–1934. Parliamentary Committee, later General Council, Trades Union Congress, 1894–1934. M.P., 1906–45.

[6] Tillett, Ben (1860–1943). General secretary, Tea Operatives' and General Labourers' Association, later Dock, Wharf, Riverside and General Labourers' Union, 1887–1921. Political secretary, Transport and General Workers' Union, 1922–30. Parliamentary Committee, Trades Union Congress, 1892–5; General Council, 1921–31. Executive Committee, Labour Party, 1901–2. M.P., 1917–24, 1929–31.

(including Tom Mann,[1] John Burns,[2] Harry Quelch, and Herbert Burrows) in extending the new organization.[3]

Success came swiftly. In June the major London companies, led by the Gas Light and Coke Company and the South Metropolitan Gas Company, acceded to petitions from their stokers for a change from two twelve-hour to three eight-hour shifts without loss of pay.[4] Subsequently, George Livesey,[5] chairman of the South Metropolitan, tried to minimize the significance of this concession, pointing out that the eight-hour day had long prevailed in Liverpool and claiming that he himself had 'suggested it to our own workmen in 1887 and 1888'.[6] But almost at once relations between the men and the companies developed from 'petition' and 'concession' to collective bargaining. On 26 June Thorne was elected first secretary of the union, and by the end of July sixty branches had been established.

Livesey was soon driven to accept changes which he was by no means ready to concede. On 4 September the union gave notice of its intention to enforce Rule 16, which required shop stewards to ensure that all new hands became members before starting work;[7] and later in the month Livesey had to reinstate a stoker dismissed for using 'unfair means' to recruit to the union.[8] On 20 September he signed an undertaking that 'members of the Gas Workers' Union shall not in consequence of such membership, and so long as they faithfully perform their duty, be intimidated or interfered with by any of the officers or foremen of the Company', and added a verbal agreement that 'non-union men and union men cannot

[1] Mann, Tom (1856–1941). Member, Amalgamated Society of Engineers. Held a number of trade union offices, prominent among them the full-time presidency of the Dock, Wharf, Riverside and General Labourers' Union, 1889–92; honorary presidency, 1893–1900; general secretaryship, Amalgamated Engineering Union, 1919–21. His political offices, equally diverse, included secretaryship of the Independent Labour Party, 1893–5; organizer of the National Democratic League, 1900–1; editorship of the *Industrial Syndicalist*, 1910–11; member of the Communist Party after 1921. He was also a member of the Royal Commission on Labour, 1891–4.

[2] Burns, John, P.C. (1858–1943). Member, Amalgamated Society Engineers. of Parliamentary Committee, Trades Union Congress, 1890–91, 1893–95. Liberal M.P., 1892–1918. President of Local Government Board, 1906–14. President of Board of Trade, 1914 till he resigned on the outbreak of war.

[3] Will Thorne, *My Life's Battles*, 1925, pp. 64–71.

[4] This change affected only the stokers. Maintenance men and labourers, who were not on shift work, obtained a reduction from 10 to 9½ hours, at least in the South Metropolitan (*Royal Commission on Labour*, C–6894–IX, 1893, Q. 26709). The absorption of increased labour costs was made easier by rapid expansion. Between 1882 and 1892 the output of authorized undertakings rose by 54 per cent. (Philip Chantler, *The British Gas Industry, An Economic Study*, 1938, pp. 6–7).

[5] Livesey, Sir George (1834–1908). Chairman, South Metropolitan Gas Company. Member of Royal Commission on Labour, 1891–4.

[6] *Royal Commission on Labour*, C–6894–IX, 1893, Q. 26789. John Rae, in *Eight Hours for Work* (1894), confirms that the eight-hour shift was already quite common in provincial gas-works (p. 86).   [7] *Royal Commission on Labour*, C–6894–IX, 1893, Q. 26794.

[8] Ibid., Qs. 26796–7.

work in the same gang, provided that the men would accept non-union gangs in the same retort-house'.[1] Nevertheless, 'within about a month after that time they succeeded in inducing or forcing every man into the Union'.[2]

On another occasion, however, when Livesey found that the men, on the instructions of their delegate, would not oil the hinges or levers of the retort lids, he was goaded into saying: ' "Well, if your Union is going to act in this way it will not last twelve months". That remark was reported all over our stations, and it was said that I had said I would smash the Union.'[3] 'Under protest', he was also forced to agree to the payment of double time from 6 a.m. to 10 p.m. on Sundays, and warned the union that 'I will take it back again as soon as I can'.[4] Understandably, Thorne became uneasy about the possible effects of these constant demands by his members; but in November he was snubbed by a delegate from the South Metropolitan works at Vauxhall when he advised a period of restraint.

By this time the London dock strike had come and gone. The example of the gasworkers affected the dockers and their leaders in several ways. Thorne had belonged to Tillett's union, and Tillett helped him to organize the gasworkers. Many of the socialists who also contributed to Thorne's initial triumph were seasoned campaigners at the dock gates, and one at least, H. W. Hobart of the London Society of Compositors, had assisted Tillett during the Tilbury stoppage of October 1888.[5] Several of the Gas-workers' strongholds were in or close to the dock areas, and they held frequent meetings throughout the East End. In those days, moreover, the gas companies paid off many of their labourers for the summer months. Each year some went into the brickyards; but others usually turned to the docks, and by August 1889 a number of Thorne's members were probably at work there.

The contemporary historians of the strike[6] emphasize the importance of the gasworkers' successes in reviving the spirits of the dockers after defeats at Tilbury had disheartened Tillett's struggling Association.

Many who had lost heart regained their confidence in combined action . . . and the men were already ripe for a contest, when, on August 12th, a dispute at the South West India Dock served as the spark which kindled the blaze. The nature of the dispute—about the division of the 'plus' on a certain cargo—is of little importance, for it was avowedly only the pretext for a revolt against all the grievances which had long rankled in the minds of the dock labourers. The men wanted to come out at once, and their leader only managed to restrain them until he had formulated their demands in writing, and sent them to the dock authorities.[7]

---

[1] Ibid., Qs. 26797–99.   [2] Ibid., Q. 26807.
[3] Ibid., Q. 26790.   [4] Ibid., Q. 26824.
[5] C. Tsuzuki, *H. M. Hyndman and British Socialism*, 1961, p. 88.
[6] H. Llewellyn Smith and Vaughan Nash, *The Story of the Dockers' Strike*, undated, but certainly 1890.   [7] Ibid., pp. 32–33.

Tillett's chief demands covered both wage rates and the system of payment. Dockers directly employed by the companies received a day wage of 5*d*. an hour (4*d*. at Tilbury); others worked for 'gangers', or subcontracting 'labour masters', under an incentive scheme. From their earnings the gang was paid a minimum of 6*d*. an hour, with a bonus out of any surplus, or 'plus', that remained, the contractor himself keeping the lion's share. The dockers now asked for an increase in the day wage to 6*d*. an hour, and the replacement of the existing contract system by an equal division of the surplus. The letter embodying these and other demands was written on 13 August and requested an answer by noon the next day.[1]

This was a bold challenge, boldly delivered; yet once it was clear that the dock companies intended to resist, the chances of success must have seemed thin. In January the seamen took the shipowners by surprise, and by June their union had had several months to prepare for a fight. Even so they could not defeat those Liverpool lines which stood firmly together. For the moment, at any rate, the gas companies had given in without a struggle; but now the dockers, virtually unorganized and without funds, were apparently taking on a hostile combination of employers with considerable resources. It soon emerged, however, that unity among them was far from complete. Indeed, many of the wharfingers and shippers with wharves of their own were willing to concede the men's terms. Only the fact that the strike committee would not at first consent to a partial settlement prevented the employers' front from cracking at an early stage.[2]

In due course the crack occurred, opening the way to a general surrender by the companies; but the issue remained in doubt for a month, during which the dispute passed through two main phases. The other factors which contributed to the dockers' victory can therefore be divided into those which made the strike effective and carried it through to the end of August, and those which renewed its solidarity and impetus at the beginning of September. Among the first were the enthusiasm of the dockers, the decision of the stevedores 'to support our poorer brothers', the assistance of the socialists, and exceptional public sympathy.

For the first few days it was possible that the strike would fizzle out, despite the initial response north of the Thames. On Saturday, 17 August, however, the executives of two well-organized stevedores' societies, the Amalgamated and the United, decided to bring in their members.[3] This gave the strikers an appropriate headquarters—the Wade's Arms in Poplar[4]—

---

[1] Smith and Nash, op. cit., pp. 21–22, 50–54; Beatrice Potter (Webb), 'The Docks', in Booth, op. cit., vol. iv.   [2] *Report on the Strikes and Lockouts of 1889*, C–6176, 1890, p. 8.

[3] In the London docks the stevedores are skilled loaders of ships. Elsewhere both loading and unloading is performed by dockers, and stevedores are contractors. In 1889 these two unions organized 50 per cent. or more of the stevedores.

[4] In Jeremiah Street, a few doors from Tillett's old headquarters, Wroot's Coffee House. The move may have helped to maintain the high spirits of the central committee.

and a body of experienced men who could help to man the committees, administer funds, and arrange picketing. The stevedores had long-established habits of acting together, and, once out, could be relied upon to stay out, thus setting an example to the dockers as a whole. It is difficult to believe that the strike could have succeeded if the decision of these key workers had gone the other way.[1]

Many of London's best-known socialists also helped to provide the leadership and the general staff which Tillett's union alone could not have supplied. The major contribution was made by the Championites, a group largely composed of members or ex-members of the Social Democratic Federation, most of them trade unionists, who supported H. H. Champion[2] in preferring immediate if limited action, industrial or political, to Hyndman's more doctrinaire approach. Of these, Burns became the most prominent of the strike's personalities as he led the famous marches through the East End which advertised the grievances of the dockers and kept up their morale. Mann's department was organization, particularly the crucial task of controlling the pickets, and Champion himself served as public relations officer.[3] Of the others, Eleanor Marx-Aveling and Annie Besant both gave valuable assistance. Whatever their brand of socialism, all had previously played some part in the organization of the less skilled, either during the strike of the match-girls in 1888 or among the gas-workers earlier in 1889.

The daily, well-disciplined marches which so moved the London public originated in a great meeting at the gates of the East India Docks on Sunday 18 August. This 'fixed the waverers once for all',[4] and led to the general extension of the strike throughout the docks. On the south side of the river, where much of the work was more highly specialized and less 'casual', a separate committee was set up, and in September Quelch began to build up the South Side Labour Protection League. However, liaison with the central committee was maintained by Mann, and during the second phase of the strike he assumed special responsibility for controlling the Surrey side on its behalf. On both banks, good weather favoured marchers and pickets alike.

A large section of the press campaigned vigorously for the dockers. In April a graphic account of their conditions by Beatrice Webb had appeared in an early volume of Charles Booth's *Life and Labour of the People in*

[1] Frederic Harrison went so far as to say that 'without the stevedores and other skilled officers, unskilled labour, even if it could be found, would have been useless in the Docks' ('Socialist Unionism', article in the *Nineteenth Century*, 1889, reprinted in *National and Social Problems*, 1908, p. 427).

[2] Champion, H. H. (1859–1928). First secretary of the Social Democratic Federation, 1884. Edited *Labour Elector*, 1888–90, 1893–4. Emigrated to Australia 1894.

[3] Champion's *Labour Elector* became the official organ of the dockers' union as well as the Gasworkers and helped to raise funds for the strike.

[4] Smith and Nash, op. cit., p. 61.

London. For the man in the street the book's 'significance was immediate and immense, and the first edition was quickly exhausted. . . . Every type of newspaper—daily and weekly, serious or sensational, at home and abroad—carried reviews and articles which provoked readers to a brisk correspondence.'[1] The impact of the strike therefore fell upon a receptive and well-prepared public opinion, and the press was quick to take up the mood. The injustices of casual labour and the brutality of life in the docks were exposed, and funds were opened. T. P. O'Connor's *Star*, on which the Fabians were influential, raised over £6,000, and at the start *The Times* itself smiled on the dockers' cause.

By the end of the first fortnight, however, they were running into serious difficulties. Apart from the limited resources of the stevedores the strike committee was dependent on outside contributions, and relief had to be provided for all the flotsam of the East End who could claim that they occasionally worked at the docks, and who might, therefore, take the place of the strikers now. But the offers of the companies were always very tempting to such men, and neither enthusiasm for the cause nor public sympathy could keep them out of the docks. That was a task for the pickets. Consequently, 'the battle [was] growing in bitterness. All processions have been stopped, and the docks are now invested by a vast silent army of pickets, through which it is almost impossible for a scab to pass.'[2]

Even if such comments exaggerated its efficiency, this intensification of picketing diminished support for the dockers; and on 28 August, finding evidence of 'intimidation', *The Times* warned them not to 'indulge in excesses or persist in immoderate demands'.[3] On the following day, however, the committee issued its 'No-Work Manifesto' (which called for a general strike in London) immediately after the companies had again rejected their 'immoderate demands'. Mann and the socialists carried the manifesto through the committee; but Tillett saw that 'it tended to alienate public sympathy'[4] and, in addition, that to summon such a strike without any assurance that other unions would respond was sheer folly. Second thoughts prevailed, and the manifesto was withdrawn on 1 September.

Engels had described the committee's original gesture as 'a declaration of despair';[5] but almost at once the outlook improved. Funds at last began to pour in, especially from Australia, where the strike had attracted the support of a radically minded population concentrated in the major ports.

[1] T. S. Simey and M. B. Simey, *Charles Booth: Social Scientist*, 1960, p. 109.

[2] *Commonweal*, 7 Sept. 1889.

[3] John Saville, 'Trade Unions and Free Labour: The Background to the Taff Vale Decision', in *Essays in Labour History in Memory of G. D. H. Cole*, 1960, edited by Asa Briggs and John Saville, p. 322.

[4] Ben Tillett, *Memories and Reflections*, 1931, p. 143.

[5] Tsuzuki, op. cit., p. 89.

Altogether the colonies sent more than £30,000,[1] and for the time being financial worries could be forgotten. Moreover, on 4 September a settlement was reached with the smaller employers, the wharfingers, the committee allowing men to return to work on condition that the extra penny on the day wage went into the strike fund. This breakthrough revived the enthusiasm of the dockers and further eased the problems of their leaders.

Simultaneously, the waning interest of the public was once more aroused by the establishment of the Mansion House Committee, which first assembled on 6 September and took upon itself the task of conciliation. This widely representative body of prominent Londoners included among its members the Lord Mayor, the Bishop of London, Sir John Lubbock, Sydney Buxton, and Cardinal Manning. Manning was able to exercise a remarkable influence over the strikers, many of whom were Catholics, and over their working-class leaders.[2] By his shrewdness, tact, and charm in dealing with both sides, he steered the Committee through some difficult negotiations to the final settlement which was signed on 14 September.

In bringing the companies to the point of agreement, Mann's pickets were also important. During the last phase of the dispute there was little movement in the port, and the shipowners put increasing pressure on the dock directors to finish the strike one way or the other.[3] Any explanation of the dockers' victory must therefore pay due regard to the restraint shown by the police.

The policy of masterly inactivity indicated by the Home Secretary served to reduce to a minimum the friction inevitable to a labour contest, which meant the turning loose into the streets of so vast and unwieldy a mass of men as the waterside labourers of London. The police kept themselves in the background as far as possible, and their conduct when action was necessary was friendly and forbearing in the extreme.[4]

The general settlement secured 'the dockers' tanner', a day wage for direct labour of 6*d*. an hour, with 2*s*. as the minimum payment for a spell of work. Subcontracting was to be replaced by a system providing for equal division among the gang of any surplus, the basic minimum here remaining at 6*d*. an hour. The union conceded protection for those who had remained at work, and accepted a delay until 4 November before the changes came into force.[5] Thereafter came separate negotiations over the demands of specialists on the Surrey side such as the iron-porters,

---

[1] The balance-sheet of the strike fund is reproduced in Smith and Nash, op. cit., appendix E. The total income was nearly £49,000. Less than £4,500 came from British trade unions as compared with almost £14,000 from the general public. The largest donation by a single trade union was £670 from the Amalgamated Society of Engineers.

[2] Tom Mann, *Memoirs*, 1923, pp. 88–89; Tillett, op. cit., pp. 91, 147–8.

[3] Smith and Nash, op. cit., pp. 128–9.   [4] Ibid., p. 115.

[5] It was the acceptance of this clause, a face-saver for the companies, which demanded all Manning's skill with the dockers.

corn-porters, and trimmers; over the lightermen's claims, settled by an arbitration award of Lord Brassey;[1] and over a general agreement for the Coal
Porters' Union, recently formed under the flamboyant Michael Henry.
These various successes were followed by the setting up of a federal
organization of waterfront unions to promote consultation and common
action, the United Labour Council of the Port of London.

The returning dockers showed considerable hostility to the men who
had replaced them, but these either joined the union or were bought out
with the remains of the strike fund. For the moment,

the fact that the trade union card has been recognised by men and dock officials
as the only passport to work, is really the foundation of the Union, and its
principal guarantee of permanence, and to have brought this about is the greatest triumph the Union has gained. Not only the casuals and the permanent
hands, but many of the foremen and officials with whom the dockers have
dealings, have joined the Union, though some of the latter have formed one of
their own.[2]

Meanwhile, there was plenty of activity among dockers in the provinces.
At Bristol 3,000 men were out between 21 and 25 October. They won an
advance and were promptly recruited by Tillett's Association, now reorganized and renamed the Dock, Wharf, Riverside and General Labourers'
Union. Fresh from its triumph in London, the new union also spread
swiftly to the East Anglian ports and to the Medway towns. In Scotland
McGhee and McHugh of the National Union of Dock Labourers 'had the
majority of labourers in Glasgow in their Union. . . . In fact the officials of
the Union were masters, instead of the stevedores themselves.'[3] On
Merseyside their union branches drew up working rules prescribing wage
rates for all classes of labour in the docks.[4] Sporadic strikes broke out early
in 1890 as the men attempted to enforce these claims, and the union's

---

[1] During the strike the lightermen claimed to be out both in sympathy with the dockers and
to enforce their own demands; but later their secretary told the Royal Commission on Labour
that 'we discountenanced strikes. . . . We were charged with striking with the docker. What
we wanted to explain was this, that when the docker did not load the barges or unload them,
the lighterman had got nothing to do, so he came out and had a walk along with the docker'
(C–6708–V, 1892, Qs. 8081–2).

[2] Smith and Nash, op. cit., p. 160. A foreman told the Royal Commission on Labour that
'the dock labourers . . . when they returned to work refused to work with foremen unless they
joined the Labourers' Union. We stood by the employers during the strike and many of us were
called upon to do manual work, and we did not quite see the force of being compelled to join
an organisation which consisted entirely of a class of men who were under our supervision. . . .
In fact, I think in the main that the foremen were heartily in sympathy with what they desired
to obtain, but we resolved to form ourselves into a union not inimical to the interests of the
employers, and we thought we should strengthen our position with reference to the labour
movement, and also should be able by organisation to make our grievances known to the employers' (C–6708–V, 1892, Q. 7355).

[3] According to George Monro, owner of a stevedoring business in Glasgow (*Royal Commission on Labour*, C–6795–V, 1892, Q. 12696).

[4] *Liverpool Weekly Post*, 25 Jan. 1890.

membership rose rapidly. As a further stimulus McGhee introduced the 'docker's button', a coloured badge which was changed every quarter and issued only to fully paid-up members.[1]

In London the Gasworkers under their socialist leaders soon spread into a number of other trades, including brickmaking and india-rubber; and Eleanor Marx-Aveling helped to organize the women rubber workers during a strike at Silvertown. At the same time the provincial gasworkers were forming branches in many places, especially the northern manufacturing towns. In Birmingham, however, a group of craft unionists had already helped to found a separate society, the Amalgamated Gasworkers, Brickmakers and General Labourers. Two Lib-Lab city councillors, Eli Bloor of the National Flint Glass Makers and Allan Granger, president of the Birmingham Typographical Printers, helped to organize the municipal gasworkers,[2] and Bloor became treasurer of the new union. The secretary was another Lib-Lab, W. F. Beston, who was also secretary of the Amalgamated Toolmakers, Engineers and Machinists, founded in 1882 for lower-paid engineers.

With the help of its sympathizers on the council, the union won wage increases and the eight-hour day before moving on into the Black Country, Coventry, and Derby, and then into Yorkshire. In Bradford contact was made with the socialists, one of whom, James Bartley, sub-editor on the *Workman's Times*, became northern representative on the executive. Here, too, the Lib-Labs provided valuable assistance, notably through Sam Shaftoe, secretary of the Bradford Trades Council and 'too good a trade unionist to stand aside from the tide of new unionism'.[3] The union's general demeanour was suitably restrained. 'The Birmingham society was not aggressive, but only sought to bring about a better understanding between capital and labour.'[4]

Another new union of a very different sort was the National Labour Federation. Started on Tyneside in 1886 by some Newcastle members of the Amalgamated Society of Engineers,[5] its special mission was to assist hitherto unorganized labour. The Federation was open to men and women of all trades and also to trade unions, which could join *en bloc* and take advantage of its supplementary strike benefit. Support was given to all strikes approved by the union of the trade concerned or, when the dispute involved individual members, by the federal executive. This hybrid organization owed something to socialist inspiration: E. R. Pease, a founder-member and later secretary of the Fabian Society, presided over

---

[1] Sir James Sexton, *Sir James Sexton, Agitator*, 1936, p. 102.

[2] *Workman's Times*, 4 July 1890.

[3] E. P. Thompson, 'Homage to Tom Maguire', in *Essays in Labour History*, edited by Brigg and Saville, p. 310.   [4] *Workman's Times*, 5 Dec. 1890.

[5] Webb Trade Union Collection E (Brit. Lib. of Pol. Science, London School of Economics), Section A, vol. xlii.

its first public meeting and acted as secretary for a short period about 1888.[1]

When the Tyneside and National Labour Union appeared in 1889, the two bodies competed locally among much the same groups—the less-skilled production workers in engineering, shipbuilding, iron and steel, chemicals, glass, and building. The initial motive behind the formation of the Tyneside and National Labour Union had been to provide protection for the platers' helpers and other assistants employed by the skilled craftsmen of the Boilermakers' Society.[2] But it soon widened its appeal, and organized dockers in the North-east whom Havelock Wilson had felt compelled to turn away.

Meanwhile, over the whole field covered by the new unionism, dozens of minor societies were springing up to cater for dockers, builders' labourers, general labourers, carters, and other transport workers. Many of them succeeded in winning a local victory and establishing a pocket of strength. A general expansion of the new unions continued, along with good trade, into 1890; and at the annual conference of the Tyneside and National Labour Union in August of that year, its secretary, William Stanley,[3] could claim that 'instead of being ordered off the premises as interlopers, your delegates' services are eagerly sought after by employers, whenever a hitch in their work occurs. Nor can it be said that they have adopted this procedure because of the pliability of your representatives.'

According to Stanley, his shop stewards and other active members were protected by a 'Labourers' Legion of Honour, namely a victimised fund'. Many disputes, however, were settled by arbitration. If expenditure on strike pay had been heavy, this was almost entirely due to disputes originated by other unions. 'Though unskilled labour is the principal driving wheel of all kinds of skilled labour . . . yet for a temporary period it can be dispensed with. Thus our members employed in building and kindred trades are at the mercy of skilled operatives.' Hence 'the immense value our society renders to its members in supplying them during lock-outs. . . . Too often in days gone by, did the employers take advantage of the helpless state of disorganised labourers in times of lock-outs, to impose fresh and terribly severe reductions of wages upon them.'

The Counter-attack begins

Where employers decided to obstruct the new unions, however, they were often successful. Indeed, they had begun to score victories even before the end of 1889. In December, for instance, the Gasworkers suffered a

---

[1] Pease stipulated 'no class barriers', and there were a few middle-class members. The Rev. Moore Ede of Gateshead was trustee and brought his curates in (Webb Trade Union Collection E, Section A, vol. xlii).   [2] Ibid.

[3] Stanley was the second secretary. The first had departed leaving financial disorder behind him, but this did not stop the union's growth.

severe setback in the provinces. They had already secured the eight-hour day at the municipal works in Manchester and Salford, and the union was spreading rapidly to other parts of Lancashire. When the district secretary served strike notices on both undertakings with the object of imposing membership on 'six men in the Manchester works who from conscientious scruples would not join any Union'[1], Thorne came up to try to prevent a stoppage. He pleaded with the local authorities to permit the union to withdraw the notices, but they replied that new staff had already been engaged. Thus the strike had to go on, and it failed miserably.[2]

Thorne then had to hurry back to London where the troubles at the South Metropolitan had come to a head, in a major attack on the union. According to Livesey, the Company started to prepare for a strike from the day when he had signed an agreement promising not to intimidate or interfere with union members.[3] Advertisements for substitute labour were drafted and distributed to the press ready for insertion on the receipt of a telegram. To accommodate the strike-breakers, beds and temporary housing were ordered. However, in the hope that there might be 'a better way out', Livesey proposed a profit-sharing scheme to the men on 30 October.[4]

Many of the maintenance staff and the yard labourers (who were weakly organized) appear to have been attracted by the scheme, but the union took exception to several of its clauses. Three of these were withdrawn, including one prescribing that the men concerned would forfeit their share 'in the case of a strike or wilful injury to the Company'.[5] There remained the requirement of a twelve-month contract which would have been crippling in view of the provision in the Conspiracy and Protection of Property Act of 1875 making strikes in breach of contract in public utilities a criminal offence.[6] To a man, therefore, the well-organized stokers refused to sign until at the end of November 'three men at Vauxhall . . . signed the agreement by stealth'.[7] The union at once invoked the promise of 20 September that its members should not be required to work in the same gang as non-unionists,[8] and threatened to strike.

The demand was refused, and the Company's plans were set in motion as Livesey brushed aside attempts at mediation.[9] When the stoppage began on 13 December practically every one of the 2,000 stokers came out; but over 4,000 replacements had already been engaged. With experience,

[1] According to Ward, the assistant secretary of the union (*Royal Commission on Labour*, C–6894–IX, 1893, Q. 24154).　　[2] Ibid., Qs. 24560–612, for Thorne's account.

[3] See p. 58.

[4] *Royal Commission on Labour*, C–6894–IX, 1893, Q. 26836.

[5] Ibid., Q. 26841.

[6] For the full text of the profit-sharing agreement, and the amended version used after the strike, see ibid., appendixes li and lii.　　[7] Ibid., Q. 26874.

[8] It is not clear that the men were expelled from the union. One union official said that they had refused to pay their contributions (ibid., Q. 28117).　　[9] Ibid., Qs. 26882–6.

and by reverting to the twelve-hour shift, their output rose and the union's chances diminished. Eventually, on 4 February 1890, a settlement was reached which provided for a return to the eight-hour day, 'except where mutually agreed to the contrary', and preference was to be granted to previous employees 'in the event of any vacancies arising'.[1] However, the agreement never came into operation, for Livesey repudiated it on reading that Thorne had 'warned the consumers of London that the men would not give seven days' notice again before striking'.[2] A declaration that 'no one who pays to, or is a member of, the Gas Workers' Union will be employed by the Company' was posted at the works, and a corresponding clause added to the profit-sharing scheme.[3]

One of the notable features of the dispute was the strong police protection for the 'free labour' imported by the company. Before the strike began, Livesey obtained assurances from the Home Secretary and the Commissioner of Police that 'everything that the police can do within the law . . . will be done'.[4] Both had recently come under criticism for their passive role during the dock strike, not only from the companies but also from *The Times*. Livesey was satisfied with the results of his own approach. 'When they were once convinced that there was danger, they acted splendidly—splendidly I say as a citizen—splendidly in the interests of London.'[5] While still critical, *The Times* also saw some evidence of improvement.[6]

Thorne himself had been manhandled, and the strikers gave the police much of the blame for their defeat.

The tolerance of the police in 1889 [wrote Sidney Webb] did much to enable Burns and Tillett to win the dock strike, and still more, the way in which the police threw themselves into the strike at the South Metropolitan Gasworks . . . on the side of Mr. Livesey, was an important factor in that gentleman's triumph. It is not too much to say that the police could if they chose absolutely prevent all picketing whatsoever, all demonstrations of disapproval of blacklegs, all strike processions and street collections, if they determined to carry out the law with vigorous strictness against the working man.[7]

The union ran into similar difficulties with the Gas Light and Coke Company. In several brief strikes the stokers attempted in vain to enforce a closed shop; and on 14 May 1890 seventy-two of them struck at Beckton against the introduction of labour-saving machinery.[8] They were replaced

---

[1] *Royal Commission on Labour*, C–6894–IX, 1893, Q. 26898. After the strike three of the company's six works elected to keep the 12-hour shift (ibid., Qs. 26902–3) which, according to Livesey, was in fact 11–11½ hours. They were paid 6s. 4d. a shift, instead of 5s. 4d. for 8 hours—a 19 per cent. wage increase for hours longer by 37–44 per cent. (ibid., Q. 26709).

[2] Ibid., Q. 26903.

[3] Ibid., appendixes li and lii.　　　　[4] Ibid., Q. 26835.　　　　[5] Ibid., Q. 26882.

[6] *The Times*, 14 Dec. 1889. See also Saville, loc. cit., pp. 322–3.

[7] *Workman's Times*, 23 Jan. 1892.

[8] *Royal Commission on Labour*, C–6894–IX, 1893, Qs. 26496–505.

within a few days by non-union men, and police protection was not withdrawn until 20 June.[1] This caused no immediate repercussions, but the Company took precautions very like those at the South Metropolitan.[2] By the beginning of October a strike was expected, and

both the Home Office and the War Department were also satisfied that the situation was a threatening one, a fact sufficiently demonstrated by the unusual magnitude and character of the assistance promised to the Company. The commander of the garrison at Chatham . . . could spare a thousand men for special duty, and these . . . were served with twenty rounds of ball cartridge each, but they were kept in ignorance of their destination, which was imparted only to the superior officers.[3]

A meeting was arranged, however, at which the directors heard Thorne's complaints. They rejected his suggestion that men should be employed only through the union, but promised 'not to interfere with Union men in regard to the payment of their subscriptions to the Union', and excused their preparations on the grounds that they had 'no notion . . . of taking aggressive steps'.[3] This seems to have been the end of the matter so far as the Gas Light and Coke Company was concerned; but Thorne said later that if the dispute with the South Metropolitan were to recur he would urge his members to strike without giving notice, thus breaking their contracts and risking criminal proceedings, both in order to avoid giving the Company time to prepare and because of 'the disadvantages that we were labouring under, through the press and the police'.[4]

The police were not always the aggressors, nor did violence necessarily mean defeat. In June 1890 the men at the municipal gasworks in Leeds struck against the council's attempt to introduce a four-month contract. The authorities imported 'several hundred blacklegs, headed by cavalry, surrounded by a double file of police, and a file of military, and followed by the Mayor and magistrates'. From a railway bridge, 'coal, sleepers, bricks, bottles and assorted missiles were hurled down by pickets and sympathisers upon the civic procession. . . . For several days the town was like an armed camp [and] hussars with drawn swords patrolled the streets.'[5] One observer noted 'the formidable sticks, many of them with hooks, spikes and nails attached, with which the gas-workers and others were armed', and recorded that 'the first attack was made by the crowd who, rushing on the police in a serried mass, actually succeeded in breaking their front rank'.[6] Whether because the replacements were inefficient, or because a

---

[1] *Report on the Strikes and Lockouts of 1890*, C-6476, 1891, p. 66.
[2] *Royal Commission on Labour*, C-6894–IX, 1893, Qs. 26530–5.
[3] *Daily Telegraph*, 4 Oct. 1890, quoted in the National Union of Gasworkers and General Labourers' *Annual Report*, 1891.
[4] *Royal Commission on Labour*, C-6894–IX, 1893, Q. 25180.
[5] E. P. Thompson, loc. cit., p. 300.
[6] When Livesey, as a member of the Royal Commission on Labour, quoted this account from

public authority cannot fight a really determined strike as effectively as a determined private employer, the council gave way and the strikers returned triumphant.

During the Leeds dispute the Gasworkers had been greatly assisted by a small band of local socialists, including Tom Maguire, Tom Paylor, and Alf Mattison, who had already helped a number of other groups to combine.[1] Many of these joined the Gasworkers, and branches were set up for maltsters, engineering labourers and machinemen, draymen, coke-burners, clay workers, quarrymen, dyers, sanitary workers, and chemical workers, as well as gasworkers and general labourers. Building labourers had come under their stimulus in June 1889, when a union was formed and a successful strike called for wage increases. 'Week after week, [they] attended demonstrations, assisted strikes, presided at the formation of new unions: tramway workers, blue dyers, corporation workers, plasterer's labourers, paviour's labourers, mechanic's labourers, axle workers.'[2] The campaign now spread westwards, with Maguire and his associates organizing the gas and clay workers at Halifax.

Elsewhere, the Gasworkers were also busy with or without socialist assistance. By the end of 1890 there were separate district organizations in Belfast, Birkenhead, Birmingham, Bristol, Dublin, Manchester, Plymouth, and Sunderland, and each of them included a variety of occupations. In Kent, however, the brickmakers now had their own district. Meanwhile, the Amalgamated Gasworkers, Brickmakers and General Labourers of Birmingham were adding to their outposts by organizing gasworkers and dyehouse labourers in the Kidderminster area, and on its home ground the union had turned its attention to the men at the Birmingham municipal waterworks.[3]

For the National Union of Dock Labourers 1890 brought a setback in Liverpool. The earlier sporadic strikes flared up into a mass stoppage when the union felt strong enough to make the wearing of its badge compulsory and requested the dock companies in future to 'employ union men in the first instance'.[4] This was curtly refused and by early March between twenty and thirty thousand men were out. Public opinion on Merseyside was not hostile to the strikers. The *Liverpool Weekly Post*, which had criticized the employers' response to the union's 'civil request', gave them a tart reminder that there were 'much worse evils than a Dock Labourers' Union';[5] and the Lord Mayor tried unsuccessfully to mediate.

the *People's Press*, of which Thorne was a director, Thorne's only comment was: 'That is not true about the sticks being spiked and nailed' (C–6894–IX, 1893, Qs. 25141–2).

[1] E. P. Thompson, loc. cit., pp. 295–300.
[2] Ibid., p. 296.
[3] *Workman's Times*, 5 Dec. 1890; 20 and 27 Mar. 1891.
[4] *Liverpool Weekly Post*, 15 Mar. 1890.
[5] Ibid., 22 Mar. 1890.

Nevertheless, substitute labour was imported from other Lancashire towns; violence ensued with the strikers, and troops had to be called in.

The union tried to retaliate by imposing a boycott of Liverpool ships in Glasgow, but this failed.[1] Work was resumed on 8 April, when the union men undertook to abandon their badge and to work harmoniously with non-unionists. The companies in return conceded a nine-hour night shift and other minor advantages. Later in the year the Birkenhead dockers, by refusing to work overtime,[2] also secured the shorter night shift. In addition, the branch won full control of local dock labour, with a code of working rules accepted by the employers and a procedural agreement for disputes.[3]

However, the most significant event of 1890, as of 1889, occurred in the London docks, but in a very different fashion. The 'Great Dock Strike' had attracted world-wide attention; yet twelve months later Tillett's union was eased out of the docks with scarcely a ripple of public interest. Its grip was first loosened by a dispute arising out of the 1889 settlement. On 16 January men at Hays Wharf struck unofficially for reversion to payment for meal-times, eliminated under the agreement. Their leaders reluctantly supported the strike;[4] but after a bitter struggle, during which the company introduced non-union labour, they had to cut their losses in May. An attempt at sympathetic action on other wharves in February lasted just over a week. Equally unsuccessful were several minor strikes in February, July, and August to enforce union membership.[5]

The major blow fell in November. A year before, Mann had signed an agreement in fulfilment of the clause in the Mansion House settlement providing for the abolition of subcontracting. The 'labour masters' were replaced by union members as gang representatives, who negotiated piece rates with the employers on behalf of their gangs. Under this so-called 'co-operative' system, the men had considerable latitude in determining the size of the gang. The companies thus became convinced that the system offered insufficient incentive, and persuaded Mann, now the union's president, of the need for a new agreement abolishing the guaranteed minimum.[6] Only if this was accepted would they continue to allow the men to control the composition of the gang.[7] Subsequently, however, hearing of a plan to use this control to get rid of all non-unionists,[8] they also proposed to curtail the rights of the gang representatives.

The dockers, who were already reluctant to give up their minimum, would not accept this additional encroachment. On 4 November, when the agreement establishing the 'co-operative' system expired, the employers

---

[1] *Royal Commission on Labour*, C–6795–V, 1892, Qs. 12801–4.
[2] *Workman's Times*, 19 Sept. 1890.   [3] Ibid., 24 Oct. 1890.
[4] *Royal Commission on Labour*, C–6708–V, 1892, Qs. 65–67.
[5] *Report on the Strikes and Lockouts of 1890*, C–6476, 1891, pp. 88–90.
[6] *Royal Commission on Labour*, C–6708–V, 1892, Qs. 4778–86.
[7] Ibid., Q. 4789.   [8] Ibid., Q. 4793.

retaliated by refusing to renew it, thus reverting to the old, pre-strike arrangements for piece-work. This was a severe setback, for it meant that the union no longer had any recognized rights over wages and conditions, other than day wages. Membership slumped everywhere except at Mill-wall, where Colonel Birt was, for the time being, 'decidedly in favour of the Union' and 'shows that by giving the dockers' delegate permission to order any man out of the dock who is not a union man'.[1] The remaining companies took a different view; and, as the strength of the union ebbed away, they gradually rid themselves of its representatives.[2]

Elsewhere, the Dockers had further failures to report. In September their Southampton members had embarked upon an unofficial strike for union recognition, and on the second day troops were called in. The strike soon collapsed, however, broken initially (according to a Dockers' official, Tom McCarthy) by conflict between the local branch and the national executive, which was unwilling to recognize the dispute. Its leader, Will Sprow, was sentenced to three months' imprisonment for intimidation. The employers then formed a 'free labour' association, with the vice-president of the chamber of commerce as honorary secretary, and forced their men to join. Before long, McCarthy had to admit that the union's position in Southampton was 'very low indeed'.[3]

In Plymouth the Dockers joined the Gasworkers and the Bristol, West of England and South Wales Operatives[4] in negotiations over unloading coal which ran into trouble about 'the working of unionists with non-unionists'. A stoppage in October was headed by Pete Curran[5] of the Gasworkers, whose arrest for intimidation led to an important legal decision.[6] 'The very rough disturbance lasted about 10 days, I should think', said one employer. 'In order that we might get men to work at all for us . . . we were obliged to go to the superintendent of the police and to make him guarantee us a certain number of men to convoy our men from the police station at about half-past five in the morning to the wharf.'[7] After the strike had collapsed, a Plymouth and District Free Labour Association

---

[1] *Royal Commission on Labour*, C-6708-V, 1892, Qs. 1007-8. Colonel Birt told the Royal Commission that 'all the little difficulties we have are from men who break the rules of the Union, and to get them put right we have to appeal to the executive of the Union. I should like to see the powers of the executive stronger even than they are at present' (ibid., Q. 6962).

[2] Ibid., Q. 996.

[3] Ibid., C-6795-V, 1892, Qs. 12163-4, 12275-8; Saville, loc. cit., pp. 325-6.

[4] This organization, founded in 1873, was a forerunner of the new unions in the type of member included. It was, however, more of a friendly society than a trade union, and may have registered in error under the wrong Act. This is the only occasion when it is recorded as having been involved in a strike.

[5] Curran, Pete (1860-1910). Organizer, National Union of Gasworkers and General Labourers, 1889-1910. Chairman, General Federation of Trade Unions, 1899-1909. Executive Committee, Labour Party, 1900-9. M.P., 1907-10.

[6] *Curran* v. *Treleaven*, [1891] 2 Q.B. 545. See p. 307.

[7] *Royal Commission on Labour*, C-6795-V, 1892, Qs. 12501-2.

was established, with the secretary of the local coal merchants' association as honorary secretary. Thus the influence of the unions was 'most materially' reduced.[1]

Meanwhile, the Dockers had won some successes to set against these failures. Having consolidated its early gains in Bristol, Tillett's union spread to South Wales. Cardiff was unreceptive, but Swansea provided a better welcome. In addition to the dockers themselves, a considerable membership was built up among the copper workers.[2] From the ports of East Anglia the union also moved north to Hull, where it secured collective agreements in the docks[3] and in the seed-crushing mills.[4]

By the end of 1890, however, the outlook was bleak. For the Seamen were embroiled in a dispute which affected almost every port in the kingdom, and caught up both the major dockers' unions in battles for which they were ill-prepared yet could not avoid. Wilson had spent twelve months trying to consolidate his initial victories. The Seamen were now established in London and claimed a total of 60,000 members. But they still had to struggle to keep them, and during 1890 itself they were involved in six strikes against the employment of non-unionists, two against the dismissal of union members, and one against the practice of signing articles on board ship under the eyes of the ship's officers.[5] Moreover, with freight rates beginning to fall[6] despite the general prosperity, the shipowners refused to take part in collective negotiations with the Seamen. Though pressed to co-operate in setting up a conciliation board, they were determined to avoid the recognition of Wilson and his union which this would entail.

Perhaps because of their refusal, Wilson lent his name as 'honorary general manager' to an organization called the 'Certificated Officers' Union of Great Britain and Ireland'. This was the outcome of a secession from the professional association for ships' officers which had the goodwill of the owners.[7] The Seamen further assisted the new union by threatening to strike against the employment of non-union officers. This was the last straw for the owners and drove them to a step which was to prove crucial to the fortunes of the seamen, dockers, and other waterfront workers. In September 1890 they formed the Shipping Federation 'for the purpose of maintaining liberty of contract and resisting the new union methods of

[1] Ibid., Qs. 12493-5; Saville, loc. cit., p. 326.

[2] *Royal Commission on Labour*, C-6894-IX, 1893, Qs. 22195-6; P. S. Thomas, *Industrial Relations*, Social and Economic Survey of Swansea and District, Pamphlet No. 3, 1940, pp. 73-74.   [3] Clem Edwards, 'The Hull Shipping Dispute', *Economic Journal*, 1893.

[4] *Workman's Times*, 28 Nov. 1890.

[5] *Report on the Strikes and Lockouts of 1890*, C-6476, 1891, pp. 86, 211-12. The union's objection was that, under these conditions, seamen might be persuaded to accept worse terms than in the less intimidating atmosphere of a Board of Trade office. In all, the union was involved in seventeen strikes during the year.   [6] Kirkaldy, loc. cit.

[7] *Royal Commission on Labour*, C-6708-V, 1892, Q. 9448.

coercion, more especially the tactics adopted by the National Amalgamated Sailors' and Firemen's Union'.[1]

The Federation established registry offices in the major ports. These issued 'Federation tickets' to any sailor or fireman 'provided he agrees to carry out his agreement on the articles . . . and to proceed to sea in any vessel in which he signs articles, notwithstanding that other members of the crew may or may not be members of any Seamen's Union'.[2] Holders of the ticket were to receive preference in employment, and, in its original form, were also entitled to membership of the Amalgamated British Seamen's Protection Society, a shadowy and highly suspect organization.[3] The union therefore 'sent out a circular to . . . the branches . . . desiring them to express their opinion as to whether this ticket ought to be accepted or not. The resolutions were unanimous from every branch . . . that all members were to refuse to take it, or to sail with men who did take it'.[4]

The Federation first showed its strength in London. In the course of a demarcation dispute with an obscure labourers' union, the Seamen had 'blocked' the ships of the firm concerned, which thereupon adopted a custom common in the North, especially in Liverpool, and began signing up crews on board ship. When other employers in London followed suit, the union objected and started to look for allies. Strikes either of seamen, dockers, or ship-repairing workers always tended to put the other two groups out of work, and sometimes touched off secondary strikes. Faced by a combination of owners, the Seamen now realized that to stop ships sailing with non-union crews they must have the full support of the men on the waterfront. On their initiative, talk of a wider federation, which had been heard for some time, gave way to action.

On 5 December 1890 the United Labour Council of the Port of London issued a manifesto from its headquarters at the Wade's Arms, calling on all members 'to abstain from doing any work, either direct or indirect, that will conduce to the sailing of the vessels of [the three lines concerned] until they give an undertaking that, for the future, they will sign and discharge their respective crews at the regular shipping offices provided by the Board of Trade, and sign no other than members of the N.A.S.F.U.'[5] With Wilson's union, the Council formed a new Federation of Trade and Labour Unions[6] connected with 'the Shipping, Carrying and other

[1] *Royal Commission on Labour*, C–6708–V, 1892, Q. 4925–38; L. H. Powell, *The Shipping Federation*, 1950, chapter 1.

[2] *Royal Commission on Labour*, C–6708–V, 1892, Q. 4946.

[3] Formed in 1872, the Society had made returns to the Chief Registrar until 1882, by which time its outstanding feature was a remarkably high proportion of expenses to total receipts. In 1881 its income was £95 with expenses of over £90. The membership in 1882 was 42, with an income of £6. 13s. 0d., and its expenses £6. 2s. 3d. It made no further returns (Saville, loc. cit., p. 335). See also p. 82.

[4] *Royal Commission on Labour*, C–6708–V, 1892, Q. 10332.   [5] Ibid., appendix xiii.

[6] By 1893 some forty-one unions with a total membership of 130,000 were affiliated.

Industries', and Clem Edwards was appointed secretary.[1] The Shipping Federation countered the manifesto by a declaration that the owners would continue to sign on board, and would not 'engage members of one particular union only', but that both unionists and non-unionists could obtain the Federation ticket and with it preference in employment.

Consequently, 'the sailors of these fleets . . . came out, and in sympathy with them came out the coalies . . . and also the shipworkers, carpenters, painters and various other trades who have formed themselves into this Labour Council . . . but . . . neither the dockers nor the stevedores'.[2] However, when the Federation recruited new 'coalies' from Kent and set them to work under police protection,[3] the strikers at once tried to bring out the dockers and stevedores as well. Mann, as president of the Dockers, told a crowd at Tower Hill on 13 January 1891 'that in three weeks' time he hoped that the dockers, the gasworkers, the watermen, the lightermen, the stevedores, the sailors, the firemen and other unions would all be federated, and then they would put down their foot and say they did not intend to work with non-union men (loud cheers)'.[4]

On 12 February, in company with officers of other unions, Mann went to see officials of the Shipping Federation in a more conciliatory mood. He told them that at present he was 'not prepared to contend for a monopoly for anyone', and that he thought both sides were making too much of the issue of signing articles on board ship. Nevertheless, no agreement could be reached, and the Federation prepared to impose its ticket on the seamen. On 25 February, therefore, the Federation of Trade and Labour Unions called out the stevedores. But the response was poor,[5] and it seems that the dockers, whose union was already disintegrating in London, did not come out at all. These failures were disastrous, and according to G. A. Laws, general manager of the Shipping Federation, the strike was 'utterly defeated'.[6]

During the dispute the Federation put into operation elaborate plans for the introduction of 'free labour'. Laws felt obliged to see the Commissioner of Police 'because it had appeared to me that in a previous great strike . . . there was not sufficient care taken to defend the free labourers before they were hurt'. This time, however, 'the most effective arrangements were made'. When the dock police showed themselves 'utterly

---

[1] Clem Edwards (1869–1938) 'worked with Tillett and the Dockers' Union from the time of the 1889 strike. He started work as a farm labourer, did other casual jobs, and then studied law, being called to the Bar in 1889. Throughout the nineties he played an important part as trade-union organiser, publicist, and labour journalist.' He was labour editor of T. P. O'Connor's short-lived paper, the *Sun*, and became Member of Parliament for Denbigh Boroughs in 1906 (Saville, loc. cit., pp. 324–5, footnote).

[2] *Royal Commission on Labour*, C–6708–V, 1892, Q. 4954. The stevedores claimed that they had not been consulted (ibid., Q. 4097). [3] Ibid., Q. 4954.

[4] *Daily Chronicle*, 14 Jan. 1891, quoted in ibid., appendix xxvi.

[5] *Royal Commission on Labour*, C–6708–V, 1892, Q. 4956. [6] Ibid., Q. 4955.

useless and inadequate to tackle' the pickets, 'the Metropolitan police cleared the docks and the work went on'.[1] Once the strike was over, the Federation opened a 'free labour' registry at the Albert Dock.

Wilson saw little of the closing stages of this dispute. He was in Cardiff, dealing with the consequences of the refusal of coal-tippers on 5 February to load the *Glen Elder* because of its non-union crew. The strike spread throughout the port, thus involving the dockers, and became a struggle for the abolition of the Federation ticket. The Seamen made full use of the technique of marches, bands, and public display which had accompanied the London dock strike of 1889. The Shipping Federation housed its 'free labour' on the *Speedwell*, and the strikers acquired an old tugboat to add naval warfare to the rough combat on land. Strike-breakers were provided by the 'crimps', or boarding-house keepers engaged in the supply of seamen to ships in contravention of the Merchant Shipping Acts. The Cardiff crimps had already set up their own Free Labour Union late in 1890, and 'declared war on the seamen'.[2] As a result of his clashes with them during the strike, Wilson was charged with 'unlawful assembly and riot' and sentenced to six weeks' imprisonment.[3]

Despite conferences with the shipowners, Wilson was unable to reach an agreement.[4] Indeed, with London as well as Cardiff in mind, the Federation decided to enforce the ticket from 23 February 1891. They refused to employ any seaman not prepared to accept its terms, and reiterated their determination to maintain the owners' right to sign up crews on board ship.[5] In some respects, however, the ticket had been revised. The original charges of 1*s*. for registration and 6*d*. for renewal were abolished. No mention was made of the Amalgamated British Seamen's Protection Society. Members of 'any seamen's trade union' could still register 'without prejudice'; and the ticket now entitled its holder 'to employment', not 'to preference of employment'.[6] Grasping at straws, the Seamen claimed a victory, and the dispute at Cardiff was called off on 14 March. But it was a victory that the local branches of the unions concerned did not long survive.

Meanwhile, strikes against the Federation ticket occurred at Newcastle, Hartlepool, and Middlesbrough, and in Scotland. In the North-east, Wilson's old union, the Sailors' and Seagoing Firemen's, was deeply involved, despite its hostility to Wilson himself.[7] At Aberdeen the seamen struck on 25 February, and the appearance of 'free labour' brought the dockers out in sympathy. On 15 March, a day later than Cardiff, they accepted the ticket, but 'many of the labourers lost their employment'.[8]

---

[1] *Royal Commission on Labour*, C–6708–V, 1892, Q. 4954.
[2] *Workman's Times*, 28 Nov. 1890.   [3] J. H. Wilson, op. cit., pp. 225–7.
[4] Ibid., p. 223.   [5] *Royal Commission on Labour*, C–6708–V, 1892, Q. 8632.
[6] Ibid., appendix lx.   [7] Ibid., Qs. 10026–7, 10472–3.
[8] *Report on the Strikes and Lockouts of 1891*, C–6890, 1893, p. 169.

Elsewhere, the picture was similar, and before the end of 1891 clashes with the Federation had also taken place in Liverpool, Shields, Leith, Hull, and Swansea. 'The central issue was the introduction of free labour, and with only minor exceptions the strikes resulted in a marked weakening of unionism among the seamen and the waterside workers all round the country.'[1]

The dockers were invariably affected, and the National Union of Dock Labourers had already suffered in the closing weeks of 1890. During a dock strike at Barrow in September the employers introduced 'free labour', and the union retaliated by blocking all ships leaving the port. The blockage was most effective in Glasgow, where relations with the Seamen were close; and in December the local dockers also blocked ships employing non-union seamen. At this point the Federation intervened, offering to support the stevedores if they would repudiate the Dock Labourers and their working rules.[2] Helped by open warfare between the union and the Glasgow Harbour Labourers, an old society whose relations with the employers were good,[3] this strategy broke the strike and the men returned to work. The resistance of the sailors and firemen was then brushed aside with ease.[4]

The final consequence of Wilson's battle with the Federation was that the Seamen had to allow their members to sign the ticket.[5] Still unrecognized by the shipowners, they could no longer attempt to enforce union membership upon men employed by lines belonging to the Federation, which claimed to represent seven million tons of shipping out of eight million in all. In May 1891, however, their journal, *Seafaring*, was still treating the battle as a victory, and went on to assert that, 'had the Seamen's Union received the support a great struggle like this entitled them to, the victory would have been more complete and lasting'.[6] They could not have been more mistaken. The result of the Seamen's action was not an isolated disaster, affecting only themselves. They had also accelerated the decline of some of their best allies.

More Defeats, 1891–3

The customary explanation of the change in the fortunes of the new unions after their initial triumphs is the return of economic depression. 'The expansion of trade which began in 1889', wrote the Webbs, 'proved to be but of brief duration, and with the returning contraction of 1892 many of the advantages gained by the wage-earners were lost. Under the influence of this check the unskilled labourers once more largely fell away from the Trade Union ranks.'[7] In fact, however, most of these early

[1] Saville, loc. cit., p. 328.   [2] *Royal Commission on Labour*, C–6795–V, 1892, Q. 12696.
[3] Ibid., Qs. 12801–4.   [4] Ibid., Qs. 12808–9.
[5] Ibid., C–6708–V, 1892, Q. 9325.
[6] 2 May 1891, quoted ibid., appendix lx.   [7] *History*, p. 420.

setbacks had occurred before the end of 1890, and were the result not of depression but of a counter-attack by the employers, who launched their offensives at the height of the boom which continued through 1890 and into 1891.

Indeed, during the summer of 1891 London road transport workers were still pressing for improvements; and about 2,500 cabmen were out at different times between April and July. This was the standard time of year for such strikes, for the men hoped to benefit from the increased trade during the summer season. The dispute began as a protest against higher charges for the rent of cabs, and developed into a general demand for reductions. Their secretary afterwards claimed that most rents had been cut by 2s. a day, though another member of the union described it as 'a drawn battle'. Whatever the gains, they were lost through the men's 'laxity in not clinging together',[1] and by 1893 their union had disappeared.

The ostensible cause of the strike of 8,000 employees of the London bus companies in June 1891 was the demand for a twelve-hour day. This was granted, and the strike ended within a week. Its real cause, however, was the new system of giving tickets to passengers in return for their fares. Previously, 'the men . . . were accustomed to take . . . what they thought was a fair amount from the average result which they were expected to produce to the company'.[2] The companies had recognized the loss of illicit earnings by raising wages 1s. a day, making a total of 6s. to 7s. for drivers; nevertheless, the men still struck. They were led by a tiny union whose president was a young barrister, Thomas Sutherst,[3] who had been assisted by William Collison.[4] When Sutherst was accused of dictatorial behaviour, the London Trades Council sent (and paid)[5] one of its members, the socialist Fred Hammill, to build up a more dependable organization;[6] but within a year or two the union had disappeared.

In 1892 London's main transport strike was among the coal-porters. After Henry had been replaced as secretary of their union by James O'Connor, 'business was carried on with very much less friction. . . . The merchants were not sorry to have a practical, responsible body of officials with whom to discuss any question affecting labour, and . . . in the early part of 1890 . . . it was agreed that the merchants should recognise the Union.'[7] Trouble subsequently arose over the enforcement of union membership, and late in 1891 the employers complained of men refusing to work with non-unionists, since the union had 'always stated that such action was unauthorised'.[8] In February 1892 a complicated dispute about

---

[1] *Royal Commission on Labour*, C–6894–VIII, 1893, Qs. 17369–72, 17823.
[2] Ibid., Q. 22915. See also Q. 22658 for the evidence of a driver on the same point.
[3] Ibid., C–6795–V, 1892, Qs. 15743–6.
[4] See p. 171.   [5] *London Trades Council, 1860–1950, A History*, 1950, p. 73.
[6] *Royal Commission on Labour*, C–6894–VIII, 1893, Q. 22691.
[7] Ibid., C–6894–IX, 1893, Q. 27741.   [8] Ibid., Q. 27748.

the hiring of an ex-foreman who was unacceptable to the union led to a stoppage. The strikers were dismissed and a general strike began on 10 February. However, unemployment was now rising, and the merchants easily found replacements. Two days later the union retreated with the assurance that old hands would be taken back as vacancies occurred; but the employers opened a 'free labour' registry.[1]

Meanwhile, in 1891 the Gasworkers had scored a Pyrrhic victory. In May they brought out 2,000 brickmakers near London and kept them out until August in order to secure an advance for the remainder of the brick-making season, which ended in September. But times were changing, and in his *Annual Report* for the year ending in March 1892 Thorne advised caution. 'As we are now entering one of those periodic depressions in trade with which we workers are so well acquainted we should therefore be very judicious . . . in treating with the employer in matters connected with work and wages, and whenever possible without loss of dignity and self-respect, all disputes should be settled in the most quiet and expedient manner.'

The Tyneside and National Labour Union had followed these precepts from the start, and they continued to yield results. The *Annual Report* for 1891 stated that the union now enjoyed direct recognition by the ship-building employers;[2] and before long they claimed to have 4,000 members in the Tyneside chemical works, where 'our official delegates have the power and privilege to enter the works on any matter of business with the *employés* at any time . . . they are not kept waiting outside the gate'.[3] The union also set out to organize building labourers throughout the North-east, and was reaching down into Lincolnshire, Sheffield, and London.[4] Its internal affairs were not so happy. After a series of squabbles involving the executive and successive conferences, Stanley, the secretary, who was alleged to be drunken and disobedient, was replaced during 1892 by A. T. Dipper, a London member who was the union's foremost exponent of socialism.

Superficially, the rival National Labour Federation seemed to be keeping pace. Its professed aim was now 'a gigantic National Labour Federation of all workers',[5] and it already included Hull and Hartlepool drillers, Sunderland trimmers and teemers, South Shields women glass-workers, Lincolnshire ironworkers, Stockton shipyard helpers, Oxford-shire farm labourers, South Wales metal-workers, as well as general labourers in Southampton and elsewhere on the South Coast. In 1892,

---

[1] Ibid., Qs. 27763–6.
[2] The shipyard labourers had previously conducted their negotiations with the platers, or other skilled men who acted as subcontractors.
[3] *Royal Commission on Labour*, C–6894–IX, 1893, Qs. 21504, 21653.
[4] Webb Trade Union Collection E, Section A, vol. xlii.
[5] *Workman's Times*, 3 Apr. 1891.

however, the Federation had £386 in the bank, whereas the Tyneside and National Labour Union, which offered accident benefit and funeral grants as well as strike pay, had £9,000.[1] Soon its branches in the North-east began to crumble, and the Tyneside union was very ready to take over their members.[2]

Since the employers' counter-attack, the Seamen and both the major organizations of dockers had been lying as low as they could. After his release from prison Wilson was much occupied by the difficulties arising from his own and his union's debts, and with his political career.[3] The National Union of Dock Labourers avoided all but minor disputes after the settlement in August 1891 of a two months' strike of 3,000 dockers in Dublin, where the corn-porters were trying to force the shipowners to employ more checkweighmen and tallymen. During 1892 Tillett's union was involved in only one considerable dispute, an unsuccessful strike for the closed shop among dockers at Swansea.[4] Try as they would, however, seamen and dockers could not keep out of trouble and in 1893 they sustained a disastrous defeat.

By this time Hull had become 'the best organised port' in the country,[5] largely because of the active sympathy for the Dockers shown by Charles Wilson, Liberal Member of Parliament for Hull West and head of the port's biggest shipping company, Thomas Wilson & Sons. The firm apparently left the Shipping Federation soon after its formation, but was prevailed upon to rejoin early in 1893.[6] In February they refused their usual co-operation in collecting arrears of union contributions, and insisted that their clerks and foremen, previously permitted to join the Dockers, should now withdraw. On 23 March a 'free labour' registry was established by the 'employers of labour in connection with the docks and shipping at Hull', who invited 'all respectable, steady workmen' to register 'and thus secure preference of employment'. On 4 April Wilsons gave their support, and free labourers were introduced the next day. By 10 April dockers, seamen, and lightermen had come out in protest against this new attack by the Federation.

Tillett and Mann had certainly not wanted a strike. Unemployment among their members was further weakening a union already undermined by hard knocks since 1890, and freight rates were now falling rapidly. Their attitude was therefore conciliatory. Yet the dispute dragged on for nearly seven weeks, until 19 May, accompanied by a good deal of violence. 'There was a considerable amount of rioting and stone-throwing. There were several large fires near the docks, some of which were said to be caused by incendiaries. Extra police and military were brought into the

[1] *Workman's Times*, 12 June 1891.   [2] Ibid., June and July 1891.   [3] See p. 277.
[4] P. S. Thomas, op. cit., pp. 75–76.   [5] Clem Edwards, op. cit.
[6] According to Clem Edwards, op. cit.

town.'[1] In such circumstances the employers enjoyed many advantages. 'Of thirty-eight magistrates, four were shipowners and nineteen others owned shares or were financially interested in shipping. Five out of fifteen members of the Watch Committee were shipowners. The Poor Law Guardians openly acted as recruiting sergeants for "free labour" when able-bodied labourers applied for relief.'[2]

Negotiations continued throughout the strike, sometimes in Hull, sometimes at York, and sometimes in the House of Commons. Havelock Wilson managed to get a debate on the conduct of the Federation which revealed the concern of the House; and Mundella, the President of the Board of Trade, intervened unofficially, but with the government's 'great sympathy and goodwill',[3] in an unsuccessful attempt at mediation. In the later stages the unions tried to use the machinery of the Federation of Trade and Labour Unions to promote sympathetic action at other ports. Exactly what happened is not clear, for the accounts vary;[4] but the strike was not extended, and there could have been no strength behind such a move. Whatever Tillett may have done at the time, his *Annual Report* for the year commented that 'the idea of a general stoppage was tabooed, as it behoves the toilers first to organise and then to sympathetically set about the task of reform'.

'At Hull, as elsewhere, the New Unionism has been defeated', said *The Times* the morning after the strike ended. 'But nowhere has the defeat been so decisive, or the surrender so abject.'[5] The final settlement was complex;[6] yet, though the unions won for their members the right to reinstatement when vacancies occurred, they failed to survive. The Dockers disappeared from the East Coast, and in 1894 the Seamen went into liquidation. When their affairs were wound up, a new National Sailors' and Firemen's Union was started with Wilson as president. This was credited with about 1,000 members in London,[7] but the Board of Trade returns ignored it completely. By 1899 Wilson had again secured a foothold in Glasgow, and it 'became impossible to muster a full [Shipping] Federation crew'[8] until a strike, which lasted from November 1899 to January 1900, was broken.

Where the Shipping Federation could not achieve its objectives directly, it relied on subsidiary organizations. When the seamen called the water-front workers to their aid, the Federation 'found itself as much engaged in the loading and unloading of ships in port as in providing for the navigation

[1] *Report on the Strikes and Lockouts of 1893*, C-7566, 1894, p. 29. See also Saville, loc. cit., pp. 328-30.

[2] Saville, loc. cit., p. 330.

[3] The phrase was Gladstone's (*Hansard*, 2 May 1893, col. 1744).

[4] J. H. Wilson, op. cit., pp. 273-4; Tillett, op. cit., pp. 161-2.

[5] Saville, loc. cit., p. 330.

[6] The terms are given in full in the *Report on the Strikes and Lockouts of 1893*, C-7566, 1894, p. 217.

[7] Booth, op. cit., vol. vii, 1896, p. 364.   [8] Powell, op. cit., pp. 13-14.

of them at sea'.[1] Thus the shipowners became involved with other port employers in local 'free labour' associations set up to supply substitute labour during dock strikes. In order to meet the needs of these associations, use was made of the Amalgamated British Seamen's Protection Society and even less reputable bodies, belonging to 'an underworld of breakaway or independent unions as well as organisations with working class names whose services were always for hire'. The improbable headquarters of this underworld was the Trafalgar Temperance Hotel in Whitechapel, and its leaders first appeared 'in the Fair Trade movement of the early eighties'.[2]

There was little incentive for the Federation to seek other allies, for these served its purpose. For their part, employers in coal and cotton could not have drawn much advantage from an alliance with the shipowners in their concurrent struggles with their own unions. In view of the later developments in engineering, however, it is worth noting that there were already rumours of an 'understanding between the shipbuilders and engineers and the newly-founded Shipping Federation'.[3] The Federation could not depend upon public support. The widespread sympathy aroused by the dock strike of 1889 had waned during subsequent stoppages accompanied, as they often were, by coercion and violence; and the generally accepted intervention of the police and the troops had favoured the employers by protecting 'free labour'. But their reaction to the disputes at Hull and elsewhere showed that neither the public nor the House of Commons believed the unions were to blame for all the disorders associated with strikes. The mood was one of uneasiness at continued labour troubles rather than general hostility to trade unions.

The Survivors, 1894–1900

There is no means of determining the precise membership of the new unions before 1892. The Board of Trade returns approach completeness only in that year; and the turnover of members was so rapid as to make any annual totals highly suspect. The peak must have occurred during 1890,

---

[1] *The Shipping Federation: Why it was formed and what it has done*, reprinted from the Federation's journal, *Fairplay*, 7 June 1895.

[2] Saville, loc. cit., pp. 331–2. One such organization was the 'General Labour Union', which boasted as its president the Marquis of Bute, owner of much of the Cardiff docks (*Workman's Times*, 26 Dec. 1890). In addition to subsidizing these organizations, the Federation maintained in London 'a depot of stores where beds, bedding, kits, cooking utensils, loading and discharging gear . . . are always kept in readiness to be dispatched at a moment's notice, with bodies of free labourers, to any district where there may be a strike . . .' (*The Shipping Federation: Why it was formed*, &c.). The *Annual Report* of the National Union of Dock Labourers for 1892 quoted 'a private and confidential' document of the Federation, reporting an expenditure of £53,420 between Sept. 1890 and Sept. 1891.

[3] *Workman's Times*, 12 Dec. 1890 ('Tyneside Notes'). See also 'Master and Man versus the New Unionism', two articles from the *Globe*, reprinted in the *Royal Commission on Labour*, C–6795–V, 1892, appendix xcii.

after the counter-attack had begun but before the unions lost their impetus. Consequently, the figures of affiliations to the Trades Union Congress in 1890, however faulty, are the best available estimate of the maximum strength of the new unions, and at that time the nine major societies allegedly totalled over 350,000.[1] According to the official returns, they

TABLE 2

Membership of major 'new unions', 1890–1900

Union	Affiliation figures 1890 Trades Union Congress	Membership figures		
		1892	*1896*	*1900*
Dock, Wharf, Riverside and General Labourers' Union	56,000	22,913	10,000	13,829
National Union of Dock Labourers	50,000	8,463	11,697	13,388
National Amalgamated Union of Sailors and Firemen	58,780	20,000	dissolved 1894	
National Union of Gasworkers and General Labourers	60,000	36,108	29,730	47,979
National Amalgamated Union of Labour	40,000	23,834	20,864	21,111
National Labour Federation	60,000	6,000	dissolved† 1894	
National Amalgamated Coal Porters' Union	7,500	12,000	4,000	4,500
Amalgamated Association of Tramway, Hackney Carriage Employees and Horsemen in General	founded 1889	2,723	4,853	9,214

† The annual conference of 1893 was told that, 'owing to bad trade', many branches had been unable to send delegates. Nearly £3,000 had been spent on strike pay in 1892, and current expenditure was very high owing to the Hull dock strike.

stood at 140,000 in 1892, when the Board of Trade's figures give a grand total for the Transport (excluding railways) and the General Labour groups of 211,000. By 1896 this had fallen to 153,000, but it recovered to 204,000 by 1900.[2]

[1] This includes both major dockers' unions, the Seamen, the Gasworkers, the Tyneside union, the National Labour Federation, the General Railway Workers' Union, the Coal Porters, and the London and Counties Labour League, which was dissolved in 1895, at 13,000. The affiliation figures also included the Bristol Gasworkers and the London Dockers at 60,000 and 56,000 respectively. Since these are the same as the national totals recorded for Thorne's and Tillett's unions, they must arise from counting these branches as separate organizations and attributing to them the membership of the whole of their societies. The General Railway Workers claimed 20,000 from their London office, but their Liverpool branch was separately affiliated on the incredible figure of 40,000.

[2] These totals include the Bristol, West of England and South Wales Operatives, who rose from 7,000 in 1892 to 9,664 in 1896 and 25,459 in 1900. The status of this body is discussed on p. 72, footnote 4.

All the survivors showed some gains in the last years of the decade, and these were mainly due to gradual geographical and industrial expansion, partly offset in most instances by further losses in the original centres of strength. As Table 2 reveals, recovery owed much to the Gasworkers, who provided over one-third of the new members; but the most spectacular growth was achieved by the provincial tramwaymen of the Amalgamated Association. The Tramwaymen are also the best example of geographical expansion. In 1892 over half the members were in Manchester, the site of their head office; and the only branch outside Lancashire and the West Riding was at Nottingham. New branches were opened at Leicester and Wolverhampton in 1894, at Portsmouth in 1895, and in 1897 at Birmingham, Cardiff, Crewe, and Newcastle-on-Tyne. In 1898 the Association absorbed local unions in Belfast and Edinburgh. In almost every case these gains were held.

From its early days on Tyneside, the National Amalgamated Union of Labour had ventured both southwards and into Scotland, but most of these initial excursions brought little return. Scotland was quickly lost; the London district struggled to maintain a few hundred members; and Lincolnshire, booming in 1891–2, was down to just over 400 by 1893. Later in the decade, however, there developed a steady move away from Tyneside. In 1893 only 3,000 of the membership came from outside the coastal area of the North-east. Over half of these were in Belfast, where the unrest among engineering and shipbuilding workers encouraged recruitment. By 1897 a district had been re-established on the Clyde, and both the Sheffield and Belfast districts exceeded 2,500. Over 7,000 out of a total of 21,000 now came from beyond the North-east, and by 1899 Sheffield, with 4,500 members, had replaced Mid-Tyne as the largest district.

Within the Gasworkers a comparable change was taking place, as the provinces gained ground at the expense of London. Districts had been opened up in the first two years over most of England and in Belfast and Dublin. But the relative balance at this time may be gauged from district contributions to the central union funds assessed on a *per capita* basis, which show that in 1891–2 London provided two-thirds of the total. By 1896 Belfast and Dublin had been lost, yet in that year a census contained in the fourth *Quarterly Report* for 1897 shows London with no more than 8,556 out of 29,730 members, followed fairly closely by Birmingham with 6,024. In 1899, moreover, a new district was established in Scotland.

The geographical shift within both the National Amalgamated Union of Labour and the Gasworkers was accompanied, and partly explained, by an industrial shift. The growth of the National Amalgamated Union of Labour in Sheffield was mainly the result of the organization of colliery surface workers. The rise of the Gasworkers in Birmingham was attributed to the establishment of the Birmingham Alliances in the metal trades with their condition that 'workers must all be trade unionists . . .'.[1] But the most important single factor in the increase in the strength of the Gasworkers between 1896 and 1900 seems to have been a determined attempt to bring in the building labourers. In July 1899 Thorne reported that no less than 13,650 of his total membership of 44,968 belonged to branches of builders' labourers. Six thousand were in London and 4,000 in Birmingham.[2]

Like its Birmingham counterpart, the Amalgamated Gasworkers, Thorne's union also turned its attention to recruiting men employed by the various local authorities, especially their labourers. The secretary of the Bristol district, for example, reported that 'we have also managed to organise the workmen of the Sanitary Authority . . . and we hope to be able by having, as times are, a fairly democratic Town Council, to keep those men good members of our organisation and by that means bring a better condition of labour for Municipal employees, which shall set a good example to private employers'.[3] In the next *Annual Report* he was able to say that the union had 'gained advances for every workman' in this department.

Defeated in London and on the East Coast, Tillett's Dockers survived in strength only in the Bristol Channel. The success of the union in Swansea was underlined by the recruitment of large numbers of tinhouse-men in 1899 after the break-up of the South Wales, Monmouthshire and Gloucestershire Tinplate Workers' Union.[4] In June of the same year, along with the other unions affected, Tillett met a newly formed employers' association to set up a conciliation board. He had been able to tell his annual conference in May that membership was at last increasing, and the total rose from 9,000 in 1898 to 13,000 a year later. The other major centre was Bristol itself, where the union had maintained a better hold on the dockers than anywhere else. In July 1900 the establishment of two concilia-tion boards, one for corn-porters and the other for dock labourers,[5] further fortified its position there.

In the North-west and the Irish ports the National Union of Dock Labourers managed to hold on without much geographical or industrial expansion. Merseyside, and especially Liverpool, remained its strongest point. The opening of the Manchester Ship Canal in 1894 led to the

---

[1] Curran's Organizer's Report in the *Quarterly Report* for Mar. 1896. For the Alliances see p. 194.

[2] Since Thorne was engaged in an old dispute with Stevenson, secretary of the United Builders' Labourers, he may have exaggerated, though his report was mainly for internal con-sumption. But the claim is at least partly confirmed by the record of strike payments in the London building dispute (*Special Auditors' Report*, 30 July 1896). Thirty branches were involved and payments were made to 1,214 members. Since by no means the whole of the London building industry was shut down, this may represent a membership two or three times as large.

[3] *Annual Report*, 1893–4.   [4] See p. 209.

[5] *Report on the Strikes and Lockouts of 1900*, Cd. 689, 1901, pp. 109–11.

formation there of a vigorous branch; but in May 1895 the Ship Canal Company set out to break it. 'At Salford from May 27th to June 22nd 350 dock labourers were out on account of the refusal of employers to engage men wearing the union badge. It was agreed that the union badge should be worn less prominently, and that union and non-union men should be engaged without distinction.'[1] Other employers in the North-west were also coming to tolerate the badge. At Liverpool in October 1893 the union had even defeated an important shipping company, Elder Dempster, both over the badge and on the issue of whether foremen should be trade unionists.[2]

This degree of success was all the more remarkable in view of the divisions, dissensions, and jealousies within the union. In 1893 McGhee and McHugh resigned as president and secretary, partly because they felt their mission was accomplished, partly because they had been handicapped by a lack of technical knowledge of the docks, but partly because of intrigues against them by office-seekers.[3] They were replaced by M. Connelly and James Sexton.[4] Sexton as secretary was a valuable acquisition, a more competent administrator than the mercurial Tillett, with something of Thorne's sturdy qualities. He was also a Roman Catholic and a Home Ruler. Though the union reflected the religious and political differences to be found among dock workers in Glasgow and Liverpool,[5] Home Rule and Catholicism were very strong in both, and this may help to explain the union's hold over its members.

Even if the Dockers and the Gasworkers had suffered serious setbacks in London, and were finding recovery easier in the provinces, the capital remained a centre of the new unionism. Its resilient cabmen not only managed to make good the loss of their previous organization in 1894, but to come out on strike 7,000 strong for a month in May against an increase in rentals. Both the London Chamber of Commerce and the London County Council offered to arbitrate but were snubbed. The parties were finally persuaded to nominate Asquith, the Home Secretary, and his award, which split the difference, was accepted. London in 1894 also saw the formation of Albin Taylor's London County Council Employés, later the Municipal Employés Association, which was looking beyond its metropolitan origins by the end of the decade.

During the nineties a number of unions had been started for the manual

---

[1] *Report on the Strikes and Lockouts of 1895*, C-8231, 1896, p. 42.

[2] *Liverpool Weekly Post*, 21 Oct. 1893.   [3] Sexton, op. cit., pp. 107-8.

[4] Sexton, Sir James, P.C. (1856-1938). General secretary, National Union of Dock Labourers, 1893-1921. National Supervisor, Docks Section, Transport and General Workers' Union, 1922-8. Parliamentary Committee, Trades Union Congress, 1900-6, 1907-8, 1909-21. Executive Committee, Labour Party, 1902-4. M.P., 1918-31.

[5] For example, the coal heavers had a society at one end of Liverpool docks which was led by an Ulster Orangeman, and another at the other end led by a Home Rule Catholic. They were irreconcilable.

employees of local authorities. Societies in Birmingham, Sheffield, Bolton, Hull, Battersea, Bristol, and Glasgow found their way into the returns along with two or three Irish organizations. A more ambitious (and comprehensive) venture was the National Municipal and Incorporated Vestry Employés, founded in London in 1891. By 1892 it had nearly 6,000 members; but these gradually slipped away, and the union was dissolved in 1900. The remnants appear to have transferred their allegiance to the Municipal Employés Association, which jumped from 650 members in 1899 to 1,500 in 1900. Thereafter, under the forceful Taylor, the Association continued to grow and to absorb other local unions.

The third of the new creations of this period was a product of Mann's erratic course through the various sections of the labour movement. In 1898 he felt the need for a fresh organization, the Workers' Union, intended primarily to cater for the less-skilled engineering workers.[1] With nearly 3,000 members by 1900, it can best be described as a southern counterpart of the National Amalgamated Union of Labour. The union's first secretary was Tom Chambers, who was also secretary of a body known as the International Transport Federation; but he was soon succeeded by Charles Duncan, a member of the Amalgamated Society of Engineers from Middlesbrough.[2]

The Nature of the New Unionism

E. J. Hobsbawm has examined the reasons for stability and growth in the more important of the new unions in these years.[3] Primarily on the basis of a close scrutiny of the branches of the Gasworkers and the National Amalgamated Union of Labour, and taking into account the spread of the Dockers in the Swansea area, he concludes that 'the General Unions, at any rate between 1892 and 1911, depended far more on their foothold in certain industries and large works, than on their ability to recruit indiscriminately'. He stresses the significance, within such industries and works, of the 'recognition' by the employers of the unions as bargaining agents; and he sums up by calling them 'alliances of local closed shops, composed of regular employees', rather than the associations of mobile, footloose labourers, ready to turn their hand to almost any unskilled task, which constitute an essential element in the myth of the new unionism.

[1] Mann, op. cit., pp. 150–2. Mann's decision may have been influenced by the engineering dispute of 1897–8 (see p. 161). One of its main issues was the attempt of the skilled engineers to prevent certain types of machine from being operated by the less-skilled workers. Having lost the dispute, and knowing that their own Society would not admit such workers, engineers like Mann and Duncan may have concluded that they must have their own union.

[2] Duncan, Charles (1865–1933). Member, Amalgamated Society of Engineers. President, Workers' Union, 1898–1900; general secretary, 1900–28. Parliamentary representative, Transport and General Workers' Union, 1928–33. Executive Committee, Labour Party, 1920–2. M.P., 1906–18, 1922–33.

[3] 'General Labour Unions in Britain, 1889–1914', *Economic History Review*, 1949.

This analysis forms a valuable part of the explanation for the survival and development of these organizations. Only relatively permanent employees could give stability, but even they might not prove stable members without some form of pressure to keep them in the union. Recognition by the employer would provide a positive incentive to join a body which could handle grievances, and might lead to his acceptance of some form of closed shop. The importance to Tillett's union of the conciliation boards for tinplate and the Bristol dockworkers[1] emphasizes the force of the argument. But for a full account—and one which covers the wider range of unions included in this chapter—a more elaborate framework of analysis is required.

Rates of industrial growth were clearly important, since it is easier for a union to organize effectively in an expanding industry than in one which is on the decline. Most of the industries from which the new unions drew their chief strength were expanding rapidly. Between 1881 and 1901, for example, the numbers engaged in gas, water, and sanitary services in England and Wales rose from 25,000 to 68,000; in docks and harbours from 43,000 to 100,000; and carmen, carriers, carters, and wagoners increased from 125,000 to 273,000. All these rates of growth far exceeded that of the employed population as a whole.

The structure of the labour market and the nature of ownership had their effect. It was more difficult to maintain membership where labour was casual, as in the docks, or semi-casual, as in building and brickmaking, than where permanent employment was customary. The attitude of local authorities to trade unionism varied greatly from one area to another; but, where the unions managed to build up some political strength, they could exert an influence which was not available in private employment. The municipal undertakings of the industrial North provided the most stable membership for the gasworkers' unions, in sharp contrast to the London companies. In Bristol and Swansea the public had a share in control of the docks, and in Swansea Tillett's union included every kind of municipal employee.

The Gasworkers and the Dockers therefore paid close attention to local elections. By 1893 the Gasworkers had 'placed 18 men and women upon the various Municipal Councils, School and Local Boards, also Boards of Guardians';[2] and in 1901 the Dockers had three councillors, one of them on the Harbour Trust, three guardians, and one vice-chairman of a school board in Swansea alone.[3] The Tramwaymen shared this interest. In 1894 their four principal officers were all local councillors. By 1891 the Glasgow Tramways Committee had made a maximum working week a condition of lease,[4] and the union was able to report substantial concessions when

---

[1] See p. 85.   [2] *Annual Report*, 1893.   [3] *Dockers' Record*, Aug. 1902.
[4] *Royal Commission on Labour*, C–6894–VIII, 1893, Q. 19035.

Sheffield in 1896, Manchester in 1897, and Hull in 1899 took over their own tramways.

Other forces were at work where the new unions recruited labourers in the craft trades. The results might be beneficial, as when membership among builders' labourers rose with that of the craft societies during the building boom.[1] But the strength and resources of the National Amalgamated Union of Labour and the Gasworkers suffered from the great engineering and shipbuilding stoppages of the period, when the decisions of the craftsmen put their members out of work. So serious was the problem that for four years during the nineties the National Amalgamated Union of Labour ran at a loss, with between 25 and 50 per cent. of its income going on dispute pay. In the end the union was forced to cut the rate of lock-out benefit.

Leadership also played its part. Both Thorne and Sexton were sensible and competent officers. The Gasworkers had perhaps the best record of all the new unions, and the National Union of Dock Labourers picked up after Sexton took over; but the Dockers were less fortunate. Tillett was summed up by Collison as 'a demagogue, with the taste of a sybarite; a voluptuary with the hide of an agitator. . . . He never knew how to labour and to wait. Ever grasping at the present shadow of fleeting popularity, he lost the substance of future greatness.'[2] Much of the time of annual conferences from 1892 to 1894 was taken up by Tillett's disputes within the union, and subsequent meetings had to cope with the problem of his debts. Mann, a more likeable person, was no better as an administrator, and often deserted the president's office to take up other jobs in the labour movement. On the other hand, the National Amalgamated Union of Labour held up well despite a disastrous run of leaders. Like his predecessors, Dipper was dismissed, for 'neglect of duty', in 1898.

If these circumstances shaped its subsequent development, what had caused the new unionism? The first explanation for the upsurge of membership in 1889 and 1890 must be the rapid revival in trade which had begun about 1887. Dramatic growth, such as that in France and the United States during the 1930's, has always occurred at times of economic recovery. Economic recovery, however, is not a sufficient condition of a sharp rise in membership. In 1889 British trade unionism had lain fallow for over a decade, and was almost completely unresponsive to the brief revival of 1882, just as trade unionism in France and the United States achieved little during the boom years of the late 1920's. Another factor is external stimulation, as by the New Deal in the United States and the Popular Front victory in the French elections of 1936. If parallels are to be found in the British political scene of 1889, they must be sought in the

[1] See p. 153.
[2] William Collison, *The Apostle of Free Labour*, 1913, p. 251.

socialist movement of the time, and in the concern for poverty and suffering which spread far wider than socialist influence.

Of the widespread and genuine character of this concern there can be no doubt. Booth's *Life and Labour of the People in London* was only the most important account of the life of the poor to arouse public sympathy. *The Bitter Cry of Outcast London*, for instance, which was published in 1883, 'originated in a sober enough endeavour on the part of the London Congregational Union to discover which districts were most suitable for missionary work, but its revelations profoundly shocked public opinion. Issue after issue was promptly sold out, and in every large city similar "commissions of inquiry" were appointed to report on conditions in the local slums.'[1] Certainly works of this kind helped to create the favourable public opinion which made so much difference to the London dock strike, whose defeat would have been a disastrous blow. Thus they provided an important element in the context of the new unionism.

The role of the socialists was also important. Not only was their agitation among the London unemployed in 1885–7 part of the immediate background to the new unionism, but in addition there were direct links: between Pease and the National Labour Federation, between Eleanor Marx-Aveling and the Gasworkers, and between the Championites and the Dockers. Even so, a number of the new unions, including the Seamen, the National Union of Dock Labourers, and the Tyneside and National Labour Union, received little or no initial help from socialists and were already in existence before the London dock strike. In London much depended upon the individualistic, self-sufficient Champion. It was he who had suggested to Mrs. Besant that she should take up the problems of the match-girls, who first came to the aid of the Gasworkers, and who financed the activities of Mann and Burns.[2] Collison said that he was 'the brains of the Dock Strike',[3] and Joseph Burgess that he was 'credited with doing a lot of the organising behind the scenes'.[4]

Both were keen observers of the dockers' struggle. On this occasion, however, Champion himself played down the importance of socialism. 'There is no doubt whatever', he wrote, 'that those Socialists who took part in the strike were welcomed not because of their Socialism, but in spite of it; not on account of their speculative opinions, but for the sake of their personal ability to help.'[5] There were also the provincial groups of socialists, such as Maguire and his friends at Leeds, who threw themselves into the organization of the less skilled. But their efforts can be matched by the work of Lib-Labs in Birmingham, Bradford, and on Tyneside; and

[1] T. S. Simey and M. B. Simey, op. cit., p. 65.
[2] Pelling, *Origins*, pp. 59–73, 83–96, and *Cambridge Journal*, 1952–3, pp. 222–38.
[3] Op. cit., p. 80.   [4] *John Burns*, 1911, p. 107.
[5] *The Great Dock Strike*, 1890, quoted in Joseph Clayton, *The Rise and Decline of Socialism in Great Britain*, 1926, p. 56.

some new unions seem to have managed without the support of either group.

Finally, and possibly most important of all, come those leaders of the new unions, such as Thorne and Tillett, who were socialists themselves. Others, however, found leaders who were not socialists. Perhaps it is sufficient to say, in explanation of the considerable number of socialists at the head of the new unions, that the type of man who was likely to come forward in 1889 was also likely, particularly in London, to have come under socialist influence. That influence was therefore probably not a major cause of the upsurge in trade union membership, though it had its effect on the course taken by some of the new organizations, and though the assistance of certain socialists may have been crucial to the success of the London dock strike and at least helpful elsewhere.

In any case, an enumeration of the causes of the new unionism cannot explain what it was. Nor is it possible to define the phenomenon in terms of the structure of the new unions, for they showed a generous variety of forms. Here the basic distinction was between those which confined themselves to a single industry, and those which straddled a number of industries. The latter can be classed as 'general' unions, but the former must be subdivided. Some of them were 'industrial' unions, like the Seamen, claiming to organize all, or almost all, workers in a given trade, and no one else. Others claimed to organize only labourers in one industry; local builders' labourers' unions, for example, were particularly common.

General unionism was probably not a form which would have suggested itself to experienced officials, and when Wilson drew up his rules with the help of such men he provided for sailors and firemen alone; but the established unions usually stood aside and allowed the new unionists to choose for themselves. Others were advised by socialists, who had been attacking the existing sectional trade unionism and demanding its replacement by 'the solidarity of the workers—employed and unemployed, skilled and unskilled'.[1] But socialist influence did not determine whether a 'new union' became a 'general union'. Some of the organizations which they helped to set up, like the Gasworkers, did so; but others, like the Leeds Builders' Labourers, founded by Maguire and his colleagues, and J. L. Mahon's Postmen's Union, did not. Similarly, not all the unions which were or became 'general' owed much to the socialists. The National Labour Federation, with its premonitions of 'One Big Union', was socialist-inspired; but the Tyneside and National Labour Union and the Birmingham Gasworkers were the creation of Lib-Lab craft unionists and middle-class Liberal well-wishers.

The most convincing explanation of the origins of the major general

---

[1] *Strikes and the Labour Struggle*, issued by the Strike Committee of the Socialist League, 1886, and quoted in E. P. Thompson, *William Morris*, 1955, p. 513.

unions—the Gasworkers, the Dockers, and the National Amalgamated Union of Labour—is that they adopted this form unintentionally. Setting out to cater for a particular group of workers—gasworkers, dockers, or shipyard labourers—they found other workers clamouring to join and let them in. As they grew and spread to new centres, in which their organizers sought members where they could find them, their industrial coverage became wider and wider. Even if socialist influence prepared them to open their ranks, socialists could not have foreseen, still less planned, the strange and complex structure which these three unions (and one or two others) were to develop over the next ten years.[1]

If structure fails to define the new unions, it is possible to turn to the group of characteristics which contemporaries and subsequent historians have put forward as their distinguishing features. These are a membership of unskilled, low-paid labourers; a militant outlook; a readiness to employ coercion against non-unionists and blacklegs; low contributions allowing for the payment only of 'fighting' benefits; an acceptance of socialism; and a tendency to look to parliamentary and municipal action to solve labour's problems.[2] Yet this is too open to objections to serve as a guide to a satisfactory definition.

The meaning of the word 'labourer', for example, varied from industry to industry. Its most clear-cut usage was to describe the unqualified assistant of the apprenticed craftsman in the engineering, shipbuilding, building, printing, and minor craft trades. In other industries, however, there were no qualified craftsmen, or only a few maintenance workers; and the word was used to cover production or service workers, regardless of the fact that they might be relatively experienced and skilled. Dock labourers, chemical labourers, and seed-crushing labourers fell into this category. Other groups caught up in the new unionist ferment, for instance, the seamen, gas stokers, carters, and tramwaymen, were not known as labourers at all, and could hardly be regarded as unskilled.

Similarly, it is an oversimplification to think of the new unionists as necessarily low paid. With average adult male earnings at something like 25s. a week, labourers in shipyards, on building sites, or in engineering shops rarely earned more than 20s. But after 1889 the dockers' minimum wage for a full week became 24s., and many specialists among them earned more than that. In 1890 Wilson gave the rates for seamen (including allowances) as 28s. to 32s. 8d. a week, and compared this with 'the average

---

[1] The original preamble to the rules of the Gasworkers used the language of the old unionism. It was the 1892 edition that adopted the terminology of the class war to justify admitting 'every kind of "unskilled" labour . . . on an equal footing'; and this was long after the event. E. J. Hobsbawm, who prints both preambles in *Labour's Turning Point, 1880–1900,* 1948, pp. 99–101, suggests that the 1892 version was probably drafted by Edward and Eleanor Marx-Aveling.

[2] Howell, *Trade Unionism, New and Old;* Tom Mann and Ben Tillett, *The New Trades Unionism: a Reply to Mr. George Shipton,* June 1890.

wage of engineers' of 'not more than 32s.'[1] More striking still, the earnings of London gas-stokers varied between 30s. and 45s. a week.

Some of the new unions displayed a flamboyant militancy; but others, like the National Amalgamated Union of Labour and the Birmingham Gasworkers, worked for good relations with employers from the start. Most of those which started as 'fighting' unions soon came to see the advantages of moderation and a conciliatory approach. Mann, for example, told the first annual conference of the Dockers in 1890 that

at the present time in every port in the Kingdom steps are being taken to enable the employers, as a class to act concertedly. I rejoice at this. . . . I yearn for industrial order to take the place of industrial chaos, and am strongly of the opinion that a complete combination of employers, and an equally complete organisation of workers are essential before even an approach can be made. . . . I am entirely in favour of such Boards [of Arbitration] if formed as the outcome of organisation on the employers' side and ours.

The switch to moderation and conciliation was hindered, however, by two things: the extreme vulnerability of the members of these unions to replacement by other workers, and the determination of the Shipping Federation to destroy the Seamen and their allies. Moreover, unions of seamen and dockers in any case faced exceptional difficulties in retaining their membership. Seamen were outside the influence of the union except when on shore, and sailors returning from a voyage of several months were under a strong temptation to lapse rather than pay their accumulated debt of contributions. The weakness of the dockers in this respect arose mainly from the system of casual hiring. Both they and the seamen therefore tried to solve their problems by enforcing the closed shop.

In other industries, however, the new unions were not so dependent on the closed shop. Their members were not casual employees, and contributions could be collected each week. Once a union had a fair following in a given place of work, and enjoyed some recognition by the employer, it could bring social pressures to bear on those still outside. Nevertheless, they were all happy enough to take advantage of the closed shop wherever they could get it; and Thorne told the Royal Commission on Labour: 'If I had my way I tell you frankly that I would make every man join a union.'[2]

These differences led to inter-union conflict. Tillett tried to put a 'ring-fence' round the docks to exclude all but members of his union. Nevertheless, he wanted to be allowed to organize in other industries. The Gasworkers retaliated with the policy of 'one man, one ticket': if members of their union could work in the docks, members of the dockers' union could work in their preserves. This controversy was one of the many difficulties

[1] Annual Report of the National Amalgamated Union of Sailors and Firemen, 1890, *Royal Commission on Labour*, C–6894–VIII, 1893, appendix clxxxviii.

[2] Ibid., C–6894–IX, 1893, Q. 24772.

that beset the feeble Federation of Trade and Labour Unions. The main consequence, however, was to drive the seamen and dockers into conflict with their employers unless the latter would grant some form of closed shop, or at least permit some such protection as the 'button' of the Liverpool dockers. Where they would not, clashes were inevitable and thus the unions were chained to their militant reputation.

Conflict was further exacerbated by the need of the new unions, once a strike had begun, for those emphatic forms of picketing which aroused criticisms of 'tyranny' and 'intimidation'. Picketing was rarely a major problem in strike action for the highly skilled workers. Among the cotton spinners or the boilermakers, both sides in a dispute knew that when work was resumed the same men would have to be taken on. But the problem of 'scab' or blackleg labour arose much more in the casual or less-skilled trades.[1] To stand a reasonable chance of success, a strike required an elaborate system of pickets which was all too likely, in the heat of conflict, to give rise to scuffles, mob excitement, or worse. For the same reason, the attitude of the police could have little effect in major cotton, coal, or craft stoppages; but it could make or break strikes of new unionists.

'Fighting' benefits only, and low contributions, cannot help to define the new unions. Admittedly Thorne wrote in his first *Half Yearly Report* that he did not 'believe in having sick pay, out of work pay, and a number of other pays, we desire to prevent so much sickness and men being out of work. The way to accomplish this, is firstly to organise, then to reduce your hours of labour or work, that will prevent illness and members being out of employment.' But the Seamen paid accident and funeral benefits from the start, and on these grounds both George Howell[2] and the Labour Department of the Board of Trade[3] excluded them from the category of 'new trade unionism'. The National Amalgamated Union of Labour, however, had also paid the same benefits from its foundation.

The Dockers introduced a funeral benefit at their annual conference in 1891 as a 'means of increasing the present membership', while many of the branches started their own sick funds. The National Union of Dock Labourers brought in a funeral grant in September 1890, and its Birkenhead branch had already taken steps to set up a separate subscription for accidents and sickness. Similarly, some of the districts of the Gasworkers soon set up their own benefit funds. More benefits meant increased contributions. The Dockers, for instance, had begun with 2*d.* a week; this was later raised to 3*d.*, and in 1890 to 4*d.* The Seamen charged 6*d.* throughout. Such rates were below those of most craft unions of the time, but not all. Yet they were above those of many established unions, including, for example, the Weavers.

---

[1] Saville, loc. cit., pp. 318–19.   [2] *Trade Unionism, New and Old*, pp. 155–7.
[3] *Report on the Strikes and Lockouts of 1889*, C–6176, 1890, p. 5.

Finally, the new unions had varying political outlooks. Socialist influence had no hand in the formation of either the Seamen, the National Union of Dock Labourers, the National Amalgamated Union of Labour, or the Birmingham Gasworkers. The National Amalgamated Union of Labour refused to join the Federation of Trade and Labour Unions because of its socialist flavour; the Seamen, on the other hand, were its most passionate advocates. Later, the National Union of Dock Labourers and the National Amalgamated Union of Labour—which declared in November 1890 that 'as a society of workmen this organisation is non-political'[1]—both acquired socialist secretaries in Sexton and Dipper. But so, for that matter, did the Amalgamated Society of Engineers. Moreover, the socialism of Thorne, Tillett, and Sexton had moved considerably towards moderation by 1900. Indeed, the new unions were not even united on state intervention for the protection of labour. Soon after the conversion of the Trades Union Congress to a statutory eight-hour day, the annual conference of the Dockers declared that the eight-hour day was unsuitable for dock work.

What, then, were the common features which distinguished the new unionism? One characteristic which they shared was heavy expenditure on administration. In 1898 just over 20 per cent. of the expenditure of the '100 principal trade unions' in Britain went on 'Working and Other expenses'.[2] In both the Gasworkers and the National Amalgamated Union of Labour the proportion was 54 per cent., in the Dockers 80 per cent., and in the National Union of Dock Labourers 81 per cent. Part of the reason for this was the practice of paying commission to branch secretaries and to collectors; but the two dockers' unions were also heavily over-staffed with full-time officers from their more prosperous years. In 1890 the Seamen had permanent secretaries in nearly every port and spent £10,000 out of £41,000 on salaries alone.

This, by itself, was not of major importance. Yet the only other common factor was that they were 'new' unions: not simply in the sense that they were founded at this time, but also because they recruited among groups of workers previously untouched by trade unionism, or among those whose previous attempts at organization had been short-lived or failed to make much headway. Two other characteristics, however, were displayed by a sufficient number of the new unions to allow the press and the public to attribute them to the whole body. These were, first, general unionism, and, secondly, the militant and coercive tactics of the waterfront strikes and some of the gas strikes. The second soon ceased to be important, whereas the general unions were to grow until eventually they absorbed the great

---

[1] *Workman's Times*, 14 Nov. 1890.
[2] *Report on Trade Unions, 1898*, C–9443, 1899. The proportion for the Amalgamated Society of Engineers was 7 per cent.; for the Durham Miners 13 per cent.

majority of the new unions of 1889 and many others as well. But at the time both naturally attracted attention.

These three characteristics—newness, general organization, and militancy—are not enough to explain the fierce battle which raged between the 'new' and the 'old' unionism in and after 1889. To account for this, it is necessary to turn to the socialists once more. In their attacks on the existing unions, they had built up an image of an 'old union' which organized craftsmen, scorned labourers, hoarded its funds to pay friendly benefits, repudiated militancy, and was permeated by middle-class philosophy and the ideals of Gladstonian Liberalism. This picture was a caricature, but some of the barbs were sufficiently near the mark to hurt. Convinced by their own artistry, the socialists saw in the new unions the antithesis of the 'old unionism': a 'new unionism', open to all, free from friendly benefits, militant, class-conscious, and socialist. For a time, this description fitted some of the new organizations well enough for the enthusiasts on both sides to ignore the discrepancies; and the battles at the Trades Union Congress over the statutory eight-hour day and the leadership of Congress were represented, sometimes even by the participants, as conflicts between these two 'ideal' and mythical types.

The myth was too far from the truth to be sustained for long, and it became less and less relevant as the new unions were forced on to the defensive. Its collapse assisted the process of their assimilation into the wider trade union movement. The survivors settled down to the tasks of finding and keeping members, of chasing subscriptions, of trying to control working conditions, and of coming to terms with employers. There was little here to distinguish new from old, and the interests and preoccupations of the officers of the new unions were those of their colleagues in the older unions. It was easy for the two to work together. Aggressive recruitment by the general unions could have led to conflict, but competition of this kind was marginal. When the new unions poached members, they poached from each other.

Consciousness of social status still had a powerful effect in the relations between the boilermaker or the carpenter and the general labourer; but there was not so much reason for the miner or the weaver to look down on the gasworker or the tramwayman, and the prejudices of their members did not necessarily determine the relations between full-time officers who were doing the same sort of job in comparable conditions for a similar salary. Thus it was not difficult for the leaders of the new unions to win acceptance at the Trades Union Congress and on its Parliamentary Committee. There remained several differences of policy and of allegiance; but these diminished as the socialists permeated other unions and revised their methods to try to win general support, and as the movement as a whole came to give a higher priority to political action.

3

Coal and Cotton

Dimensions

IMPORTANT as the 'new unions' were, their emergence made no significant difference to the size of the movement. From about 750,000 at the
beginning of 1889, trade union membership rose to 1½ millions in 1892 and
2 millions in 1900. It is possible that for a moment in 1890 the proportion
organized by the new unions was substantial, but by 1892 their combined
strength was probably under 200,000, and at the end of the decade they
certainly covered less than one-tenth of all trade unionists. On the other
hand, the four industrial groups which had provided nearly three-quarters
of the total in 1888—Metals, Engineering and Shipbuilding, Mining and
Quarrying, Textiles, and Building—still provided over two-thirds in 1900,
even though they included no more than between 40 and 50 per cent. of
the country's manual workers.[1] In 1900 itself, metals, engineering, and
shipbuilding employed well over one-tenth of these workers; textiles
rather more than one-tenth; and both building and mining and quarrying
rather less.

The period had seen some changes. In 1888 the labour force in textiles
was the largest of the four, but subsequently it remained more or less
constant whereas each of the others expanded faster than the total labour
force. The contributions of the major groups to trade union membership
also changed. Textiles fell from about 16 to about 13 per cent. More
notably, metals dropped from about 25 to about 17 per cent., while mining
climbed from about 20 to about 26 per cent. to occupy the leading position.[2] Quarrymen and miners of minerals other than coal formed only a
negligible fraction of the mining group. Cotton, with about half the workers
in textiles, provided three-quarters of the group's trade unionists in 1888

[1] The industries concerned employed about four million workers by 1897 (calculated from
figures given in the *Report on Changes in Rates of Wages and Hours of Labour in 1897*, C–8975,
1898, p. xii). The Board of Trade's *Ninth Report on Trade Unions* for 1896 offered as estimates
of 'the adult population of the United Kingdom belonging to classes eligible for Trade Union
membership' the tentative figure of seven million adult males and the less tentative one of one
million adult females. The Webbs' estimate for 1891, however, had been seven million men and
'between two and three' million women (*History*, p. 424). But this covered 'all adult female
wage-earners engaged in manual labour', including domestic servants.

[2] See Table 6, p. 468. The growth in the relative importance of mining was even more
impressive than these proportions suggest. The membership figures for 1888 include the
South Wales 'sliding-scale associations', and by 1900 these had become militant, bona fide
unions.

and four-fifths in 1900. Thus the declining share of textiles as a whole masks a tightening of the grip of the cotton unions on their industry second only to that of the coal-miners.

Despite the stir caused by the new unions, the same four groups dominated the disputes of the nineties, accounting for 90 per cent. of the strikers and 93 per cent. of the working days lost between 1893 and 1900. Mining was far ahead with 60 per cent. of the working days lost; metals ran second with 17 per cent.; and textiles and building came third and fourth with 10 per cent. and 6 per cent. respectively.[1] Since the Board of Trade's wage statistics excluded several important industries,[2] these four provided more than half of the labour force covered. This, however, cannot explain their predominance in the recorded changes in wages from 1893 (when systematic statistics began) to 1900. They held undisputed leadership both in the period of cuts down to the end of 1895 and in the increases of the last five years of the century, accounting for over nine-tenths of the workers affected. There are no solid grounds for supposing that their share in the boom years from 1889 to 1891 was not equally impressive. Mining again led with 60 per cent. of the total; metals had 19 per cent.; and building and textiles each took 8 per cent. The rest were nowhere.[3]

These figures are decisive enough to show that the central story of industrial relations in the last decade of the nineteenth century must be told in terms of the established craft societies in engineering, shipbuilding, and building, and the flourishing unions of coal-miners and cotton operatives. It is also clear that among them the miners should come first.

The Miners' Federation

The Miners' Federation of Great Britain developed out of a series of meetings of delegates from the central coalfields which co-ordinated wage claims in the autumn of 1888 and during 1889; but the decision to found a permanent organization was not taken until November 1889 at a conference at Newport after it had finally become apparent that the Miners' National Union could not be transformed into a militant, broad-based body with industrial as well as legislative objectives.[4] The initial impetus came from Yorkshire and Lancashire, whose secretaries, Ben Pickard and Thomas Ashton, had worked in informal collaboration since the early eighties. During the summer of 1888, as the price of coal began to rise, Lancashire called for a national conference on wages, and in September Yorkshire invited representatives of 'all miners now free from sliding scales' to discuss 'the best means of securing a 10 per cent. advance . . . and

---

[1] *Twelfth Abstract of Labour Statistics, 1906–1907*, Cd. 4413, 1908, pp. 98–99.

[2] Lack of adequate data about seamen, agricultural labourers, and railway servants led the Board to deal separately with these groups in its reports.

[3] *Report on Changes in Rates of Wages and Hours of Labour in 1900*, Cd. 688, 1901, pp. lxviii–lxix. [4] Page Arnot, *The Miners*, vol. 1, pp. 82–87, 94–95.

of trying to find common ground for action'.[1] Twelve months later the success of the subsequent campaign made possible the conclusion of a formal alliance, and in January 1890 Pickard could declare that 'this Federation has sprung out of the recent wage agitation'.[2]

The most important constituent was the Yorkshire Miners' Association, which covered most of one of the five major coalfields.[3] Along with Northumberland and Durham in the North-east, East and West Scotland, South Wales and Monmouthshire, and Lancashire and Cheshire, York-shire produced four-fifths of the country's 177 million tons of coal in 1889 and employed four-fifths of its miners. Lancashire was the only other coal-field among the big five to join the Federation at the outset, and it could not challenge Yorkshire's predominance in output, numbers employed, or the degree of trade union organization. The remaining one-fifth of the labour force was shared between a dozen minor districts, nearly all of which joined the Federation, so that from the start it could claim to repre-sent about half the industry. Meanwhile, production was expanding rapidly but unevenly, thus altering the relative importance of the major districts. By 1900 Yorkshire had overtaken the North-east; South Wales and Monmouth remained in third place in front of Scotland; while Lanca-shire had fallen further behind.

The first years of the Federation's growth cannot be accurately charted. In 1886, at the depth of the depression, the Yorkshire Miners' Association had only 8,000 members, and there were another 7,000 in the Lancashire and Cheshire Miners' Federation.[4] But a rapid rise began in 1888 and at the end of the following year the new Federation covered 75,000–100,000 miners. By the beginning of 1892 trade union membership in the industry was approaching 300,000, more than half of whom were in the Federation. Of these Yorkshire provided 55,000, Lancashire and Cheshire 30,000, and Nottingham and Derbyshire 35,000 between them. Some 40,000–50,000 others were spread over the rest of the Midlands, Bristol and Somerset, North Wales, and parts of Scotland. Still outside the Federation stood Durham with 50,000 members and Northumberland with 17,000. A further 50,000–60,000 miners remained in unaffiliated unions in Scotland, Lancashire, and the minor districts, and in the South Wales 'sliding-scale associations'.

None of the Federation's constituents had evolved a system of collective bargaining with the employers to equal those now long established in the North-east.[5] From time to time Yorkshire supplemented its county-wide

---

[1] Ibid., p. 92.

[2] Ibid., p. 109. Pickard, who had been vice-president of the Miners' National Union since 1877, did not commit himself to the need for a new organization until Oct. 1889 (ibid., p. 110).

[3] As a statistical unit the Yorkshire coalfield covered Nottinghamshire and Derbyshire, although these counties had their own unions.

[4] Ibid., p. 74.   [5] See p. 19.

negotiations on general wage changes by *ad hoc* joint committees for South and West Yorkshire. These dealt with pit disputes which could not be settled on the spot between the colliery management and union deputations. The committees might appoint an umpire, but they lacked written rules and could be set up only by consent of both parties.[1] In Lancashire, the Coal-owners' Association told the Royal Commission on Labour, there were 'constantly little disputes going on'; but they did not want a joint committee or a conciliation board,[2] and local disputes were left to the pit, where the miners could usually insist on bringing their 'agent' into the discussion when they needed him. Joint meetings were held only to determine changes in wages for the county as a whole.

This pattern was repeated in most of the other Federated coalfields, but complications could occur. In South Staffordshire the men continued to prefer their wages board with its sliding scale to the new philosophy of direct negotiation. Consequently, when the Midland Federation of North and South Staffordshire, Cannock, and Shropshire followed the lead given by Lancashire and Yorkshire in 1888, South Staffordshire seceded.[3] In Nottinghamshire difficulties were caused by the 'butty' system. The butties had once been subcontractors operating a whole face or even a complete pit, but their status had declined until they now ranked as superior workmen rather than as employers. They were the driving force behind the union, electing checkweighmen and dominating policy. The day-wage facemen employed by the butties could also become members, and inevitably interests sometimes clashed.[4] The influx of day-wage men and others into the union during 1889 and two or three years thereafter began to change its outlook on wages. Increases were sought for the 'banksmen', and recognized price lists for the 'boys'.[5]

The Federation also claimed jurisdiction in Scotland, though the only stable organization among the remnants of Keir Hardie's[6] Scottish Federation remained aloof. This was the Fife union with its 'respectable and responsible executive',[7] and a membership of 7,000 in a labour force of 9,000. Its leaders met the local owners in conferences on county questions, but there was no joint committee for pit disputes. Elsewhere, barely 10 per

---

[1] *Report on the Strikes and Lockouts of 1894*, C–7901, 1895, p. 264.

[2] C–6708–IV, 1892, Qs. 5867, 5971.

[3] Alan Fox, *Industrial Relations in Birmingham and the Black Country, 1860–1914*, B.Litt. thesis, Oxford, 1952. The Midland Federation had been founded in 1881.

[4] A. R. Griffin, *The Miners of Nottinghamshire*, vol. i, 1955, p. 110.

[5] Ibid., pp. 76–77, 139.

[6] Hardie, J. Keir (1856–1915). Lanarkshire miners' county agent, 1879–81. Secretary, Ayrshire Miners' Union, 1886–90. Secretary, Scottish Miners' Federation, 1886–7. Chairman, Scottish Labour Party, 1888–93. Chairman, Independent Labour Party, 1893–1900, 1913–15. Executive Committee, Labour Party, 1900–15. M.P., 1892–5, 1900–15. Founder and editor, *Labour Leader*, 1894–1904.

[7] *Royal Commission on Labour*, C–6795–IV, 1892, Q. 13762.

cent. of Scotland's 70,000 miners were organized in eight separate unions. The employers' attitude was one of 'haughty indifference'[1] and they refused any kind of recognition.[2]

This varied collection of bargaining procedures was given coherence by the wage policy of the Federation, whose twin aims were a substantial increase in the miners' rates untrammelled by any kind of sliding scale, and 'an eight hours' day from bank to bank in all Mines for persons working underground'. In pursuit of the latter its leaders were ready if necessary to turn to political action, but to achieve the former they relied on industrial solidarity. 'By Unity we got the advance, and by Unity we may preserve it', said Pickard in October 1888, after the first victory in the campaign which produced the Federation;[3] and this attitude was enshrined in the famous Rule 20, adopted at Newport, which laid down that 'whenever any County, Federation or District is attacked on the Wage question or any action taken by a general Conference, all members connected with the Society shall tender a notice to terminate their contracts—if approved of by a Conference called to consider the advisability of such joint action being taken'.

It was fortunate for the Federation that it came into being during an economic recovery, and that none of the owners' associations chose to test the miners' solidarity before the new organization had been able to build up its strength. Later the opposition to sliding scales was to express itself in the defence of a minimum wage in the face of falling prices, but now prices were rising fast and the immediate objective was 'a living wage'.[4] Following on the single 10 per cent. of 1888, in 1889 all the Federated districts of England and Wales received two further 10 per cent. increases on the 'standard' wage rates of 1888. By February 1890, however, the average pithead price of coal had risen by 71 per cent. since 1887, and a special conference decided to demand a fourth increase of 10 per cent.

Strike notices were to take effect on 15 March. Pledging their organizations 'to act jointly and unitedly', the delegates also resolved 'that if the advance be not conceded all round, no district, county, or federation be allowed to accept the advance of wages asked for'.[5] Faced with this challenge, the employers of the Federated districts formed their own combination. Alfred Barnes, a Derbyshire coal-owner and Liberal Unionist

---

[1] *Report on the Strikes and Lockouts of 1891*, C–6890, 1893, p. 494.

[2] In 1893 the Federation accepted a novel recruit—the Seamen. They were admitted 'as part of the Federation on the lines of mutual help, but to be governed by rules or regulations drawn up by the two Committees of the two Associations' (Page Arnot, op. cit., vol. i, p. 226). The union was already disintegrating and nothing came of the arrangement. Less surprising was the admission of another new union, the Coal Porters, in 1892 (ibid., p. 217).

[3] Page Arnot, op. cit., vol. i, p. 94.

[4] In July 1893, on the eve of the great lock-out, Ashton told the coal-owners that the Federation 'was established to get and keep a comfortable living rate of wage for its members' (ibid., p. 259). [5] Ibid., p. 114.

Member of Parliament, took the lead, saying that, as against the Miners' Federation, individual owners or even districts 'must be powerless'.[1] The owners resolved unanimously that the demand 'should be resisted to the utmost', but the miners, 'in order that the present wages deadlock may pass away',[2] split their claim into 5 per cent. at once and 5 per cent. in July. Though a strike could not now be averted,[3] this offer provided the basis of an early settlement. The employers asked for a conference with the Federation on 20 March and a compromise was reached on August as the date for the second 5 per cent. But even more important than this further increase was the principle of joint negotiation on wages for the whole of the Federated area, which brought the Miners' Federation a long way towards realizing one of their principal aims—a uniform wage policy. So long as the employers' associations of the area were prepared to rely on such negotiations, Rule 20 would not be needed, for each section of the Federation would receive the same treatment under a common agreement.

The Federation was ably led. Its president, the domineering Pickard, was 'stubborn as a mule', a powerful speaker, and 'a most skilled negotiator', who believed that the new alliance would best be served by 'spirit and aggressiveness'.[4] Ashton, the secretary, was 'very methodical and persistent, careful and exact', as well as 'very apt with his pen'.[5] However, it was not only efficient and forceful leadership which brought success where the Amalgamated Association of twenty years before had failed.[6] Economically, the original area covered by the Federation was relatively homogeneous. The great bulk of its output went into the home market, and prices fluctuated less than those of the North-east and South Wales, which produced by far the larger part of the thirty-one million tons exported in 1891. It is perhaps also of significance that in Scotland Fife was the main exporter. Thus to apply the Federation's wage policy in the central coalfields alone, and in three successive years of rising prices, was to apply it in the most propitious circumstances.

The Non-federated Areas

Outside the Federation, Northumberland, Durham, and South Wales, like Fife and South Staffordshire, pursued their independent courses. With the possible exception of Yorkshire, Northumberland and Durham were the only mining districts which could boast any machinery for joint regulation worthy of the name. The difference no longer lay primarily in their

[1] J. E. Williams, *The Derbyshire Miners*, 1962, p. 298.

[2] Page Arnot, op. cit., vol. i, p. 114.

[3] 107,000 miners in Yorkshire, Lancashire, Derbyshire, Nottinghamshire, and Leicestershire were out for seven days (*Report on the Strikes and Lockouts of 1890*, C-6476, 1891, p. 7).

[4] Page Arnot, op. cit., vol. i, pp. 103, 110.

[5] Ibid., p. 63. In contrast to Pickard and nearly all the other miners' leaders, who were ardent Liberals, Ashton was a Conservative. [6] See p. 18.

handling of county-wide wage adjustments, for by the summer of 1889 both associations had abandoned sliding scales. This move was opposed by the leaders, whose views on industrial relations[1] did not change overnight; but henceforward they had to proceed, like their colleagues of the Federated area, by direct negotiation. The main difference now lay in the treatment of pit disputes. Those which could not be settled by meetings on the spot with the management were referred to a joint committee, with specific provision for arbitration.[2] Moreover, a criterion for determining colliery piece rates was available in the accepted standards of average earnings for all classes of workmen in each county, and rates were adjusted up or down on application by either side by reference to these recognized standards.

This machinery extended to all colliery workers, for the North-east demonstrated its advanced stage of development in this as in so many other respects. Deputies, cokemen, and colliery mechanics were well organized in their own separate unions, which had been founded during the seventies. The enginemen and boilermen were also active, as indeed they were in all coalfields, almost every district having its own small organization.[3] Each of these bodies dealt independently with the special circumstances of the occupation it represented, but in matters of common interest mining unions in the North-east acted jointly through county federations, formal in Durham and informal in Northumberland.[4]

Both before and after the formation of the Miners' Federation, the two counties were the backbone of the cautious and conservative Miners' National Union; and it might have been expected that their stable organization and traditions of 'respectability' and 'moderation' would have kept them free from any taint of the 'new unionism'. For two reasons, however, the North-east, hard-hit by the depression of the mid-eighties, showed more signs of infection than any other coalfield. The first arose out of a strike by the Northumberland miners in 1887 against the employers' demand for a cut of 15 per cent. as a condition of renewing the sliding-scale agreement. They stayed out for seventeen weeks, and the bitter conflict attracted the attention of the various socialist sects who were beginning to compete for working-class support. Setting aside sectarian jealousies, trade unionists like Tom Mann, J. L. Mahon, and James Macdonald helped to organize the North of England Socialist Federation, which flourished for a time and left behind a ferment of ideas in both counties.[5]

---

[1] See p. 19.

[2] *Report on the Strikes and Lockouts of 1894*, C–7901, 1895, p. 263. Unlike the *ad hoc* committees in Yorkshire, this machinery did not require the consent of the colliery management concerned before it came into operation. The union could thus compel the management to come before an independent tribunal (ibid., p. 264).   [3] See also p. 211.

[4] Webbs, *Industrial Democracy*, p. 126 and footnote; Page Arnot, op. cit., vol. i, pp. 65–66.

[5] Dona Torr, *Tom Mann and his Times*, vol. i, 1956, pp. 242–4; E. P. Thompson, op. cit.,

The other factor was a change in leadership. Even though Northumberland insisted upon rejecting its sliding scale at the end of 1887 and voted to terminate the secretary's parliamentary salary, Burt managed to survive the new discontent. The hostile vote was soon overruled and Burt was able to maintain his authority. But Crawford died in 1890, the year after Durham had also abandoned its sliding scale, and his successor, W. H. Patterson, was a far weaker man who tried to follow where Crawford would have led. During Crawford's long illness, unrest in the union had already begun to mount, and now indiscipline ran riot. Unofficial strikes had never been so frequent; the conciliation machinery was overloaded with disputes; and the employers lamented the union's loss of control.[1]

They held their hand, however, until prices began to fall. As always, the exporting districts were the most sensitive to changing market conditions, and the Durham coal-owners asked for a 10 per cent. reduction at the beginning of 1892. Patterson urged acceptance but was brushed aside. The men voted overwhelmingly for a strike and against either negotiation or arbitration. The owners locked-out and made the most of their ascendancy, increasing the harshness of their demands as the dispute continued and rejecting every offer from the miners. At first they even refused to revert to their original proposal of a 10 per cent. cut; but, after twelve weeks, mediation by the Bishop of Durham led to an agreement to open the pits on these terms.

The Miners' Federation, hoping to secure Durham's affiliation, contributed liberally to the strike fund. Almost £50,000 was raised outside the county and more than two-thirds came from Federation donations, most of the remainder being supplied by Northumberland.[2] In the short run this generosity brought results. Durham affiliated in June 1892, and the Federation's missionaries, appealing to the lodges over the heads of their leaders, brought Northumberland in soon afterwards. Unification was made easier because the abandonment of sliding scales had removed the major disagreement over wage policy, though the leaders of the North-east retained something of a 'sliding-scale mentality', and from experience were much less convinced of the virtues of an irreducible minimum than Pickard and his colleagues soon showed themselves to be.

On the second great aim of the Federation the two sections were still far apart. In 1890 the Federation began its long struggle for the enactment of a statutory eight-hour day. The hewers of the North-east, however,

pp. 512–25. The socialist missionaries did not find the soil entirely unprepared; for Lloyd Jones, a Welsh fustian cutter turned journalist and first secretary of the Labour Representation League, had helped the North-east miners in several arbitration cases, and had for many years preached Owenite socialism to them. His teaching influenced Crawford to some extent, but left Burt's Liberalism apparently untouched (Welbourne, op. cit., pp. 203–4, 233, 255).

[1] *Royal Commission on Labour*, C–6708–IV, 1892, Qs. 595, 1937–41, 1987.
[2] Page Arnot, op. cit., vol. i, p. 217.

were convinced that an Eight Hours Act would worsen their conditions. This fear arose from the methods of productive organization adopted in the area. The hewers worked in two seven-hour shifts, served by one long shift—about ten hours—of the less-skilled men, the 'putters' and 'transit' workers. If an Eight Hours Act was passed, the owners could adopt one of three courses. They might run one eight-hour shift of putters. Less coal would then be shifted and many hewers would lose their jobs. Secondly, the owners could run two eight-hour shifts for both putters and hewers, thus increasing the hewers' work. Thirdly, they might balance two eight-hour shifts of putters by introducing a three-shift system for the hewers. Each of these courses would be against the interest of the hewers, and the hewers dominated the unions.

Given this crucial divergence, the leaders of the North-east found it possible to persuade their members to return to their old isolation when the Federation decided to resist the challenge of the employers in 1893. In any case, the Durham men had little heart for another struggle so soon after their defeat in the previous year. Patterson was ill, and was already being pushed aside by John Wilson,[1] a powerful autocrat in the Crawford tradition who hankered after a return to sliding scales. Wilson quickly re-established the authority of the association over its lodges, and succeeded to the official leadership when Patterson died in 1896. When Durham was expelled by the Federation in August 1893, Northumberland also withdrew, though the decision to do so was based on a resolution carried only by a small majority of the membership.[2]

Even in South Wales the Federation had an impact. The chief influence in Monmouthshire was William Brace's[3] union, which had been affiliated to the Federation from its foundation. Brace began to build up a following in the Rhondda in his efforts to break the hold of the Welsh-speaking leaders over the local mining communities. The power of men like Mabon did not rest on the strength of the so-called unions whose agents they were, for these organizations were small, shadowy, feeble, and disunited.[4] It rested rather on their personal ascendancy as Welshmen, and on Welsh

[1] Wilson, John (1837–1915). Treasurer, Durham Miners' Association, 1882–90; financial secretary, 1890–6; general secretary, 1896–1915. Parliamentary Committee, Trades Union Congress, 1890–3. Liberal M.P., 1885–6, 1890–1915.

[2] Page Arnot, op. cit., vol. 1, pp. 230–1.

[3] Brace, William, P.C. (1865–1947). President, South Wales Miners' Federation, 1911–19. M.P., 1906–20. Parliamentary Under-secretary for the Home Office, 1915–18. Chief Labour Adviser to Department of Mines, 1920–7.

[4] See p. 18. According to the Webbs, 'by far the largest and most important miners' union in South Wales has no other subscription than [the compulsory sliding scale deduction] and is without lodges, branch officials, or other organised machinery' (*Industrial Democracy*, p. 211). Each colliery under the sliding scale had its pit committee, but this had no real power and outspoken members were soon victimized. 'Deputations . . . were rather infrequent. When they did take place, all the men had to stand during the whole of the proceedings, with their caps in their hands' (J. E. Morgan, *A Village Workers Council*, 1956, p. 17).

resistance to the domination of English ideas and policies. Nevertheless, the leaders never succeeded in securing complete quiescence. Occasionally the local associations had come to life to fight against encroachments on established rights, and now they demanded a more active wage policy, even winning some advances outside the terms of the sliding-scale agreements.[1]

In 1893, as depression deepened, Brace tried to defy the pressure of falling prices by seeking a 20 per cent. advance. This failed to attract the faceworkers but won the support of the hauliers in many of the sliding-scale pits. Brace determined to use them as a lever to break the sliding-scale system. A hauliers' strike was called, and meetings of hauliers refused to listen to the sliding-scale representatives. But in trying to take on the owners, the old leaders, and the trade cycle, Brace wildly over-estimated his strength. Even before the strike most employers had refused to allow him to accompany deputations, and victimized men who declared for the Federation. Now the owners co-operated with Mabon and his colleagues to defeat Brace and the hauliers. All communications from them were ignored, while the faceworkers stayed at work and kept the haulage systems going. After some ugly violence in Ebbw Vale and elsewhere, the strike petered out.[2] But discontent remained, and at the end of the year Brace claimed forty-eight lodges and 10,000 members, some two-fifths of the organized miners in the coalfield.

The 1893 Lock-out

When the boom gave way and prices fell, the Federation's response was a 'stop week' in March 1892 intended to clear away 'the surplus coal in the markets and thus maintain [prices and] the miners' wages'.[3] Whatever effect this may have had on prices was short-lived, but it was an impressive demonstration of strength achieved at little cost to the Federation—for a week's stoppage hardly strained its resources. The comment of one employer was that 'the Miners' Federation proved that they were perfect masters of the position'.[4] Perhaps because of this, the coal-owners of the Federated area made no concerted attempt to secure a reduction until the following summer. Instead they tried to undermine the solidarity of the Federation where it was weakest. In the spring of 1893 reductions were demanded in sections of the smaller coalfields. By March the Midland Federation had to ask for assistance for its locked-out members, and a conference of the national Federation decided to give full financial support but to keep Rule 20 in reserve.

[1] E. W. Evans, *The Miners of South Wales*, 1961, pp. 142–7.
[2] Ness Edwards, op. cit., pp. 108–18.
[3] Federation circular, quoted in Page Arnot, op. cit., vol. i, p. 209.
[4] Sir Joseph Pease, M.P., speaking for a deputation to Gladstone, ibid., p. 211.

By June the employers had decided that they could afford to open a general offensive. At a joint conference they asked for a 25 per cent. reduction[1] and offered to submit their demand to arbitration. All the constituents of the Federation rejected both arbitration and a reduction, except for Durham, which preferred arbitration, and Northumberland, which had already voted not only against a strike but also against a levy in support of those who might come out. A conference thereupon decided to counter the employers' demands with a notice for an equivalent advance for all those districts which had suffered reductions in wages during the past two years. In the last week of July battle was joined.

The Federation was now required to defend the principle of the 'living wage', which its vice-president, Sam Woods[2] of Lancashire, had put into these words: 'Notwithstanding all the teachings of political economists, all the doctrines taught by way of supply and demand, we say there is a greater doctrine overriding all those, and that is the doctrine of humanity. We believe that the working man is worthy of his hire, and hold at the present moment that wages are as low as they ever ought to be.'[3] The result was by far the largest dispute the country had ever seen, for the lock-out lasted sixteen weeks, brought out 300,000 miners, and cost over twenty-one million working days. As it proceeded, the growing shortage of coal gradually took effect in many other industries, and an increasing number of workshops and factories were stopped or put on short time.

Meanwhile the dispute aroused a greater degree of public interest than any episode in industrial relations since the London dock strike of 1889, which it dwarfed in size. In addition to offering a dramatic demonstration of the Federation's power, the conflict, by bringing prolonged suffering to the miners' families, caught the public's sympathy, and gave rise to much anxious discussion not only of the conditions of the workers but of class relationships as well. Subscription lists and collections for relief benefited accordingly.[4] As the suffering intensified, sporadic violence broke out here and there. Early in September the troops called in by a local coal-owning Justice of the Peace fired on a crowd of miners at Featherstone in

---

[1] Since the miners had received increases totalling 40 per cent. on the 1888 'standard', the 25 per cent. reduction now demanded would still have left them 15 per cent. above the 1888 level of rates. In terms of current earnings, the owners' demand represented a cut of 18 per cent.

[2] Woods, Sam (1846–1915). President, Lancashire and Cheshire Miners' Federation, 1881–1915. Vice-president, Miners' Federation of Great Britain, 1889–1909; honorary vice-president, 1909–15. Secretary, Parliamentary Committee, Trades Union Congress, 1894–1904. M.P., 1892–5, 1897–1900.

[3] Page Arnot, op. cit., vol. i, p. 205.

[4] The *Daily Chronicle*, whose editor, A. E. Fletcher, later became a member of the Independent Labour Party, played a leading part, and its accounts of relief work are quoted at length in Page Arnot, op. cit., vol. i, pp. 241–3, 256. £24,000 was subscribed to the Relief Fund by the general public in addition to nearly £10,000 from Durham and £2,000 from Northumberland, both of which had broken with the Federation (ibid., p. 260).

Yorkshire after a reading of the Riot Act. Two men were killed and others injured.[1]

By October businessmen were becoming alarmed at the economic effects of the lock-out. The mayors of several of the main mining towns made the first major attempt at conciliation. When they failed their place was taken by A. J. Mundella, President of the Board of Trade, who brought the two sides together at the beginning of November.[2] Both the coal-owners and the Federation were ready to establish a conciliation board to regulate the adjustment of wages in future; but the owners remained firm for a reduction before work was resumed, and the Federation was equally steadfast in its determination to go back at the old rates. Moreover, the miners' leaders added a significant rider, demanding henceforward 'that the minimum or standard rate of wages be 30 per cent. above the wage rate of January 1st, 1888'.[3] After lasting for more than two days, the meeting ended in deadlock.

The government decided that it could not let the matter rest and, after private feelers had been put out, Gladstone formally approached the parties by writing a letter on 13 November suggesting a further conference 'under the chairmanship of a member of the Government . . . Lord Rosebery has consented, at the request of his colleagues, to undertake the important duty which such position involves'.[4] This was the first instance of intervention by the Prime Minister or the Cabinet in an industrial dispute. The offer was accepted at once, and the conference took place on 17 November, reaching agreement at its first session. That morning, while recognizing that the dispute had been 'the gravest and most disastrous this country has ever known', *The Times* had called the ministry's 'interference . . . a doubtful step'.

The settlement provided for a conciliation board covering the Federated area, with an independent chairman who would have a casting vote. The board was to last for one year in the first instance, and to have power to determine wages from February 1894. Until then the miners were to receive the rates prevailing before the stoppage. Understandably, the Federation leaders greeted this as a triumphant vindication of their policies. Pickard's next presidential address claimed that

South Wales had gone down, Durham had gone down, Northumberland had gone down, and Scotland had touched the flat bottom; yet with all the

[1] Asquith, as Home Secretary, had transmitted to the War Office the request from the local authorities for troops. This he was obliged to do, but the 'Featherstone Murders' were to dog his reputation in mining areas for years to come.

[2] Mundella had already attempted earlier in 1893 to mediate, with the government's 'great sympathy and goodwill', in the dispute at Hull (see p. 81); and on 31 July he had brought in a Bill, which later proved abortive, authorizing the Board of Trade to take the initiative in encouraging the establishment of conciliation boards.

[3] Quoted in Page Arnot, op. cit., vol. i, p. 247. [4] Ibid., pp. 249–50.

fluctuations of trade and all the beating of the waves against the shores of the Federation, you had kept up your wages. . . . You were told and I was told that, when bad trade set in, the experiment we had been trying would be thoroughly tested. Only let bad trade appear, let fluctuations in prices dominate the market, then where would be your Federation and its principles? Well, the Federation, although buffeted and tossed about by the unsettled condition of trade in other localities, yet remains firm as a rock.[1]

Certainly it seemed at first sight that the Federation had disproved the principle that no miners' union could survive unless it learned to accept wage reductions when prices fell. It is possible, however, to recognize the Federation's achievement without accepting all Pickard's claims. In the first place, his comparisons were unfair, for prices had fallen further in the exporting areas than in areas serving the home market. It was perhaps fortunate for the Federation that the adherence of Northumberland and Durham had lasted only a few months, for had it been called on to apply Rule 20 on behalf of the North-east the outcome might not have been the same. Secondly, the effect of such a large and protracted stoppage was to raise the price of coal to a level at which coal-owners became anxious for a return to work at the old wages in order to recoup some of their losses.

According to the returns of the Federation, 60,000 of its members were already back at work at the old rates by the beginning of October, and the figure rose to 88,000 at the end of the month.[2] With a levy of a shilling a day they were able to pay the strike benefit of almost an equivalent number of strikers. By November, when prices had climbed still further, the coal-owners were losing nothing by promising to maintain wages for another three or four months. In due course prices resumed their downward trend, and the Federation had to concede a 10 per cent. reduction[3] after negotiations on the new conciliation board in July and August 1894, when the price of most types of coal had dropped back below their levels at the start of the lock-out twelve months before.

On this occasion, an important new principle of wage-fixing was introduced. Following a suggestion by one of the coal-owners, it was agreed that while wage rates should remain constant until January 1896, from then until August 1896 they should rise no higher than 45 per cent. above 'standard', and fall no lower than the minimum proposed by the Federation at the time of the deadlock in November 1893, 30 per cent. above 'standard'. Both sides were conscious of pioneering, and the miners' leaders were delighted. 'It was a great scheme; it was a new departure, we took very great responsibilities', said Sam Woods.[4] But it is hardly surprising that in a few districts the owners accepted the idea of a minimum only under strong protest.[5]

---

[1] Ibid., pp. 253–4. [2] Ibid., pp. 244–6.
[3] 7 per cent. off current earnings. [4] *Minutes of the Conciliation Board*, 31 Aug. 1894.
[5] In West Yorkshire they rejected the proposal at first by a large majority; Cannock Chase

The coal-owners also agreed reluctantly to lay down certain terms for some underground day-wage men and some surface workers. Pickard, confessing astonishment that his Federation included so many surface workers, disclaimed any sympathy for, or interest in, their problems. He pointed out, however, that in certain parts of the country the general unions were organizing such men and getting agreements with the employers, sometimes striking in the process and so putting hewers out of work. A settlement between the Federation and the owners was therefore necessary if this 'outside influence' was not to 'land us in serious difficulties'.[1]

After 1894, with the position of the Federation protected by its new form of agreement, coal prices continued to fall gradually for two more years. The average pithead price was 6s. 7d. in 1894, 6s. in 1895, and 5s. 10d. at its lowest point in 1896. The figure for 1896, however, was still 20 per cent. above the 1887 price of 4s. 10d. Wage rates in the Federated area could hardly have ended the trade cycle 30 per cent. above the original standard of 1888 if prices had fallen back to the 1887 level. Nevertheless, whatever share in its successes should be assigned to good fortune in the early days, the Federation survived and achieved such a grip on the districts that, when the tide began to turn twenty-five years later, the alliance showed itself to be indestructible. But this was not only because of the good management as well as the good luck of the Federation itself. It was also because the Federation's achievements gave its constituents sufficient time and opportunity to achieve control of the local mining communities.

This control had two important aspects. First, pit negotiations were almost as important as general wage adjustments in determining the earnings of miners. The wage changes negotiated by the Federation were percentage alterations of the rates prevailing in 1888. For hewers these rates were almost invariably piece rates, and piece rates required frequent alteration, or supplementation, as conditions at the coalface changed. New faces required new rates. Outside Northumberland and Durham, the miners had established little control over these changes before 1889, and only in those counties were there any general standards. Elsewhere piece-prices varied not only from colliery to colliery but even from face to face. At most pits no formal price lists were published, much less agreed with the union representatives. There was usually a customary day-wage for faceworkers by which a man could assess the 'fairness' of a particular rate, but this was only the roughest of criteria.

rejected it unanimously. There was also very strong opposition from some large owners in the districts which assented. Most districts carried it, however, by large majorities, and friction was small when the agreement came to be applied, though local strikes were necessary in a few places (*Minutes of the Conciliation Board*, 19 July and 31 Aug. 1894).

[1] Ibid., 31 Aug. 1894.

Such partial and fragmentary regulation as did exist in 1889, moreover, applied only to the faceworkers, who dominated the unions at that time. The other underground workers, and nearly all surface workers, were paid by time. Before 1889 they were almost totally unorganized, and their rates were normally adjusted at the discretion of the colliery management. Several years of Federation control made profound alterations in this system of wage settlement. The lodges secured a share in the fixing of piece rates by means of local negotiations, and these negotiations were extended to cover day wages for other underground workers. The Derbyshire miners, for example, began a campaign in 1889 'for the introduction, at every colliery, of agreed price lists which would become part of the contract of employment and could, if necessary, be enforced in the courts'.[1] By January 1892 their agent was able to say that the principle of a price list had been accepted at every colliery. In Nottinghamshire there were ten colliery disputes between 1896 and 1899 in which the union representatives negotiated lists of piece rates or improvements in existing lists with colliery managers. As a result, rates 'at other collieries were being revised in the men's favour'.[2]

The second aspect was closely associated with the first. As the miners' lodges increased their control over the affairs of the pit, they won a position of authority in the mining communities. All over the world these communities are marked by special characteristics through which sociologists have tried to explain the unique features of industrial relations in coal-mining. Miners are distinguished from other men because they work underground in dirt and danger. Usually, though not in Lancashire and North Staffordshire, for instance, they were also isolated geographically, and many mining towns and villages were worlds of their own. Consequently, they developed unusually powerful loyalties and strong social sanctions against those who flouted them.[3]

Thus, once the union had established itself in the community, it could rely on the community to maintain its membership. In addition to the solid advantages he derived from effective organization, the miner feared the wrath of his fellows and his family as much as that of his employer. By these means the Federation was able to put an end to the violent fluctuations in membership figures which had been typical of nineteenth-century trade unionism in the coalfields, and to begin the task of making the industry 'blackleg-proof'.

---

[1] J. E. Williams, op. cit., p. 302. [2] Griffin, op. cit., pp. 121–5.
[3] In South Wales, for example, 'one of the non-unionists residing at . . . Maesteg . . . went to the door of his residence in his shirt-sleeves and a number of women rushed upon him, tore his shirt off . . . and dragged him out into the street. There some of them belaboured him with brooms while others threw dirty water upon him to the accompanying shouts of "blackleg". At length he pleaded for mercy, and said that any of the men could go to the colliery office for him and get £1 to pay his subscription' (quoted in Evans, op. cit., p. 180).

Spinning Lock-outs and the Brooklands Agreement

The depression years between 1891 and 1893 also proved to be a testing-time for the other major group of non-craft unions, the cotton amalgamations, and above all for the tightly organized Spinners. Upon these aristocrats of the industry the new spirit of 1889 could have little effect. Their own organization was nearly perfect already, and they did not lack militancy. Moreover, they held their assistants, the piecers, in sufficiently firm subjection to suppress any move towards the establishment of independent unions. At least two such attempts were made under socialist inspiration, one in each of the main centres of spinning. In Oldham J. R. Clynes[1] took the lead at the end of the eighties,[2] and in 1890 the piecers of Bolton made their bid for freedom.[3] Both failed.

The Cardroom Operatives, however, had room to expand. From its foundation in 1886 their amalgamation grew gradually until it could claim 15,000 members in 1889. At this stage the union felt sufficient confidence to indulge in a dispute of its own at Oldham, the focus of its strength. In 1888 the Oldham employers had agreed to discuss a new list of piece-prices for cardroom workers provided that the occasion was not used to extract a general increase. They held that cardroom earnings were rising faster than those of the spinners, and were higher in Oldham than elsewhere in Lancashire, so that such an increase could not be entertained. During the following year, negotiations came to a standstill on this question of the level of earnings, and as a consequence three mills were struck in June. Having vainly canvassed support from other cotton towns, the masters decided to hit back by running their mills for three days a week only.[4]

Shortly afterwards, the dispute was complicated by the decision of most employers in spinning to work short time for a very different purpose. By cutting their output they hoped to break an attempt on the part of the Liverpool merchants to corner raw cotton. This move had the full support of the spinners' amalgamation, which forced laggard employers into line. Thus, though short-time working had begun as an attack on the Cardroom Operatives in Oldham, the Spinners now used their strength to make it universally effective. The corner collapsed in September and the cardroom

---

[1] Clynes, J. R., P.C. (1869–1949). Organizer, National Union of Gasworkers and General Labourers, 1891–6; secretary for Lancashire district, 1896–1914; president, 1914–37 (the union becoming successively the National Union of General Workers and the National Union of General and Municipal Workers). Executive Committee, Labour Party, 1904–39. M.P., 1906–31, 1935–45. Parliamentary Secretary to the Ministry of Food, 1917–18. Food Controller, 1918–19. Lord Privy Seal, 1924. Home Secretary, 1929–31.

[2] J. R. Clynes, *Memoirs*, 1937, vol. i, pp. 47–49.

[3] S. J. Chapman, 'Some Policies of the Cotton Spinners' Trade Unions', *Economic Journal*, Dec. 1900.

[4] Presumably because the mills were stopped only three days a week, this dispute did not rank as a strike or lock-out in the records of the Board of Trade.

operatives agreed to return to work on their previous earnings while a list was agreed for the three mills which began the dispute. In 1890 a new general list was drawn up for Oldham which appears to have given increases to most cardroom operatives. Thereafter recruitment continued apace and by 1892 the amalgamation had over 30,000 members.[1]

In 1890 the cardroom amalgamation considered itself sufficiently established to undertake negotiations for a federation with the spinners' amalgamation. Their main concern was to avoid being dragged willy-nilly into every dispute of the Spinners without a share in the negotiations, as had happened in 1885,[2] or any assurance that the Spinners would come to the assistance of the Cardroom Operatives when they struck. The federation was therefore designed to provide a common pool from levies paid by both amalgamations, and to give pledges of mutual support in mill disputes. The resources of the two unions were too unequal, however, and the federation 'did not work out in practice and was subsequently abandoned'.[3]

The major development in organization in spinning was on the employers' side. In 1888 the Oldham spinners had demanded a 5 per cent. advance, and the masters had responded in their usual fashion by touring the county to secure support for an employers' federation to oppose wage demands. On this occasion, however, they were favourably received and managed to establish the United Cotton Spinners' Association. This body accepted affiliations both from local associations and from individual firms where such associations did not exist; but from the first it was ineffective, and the Spinners' 5 per cent. advance had to be granted.

In 1889 the best that the new Association could do in the Oldham cardroom dispute was to advise the masters to introduce non-union labour. Several attempts were made to organize short-time working, but their only success was in the conflict with the Liverpool merchants, when the enforcement was due to the strength of the spinners' amalgamation rather than the sanctions of the Association. A proposal for a joint conciliation committee with the two operatives' amalgamations proved abortive, for the committee never functioned and may not even have been formed. Not surprisingly, when in 1891 the General Council of the Association advised the concession of a further 5 per cent., at a time when margins were beginning to decline, the Oldham masters started to cast about for a stronger alliance.

Coarse spinning, of which Oldham was the centre, was then suffering from a rash of 'bad spinning' disputes. The development of production

[1] The Royal Commission on Labour estimated that its 25,000 members in 1891 constituted 42 per cent. of the labour force in the preparatory stages of spinning (C–7421–I, 1894, p. 252).

[2] See p. 30.

[3] The Amalgamated Association of Card, Blowing and Ring Room Operatives, *After 50 Years* (Golden Jubilee Souvenir), 1936, pp. 9–10.

overseas, especially by the rapidly expanding Indian industry, was providing strong competition in coarse yarns. One of the ways in which British employers met this was by running their mules at higher speeds, and the *Cotton Factory Times* reported that in Oldham the increase had been over 20 per cent. since 1871.[1] Generally the spinner's earnings rose as a result, but higher speeds put a greater strain on the yarn and thus made breakages, and therefore loss of time, more likely. Since difficulties arising from running the machinery too fast were not always easy to distinguish from those caused by poor materials, the custom was for the spinner with a grievance to make a general complaint of 'bad spinning'. Such complaints mounted, and led to a number of strikes.

The normal practice of the men was to claim compensation for bad spinning, and by 1891 they were becoming anxious to secure payment retrospective to the date of the claim as well. During the early months of the year, a particularly intractable dispute over such compensation dragged on at Stalybridge,[2] and eventually the mill concerned was struck in September. At this point the Ashton employers' association extended its boundaries to include Stalybridge, Hyde, Mossley, and Droylsden, 'to counter the threats and violent action recently undertaken by the operatives and their Unions'.[3] Compensation was paid to the stopped mill, and the Ashton employers joined with Oldham in a new attempt to form a satisfactory federation in which the moving spirits were Arthur Rayner of Ashton, J. B. Tattersall of Oldham, and Charles Macara,[4] a Manchester man and more a merchant than a manufacturer.

By late 1891 they had succeeded, and the Federation of Master Cotton Spinners' Associations was established on the basis of district affiliations. Its constituents were Ashton, Bury, Darwen, Glossop and Hyde, Heywood, Manchester, Oldham, and Rochdale. With seventeen million spindles, the Federation covered nearly half of the spinning section of the industry. Of this seventeen million Oldham provided over half, and Ashton half the remainder. Bolton, the fine-spinning centre, stood apart once again, having refused the suggestion of two federations, one for each branch of spinning, with provision for joint action.

Meanwhile the Stalybridge dispute defied all attempts at a settlement. Successive mayors intervened; formulas were drawn up and tests arranged; but the spinners were determined to secure some concession on the question of retrospective compensation for bad spinning. In the end the new

---

[1] 19 Feb. 1886.   [2] Stalybridge is in Cheshire, about 4 miles south of Oldham.

[3] Ashton Employers' Association, *Minutes*, 22 Sept. 1891, quoted in Roland Smith, op. cit. Ashton is adjacent to Stalybridge.

[4] Macara, Sir Charles (1845–1929). President, Federation of Master Cotton Spinners' Associations, 1894–1914. Elected president, Cotton Employers' Parliamentary Association in 1902. President, Employers' Parliamentary Association, 1912–16. Member, Industrial Council, 1911–13.

Master Spinners' Federation imposed a lock-out, and the mills closed down on 15 April 1892, leaving idle about 60 per cent. of the membership of the spinners' amalgamation in South-east Lancashire. More than a month later an agreement was reached providing that work should start on 29 May, and laying down that, where bad spinning was proved, the men were entitled to compensation until the fault was corrected. The Stalybridge Mill Company were 'to re-employ all the hands they could find work for'.

This was by no means a clear victory for the employers, but the Spinners generally gave the agreement a cold reception. No clear yardstick of bad spinning had been established, and full reinstatement had not been guaranteed either to the spinners themselves or to the cardroom operatives. The *Cotton Factory Times*[1] reported many protests from branches, especially in the Oldham province.

By this time the boom which began in the late eighties was ending, and even before the Stalybridge dispute had reached the stage of a county lock-out, the Master Spinners' Federation had unsuccessfully approached the North and North-east Lancashire Cotton Spinners' and Manufacturers' Association[2] with a proposal for a joint 5 per cent. reduction. The suggestion was repeated in the summer of 1892, but in September the Federation decided to go ahead by itself, the executive committee resolving by an overwhelming majority to approach the unions and, if necessary, to give a month's notice. Stocks had not been cleared by the Stalybridge dispute and the unions took the view that only short-time working could bring improvement. 'Trade was in a bad condition, but no tinkering with wages would assist', wrote James Mawdsley,[3] the secretary of the spinners' amalgamation, in his *Quarterly Report* for September. Accordingly, the employers closed down the mills on 1 November 1892, and both sides prepared for a long and stubborn conflict.

By the end of November twelve million of seventeen million federated spindles were stopped, and four million were running out their contracts under penalties imposed by the Federation. Two months later the stoppage was virtually complete so far as the federated firms were concerned. But the attempt of the Oldham masters to spread the responsibility for giving a lead in the adjustment of wages had been only moderately successful, for of the 7,000 spinners locked out 4,600 were in Oldham. The total number of operatives involved was about 50,000, of whom 16,000 were

[1] 13 and 27 May 1892.

[2] This organization dealt primarily with weaving, but also represented most spindles which were not in the Federation or in the Bolton Association. See p. 28.

[3] Mawdsley, James (1848–1902). Assistant secretary, Preston Spinners' Association, 1875–8. General secretary, Amalgamated Association of Operative Cotton Spinners, 1878–1902. Parliamentary Committee, Trades Union Congress, 1882–3, 1884–90, 1891–7. Member of Royal Commission on Labour, 1891–4.

piecers and the rest cardroom operatives and winders. In strong contrast to 1885, the cardroom operatives locked out were now mostly union members, but by December their funds were spent and they had to approach trade unionists elsewhere for assistance.[1]

The employers also sought support. The Federation appealed to non-federated firms in South-east Lancashire to close, but with limited success. The Cotton Spinners' and Manufacturers' Association and the Bolton Association were also asked to help, and in February 1893 Bolton agreed to work a three-day week. Among the operatives, the ranks remained unbroken. Picketing was unnecessary, for the masters could not hope to import labour on a scale sufficient to break this stoppage. Offers of arbitration came both from civic authorities and the Church. Talks were started in January 1893, and by the end of February Mawdsley was willing to discuss reductions in wages, but his offer proved unacceptable to the Federation.

Tempers were now fraying. In his *Quarterly Report* Mawdsley complained that

recently there has arisen a new class of capitalists. These are the men whose sole capacity consists in sticking to whatever gets into their fingers. . . . Their best friends never accuse these men of having brains, but nevertheless having got some money, and being put on the directorate of three or four mills, at one of which they are probably the manager, they at once begin to consider how they can justify their entrance into middle-class rank by jumping on the men whose labour has placed them where they are. . . . It is this class of men who are mainly at the bottom of the present struggle.[2]

This was a reference to the managers of the 'Oldham limiteds', the joint-stock companies which for twenty or thirty years had been encroaching on the old family firms and had provided the moving spirits in the drive to create an effective employers' federation.

The activities of such men do not, however, provide the only possible explanation for the tendency of spinning conflicts to centre on Oldham. It is generally held that coarse spinning, which is Oldham's speciality, is a more arduous and aggravating task than the fine spinning of Bolton. Thus tempers are said to be shorter in Oldham. What is certain is that Tattersall, a self-made Oldham master spinner, did not see eye to eye with Macara, the Manchester merchant, who wanted to settle the dispute by establishing central negotiating machinery which he thought would put an end to strikes and lock-outs. It is therefore of some importance that both Tattersall and Rayner were ill during the final stages of the dispute, and Macara was left in control.

On the union side Mawdsley was still in charge. He was an able leader

---

[1] Among the spinners, heavy levies were imposed on trade unionists still at work. In the Oldham Spinners' Association the figure was 6*d*. a day.

[2] *Cotton Factory Times*, 17 Mar. 1893.

and a skilful negotiator with a powerful and autocratic personality.[1] He could be relied upon to drive the hardest possible bargain with the employers, but at the same time he was unlikely to overlook the value of a central procedure for dealing with disputes as a means of increasing the power of the spinners' amalgamation over its constituent associations. In this respect he shared the views of some of the leaders of the craft societies in other industries who, as will be shown in the next chapter, were beginning to see the advantages to themselves of joining with the employers in setting up national negotiating machinery as a device for curbing the independence of their branches.

Several joint meetings took place in March, and on the 23rd the leaders of both sides assembled at the Brooklands Hotel, a country inn outside Manchester, to escape the attentions of the press. After an all-night sitting, agreement was reached early the following morning.[2] A reduction of 7*d.* in the pound, or 2·9 per cent., was accepted by Mawdsley for the Spinners and by W. Mullin, secretary of the cardroom amalgamation. Of more importance for the future than the reduction itself were the clauses of the 'Brooklands Agreement', which for the first time provided the spinning section of the industry with central and systematic machinery for negotiation with the employers. General adjustments in wages were to take place only once a year and were to be limited to 5 per cent. in either direction. A procedure was agreed for referring unsettled mill disputes to the local associations, and thence, if need be, to the federal bodies. Concessions were made by both sides—the masters, for instance, gave up their demand that trade unionists should work amicably with non-unionists.[3]

The cost of the stoppage to the Spinners was £152,000. The whole of this sum was raised from the funds of the amalgamation and its local associations, including the proceeds of the levies. 'There was no sending round the hat to other trades on the part of the Operative Cotton Spinners.'[4] The amalgamation alone returned an expenditure per head of almost £7 for 1892 and almost seven guineas for 1893. It was an achievement beyond the resources of any other major union.

The Weavers' Uniform List

Meanwhile, the weaving section of the industry had at last achieved an ambition which had been pursued for many years both by the employers

[1] Like his fellow townsman from Ashton, Thomas Ashton of the Miners' Federation, Mawdsley was now a Conservative in politics.

[2] The Webbs quote a full account of this encounter in *Industrial Democracy*, pp. 200–3.

[3] The Spinners had allegedly organized a drive against non-unionists in 1891 and ordered their members to cease working with them (*Workman's Times*, 2 Jan. 1892). When, however, the employers complained of this practice to the Royal Commission on Labour, Mawdsley, who was a member of the Commission, denied that pressure was used, and forced the employers to withdraw their allegations for lack of evidence (C–6708–VI, 1892, Qs. 720, 2148–67, 2697–2710).   [4] *Workman's Times*, 9 June 1894.

and by the union. This was a uniform piece-price list for 'plain' weaving, the main sector of the trade. Progress had been slow.[1] For a time it seemed likely that the efforts of the joint committee which had been established in 1886 would founder on the old objection that uniformity must bring wage reductions to some weavers or cost increases to some employers. As good trade returned, the Weavers became impatient. On 15 March 1890 they threatened to 'secure a Uniform List by deliberate action'.[2] Prosperity, however, diminished the employers' objections to the only kind of list acceptable to the unions: a list that avoided serious wage cuts. Prices were rising and the spinners were already receiving wage increases. Even so, the negotiations still moved slowly.

Fortunately for the Weavers, the last obstacles were cleared away before serious depression returned to the industry. The Uniform Plain Cloth List was signed in May 1892 and was to come into force in two stages, in August and November of the same year. In its methods of calculation the new list was a compromise between the Blackburn and Burnley lists. On average, weavers gained from its introduction: more in the Burnley area than elsewhere, and more in fine goods than in coarse. Consequently, the year saw the biggest influx of members that the amalgamation had known, and its strength rose from 49,000 to 65,000. The total number of organized weavers was even higher, for some local associations were not affiliated to the amalgamation and others did not affiliate on their full strength. The Board of Trade returns show 94,000 trade unionists in weaving at the end of 1892—more than half the total labour force.

Over the next few years central negotiations were mainly concerned to fill in the details of the Uniform List, which was extended to cover exceptionally coarse wefts, and subsidiary uniform lists dealt with special products. But piece rates were not the only question to occupy the union. The growth in the number of looms per weaver—which had brought a rapid increase in earnings in the seventies—was now falling off. Between 1886 and 1906 the average rose only slightly, from 3·3 to 3·44.[3] In 1885 some Burnley employers had already begun to experiment with six looms to a weaver, a system which was to cause violent conflicts over forty years later; but at this early stage immediate opposition from the amalgamation confined the experiment to Burnley and Nelson. Speeds, however, were still increasing, and since, as in spinning, the problems arising from higher speeds could not easily be distinguished from those caused by poor materials, the Board of Trade classified disputes arising from both causes under the heading of 'bad materials'. In the cotton industry as a whole, 64 out of 137 strikes were included in the category in 1889, 48 of them in weaving. The total fell to 43 out of 135 in 1890 and to 57 out of 156 in 1891. This remained the largest single class of disputes,

[1] See p. 30.   [2] Roland Smith, op. cit.   [3] Wood, op. cit., p. 30.

but fines for lateness, indiscipline, and inferior work were another frequent source of conflict, and there were also constant complaints and a number of strikes against 'driving' by overlookers.

The latter problem was aggravated by the spread of the practice of paying the overlookers by results. The lower his 'poundage'—and it was 1s. 3d. in Burnley and 1s. 4d. in Blackburn as compared with 1s. 9d. in Ashton[1]—the more the overlooker was tempted to 'drive' the weavers, or to use the 'slating' system by which the output of the weavers was publicly recorded.[2] In 1890 seven strikes were recorded as caused by dissatisfaction with the conduct of officials, unpopular orders, and the discharge of a weaver 'for being under average with his work'. In 1893, therefore, the amalgamation instructed its districts that 'should any tackler [overlooker] speak to a weaver about his earnings at any time or place, or speak unjustly when fetched to tackle [repair] a loom, we request such weaver at once to report the same to a member of the Weavers' Committee, and if such tackler be found guilty of doing so action will be taken against him immediately . . .'. Members were advised, however, 'not to use any uncivil language to your employers'.

These difficulties did not mean that relations between individual over-lookers and weavers, or between their organizations, were generally bad. The overlooker was a skilled mechanic more than a foreman, and the weavers relied on him to keep their looms running. The unions also worked together. The overlookers expected help from the weavers if one of their number was victimized, and the weavers relied on the overlookers to help them recruit members and prevent strike-breaking. During the great strike of 1878 the two organizations had established a Joint Association of Overlookers' and Weavers' Associations for North and North-east Lancashire. Henceforward it conducted joint negotiations with the employers.[3] The local secretaries of the two unions would therefore be anxious to settle cases of 'driving' as quickly and smoothly as possible.

Industrial Peace, 1895–1900

The last years of the decade presented a strong contrast to its stormy opening. In the cotton industry the total number of recorded disputes fell from 135 in 1890 and 156 in 1891 to 52 in 1898 and 44 in 1899. Moreover, there was no dispute of any size in the industry between 1894 and 1900. Only three strikes brought out more than 1,000 operatives, and these did not last more than a few days. Conditions were favourable. Though depression continued through 1894 and into 1895, with wage reductions in many industries, the cotton employers demanded no further cuts after the

---

[1] *Royal Commission on Labour*, C–6708–VI, 1892, Qs. 898, 905, 1100.

[2] Ibid., Qs. 898–901.

[3] A federation of the weavers' amalgamation and several of the specialist unions in the weaving section was formed in 1897, but broke up in 1899.

Brooklands settlement. Meanwhile earnings continued their upward trend. The Uniform List had set the seal on good relations in weaving, and both sections of the industry now had a general procedure for the settlement of disputes.

It is true that the Brooklands Agreement did not give universal satisfaction. Mawdsley asserted that 'it was generally recognised by both sides' that though the agreement 'was lacking somewhat in regard to general disputes . . . it was satisfactory enough in small matters'.[1] Many operatives, however, took a different view. Whereas they had once been able to settle a local grievance on the spot, they had now to wait for the procedure to settle it for them. They no longer enjoyed the opportunity 'for taking prompt and effective measures for defending themselves', since the Agreement had tied them 'hand and foot' and 'fettered their freedom and policy'.[2] In 1897 a number of amendments were made, the most important of them being intended to reduce delay. But at least the machinery effectively prevented a recurrence of the Stalybridge affair. For their part, the local spinners' associations were bound to refer an unresolved dispute to central negotiations, and the Master Spinners' Federation had learned what it cost to teach their men a lesson.

The weavers' associations continued to thrive and in 1900 they claimed a membership of 109,000, 81,500 of them in the amalgamation. The Spinners had fallen from their peak of 19,662 in 1891 to about 18,000; but whether or not Mawdsley was correct in claiming a union density of over 95 per cent. in 1891, cotton spinning was certainly one of the best-organized trades in the country.[3] The membership of the cardroom associations fluctuated around 25,000, with about 20,000 in the amalgamation. The number of organized piecers went unrecorded, for the spinners' associations in which they were subordinate members excluded them from their returns; but the total in 1900 was probably some 20,000. By 1896 the Bolton province included 8,800 piecers as against 4,400 spinners, which suggests virtually complete organization, but this was exceptional.[4]

By a decision of the spinners' amalgamation, the slowly increasing numbers of women employed on ring-spinning were left to the cardroom associations to organize. The returns of these unions and those in weaving are all the more impressive because the majority of their members were women. By 1900 the proportions were 80 per cent. in the cardroom and 70 per cent. in weaving. Moreover, the degree of organization here was not much less among the women than among the men. This was a startling

---

[1] *Cotton Factory Times*, 24 Mar. 1899.   [2] Ibid., 27 Oct. 1899.

[3] The Royal Commission on Labour, of which Mawdsley was a member, had estimated the degree of organization to be 92 per cent. (C–7421–I, 1894, p. 252).

[4] The piecers continued to agitate for a union of their own to extract higher earnings from the spinners, but they found few friends. Even the liberal-minded *Cotton Factory Times* warned them bluntly that piecers who took this course would never become spinners (12 May 1899).

contrast to the situation in almost every other industry, and in 1900 the cotton unions supplied three-fifths of the country's female trade unionists.

The means by which all this was accomplished were not recorded, and the men who dominated the unions seem to have taken it for granted. Given that they had some strength, the unions could acquire more through family influence.[1] The men who took the lead in the affairs of the weavers' associations, or as overlookers, or as strippers and grinders in the cardroom associations, could recruit their wives, sisters and daughters. Lancashire cotton towns may not have been quite such cohesive communities as mining villages, but social pressure could be a powerful influence all the same. Once the unions had established their place in the community, the head of the household, even the lordly spinner who would not accept women into his own organizations, might be ashamed to admit to a non-unionist in the family. This social pressure could be further exploited by the door-to-door collection of union dues practised by all the cotton unions. The non-unionist could not hope to conceal his defection either from his family or from his neighbours.

The period of quiescence seemed likely to end in 1897 when the North and North-east Lancashire Spinners' and Manufacturers' Association canvassed, on behalf of its spinning membership, a proposal for a general reduction in spinners' wages; but the Association received no support from the Master Spinners' Federation. Moreover, as prosperity returned in the following year and brought applications for advances, the negotiations showed no sign of running into trouble. The Weavers' claim for 10 per cent. was lodged first, but it appears that they were content to wait on the Spinners, who had asked for a restoration of the 1893 cut. The *Cotton Factory Times* reported that the 'investing public' felt satisfied that the claim was reasonable, and that the 'trading community' had lost interest.[2] Thereafter the employers made a half-hearted attempt to send the claim to arbitration, and the restoration was granted in March 1899. The weaving employers followed with a 2½ per cent. increase in May.

Further increases followed for the Spinners in 1900. In February the Bolton spinners had their first increase since 1890, of 5 per cent.; and in April all operatives not on the Bolton list received 5 per cent., with 10 per cent. for male cardroom hands. This last concession involved a formal alteration in the Brooklands Agreement. Henceforward the limitation to a 5 per cent. alteration in any one year applied only to the spinners. At the same time, the cotton unions had begun to pursue a further reduction in their hours of work by agitating for twelve o'clock closing on Saturdays. This, however, was not a matter for direct negotiation with the employers, for the unions used their traditional method of persuading Parliament to make a suitable amendment to the Factory Acts.

[1] See pp. 29–30.   [2] 27 Jan. 1899.

During the negotiations of 1899 both the employers' federations had made suggestions for improving the procedure for making general adjustments in wages. The Master Spinners began with a proposal for arbitration which was promptly rejected.[1] They then put forward a plan for a sliding scale to regulate wages in relation to variations in 'standard profits'.[2] Discussions continued into 1900 and finally broke down, as might have been expected, on the definition of standard profits and the methods of calculating them. Nevertheless, the Spinners' report on these negotiations spoke warmly of the possibility of some 'automatic' system which would 'work equitably for operatives and employers'.[3]

The Organization of the Scottish and South Wales Coalfields

In coal, the Federated area ended the century in a peace almost as profound as that of cotton. The agreement of 1894 ran its two years undisturbed, and in 1896 the conciliation board had met to hear the owners' request that the guaranteed minimum be reduced from 30 to 20 per cent. above the 1888 'standard'. But the Federation stood firm and the owners had no desire for another trial of strength. Prices, moreover, were beginning to turn. Although the agreement was not renewed, the owners took no steps to enforce a reduction. In 1898 the Federation was on the offensive again, and a new conciliation board was set up with the same 30 per cent. minimum and 45 per cent. maximum. By January 1900 successive increases had brought rates to the maximum, and a new limit of 60 per cent. above standard was introduced from 1 January 1901[4] and reached two months later.

The North-east also kept the peace, but not with quite the same ease. The two counties had added yet another to their list of experiments in wage-fixing machinery when they set up conciliation boards on the Federation model for Northumberland in 1894 and Durham in 1895. Neither, however, provided for a minimum wage. This concern with flexibility reflected the requirements of a sensitive export trade, but it convinced the rank and file that conciliation was 'but a device for maintaining the hated sliding scale'.[5] As prices fell, reductions negotiated by the boards had sharpened discontent, and feeling became so strong that the unions withdrew from the boards at the low point of the depression in 1896. They were not reformed until the boom of 1899 had made the renewal of organized contacts desirable for both sides. It now became clear, however,

---

[1] Before the Royal Commission on Labour all cotton trade union representatives, and all but one cotton employer, expressed strong preference for direct dealings and rejected arbitration by an outsider (C–6708–VI, 1892, Qs. 444–52, 556, 723–7, 774–6, 1018–19, 1709–13).

[2] The proposal was that a 2 per cent. alteration in 'standard profits' should warrant a $2\frac{1}{2}$ per cent. alteration in wages, with a 10 per cent maximum.

[3] L. L. Price, 'Conciliation in the Cotton Trade', *Economic Journal*, June, 1901.

[4] For the first time, surface workers were specifically included in the wage increase conceded by this agreement.   [5] Welbourne, op. cit., p. 295.

that producing for export had its compensations. By the end of 1900 wage rates in Northumberland were 34 per cent. over December 1893, and 32 per cent. in Durham. The comparable figure for the Federated area was 7 per cent.[1] Moreover, membership was equally buoyant. With 80,000 members in 1900, Durham had once more left Yorkshire well behind, and Northumberland had risen to a new peak of 24,000.

These figures of growth, however, were dwarfed by the startling results achieved in Scotland and South Wales. Despite their weakness, the Scottish miners under the leadership of Robert Smillie[2] had decided to resist a wage cut imposed by the coal-owners in 1894. No negotiations preceded the dispute, for the owners outside Fife still refused to recognize the unions. About 70,000 miners came out, only a minority of them trade unionists. The Federation, which contributed over £76,000 to the strike funds from levies imposed throughout its districts,[3] had pressed for greater unity. Consequently, while the strike was still in progress, the local unions formed the Scottish Miners' Federation, which was duly admitted into the national Federation. With weak organization and a falling market, however, the strike could not succeed, and the men had returned on the employers' terms to face further reductions in 1895 and 1896. By the end of 1897 less than one-fifth of the underground workers were organized,[4] and the overall proportion must have been smaller still.

Meanwhile, the Fife miners, having preserved their union, had tried to solve their problems by settling for a sliding scale which included a minimum rate. This came into operation in 1895 and worked fairly smoothly for the next three years. In 1898 trade had begun to improve and Scotland was particularly affected by the prolonged strike of the South Wales miners. The sliding scale, however, did not yield such large increases to the Fife miners as were forthcoming elsewhere, and they gave notice to terminate the agreement. Thereafter prices had continued to rise, and by the end of 1900 wages in the West of Scotland stood at 33 per cent. above 1893 and in Fife 44 per cent. above 1893. Compared with 1896, the increase was even more remarkable. In four years wages in the West of Scotland rose by 87·5 per cent., and in Fife by 97·5 per cent. This was a golden opportunity for Smillie's Federation. In July 1899 a conciliation board was established with a minimum of $31\frac{1}{4}$ per cent. above the standard of 1888 and a maximum of 75 per cent. Even this maximum had to be exceeded in the following year.

[1] These figures are percentages above the actual rates of 1893, and not the increase in relation to the 'standards'.

[2] Smillie, Robert (1857–1940). President, Scottish Miners' Federation, 1894–1918. Vice-president, Miners' Federation of Great Britain, 1909–12; president, 1912–21. Parliamentary Committee, Trades Union Congress, 1918–19; General Council, 1921–7; M.P., 1923–9.

[3] Page Arnot, op. cit., vol. i, pp. 261–3.

[4] Page Arnot, *Scottish Miners*, pp. 89–90.

Between 1897 and 1900 the membership of the Scottish unions rose from 17,000 to 60,000 and affiliations to their Federation from 15,000 to 50,000. In South Wales, however, Brace had been able to reap an even larger reward from his loyalty to the national Federation, though not without a struggle. He had advised his supporters to pay the sliding-scale levies in order to gain the right to attend sliding-scale conferences, where they then 'made every effort to undermine the sliding scale from within'.[1] Slowly the principles of genuine unionism gained ground. By the time trade turned upwards again in 1897, the local mood was ripe for substantial changes, and the coal-owners were at last obliged to recognize Brace and his union. They thereby greatly increased his access to local meetings and to the ear of the miners.

Before long, conferences and ballot votes to determine policy had begun to undermine the autocratic power of Mabon and his sliding-scale colleagues. Early in 1898 they were instructed to give notice to end the sliding-scale agreement and to demand an advance of 10 per cent., together with a minimum wage. The coal-owners, taking alarm at the growth of this movement for independence, tried to prop up the tottering authority of the sliding-scale leaders by refusing to negotiate unless they were given plenary powers to conclude a settlement. The miners proceeded to vote heavily against the granting of such powers and renewed their condemnation of sliding scales.[2] The existing agreement expired on 9 April 1898, when the owners locked-out, but many miners had anticipated the stoppage by ceasing work from 1 April.

The South Wales miners were in poor shape for a hard fight. Even with the national Federation contributing £10,000, their resources were hopelessly inadequate.[3] Out of a total of somewhere between 120,000 and 140,000 miners, there were perhaps 18,000 unionists in 1897. After some weeks of widespread distress and hardship, a conference voted plenary powers to the leaders, and negotiations began. The owners held their ground, and even rejected the services of a conciliator appointed by the Home Secretary. An agreement was finally signed on 1 September 1898. This conceded a 5 per cent. advance, but retained the sliding scale, though the men could give notice to terminate it at any time after September 1899 if wages fell below $12\frac{1}{2}$ per cent. above the standard.

The stoppage was perhaps the most exhausting of all the great coal strikes of the decade. It lasted five months, even longer than the lock-out of 1893, and caused a loss of nearly twelve million working days.[4] Yet far

---

[1] Evans, op. cit., p. 157.

[2] Brace, in a speech supporting the miners' stand, declared that he 'did not believe that workmen's families should have their stomachs measured by the state of feeling on coal exchanges' (quoted in ibid., p. 172).   [3] Ibid., p. 173.

[4] Otherwise the mining industry was unusually peaceful from 1895 to 1900. From 1892 to 1894, with the Durham lock-out, the Federated lock-out, and the Scottish lock-out, mining

from crushing independent unionism in South Wales, the dispute added immensely to its strength. The South Wales Miners' Federation was formed, with a central fund, and members poured in, reaching a total of 60,000 by the end of the year. The Federation took over the negotiating functions from the old sliding-scale committee, and was able to reap the benefit of a series of wage increases almost as startling as those in Scotland. By 1900 the wages of the Welsh miners were 45 per cent. above the figure for 1893 and had increased by 64 per cent. since 1896.

There was no mistaking the temper of the new recruits. In January 1899, when Mabon and Brace, once bitter enemies, led a deputation to the annual conference of the national Federation to seek admission, Mabon said of himself and his colleagues that 'they came as penitent Welshmen'.[1] Having attempted to make sure that Mabon understood the conditions,[2] the delegates decided in favour of the application, judging that they stood a better chance of ending the sliding scale with the Welshmen in their organization than outside it.[3] Two years later the membership of the South Wales and Monmouthshire Federation stood at 128,000 and provided over one-third of the membership of the national Federation. Thus Scotland and South Wales together constituted fractionally less than half the total membership of the Miners' Federation in 1900. This was a magnificent victory for the Federation and its principles, but it may well have caused Pickard and his colleagues to wonder whether those principles would withstand the test of adversity in these new areas as successfully as they had in the Federated area in 1893.

lost 36½ million working days out of 57 millions in the country as a whole. In 1898 the figure was 13 millions out of 15 millions, but from 1895 to 1900 *excluding 1898* it was only 5 millions out of 25 millions. [1] Ness Edwards, op. cit., p. 12.

  [2] The Welshmen pledged themselves to abolish the sliding scale when their new agreement expired in 1902 (Evans, op. cit., p. 176); to support the minimum wage policy; and to back the Eight Hours Bill (Ness Edwards, op. cit., p. 12).

  [3] Page Arnot, *The Miners*, vol. i, pp. 287-8.

4

The Craft Unions and the General Counter-attack

The Boom Years, 1889–91

THE boom which began in 1888 brought no changes in the craft societies to equal the upheaval among waterfront workers and general labourers, or the development of the Miners' Federation and its machinery for collective bargaining. Nevertheless, these were years of growth and prosperity for almost all the craft societies.

In its *Annual Report* for 1889 the Amalgamated Society of Engineers recorded that 'wages have advanced two to three shillings a week, and improved rates of payment for overtime have been conceded in many places, and in only two or three instances have we had to leave work to enforce our just claims'. A year later they could declare that 1890 would be remembered especially for its wage increases achieved without serious resistance from the employers. Among shipbuilding workers, the Labour Department reported that unemployment had fallen from over 21 per cent. in 1887 to under 1 per cent. by March 1890;[1] and shipyard wages rose once in 1888, twice in 1889, and again in 1890. In 1890 and 1891 the Amalgamated Society of Tailors presented wage demands in twenty-three towns. Of these all but one were successful, and only one or two involved strikes.[2] In building, 'movements to increase wages or reduce working hours were frequent all over the kingdom' during 1891 and 1892.[3] By 1892 at least half the branches of the Typographical Association had secured an advance in wages or a reduction in hours, and some had gained both.[4]

Though the great majority of such benefits were won without stoppages of work, there were several strikes which deserve comment. For example, brief but widespread stoppages were caused by the agitation of the engineering unions in the North-east for a reduction of hours from fifty-four to fifty-three a week, and for a curtailment of overtime. The first of these demands led in March 1890 to a strike of 20,000 men throughout

---

[1] *Report on the Strikes and Lockouts of 1889*, C–6176, 1890, p. 4.
[2] *Workman's Times*, 25 Sept. 1891.
[3] *Report on the Strikes and Lockouts of 1892*, C–7403, 1894, p. 24.
[4] *Royal Commission on Labour*, C–6894–IX, 1893, Q. 22893.

the area, and ended in a victory for the unions which inspired the Humber ports and Manchester to follow suit.[1] During the subsequent year the Engineers banned the working of overtime in order to persuade the local employers' associations to reduce the practice. The employers countered with a 25 per cent. lock-out, and the union called out all its members in the North-east. As a result, a settlement laid down a limit of eighteen hours overtime a month for each worker.[2]

In 1891 the unions represented by the London United Trades Committee of Carpenters and Joiners also brought a lock-out upon themselves by striking three firms to enforce their claim for higher wages and an eight-hour day. The stoppage affected 4,000 men and lasted six months. In October the President of the Royal Institute of British Architects agreed to arbitrate, and awarded a reduction in maximum hours from $52\frac{1}{2}$ to $51\frac{1}{4}$, better rates for overtime, and several minor improvements.[3] Later in the same year, London saw another attempt to win the eight-hour day, this time by societies of bookbinders, because they wanted 'to counter the displacement of men by machinery'.[4] Disunity among the employers precluded any general agreement; some firms gave way, and the rest were struck. By March 1892 the Vellum Account-Book Binders were broken and out of the dispute. In April the three survivors secured a nominal forty-eight-hour week, but overtime up to fifty-four hours was to be paid only at plain time rates. Piece-workers, however, received a 10 per cent. increase.

Back in 1889 the Scottish Operative Bakers had called a strike of over 4,000 men, mainly for a fifty-five-hour week. Settlements were made with the individual employers, the last a month after the stoppage had begun.[5] The secretary of the union claimed 'a general success over Scotland with the exception of the large firms in Glasgow, who defeated us, and some of the large firms in Edinburgh'.[6] Glasgow and Edinburgh might appear to be gaping holes in the front of any Scottish union; but the Bakers had obtained a firm hold elsewhere and were later able to pick off the big

---

[1] By Jan. 1892, engineering firms in fifty-four towns were working the fifty-three hour week (*Workman's Times*, 9 Jan. 1892). In Birmingham one employer had replied to the claim in these words: 'it has pleased God that the masses of the inhabitants of the world should be hewers of wood and drawers of water. . . . You want reduced working hours, the men don't. They want more money for drink' (ibid., 6 Mar. 1891).

[2] During the dispute the union's branches had established a 'United Grand Committee of the Tyne, Wear, Hartlepool and Tees' to deal with the employers as a whole instead of leaving each town or district to act on its own. The employers asked them to set up a conciliation board, but this was refused, the union preferring to retain complete freedom of action (*Royal Commission on Labour*, C–6894–VII, 1893, Qs. 25233–4).

[3] Ibid., C–6795–VI, 1893, appendix xxxiv.

[4] E. Howe and J. Child, *The Society of London Bookbinders*, 1952, p. 220.

[5] *Report on the Strikes and Lockouts of 1889*, C–6176, 1890, p. 62.

[6] *Royal Commission on Labour*, C–6894–IX, 1893, Q. 27554; also Tom Johnston, *A History of the Working Classes in Scotland*, 1921, pp. 329–30.

employers at their leisure.[1] Their English counterparts, the Amalgamated Operative Bakers and Confectioners, were less effective. When 150 London bakeries were struck for a ten-hour day in 1889, most of the employers gave in for the time being; but the previous working day was gradually restored as union membership ebbed away. The English Bakers also organized the provinces, and from 1892 onwards claimed about 5,000 members.

Demarcation Disputes and Inter-union Conflict

Not all the conflicts of these prosperous years were with the employers. Indeed, some of the craft societies seemed bent on proving that their main quarrel was with one another. The major centre of the trouble was the marine engineering and shipbuilding industry on the North-east coast. 'Within the space of thirty-five months' between 1890 and 1893, 'there were no fewer than thirty-five weeks' in which one or other of the most important sections of skilled men on Tyneside were idle because work to which they laid claim was being done by others.[2]

This fierce and persistent competition owed much to a change in the nature of the product. Specialization in shipping was increasing rapidly. The introduction of luxurious passenger liners and 'special purpose' vessels, such as refrigerated ships and oil-tankers, all requiring much elaborate equipment, made the operation of fitting-out more complex than ever before. Quite apart from its effects on those engaged in the construction of the hull, this created work for a wide variety of crafts which fought each other savagely to establish their overlapping or conflicting claims.

Thus the industry had the misfortune to be the meeting ground of many well-organized crafts during a revolution in its technique, and to offer an expanding range of new jobs which lent themselves to much hair-splitting debate. The situation was further complicated by the competition of unions within the various crafts. This applied most of all to the engineering trades, where the Amalgamated Society of Engineers at one time or another fought not only the plumbers, boilermakers, shipwrights, joiners, brassworkers, and tinplate workers, but also the fitters, turners, and others who were organized by the Steam Engine Makers' Society, the National United Trades' Society of Engineers, the United Machine Workers' Association, and the Amalgamated Society of Metal Planers, Shapers and Slotters. All of these had members in the North-east working in the same shops and on the same materials as members of the Amalgamated Society of Engineers.

Almost as important, however, as the changing nature of the product

[1] In 1898 the union set up an arbitration board with the employers (W. H. Marwick, *Labour in Scotland*, n.d., p. 15), and by 1900 claimed 4,500 members. In 1891 its secretary had estimated that there was a total of 6,000 bakers in Scotland (*Royal Commission on Labour*, C–6894–IX, 1893, Q. 27550).   [2] Webbs, *Industrial Democracy*, p. 513.

was the special problem of the Shipwrights. The rise of iron shipbuilding had been the making of the Boilermakers, who now also recruited platers, riveters, angle-iron smiths, caulkers, and holders-up. The main losers were the Shipwrights, who had ruled the industry when wood was the predominant material. But enough wood was still used to keep them in existence, and the Associated Society tried to recoup some of their losses at the expense of the ships' joiners, who were organized by the Amalgamated Society of Carpenters and Joiners. Joiners had played little part in building wooden ships, but with the growing elaboration of superstructure, equipment, and fittings, a considerable amount of work appeared to which they could lay claim and for which the shipwrights were prepared to do battle.[1] In Scotland the position was exacerbated by the presence of a rival 'Associated' union, which also included ships' joiners; and the Clyde was almost as frequent a scene of conflict as the North-east coast.

Indeed, scarcely a port in the country escaped demarcation disputes once shipbuilding rose with 'amazing suddenness' out of the depression of the mid-eighties into the 'unexampled prosperity' of 1889–90.[2] These conflicts were not blind, insensate struggles, but were dictated by the logic of craft organization. The skilled men in each craft had come together to protect the customs which gave them their standing, and to strengthen their position by the elaboration of rules and, if need be, by agreements with the employers. Their privileges might be destroyed by direct onslaught or by the introduction of new methods which relied on unskilled labour, but they could also be undermined by changes in technique which called for new or different skills. Without privileges to defend there would be no craft unions, and if privileges were to be preserved they must be defended against all comers, whether employers, unskilled workers, or other crafts.

It is also true, however, that both the leaders of the societies, with their central funds to protect, and the employers had an interest in preserving peace. On Tyneside, for example, repeated attempts were made to end the battle between shipwrights and joiners. During the eighties a joint committee had tried in vain to lay down a satisfactory division of work. After prolonged negotiations with the employers' association, the dispute was referred to the arbitration of Thomas Burt, who made an exhaustive inquiry and drew up a detailed schedule defining the contestants' rights. When the employers proceeded to apply it in 1890 the joiners came out on strike. The issue was then put before a conciliation board composed of representatives of all the shipbuilding crafts, with an independent chairman. A temporary peace was patched up, but much bitterness remained.[3]

---

[1] *Royal Commission on Labour*, C–6894–VII, 1893, Qs. 22010–14.
[2] *Report on the Strikes and Lockouts of 1889*, C–6176, 1890, p. 4.
[3] *Royal Commission on Labour*, C–6894–VII, 1893, Qs. 21437–8.

Subsequently a 'referee court' was created in a fresh attempt to find some solution, and in 1893 there followed a standing committee, representing the employers and both the unions, to deal with disputes as they arose.[1] This worked quite well, largely because returning depression, while intensifying their fears and sense of insecurity, reduced the workers' ability to express these reactions in strikes.

The employers naturally found conflicts of this type particularly exasperating. Sometimes they claimed a right of final decision, and in a clash between the fitters and the plumbers in 1890–1 they resorted to a general lock-out to compel the unions to reach a settlement. Increasingly, however, employers in the North-east, on the Clyde, and on the Mersey sought to protect themselves by drawing up agreements with the various pairs of contestants in which work rights were defined and accepted. These were supplemented by other agreements which laid down a procedure for referring disputes to standing committees representing both the competing societies and the employers, with provision for final decision by referees.[2] By 1900 there were seven permanent boards of the kind in the major centres.[3]

On the workers' side the main contribution to a solution came from Robert Knight, secretary of the Boilermakers, who in 1890 brought together thirteen unions[4] in the Federation of Engineering and Shipbuilding Trades. This body was intended partly as a counterweight to the Shipbuilding Employers' Federation which had been formed in the previous year.[5] Its rules tried to ensure that disputes with the employers would be referred to arbitration, but also gave the Federation power to call out all affiliated societies to support any of its constituents involved in a dispute which raised issues of trade union principle. These objects, however, were subsidiary to the main aim of resolving inter-union conflicts. Problems of demarcation were to be referred to a court of arbitration composed of two members from each side and an independent 'umpire' who could issue a binding award if necessary.

In some cases this machinery was successful, but not in all. 'We found a difficulty in getting it to work',[6] said Alexander Wilkie[7] of the

---

[1] *Report on the Strikes and Lockouts of 1895*, C–8231, 1896, p. 232.

[2] *Second Report on Rules of Voluntary Conciliation and Arbitration Boards*, Cd. 5346, 1910, pp. 195–210.

[3] *Report on the Strikes and Lockouts of 1900*, Cd. 689, 1901, p. liii.

[4] The Boilermakers, Steam Engine Makers, Ironfounders, Scottish Moulders, Associated Blacksmiths, Co-operative Smiths (Newcastle), General Union of Carpenters, Shipwrights, Metal Planers, United Machine Workers, Patternmakers, Plumbers, and National Engineers Trades Society.   [5] See p. 151.

[6] *Royal Commission on Labour*, C–6894–VII, 1893, Q. 21455.

[7] Wilkie, Alexander (1850–1928). General secretary, Ship Constructive and Shipwrights, Association, 1882–1928. Parliamentary Committee, Trades Union Congress, 1890–1, 1895–1903, 1904–9. Executive Committee, Labour Party, 1900–4. M.P., 1906–22.

Shipwrights, whose views coincided with Knight's on many matters. The Federation was much weakened by the aloofness not only of the Carpenters and Joiners but also of the Engineers, whose absence made it of little value for concerting policy among the engineering trades. As the major union in engineering, the Amalgamated Society of Engineers had the largest front exposed to attack, and its branches needed a free hand to fight the technical innovations which were gradually differentiating the functions of the fitters and turners into separate, specialist tasks and which tended to give rise to sectional societies. Defence of their privileges would be impossible if they joined an organization in which each of their smaller rivals had an equal voice with the Amalgamated Society itself.

The Engineers had therefore refused to enter the Federation except with sufficient voting strength to allow them to dominate the smaller societies. To this, of course, the latter could not agree. Moreover, the Society regarded the sectional unions as 'these small and unnecessary . . . absurd and irritating institutions'.[1] To join the Federation at all would be to recognize the right of the Steam Engine Makers, the Patternmakers, and the smaller societies to an independent existence. Despite the increasing number of such specialist organizations, the Engineers still preferred to hope that one day, and the sooner the better, they would be able to absorb them all.

Yet however strongly they might wish to deny the right of sectional unions to exist, the Engineers found it convenient to promote local co-operation from time to time, and temporary joint committees were formed in many centres when trade movements[2] were launched. Sometimes these worked smoothly and fruitfully, but more often dissension and recrimination were the result.[3] The Amalgamated Society was apt to assume the leading role, plan the operation, and then hustle the sectionals into acquiescence.[4] This tended to arouse hostility from their leaders, who resented the contempt and impatience reflected in such tactics. Participation by the Engineers in any more formal structure for joint negotiation remained unthinkable. In 1889 the sectional societies on Tyneside formed a Federal Board, but the Engineers refused to associate with it.[5] Four years later the same unions invited the Amalgamated Society to join them in forming a Central Wages Board to oppose wage reductions,[6] but the Engineers' executive told the Sunderland District Committee that 'we do not

---

[1] Amalgamated Society of Engineers, *Quarterly Report*, Mar. 1893.

[2] A 'movement', or 'trade movement', was the term used by trade unionists to cover the whole process of deciding upon a claim, promoting the necessary support, submitting the claim to the employers, negotiating and, if need be, applying sanctions.

[3] W. Mosses, *The History of the United Pattern Makers' Association*, 1922, pp. 106, 123.

[4] Ibid., p. 87.

[5] Ibid., pp. 87, 92.

[6] Ibid., p. 106.

recognize that the time has yet arrived when our power has diminished to such an extent as to warrant handing over our authority to another body'.[1]

In their dealings with the smaller unions which organized men doing certain preparatory jobs in the shipyards, the Boilermakers displayed an attitude similar to that of the Engineers. In London, for example, they claimed the work of the drillers for their own riveters, and that of the chippers for their own caulkers. The drillers and chippers formed a union to fight back, but this gradually lost ground. Realizing that they must be defeated if the unequal struggle continued, the drillers came to terms. They broke with the chippers, reached an understanding with the London boilermakers on work rights, and abandoned the chippers to their fate. Then, with the chippers at their mercy, the boilermakers closed most of the shops to them.[2] Meanwhile, as the United Society of Drillers, the London drillers had adopted the rules and customs of the Boilermakers and henceforward worked under their 'protection'.

The drillers came together in many other places as well, and in 1892 the National Society of Drillers was founded. The policy of the Boilermakers' national leaders was to bring them into the union rather than to allow them to remain as potential enemies in their own separate organizations. But in the branches the rank and file rejected this policy, for they were unwilling to admit the lowly drillers into membership. Eventually, in 1900, the leaders' fears were realized when the National Society took its 2,000 members in the provinces into an amalgamation with the Shipwrights.

The organization of shipyard labourers by the National Amalgamated Union of Labour and other general unions also offended the Boilermakers. Many labourers were employed by members of the society, and Knight's view was that there would be no divergence of interest between platers and their helpers 'if we could only get the labourers to keep their places. . . . The helper ought to be subservient and do as the mechanic tells him.'[3] The helpers, however, had their own grievances. They resented the platers' power of summary dismissal, and considered themselves exploited, and sometimes even cheated, by their masters. Moreover, helpers were debarred from entry into plating, which was recruited by apprenticeship. With a union behind them, the helpers began to engage in disputes with the platers. Not only in the North-east, but also in South Wales and elsewhere, agreements were obtained both with the employers' associations and with the Boilermakers. The helpers' rights were formally recognized, and it became increasingly common for them to be paid from the firm's office and not by the platers.

---

[1] Amalgamated Society of Engineers, *Quarterly Report*, Dec. 1893.
[2] Booth, op. cit., vol. v, 1895, pp. 325–6.
[3] *Royal Commission on Labour*, C–6894–VII, 1893, Qs. 20801–2.

Shipbuilding and engineering were not the only industries to be troubled by demarcation disputes and inter-union conflict. Besides taking their share of the struggles in the shipyards, the societies of building craftsmen fought among themselves for building work. The London and Manchester Orders of Bricklayers battled with each other for members, and with other unions for work. In 1896 they began a prolonged struggle with the Plasterers over the laying of floors and the fixing of tiles.[1] Meanwhile, the Plumbers fought everyone. The hot-water and gas-pipe fitters formed their own association, the Heating and Domestic Engineers, more to defend themselves against the Plumbers than to resist the employers.[2] As in shipbuilding, various methods of settling these disputes were tried, with very limited success.

The conflicts of the printing unions, on the other hand, were comparatively mild. The most important was that between the provincial Typographical Association and the London Societies of Compositors and Printing Machine Managers. As the Typographical Association built up its southern branches, competition developed for membership on the outskirts of London.[3] Behind the clash lay the problem of the London differential. The metropolitan societies feared that undercutting would follow the encroachment of provincial rates, whereas the Typographical Association could not see why it should struggle to establish a higher rate for branches in the Home Counties than for its other members.

This fear of jeopardizing the differential also kept the two London unions out of the Printing and Kindred Trades Federation, which had been formed in 1891 at the instance of G. D. Kelley,[4] secretary of the Lithographic Printers, whose headquarters, like those of the Typographical Association, were in Manchester. Kelley's main intention was to concert trade policy and trade movements; but, without central funds or the power to take decisions except after reference back to the constituent societies, the Federation proved of little value.[5] Local federations, however, had shown themselves to be of considerable importance in co-ordinating claims at the beginning of the decade, and London formed its own in 1894.

Tailoring

Demarcation disputes were not the only consequence of the impact of new methods of production upon the customs and conventions of the craft unions. At least as dangerous to the established societies was the erosion of power and privilege within areas which had once been regarded

---

[1] Postgate, op. cit., p. 363.   [2] Ibid., p. 356.   [3] Musson, op. cit., pp. 270–2.
[4] Kelley, G. D. (1848–1911). General secretary, Amalgamated Society of Lithographic Printers, 1881–1911. General secretary, National Printing and Kindred Trades Federation, 1891–1911. Parliamentary Committee, Trades Union Congress, 1871–2, 1883–4, 1887–8, 1890–2. M.P., 1906–10.   [5] Ibid., p. 290.

as the exclusive province of one great craft or another, and the years of depression were soon to show how far such erosion had gone. Indeed, the Amalgamated Society of Tailors were forced to face this problem even before the tide of prosperity had turned.

There were now three main types of production in the clothing industry. The handicraft tailors, still squatting cross-legged and using almost no machinery, served the master tailors of the retail bespoke trade. Most of them worked on the employers' premises, but some took work home and might employ their own subordinate labour. Outside the very highest quality trade, women were engaged to sew, sometimes using machines, and to work as tailoresses on the simpler garments. Secondly, there was a growing number of workshops supplying the wholesale ready-made and the wholesale bespoke trades, which also took jobs on sub-contract from some of the master tailors. The characteristics of this section were tighter organization, a greater division of labour, and the employment of men and women on similar work. Many of these 'subdivisional' shops were staffed and run by Jews.[1]

The chief producers for the expanding wholesale market, however, were the factories, which were characterized by extreme division of labour, mechanical methods, and a labour force which, apart from a minority of skilled male cutters and pressers, was predominantly female. They were supported by a mass of subcontractors and individual homeworkers operating at cut rates and dealing with the 'excess backlogs of the clothing factories'.[2] Everywhere the handicraft tailor was having to give way in all but the finest bespoke work before the subdivisional shop, with its superior management and more efficient use of skill; and in turn the subdivisional shops themselves were spurred on by the competition of the factories. Both these sections were growing, and with them the army of homeworkers.

Long before the rise of the factory and the subdivisional shop, the handicraft tailors had built up an exclusive unionism which still had considerable power in the highest classes of the trade. The Amalgamated Society of Tailors had by now absorbed practically all the local trade clubs in England. From a strength of 14,000 in 1888, the society grew to well over 17,000 by 1891, and its Scottish counterpart, the Scottish National Operative Tailors, had a membership of about 4,000. Wherever they could the two societies resisted the employment of women, the increased division of labour, and the use of subcontractors and outworkers,

[1] Mass immigration brought the Jewish population in Britain from 65,000 in 1881 to between 250,000 and 300,000 by 1914 (V. D. Lipman, *Social History of the Jews in England, 1850–1950,* 1954, p. 103). The 1901 Census showed that 40 per cent. of the 24,000 male and 50 per cent. of the 5,000 female Russians and Poles 'gainfully occupied' in London were employed in tailoring (ibid., p. 107).

[2] L. P. Gartner, *The Jewish Immigrant in England, 1870–1914,* 1960, p. 89.

all of which were thought to undermine the wages and conditions of craftsmen and their control over productive methods.[1] Wages were regulated by local piece-price lists, or 'logs', some agreed with the master tailors and others enforced by the union alone. When coercion was necessary, the Tailors adopted the common craft technique of singling out one town for a strike, concentrating their resources to ensure victory, and then bringing other centres into line.[2]

By 1890 the twin pressures of craft control and competition from the new methods of production had driven the master tailors of England, Scotland, and South Wales to combine in the Master Tailors' Association of Great Britain, later the National Federation of Merchant Tailors. Their aims were to rid themselves of restrictions on the organization of work and the engagement of women; to introduce a uniform national log which would prevent the Tailors from playing off their local associations against one another; and to persuade the union's branches to join in setting up arbitration committees which might limit the use of the strike. Early in 1891, when the Southport and Liverpool branches struck against the employment of women and outworkers, the Master Tailors further resolved to meet future action of this type with the full weight of their new Association.

In the same year an approach to the union's executive led to the establishment of a national joint conciliation committee.[3] All disputes not settled locally were to be referred to this body for conciliation and, if need be, arbitration. Suitably encouraged, the employers proposed that the committee should also negotiate a national log. The national leaders of the Tailors were by no means hostile to this development. The Society already had a rule by which any local dispute was to be referred, if possible, to a joint committee on the spot;[4] and such committees often dealt with difficulties arising out of the existing logs. Since it would enhance their authority over the branches, a national committee to complete the structure was perfectly acceptable to the union's leaders.

They were quickly brought to heel. Branches in the stronger and best-paid districts had no intention of opening the way to a national log, which was bound to level down the higher piece rates; nor did they wish to commit themselves to referring all unsettled disputes to a national committee. Especially where vital craft principles were concerned, they preferred to be free to impose their own terms. Consequently, at the next triennial conference of the Society in July 1891, the agreement was condemned,[5] and the union's leaders were forced to withdraw from the

[1] *Royal Commission on Labour*, C–6795–VI, 1893, Qs. 14193, 14256–8.
[2] S. P. Dobbs, *The Clothing Workers of Great Britain*, 1928, p. 130, footnote.
[3] The Scottish union took part in the early negotiations, but subsequently withdrew.
[4] *Royal Commission on Labour*, C–6795–VI, 1893, Qs. 14197, 14714–15.
[5] Ibid., Q. 14246.

national committee, thus allowing the employers' president to complain that they had 'broken off relations with us, which we had entered into, and refuse to recognise us, and will not admit our interference in any dispute'.[1]

In 1892 events in Liverpool precipitated a crisis. The local branch of the Tailors circularized their employers 'requiring' them to abandon all outwork. Some complied, with or without protest, and the remainder were struck. The Master Tailors' Association then sought national negotiations with the union, but they were rebuffed because the Liverpool branch, confident of its strength, insisted that the matter must be settled locally. The Master Tailors, fearful that a defeat of their Liverpool members would weaken the chances of breaking down craft restrictions throughout the country, continued to demand that the issue should be resolved nationally. Eventually the union consented to national meetings, but these failed to end the deadlock. About 180 of the Association's 800 members thereupon locked out some 1,800 trade unionists.

'Keep before you', declared an employers' circular, 'the plain issue which the men's conduct has raised, viz.; whether employers shall have reasonable liberty to conduct their businesses free from the dictation and tyranny of their union, or from henceforth, be subjected to their orders and exactions, however unreasonable such may be.' Most employers, however, paid no attention to this appeal. Many 'high class' masters felt that the struggle over outwork was not their battle since they did not put work out. Nor did the Scottish masters offer any support. Though they faced problems similar to those of their English colleagues, pressure to break down craft restrictions had not yet built up as it had in England.[2] Faced with this poor response, the Association had no choice but to bring the lock-out to an end and leave the dispute to be settled in Liverpool itself.

This success flattered the union's strength, and there were limits to what the Tailors could achieve by the use of craft controls. Later in 1892, for example, the employers called their leaders into conference concerning the Society's unilateral imposition of a rule prescribing that 'during slack seasons a fair equitable division of trade should be compulsory in all shops'. The employers were willing to grant that work ought to be shared in such circumstances, but the union was forced to concede that the new rule did not imply 'the distribution of the work in turns, nor are the employers called upon to surrender the discretion they have always exercised in the selection of workmen for the different classes of work'.[3]

The union and the employers were not always in conflict, and there

[1] *Royal Commission on Labour*, C–6795–VI, 1893, Q. 14175.

[2] The continued growth of the Scottish union during the nineties may indicate that the trend away from the handicraft tailoring had as yet had less effect than in the south. The employers' challenge in Scotland was to come later. See p. 348.

[3] *Report on Collective Agreements*, Cd. 5366, 1910, pp. xxvii–xxviii.

were occasions when the two sides worked together. In particular, they often joined forces politically to fight against the growing tendency of local authorities to award contracts for the uniforms of police, fire, and other services to non-federated (and non-union) firms using the cheaper subdivisional methods. Nevertheless, conflict had become more and more the dominant feature in their relationship. Between 1891 and 1900 the union spent £30,000 on disputes, and only in one year did the sum fall below £1,000. Yet in the previous decade annual expenditure on strike pay had never risen as high as £1,000. 'In the good old days it was come out and it was over in most towns', declared the union's journal, 'to-day it is come out and at the end of the first month both parties have settled down to a desperate and determined struggle.'[1]

In addition to this friction, there was a gradual decline in the union's membership, which began in 1892 and continued as the subdivisional shops increased their share of the market. Consequently, the thoughts of several leaders turned towards reorganization. If the Tailors could open their ranks to the rest of the industry, they might not only win new members but also reduce the pressure on the craftsman by improving the wages and conditions of those who were undercutting him. With these possibilities in mind, the socialist James Macdonald evolved a programme which was an ingenious blend of the 'new unionist' approach with craft conservatism, especially designed to gain support in London, where he was district secretary. The London tailors, an aristocracy of craftsmen with high piece rates, thought the union was doing too little to protect them. Macdonald therefore combined proposals for a wider solidarity among the workers, which meant lowering craft barriers to let in other sections of the trade, with a demand for full local autonomy, which was expected to appeal to the traditions—and self-interest—of the London branches.[2]

At the conference in 1891, however, the London delegates had failed to carry this programme. The conference agreed to set up a special class of members with low contributions in the hope of bringing in the Jews of the subdivisional shops; but proposals to admit women and factory workers, and to give the branches complete control over trade policy and trade funds, were both rejected. There then developed a complicated quarrel between the district and the Society's executive which led to Macdonald's expulsion in 1892 and the resignation of the West London District Committee *en bloc*.[3] Despite these setbacks, the new London secretary, T. A. Flynn,[4] continued Macdonald's policy, and in 1893 he co-operated with

---

[1] Amalgamated Society of Tailors and Tailoresses, *Journal*, Feb. 1902. The figures of expenditure on disputes are taken from ibid., Nov. 1901.

[2] *Workman's Times*, 14 Nov. 1891.   [3] Ibid., 12 Mar. 1892.

[4] Flynn, T. A. (1858–1925). Secretary, London district, Amalgamated Society of Tailors and Tailoresses, 1892–4; general secretary, 1894–1925. Parliamentary Committee, Trades Union Congress, 1916–18.

several small unions of machine operators, women, and Jews to form the London Tailors' Federation. This body, which was open to all clothing workers, set out to fight sweating,[1] and soon began to organize Jewish branches in Manchester.

The leaders of the Society, the president, J. Hollings, and the secretary, G. Keir, had no sympathy with the demand for an increase in local autonomy, which caused them enough trouble as it was; but they were in favour of the rest of the London programme. To any far-sighted person, whether a socialist or not, the organization of subdivisional shops, factories, and outworkers offered the only real hope of maintaining the Society's strength. To most of the craftsmen in the branches, on the other hand, it appeared that the new policy would not only legitimize the productive methods of the employers who were undermining their privileged position, but might also lead to the introduction of those methods into their own section of the trade. As the result of such fears they preferred to fight a rearguard action against change.

In 1893 the 'progressives' managed to persuade the conference to accept the principle of organizing all male and female workers in the industry, and a special committee was instructed to draw up a detailed plan. Their scheme was approved by a ballot of the Society in 1893 and again in 1894; but on both occasions the executive decided that the total poll was too small to justify so radical a change. When the scheme was revived in 1899 the outcome was the same. Membership was still declining, however, and the executive were now convinced at least of the need to recruit women. In 1900 they set up a Female Section with low contributions, and the Society's title was changed to include the Tailoresses.[2]

Engineering

A similar controversy had developed within the Amalgamated Society of Engineers, and for much the same reasons. Competition in engineering was quickening both at home and abroad. Some foreign producers, especially in Germany and the United States, had already overtaken the British lead. At home new methods of production were putting a double pressure on the craftsmen. Where these methods were introduced, they destroyed craft customs and privileges, and the competition of their products tended increasingly to force other firms to follow suit.

Pattern making, foundry work, blacksmiths' work, and boilermaking all saw the appearance of minor labour-saving devices; but the most fundamental and rapid changes were taking place in the machine shop,[3] which, with its fitters and turners, was the heart of the Engineers' empire.

---

[1] *Workman's Times*, 1 and 22 July and 5 Aug. 1893.
[2] Amalgamated Society of Tailors and Tailoresses, *Journal*, Mar. 1900.
[3] Rowe, op. cit., pp. 89–103.

About 1890 came the capstan and turret lathe, the vertical, horizontal, and later the universal milling machine, the external and surface grinder, the vertical borer, and the radial drill. Work on these specialist machines did not require the all-round competence of the craftsman, and many of the men put on to them, at wage rates below craft standards, had neither served an apprenticeship nor picked up a broad experience on the shop floor. The fitters and turners were soon faced with a growing threat from the 'dilution' of their skills, which was sharply underlined when unemployment rose from 2 per cent. in 1890 to 11 per cent. in 1893. Moreover, as improvization gave way to planning, works engineers, planners, inspectors, rate-fixers, and progress men appeared. The latitude once allowed to the good craftsman was reduced by detailed specification, close inspection, and tighter supervision, while speeding-up was encouraged by the growth of payment by results.[1]

When their privileged position was threatened, the Engineers reacted, like the Tailors, by trying to strengthen their traditional defences. At first, for example, they attempted to maintain a complete ban on piece-work except in shops where it was long established. The old 'piece-master' or subcontracting system had already been brought under control (and out of favour) by a rule that the earnings of a gang must be divided in proportion to their basic rates.[2] But the rule against straight piecework was less successful, and had the disadvantage that if an employer managed to evade it his shop had to be left to non-unionists. In 1892, therefore, the Society beat a reluctant retreat. Subject to the approval of the executive, district committees were allowed to regulate piecework in the light of local conditions. Some continued to prohibit the system altogether, but others accepted it so long as the worker drew at least his time rate plus 25 per cent., whatever his output.[3] Manchester worked out a code of rules to check rate-cutting, and shop committees were set up to negotiate piece-prices.

Shop lists, however, were the peak of achievement. In contrast to the prolonged agitation for the 'standard district rate',[4] no attempt was made to introduce district piece-price lists,[5] or to set up conciliation machinery to settle local disputes over prices. Instead the Manchester District Committee were snubbed by the executive for spending their time protecting piece-workers.[6] In 1894 the executive declared that 'the last Delegate Meeting did not sanction piece-work for the purpose of guaranteeing to some members an increased wage for the rate of contributions which is paid by those compelled to be content with day-work wages, and therefore

---

[1] See Phelps Brown, op. cit., pp. 90–98, for a sympathetic study of the craftsman's response to these changes.   [2] *Royal Commission on Labour*, C–6894–VII, 1893, Q. 25740.
[3] Webbs, *Industrial Democracy*, p. 297.   [4] See p. 11.
[5] *Report on Standard Piece Rates of Wages and Sliding Scales*, Cd. 144, 1900, p. xiii.
[6] Amalgamated Society of Engineers, *Quarterly Report*, Dec. 1893.

shop rates of piece-work must be regulated voluntarily by those engaged in the system'.[1]

To protect its empire, the Amalgamated Society still relied upon the traditional devices of controlling entry through apprenticeship and limiting overtime. With the strength brought by the boom years of 1889–91, many districts felt able to challenge what seemed to them too rapid an increase in the number of boys and learners taken on by particular firms. The Society's rules laid down no specific ratio and local practice varied, but opinion among the leadership favoured one apprentice to three journeymen.[2] There were also several campaigns to limit overtime, though what success these enjoyed usually proved temporary. In 1891, for example, gains were made in the North-east;[3] but the agreement had hardly been signed before union members were yielding to the temptation to increase their earnings by breaking it.

Even a well-devised system of local bargaining might have proved inadequate to solve these problems. In many large towns it was becoming the practice of the branch officials or the district committee to negotiate with the local employers' association. But there was nothing automatic about the process, and most local movements still began with a circular to individual firms, even where these were associated. In some centres, moreover, including London, the employers remained unorganized. Union leaders normally encouraged joint conferences, and they were prepared to advocate conciliation boards and even arbitration when unemployment mounted in 1892;[4] but in general their members preferred to meet any violation of craft rules by a peremptory demand for the employer to mend his ways, followed if necessary by a strike.

Payment by results, if growing, was still far less common than payment by time, which was governed by the all-important standard district rate. Though advances and reductions were increasingly negotiated by local conferences, the rates themselves were not subject to agreement. Engineering employers almost everywhere insisted on their right to pay some workers more and others less than the local standard, and they refused to commit themselves formally to anything in the nature of a minimum. On their side, the district committees were left free to fix their own standard rates, and to try to win for them the tacit recognition of the employers. The only interference from head office was a gentle prodding towards the levelling-up of the lower-paid districts.[5]

---

[1] Jefferys, op. cit., p. 139.

[2] *Royal Commission on Labour*, C–6894–VII, 1893, Q. 22762. Here and there agreements were eventually secured, laying down apprenticeship regulations, as with the Port Employers' Association at Swansea in 1899 (Amalgamated Society of Engineers, *Journal and Monthly Record*, Aug. 1899).   [3] See p. 126.

[4] Amalgamated Society of Engineers, *Monthly Report*, Apr. 1892 and Apr. 1893.

[5] *Royal Commission on Labour*, C–6894–VII, 1893, Q. 22807. Variations in the standard

Among the smaller engineering unions, the ironfounders' societies had in some areas advanced further in collective bargaining. In Scotland the Associated Ironmoulders had 'for the last 10 years' been working under an agreed procedure with two employers' organizations covering the West and the North-east respectively. Stoppages were prohibited except after a month's notice, during which 'generally conferences are held between representatives and arrangements come to amicably'.[1] In the North-east of England, after a prolonged and unsuccessful strike for a wage increase in 1894,[2] the Friendly Society of Ironfounders accepted a proposal by the associated employers of the Tyne, Wear, Tees, and Hartlepools districts for a conciliation board with a standing committee and a rule which forbade stoppages. Encouraged by the success of this board, employers in the North-east persuaded the United Patternmakers' Association to set up another in 1896. But the union's members viewed the board with characteristic craft suspicion, and the annual vote for its continuance sometimes produced only small majorities in its favour.[3]

Meanwhile, the return of heavy unemployment by 1892 had led most districts of the Engineers to intensify their efforts to restrict apprentices and exclude non-unionists. In addition, some of them—Glasgow and Manchester, for example—imposed upper limits on earnings from piece-work and fined the transgressors.[4] Tension was further increased by 'the machine question'. In an attempt to maintain its old control by 'following the work to the new machines',[5] the Amalgamated Society tried to insist that any machine performing work which had previously required a skilled man must be operated by a skilled man paid at the full craft rate. Feelings ran so high that in some shops there were strikes against the introduction of machines on any terms, though this was not official policy. 'The proportion of machine to hand work is an increasing one', declared the executive. 'If skilled engineers are to retain a position in the trade, they must follow the work to the machine.'[6]

These were orthodox responses by an aristocracy of craftsmen, menaced by change. But among the Engineers, as among the Tailors, there was also the unorthodox view, inspired by socialist and 'new unionist' notions,

district rate ranged from 27s. to 40s. a week (ibid., pp. 468–9). Individual rates also varied widely (Rowe, op. cit., p. 82).

[1] *Royal Commission on Labour*, C–6894–VII, 1893, Qs. 23460–4, 23491.
[2] H. J. Fyrth and Henry Collins, *The Foundry Workers*, 1959, pp. 101–2.
[3] Mosses, op. cit., pp. 121 2.
[4] R. O. Clarke, 'The Dispute in the British Engineering Industry, 1897–1898', *Economica*, May 1957. In the *First Series of Examples of Restriction and Interference* (Federation of Engineering and Shipbuilding Employers, 4 Nov. 1897), a Clydeside firm reported several cases where shop stewards 'repeatedly checked one of the turners for turning out too much work'. Manchester offered similar instances (Webb Trade Union Collection E, Section B, vol. lix).
[5] Jefferys, op. cit., p. 142.
[6] Amalgamated Society of Engineers, *Annual Report*, 1897.

of those who believed that change must be accepted, mastered, and, if possible, exploited. Since the mid-eighties John Burns and Tom Mann, both skilled engineers and members of the Amalgamated Society, had been attacking the 'old' unions for their alleged lethargy and conservatism. Burns stressed the importance of political action and urged the running of independent labour candidates for Parliament. Mann agreed but also emphasized the need for the Society to become more militant, to take in the new sections of engineering workers, and to reform its government and administration to meet changing conditions. From 1888 onwards, in the recruiting campaigns of the boom years, he set about rallying the younger members behind this programme.

When Robert Austin, the 'cautious and traditional'[1] secretary, died in 1891, Mann threw up his full-time post as president of the Dockers and ran for the vacancy. His main opponent was John Anderson, an assistant secretary since 1883. Anderson was against broadening the membership, against the 'new-fangled idea of piling up money for fighting the capitalists',[2] against political action, and against any re-casting of union organization. Thus the conflict

reflected the difference in outlook and policy of the conservative elements and those who wished to make a decisive break with the past. It was not merely the most hotly contested election ever held in the Society, it also excited wide interest in the broader labour movement and the press. For the first time both candidates addressed meetings up and down the country and members in different localities formed election committees to support their candidate.

In the end Anderson was elected by the narrow margin of 18,102 votes to 17,152 in a poll of over 50 per cent.; 'by far the largest vote ever cast' in the Society.[3]

Though contained at the polls, unorthodoxy triumphed at the Leeds Delegate Meeting of 1892, the first since 1885. There the forces which had been rallied by Mann succeeded in remoulding the Society.[4] The conference lasted through ten weeks of heated argument and keen voting. The old local executive, composed since 1851 exclusively of working representatives of the London branches, was replaced by an executive of

---

[1] Jefferys, op. cit., p. 111. But see p. 293, footnote 2.   [2] *Workman's Times*, 4 June 1892.

[3] Jefferys, op. cit., p. 113. It should be added, however, that Mann's candidature did not depend solely upon 'progressive' support. Apparently his nomination was endorsed by Thomas Burt, Robert Knight, and Edward Trow of the Associated Iron and Steel Workers (D. W. Crowley, *Origins of the Revolt of the British Labour Movement from Liberalism, 1876–1906*, Ph. D. thesis, London, 1952). At the time Burt and Trow were Mann's colleagues as members of the Royal Commission on Labour.

[4] One of the delegates was George Barnes, a socialist who had followed Burns as member of the executive and later became secretary of the society. A member of a voluntary organizing committee, he had addressed meetings all over London propagating Mann's ideas, and was secretary of the London committee which promoted his candidature in 1891 (Barnes, op. cit., pp. 36–38).

full-time officials elected by eight electoral districts. Six full-time organizing district delegates were to be elected as organizers and negotiators, and as intermediaries between the executive and the district committees. In future the Delegate Meeting was to assemble every four years, and the rules governing union membership were somewhat relaxed. Full membership was granted to roll turners, electrical engineers, drop forgers, press toolmakers, and other minor groups. Special membership was also available for workers who were ineligible for full membership because of age or infirmity or because they received a lower rate of wages.

The *Workman's Times* described this victory as 'one of the most encouraging signs of the progress of Socialist thought and action in trades unionism';[1] and the 'progressives' did their best to ensure that the changes were implemented in what they regarded as the right spirit. The Manchester district formed a Progressive Party to hold regular meetings, to further co-operation and amalgamation between engineering unions, to disseminate the 'true principles' of trade unionism, and above all, to organize the voting for members of the executive and district organizers.[2] Similar steps were taken in Hull, and the Belfast Progressives called meetings to do 'all that is possible towards the ultimate election of officers who are in entire sympathy with the changes which have been made in the rules'.[3]

Something was achieved. Voluntary organizing committees were formed up and down the country to assist the full-time district organizers, and recruitment rose in Scotland, South Wales, London, and the Eastern Counties. But generally the results were disappointing. In some districts the newly appointed officers had a frigid reception, which made their work difficult. 'Many influential members . . . had a deep-rooted prejudice against the new order', and looked upon the appearance of its local representatives 'as almost a personal affront'.[4] One of them referred later to 'that fatal Leeds Delegate Meeting' which ushered in the 'new unionism', with its 'wretched dogmas and its mischievous and meddling organisers'.[5] Moreover, the attitude of the craftsmen towards bringing in the new sections of engineering workers remained for the most part exceedingly orthodox. By January 1898 there were only 4,500 members in the special groups, out of a total membership of over 91,000.[6]

Printing and Shipbuilding

The spirit of change also affected the London Society of Compositors one of the most exclusive and conservative of craft unions. Infected by

[1] *Workman's Times*, 20 Aug. 1892.   [2] Ibid., 19 Nov. and 26 Nov. 1892.
[3] Ibid., 3 Dec. 1892.
[4] Amalgamated Society of Engineers, *Journal and Monthly Record*, Jan. 1897.
[5] W. Harmston, *Election Address*, 9 Mar. 1898. See also the election addresses of H. Barton and W. Cooper, 1898.   [6] Jefferys, op. cit., p. 138.

the 'new unionism' and critical of the Society's leaders, especially the secretary, C. J. Drummond, a Conservative in politics who had the reputation of being distant and unapproachable,[1] a minority founded the London Society of Compositors' Reform League in 1891 to promote 'honest and legitimate opposition' to the existing leadership. More specifically, the League set out to 'fight the bastard trade unionism' of Drummond and his colleagues, to secure the election of new men to the executive, and to break up the 'gifts'.[2] These local cliques each had a limited membership, admitted only after careful scrutiny,[3] and existed to get work for their members and to supplement union benefits.[4] Each gift kept its own call-book and tried to maintain a monopoly of the jobs available in the district. Their nominees dominated the executive, and they were understandably unpopular with the rest of the Society.

The Reform League enjoyed swift and striking success, winning three places on the executive early in 1892.[5] The chairman of the Society promptly resigned, followed by Drummond, who made his farewells at the annual conference in March. 'He was not in sympathy with what was known as the new unionism, and as the members had placed on the committee three representatives of a policy with which he could not agree, he felt himself unable to carry out their instructions.'[6] Drummond's successor was the Fabian C. W. Bowerman,[7] who may have had more sympathy for the League's ideas; but in 1893 nominees of the gifts managed to hold all the seats on the executive that they had retained the previous year. Though it was still able to carry a ballot in favour of excluding members of the gifts from the Society, the League's impetus was flagging and before long it was disbanded, ostensibly to set an example to the gifts, which they did not follow.

In the provincial Typographical Association there were no gifts, and reformers concentrated upon criticism of the union's government. They objected to an executive drawn only from the Manchester branch, to its reluctance to summon delegate meetings—the last had been held in 1877— and to the reliance on frequent ballots.[8] Delegate meetings took place in 1891 and 1893, but all that the 'progressives' managed to achieve was a decision to hold them every five years in future and to introduce an

---

[1] *Workman's Times*, 12 Mar. 1892.   [2] Ibid., 20 Aug. 1892.
[3] *Report on Agencies and Methods for dealing with the Unemployed*, C–7182, 1893, pp. 48–49.
[4] Child, op. cit.
[5] One of their successful candidates was H. W. Hobart (see p. 59).
[6] *Workman's Times*, 26 Mar. 1892. When it was proposed that Drummond should be presented with a purse of 100 guineas in recognition of his services, the conference 'declined to entertain the proposal, and the motion was declared lost'. He joined the Labour Department of the Board of Trade on its reconstruction in Jan. 1893.
[7] Bowerman, C. W., P.C. (1851–1947). General secretary, London Society of Compositors, 1892–1906. Parliamentary Committee, later General Council, Trades Union Congress, 1897–1923; secretary, 1911–23. M.P., 1906–31.   [8] Musson, op. cit., pp. 141–2.

annual Representative Council, which soon proved a clumsy failure. Here, too, the demand for change ebbed away as both societies went from strength to strength.

The established leaders may have been spurred on by the opposition of the militants; but the industry was expanding rapidly in the nineties, and union growth was almost continuous throughout the decade. The Typographical Association rose from 8,000 to 16,000 members, and the London Society of Compositors from 8,000 to 11,000. Of the other unions, the provincial Bookbinders and Machine Rulers grew from 3,000 to 4,000, and the Lithographic Printers from 2,000 to 4,000. Most of the smaller societies kept pace. Among employers, the response to the advance movements of 1889–91 had been the same as in so many other industries, and various organizations were founded or revived. The most important, the London Master Printers' Association, in abeyance since the early seventies, was re-established in 1890.[1] Soon most provincial centres were following suit, and by 1901 there were thirty-six local associations.[2]

Joint conferences and collective agreements, which had hitherto been rare, could thus become more frequent and widespread, supplementing the unilateral regulation of the craftsmen. Like their colleagues elsewhere, the leaders of the printing unions were not sorry to see this development, for it tended to increase their authority over the branches. The chapels and branches continued to take the initiative, but the societies insisted that no coercive action should be taken before the executive had investigated and sought a peaceful settlement. Beyond this, the leaders gave cautious encouragement to arbitration where no question of principle was at stake.[3] Central control was limited, however, by the considerable funds at the disposal of the larger branches, some of which employed their own full-time officers.

Their growing strength enabled the societies to apply traditional restrictions more effectively, notably upon entry to the trade. The dangers of labour abundance still worried them, however, and the Typographical Association regarded unemployment as its greatest problem. Since the industry was partly seasonal, many craftsmen faced some months on short time every year. Between one-fifth and one-eighth were only 'casually employed' in times of prosperity, and up to a third during depression.[4] Consequently, more apprentices now might lead to more unemployment later; and the unions were acutely aware of the constant threat from 'unfair' firms which used large numbers of boys in their attempts to undercut the market. The Typographical Association tried to limit each establishment

---

[1] The London Master Printers had been meeting the London Compositors at intervals since 1793 to revise piece-price scales. In 1871 nearly half the printers of England and Wales were in London, and in 1891 two-fifths.

[2] Child, op. cit.   [3] Musson, op. cit., pp. 171–2.   [4] Ibid., p. 103.

to three apprentices regardless of its size, thereby producing a crop of strikes. The Scots fought hard to enforce their rule of one apprentice to three journeymen, and in 1894 the London Compositors voted to cut their ratio to one in six, though members were warned by the executive against 'precipitate action' in applying the new rule.

From time to time the employers tried to introduce women 'because the subdivision of labour and the application of mechanical power had created simple processes; because they were willing to accept low wages; and because, unlike the men . . . they made no efforts to interfere in the management of the works'.[1] In the seventies an attempt to establish female compositors in London had not prospered; but in Edinburgh they were brought in to replace the men during a strike in 1872. When the union subsequently failed to dislodge them, the practice spread to other Scottish towns.[2]

The official policy of all three societies towards organizing women was defined in a proclamation of 1886 admitting them as members so long as they were paid the rate for the job. But in fact women were only employed if they accepted lower rates, and, as the secretary of the Typographical Association said, 'if you organise women, you recognise their conditions. You then establish a minimum wage for women that is lower than ours.'[3] During the nineties the unions were well able to prevent any further encroachment, but the problem of Edinburgh remained. In 1898 the Edinburgh Female Compositors' Society was formed under the auspices, and with the financial assistance, of the local branch of the men's union. It lasted only a few months.[4]

Despite these restrictions on the engagement of boys and women, un-employment relief continued to be expensive. The societies applied all their old remedies, such as tramping benefits, the use of 'call-books', and grants for both removal and emigration. In addition, they sought to spread work by reducing hours and limiting overtime. By 1893 pressure for shorter hours had brought the newspaper offices down to between fifty and fifty-two a week, and book and jobbing work averaged not more than fifty-three.[5] A campaign to limit overtime, launched by the London Compositors during 1898, had achieved an informal understanding with the London master printers by 1900.[6] Generally speaking, however, limitation was not effective, and more success was attained in securing higher rates for the hours of overtime worked.

[1] *Women in the Printing Trades*, edited by J. R. Macdonald, 1904, p. 27.

[2] S. C. Gillespie, *A Hundred Years of Progress, The Record of the Scottish Typographical Association*, 1953, p. 105.   [3] Musson, op. cit., p. 121.

[4] The women 'employed in the actual printing processes do not seem to have regarded their work as their permanent means of livelihood to the same extent' as those employed as folders in bookbinding (Macdonald, op. cit., p. 29).

[5] *Royal Commission on Labour*, C–6894–IX, 1893, Qs. 22797–8.

[6] E. Howe and H. E. Waite, *The London Society of Compositors*, 1948, p. 300.

There were also rules to prevent the interchange of men between one type of job and another, and to prescribe manning ratios for most machines. Nevertheless, the societies' control over printing machines was far from complete.[1] In London the Compositors left them to the Printing Machine Managers, the Platen Machine Minders, and the Amalgamated Pressmen; but in the provinces and in Scotland the two typographical associations claimed jurisdiction without, however, managing to persuade all their branches that machine operators were fit members for a craft union. Platen and rotary machine minders, or 'managers', were particularly neglected. Moreover, many firms refused to recognize that societies of craftsmen had any rights in the machine room even where the local branches tried to assert them.[2]

The greatest test of the unions' capacity for maintaining their authority came with the introduction of mechanical typesetting to replace hand-composing, at first mainly on newspaper work. Linotype and other similar machines had been brought in twenty years earlier, but not until the end of the eighties did their use become sufficiently common to present a serious challenge to the craftsmen. The prime concern of their societies was to get full control of the new machines and those who manned them, and to see that as few hand-compositors as possible were displaced. During the early nineties, therefore, agreements were signed both with individual firms and with local employers' associations, defining the terms under which machinery was to be installed and operated.

In 1894, for instance, a general agreement with the daily newspapers gave the London Compositors exclusive control over the machines and a scale of piece-prices which produced extremely high earnings. The employers tried to reduce these rates in 1896, but their gains were small. After the Society had succeeded in getting the new arrangements extended to weekly newspapers and to book-work, many firms in London turned to payment on 'stab', or time rates.[3] In the provinces, keen bargains were driven by the Typographical Association. Many branches were worried by the displacement of hand-compositors, especially among the older men, and organized restriction of output to slow down the process. The employers wanted piece-work, hoping to tempt operators into the higher output of which the machines were capable; but in return the union demanded prohibitively high rates. Before long most provincial linotype work was also being done on stab.[4]

---

[1] Musson, op. cit., pp. 51, 99, 249–55.

[2] Ibid., p. 255. In Scotland the problem was further aggravated by breakaways (Gillespie, op. cit., pp. 122–5). In London, the Platen Minders and Pressmen continued to operate on the traditional craft basis, establishing their wage minima and craft rules by 'individual house movements'. As small and not very strong societies, they would have preferred collective agreements, but the London Master Printers would not recognize them for bargaining purposes (C. J. Bundock, *The National Union of Printing, Bookbinding and Paper Workers*, 1959, pp. 235, 239, 245, 258, 277–8).   [3] Child, op. cit.   [4] Musson, op. cit., pp. 233–4.

The Linotype Company took up the struggle with the craft societies, fearing that demands for high wages and restrictions on training would discourage the use of their machine.[1] Schools were set up in London and Manchester during 1893–4 for the instruction of operators on a large scale.[2] This threat was more effective in the provinces than in London, and forced the Typographical Association to relax its rules on the period and conditions of training. In 1894, after a conference with the Company and several users of linotype, the union also reduced its requirements for piece-work. A complicated series of local negotiations followed and fresh agreements were made; but rates remained, as the Association itself boasted, 'high and almost prohibitive'.[3]

Like their London colleagues, the provincial newspaper proprietors tried again in 1896, and in so doing pioneered national negotiation in printing. They formed the Linotype Users' Association and approached the Typographical Association for a general agreement, in the 'interests of peace and equity'. A conference was held in 1897, and in 1898 there followed the first national agreement.[4] This could hardly have been more favourable to the union. All linotype operators were to be members of the Typographical Association; working hours were to be forty-eight on day-work and forty-four on night-work; stab rates were to be $12\frac{1}{2}$ per cent. above those for hand-composing; and prices for piece-work were left to local negotiation. Then, to the disgust of the employers, the union insisted on treating these terms as a minimum, and in several instances achieved even more.

There were few important developments in other sections of the industry. Both sides tended to accept the lead of the compositors in settling wages and conditions, and no major technical innovations disturbed their relationship. The exception was London bookbinding,[5] where the unions had to cope with the substitution of cloth for leather and with the mechanization of cloth case-making. In addition, mass production of standard works such as bibles and prayer books favoured subdivision of labour and the use of new machinery. These changes permitted employers to replace craftsmen by machine operators, and thus allowed women to advance beyond their traditional tasks of folding and stitching. By 1891 women constituted over 60 per cent. of the labour force in bookbinding, stationery, paper, box- and bag-making; and during the next ten years

---

[1] On a visit to Herbert Spencer, the apostle of *laissez-faire*, Beatrice Webb found that 'all his savings are in the Linotype Company, in which he invested in order to break the trade union' (Beatrice Webb, *Our Partnership*, 1948, p. 187).

[2] Musson, op. cit., pp. 231–2.

[3] Ibid., p. 240.

[4] It did not cover Scotland, where linotype operation continued to be covered by separate agreements with individual employers (Gillespie, op. cit., p. 113).

[5] See also p. 127.

their numbers grew by 40 per cent. as against an 18 per cent. increase in male workers.

In 1885 the men's unions had set up a joint trade committee to determine the jobs to be reserved for craftsmen. They were able in 1893 to reach an agreement with the employers which included a schedule of journeymen's work, defined some of the women's operations, and laid down piece-prices for case making.[1] No real effort was made to recruit women, but among those employed in folding and binding 'we find much greater collective activity and closer co-operation' than existed among women in printing.[2] Several women's unions were already in existence, and others were established both in London and the provinces. As important as these small local unions, however, were 'the frequent and persistent efforts of women to act jointly without establishing a permanent organisation', and on a number of occasions they acted with the men. This feature of the trade was 'almost entirely due to the fact that women's labour in bookbinding, e.g. in folding, was accepted by the men, and that in all workshop matters women were the fellow-workers and not the rivals of the men'.[3]

There was some development of organization among the less-skilled male workers. The new printing machinery required machine 'assistants' (not to be confused with machine managers) who founded the Printers' Labourers' Union in London during 1889. The London master printers decided in 1893 to support any firm attacked by the new union, and in 1894 sought the help of William Collison's National Free Labour Association.[4] But the union survived, and in 1899 it was negotiating with the London Master Printers' Association on behalf of its 2,000 members under the title of the Operative Printers' Assistants' Society. No agreement, however, emerged. 'Stirred into action by the noble example shown by the Printers' Labourers' Union and also by the dockers',[5] London warehousemen and cutters formed another new union in 1889. At the end of the nineties this body amalgamated with an old and conservative group of London warehousemen, and declared itself open to 'bench hands' throughout the whole of the printing and paper trades.[6]

In turning new developments to their own advantage, the societies of printing craftsmen were emulated by the United Society of Boilermakers and Iron Shipbuilders, 'one of the most powerful and best-conducted of English trade societies'.[7] In an expanding industry, the union's strength grew from 30,000 in 1889 to 48,000 in 1900; and its well-paid members were little threatened by technical change or the encroachment of other

---

[1] This was the only negotiated uniform list in bookbinding. Prices elsewhere varied from shop to shop both in London and the provinces (*Report on Standard Piece Rates*, C–7567–1, 1894, p. 178).
[2] Macdonald, op. cit., pp. 29–30.
[3] Ibid., p. 29.
[4] See p. 171.
[5] Bundock, op. cit., pp. 111–12.
[6] Ibid., p. 124.
[7] Webbs, *Industrial Democracy*, p. 28.

crafts. These circumstances appeared to justify the autocratic rule of the secretary, Robert Knight, who continued to exercise a domination which few other union leaders could hope to equal. His membership was unified and well-drilled,[1] men even being fined for bad work. Knight still followed the principle that wages must fluctuate with the state of trade, and the employers assured the Royal Commission on Labour that they much preferred to deal with him rather than with the Engineers, whose executive they could not get to 'bring their influence to bear' upon the districts. With the Boilermakers, however, they could 'always command the immediate attention' of the 'powerful body at headquarters that has considerable control over their branches'.[2]

Negotiations with the local employers' associations were now normal on the Tyne, the Wear, and the Tees, where the district committees had the assistance of a full-time district delegate. In 1894 Knight was able to systematize and strengthen these arrangements by an agreement covering the whole North-east which laid down a minimum period of six months between general wage changes, and a maximum change of 5 per cent. at any one time. Any change required a month's notice, and had to be referred to a joint conference. Joint standing committees were to deal with issues affecting only one river. Minor disputes were to come first to the consideration of an employers' agent and the Society's district delegate, and then to a joint committee of employers and union officers. There were to be no stoppages, and the agreement was to last five years, and thereafter be terminable by six months' notice.[3]

With the approval of the executive, Knight's scheme for the North-east was brought into operation by a majority vote of the whole Society against the opposition of most of the branches whose affairs it was to govern.[4] Partly, perhaps, because 1894 was a year of depression, the branches carried their hostility no further. On Clydeside, however, where joint settlements were more recent, members were less obedient to the leadership. The employers' association had not recognized the union until 1888, and the area had a history of long and bitter conflict. The shipbuilding boom of 1889–90 compelled the local employers to come to terms, and there slowly developed a bargaining structure similar to that in the North-east. But old attitudes died hard and Clydeside, 'not having been disciplined into the new system',[5] was far more unruly than elsewhere, striking in 1891 against a wage reduction negotiated by the Society's executive after district bargaining had failed.[6]

---

[1] In 1889 and 1891 Knight had little difficulty in subduing attempts on Clydeside to form a breakaway Scottish union (Webbs, *Industrial Democracy*, p. 82; also Trade Union Collection E, Section A, vol. xxxiii).   [2] C–6894–VII, 1893, Qs. 25559, 26332.
[3] Cummings, op. cit., pp. 190–1.   [4] Ibid., p. 134.
[5] *Royal Commission on Labour*, C–6894–VII, 1893, Q. 20712.
[6] *Report on the Strikes and Lockouts of 1891*, C–6890, 1893, p. 5.

Employers in these two principal centres of shipbuilding had already begun to show an interest in securing an industry-wide uniformity in wage movements. In 1889 they set up the National Federation of Shipbuilding and Engineering Employers, 'to arrange for alterations of rates of wages in all districts taking place for stated periods and at fixed dates'. The Federation covered shipbuilders in the North-east, on the Clyde, and in Belfast. Its other objects included 'mutual support in resisting interference by workmen's associations with free contract work, number of apprentices engaged etc.', and assistance for any firm or employers' association in bringing 'any unreasonable strike to an end'.[1]

In South Wales, which was outside this grouping, the Society was well-organized in the shipbuilding and repairing yards of Cardiff, Newport, and Swansea, but weak in the great iron and steelworks in the valleys, where resistance to recognition was unyielding and wages were governed by sliding scales. Even here, however, the Boilermakers were extending their influence. In 1892, along with other craft unions, they began a stoppage which lasted for fourteen months. To assist the strikers, the Society boycotted iron and steel plates from Dowlais and the repair of vessels carrying ore to the works concerned. The Shipping Federation, whose members were hard hit by this decision, tried to get repair-dock owners to lock out. When this failed, they brought pressure to bear on the iron and steel companies to settle. Within two months three of the major firms had capitulated, conceding a large increase in wages and abolishing the sliding scales.[2]

As the decade progressed, district negotiation became the rule, and agreements were signed in Hull, Liverpool, London, Manchester, Newport, Southampton, and elsewhere. Bargaining was a complex affair, mainly because of piece-work arrangements.[3] For some operations, such as plating and angle-iron work, local lists were supplemented by individual bargaining for each gang in the shipyards. Others, such as riveting, lent themselves more readily to the negotiation of district uniform lists, and the coverage of these lists was steadily extended during the period. In 1898 the Society negotiated a list for Clydeside riveters over the heads of the rank and file, who struck against it. Their protest was ignored until they returned to work, but amendments were then made.[4]

Meanwhile, the Boilermakers did not neglect the control of hours or overtime, and the regulation of apprenticeship led to their first national agreement. The Shipbuilding Employers' Federation had, in the event,

---

[1] Associated Society of Shipwrights, *Annual Report*, 1890, quoted in British Steel Smelters' *Monthly Report*, May 1890. 'With this new departure on the part of employers, we . . . should draw ourselves a little closer together' (ibid.). See also *Royal Commission on Labour*, C–6894–VII, 1893, Qs. 26183–7.   [2] Cummings, op. cit., pp. 130–1.

[3] *Report on Standard Piece Rates of Wages and Sliding Scales*, Cd. 144, 1900, pp. 35–53.

[4] Ibid., p. 42.

become more concerned with craft questions than with wage movements. In January 1893 the Society tried to enforce its ratio of one apprentice to five journeymen by the issue of apprentice cards. The Federation at once asked for a national conference at which the union leaders agreed to withdraw the cards in return for an agreement on a ratio of 2 to 7.[1] A further major settlement followed in 1894 when all the unions concerned in ship-repairing, including the Engineers, agreed with the Ship Repairers' Federation on the terms of employment for their members working on oil-tankers.

The second of the two most important shipbuilding unions, the Associated Society of Shipwrights, grew even more rapidly than the Boiler-makers, increasing from 4,000 in 1887 to over 18,000 in 1900. Collective bargaining developed on lines roughly parallel with those of the Boiler-makers, though boilermakers tended to keep themselves aloof, whereas shipwrights were more ready to co-operate with the smaller unions. On the Wear, for example, a conciliation board had been established in 1885 which covered the shipwrights, smiths, joiners, drillers, and painters, and dealt with inter-union disputes as well as differences with the employers.[2] The board was successful in avoiding serious stoppages, but found no imitators.[3]

A weak spot for the societies of shipbuilding craftsmen lay in the Admiralty dockyards. There were several wage advances for dockyard workers during this period, and an example was set to private industry by the granting of a forty-eight-hour week in 1894; but the Lords of the Admiralty consistently refused to recognize the unions. The only remedy for the men lay in petitions through their departmental chiefs: 'it is thought subversive of discipline', explained the Financial Secretary, 'if the communication is made through anyone outside the dockyards.'[4] In order to call attention to their grievances, the Shipwrights brought pressure to bear on Members of Parliament for the dockyard constituencies, complaining of rates lower than those in private yards and the absence of any share in the fixing of piece-prices.[5]

---

[1] The agreement also laid down a five-year apprenticeship and minimum rates for the apprentices. In 1894 it was countersigned by J. Muirhead, secretary of a Joint Committee of Members of the Federation and Non-Associated Employers, covering most of the firms in the United Kingdom. Another, less favourable, arrangement with the Iron Trades Employers' Association (see p. 12) applied to the boilershops.

[2] *Royal Commission on Labour*, C–6894–VII, 1893, Qs. 25712–20.

[3] Except on the Clyde, where a strike of ships' joiners in 1894 led to a conciliation board; but its life was short. In the same year the umpire gave an award against the men, and they gave notice to terminate the board.

[4] Ibid. Q. 25968.

[5] Ibid., Qs. 21961, 21967, 25875–6. In the dockyards a separate Ship Constructive Association competed with the Shipwrights and there were many local associations catering for other shipyard craftsmen. All lost membership during the nineties.

Building Craftsmen slip the Leash

Cyclical fluctuations in building have generally followed a course of their own, divorced from the trade cycle which governs activity in most other industries. Thus throughout the years 1889–1900 building experienced an unbroken expansion,[1] and this was followed by a prolonged slump which persisted until 1911. A further contrast with many other craft trades during the nineties was the absence of any technical changes of importance apart from the continued substitution of brickwork for masonry. Up to the turn of the century, therefore, the societies of building craftsmen had an opportunity for extending their control even more favourable than that enjoyed by the printing and shipbuilding unions. It was taken up, but with this difference. In printing and shipbuilding, union leaders were able to use the opportunity to strengthen the central authority of their executives. In building, the branches broke ranks in what amounted to a free for all.[2]

Prosperity was reflected in the growth of the leading societies. Between 1888 and 1900 the Stonemasons rose from 10,000 to 19,000; the Carpenters and Joiners from 25,000 to 65,000; the Bricklayers from 7,000 to 39,000; the Plasterers from 1,500 to 11,000; the Plumbers from 4,000 to 11,000; and the largest body of painters from 2,000 to 10,000. Almost every major craft had its own Scottish society, and these, together with the minor craft organizations and many unions of builders' labourers, rose at a comparable pace. Understandably, strikes were common, and their number increased as the tempo of the industry mounted.[3] Some were official, but many were not, for branches forged ahead with claims as they thought fit. If the employers resisted, they could usually raise their own levies to finance a strike;[4] but with building demand running high there might be no need of a stoppage at all.

Agitation for higher wages and better conditions sometimes elicited

[1] The Board of Trade declared that 1893, 1894, and 1895, years of depression in other industries, had been remarkable in building both for advances in wages and for a low level of unemployment (*Report on Changes in Wages and Hours of Labour in 1894*, C–8075, 1896, p. xvi). This low level of unemployment is even more impressive when the growth of the industry is taken into account. In 1891 there were 900,000 employers, craftsmen, and apprentices. To these should be added not less than 250,000 labourers (Clapham, *Economic History of Modern Britain*, vol. ii, p. 120). By 1901 the total had risen to 1,272,000, together with perhaps 350,000 labourers.

[2] This development seems to have gone all but unnoticed by the historian of the building unions, R. W. Postgate (op. cit.). Indeed, though his is one of the most readable of union histories, most of the developments of the decade seem to have escaped him. Two of the more startling sub-headings in the chapter on the period ('The Building Trades Isolated') are 'Decay of the Lodges' and 'No Trade Activities'.

[3] The number of stoppages rose almost annually after 1890, being 131 in 1893 and 193 in 1897. The total then remained at around 180 for the next two years (*Second Annual Report of the Labour Department of the Board of Trade*, C–7900, 1895, p. 62; *Ninth Abstract of Labour Statistics*, Cd. 1755, 1903, p. 88).

[4] *Royal Commission on Labour*, C–6795–VI, 1893, Qs. 17296–7.

local co-operation between the crafts. In London the carpenters' lock-out of 1891[1] was followed in 1892 by a general forward movement led by the bricklayers, who handed in their notices early in the summer. The employers proposed delay until the autumn (when the seasonal slackening was apt to weaken the unions' position) and the elaboration of an agreement for all trades. The societies responded by forming a federation which negotiated an immediate settlement for most of the crafts except the stonemasons.[2] Other centres also set up federations, and by 1895 there were twenty-five. By and large they were welcomed by the weaker societies, while the stronger stood aloof or withdrew when it suited them.[3] The federations tended to develop an independence which further undermined the authority of the union executives, who therefore showed no liking for them; and it was often tempting for local leaders of the stronger societies to pull out of a joint movement and make their own terms.

In the field of collective bargaining,[4] development over the decade was basically more durable and far more widespread, though some districts still relied upon unilateral action by the union branches. In 1892 the National Association of Master Builders had submitted tables of wages and hours to the Royal Commission on Labour which contained figures for 126 towns and cities.[5] The probability is that this represented the full extent of collective bargaining at the time, though it does not follow that there were 'working rules' covering every craft in all these places. However, of the 173 new collective agreements reported to the Board of Trade in 1899, no less than 141 concerned the building trades,[6] and in the industry as a whole there were now nearly 500 such agreements in operation in some 260 towns and cities.[7]

Towards the end of the century some of these included an 'authority of employers' clause which bore witness to the nature of the conflicts then reaching their climax. 'Each employer shall conduct his business in any way he may think advantageous in all details of Management, not infringing on the individual liberty of the Workmen or the rules.'[8] Many agremeents also included a 'conciliation and arbitration' clause, though branches in a strong bargaining position might well ignore its provisions. It usually forbade stoppages, and provided for all disputes to go to a joint conciliation committee, the decisions of which would be binding. In the event of deadlock, a dispute was to be referred either directly to a neutral

---

[1] See p. 127.

[2] Despite this show of unity, however, the plumbers secured superior terms and the painters no terms at all.

[3] Postgate, op. cit., pp. 359–60.   [4] See p. 13.

[5] C–6795–VI, 1893, appendix xxx.

[6] *Report on Changes in Rates of Wages and Hours of Labour in 1899*, Cd. 309, 1900, p. 206.

[7] Ibid., appendix iii, pp. 236–61.

[8] Ibid., p. 209. The similarity of wording in such cases suggests that the National Association of Master Builders had circulated a formula among its members.

umpire or to two arbitrators, one from each side, and thence, if still un-
unsettled, to an umpire.[1] Only the Plumbers went beyond local or district
arrangements, when in 1897 they reached an agreement with the Master
Plumbers under which a national conciliation board was set up to deal
with disputes referred to it by the localities.

Scotland provided two of the best-established systems of joint regulation. Since 1884 the Scottish United Operative Masons and the Glasgow
Master Masons' Association had met every year to settle wages, hours,
and other questions for the Glasgow area for the ensuing twelve months.
A standing joint committee dealt with minor disputes, and no stoppage
was permissible until a dispute had been referred either to the committee
or to the annual conference.[2] In 1888 a separate organization, the Aberdeen
Operative Masons' and Stonecutters' Society, and the employers of the
Aberdeen Granite Association had signed a remarkable agreement which
had features in common with the Birmingham Alliances of the nineties.[3]
Members of the Association were to employ only members of the union,
and members of the union were to work only for members of the Association.[4]

In building, however, as in so many other craft trades, collective bargaining was no more than half the story, for the societies also took advantage of every opportunity to enforce craft controls. Prominent among the
objects of their attack was piece-work, which had been condemned in a
joint resolution of 1867 by the carpenters and joiners of both the Amalgamated Society and the smaller General Union as having a tendency to
reduce wages and produce bad workmanship. Thereafter the Amalgamated Society 'gave tacit support and encouragement to the branches
individually to resist it',[5] until in 1892 a rule banned the system altogether.
Equally hostile were the Stonemasons, the Bricklayers, the Plumbers, and
the Plasterers.

Usually, however, piece-work in building meant sub-letting the hiring
and supervision of labour, a practice which the unions similarly opposed.
With their secretary's approval,[6] the Plasterers' branches raised local
levies to finance strikes against it, and the London Building Trades
Committee was formed specially to deal with the problem.[7] This body

---

[1] Among the societies themselves, the Carpenters and Joiners inherited a bias in favour of
arbitration; the Stonemasons were traditionally hostile; and the Manchester Bricklayers gave
their branches complete discretion.

[2] *Royal Commission on Labour*, C-6795-VI, 1893, Qs. 17892–904. The system was embodied
in a formal agreement in 1891.   [3] See p. 194.

[4] K. D. Buckley, *Trade Unionism in Aberdeen, 1878–1900*, 1955, p. 36. The union enjoyed
virtually 100 per cent. membership by the mid-nineties.

[5] S. Higenbottam, *Our Society's History*, 1939, p. 139.

[6] *Royal Commission on Labour*, C-6795-VI, 1893, Q. 17295–6.

[7] The committee, under the secretaryship of George Dew, London secretary of the Carpenters and Joiners, had been formed in 1888 partly in consequence of the allegedly 'apathetic

persuaded the London School Board and later the London County Council to insert a clause in all their contracts prohibiting sub-letting. With the support of the Trades Union Congress, the Committee also turned its attention to government contracts, sending deputations to the First Commissioner of Works and arranging for sympathetic Members of Parliament to raise questions in the House.[1]

In all these efforts the societies were hampered by their failure, even in favourable circumstances, to include more than a minority of the craftsmen. This was true especially in London,[2] where their chief difficulty lay in organizing the multitudinous small firms scattered throughout the area. The presence of non-unionists was a constant source of resentment, but action against them was always likely to fail since there were so many non-unionists who could be called in to break a strike. The frustration of the branches was aggravated by the employers' determination to exploit the situation. In 1890, when the societies of carpenters and joiners began negotiations with the Central Association of Master Builders of London, the employers complained that the men's delegates were all trade unionists, whereas non-unionists were in a clear majority in London. The societies were therefore forced to bring some non-unionists into their delegation.[3]

This became the general policy recommended by the National Association of Master Builders, whose president in 1891 advised employers everywhere to insist upon dealing with non-union as well as union men.[4] The National Association was growing rapidly,[5] and before long there were proposals to establish a central fund. These were rejected by the members;[6] but the search for devices to counter the pressure of the unions continued. In 1896, for example, the London Master Builders attempted to secure the universal adoption of the 'discharge note', which would have meant that no worker could be engaged without a reference signed by his previous employer. Such a system, however, was not likely to be successful at a time of severe labour shortage, and the proposal was dropped.[7]

The natural response of craft employers faced with a shortage of labour is to increase the number of apprentices and learners. But the use of this

manner in which the [Building Trades Department of the] London Trades Council had dealt with the interests of the building trades' (*The Builder*, 28 June 1890). The Committee was absorbed by the London Building Trades Federation formed in 1892 (see p. 154).

[1] *Royal Commission on Labour*, C–6795–VI, 1893, Q. 17381; *The Builder*, 28 June 1890. See also p. 255.

[2] N. B. Dearle, *Problems of Unemployment in the London Building Trades*, 1908, pp. 152–7.

[3] *Royal Commission on Labour*, C–6894–IX, 1893, Q. 32315.

[4] *The Builder*, 7 Feb. 1891.

[5] By 1891 the accession of local associations had brought the total membership up to 1,300 firms, all contractors. Speculative builders were excluded (*Royal Commission on Labour*, C–6795–VI, 1893, Qs. 18433–41).

[6] National Association of Master Builders, *Minutes*, 28 May 1894 and 22 Jan. 1895.

[7] Ibid., 29 Jan. and 28 July 1896.

remedy was obstructed by the growing insistence of union branches upon limiting the intake, and they had already achieved a fair measure of success. In 1898 the National Association circularized its members in 170 towns in order to discover the extent of restriction on the number of apprentices. Eighty-five replies were received, and about seventy showed that the societies had succeeded in imposing a restriction in one or more of the crafts, in some cases getting limitation written into the agreed working rules. Firms were even fined for overstepping the limits laid down.[1]

Faced with this challenge, the exasperation of the employers mounted. Early in 1898 the president of the National Association declared that there must be absolute resistance to the limitation of apprentices, which would 'trench upon the just and inalienable rights of the employer and would be a national calamity'.[2] If a solid front was to be formed, the first step was to organize the local associations of master builders into regional federations. These had begun as a spontaneous development in the provinces during 1897, but once the movement had begun it was strongly supported by the National Association. Later in 1898, its Council reported on the early stages of a campaign in several towns 'for the removal of this restriction, which is severely handicapping employers generally', and promised that 'when federation all over the country is properly in order [the Council] will have great pleasure in taking up the matter'.[3]

Thus the struggle over apprenticeship brought both a sharpening of mood and a consolidation of organization among employers which made large-scale conflict increasingly likely. The clash came in plastering, where the shortage of labour was particularly acute, and where relations were worse than in any other craft. 'The plasterers were probably the most impudent and independent class of men in the building trade', complained a Leicester employer in 1897,[4] and a London builder asserted that 'the masters were in the hopeless position of being obliged to accept almost any terms that the Plasterers made with them'.[5] In 1896, moreover, the careful and hard-working Arthur Otley, who had built up the society from a low point of financial weakness and internal dissension in 1885, was replaced as secretary by the 'forceful . . . domineering . . . overbearing and intolerant' Michael Deller.[6]

As so often, the immediate cause of conflict was a relatively minor

[1] In Nottingham, for example, employers paid fines of up to £50 for transgressing union rules on apprenticeship and demarcation (*Royal Commission on Trade Disputes and Trade Combinations*, Cd. 2826, 1906, Q. 3060).

[2] National Association of Master Builders, *Minutes*, 25 Jan. 1898. The Liverpool Master Builders urged 'that . . . no limitation of apprentices be conceded to any branch of the building trade and that no arbitration be accepted on the question' (ibid., 26 July 1898).

[3] Ibid., 19 Oct. 1898.

[4] Ibid., 26 Jan. 1897.   [5] Ibid., 20 July 1897.

[6] 'Onlooker', *Hitherto, The Story of an Association*, 1930, p. 50.

matter. In London, contractors had tried to find an alternative to subletting as a means of controlling labour by appointing 'managing foremen' with special disciplinary powers.[1] The Plasterers' branches countered by compelling the foremen to join the union, and there was an unofficial strike at the end of 1898 when three of them refused. The London Master Builders then approached the National Association, which at once resolved that the Council should 'form a special committee to confer with [the London Association] as to the best means of dealing with the attack of the plasterers, and that the same committee . . . be empowered to deal with the whole question of plasterers throughout the country'.[2]

The new regional federations were only prepared to support London on the condition that any agreement which might result from joint action must apply to the whole country. Consequently, it was decided that all local associations should simultaneously demand, on pain of national lock-out, the immediate ending of certain restrictive practices by the Plasterers. The society was to abandon coercion of foremen, the limitation of apprentices, and the enforcement of union membership by boycott. In addition, they would be expected to accept the employer's decision in any difficulty over demarcation, and to seek a peaceful settlement of all disputes before resorting to strike action.

The Plasterers' reply to these demands was considered unsatisfactory and evasive, and a national lock-out began on 6 March 1899. Except in Yorkshire, Lancashire, and Cheshire, however, the response of the local employers' associations was poor. The Scottish Master Plasterers refused to join the lock-out at all, and even London's showing was far from impressive. Three weeks after the stoppage had begun the total number of plasterers locked out was only 3,000, and many of these were promptly taken on by speculative builders, who were not admitted as members of the National Association. Nevertheless, the dispute still dragged on.

Meanwhile, the National Association took up the idea of requiring a monetary guarantee from the society against the breach of any subsequent agreement. Such a provision would have put pressure on the leaders to discipline the rank and file in order to avoid unofficial strikes and other forms of default. When the proposal was put to them at a joint conference on 6 April 1899, the leaders replied that while they did not want, for example, non-unionists to be coerced, they could not undertake that their members would stop at persuasion.[3] The employers therefore decided to extend the dispute; and at the end of April the other building unions were threatened with a general lock-out unless they withheld support from the Plasterers. This was met by an unusual show of solidarity

---

[1] 'Onlooker', op. cit., p. 54.
[2] National Association of Master Builders, *Minutes*, 22 Nov. 1898.
[3] Ibid. (Joint Conference), 6 Apr. 1899.

at a meeting called by the Carpenters and Joiners from which only the Stonemasons held aloof.[1]

Despite these brave demonstrations, neither side had the stomach for an all-out struggle. Suggestions put forward by the London *Daily News* were accepted as the basis of a settlement, and a conference on 30 May 1899 soon arrived at agreement.[2] In future there was to be no stoppage until a dispute had passed through a formal procedure culminating in a national joint committee; the society gave assurances that foremen and non-unionists would not be coerced; and a special committee was appointed to examine the question of apprenticeship. Before long, however, this body reached deadlock, and had to fall back on a vague formula devised by the editor of the *Daily News*.

The mood of the branches seemed more recalcitrant than ever, some even demanding an increase in wages before returning to work,[3] and few showing any concern for the new agreement. The society's leaders declared that their members would not work with men who had failed to come out. Stung into retaliation, the employers reverted to the threat of a general lock-out in the hope of salvaging something of their gains. The unions replied with a proposal for a national conciliation board, drawn up by the Carpenters and Joiners and presented to the National Association in July 1899 by a committee representing virtually all the societies of craftsmen and three unions of builders' labourers.[4] But the employers remained more interested in combating craft controls than in setting up machinery for settling disputes; and they would only accept the new scheme if a monetary guarantee were included to force the societies to curb their branches. On this point all the unions shared the misgivings of the Plasterers' leaders, and the discussions came to nothing.

Furniture

By the end of the decade, the boom in building had also contributed to a considerable growth in the furniture trades. Membership rose in the major unions: the national Alliance Cabinet Makers' Association, the Amalgamated Union of Cabinet Makers centred on Manchester and Liverpool, the Scottish United Operative Cabinet and Chair Makers, and the Amalgamated Society of French Polishers, all of whom set about strengthening their craft controls. At the same time, competition within the industry was intensified by the growing number of small masters who specialized in one type of furniture and produced low-quality goods with

[1] Postgate, op. cit., p. 367.
[2] The parties were brought together 'through the good offices of Clem Edwards, of the *Daily News* staff [see p. 75, footnote 1] . . . and his chief, Mr. E. T. Cook (later Sir Edward Cook)' (J. R. Newman, *The N.A.O.P. Heritage*, 1960, p. 12).
[3] 'Onlooker', op. cit., p. 57.
[4] Higenbottam, op. cit., pp. 144–6.

cheap labour.[1] Squeezed between these two forces, the employers of craftsmen sought refuge in combination.

In England, the diversity both of firms and of markets prevented anything more than local organization; but the Scottish Furniture Manufacturers' Association covered all the main centres except for Aberdeen and Edinburgh. In 1898 the Scottish Cabinet Makers, whose leader, A. G. Gossip, was a militant socialist, presented a wage claim at Beith near Glasgow. This was refused, and the Association presented a list of demands designed to break down craft restrictions in most Scottish centres of the trade. In future there was to be no limitation of output; manufacturers were to have full discretion in deciding between piece-work and time-work; union members were to work with non-unionists; and the society was to relax its rules on overtime.

When these terms were rejected, the employers enforced a lock-out of some 1,700 furniture workers which lasted ten months and cost half a million working days. To meet the challenge of the Association, the Scottish Cabinet Makers came together with the Alliance and the Amalgamated Society of Upholsterers, who also had members involved in the dispute, to form a Scottish federation. After many unsuccessful meetings with the employers, a three-day conference produced a compromise on piece-work and overtime, but the societies were compelled to give way on non-unionists and the limitation of output.[2] At a time of prosperity this was a notable setback.

In England the unions came under no such concerted attack from the employers. Conflicts remained for the most part small-scale and local; the craftsmen lost some and won others, but in general managed to increase their hold on the industry. The Alliance Cabinet Makers claimed that by the end of the nineties subcontracting had been eliminated in the organized sector of their trade, and that the fight against piece-work had been pressed hard. Even more successful were the French Polishers, who had linked up the London clubs in 1894. The Upholsterers were also an amalgamation of local clubs, but they were far less effective, for the trade had been invaded by women and attempts to organize them met with little success.

A number of local employers' associations were willing to meet the unions, and by 1900 those in Manchester, Liverpool, Birmingham, and London (where a Cabinet Trades Conciliation Board was established) had signed agreements with one or more societies which covered apprenticeship ratios and procedures for avoiding disputes as well as wages, hours, and rates for overtime. Many organized sections, however, still

---

[1] Booth, op. cit., vol. v, 1895, pp. 180–3.

[2] N. Robertson, *A Study of the Development of Labour Relations in the British Furniture Trade*, B.Litt. thesis, Oxford 1955.

relied on old-style shop agreements, and regulation of any kind was confined to the high-quality firms. Elsewhere, employers treated the unions with contempt or discouraged them by intimidation.[1]

The Engineering Lock-out

The crisis in building had been preceded in 1897 by a greater crisis in engineering. Faced by the opposition of the Engineers to the introduction of lower-paid, semi-skilled labour on the new machines, employers in the North-east, led by Armstrong-Whitworths of Elswick on Tyneside, formed a standing committee in March 1894 to deal with all disputes. This was the prelude to a more decisive step: the establishment two years later of the Employers' Federation of Engineering Associations, after the initiative had been taken by an informal alliance of the North-east, Clydeside, Belfast, and Barrow. The objects of the Federation's promoters were 'in particular, to protect and defend [their] interests against combinations of workmen seeking by strikes or other action to impose unduly restrictive conditions upon any branch of the engineering trades'; and to 'secure mutual support . . . on such questions as interference with foremen, unreasonable demands for wages, minimum rates of wages, employment of apprentices, hours of labour, overtime, limitation of work, piecework, demarcation of work, machine work, and the employment of men and boys on machines'.[2] Within a few months of the Federation being set up in June 1896 other local associations had been absorbed, notably that of Manchester; but its origins indicate that the spearhead of the counter-attack was provided by the employers of the principal marine engineering centres, many of whom were already members of the Shipbuilding Employers' Federation.[3]

The successful launching of the new movement owed a good deal to a tangled dispute in the Belfast and Clyde districts during 1895–6. At the height of the struggle, in November 1895, the employers' associations on Clydeside and at Belfast invited their colleagues both in Barrow and in the North-east to consider joint action on a wider scale.[4] The subsequent discussions led directly to the setting up of the Federation, with Colonel Dyer, managing director of Armstrong-Whitworths, as its first president.

The dispute arose out of claims for wage increases which the Engineers submitted separately in each district. The two employers' associations entered into a compact to support each other in resisting them, and stood by it throughout the conflict. When in October a compromise was reached on the Clyde but the Belfast men struck, the employers refused to negotiate

---

[1] *Royal Commission on Labour*, C–6795–IX, 1892, pp. 130–1.

[2] The Employers' Federation of Engineering Associations, *Conditions of Federation*, 1896. The new body effectively replaced the old Iron Trades Employers' Association, which was wound up in 1900.   [3] See p. 151.

[4] *Report on the Strikes and Lockouts of 1895*, C–8231, 1896, p. 34.

except 'through the joint association, centred in Glasgow'.[1] After a conference with the Engineers' executive had failed to arrange terms acceptable to the Belfast strikers, the employers decided on a lock-out by stages on the Clyde. Finally, in January 1896, when the Clyde engineers, having replied to the first stage of the lock-out by striking in a body for their original demands, once more agreed to accept an offer, their employers refused to open their works until the Belfast men gave in. Deadlock was ended only when the Engineers' executive ordered the protesting Ulstermen back to work over the heads of their district committee and suspended all friendly benefits to enforce their decision.

Within the Society the weaknesses revealed by the conduct of the strike strengthened the militants. Their main objection was to Anderson's 'pacifism', but they were also able to draw on local resentment at the assumption of authority by the executive. Ordering payment of the benefits which had been withheld, the Delegate Meeting in May 1896 condemned 'the policy of yielding when a complete victory was possible',[2] and passed a new rule depriving both the executive and the district committees of power to close a dispute without the consent of two-thirds of the members concerned.[3] By August the militants were clamouring for blood, and the executive 'considered it necessary' to dismiss Anderson for 'wilful neglect of duty'.[4] Shortly before the stoppage, George Barnes[5] had followed in Mann's footsteps by challenging Anderson for the secretaryship at the triennial elections and had been narrowly beaten. Now Barnes won with 17,371 votes, over 8,000 more than Anderson, who had stood again.[6]

The new Employers' Federation soon faced its first test on 'the machine question'. In January 1897, after a nine-months' strike at a marine engineering and shipbuilding firm in Hull, members of the Society 'forced recognition of the principle that machines which supersede hand-skilled labour should be manipulated by skilled and full-paid men'.[7] When similar

---

[1] *Report on the Strikes and Lockouts of 1895*, C–8231, 1896, p. 32. The account given here differs in some important details from that in Jefferys, op. cit., pp. 140–1.

[2] Jefferys, op. cit., p. 141.

[3] Webbs, *Industrial Democracy*, p. 96.

[4] Jefferys, op. cit., p. 141. Anderson's supporters later asserted that these 'astounding allegations' were quite unfounded; he himself spoke of 'relentless persecution' (*Election Addresses* for the 1898 election).

[5] Barnes, G. N., P.C. (1859–1940). Assistant secretary, Amalgamated Society of Engineers, 1892–6; general secretary, 1896–1908. Parliamentary Committee, Trades Union Congress, 1906–8. M.P., 1906–22. Minister of Pensions, 1916–17. Minister without Portfolio in War Cabinet, 1917–18. Remained in Cabinet 1918–20, resigning from Labour Party 1918. Resigned from government, 1920, and from Parliament, 1922.

[6] The executive's sacrifice of Anderson was timely. Three of its members had stood for re-election in 1896; all were returned, though with tiny majorities (Jefferys, op. cit., p. 142).

[7] Amalgamated Society of Engineers, *Journal and Monthly Record*, Jan. 1897. Barnes recommended this policy, 'maintained with a pertinacity beyond all praise', to other districts where 'great laxity has been the rule'.

demands were made at Sunderland and Barrow, the Federation intervened and posted lock-out notices. Knight's Federation of Engineering and Shipbuilding Trades then withdrew the machine operator (a member of an affiliated union) whose employment had caused the dispute at Sunderland, and so made possible a conference between the Employers' Federation and the Engineers. The employers rejected the Society's proposed compromise of local joint committees, with independent referees, to settle wage rates for men working on the machines, asserting that such bodies 'would practically control the management of the employers' works'.[1] Nevertheless, a lock-out was averted—for the moment.

Meanwhile, a committee had been set up in London by branches of the Engineers, the Boilermakers, and five smaller unions, to co-ordinate a campaign for the eight-hour day. In May 1897, when about 800 firms were approached, over a hundred conceded the claim almost at once; but many others responded to the canvassing of the Employers' Federation and took part in the formation of the London Employers' Association, which affiliated to the national body. In July, when the joint committee struck three London firms to force them into line, the Federation countered with a lock-out of 25 per cent. of the unions' membership employed by its constituents throughout the country. By this time the Boilermakers had instructed their London district to abandon the campaign,[2] and the Patternmakers decided 'that the time was inopportune' for a battle.[3] The Engineers would not give way, however, and replied to the lock-out by withdrawing their remaining members from the federated firms.

The stoppage was by no means universal, for at no time were more than 47,500 workers affected—35,000 directly, including 27,000 engineers, and the rest indirectly. Nevertheless, six million working days were lost in 1897 and a further million in 1898. In a number of places 'free labour' was supplied by Collison's National Free Labour Association;[4] and in at least one district the Poor Law Guardians combed their workhouse for engineers and handed them over to local employers.[5] It was found, however, 'in Sheffield, Manchester, London and elsewhere . . . impossible to carry on the work with willing labour unless the willing labour was

---

[1] *Report on the Strikes and Lockouts of 1897*, C–9012, 1898, p. liv.

[2] The Boilermakers' leaders had previously told the Engineers that they were not pledging the union 'to fight this question to the end in London alone'. They now asked if this was what the Engineers wanted, or whether they would join the Federation of Engineering and Shipbuilding Trades in a national campaign, as had been suggested in 1896. The Engineers gave no satisfactory answer, and the Boilermakers stood aside (Amalgamated Society of Engineers, *Notes on the Engineering Trade Lockout, 1897–1898*, appendix, pp. 22, 88–89). Some London boilermakers had already enjoyed the eight-hour day for some years (Cummings, op. cit., p. 149). [3] Jefferys, op. cit., p. 145.

[4] See p. 171. The Engineers took this lightly. 'Collison's army of 180,000 brawny freemen have either lost their way or found a free canteen. In any case they are not shifting much, unless it may be rations' (Amalgamated Society of Engineers, *Journal and Monthly Record*, Nov. 1897). [5] Ibid.

protected either by the local police or by a private police. In many cases the local police refused to act', owing 'to the desire of the watch committee not to bring themselves into bad odour with the unions'.[1] Employers had less to complain of, however, in the attitude of magistrates, who were congratulated by one engineering trade journal for 'praiseworthy courage in punishing picket violence. . . . [They] have . . . passed sentences of imprisonment in place of fines. . . . It is a virtue that has not always been displayed in the past.'[2]

Many of the public arguments on both sides centred round the claim for an eight-hour day; but the crucial issue for the employers was the unions' attitude towards technical change and its consequences.[3] They condemned the Engineers' challenge on these questions as an encroach-ment upon managerial prerogatives, and their mood was made the more dangerous by current fears of declining industrial efficiency in the face of German and American competition.[4] For most of them, therefore, the 1897 lock-out was primarily an intensification of the struggle which had begun earlier in the year in the northern counties; and they were spurred on by the belief that the challenge was directly inspired by socialist militancy. 'The degrading doctrines of the new unionism', said the chairman of one of the largest firms on Tyneside, 'have so poisoned the A.S.E. as to make them as a class fully 20 per cent. less valuable than they ought to be.'[5]

The union leaders naturally did their best to focus attention on the eight-hour day. 'We have averted the fight upon an unpopular issue', wrote Barnes, 'and have shunted it on to a question upon which we ought to get . . . the support of our fellow workmen.'[6] Working-class support was evoked even more by the impression that the employers were trying to destroy the unions, though they often denied this.[7] Colonel Dyer, however, wrote to *The Times* to say that members of the Federation were 'determined to obtain the freedom to manage their own affairs which has proved to be so beneficial to the American manufacturer';[8] and Alexander

---

[1] *Royal Commission on Trade Disputes and Trade Combinations, Minutes of Evidence*, Cd. 2826, 1906, Qs. 3360–2. In Sheffield and Leeds employers formed their own private police forces, and in Leeds some of these private policemen were sworn in as special constables (Qs. 3362–4).   [2] *Engineering*, 24 Sept. 1897.
[3] F. W. Hirst, 'The Policy of the Engineers', *Economic Journal*, Mar. 1898.
[4] Union restrictions had 'so increased the cost of production', wrote the Federation to the Board of Trade (27 Oct. 1897), 'that important orders for engineering work have been placed in foreign hands, British competitors being underbidden even for machinery and plant for use in this country. . . . The keenness of foreign competition is increasing every day' (*Notes*, appendix, p. 125).
[5] Jefferys, op. cit., p. 145. *The Times* warned its readers that the Engineers had recently 'fallen under the domination of an extremely aggressive set of leaders' (Clarke, loc. cit.).
[6] Letter to *People's Journal*, Dundee, 7 Aug. 1897 (*Notes*, appendix, p. 75).
[7] Thus causing *Engineering* to criticize them for 'unnecessary hypocrisy. Trade unionism as now practised in . . . British engineering . . . has to go' (24 Sept. 1897).
[8] 5 Sept. 1897. See also p. 172.

Siemens, leader of the London Employers' Association, declared that the societies would be ignored in the settlement of the dispute, and that the men would have to come back individually on the employers' terms.[1] As a result, the first reason given by the Parliamentary Committee of the Trades Union Congress when sponsoring the appeal for financial aid was that 'the Employers have intimated that their object is to crush the Engineers' Trade Union'.[2]

Initially, the response was good, and subscriptions to the strike fund reached a total of £116,000. £23,500 passed through the hands of the Parliamentary Committee,[3] while £28,000 came from colonial and continental unions, over half from Germany alone.[4] Nevertheless, as the dispute dragged on, one of the main problems for the strikers was how to broaden the basis of their support. The Parliamentary Committee now grew cautious, and in December refused a request to organize a conference to muster further assistance.[5] The London Trades Council did call a meeting, which was 'enthusiastic' and decided 'that all trade unions represented should levy their members'. But the decision brought no increase in subscriptions and the financial situation became critical.[6] A last-minute attempt by the Engineers to affiliate to the Federation of Engineering and Shipbuilding Trades met with a cold reception. Most of the federated societies, including the Boilermakers, the Ironfounders, and the Patternmakers, had remained at work. If challenged, they could point to the many occasions on which the Engineers had preferred to 'go it alone'.

By contrast, the employers eventually achieved a remarkable unity. At first the incompleteness of the stoppage persuaded the Engineers and their allies that victory could not be long delayed; but the membership of the Employers' Federation grew from 180 at the beginning of the conflict to 702 at the end.

Throughout August and September the area of the dispute continued to expand, lockout notices being posted in the districts of Sheffield, Oldham, Keighley, Ipswich, Heywood, Edinburgh, Leith, Aberdeen, Dumbarton, Dundee, Bristol, Hanley, Blackburn, Ashton, Carlisle, and Otley, which at the outset had held aloof. On the other hand in London there was no material increase in the number of men employed under the eight hours' system, and at the beginning of October there were several cases of reversion to longer working hours. On October 7th the Ship Repairers' Association gave one week's notice of their intention to revert to the nine hours' system.[7]

---

[1] *Daily News*, 7 Oct. 1897.
[2] *Notes*, appendix, p. 111; Parliamentary Committee, *Minutes*, 13 Oct. 1897.
[3] Trades Union Congress, *Annual Report*, 1898.   [4] Jefferys, op. cit., p. 146.
[5] Ibid., p. 138. For its stated reasons see Trades Union Congress, *Annual Report*, 1898, and Roberts, op. cit., p. 161.   [6] Jefferys, op. cit., p. 147.
[7] *Report on the Strikes and Lockouts of 1897*, C–9012, 1898, pp. lvi–lvii.

For the leaders of the Federation thus to extend the scope of a lock-out, particularly at a time of improving trade, was a difficult if not unique operation. Their success was powerful testimony not only to the strength of their feelings but also to a lack of fastidiousness in their methods. The economist, F. W. Hirst, in a contribution to the *Economic Journal* markedly unsympathetic to the unions, observed that 'the organisers of the Employers' Federation have exercised pressure of the most extraordinary kind upon employers who did not wish to join them, and had no complaints against their workpeople', and he 'expected that some of the small firms which have been forced into the lock-out will be ruined'.[1] To encourage such laggards, many of the large firms, who bought considerable supplies from other engineering employers, threatened to give their contracts only to those who supported the Federation.[2]

By the end of November 1897 the unions were ready to sue for peace. In September an early feeler by the Board of Trade had been accepted by the Engineers but rebuffed by the Federation. The Board renewed its efforts late in October; after lengthy preparation in private, the two sides were finally brought together in a conference which lasted from 24 November to 3 December. These negotiations produced proposals which the societies agreed to submit to a ballot of their members. The terms gave strong support for the view that the employers' aim was 'to crush' the Engineers and their associates, for they prescribed individual bargaining on wage rates, piece-prices, and overtime, with almost no formal functions left to the unions. Understandably, the strikers rejected them almost to a man.[3]

There were a number of public protests against the demands of the Federation. Fifteen Oxford dons (including H. A. L. Fisher, Sydney Ball, Arthur Sidgwick, Edward Caird, and Henry Rashdall) wrote to the *Daily Chronicle* insisting that 'it cannot be held that, *prima facie* at least, the ultimatum is anything but a deliberate attempt to overthrow the principle of collective bargaining'.[4] A Loan Fund had already been launched by middle-class Liberal sympathizers to safeguard the union's capacity to pay friendly benefits. Now its honorary secretaries, C. P. Trevelyan and R. C. Phillimore, issued a fresh appeal. So far guarantees totalling about £17,000 had been received, but more was needed as a result of what the sponsors regarded as the Federation's new threat to trade unionism.[5] On

---

[1] Hirst, loc. cit.

[2] Amalgamated Society of Engineers, *Journal and Monthly Record*, Aug. and Sept. 1897.

[3] The voting was 752 for acceptance, 68,214 against.

[4] 13 Dec. 1897, reprinted in *The Times*, 14 Dec. 1897. Sir Frederick Pollock also wrote identifying himself with the Oxford signatories (*The Times*, 15 Dec. 1897). From Cambridge, on the other hand, Alfred Marshall wrote to Caird, the Master of Balliol: 'I want these people [the strikers] to be beaten at all costs' (Clarke, loc. cit.).

[5] Webb Trade Union Collection E, Section B, vol. lix.

10 December Beatrice Webb recorded in her diary that 'this morning we . . . wrote private letters to the leading officials of the great unions begging them to take the matter up on the ground that collective bargaining is attacked'.[1]

The Federation had gone too far, and their terms were revised at a conference on 14 December 1897. This time Barnes himself was willing to say that 'the right of the unions to collective bargaining . . . is maintained';[2] but his members again refused their approval. Another meeting in January 1898 drew further concessions from the employers, provided that the Engineers would withdraw their claim for the eight-hour day. With these amendments, the revised terms received a two-to-one majority. By their intransigence, the strikers had secured the acceptance of collective bargaining on general wage changes, and a recognition of the right of the societies to handle claims through the formal procedure for disputes which the Federation wished to establish. In most other respects, however, the settlement gave the employers 'all they could reasonably ask for'.[3]

The unions were forced to grant them 'the right to introduce into any Federated workshop . . . any condition of labour under which any members of the Trade Unions here represented[4] were working at the commencement of the dispute in any of the workshops of the Federated Employers'.[5] Firms obtained a free hand in the employment of non-unionists; power 'to appoint the men they consider suitable to work' on the new machines; the right to employ men 'at such rates as should be mutually satisfactory'; virtually unrestricted overtime; freedom to introduce piece-work, at prices fixed 'by mutual arrangement'; and the abandonment of limits on the number of apprentices. Under the 'Provisions for Avoiding Disputes', the employer was first to receive a deputation from those directly affected by any grievance. If unresolved, the issue was to be discussed by the local employers' association and local union officers, and could then be referred to a Central Conference of the executives of the Federation and the union or unions concerned. There was to be no stoppage until this procedure had been completed.

These requirements represented a major set-back to the authority and pretensions of the unions of craftsmen involved in the lock-out, and promised to relieve the employers of many of their difficulties. The policy of the promoters of the Federation seemed to have triumphed, largely at the expense of the Engineers, who soon found that the settlement could even affect the internal working of their society. Among the first Central

---

[1] *Our Partnership*, p. 54.   [2] *Notes*, appendix, p. 142.

[3] Clarke, loc. cit.

[4] The parties to the settlement were the Engineers, the Steam Engine Makers, the United Machine Workers, the Amalgamated Toolmakers, the United Smiths and Hammermen, and seven small London engineering unions.

[5] This clause did not apply to wages and hours.

Conference decisions was an agreement that organizers[1] might take part in local conferences, but not in central conferences, except in a purely consultative capacity which did not involve their presence in the conference room.[2] This blow to the local spirit and practice of the union drove two organizers to revolt. One of them, J. Ratcliffe of the Northeast, later apologized; the other, F. H. Rose of the North-west, was discharged from office but finally reinstated.[3]

The employers had won their victory, but though the Engineers had suffered considerable financial damage, the '*sauve qui peut* stage was . . . never reached'.[4] Membership, which had risen from 61,000 in 1889, fell from 91,500 in 1897 to 83,500 in 1898, but was back to 87,500 by 1900. All the other engineering unions also expanded over the period. Between 1889 and 1900 the Ironfounders increased from 14,000 to 18,000, the Steam Engine Makers from 5,500 to 8,500, the Patternmakers from 2,000 to 4,500, and the smaller organizations kept pace. These rates of growth, however, fell far behind those of the societies of building craftsmen. The difference is only partly explained by the lower rate of expansion in the engineering labour force, which rose from 900,000 in 1891 to 1,150,000 in 1901. The effects of depression in the industry, as well as those of the lock-out, must also play a vital part in the explanation.

The Nature of the Counter-attack

The two most significant developments in the craft trades during the last years of the nineteenth century were the growth of employers' associations, both local and national, and the establishment of collective bargaining. In most instances, moreover, the elaboration of procedures followed the large-scale organization of employers. Both resulted from the impact of technical and economic change on craft controls. Such controls might be tolerable to the employers so long as conditions were stable or innovations gradual; but they became intolerable when the rate of change increased. In a competitive world employers had to accommodate their businesses to change or go under. Craft controls were peculiarly exasperating obstacles. The craftsmen were apt to regard them as principles which they must never willingly submit to negotiated compromise, and where their societies were strong there was no way round. Consequently, the employers banded themselves together in order to break through.

---

[1] The organizing district delegates (see p. 143).

[2] 23 Apr. 1898 (*Decisions of Central Conference, 1898–1925*, Engineering and Allied Employers' National Federation, 1926, p. 66).

[3] There was strong feeling on this issue, as always. Later that year the member of the executive for the North-east was refused re-election at the end of his term of office—the first time in the Society's history that this had happened. His opponent won on the 'local autonomy' ticket (Amalgamated Society of Engineers, *Journal and Monthly Record*, Oct. and Dec. 1898, Jan. 1899).

[4] E. Aves, 'The Dispute in the Engineering Trades', *Economic Journal*, Mar. 1898.

The original purpose of the amalgamation of local clubs into national societies was to increase the capacity of the craftsmen to impose their will on employers. So long as the branches could limit the area of conflict and pick off one firm or one town at a time, a society's headquarters could afford to leave trade policy to them and concentrate on providing the benefits which financed disputes and retained members. When the employers began to fight back, however, the drain on funds might become severe and the union leaders had to intervene. The 'new model' pattern of control by financial centralization was seldom fully effective, for most branches had enough money at their disposal to start a conflict, if not to finish it. Once a strike or lock-out had begun, it was difficult for the executive to withhold support; the only remedy then was to secure a settlement, but this meant negotiating with the employers.

Most union leaders could see the advantages of an established procedure for conciliation which would give them the opportunity to intervene before a stoppage began. Thus both employers and union leaders had an interest in devising arrangements which would facilitate change, and in this respect they differed from the branches. There were, of course, various types of procedure to which the three groups had different reactions. Many branches accepted local conciliation because they retained the last word: at the end of any negotiations they could decide to strike, or to stonewall. National conciliation, on the other hand, strengthened both the employers and the society's headquarters against them. Since acceptance of arbitration at either level meant surrendering the last word, the branches usually rejected it. The national leaders might be less hostile, and the employers could hope that few arbitrators would have much sympathy with the more restrictive of craft practices.

Without an agreement of any kind, no craft restriction could be ruled out of order; but an agreement might outlaw some practices and provide the means of changing others. The employers' ideal, no doubt, was complete managerial freedom. Where this could not be had, they strove for an agreement which would not only establish a means of securing orderly changes in wages and conditions of work as they were required but would also ban the more objectionable restrictive practices. Here, however, union leaders were at one with the branches in desiring the maximum freedom of action on their part.

Conditions in printing and shipbuilding allowed the leaders to utilize the needs both of the branches and of the employers to enhance their own authority. The employers wanted arrangements for local conciliation and, if possible, national agreements, while the branches demanded firmer protection of craft privileges. Robert Knight therefore wrote the Boilermakers' rules on apprenticeship into a national agreement, and the Typographical Association protected the provincial compositor by a national agreement bringing the linotype machine securely under its control. In building, the leadership was less successful, for prolonged labour shortage in an industry safe from foreign competition and technically conservative gave the branches such power that they could defy both the employers and their leaders. By contrast, engineering was changing rapidly and pressure was concentrated on the machine shop, the preserve of the mightiest of craft unions. Collective bargaining was little developed and the Society's rules were among the most restrictive. Its leaders had no hope of playing off the branches against the employers, and sided with them over the 'machine question'. A battle was thus unavoidable, but the employers' victory increased central control within the union.

These various patterns were mirrored time and time again in the minor crafts. Basket workers, leatherworkers and hand papermakers maintained their traditional controls, while the coopers' clubs, linked in a national federation some 5,000 strong, had already developed advanced methods of local bargaining.[1] But most of the smaller societies had to face serious challenges in the last years of the century.

Machine-made products forced the Sheffield cutlery clubs and the cordwainers to retreat, and drove the London clubs of sheet-metal workers and their employers into a protracted series of negotiating committees from which there emerged in 1900 a new book of piece-prices to meet the new conditions.[2] Other societies were threatened by female labour. The cigarmakers met the challenge by amalgamating with the women's union and the Lancashire felt-hatters by prohibiting the women from some departments and organizing those in other departments in a subordinate union; but the Warwickshire felt-hatters failed to prevent a large influx of unorganized women during a disastrous strike in 1892,[3] and the brushmakers were also losing ground to women.[4] In the silver trades it was boy-labour together with an increased subdivision of work which threatened the craftsmen.[5] Finally, apprenticeship was responsible for the most important dispute among the minor crafts. In 1892–3 the Yorkshire glass-bottle employers locked out 5,000 men when the union refused to accept a reduction in wages and an abolition of its restriction on apprentices, and the conflict spread to Lancashire. After four months the masters capitulated.[6]

If the combination of characteristics which constituted craft unionism

[1] *Royal Commission on Labour*, C–6795–VI, 1893, Qs. 20371–84.

[2] A. T. Kidd, *History of the Tinplate Workers' and Sheet Metal Workers' and Braziers' Societies*, 1949, pp. 49–52.

[3] Barbara Drake, *Women in Trade Unions*, 1920, pp. 40, 146. The silk hat-makers were much weakened when a major London firm shook off their control during a strike in 1894 (Booth, op. cit., vol. vii, 1896, pp. 28–29).

[4] *Select Committee on Fair Wages, Minutes of Evidence*, Cd. 4423, 1908, Qs. 1977–84, 3704–8.

[5] *Royal Commission on Labour*, C–6795–IV, 1892, Qs. 19012–18.

[6] *Workman's Times*, 24 Dec. 1892 to 6 May 1893.

was unique, other unions shared some of them and in this period of expansion they evoked similar reactions from their employers. The attempt to impose union membership, a common feature of craft societies, had been the origin of the counter-attack by the Shipping Federation which had defeated and nearly destroyed the waterfront unions. The methods of the cotton spinners bore an unusually close resemblance to those of the craftsmen, and they had driven the master spinners to federate. Comparable pressure by the National Union of Boot and Shoe Operatives produced much the same result.[1] The success of the Miners' Federation had led to counter-organization, and the extension of the Federation into South Wales attracted a particularly bitter response from the local coal-owners.

Consequently, attempts were made to form a national organization among employers; and their first common efforts were aimed at prompting an alternative to trade unionism. They were able to build on the foundations laid by William Collison, a man of considerable shrewdness and organizing ability,[2] who improved upon the various strike-breaking bodies established during the 'new unionist' period[3] by setting up the National Free Labour Association in 1893. Collison affected respect for what he deemed the 'old' unionism, declaring in his *Free Labour Gazette*[4] that 'workmen can obtain by combination what they could obtain in no other way'. But he had decided to dedicate his life to protecting 'the general body of Labour from the tyranny and dictation of Socialistic Trade Union leaders'. The 'new unionism' had transformed the movement into 'a despotism for the enforcement of admittedly false and subversive doctrines', which included intimidation, boycotting, and unlawful picketing, 'undue restriction of the hours of labour and an arbitrary limitation of the output—a curtailment . . . of human industry . . . and a restriction of productive power in the working of mechanical appliances'.[5]

Collison was coy about naming his original backers, but they were almost certainly the shipping and dock interests, and probably George Livesey of the South Metropolitan Gas Company.[6] Sir William Lewis, the South Wales industrialist and another unrelenting enemy of trade unionism, also made use of Collison. The railway companies helped to

[1] See p. 200.

[2] He was born in 1865, the son of a policeman. After varied experiences as soldier (1881–3), bricklayer's labourer (joining the General Labourers' Amalgamated Union in 1884), and casual waterfront labourer, he became an omnibus driver and in 1889 helped to form the London and County Tramway and Omnibus Employees' Trade Union, of which he became a full-time official, resigning after a quarrel with Thomas Sutherst, its middle-class president (see p. 78).

[3] See p. 82.   [4] Dec. 1895.

[5] Collison, op. cit., pp. 88–89.

[6] Two usually reliable contemporary observers, the Frenchmen Mantoux and Alfassa, state that the National Free Labour Association developed from the 'free labour' exchanges set up by the shipowners in and after 1890 (*La Crise du Trade-Unionisme*, 1903, p. 213). Collison described Livesey as 'one of the best friends Free Labour has ever possessed in this country' ibid., p. 96). On the Association's finances see also p. 175, footnote 3.

finance him, and he was called into disputes in engineering, shipbuilding, and iron, among many others. Collison's was not the only organization of its kind,[1] but he succeeded better than his imitators because his Association was more reliable, better financed, and had some pretensions to respectability. He was very anxious, for example, to dissociate himself from the Graeme Hunter Association, whose dubious methods involved Hunter in a number of well-publicized cases of litigation. 'Graeme Hunter is not of the class of men from whom we elect our officials', wrote Collison in 1896, '. . . it is vultures of the Graeme Hunter type who bring discredit upon the Free Labour Movement.'[2]

Even the National Free Labour Association, however, was of only marginal value to employers in the craft industries—or, for that matter, to those in coal or cotton. Collison could successfully replace unskilled or semi-skilled workers in relatively small strikes. His main service was to groups of employers, like the Shipping Federation or the railway companies, who were trying to keep weak unions out rather than to defeat established societies. In 1894 the London Master Printers used his organization against the Printers' Labourers' Union which at that time they refused to recognize, and this is a fair measure of his value to craft employers. The use of his men by engineering firms in 1897 had very little effect on the outcome of the dispute.[3]

Nevertheless, some leading employers in engineering would have used Collison to smash the unions if they could. Colonel Dyer drew this lesson from his visit to the Carnegie works at Pittsburgh, of which he wrote that 'for perfection of machinery, organisation, and completeness of installation, there is nothing in Europe to compare with them'. Originally the plans of the Carnegie management had 'been strenuously opposed by the Trade Unions . . . until at length, driven to desperation, the managers determined to manage their business as their experience and intelligence directed, and to free themselves entirely from the dictation of the Trade Union leaders'.[4] Editorial opinion often went a long way to support his views. *The Times*, especially, castigated 'the persistent deterioration of the efficiency of English labour which is inculcated by the trade unions',[5] and urged that, 'if the conflict is to end in the victory of the employers, the battle must be fought with unflinching determination and with every available resource'.[6]

The positive side of 'free labour', however, also had its appeal. Another critic of the alleged tyranny of trade unionism, W. V. Osborne,[7] though

---

[1] Several others are mentioned in Phelps Brown, op. cit., pp. 166–7.

[2] *Free Labour Gazette*, Feb. 1896.   [3] Jefferys, op. cit., p. 146.

[4] *The Times*, 5 Sept. 1897. A dozen men were killed and many seriously injured in what amounted to a private war (John R. Commons, *A History of Labour in the United States*, vol. ii, pp. 495–7).   [5] *The Times*, 30 Aug. 1897.

[6] Ibid., 21 Aug. 1897.   [7] See p. 413.

convinced that Collison's basic purpose was 'to organise an army of professional strikebreakers', attributed to him the professed aim of creating 'an association of free labourers who objected to Trade Union restraint and who desired to follow their own employment in their own way', a desire which 'deserved nothing but respect'.[1] For some of Collison's backers this more positive aim was the important one, and they expressed uneasiness about the other aspects of his organization. Lord Wemyss, for example, perhaps the most persistent advocate of 'free labour',[2] apparently 'objected to the open warfare of strikebreaking';[3] Lord Dysart shared this objection, and hoped that educational methods would suffice; Lord Avebury, a third supporter, conducted a long correspondence with Collison on whether strike-breaking could be avoided.[4]

Both these attitudes played their part in the formation of the Free Labour Protection Association in July 1897 at a meeting of influential employers and representatives of their principal organizations under the chairmanship of Lord Wemyss. Among those present were Colonel Dyer, G. A. Laws, Sir William Lewis, George Livesey, T. F. Rider of the National Association of Master Builders, and Alexander Siemens. The stated objects of the Association were to test the existing laws concerning protection of non-unionists, to ensure observance of the law during stoppages, and to watch legislation on trade and industry.[5] According to *The Times*, however, the new organization was also intended to supply free labourers and to recruit a corps of able-bodied men to protect them.[6] Frederick Millar, a protégé of Lord Wemyss, was appointed secretary.[7]

At this stage, as the engineering lock-out approached its peak, *The Times* seems to have lost all sense of proportion in extolling the virtues of individual bargaining and 'freedom from trade union interference'.[8]

---

[1] W. V. Osborne, *Sane Trade Unionism*, 1913, p. 73.

[2] As Lord Elcho, Wemyss had been a member of the Royal Commission on Trade Unions in 1867 and had taken a liberal view of them, but time had wrought a change. He now sponsored the Liberty and Property Defence League and *The Liberty Review*, edited by Frederick Millar.

[3] Collison, op. cit., p. 309. This is almost the only reference to Wemyss in Collison's autobiography, but there is every suggestion of a fairly close association in Mantoux and Alfassa, op. cit. The authors interviewed both Collison and Wemyss and published the record of the interviews as appendixes.

[4] Ibid., pp. 309–10. For other activities of Avebury, previously Sir John Lubbock, see p. 226.

[5] W. J. Shaxby, *The Case against Picketing*, 1897, pp. v–vi. It had been intended to keep the scheme secret until all the employers' organizations had been persuaded to affiliate, but a workman in one of the firms approached 'obtained possession of private and confidential circulars' and at once published them.   [6] 9 Oct. 1897.

[7] With the engineering employers' experience during the 1897-8 lock-out in mind (see p. 164), 'the first step taken by the Labour Protection Association was to distribute among the leading employers, the magistrates, and chief constables throughout the country, copies of a handbook entitled *The Case against Picketing*' (Millar's evidence, *Royal Commission on Trade Disputes and Trade Combinations*, Cd. 2826, 1906, Q. 3208). This produced results: 'a more wholesome and satisfactory method of interpreting the law [towards picketing disturbances] was adopted. . . . Imprisonment with hard labour soon became the rule' (Q. 3208). The 'handbook' was presumably Shaxby's.   [8] 1 Oct. 1897.

Editorials asserted that heavy dispute expenditure by the Engineers would compel the Society to repudiate its benefit liabilities,[1] and attacked any suggestion of conciliation by the Board of Trade.[2] All employers were enjoined to combine 'to stop the growing demoralisation of labour and to avert disaster from the nation as a whole',[3] for the lock-out was delaying the Royal Navy's shipbuilding programme and, if it continued, would soon menace British naval supremacy.[4]

This last theme was taken up again during the coal strike of 1898 in South Wales. Since the valleys supplied the top-grade steam coal on which the Navy relied, the dispute threatened 'like the last, to lame the efficiency of our Imperial defences. While we are struggling to recover the ground lost in naval construction during the strike in the engineering trade, a strike in the Welsh coal trade has begun which must rob our fleets of an assured supply of the fuel best adapted for naval consumption'.[5] When Goschen as First Lord announced in the House of Commons that the shortage of steam coal had compelled the Admiralty to cancel its annual manœuvres, the stoppage became 'a national calamity, parallel within its limits to pestilence or to famine. . . . The nation has no security that a similar strike might not occur in time of public peril, when the prompt action of every ship might be a matter of cardinal necessity.'[6]

Though the engineering lock-out had now been settled, the Employers' Federation[7] invited Lord Wemyss and the Free Labour Protection Association to a conference in September 1898 to 'consider a proposal to accept into the Federation . . . all cognate trades having . . . grievances with tyrannical Trade Unions'.[8] Their intention was to maintain 'absolute freedom of contract between employers and employed' and the right of 'managing their . . . business without interference from Trade Unions'. Any member firm or firms engaged in a dispute would be guaranteed average profits, and all negotiations would be handled by the Federation. The conference, however, took no decision about this part of its programme, resolving instead on the more modest aim of forming a Parliamentary Committee (later Council) to watch over legislation 'affecting the interests of trade, of free contract and of free labour'.[9]

'Those who profess through labour organisation to speak collectively

---

[1] *The Times*, 13 Sept. 1897.
[2] 13 Nov. 1897. 'There is no room for the namby-pamby methods of the arbitrator.'
[3] 18 Nov. 1897.   [4] 7 Oct. 1897.   [5] 8 Apr. 1898.
[6] 18 July 1898.
[7] Colonel Dyer had died earlier in the year and Sir Benjamin Browne was now their president.
[8] Richard Bell, *Trade Unionism*, 1907, p. 30.
[9] The Free Labour Protection Association had but a short and insubstantial life. Millar claimed to have a force of a thousand ex-policemen and soldiers to protect free labour when required, but they were put to little use and by 1904 the Association did 'not exist as an active body' (*Royal Commission on Trade Disputes and Trade Combinations*, Cd. 2826, 1906, Q. 3416).

in the name of labour are listened to', wrote Lord Wemyss to *The Times*, 'while employers, as a body hitherto having no corporate organisation, are consequently not listened to.'[1] The new association could 'make members of Parliament—even Governments—and the Board of Trade see that in Labour and trade questions there are possibly two sides'.[2] The Parliamentary Council, complete with an Executive Committee, was duly constituted at a meeting on 15 November at which the industries represented included engineering, coal, cotton, building, printing, furniture, baking, boot and shoe manufacture, tailoring, and glass-bottle manufacture. In the eyes of its founders at least, 'the Council was to become to the employers what the Trades Union Congress was to the working class, and the relation between the Executive Committee and the Council would reproduce that which obtained between the Parliamentary Committee and the Congress'.[3]

What had the employers' counter-attack achieved? In so far as it was their intention to convert unilateral regulation of working conditions by the craft societies into joint regulation by collective bargaining, the engineering agreement of 1898 crowned a series of successes; yet in terms of crippling the unions its accomplishment was negligible. This was partly due to the strength and resilience of the Engineers, but it was also due to the opposition of public opinion. The letter of the fifteen Oxford dons[4] was much closer to the general reaction to Dyer's statement of aims than were the editorials of *The Times*; and George Barnes probably hit the mark when he replied to Dyer's praise for Carnegie's methods by saying that 'enlightened public opinion in this country would resent the introduction here of the "Boss" system, with its attendant unrestrained brutality and lawlessness'.[5]

There were many indications that Dyer's Federation was not wholly representative of the employers, even in the engineering and shipbuilding industries. Indeed, the proposal to form a comprehensive national organization and link it up with the Free Labour Protection Association had fallen through because 'many . . . firms . . . did not at all care about being tied to the tail of Wemyss & Co.'[6] In 1895, before the Federation's foundation, an Industrial Union of Employers and Employed had been established in the belief that there was a need for an association which, while adopting as a fundamental principle the recognition of combination, would 'emphasise the underlying common interests of both classes . . .

---

[1] *The Times*, 18 Nov. 1898.   [2] Ibid., 8 Nov. 1898.

[3] E. Halévy, *A History of the English People in the Nineteenth Century*, vol. v, 1951 edition, p. 256. What relationship was established between the Council and Collison is not clear; but in 1902 Wemyss told Mantoux and Alfassa that the National Free Labour Association received 'almost all' its funds from the Council, and that 'we have tried to give it the appearance of a life of its own for the benefit of public opinion' (op. cit., p. 213).

[4] See p. 166.   [5] *The Times*, 9 Sept. 1897.   [6] Bell, op. cit., p. 34.

and cultivate the feeling of goodwill on both sides'.[1] The provisional committee appointed at a preliminary meeting in 1894 consisted of employers and trade unionists from the major industrial centres, including David Dale, the ironmaster, on the employers' side, and on the union side W. J. Davis of the National Society of Amalgamated Brassworkers and Edward Trow of the Associated Iron and Steel Workers.[2]

The Industrial Union faded out in 1896;[3] but in 1900 there came into being the more impressive National Industrial Association, 'a National Association of Employers' Associations and Trade Unions' with much the same objects. On the employers' side it included G. B. Hunter, a Wallsend shipbuilder, George Bean, a Birmingham engineer, and J. W. Meldrum, a Manchester engineer; on the union side Richard Bell of the Railway Servants, Wilkie of the Shipwrights, and Kelley of the Lithographic Printers.[4] Immediately after his retirement in 1900 Robert Knight himself was proselytizing on its behalf, and many other leaders expressed a sympathetic interest. The General Federation of Trade Unions, though critical of the constitution and machinery of the Association, thought that some such organization was necessary 'if Britain is to be freed from the irritating and unbusinesslike stoppages which periodically hamper her productivity'.[5]

If opinion generally was unfavourable to any attempt to smash the unions, recent events had nevertheless aroused a good deal of disquiet about some aspects of trade unionism. L. L. Price, an Oxford don and a student of industrial relations, gave expression to this in a paper to the British Association in September 1898. 'During recent years', he wrote, 'an unquiet spirit has been abroad, which . . . is inimical to industrial peace. . . . The rumours, spread with more or less authority, of the attempted or accomplished capture of unionism by socialistic propaganda, have not proved destitute of confirmation. . . . The older unions have not failed to catch some of the contagion of the new spirit. They have endeavoured to gain greater control over the technical side of industry.' These socialistic ambitions had prompted some 'reversion to old practices . . . by the most skilled workmen of the country . . . in some cases at least'; and this was 'particularly inopportune at a moment when masters and men are likely to be put on their mettle to meet the competition of foreign countries'.[6] For all their cautious phrasing, these judgements seemed to support Livesey's dictum that 'Socialism can be proved to be the very essence of present day unionism'.[7]

---

[1] Extracts from a paper read to the Preliminary Conference on 16 Mar. 1894 by T. W. Bushill (Webb Trade Union Collection E, Section B, vol. xxviii).

[2] Ibid., vol. xxviii.   [3] *Daily Express*, 22 Dec. 1900.

[4] Webb Trade Union Collection E, Section B, vols. xv and xvi.

[5] *Annual Report*, June 1901.

[6] 'Industrial Conciliation: A Retrospect', *Economic Journal*, Dec. 1898.

[7] *The Times*, 28 Oct. 1897.

This kind of analysis led to two sets of proposals for legislation: one on the means of determining wages and conditions of work, and the other on the legal status of the unions. The first sought for some new system of regulation which would avoid the massive trials of strength between employers and the unions that had caused so much industrial disruption and aroused so much public concern during the past decade. The Conciliation Act of 1896[1] and the Labour Department of the Board of Trade were widely held to have failed in this respect. Many employers took the view that the Department usually intervened to try to patch up a settlement just when it was essential in the country's interest to fight to the bitter end the attempts of the unions to usurp the powers of management. That strikes had not been averted by the Act was evident to all, and there were many suggestions for its amendment. Only one attracted serious attention: Ritchie's outline for a National Conciliation Board first put forward in December 1898.[2] This was welcomed by many union leaders, at least in principle; but the employers treated it with contempt.

Experiments of a different kind, however, had been tried in the Antipodes. In New Zealand an Act of 1894 had established a system of compulsory arbitration for industrial disputes. Two years later the state of Victoria in Australia had tackled the problem of sweating by setting up wage boards empowered to fix minimum rates enforceable at law. The Bishop of Hereford wrote to *The Times* that the demand for 'authoritative legal control' of this kind was being made 'on all sides by those who long to see the spirit of Christianity made more effective'.[3] They had the additional advantage of providing for the ill-organized trades which were unprotected by the unions. The Webbs took the same view. 'We do not believe that trade unionism, by itself, can supply the solution of this problem. . . . We regard the legislation of Victoria and New Zealand as pointing a more excellent way.'[4]

From the trade union side George Barnes provided further support. In an editorial in the Engineers' *Journal* he wrote that public opinion, becoming better informed, 'will resent indulgence by either side of mere "wild cat" tactics'. There should be machinery for 'finding out what is right as well as what is practicable, and applying it'; and this would be accomplished only 'when the community fully realises that it has a right to be regarded as the arbiter in the maintenance of social peace'.[5] On more than one occasion the issue was debated in the House of Commons; but in the end nothing came of it because the unions, on balance, were opposed, despite the efforts of Ben Tillett,[6] and the employers were strongly hostile.

---

[1] See p. 263.   [2] See p. 265.   [3] *The Times*, 23 Dec. 1898.   [4] Ibid., 6 Dec. 1901.
[5] Amalgamated Society of Engineers, *Journal and Monthly Record*, Feb. 1899.
[6] See p. 265, footnote 4.

There remained the second proposal for statutory intervention: the revision of the legal status and powers of the unions. The final comment of *The Times* on the engineering lock-out had stressed the need for such a revision.

> It is high time . . . that unions should cease to be extra-legal in character, and an Act for their due regulation need not be either cumbrous or complicated. . . . Funds subscribed for provident purposes should surely be earmarked . . . and secured [by law] against misapplication to other ends than those for which they were originally contributed. The time has come also for placing upon the unions a proper amount of corporate responsibility for illegal acts which inflict injury upon employers or upon non-unionists.[1]

The Employers' Parliamentary Council took up this programme with enthusiasm, and it was not long before startling successes were achieved in the courts, if not in Parliament itself.

Finally, the counter-attack had one consequence which its promoters can hardly have intended: the unions were provoked into considering ways and means of strengthening their defences. In his presidential address to the Trades Union Congress of 1898 the socialist James O'Grady of the Alliance Cabinet Makers tried to assess the significance of the engineering lock-out for the movement. He saw the Employers' Federation as 'a mammoth combination of military-led capital, whose object, as openly stated by its leader, was to cripple, if not crush, the forces of trade-unionism'. Colonel Dyer and his colleagues had brought 'into existence an organisation that fought scientifically, that never missed a point in the game, and took advantage of every little opportunity, and went intelligently to work to compass their end. And though not wholly successful, it was a very fair beginning, tried as it was against our brigade of guards in the industrial army.' For him the moral was the need both for industrial federation and for independent political organization.

[1] 29 Jan. 1898.

5

Patterns of Industrial Relations

DESPITE considerable fluctuation in their rates of growth, the three groups which have so far been discussed—the 'new unions', coal and cotton, and the craft societies—included three-quarters or more of the membership of British trade unions at any time between 1889 and 1900. About half of the remainder were to be found in organizations which relied heavily upon parliamentary action, and so form part of the next chapter. Thus about one-eighth of the total was provided by a large number of unions, most of them small, which normally fell into one of two main categories. Either they were too weak to cut much of a figure at all, or their industries provided unusual opportunities for collaboration with the employers. And in the first group the three most important were the unions in agriculture, wholesale clothing, and wool.

Agriculture and Fishing

For a brief period after 1889 life returned to agricultural trade unionism. Joseph Arch's National Agricultural Labourers' Union enjoyed a revival, notably in Norfolk, and rose from 4,000 members in 1889 to 15,000 in 1891. In 1890 there appeared the Eastern Counties Labour Federation, centred on Suffolk, which claimed as many as 17,000 members in 1892. The Federation was inspired by the 'new unionism', but a smaller organization, the Norfolk and Norwich Amalgamated Labourers' Union, founded in 1889–90 by George Edwards,[1] was 'in the main an attachment of the Liberal Party'.[2] Like Arch, Edwards received help from Liberals who saw agricultural trade unionism primarily as an instrument for organizing the rural vote.[3] Conservatives in East Anglia therefore employed A. L. Edwards and other agents to 'get the labourers divided so that they may get a political advantage at the next General Election',[4] and the Labourers' Independent Federation formed for this purpose supplied 'free labour'.

Among the remaining bona fide unions was the London and Counties

---

[1] Edwards, Sir George (1850–1933). General secretary, Eastern Counties Agricultural Labourers' Union (later National Union of Agricultural Labourers), 1906–14. Parliamentary Committee, Trades Union Congress, 1912–13. M.P. 1920–2, 1923–4.

[2] R. Groves, *Sharpen the Sickle!*, 1949, p. 87.

[3] See p. 36. Arch had been lionized by the Liberal Party and the process had not improved his performance as a trade union official (Selley, op. cit., p. 101).

[4] G. Edwards, *From Crow-scaring to Westminster*, 1922, p. 78.

Labour League, which in 1892 claimed over 10,000 members, mainly in Kent and Sussex; and in half a dozen other counties in the South and South Midlands there were small associations whose existence owed much to village campaigns by the Land Nationalization Society and the Land Restoration League between 1890 and 1893. Within reach of London, part of the stimulus to growth had come from the Dockers and the Gasworkers, both of which feared the farm labourers as potential blacklegs.[1] This influence, however, disappeared with the decline of the 'new unions'. In the North, in Wales, and in Ireland, agricultural trade unionism was non-existent. In Scotland, on the other hand, there were two local organizations in areas where the crofters' movement was active, while in 1892 the Scottish Ploughmen's Federal Union had 6,000 members spread over sixteen counties.[2]

Since most of the agricultural unions also organized other groups of labourers, not all their nominal membership of 50,000–55,000 in 1892 consisted of farmworkers; but even if these dubious figures are accepted at their face value they represent only a tiny fraction of the 1,200,000 persons returned in the 1891 Census as employed in agriculture in the United Kingdom. In any case, by 1892 the unions were beginning to disintegrate. Arch's society repudiated its liabilities for sick and provident benefits, and then dissolved in 1895, followed by the Eastern Counties, the Norfolk and Norwich, and the London and Counties. Most of the others went the same way, though in Scotland the Federal Union clung on until 1900, and in 1897 the Wiltshire association took 200 members into the Gasworkers. At the end of the decade the Workers' Union[3] had some scattered success among farmworkers, but this was short-lived.

The upsurge of agricultural unionism in 1871–4 had come at the peak of twenty years of prosperity for British agriculture, with prices still rising and imports still checked by the inability of foreign producers to export on a grand scale. But the subsequent influx of cheap grain sent a major part of the industry into sharp decline; and it was precisely the big corn-growing farms, with their relatively large staffs of regular employees, which had provided the most promising environment for trade unionism. As depression deepened, the shift from arable cultivation to permanent pasture reduced the demand for labour and earnings fell. Thus the brief

[1] The dockers' strike of 1889 had taken place during the harvest, when 'employers could not easily obtain blackleg labour from the country' (Selley, op. cit., p. 77). During 1890 and 1891 the union sent organizers into Oxfordshire, Buckinghamshire, and Lincolnshire villages and gave financial help to strikes, some of them successful, for higher pay (ibid., p. 78, and *Royal Commission on Labour*, C–6894–XXV, 1894, pp. 148, 151). 'One gratifying feature of the movement in Oxfordshire has been that university students have been assisting' (*Workman's Times*, 20 Mar. 1891). Prominent among them was a future Liberal cabinet minister, Herbert Samuel (Viscount Samuel, *Memoirs*, 1945, pp. 15–17).

[2] *Royal Commission on Labour*, C–6894–XV, 1893, pp. 29, 138, 162.

[3] See p. 87.

union revival of 1889–92, confined as it was mainly to the corn-producing areas of East Anglia and the South, had no stable foundation; and the death-blow came when grain prices took 'their final plunge to the absolute minimum of 1895'.[1]

Well before this, however, the farmers had shown that they could brush the unions aside with ease. In 1891 they formed a Federation in East Anglia which forbade each member to alter wages 'without the sanction of the committee of the district to which he belongs'.[2] Arch managed to secure a conference with its Norfolk representatives in 1892, but failed to persuade them to join his union in setting up a wages board.[3] In 1892–3 there was a series of strikes against members of the Federation, some of them prolonged, but nearly all were unsuccessful.

In the fishing industry a few small unions had survived from the seventies, and a National Federation of Fishermen, founded in 1890, was able to win some concessions from the employers before it disappeared in 1894. With the introduction of steam-trawling a further crop of local organizations appeared along the East Coast, and the end of the nineties even saw the beginning of collective agreements. In 1899, for example, the Hull fishermen negotiated a settlement with their employers' association which covered wages and bonuses for all grades except captain and mate.[4] At this stage perhaps 4,000 out of 62,000 workers were organized, a proportion considerably higher than that attained in agriculture.

Wholesale Clothing

In clothing the market for hand-tailored goods was being eaten into by the 'subdivisional' workshops, to the detriment of the craftsmen of the Amalgamated Society of Tailors.[5] In the wholesale sector of the industry, competition between the subdivisional shops and the factories weakened such trade unionism as existed within these two groups.[6] The Jewish shops were often identified with the 'sweating dens' which aroused an intermittent agitation from the eighties onwards. This was only partly justified, however. Piece rates were well below those of the handicraft tailors, but earnings were sometimes as high as theirs because of the absence of craft restrictions and the more efficient organization of production. Indeed, sweating was often due to the efforts of less competent employers to compete with the Jewish masters, for prices which could

---

[1] Clapham, op. cit., vol. iii, p. 78. Between 1879 and 1896 there was a drop of 38 per cent. in the wholesale price of wheat (Bellerby, op. cit., pp. 57–58).

[2] *Royal Commission on Labour*, C–6894–III, 1893, p. 71.

[3] Ibid., C–6894–XXV, 1894, p. 152.

[4] *Report on Changes in Rates of Wages and Hours of Labour in 1899*, Cd. 309, 1900, p. 218.

[5] See p. 134.

[6] It was difficult for the workers in the subdivisional shops and the factories to pursue common objectives because orders let on subcontract from the factories to the shops depended on the latter's cost-advantage in that type of work.

yield an adequate income to the male worker in a subdivisional shop might be totally inadequate for the female homeworker.

The Jewish workers made repeated attempts to organize, forming not less than fifteen local unions between 1892 and 1901. These were all small—the two largest, at Leeds and Manchester, each having about 1,000 members in 1900; but a few of them had managed to win at least temporary gains. In the East End, immigrant workers[1] struck in 1889 in the hope of capitalizing the sympathy evoked by the revelations of the House of Lords' Select Committee on Sweating. Despite their shortage of funds the stoppage lasted for five weeks until a negotiated settlement was brought about by the Jewish millionaire and Liberal Member for Whitechapel, Samuel Montagu.[2] Through a similar strike in 1890 the Manchester Jewish Machinists, Tailors and Pressers also secured a collective agreement after arbitration by the Lord Mayor.

In both cities, however, the unions were too weak to enforce the agreement, which consequently soon came to be ignored. In Leeds, where Jewish workers were better off and sweating was less common, a union had appeared as early as 1880. It disappeared after an unsuccessful strike in 1888, but a new union formed in 1893 grew rapidly and 'was effective in improving conditions of work',[3] exhibiting 'a strength and continuity without parallel elsewhere in the Jewish immigrant communities'.[4] It enjoyed an advantage in that the Leeds workshops, 'at work on substantial orders from clothing factories', were fewer, larger, and more mechanized, and maintained a higher productivity than in London and Manchester, where there were 'many little workshops producing for many clothiers'.[5]

Nevertheless, most of the movements by Jewish workers proved unstable and broke up once the stimulus of brisk trade had passed. After many disappointments, leaders of the Tailors who had tried to organize or co-operate with them[6] became convinced that the immigrants, while fully capable of collective militancy at boom periods, could not sustain any permanent organization. Such beliefs, added to linguistic and cultural barriers, craft snobberies, and anti-semitism, hampered joint action in London and elsewhere.[7] When, for example, about 9,000 Jewish and other

[1] Gartner (op. cit., p. 122) gives the number as 10,000; the Board of Trade's *Report on the Strikes and Lockouts of 1889* (C–6176, 1890, pp. 42, 78) as 2,000.

[2] The masters conceded a reduction in hours to twelve a day, a limitation on overtime, and higher rates for it (Gartner, op. cit., pp. 122–6). Together with Lord Nathaniel de Rothschild, Montagu contributed a quarter of the total strike fund of £400.

[3] Joan Thomas, *History of the Leeds Clothing Industry*, 1955, p. 31 (Yorkshire Bulletin of Economic and Social Research, Occasional Paper No. 1).

[4] Gartner, op. cit., p. 121.

[5] Ibid., pp. 89, 91.

[6] One instance of such co-operation was the formation in 1896 of the Jewish Garment Workers' Federation, uniting several small Jewish unions with some Jewish branches of the Amalgamated Society.

[7] The growing influx of 'foreign pauper labour', which went mainly into the clothing,

immigrants in the East End struck in 1891 for the abolition of sweated outwork, they received practically no support from other unions, and the strike collapsed after three weeks.[1]

The explanation was not, however, that Jews were inherently inferior as trade unionists:

the reasons . . . are to be found in the nature of their trades. The Jewish labour force was constantly shifting, for new immigrants were always arriving while others were leaving for America. . . . In London, workshops were constantly opening and closing; slack seasons were periods of demoralization. . . . Skilled workmen moved in and out of entrepreneurship. . . . Where there were larger and stabler producers, as in Leeds, Jewish trade unions also became effective instruments.[2]

In the factories, which employed mainly women and girls, trade unionism was largely confined to the skilled male cutters and pressers. In 1894 local organizations in Bristol and Leeds combined to form the Amalgamated Union of Clothiers' Operatives; by 1900 they were expanding into other areas and other classes of workers, including female finishers, and had achieved a membership of 1,400. A few firms were prepared to tolerate the union, and approaches to individual employers even brought increases in wages.[3] Some branches made use of an old trade union device by recommending to co-operative societies and public authorities as 'fair shops' those which were ready to meet the union, pay an agreed wage, and accept regulation governing apprenticeship among cutters and pressers. The union made its way only slowly, however, being driven from Plymouth, for example, by a lock-out.

One of the few instances of independent organization among the female factory workers occurred at Leeds, where about 800 women and girls, helped by the trades council and the socialist Tom Maguire, struck in 1889. The strike itself failed but resulted in the formation of the Leeds Tailoresses' Union, which survived to play a minor part in getting the 'particulars clause' of the Factory and Workshops Act of 1895 extended to wholesale clothing.[4] Yet, if trade unionism was weak among women in the factories, it was 'negligible among the hundreds of thousands of seamstresses, dress-makers, milliners and all the stitching trades, with their small business units, their upstairs gentility and their echoes of the Song of the Shirt down all the lower corridors'.[5]

furniture, and boot and shoe trades produced resolutions at the Trades Union Congress in favour of legislative restrictions on immigration in 1892 and 1894.

[1] *Workman's Times*, 3 Apr. 1891 to 26 June 1891.
[2] Gartner, op. cit., p. 119.
[3] Amalgamated Union of Clothiers' Operatives, *Half-Yearly Reports and Balance Sheets*, 1898–1900.
[4] Leeds Independent Labour Party, *Forward*, July 1898. For the particulars clause see p. 244.
[5] Clapham, op. cit., vol. iii, pp. 331–2.

Wool and Minor Textiles

During the nineties the contrast between trade unionism in cotton and wool[1] became even more striking. Union membership and joint regulation continued to grow in Lancashire, but in Yorkshire most of the puny gains of the 'new unionist' period were soon lost. In 1900, having brought in a few spinners and others, the West Yorkshire Power-loom Weavers changed their name to the General Union of Textile Workers. The union had increased from 700 members in 1888 to 4,700 in 1892, only to fall back to 1,800 by 1900. Its leaders, Ben Turner,[2] Allen Gee,[3] and W. H. Drew, struggled on with little encouragement. For all the improved organization of gasworkers, general labourers, and other 'new unionist' groups in the West Riding,[4] and despite the political ferment which made Yorkshire the centre of agitation for independent labour representation, Turner could still speak despairingly of his union's lack of progress. Bradford was 'the most heartbreaking district for Trades Union organising that ever I came across'; Halifax was a 'hopeless area', where men joined the union when trouble arose but lapsed immediately afterwards; while Keighley, a 'blackleg area', was equally discouraging.[5]

Among preparatory workers the Bradford and District Woolsorters, a skilled group, were hit by growing imports of colonial wool needing little or no sorting, which led to a severe depression in their trade.[6] Simpler methods made sorting easier to enter and so reduced its status. Moreover, the union was split by a conflict between piece-workers and the day-wage men; virtually nothing was achieved, and its numbers were well under 1,000 in 1900. Labour-saving improvements also undermined the position of the machine woolcombers, and their weakness was aggravated by the fact that many married women were 'driven through the low wages to supplement the earnings of the husband'[7] by seeking jobs as combers themselves. The Bradford Machine Woolcombers' Association attained some strength early in the decade, but had almost disappeared by 1900.

The only unions to maintain a significant degree of organization and influence were those of the supervisors and the highly specialized craftsmen such as the warp dressers, twisters, and drawers. The Bradford and District Power-loom Overlookers actually increased their membership

[1] See p. 33.
[2] Turner, Sir Ben, P.C. (1863–1942). President, General Union of Textile Workers, later National Union of Textile Workers, 1902–33. General Council, Trades Union Congress, 1921–9. Executive Committee, Labour Party, 1903–4, 1905–21, 1930–2. M.P., 1922–4, 1929–31. Parliamentary Secretary for Mines, 1929–30.
[3] Gee, Allen (1853–1939). General secretary, General Union of Textile Workers, 1888–1922. Chairman, General Federation of Trade Unions, 1910–12. Executive Committee, Labour Party, 1900–5.　　　　[4] See p. 70.
[5] Ben Turner, *Short History of the General Union of Textile Workers*, 1920, pp. 124, 153, 155, 156.　　　[6] *Royal Commission on Labour*, C–6708–VI, 1892, Qs. 6213–17.
[7] Ibid., Q. 6126.

from 698 to 748 out of an estimated total of less than 1,000 supervisors in the area. The Leeds and Huddersfield overlookers' associations were no more than friendly societies, but those of Bradford and Halifax enforced restrictions on entry and other traditional craft controls, though without much regular contact with the employers.[1]

There was little collective bargaining anywhere in the industry. In 1883, during a weavers' strike in Huddersfield, the manufacturers had agreed to meet representatives of the Huddersfield (later the West Riding) Power-loom Weavers to discuss a uniform piece-price list, but this was described as an 'act of condescension' on their part.[2] In the end the employers imposed their own list which continued to form a rough basis for the district, though it was issued as a maximum not a minimum scale and many paid less. In general, each mill-owner was able to impose his own piece-prices and to reduce them whenever he chose without meeting effective resistance. The two or three years after 1889, however, brought many strikes by unorganized as well as organized workers against such reductions. Some were followed by meetings between individual employers and union officials, and a few mill lists were negotiated; but there was no development of machinery for negotiating district lists. Even though some of the larger Huddersfield firms allowed the election of 'mill committees' to mediate between management and workers, these had no connexion with the union.[3]

With returning depression, the few negotiated lists were gradually undermined, and the only lasting testimony to the influence of the General Union was its successful opposition to the two-loom system which some Huddersfield employers tried to introduce early in the decade. Since this was a more general threat than the whittling down of individual piece rates, it was easier for the union leaders to rally the weavers to resist. They secured a meeting with the employers at which no agreement was reached; but the mill-owners did not proceed with their plans.

Their failures and disappointments made the leaders of the General Union exceedingly cautious. 'The governing body were afraid to spend sixpence to make a shilling for the union', wrote Turner. When the West Country workers sought inclusion, 'our Union officials had not then imagination (or pluck enough) to strike out and make our Union the National Union for Woollen Workers.'[4] Nevertheless, in 1894 the Yorkshire Textile Workers' Federation brought together the General Union, the Bradford

---

[1] From a manuscript lent to us by Mary J. Taylor of Leeds.

[2] The weavers' comment was: 'Just fancy . . . talking of "condescending" to meet the very weavers among whom they must look for many of their nearest relations' (Turner, op. cit., p. 49).

[3] *Royal Commission on Labour*, C–6708–VI, 1892, Qs. 5048–54.

[4] Turner, op. cit., pp. 164, 178. The West Country workers were advised to form their own organization, which collapsed in 1895.

Woolsorters and Combers, a couple of local unions in Leeds and Yeadon, and some small groups of carpet weavers, blanket workers, and others for parliamentary agitation on such issues as the Truck and Factory Acts. Membership of this pale shadow of the United Textile Factory Workers' Association[1] fluctuated around the 4,000 level, the societies of craftsmen and supervisors remaining aloof.

One important reason for the continued weakness of trade unionism in wool was that the industry was suffering from an excess of labour, especially male labour. Figures of output and the consumption of raw materials still showed a steady rise, but the pace and capacity of the machines also increased. The number of woollen spindles fell by 16 per cent. between 1889 and 1904, and woollen looms by 19 per cent. Despite a change in fashion in favour of worsted cloth, worsted looms also fell, by 22 per cent. The only increase, of 22 per cent., was in worsted spindles,[2] but worsted spinning was mainly a job for girls. Since weaving, too, was increasingly a woman's occupation,[3] the balance of the labour force shifted towards the female workers. J. H. Clapham, writing in the early years of the new century, considered that the ease with which all-male night shifts could be recruited in emergencies was convincing evidence of a 'surplus body of reasonably qualified workers'.[4]

Wage levels remained well below those in Lancashire. Some male woollen spinners, along with overlookers, specialists, and some sorters, might receive as much as 30*s*; but the girls in worsted spinning were paid no more than 10*s*. a week. Male cotton spinners, by contrast, averaged around 40*s*. Among worsted weavers, earnings of 14*s*. were typical and the maximum for men on the best class of work was 24*s*.; in wool, the weavers' earnings ranged from 12*s*. to 21*s*.[5] By comparison, in cotton weaving women averaged nearly 20*s*. and men perhaps 25*s*. Thus the relative poverty of Yorkshire was a further hindrance to the development of trade unionism.

While industrially backward, some at least of the West Riding textile workers were politically advanced. This was reflected in the columns of the *Yorkshire Factory Times*, founded by John Andrew in 1889 as the counterpart to his *Cotton Factory Times*. In Yorkshire, as in Lancashire, he relied upon trade union officers to contribute local news. 'But the contrast between the two types of union organisers, in Lancashire well established and conservative, in Yorkshire precarious and politically advanced, made all the difference between the politics of the two papers. Moreover, the editor of the Yorkshire paper was Joseph Burgess . . . a pioneer of

[1] See p. 245.
[2] Clapham, *The Woollen and Worsted Industries*, pp. 8–9.
[3] *Royal Commission on Labour*, C–6894–XXIII, 1893, p. 100.
[4] Clapham, op. cit., p. 184.
[5] Ibid., pp. 192–202.

independent labour representation.'[1] Like Burgess, Turner, Gee, and Drew were socialists of some sort, and all were correspondents for his paper.[2]

The defeat of the future General Union in the most important woollen dispute of the period added to the strength of the political movement. The McKinley tariff imposed by the United States early in 1890 had the intended effect on Yorkshire's export trade, and in December Samuel Lister provoked a stoppage by announcing cuts in wages at his family's Manningham Mills in Bradford. 'Contrary to the general impression, it was not the most-depressed but the better-paid workers—velvet and plush weavers—who initiated the strike. The several thousand unskilled women and girls who later thronged the streets came out in sympathy or were forced out by the firm in order to embarrass the strike fund.'[3] The mills had not been organized, but the union's officers were called in when the dispute began. Lister ignored them, however, and declared a lock-out which lasted for five months. A strike committee, over half its members women, issued appeals, made collections, and arranged demonstrations;[4] but in the end, in April 1891, 'Sam Lister won. He was, as a consequence, one of the most hated men of the period.'[5]

The 'new unionism' had already inspired in the West Riding a considerable agitation in favour of independent political action. The anger and resentment caused by the dispute at Manningham Mills added to its supporters and led to the foundation in May 1891 of the Bradford Labour Union, whose independence of both the existing parties 'made it the pioneer of a new type of local political organisation'.[6] This move had the enthusiastic backing of the *Yorkshire Factory Times*, and all the leaders of the General Union were involved, Drew becoming first president of the Labour Union. Thirty years later, Turner insisted that the Manningham stoppage had thus played a considerable part in 'paving the way for the present Labour dominance on the public bodies and public life of Bradford'.[7] In 1893, when the city was chosen as the venue for the inaugural conference of the Independent Labour Party, over one-third of the delegates came from the West Riding, nearly all from the woollen districts.

Meanwhile, the underlying causes of the weakness of Yorkshire textile

[1] Pelling, *Origins*, p. 99.

[2] E. P. Thompson, loc. cit., pp. 289, 306. The new venture may have contributed to their union's growth between 1889 and 1892. 'The establishment of that paper', wrote Turner, 'made our union prosper' (op. cit., p. 66).   [3] Ibid., p. 306.

[4] The local authorities threatened to prohibit open-air meetings, and brought in special police and troops to break up one of them (Turner, *About Myself*, 1930, pp. 113–15).

[5] Turner, *Short History*, p. 137. Lister later became Lord Masham, and Turner commented that 'even his title did not redeem him in the eyes of the working-class public'.

[6] Pelling, op. cit., pp. 100–1.

[7] Turner, *Short History*, p. 129. See also Fenner Brockway, *Socialism over Sixty Years*, 1947, pp. 37 ff.

unions continued to escape not only outside observers but also the leaders of the General Union. When questioned before the Royal Commission on Labour by James Mawdsley, Drew could think of no more convincing explanation for the unorganized state of woollen workers than 'their want of education and their fear of the employers'.[1] Mawdsley, secretary of the Cotton Spinners as well as a member of the Commission, was both patronizing and disparaging, scarcely bothering to conceal his opinion that the basic reason was the short-sighted folly of the Yorkshire workers as compared with those of Lancashire. 'It would not be correct', he asked, 'to say that another cause was that they preferred to stick to their money than to pay it into a society?'[2]

Compared with this humiliating state of affairs, trade unionism in the jute and linen industry of Dundee, Forfar, and Brechin was more impressive. Indeed, these Scottish textiles made a larger contribution to female union membership than any industry except cotton, totalling 9,000 in 1896 and 10,000 in 1900. There were eight local unions in 1892 and fourteen in 1900, five more having failed meanwhile. The largest was the Dundee and District Mill and Factory Operatives, under the presidency of a Radical Unitarian minister, the Reverend Henry Williamson, who had been approached by the women in 1885 to act as their spokesman when they struck against a wage reduction. The rest of the officers were almost all women but, since they feared victimization, such meagre contacts with the employers as took place were left entirely to him.

There was no development of joint machinery for negotiation and the settlement of disputes, either at Dundee or elsewhere. The committee of large employers in Dundee which periodically discussed labour matters firmly defended their right to dictate wages. On the union side Williamson tried to discourage strikes. Combined with his position as a minister and his tendency to secrecy in administration, this aroused the suspicions both of the Dundee Trades Council and of the Parliamentary Committee of the Trades Union Congress. In 1895 he could not prevent a strike which spread throughout the district and ultimately included 32,000 workers. The employers responded by binding themselves, under penalty of £500, not to raise the existing rate of wages. This agreement was signed by forty-seven firms, and the strike collapsed.[3] The union survived, however, and in 1900 claimed 7,000 members, 6,000 of them women.

In Northern Ireland the employers of the Linen Merchants' Association met all attempts to organize women by the threat of a lock-out;[4] but some of the male specialists had their own associations. By 1892, for example,

[1] *Royal Commission on Labour*, C–6708–VI, 1892, Q. 5536.   [2] Ibid., Q. 5537a.
[3] *Report on the Strikes and Lockouts of 1895*, C–8231, 1896, pp. 40–41.
[4] 'In the Belfast district there is a general understanding among the manufacturers to act together in raising or lowering wages' (1906 Board of Trade Earnings Enquiry, *Textiles*, Cd. 4545, 1909, p. liii).

the Lappers, who measured, examined and folded the finished linen, had recruited 400 out of a total of 600 men in the trade. But their demands for uniform wages and working hours were defeated by a lock-out, and membership languished. In silk, which in 1901 employed a mere 35,000 compared with the 120,000 of 1851, trade unionism was as feeble as in wool. There were a few tiny unions, most of them 'discouraged organizations among handworkers',[1] in Macclesfield and Leek; but the Macclesfield Silk Weavers still managed to maintain for the factory hand-loom weavers piece-price lists based on an agreement with employers in 1849.[2]

Industrial Collaboration

Other textile trades displayed a very different picture in the degree of organization attained, the development of collective bargaining, and the attitudes of employers. In the West Riding the most notable case was that of the dyeing of woollen and worsted cloth. This was a man's occupation, and the dyers made excellent use of their strategic position in the productive process, confirming the view 'that producers of any sort who are concerned only with a single essential process, and whose earnings do not form an important part of the selling price of the finished goods, have special opportunities for securing by combination what appears to them a reasonable reward'.[3]

The two unions of skilled men—the Huddersfield, Bradford, Barnsley and District Dyers and Finishers and the Bradford and District Amalgamated Society of Dyers—dated back to 1851 and 1878 respectively, and after 1890 the less skilled were organized by the Gasworkers. Until 1891 keen competition had prevailed among the employers, but in that year they formed the West Riding Dyers' and Finishers' Association to fight a campaign by the unions for a shorter working week.[4] Thereafter two conciliation boards were established, one in 1892 for Huddersfield and the other in 1893 for Bradford. In the same year a number of the large piece-dyeing firms formed a combine, the Yorkshire Piece Dyers' Association, to regulate prices. In 1894 this body made a remarkable agreement with the Amalgamated Society and the Gasworkers which laid down the terms of an alliance to eliminate competition for the benefit of both sides of the industry.

In future, a joint board would determine wage rates and selling prices, linking them together by means of a sliding scale, and was to be responsible for regulating relations between the firms in the combine and their workers. The unions were granted a closed shop, and in return were to

---

[1] Clapham, *Economic History of Modern Britain*, vol. ii, p. 168.
[2] *Report on Standard Piece Rates and Sliding Scales*, Cd. 144, 1900, p. 150.
[3] Clapham, op. cit., vol. iii, pp. 230–1.
[4] Taylor, loc. cit.

strike against any firm which broke away.[1] In 1896 these arrangements for collaboration were amended, for the combine had not proved sufficiently universal to ensure their success. A new board was therefore set up to cover the Huddersfield union as well as the others,[2] and a monetary penalty now bound each side to abide by its decisions.

There were changes in the content as well as the scope of the agreement. The provisions for a closed shop were modified to allow non-unionists to be engaged if the unions failed to supply labour; but such men 'shall be requested to become members of one of the men's societies'. Any existing member who lapsed from his union was to be required by his works director to 'resume his membership'. No worker could leave any firm in the combine without the permission of his employer or the board, and the conditions on which an employer could dismiss a man were defined. Finally, the sliding scale was replaced by standard rates which all firms had to observe provided that they had made a profit of 5 per cent. over the previous three years.

Efforts to strengthen the combine still continued, however, and in 1898 it was re-formed as the Bradford Dyers' Association, which came close to monopolizing piece-dyeing in the West Riding.[3] The Association's agreement with the unions in 1899[4] followed the pattern set three years before. With this added assistance, the Amalgamated Society had risen to almost 5,000 members by 1900, and the Huddersfield union to nearly 1,500. They were now much stronger than their counterparts in Lancashire, where the employers were unable to establish the control over prices which made such agreements possible.

It was not only in the securing of collective agreements that the Yorkshire dyeing unions were remarkable. The Bolton Amalgamation of Bleachers, Dyers, and Finishers fluctuated between 4,000 and 5,000 members, but they received lower wages and enjoyed less advantageous conditions than those prescribed on the other side of the Pennines. This contrast is almost as noteworthy as the reverse contrast in the main sections of spinning and weaving but has received far less attention. Conscious of their growing strength, the Yorkshire unions persuaded the Bolton organization to form a federation in 1896 which they hoped might ultimately lead to full amalgamation.[5]

[1] Four firms did break away during 1894–5. Three were struck, the men receiving financial help from the combine. One of the strikes succeeded, the other two were broken by substitute labour introduced under police protection (Taylor, loc. cit.). [2] Ibid.

[3] F. Hooper, 'The Woollen and Worsted Industries of Yorkshire', in *British Industries*, edited by W. J. Ashley, 1903, p. 114.

[4] *Report on Collective Agreements*, Cd. 5366, 1910, pp. 221–2.

[5] This federation also included two hosiery dyeing unions which participated in two boards of conciliation and arbitration in the Leicester area (*Report on the Strikes and Lockouts of 1897*, C–9012, 1898, p. 109; and *Report on Changes in Rates of Wages and Hours of Labour in 1899*, Cd. 309, 1900, p. 268).

In contrast to these developments in the West Riding, collaboration in the Midlands between employers and the unions in both hosiery and lace had become increasingly difficult. What survived of earlier systems of joint regulation was still being undermined by technical change and competition. This was particularly marked in hosiery. Since the break-up of the boards,[1] the unions had striven to maintain the old piece-price lists and to preserve collective bargaining of some sort. In Nottingham, therefore, 'statement prices' continued to be paid for some high quality work in hand-knitting, and a spokesman for the power-machine workers at Leicester declared that 'if any dispute arises there is no difficulty whatever in the two sides meeting and adjusting the differences before a strike takes place. . . . We have met upon several occasions and re-arranged prices without any strike at all.'[2]

In general, however, the weakened unions were less successful. The Leicester list for power-machine work still 'guided' the local industry but governed it only 'in some branches'.[3] For the hand-knitters engaged on government contracts, 'the old statement of prices has been encroached on terribly'.[4] On their side, the employers saw serious obstacles to any revival of joint regulation. In the Nottingham power-machine section, for example, the factory owners now asserted that 'if they were to agree to a board tomorrow, the next day some of the members would run away from the arrangement'.[5] These setbacks were all due to heightened competition, not only between hand- and power-knitting but between town and country as well. Indeed, rural employers in Nottinghamshire, Derbyshire, and Leicestershire stamped out incipient trade unionism wherever they could in order to retain their advantage in labour costs.[6]

Nevertheless, in 1888 workers in the Ilkeston district of Derbyshire managed to form a union which soon spread to Belper and Heanor. By the end of 1891 they had won acceptance by the employers and a much improved list of piece-prices.[7] In Leicestershire about 2,000 men and women struck at Hinckley in April 1891 for the right to join the Leicester and Leicestershire Amalgamated Hosiery Union. Though they declared themselves ready to accept a district list, the employers insisted upon dealing only with a local union, for they feared that the Leicester union would seek to level up rural conditions and so weaken their competitive advantage. The strike ended in June when the employers recognized the newly formed union as a branch of the Leicester amalgamation. Prices were then negotiated which conceded some advances of between 20 and

---

[1] See p. 24.
[2] *Royal Commission on Labour*, C–6795–VI, 1893, Q. 12744.
[3] *Report on Wages and Hours of Labour*, Part II, C–7567–I, 1894, p. 43.
[4] *Royal Commission on Labour*, C–6795–VI, 1893, Q. 13603.
[5] Ibid., Q. 13031.   [6] Wells, op. cit., pp. 196–7.
[7] *Workman's Times*, 26 June and 7 Aug. 1891.

40 per cent.,[1] but in general the list was still below that for Leicester itself.

The Midland Counties Hosiery Federation, a loose grouping formed in 1889 by the Leicester, Nottingham, and Derby unions, now began to talk hopefully of a uniform list for all the competing districts, and in 1892 a delegate meeting got as far as electing a committee to draw it up.[2] In 1895, however, the Leicester employers demanded reductions in piece rates to enable them to meet competition from the country-side. After a strike affecting 4,000 workers[3] a compromise was reached; but the dispute drove a wedge between town and country branches of the union, and two of the rural districts, Hinckley and Loughborough, broke away to set up their own organizations. Competition between town and country intensified, and eventually caused joint regulation in Leicester to break down altogether, thus forcing the union in one main centre of the trade to deal with each employer individually.

In 1892 the unions had claimed about 5,000 out of a total of 50,000 workers in the industry, a quarter of them in the small unions affiliated to the Hand Framework Knitters' Federation, which covered both Scotland and the Midlands, and three-quarters in the unions of machine workers affiliated to the Midland Counties Hosiery Federation. As a result of the break-up of the Leicester amalgamation, the number of unions rose and their aggregate membership fell slightly. In particular cases the fall could be more serious, for the little Ilkeston union, whose members were once more subjected to systematic victimization, lost nearly half its strength after 1895.

In lace, the hand-workers had never been organized, and it was the growth of machine production which provided the opportunity for joint regulation.[4] An arbitration board had been established at Nottingham in 1867, and strong unions of the skilled male operatives took advantage of the profitability of the industry in its early stages to negotiate favourable piece rates.[5] Before long Nottingham began to feel competition from Derbyshire and from the rural areas of Nottinghamshire, and in 1874 this led to a dispute over the rates agreed. When an arbitrator, Rupert Kettle, awarded the reductions which the employers now wanted, the unions joined forces in the Amalgamated Society of Operative Lacemakers. The new organization retained some strength in Nottingham itself, but efforts to establish branches in the competing districts were usually

---

[1] *Workman's Times*, 24 Apr. and 19 June 1891.

[2] Ibid., 8 Oct. 1892.

[3] *Report on Changes in Rates of Wages and Hours of Labour in 1895*, C–8374, 1897, p. 163.

[4] By 1901 the change to the machine was almost complete and there remained only 2,000 hand-workers in an industry employing over 36,000.

[5] *Select Committee on Home Work*, H.C. 246, 1908. Evidence of W. A. Appleton, secretary of the Amalgamated Society of Operative Lacemakers, Qs. 3363–5.

frustrated either by victimization or by a lock-out.[1] Meanwhile, the board fell into disuse.

In 1889, a year of unusual prosperity elsewhere, the Nottingham employers demanded the setting-up of a new conciliation board to negotiate a further reduction in rates. At a time when the Lacemakers had about 3,500 members, the men of seventy-five firms struck in vain against this proposal. The employers, having secured the reductions they required, were prepared to agree to a more thorough-going system of joint regulation. A committee was formed to settle disputes, with provision for arbitration as the last resort. Financial penalties were laid down for breaches of the agreement, and the employers' association was to pay half the cost of a strike against a defaulting employer.[2] Yet, whatever its merits, the settlement could not solve the problem of competition from the low-wage areas, for they met reduction with reduction. A further effort by the union at about this time to organize the workers in one such area, Long Eaton, was crushed by a lock-out lasting seven to eight months.[3]

Thus, though it survived, collaboration in Nottingham remained uneasy. The Lacemakers' leaders did their best to minimize any concessions demanded from their members by the careful timing of negotiations,[4] and they even managed to extend their craft-type rules. Hitherto some of the men had each employed a number of boys and had therefore been able to operate several machines. During the nineties, however, the union succeeded in imposing a restriction of one boy to every seven men, a four years' apprenticeship, and a limit of two machines per man.[5] This, of course, did nothing to improve either the competitive position of Nottingham or relations with the employers.

The carpet industry also preserved a measure of joint regulation. A dwindling body of hand-loom weavers, thinly scattered over Yorkshire, Lancashire, Durham, and Scotland, still managed to retain the custom of annual meetings with the employers to settle wages for the coming year;[6] but union membership had shrunk to a couple of hundred by 1900. Of the three organizations of power-loom weavers, the Kidderminster Power-loom Carpet Weavers were the most powerful, and they successfully maintained an agreed price list[7] and a standard wage of 35s., even though similar work was being done in Yorkshire by women for 15s. a week.[8]

---

[1] N. H. Cuthbert, *The Lace Makers' Society*, 1960, pp. 54–55.

[2] *Report on the Strikes and Lockouts of 1889*, C–6176, 1890, pp. 136–8.

[3] Industrial Council, *Inquiry into Industrial Agreements*, Cd. 6953, 1913, Q. 10695.

[4] 'It was comparatively easy to watch the markets . . . and to take care that the acute stage in the negotiations came on at the commencement of the busy time' (*Select Committee on Home Work*, H.C. 246, 1908, Q. 3361).

[5] Industrial Council, *Inquiry into Industrial Agreements*, Cd. 6953, 1913, Q. 2931.

[6] *Royal Commission on Labour*, C–6795–IX, 1892, p. 185.

[7] *Report on Standard Piece Rates and Sliding Scales*, Cd. 144, 1900, p. 153.

[8] *Royal Commission on Labour*, C–6894–XXIII, 1893, p. 140.

Despite the importance of industrial collaboration in some textiles, the most advanced type was first developed in the metal-working trades of Birmingham. In 1889 the largest strike hitherto recorded for the city led to the formation of the Bedstead Workmen's Association.[1] The making of metal bedsteads was highly competitive, and an employer, E. J. Smith, evolved a scheme for a close alliance between the union and the associated manufacturers which was designed to safeguard the interests of both. Founded in 1891, his Bedstead Alliance combined the principle of joint regulation with that of an industrial cartel. Members of the union agreed to work only for members of the employers' association, and in return the union enjoyed the advantages of a closed shop and equal representation on a wages board. Selling prices were fixed by the manufacturers' cartel, with the board's agreement, and any employer failing to comply was penalized by a strike financed by both sides.[2] Wage rates were linked with prices, a bonus being paid for every increase secured by the cartel.

The Alliance provided the model for the West Riding dyeing agreement of 1894, and Smith was convinced that his formula for a well-ordered industry was capable of wide application. He received support from W. J. Davis, secretary of the National Society of Amalgamated Brassworkers, who had long been struggling with the difficulties of regulating the Birmingham trades with their many firms, small masters, diversity of products, ease of entry and back-alley workshops.[3] Davis had learnt that a union's capacity to control the smaller, price-cutting employers helped to determine not only the concessions which could be extracted from the larger firms but also their readiness to tolerate the union and collective bargaining. He was thus prepared to welcome any scheme which promised to restrain the competitive forces which had so handicapped trade unionism in the city.

In 1896 Davis helped Smith to set up Alliances in the brass and iron fender trade, coffin furniture, cased tubes and stair rods, bedstead mounts and fender supports, china fittings, bricks and fire-clay, and metal rolling and wire drawing. An Alliance for the pin trade had begun a year earlier, and a Cycle-tube Alliance followed in 1897. Altogether about a dozen minor trades adopted the system, covering between them 500 employers and 20,000 workers.[4] In many cases Davis occupied the position of operatives' secretary to the board, but Smith's main task was complete once an

---

[1] This ten-day strike of 4,000 men for a 15 per cent. wage increase was settled by an arbitration award giving an immediate rise of 10 per cent. with a further 5 per cent. to follow in Mar. 1890 (*Report on the Strikes and Lockouts of 1889*, C–6176, 1890, pp. 130–1).

[2] Brief references to such strikes can be found in the *Birmingham Weekly Post* of 6 May and 21 Oct. 1899, and 25 Aug. 1900.

[3] The basic principles of the Alliance were adumbrated in union reports as early as 1885 (National Society of Amalgamated Brassworkers, *Annual Report*, Birmingham, 1885).

[4] H. Macrosty, *The Trust Movement in British Industry*, 1922, p. 80.

Alliance had been launched. When called in to 'organize' a trade, he worked out the average costs of all the manufacturers, added a percentage profit, and then issued the first list of selling prices.

Some observers had already suggested that conciliation boards might 'lead employers and employed to . . . exclude competition', and 'to follow the example set them by many medieval guilds of hardening themselves into organised conspiracies for promoting the well-being of the privileged few at the expense of the great mass of the people'.[1] Many union leaders took a different view. 'The curse of our trade', wrote Davis, 'is the under-cutter who by the most dastardly means brings down wages and prices, and so filches orders from those who conduct their business in a fair and honourable way. The upright manufacturers . . . have always wished well to our Society, and their only complaint against it has been that it was unable to protect them completely from the mischief these harpies were doing.'[2] In the same spirit, during negotiations in 1899, he told the employers that 'we meet . . . to rescue our trade, and to make secure the property of employers as well as of workmen'.[3]

Some of the Alliances produced results, and Davis could speak of employers 'who recognise in the new principle . . . a revelation of a happy future in which industrial strife shall cease, and when that always regret-table mode of warfare, the strike, shall be remitted to a barbarous past'.[4] By 1899 prices and wages in the bedstead trade were double what they had been in 1891.[5] But success undermined the Alliance, for the number of manufacturers rose from forty to fifty-six;[6] furniture stores switched to wooden bedsteads, and foreign competition appeared. These develop-ments put a severe strain on loyalty to the cartel. Despite the use of private detectives to control evasion, many employers found ways of enlarging their share of the market by concealed price cuts. At last three firms re-volted, and the expense of maintaining their workers on strike depleted the common fund. In August 1900 the Bedstead Alliance was dissolved, and others which still survived soon followed. The 'once famous Birming-ham Alliances', wrote one economist, were now 'happily defunct, never, it is to be hoped, to reappear in British industry'.[7]

In brassworking, which was Davis's chief concern, the leading employers had refused to set up an Alliance, fearing that it could never control the whole industry and would therefore handicap them competitively. Regu-lation of the trade was beset by problems such as subcontracting, an abundance of small masters, easy entry, boy labour, and a product range

---

[1] The economist Alfred Marshall, in the preface to *Industrial Peace*, L. L. Price, 1887.

[2] Quoted in Dalley, op. cit., pp. 186–7.

[3] Ibid., p. 189.   [4] Ibid., p. 128.

[5] Macrosty, 'The Trust Movement in Great Britain', in *British Industries*, edited by W. J. Ashley, pp. 202–3.

[6] Macrosty, *Trust Movement*, p. 81.   [7] Ibid., p. 79.

of enormous size and complexity. But these difficulties were less severe in the high-quality sector, and some degree of joint regulation had already been achieved through conventional conciliation boards. Piece-price lists had been drawn up by special conferences or by the Amalgamated Brass Trades Board of Conciliation, established in 1891; and these covered a multitude of operations and products.[1]

Davis was resourceful in his attempts to strengthen control. In 1896 he persuaded the employers to grant a 5 per cent. bonus to his members only. As a result, 4,000 flocked into the union within the space of a few weeks, and membership, which had remained at 5,000–6,000 between 1892 and 1895, leapt to over 10,000. 'The one thing wanted', wrote Davis, 'was a lever, such as this new arrangement gives us, to bring pressure to bear upon—we will not say unworthy, but thoughtless—workers who remained outside.'[2] This unique policy lasted only four years, for it did not solve the problem of the price-cutting, low-wage 'garret-masters'. In 1900 the 'arrangement' was ended at the behest of the employers by an arbitration award. The bonus remained but was now to be paid to non-unionists as well.

The union had begun as an association of piece-working contractors, but day-wage men, including those employed by the contractors, were allowed to join and had grown steadily in number. Davis showed considerable agility in riding an internal conflict between the two groups. The contractors were anxious to hold down the wages of their employees; the day-wage men, on the other hand, whether employed by contractors or by the firms direct, wanted to establish a minimum wage at the highest possible level. During the nineties, as the latter gradually won control, this replaced piece-prices as the union's main concern; but in 1892 the opening of the minimum wage campaign was followed by the exodus of 30 per cent. of the Birmingham members.

The campaign culminated in arbitration by Sir David Dale in 1900. In addition to a minimum wage, the union demanded the regulation of boy labour, the limitation of subcontracting,[3] and other concessions. These claims were now openly opposed by some contractor members of the union.[4] Dale awarded only the minimum wage—at a much lower level than the union had sought—and a few of the minor claims. Birmingham membership suffered a further sharp decline, but meanwhile the union had spread to many other centres in the Midlands and the North.[5]

[1] In many sections, however, the constant succession of new products made standard lists impossible. Here Davis resorted where he could to one of two methods of control: either the employers sent the product to his office to be priced, or the price was negotiated by workshop committees.

[2] National Society of Amalgamated Brassworkers, *Annual Report*, Birmingham, 1897.

[3] Some contractors employed only two or three boys and presented little threat to the union, but others ran large teams based on elaborate subdivision of labour and were difficult to control.

[4] *Report on the Brass Trades Minimum Rate Arbitration*, Birmingham, 1900.

[5] Total membership, 6,548 in 1892, fell from a peak in 1897 of 10,784 to 8,675 in 1900.

Davis was not the only union leader in his area to propagate the Alliance philosophy. For a time it became the accepted doctrine of most of the tiny organizations affiliated to the Midland Counties Trades Federation, whose secretary was Richard Juggins, the leader of the National Society of Nut and Bolt Workers, a hand-workers' union in a keenly competitive trade. Juggins joined the employers in setting up the South Staffordshire Bolt and Nut Trade Wages Board, which negotiated piece-price lists and hired auditors to check the employers' books. If an employer was found not to be paying the standard rates, his workers were called out by the Board and paid from a joint fund.[1]

At one time it seemed as if an Alliance might also be formed in the pottery trade, where conciliation had a long history. Arbitration had been accepted since 1850, and a board was established in 1868; but a series of adverse decisions undermined the men's faith in the system. During the eighties the board was reconstituted, and a new rule permitted the umpire to verify evidence by examining the employers' books 'through the sworn accountant appointed by and responsible to the umpire', provided that his findings 'shall be disclosed to no other person'.[2] But faith was not easily restored. In 1890, when the unions claimed an increase in wages of 10 per cent., the employers delayed until the boom had passed its peak.[3] When the case was heard in 1891 they persuaded the umpire to reject the claim on the evidence of their own accountant.[4] The men accepted the award but refused any further part in the board unless it applied the rule permitting full investigation of the employers' books.

Early in the following year, several local stoppages occurred over the limitation of apprentices and the dismissal of certain union members. In addition, mass meetings demanded monthly contracts as against the traditional practice of yearly contracts renewed annually at Martinmas on 11 November—a bad time if the unions chose to strike. The employers countered with a general lock-out of 20,000 men and women which lasted from 2 May to 21 May 1892. The settlement provided for the reinstatement of the men dismissed, yearly contracts renewed on 25 March, and the establishment of a board of conciliation, without any arrangements for arbitration.[5]

Thereafter, from 1892 to 1898, the energies of the unions were divided between an experiment in co-operative production[6] and their attempt to

[1] *Royal Commission on Labour*, C–6795–IV, 1892, Qs. 17893–904.

[2] Ibid., C–6894–IX, 1893, Qs. 30401–2. This followed a hint by Lord Brassey, in an arbitration in 1880, when he said that 'in the absence of more independent sources of information we must take into consideration, in the first place, the assertions of the employers themselves'.

[3] *Workman's Times*, 8 Aug. 1890 to 5 June 1891.

[4] *Royal Commission on Labour*, C–6894–IX, 1893, Qs. 30402–5.

[5] *Workman's Times*, 20 Feb. 1892 to 21 May 1892.

[6] The Brownfield Guild Scheme (W. H. Warburton, *History of Trade Union Organisation in the Potteries*, 1931, pp. 210–11).

form an Alliance. In 1890 and 1891 they had already approached the employers to discuss methods of controlling selling prices,[1] but without success. In 1895, however, an Alliance was established in the china furniture and electrical fittings trades, and three years later 'Bedstead' Smith was called in to explain his formula to the earthenware manufacturers and their operatives. An agreement for an Alliance was drawn up with the strong support of the unions and 'many of the chief employers';[2] but the scheme foundered on the opposition of those manufacturers who preferred to retain their competitive freedom. Thus, when prosperity returned, there was no obstacle to renewed conflict. In February 1900 the various societies asked for increases in wages and their requests were refused. By April 20,000 workers were on strike, and the stoppage continued until advances of 5–8½ per cent. were granted late in May.

Over a decade of erratic development trade unionism in pottery increased its strength from 5,000 to nearly 6,000 members, though the total fell below 3,000 in 1897. One major reason for fluctuations in membership was rapid technical change. 'Our trade is in a state of transition, for mechanical appliances are being brought to bear upon it and potters' lathes are being driven by steam.'[3] Consequently, the unions presented a shifting pattern of dissolutions, new ventures, and amalgamations. The principal body in 1900 was the Hollow-ware and Sanitary Pressers, Mould Makers, Flat Pressers and Clay Potters with 2,500 members, several hundred of them a legacy from the National Order of Potters, now extinct but 1,000 strong in 1892. The only other organization of note was the Printers, Transferrers and Female Decorators, founded in 1898, which had 1,750, nearly three-fifths of them women. With machinery had come an 'influx of low-paid female labour',[4] and between 1899 and 1902 the new union recruited some of these women. But they could not hold their gains.

The Boot and Shoe Trade

These examples of industrial collaboration, or of its failure, support the view that collaboration thrived in highly competitive trades where the unions were strong enough to take a major share in limiting competition by enforcing minimum wages and possibly minimum prices as well. Granted these conditions, employers might be willing to work with the unions and even to strengthen them by encouraging the closed shop. On the other hand, collaboration was weakened wherever the unions failed to

---

[1] *Royal Commission on Labour*, C–6894–IX, 1893, Q. 30440. 'Throughout their history the policy of the organised working potters was, on the whole, to favour the regulation of selling-prices and the existence of a strong manufacturers' association to enforce such regulation' (Warburton, op. cit., p. 200).   [2] H. Owen, *The Staffordshire Potter*, 1901, p. 250.

[3] *Royal Commission on Labour*, C–6894–IX, 1893, Q. 30443.

[4] Warburton, op. cit., p. 199.

control the whole of their labour market, thus permitting competition to undermine the basis of their good relations with the employers. However, neither of what have since proved to be the outstanding instances of amicable co-operation—the boot and shoe trade and the iron and steel industry—fits completely into this mould.

The boot and shoe trade was certainly competitive, and the National Union of Operative Boot and Shoe Rivetters and Finishers was firmly established by 1889; but this did not ensure good relations. Indeed, the first years of the nineties were spent in working up towards a major conflict.[1] In 1889 itself 2,000 riveters and finishers in Bristol struck unofficially for a 10 per cent. increase in wages and resumed work only on the promise of a uniform piece-price list. When the list had been negotiated, further disputes arose over its application. The employers tried to restore discipline with a general lock-out of 10,000 men, which lasted into 1890, and the eventual settlement included provision for an arbitration board.[2]

Wage issues, however, were the least fundamental of those currently disturbing the trade. The first wave of technical change, which created a new wholesale industry in the fifties and sixties by replacing the handsewing of soles and uppers with machinery, was now being succeeded by a second, which partly mechanized the lasting and finishing processes and was accompanied by a greater use of boys, a more elaborate subdivision of labour, and a fuller use of subcontracted outwork. The union was hostile to all these changes, and its policy was to limit the employment of boys,[3] to abolish outwork, to prevent any further subdivision of labour, and to connive at local resistance to mechanization by restriction of output and demands for penally high piece rates.

For all this, the national and most branch leaders were anxious to preserve the local machinery for joint regulation through which the union had consolidated its position.[4] Their attitude, however, was not wholly shared by the members, some of whom were induced by their fear and resentment at change to listen to militants who sought to intensify resistance by the use of socialist arguments. By 1890 these militants were denouncing the leaders' attachment to conciliation and arbitration, and trying to substitute a strike policy. Moreover, in their attempts to oust the moderates from office they set out to demoralize them by personal attacks. As a result, the union had four presidents and two treasurers between 1890 and 1893; in 1891 the entire leadership of the Leicester branch

---

[1] Fox, *Boot and Shoe Operatives*, section iv.

[2] *Report on the Strikes and Lockouts of 1889*, C–6176, 1890, p. 113.

[3] The campaign for limiting boy-labour was further stimulated by the extension of union organization to the 'clickers', who were seeking a defence against the breakdown of apprenticeship in their department. Their inclusion in 1890 was the reason for the change of title to the National Union of Boot and Shoe Operatives. [4] See p. 25.

resigned, as did Leicester's executive member;[1] and in 1894 five North-ampton officials resigned in seven months.[2]

Though they acquired a considerable following in Leicester, London, and Bristol, and won a seat on the executive, the militants nevertheless failed to capture control of the union; but they were able to exploit the feelings of the rank and file in order to influence its policy. Faced with this menace, the local employers' associations formed a national federation in 1890,[3] and the union leaders responded by pressing for national nego-tiation on the major issues in dispute. The federation tried to resist, but in 1892, when the union threatened to strike, they agreed to national negotiation on the claim for a limitation of boy labour and various other questions, with provision for reference to an umpire in the event of any disagreement. Disagreement there was, and the umpire, Sir Henry James,[4] awarded a limitation of one boy to every three men.

The conference in 1892 also drew up *Rules for the Prevention of Strikes and Lockouts*, which consolidated the existing pattern of local boards of conciliation and arbitration, made good any gaps, and prescribed a national conference at least once a year. Without exception, all disputes were to be settled through this machinery, and their acceptance of the *Rules* may be seen in part as an attempt by the employers to bolster up the authority of the more moderate among the union leaders. Unofficial strikes had increased, and resistance by the branches to the new techniques of pro-duction was becoming more open, despite the anxiety of national leaders to play it down.

Some stoppages were of considerable importance. In London, for example, 10,000 operatives struck in 1890 for the abolition of outwork, winning a success which lasted, however, only until bad trade returned. In Leicester 3,000 struck in 1892 to achieve the same object and thereafter managed for the most part to hold their gains. In Leicestershire 4,500 came out for certain 'extras' on their piece-price list. The dispute went to arbitration, the award going in the men's favour. At Bristol, also in 1892, there was another mass lock-out, this time of 15,000 men, when workers objected to the employers' interpretation of an award by the local board. This, too, went to arbitration and was won by the union.[5]

Despite his ability and personal influence, the secretary, William In-skip,[6] was unable to hold back his members, mainly because of the absence

---

[1] Fox, op. cit., pp. 168–70.   [2] Ibid., p. 211.

[3] Some important centres, for example Norwich, held aloof.

[4] James, Sir Henry, P.C., Q.C., later Lord James of Hereford (1828–1911). Liberal and Liberal Unionist M.P., 1869–95. Attorney-General, 1873–4 and 1880–5; Chancellor of Duchy of Lancaster, 1895–1902. Chairman of Conciliation Board of English Federated Coal-mining Area,1898–1909.   [5] *Report on the Strikes and Lockouts of 1892*, C–7403, 1894, p. 85.

[6] Inskip, William (1851–99). Treasurer, National Union of Operative Boot and Shoe Rivetters and Finishers, later National Union of Boot and Shoe Operatives, 1880–6; general secretary, 1886–99. Parliamentary Committee, Trades Union Congress, 1887–99.

of any constitutional means of restraining the large branches which had their own funds and full-time officers. After two years of continued conflict, which destroyed several of the local boards,[1] the employers decided to take a sterner line. The immediate reason for their decision was a sudden jump in the volume of imports from the United States, which rose by twelve times in 1894. As early as 1887 the principal trade journal was saying that 'the rapid development of the import of foreign boots and shoes continues to give cause of serious apprehension'. In 1891 a series of articles emphasized the superiority of American productive methods and warned that failure to imitate them would create 'an enormous foreign competition'. Three years later the 'American Invasion', as the industry was later to call it, had begun.[2]

The employers' federation now presented the union with its demands. There was to be a standstill on wages for two years, a free hand for employers over machinery and the organization of production, and the abandonment by workers of all restriction of output. Use of the local boards was to be limited to disputes arising from the application of existing piece-price lists and day rates, and national bargaining was to be abolished. Even the most moderate of union leaders could not consider accepting such terms, and a few months later, early in 1895, a strike in Northampton gave the employers the opportunity for which they had been waiting. A general lock-out was declared in all the federated centres which involved about 46,000 workers and lasted for over five weeks.

The dispute, which attracted nation-wide attention, bore a number of similarities to the engineering lock-out which was to follow two years later. The cause was essentially the same—the workers' resistance to technical change. The employers' federation, like its engineering counterpart, put strong pressure on firms reluctant to join in the fight, even threatening to have orders withdrawn.[3] Like the engineering employers, they made great play with socialism as a major factor in precipitating the crisis. 'The struggle is not with the men', said one prominent London manufacturer, 'or with Trade Unionism as such, but . . . against the pernicious and most outrageous doctrines that are being disseminated by the extreme Socialistic party . . . that section has managed to capture and lead the Executive at Leicester.'[4]

After rejecting many outside offers of mediation, the federation was finally persuaded by the Permanent Secretary of the Board of Trade, Sir Courtenay Boyle, to accept a settlement with the union, which was by now financially weakened. The proposed standstill on wages was dropped, but

---

[1] The Webbs seem to have supposed that it was the bargaining machinery itself which caused the trouble. 'The boards have been the cause of endless friction, discontent, and waste of energy among workmen and employers alike' (*Industrial Democracy*, p. 187). They had worked smoothly enough, however, until overtaken by the conflict over machinery and other aspects of productive organization.   [2] Fox, op. cit., pp. 208–9.   [3] Ibid., p. 227.   [4] Ibid., p. 228.

otherwise the agreement gave the employers most of what they wanted. The jurisdiction of the local boards was strictly limited to exclude all the issues on which the branches had been challenging the employers, including the manning of machinery, productive organization, discipline, and hiring and firing. Such conditions of employment as were not excluded were left, along with wages, to be regulated by the boards. In addition, a guarantee fund was established to penalize any breach of the agreement, thus forcing the union to exercise greater control over local strikes. Each side paid £1,000 into the fund, and an umpire was to decide when a breach had occurred and to impose an appropriate fine.

On the eve of the lock-out in 1895 the union had reached a membership of 44,000, but by 1900 this had fallen to 28,000. The outcome of the dispute was only one of the causes of decline. Mechanization continued apace, and young workers were substituted for old; there were several years of poor trade; an eight-months' strike at Norwich in 1897 ended in failure; and in 1899 the London clickers seceded. Thus at the end of the nineties there was little reason to forecast a future of good relations in the industry. Aided by fortuitous circumstances, the employers had seriously weakened the union and imposed a measure of discipline in the trade;[1] but the union might be expected to challenge them anew in more favourable conditions.

Iron and Steel

The background to the development of industrial relations in iron and steel was the continued change-over from iron to steel. From 2,800,000 tons in 1882 the production of wrought-iron had fallen to an annual average of one million tons by the first decade of the twentieth century, whereas steel of all types rose from two million tons in 1885 to nearly five millions in 1901. Over the same period the output of Siemens 'acid' steel alone soared from 600,000 tons to nearly three millions.[2] The response of the leaders of the Associated Iron and Steel Workers, the ironworkers' union, was to cling more passionately than ever to their established system of regional conciliation boards determining wages according to sliding scales.[3] Amid the stresses and strains of a contracting industry, they proved able to preserve both the system and their own authority.

The union itself still lacked any formal status on the boards. The employers were convinced that formal recognition would make it impossible to resist the claims of craft societies involved in the iron trade;

[1] During 1895 and 1896 there had been some talk within the federation of setting up a free labour association, and a committee had been appointed to draw up a scheme. Nothing came of it, however (Fox, op. cit., pp. 236, 242).

[2] Clapham, vol. ii, p. 58, and vol. iii, pp. 147, 150.

[3] See p. 21. and also the evidence of William Aucott, the president, and Edward Trow, the secretary, before the Royal Commission on Labour (C–6795–IV, 1892).

and they feared that if representatives of the fitters, bricklayers, and others came on to the boards their divergent interests would threaten the smooth working of the whole system. Edward Trow and his colleagues, confident in their ability to control the operatives' side through the union's domination of the works, chose not to disturb their harmonious relationships with the employers by enforcing a change. Similarly, they remained firmly attached to the principle of the sliding scale.

In 1903 W. J. Ashley explained this attachment—which contrasted sharply with the fierce opposition of the great bulk of the miners—by two considerations. In the first place, sliding scales in coal had always been prejudiced by 'selling ahead'. In times of depression, competition for forward contracts was thought to accentuate reductions in prices and therefore in wages also. In iron and steel, however, forward contracts were not used. According to James Cox, Trow's successor as union secretary, this was mainly because fluctuation in prices of the raw material made them too dangerously speculative. Secondly, the ironmasters were thought to have been more successful in maintaining selling prices than had the coal-owners.[1]

These explanations were accepted both by Cox and by Daniel Jones, the employers' secretary of the Midland Board; but they are not convincing. Both arguments presuppose that the price of iron fluctuated less than that of coal. So far as the exporting coalfields were concerned—and it was in districts such as Northumberland, Durham, and South Wales that selling prices fluctuated most and sliding scales persisted longest—this was not so. Between 1888 and 1890 average pithead prices in Northumberland rose by 74 per cent.; by 1893 they had fallen by 23 per cent. In South Wales and Monmouthshire the average for those classes of coal selected to govern wages rose by 29 per cent. in the first period and fell by 27 per cent. in the second. Over the same periods the 'mean ascertained' price of iron in the North-east rose by 33 per cent. and fell 23 per cent.; in the Midlands, where the figures for 1888 are not available, the fall was 19 per cent.[2]

These differences do not support the hypothesis that selling prices in iron offered a notably more stable basis for wage rates than in coal. Moreover, it was not the experience of the coal industry that relatively stable prices brought acceptance of sliding scales: union opposition was strongest in the central coalfields, which produced for home consumption and where prices fluctuated less than in the North-east and South Wales. In fact, a better explanation is to be found in the attitudes of the leaders and their relations with the rank and file.

There was nothing in the sliding-scale system itself to attract union

[1] Ashley, *The Adjustment of Wages*, pp. 149–50.
[2] *Sixth Abstract of Labour Statistics*, 1898–9, Cd. 119, 1900, p. 90.

leaders, for its intrinsic advantages were obvious only to employers. Iron-masters had been attracted to it, had experienced it, and found it good. They wanted no change. The leaders of the Ironworkers had realized that the employers' acceptance of the union and of joint regulation depended upon their readiness to admit the principle that wage rates should fluctuate in sympathy with selling prices. It is true that this connexion might not be so obvious to the rank and file; but the leaders also appreciated that the whole system of the boards fortified their powers over the members. These rested on three main supports.

In the first place, Trow, the union secretary, was secretary of the North of England Board, and Aucott, the president, was secretary of the Midland Board. These positions provided them with salaries which reduced the need to attend to the whims of their followers.[1] Secondly, the disciplinary powers of the boards were at their disposal and could be turned against troublesome members. A worker refusing to accept a decision of the boards was discharged, and the union joined with his employer in finding a substitute.[2] Thirdly, the union was largely composed of contractors. Their relatively high earnings may have rendered them less sensitive to short-run fluctuations in wages than lower-paid workers, and the fear of losing their positions certainly increased their respect for the boards. The union leaders could rely on senior members such as the head rollers to curb local hot-heads. The contractors in their turn had power over the 'underhands' whom they employed in their teams, and who were admitted to the union only on subordinate terms.

In coal the sliding scale could not secure permanent support from both sides of the industry. In the central coalfields the owners did not require such large and frequent reductions in wages during bad years as did those of the exporting districts. Consequently they had less affection for sliding scales. Some of the unions in what later became the Federated area had turned to them in periods of weakness as the only available means of joint regulation, but this was a counsel of desperate necessity. As their organizations grew stronger, the leaders repudiated the whole philosophy of the inescapable link between wages and prices without meeting much resistance. Owners in the exporting districts, however, were more insistent on the virtues of sliding scales, and Burt of Northumberland and Crawford of Durham had as much reason as Trow and Aucott to see that they could bring better relations and greater security for the union. But the

---

[1] Their independence can be seen in Trow's statement to the Royal Commission on Labour: 'with our decaying trade our board has had a most stupendous task to . . . prevent the employers on the one part . . . or the men on the other . . . trying to take advantage' (C–6795–IV, 1892, Q. 15169).

[2] A 'blue bill' was posted in the works to the effect that the union would not regard the man who took his post as a blackleg (Industrial Council, *Inquiry into Industrial Agreements*, Cd. 6953, 1913, Q. 8820).

miners' leaders did not enjoy the exceptional sanctions possessed by their colleagues in the Ironworkers, and in the end their members forced them to terminate the scales.

Even in iron, sliding scales could not relieve the union leaders of all their problems. Rising prices brought membership from under 4,000 in 1880 to 8,500 in 1890, but in the subsequent depression the total fell to 5,000 by 1895. Trouble was particularly apparent in the Midlands. Though the transfer to steel in the North-east made the Midlands, along with the West of Scotland, the major producer of iron,[1] its board still continued to follow the wage leadership of the North-east, as did the smaller districts.[2] Regulation remained somewhat less stable and effective, however, than in the North-east, and an attempt was made to strengthen it by making membership of the board compulsory on all workers. The North of England Board also adopted the practice[3] and, with economic revival, union membership rose to 8,000 in 1900.

The switch from iron to steel was not a total loss to the Ironworkers, for they retained control of some of the works which changed over; but this only cushioned the union's slow decline. Some works shut down for good; in those which were converted, steel usually required fewer workers; and among the steelworkers they faced the aggressive competition of the British Steel Smelters' Amalgamated Association, a very different type of union from their own.

This difference arose from the contrast between the two systems of organizing production. In both iron and steel the contractors were paid by the ton; but whereas in iron the contractor was the leading man on each process, employing the less-skilled day-wage men, in steel he ran a whole melting shop, which normally contained a number of furnaces each with its complement of leading and subordinate hands, all of whom were paid day wages. In the forges and rolling mills he might contract for one, two, or three mills, each with its team of workers. The steel unions— for this applies also to the Associated Society of Millmen—were at first composed almost entirely of day-wage men with a direct interest in abolishing the contract system. They thus started life with a radical and egalitarian approach which contrasted sharply with the aristocratic conservatism of the Ironworkers.

Their objective was to get rid of the contractor and to be paid directly by the firm on the basis of tonnage rates instead of day rates. This claim met with some sympathy from management, for technical improvements

---

[1] H. G. Roepke, *Movements of the British Iron and Steel Industry, 1720–1951*, 1956, p. 82.
[2] When the Midland sliding scale yielded rates lower than those paid in the North, the Board either manipulated the scale to yield the Northern rates or, if this proved technically difficult, suspended the scale altogether. 'By common consent it had long been admitted that a specified relationship should be maintained . . .' (A. D. Evans, 'An Iron Trade Sliding Scale', *Economic Journal*, Mar. 1909). [3] Webbs, *Industrial Democracy*, p. 211.

did not always bring the anticipated results, and this could be attributed to failure of the contract system to offer an incentive to anyone but the contractor. This factor enabled John Hodge, the secretary of the Steel Smelters, to achieve an early success with the Steel Company of Scotland, the acknowledged leader of Siemens steel production in Scotland, and other firms soon followed.[1] By the mid-nineties the contract system had lost much ground and could be found on a major scale only in the Sheffield area,[2] though 'it was a long time a-dying and succumbed piecemeal'.[3]

But success itself began to alter the character of the union. Since output was rising, the tonnage rates provided steadily increasing earnings.[4] The earnings of melters in particular were high and, since earnings were divided between members of the team according to their status, those of first-hand melters were very high.[5] Fearing that this disparity of income might weaken unity, Hodge developed the idea of replacing the two twelve-hour shifts with three eight-hour shifts. Tonnage rates were to be adjusted so as to share earnings among the three shorter shifts, and to level up the incomes of second and third hands; and the change would also strengthen the demand for labour. Hodge's scheme was approved by the branches, but quietly killed by its opponents on the executive.

One reason why this and other high-handed acts by national leaders aroused no revolt among the membership was the regulation of promotion by seniority which had been one of the earliest preoccupations of the union. Since high earnings depended on promotion, over which the union rapidly achieved effective control, the leaders had a powerful weapon with which to discipline their members. Indeed, in addition to this point of similarity with the older union, Hodge had by now developed a philosophy very like theirs. He believed in collaboration with the employers, and in accepting technical change, 'provided we got a fair share of the plunder'.[6] Stoppages were condemned because they reduced profits, 'consequently, there must be less to divide between capital and labour'.[7]

Where the earlier steelworkers, the Bessemer men, had joined the Iron-workers, their terms of employment were regulated by sliding scales for each individual works, either arranged by the North of England Board or set up on their model. Such scales existed at Eston, Consett, and Jarrow in the North-east, and Barrow in the North-west. Joint committees at works level settled minor disputes.[8] In the Siemens open-hearth section

---

[1] John Hodge, *From Workman's Cottage to Windsor Castle*, 1931, pp. 83–86.

[2] *Royal Commission on Labour*, C–6795–IV, 1892, Qs. 16423–4.

[3] Burn, op. cit., p. 142, footnote.

[4] British Steel Smelters' Amalgamated Association, *Monthly Report*, July 1898.

[5] The average weekly earnings of first hands in thirteen important British works in 1906 were £7. 6s. 0d.; of third hands £3. 11s. 6d. (Burn, op. cit., p. 142, footnote). See also p. 481.

[6] Hodge, op. cit., p. 91.

[7] Ibid., p. 69. In 1891 he suggested an Alliance on the Birmingham model, but nothing came of it.   [8] *Royal Commission on Labour*, C–6795–IV, 1892, Qs. 14855–76, 14922–40.

of the industry, however, contact with the employers was for some years limited to the works level, though Hodge found little difficulty in persuading management to accept his presence alongside deputations of his members.

In 1889 the North-eastern steelmasters met the men's representatives on the question of abolishing Sunday working. One representative of the employers and one workmen's delegate attended from each firm participating in the conference. These district contacts were soon superseded by something akin to industry-wide bargaining when in 1890 a large conference representing the steelmasters of the West of Scotland and the North-east and their men met at Newcastle and negotiated a wage reduction, Hodge putting the men's case. Similar meetings followed later in the year and again in 1891. The union continued to make settlements with individual firms outside the North-east and Scottish districts, but these generally followed the major agreements.

By this time the employers were pressing for a board and a sliding-scale agreement, but Hodge was ready to accept a board only if it embodied formal recognition of the union. By now he led a unified and compact group;[1] the industry was expanding rapidly; and he had obtained direct recognition from the employers. Consequently, he did not have to concede a sliding scale to win their acceptance of the union. The employers, on the other hand, suspected that a board on Hodge's lines would be used by the workers' side to enforce complete union membership, and did not find the prospect appealing.[2] On this point, therefore, negotiations for a board broke down. Meanwhile, at the works level the union was building up a procedure for settling minor disputes. If direct negotiations failed, a committee of two neutral employers and two branch nominees dealt with the matter, selecting an umpire if they failed to agree.

Like the Smelters, the Associated Society of Millmen, which was concentrated in the Scottish Siemens steel industry, was opposed to the contract system. At the beginning of the decade the union was so weak that it sought to amalgamate with the Ironworkers, but this fundamental difference in policy proved insuperable. An approach to the Smelters was contemptuously rejected.[3] By 1893 the union had less than 800 members, and its leaders turned in desperation to the unorganized forges and mills of the Scottish iron trade, taking in both contractors and day-wage workers.

Meanwhile, their weakness had obliged them in 1890 to accept a board covering the Scottish steel-rolling departments which was precisely

[1] Out of 5,000 men employed in the relevant departments in the main centres, the union had recruited about 3,000.

[2] *Royal Commission on Labour*, C-6795-IV, 1892, Qs. 16414-16.

[3] 'A lame man looking for a crutch' was the opinion of one of the Smelters' leaders (*First Triennial Conference Report*, 1894).

similar in constitution to the North of England Manufactured Iron Board. Board control was very imperfect; little more than half the millmen were covered, and the Board was sometimes ignored even by employers who belonged to it.[1] But it did yield some degree of collective regulation.

The Millmen were now obliged to build up regulative machinery for the ironworkers. To some extent the Scottish iron trade followed the leadership of the North of England Board, but this applied only to puddlers.[2] Millmen handling iron were quite unregulated. Yet another board, therefore, was set up in 1897 for the Scottish Manufactured Iron Trade, with about twenty works and 3,000 'operative subscribers'. The fact that the board concerned itself, *inter alia*, with the 'remuneration of underhand puddlers'[3] reflected the Millmen's interest in recruiting them. This broadening of scope expressed itself in a change of name, the union becoming the Amalgamated Steel and Iron Workers, and in an increase of membership to nearly 10,000 by 1900.

Meanwhile Hodge, too, was finding new outlets for expansion. The application of the Gilchrist–Thomas process to the Siemens open-hearth method had permitted the use of phosphoric iron ores, and a small 'basic' steel industry was developing in Lincolnshire, Lancashire, and the Midlands. Hodge negotiated an agreement to cover its workers. Another opportunity arose in the South Wales tinplate trade, which employed about 25,000 workers. The industry was widely scattered and subject to sharp fluctuations, many firms were small, and the employers were at once autocratic and paternalistic. Language formed a barrier between Southeast and South-west Wales; the local and powerful Methodism was generally anti-union; and the leading workers were closer in status and sympathies to the masters than to the other workers.[4]

Nevertheless, a union formed in 1871 maintained an intermittent existence in South-west Wales and had some fleeting success, which culminated in the emergence of the 1874 uniform piece-price list. This had 'governed' the industry in the west, more honoured in the breach than the observance, ever since. Unrecognized and largely ignored by both sides, the union's nominal survival to 1887 rested on a mere handful of devotees.[5] Its final disintegration was hastened by a change in the nature of the product—the substitution in the early and middle eighties of steel for iron as the basis of tinplate. Previously the iron forge, the tinplate rolling mill, and the 'tinhouse' or finishing department were linked together in one factory, but

---

[1] *Royal Commission on Labour*, C–6795–IV, 1892, Qs. 15938–40, 16046–51.

[2] A. Pugh, *Men of Steel*, 1951, p. 226. Everywhere in the manufactured iron trade, puddlers tended to be more unified and vigilant than the millmen, just as the melters were more unified than the millmen in steel (Fox, *Industrial Relations in Birmingham and the Black Country*).

[3] *Report on the Strikes and Lockouts of 1897*, C–9012, 1898, p. 119.

[4] W. E. Minchinton, *The British Tinplate Industry*, 1957, pp. 114–15.

[5] Ibid., p. 118.

now the steelworks making bars for tinplate became separate and distinct units.[1] After 1886 workers in these plants had found a more appropriate and stable home with the Steel Smelters.

The tinplate union's successor, the South Wales, Monmouthshire and Gloucestershire Tinplate Workers' Union, formed in 1887 of millmen and tinhousemen only, brought together the workers of South-east and South-west Wales for the first time. By 1889 it achieved some success, but the McKinley tariff of 1891 hit the trade severely and cyclical depression intensified the damage. Unemployment rose; wage reductions followed which the union was too weak to control; and the output restriction with which the workers tried to meet the falling market was soon broken down by employers seeking to reduce costs by raising output per shift.[2]

Another effect of the McKinley tariff was to create a schism between the millmen and tinhousemen. A trade in untinned sheets developed which, because it did not require tinhouse labour, came under attack by the tinhouse workers.[3] Many millmen, scenting collapse, applied for admission to the Steel Smelters. Hodge, however, wanted full amalgamation. For some years he had been pressing the tinplate leaders to co-operate with him in seeking ways of mutual help.[4] Since imported American tinplate bars threatened the steel trade, Hodge sought control over the tinplate millmen with the object of getting them to refuse to work imported bars.[5]

In 1896 the tinplate employers' organization disbanded, declaring that no agreements were enforceable, and the union collapsed two years later. A number of rival unions at once descended to plunder the corpse. Hodge took in the majority of the millmen; the tinhousemen, determined to go their separate way, turned to Ben Tillett's Dockers. Day-wage and maintenance men joined either the Welsh Artizans' Union or the Gasworkers. The Engineers also recruited a few members.[6] Some of the millmen resisted Hodge's allurements, fearing to be a weak section of a strong union and suspicious of Hodge's motives in seeking control of the tinplate mills.[7] These formed the Tin and Sheet Millmen, led by the secretary of the defunct union. Hodge's repeated efforts to get them to amalgamate were consistently rebuffed.

The task of re-creating machinery for joint regulation was greatly eased by a long period of prosperity in the industry which began in 1899. 'Wages were stabilised . . . and conciliation machinery was set up which brought to an end the guerrilla warfare of the nineties and led to a long period of industrial peace.'[8] The employers re-formed their association and set up

---

[1] J. H. Jones, 'Trade Unions in the Tinplate Industry', *Economic Journal*, June 1909.
[2] Minchinton, op. cit., p. 123.
[3] J. H. Jones, loc. cit. [4] Hodge, op. cit., pp. 128–30.
[5] British Steel Smelters' Amalgamated Association, *Monthly Report*, Oct. 1901.
[6] Minchinton, op. cit., p. 126.
[7] J. H. Jones, loc. cit. [8] Minchinton, op. cit., p. 125.

a conciliation board in collaboration with Hodge, Tillett, the Tin and Sheet Millmen, and the Gasworkers. Tillett and Hodge tried to persuade the employers to use the board as the basis for an Alliance on the Birmingham model, but even in prosperity unity among the employers was not strong enough for that.

South Wales also provided an opportunity for a display of union discipline by Hodge. In the steel plants there he had from the start organized millmen as well as melters because the area was outside the sphere of the Ironworkers. Wide disparities in earnings between works, as well as within them, were causing trouble, and in 1899 Hodge proceeded to negotiate uniform standard rates in the teeth of strong opposition from the top-paid men. When some of them came out on strike Hodge left them to their fate. 'After some months of . . . labour', said an employer later, 'we were enabled to arrive at an arrangement which to a considerable extent gave uniformity of wage rates in the trade.'[1]

These developments did not touch the great integrated coal and steel plants at Dowlais, Ebbw Vale, Tredegar, Cyfartha, and Blaenavon, where sliding scales had been introduced in 1890 to cover all employees, including the maintenance craftsmen. Superficially they resembled those in the North-east and the Midlands, but the workers were organized by a 'company union', the Amalgamated Association of Iron and Steel Workers and Mechanics of South Wales and Monmouthshire, and there was no provision for any kind of appeal outside the board. The policy of the Steel Smelters was to increase their membership so as to take control of the workers' side of the board,[2] and by 1900 they had won some recruits at the Ebbw Vale works.

The blastfurnacemen had fallen behind in union organization. At first the Ironworkers had included them, but as a minority group of a relatively low status their interests tended to be ignored[3] and their isolation was confirmed by technical developments which made the blastfurnace a separate unit in the economic structure of the industry.[4] The Cleveland men had broken away from the Ironworkers in 1878, and set up their own joint regulation machinery in exact replica of the system in wrought-iron, with a board, a sliding scale linking wages with pig-iron prices, and a joint committee for resolving minor disputes.[5] The Cumberland workers, who had their own local association and machinery for joint regulation, joined with the Cleveland Association to form the National Association of Blastfurnacemen. Other districts followed, and by 1892 the union, which was

---

[1] British Steel Smelters' Amalgamated Association, *Monthly Report*, Nov. 1901.

[2] There were some other places where the writ of the union did not run. In 1899–1900 there was a bitter struggle for recognition at the Mossend Works in Scotland, and the management employed Graeme Hunter's Free Labour Association.

[3] J. Owen, *Ironmen*, 1953, pp. 9–10.

[4] Pugh, op. cit., p. 10.   [5] Owen, op. cit., pp. 11–15.

really a federation of largely autonomous local associations, covered Cleveland and Durham, Cumberland, North Lancashire, Nottinghamshire, Derbyshire, North Staffordshire, Shropshire, Lincolnshire, and Scotland, with a total of 7,000 members.

The union's first concern had been to reduce working hours, which were eleven on days and thirteen on nights on alternate weeks, with a twenty-four hour 'long turn' every fortnight.[1] Most North Lancashire works, however, had operated three eight-hour shifts per day since the late seventies.[2] In 1890 the practice was extended to Cumberland with some sacrifice in wages.[3] The task of shortening the working day was made easier for the Cumberland leaders by the fact that their members were on time rates; in Cleveland it was complicated by some men being on tonnage rates and nervous of a sharp fall in earnings.[4] In 1894, however, some Cleveland firms conceded an eight-hour day, and in 1897 the agreement was extended to the whole district.

Outside Cleveland, Cumberland, and North Lancashire the union was relatively weak. In Scotland the ironmasters refused to recognize it, and the workers themselves were divided by nationality and religion, since there were a considerable number of foreigners.[5] An attempt in 1890–1 to get 'time and a half' for the Sunday shift, the general practice in the North of England, involved the men in a strike lasting nearly six months. Defeat greatly weakened the local association, which expired altogether later in the nineties.[6] This loss was balanced by the organization of a few plants in South Wales, and by 1900 the union membership had grown to over 8,000.

In addition to these major unions, there were one or two minor organizations of production workers in iron and steel. Labourers not directly engaged in the productive process were organized, if at all, by such unions as the Gasworkers and the Dockers, and the maintenance workers by the craft societies. The industry also employed a large number of enginemen, firemen, boilermen, and cranemen, who were found in many other industries as well. By the nineties, for example, almost every coalfield had its small district—sometimes colliery—unions of winding enginemen, far too numerous to warrant separate mention. But in addition to these colliery unions and similar specialist groups employed in textile factories, unions were formed for enginemen employed in iron and steelworks together with others from shipyards, docks, public utilities, and large factories.

One of these was the Amalgamated Enginemen, Cranemen, Boilermen and Firemen, formed in 1889. In 1893 this split into two competing unions the National Amalgamated Enginemen and the Northern United

---

[1] Ibid., p. 23.
[2] *Royal Commission on Labour*, C–6795–IV, 1892, Q. 14418.
[3] Ibid., Qs. 14422–6.
[4] Ibid., Q. 14041.
[5] Ibid., Qs. 14451–9.
[6] Owen, op. cit., pp. 18–19.

Enginemen. Both were based in the North-east and extended into most of the northern counties and into Scotland. Bargaining was principally with individual firms, though in the West of Scotland the National Amalgamated was represented on a conciliation board covering the steam, electrical, and hydraulic service of the steel trade. A National Amalgamated publication declared that 'in Scotland we have been accustomed to rise in wages with the price of material [steel] and fall accordingly. In England we have mostly an arrangement to rise and fall in wages with the Amalgamated Society of Engineers.'[1]

Soon other rivals were springing up—principally the National Amalgamated Enginemen, Cranemen and Hammer Drivers, formed in Rotherham in 1895, which also quickly pushed out far beyond its place of origin. In addition to these unions with national aspirations there were a score or more of local unions organizing the same classes of workers. The Gasworkers and Dockers also included them where they could. All three national unions prospered over the decade. By 1900 the North Eastern National Amalgamated Enginemen had nearly 4,000 members, and the Rotherham union over 6,000. By this time they were signing agreements among themselves and with the Gasworkers and Dockers to limit competition for members.

Iron-ore miners were divided between two powerful local unions, one covering Cleveland and North Yorkshire, and the other Cumberland and North Lancashire. By 1900 the Cleveland union included 7,500 out of a total of 9,000 workers, and the Cumberland membership was over 4,000. The Cleveland miners switched from a system of arbitration to a sliding scale in 1879, and abandoned the scale for *ad hoc* negotiations in 1889, though selling prices of pig-iron were still recognized as the major determinant of wages.[2] There was no formally constituted conciliation board, but the close links between both sides of the industry and the owners and miners in the Durham coalfield resulted in the use of similar methods. All issues which could not be settled in the individual mine were referred to a joint committee with provision for an umpire in case of need.

The Penrhyn Dispute

Quarrying, though not in general well organized, provided the bitterest conflict of the whole period. The North Wales Quarrymen's Union, with a peak membership of 7,000 in 1897, had been involved in an intermittent battle with the major local employer, Lord Penrhyn, since 1865. After 1874 a union committee had negotiated with the Penrhyn management concerning the complex piece-rate structure of wages, but in 1885 a new Penrhyn took over[3] and withdrew recognition. The union made a series

[1] National Amalgamated Society of Enginemen, *List of Concessions, 1898 to 1902*, p. 19.

[2] Industrial Council, *Inquiry into Industrial Agreements*, Cd. 6953, 1913, Q. 13218.

[3] It is probable that his attitude was affected both by politics and by religion. He had been

of attempts to regain its position, and in 1896 called out 2,800 of Penrhyn's employees for higher wages and union recognition.

After eight weeks they appealed to the Board of Trade for help under the new Conciliation Act.[1] The Board tried to promote a joint conference, but Penrhyn rejected this 'outside interference with the management of my private affairs'. Sir Courtenay Boyle replied that 'the Board cannot admit that the settlement of a prolonged dispute affecting some thousands of men and their families can be rightly regarded as a matter of private interest only'.[2] But the Board had no powers under this or any other Act to compel Penrhyn to modify his attitude.

Towards the end of the year the quarries were reopened, but the quarrymen stood firm and it was not until August 1897 that a settlement of sorts provided for a return to work, without protection for the union. Thereafter victimization was common, and in 1900 smouldering conflict broke out into another open battle which lasted into the following year with a further display of bitterness and vindictiveness almost unequalled in other disputes. In 1896 this one stoppage of less than 3,000 men lost almost 800,000 working days—in these terms the largest strike of the year. The stoppage in 1900 accounted for another half million and was the second largest strike that year.

No other dispute of the nineties brought into sharper focus the opposing attitudes in the country towards trade unionism, collective bargaining, and the state's role in industrial relations. The unions rallied to the support of the quarrymen, seeing Penrhyn as the spearhead of the employers' counter-attack.[3] Extremists among the employers cheered Penrhyn's refusal to recognize the union or to permit the Board of Trade to intervene.[4] The inability of the Board to find a solution demonstrated that the state, while committed to approval of the collective regulation of industrial relations, was committed to the encouragement of a *voluntary* system only.

Defending the Board's intervention, C. T. Ritchie, its Conservative President, told the House of Commons that its principal object had been to persuade the parties to settle the dispute themselves. The Liberal opposition doubted whether this was enough:

turned out of his Caernarvonshire seat in 1868 by a Liberal, and was beaten again in 1880; and there was a strong local movement for disestablishment (W. J. Parry, *The Penrhyn Lockout*, 1901, pp. 35–36).

[1] See p. 263. [2] Parry, op. cit., p. 122.

[3] In 1903 trade unions and other sympathizers contributed towards establishing the North Wales Quarries Ltd. to employ the Penrhyn strikers. It began under the chairmanship of Richard Bell, who set up a conciliation board with the employees (*Report on the Strikes and Lockouts of 1904*, Cd. 2631, 1905, p. 42). Hodge took over in 1905. From 1909 to 1913 the Steel Smelters carried on the business as sole proprietor (Pugh, op. cit., p. 180).

[4] The Board's efforts at peacemaking had been found irksome by the employers in other disputes also. See pp. 81, 201.

You have in the Board of Trade [said Sir William Harcourt] a very useful instrument of conciliation. Are you going to destroy it by encouraging the line that Lord Penrhyn has taken? . . . Are you going to make war on the trade unions? Are you going to . . . make war upon that . . . method of conciliation by which it is competent for trade unions to appoint representative men to deal with their employers? If so, you are preparing for yourselves a very evil future.[1]

[1] *Hansard*, 29 Jan. 1897, cols. 691–760.

6

Parliamentary Action and the
Trades Union Congress

Government Employees

THE unions described in the previous four chapters relied primarily upon industrial action, in the form either of unilateral control by craft methods or of joint regulation by collective bargaining; but there were others for whom political action came first. Prominent among them were the organizations of government employees over whose wages and conditions Parliament had final authority. Since the departments refused to recognize their unions and responded reluctantly to departmental petitions of the traditional type, the most effective means of redress was found to lie in a direct approach to the House of Commons.

This was the experience of those who worked for the largest employer, the Post Office, which also had the most conspicuous problems. The first stable organization of postal employees was formed by the telegraphists in 1881, and the second by the provincial sorting clerks in 1887. The sorting clerks had been generously treated in the scales of pay introduced in 1881 by the Liberal Postmaster General, Henry Fawcett, the blind economist; but at the end of the decade, J. H. Williams, one of the London sorters who had once been an aristocracy among postal workers, decided that he and his colleagues were being denied further concessions intended by Fawcett. Williams and W. E. Clery therefore formed the Fawcett Association[1] to agitate for the London sorters' rights. Raikes,[2] the Conservative Postmaster General, agreed to meet them, and to refer any disputed points to a departmental committee. In March 1890 the committee found against the sorters on every issue which they had raised, whereupon the Association drew up a list of direct claims and a deputation presented them to Raikes.

Meanwhile the London postmen had been affected by the 'new unionism'. In September 1889, at a meeting in Clerkenwell, the Dockers, the Coal Porters and the Gasworkers supported the formation of a General

---

[1] The Association was unique among British trade unions in using the name of an individual in its title.

[2] H. C. Raikes (1838–91), who had been Postmaster General since 1886, was a Tory Democrat. He had been prominent in all attempts to build up working-class support for Conservatism, and a prime mover in the formation of the National Union of Conservative and Constitutional Associations in 1867.

Postmen's Union,[1] whose leaders were Tom Dredge, a postman dismissed for calling a departmental meeting without permission, and the ubiquitous J. L. Mahon, an associate of H. H. Champion.[2] Their programme demanded increased wages, an eight-hour day, overtime at time and a half, abolition of the rule prohibiting postal servants from holding meetings in public, and recognition of the union. In contrast to the Fawcett Association, the new union decided to rely on the leadership of outsiders, who would not be subject to Post Office discipline, and to make use of the strike weapon. Accordingly Mahon was elected secretary, and the committee included both outsiders and postmen in an uneasy alliance.

Tension mounted as the Postmen drew attention to their case by public meetings, and the department suspended or fined a number of those known to have taken part. In July 1890 the union determined to fight the introduction of new staff who were apparently being engaged as an insurance against any emergency. Clery made it plain that the Fawcett Association would not support a strike; but Mahon, under pressure from his members at Mount Pleasant, threatened the Post Office with a stoppage on 10 July unless the 'blacklegs' were dismissed. The department refused to have any dealings with him as an outsider, and prompt disciplinary action turned the strike into a rout. Only in the East End did the men come out in any numbers. Further suspensions and dismissals brought the total to 435,[3] and the union collapsed.

Since the spring Raikes had been working on a general review of wages and conditions in the Post Office. By the end of the year he was able to publish proposals for telegraphists, London and provincial sorting clerks, and his suggestions for postmen followed in 1891. Considerable concessions were made to each group. The whole service received longer holidays and full pay during sick leave. There were increases in salary for certain grades, and in future postmen were to be paid for Sunday work and for overtime.[4] No group was satisfied with the Raikes scheme, however, and before long the Fawcett Association presented a new petition to Sir James Fergusson, a martinet who had succeeded Raikes on his death in August 1891. When their claims were twice rejected it was clear the department would make no further concessions.

---

[1] H. G. Swift, *A History of the Postal Agitation*, 1929 edition, pp. 199–200.

[2] A member of the Social Democratic Federation, the Socialist League, and later of the Independent Labour Party, Mahon had founded his own Labour Union at nearby Hoxton in 1888 to promote Champion's policies (Clayton, op. cit., pp. 67–68).

[3] After personally investigating their cases, Raikes reinstated fifty, and subsequent pressure from Members of Parliament (especially George Howell) led to further reinstatements.

Raikes also stopped the promotion of eight Cardiff sorters, and transferred them to other offices, for communicating their grievances to the press, contending that 'it was not intended as a punishment, and was ultimately for the men's own good' (Swift, op. cit., p. 220).

[4] It had previously been held that if postmen were paid for overtime they would spread out their work.

Clery therefore persuaded the Association to turn its attention to the House of Commons, whereupon Williams, who was opposed to parliamentary action, resigned the chairmanship. Clery replaced him and W. B. Cheesman succeeded Clery as secretary. Since their policy was to demand pledges at the 1892 election, Fergusson laid down that it 'would be improper for [Post Office employees], whether in combination or otherwise, to extract promises from candidates . . . with reference to their pay and position'.[1] Clery and Cheesman evolved a form of words which appeared to avoid any such reference; but Fergusson found time after the election, and before the government resigned, to dismiss the two officers, brushing aside their defence that because the Association had directed their action they were no more guilty than any other members. Arnold Morley,[2] the new Liberal Postmaster General, refused to reinstate them, and to meet deputations which included them, on the grounds that they were no longer Post Office employees.

A new organization for postmen, the Postmen's Federation, had been established in 1891. This time they did not seek outside leadership, and a London postman, C. Churchfield, became secretary. Under his guidance the union proceeded moderately and circumspectly, reaping its reward in a rapid growth both in London and in the provinces. Along with the Telegraphists and the two unions of sorting clerks, the Federation concentrated on parliamentary action. The lead continued to be taken by the Fawcett Association but on many issues the four unions worked together, and in 1898 they formed a National Joint Committee of Postal and Telegraph Associations. Calling the London Trades Council and the Trades Union Congress to their aid,[3] they sought the establishment of a parliamentary inquiry through their friends in the House, who varied the attack from time to time by demanding reinstatement for Clery and Cheesman.

In this campaign, which began with the session of 1893, the postal workers secured the assistance of a wide range of Members of Parliament. They could rely on one Conservative, Sir Alfred Rollit, chairman of the London Conciliation Board[4] and a well-known enthusiast for improving industrial relations. Among the Liberals were John Morley, a cabinet

---

[1] *Post Office Circular*, 17 June 1892, quoted in Swift, op. cit., p. 253.

[2] Arnold Morley (1849–1916) was a son of the Radical philanthropist, Samuel Morley, and Liberal chief whip from 1886 to 1892. He shared Schnadhorst's views on the need for Liberal attention to working-class demands and labour representation (see p. 279).

[3] At the 1893 Trades Union Congress, Clery complained of neglect by the labour Members, 'many of [whom] had supposed the civil servants to be a snobbish body'. With justification, Burns and Fenwick denied the charge, Fenwick saying that 'instead of coming to the Labour Members, Mr. Clery had passed them by, and then denounced them on platforms for dereliction of duty. (Loud applause).' The complaint may, however, have helped to stimulate activity. *Hansard* shows that, as the nineties progressed, postal issues were concentrated more and more in the hands of labour Members, notably Woods and Steadman.

[4] See p. 288, footnote 5.

minister between 1892 and 1895; two professional leftists, C. A. V. Conybeare, an associate of Cunninghame Graham, and James Rowlands of the Metropolitan Radical Federation; E. H. Pickersgill, an old postal employee and one of the Members for Bethnal Green; and Hudson Kearley,[1] Member for Devonport and a strong advocate for dockyard workers. Among the Lib-Labs were the Londoners, Cremer, Howell, and Steadman,[2] who was described as 'the most persistent and the most pushful';[3] and the successive secretaries of the Parliamentary Committee of the Trades Union Congress, Fenwick and Woods.

In February 1895 Woods drew attention to the grievances of postal servants by moving an amendment to the Address which he failed to carry by only eight votes, and in May, when Kearley moved for a parliamentary inquiry, Arnold Morley agreed to appoint a departmental committee. Its chairman was the Lord Privy Seal, Lord Tweedmouth, but the other members were all secretaries of government departments with the exception of Llewellyn Smith,[4] who was Commissioner for Labour at the Board of Trade. The postal unions were discouraged by the composition of the committee, and still more by its proceedings. From the start Tweedmouth ruled questions of civil rights and reinstatement to be out of order; the Secretary of the Post Office, Spencer Walpole, was a member of the committee and played a large part in the cross-examination of witnesses; and other departmental officials were present at the hearings.

The Tweedmouth report, which appeared in March 1897, proposed a number of improvements in conditions of work, but refused to consider the question of pensions, which had been pressed by the unions; recommended only meagre increases in pay; and acquitted the department of imposing excessive punishments for breaches of Post Office rules. Continued agitation, however, led in July 1897 to the Norfolk–Hanbury conference,[5] which was attended by the main parliamentary advocates of the unions and was followed by some additional concessions early in 1898. The unions were not satisfied and Steadman moved an amendment to the Address in February 1899, but it was too soon to begin the battle again.

The early struggles of the postal unions reveal how many different rights

[1] Hudson Kearley (1856–1934), a successful tea merchant of humble origins, first entered the House in 1892. Later, as Lord Devonport and chairman of the Port of London Authority, he was to come into bitter conflict with the dockers' unions.

[2] Steadman, W. C. (1851–1911). General secretary, Barge Builders' Union, 1879–1908. Parliamentary Committee, Trades Union Congress, 1899–1911; secretary, 1905–11. M.P., 1898–1900, 1906–10.

[3] Swift, op. cit., p. 298.

[4] Smith, Sir Hubert Llewellyn (1864–1945). Commissioner of Labour, Board of Trade, 1893–1903. Controller-General, Commercial, Labour and Statistical Department, Board of Trade, 1903–7. Permanent Secretary, Board of Trade, 1907–19. Chief Economic Adviser to the Government, 1919–27.

[5] The Duke of Norfolk was now Postmaster General and R. W. Hanbury was Secretary to the Treasury.

are included in the deceptively simple term 'recognition'. In private industry everything implied by recognition may be conceded at once; in the Post Office the process had several stages and each was dragged out over several years. In 1873, for example, a charge of conspiracy was in preparation against the leaders of a temporary postmen's union;[1] but no legal action was taken against later associations, and by 1889 it was accepted that 'civil servants had a right to combine for mutual benefit'.[2] In 1881 Fawcett had been the first Postmaster General to meet representatives of a union—the Telegraphists—and he also allowed departmental meetings to be held on application provided they were on Post Office premises. Raikes raised the ban on public meetings in 1890, in the first instance to permit the foundation meeting of the Fawcett Association. But official reporters were still sent to meetings held off the premises, and they even attended annual conferences.

After the return of the Liberals, this last restriction on freedom of assembly was removed, the government's decision being announced by Gladstone himself.[3] According to the Fabians, however, Arnold Morley 'reinstated only some, not all, of the dismissed trade unionist postmen and telegraphists, thereby effectually maintaining the old official intimidation of Trade Unionism', even after he had admitted 'the right of his staff to hold meetings without official spies'.[4] In 1894, moreover, several delegates to the annual conference of the Postmen's Federation were at first refused leave of absence. When the union complained, Spencer Walpole replied that 'under the circumstances' leave had been granted.[5]

Despite the grudging attitude of officialdom, these changes in Post Office regulations gave its employees scope to build up strong organizations, and the decision of the Tweedmouth Committee to hear only those witnesses who represented associations of postal servants aided recruitment and encouraged the formation of new societies representing sub-postmasters and other special groups. The department, however, still refused to meet or correspond with union officers who were not postal servants, and held out against any kind of collective bargaining. In 1899 Norfolk agreed to receive representations from the unions so long as they were made through the usual channels and by officers directly concerned. A year later his successor, Lord Londonderry, restricted these to issues

---

[1] Swift, op. cit., pp. 74–77.   [2] Ibid., p. 181.

[3] Gladstone also emphasized that 'as regards the Parliamentary franchise, there can be no question that its exercise is absolutely free from external interference' by the department (*Hansard*, 28 Aug. 1893, col. 1218).

[4] 'To Your Tents, O Israel!', *Fortnightly Review*, Nov. 1893, reprinted in Fabian Tract 49, *A Plan of Campaign for Labor*, 1894, p. 4. The most important cases were those of Clery and Cheesman.

[5] *The Postmen's Case for Enquiry, A Verbatim Report of Evidence Given Before Lord Tweedmouth and the Committee by the Representatives of the Postmen's Federation*, published by authority of the Federation for private sale, p. 23.

affecting a whole class of employees, thus excluding individual grievances; and there was no question of collective agreements in decisions concerning pay or conditions.

Excluded from responsibility, the unions were at least free to condemn every concession as inadequate, and to agitate at once for something better. They naturally tried to exploit their electoral opportunities. In 1892 John Morley's majority of 1,539 at Newcastle was said to be partly due to 'five hundred Civil Service voters', for whose demands he had promised support;[1] and in the victory of their champion Steadman by 20 votes at the Stepney by-election of 1898, postal workers may have been 'the turning balance'.[2] But such opportunities were rare. If most of their parliamentary spokesmen sat for metropolitan constituencies, this is to be explained by the strength of London Radicalism rather than the concentration of postal workers in the area. The political influence of the unions rested mainly on their ability to find sympathizers in the House. They could rely on labour Members to handle specific grievances and for support on broader issues like recognition; and the civil and political rights of the working man was an old cause of left-wing Liberalism.

To make parliamentary action effective the unions also sought to build up public sympathy through the press. Reporters were smuggled into meetings on Post Office premises, and Clery, already well known as a journalist, made full use of the freedom which resulted from his dismissal. Little more was heard of industrial action after the Postmen's strike; but the Telegraphists took ballots in favour of a ban on overtime in order to bring pressure to bear on Raikes in 1890 and again on Norfolk in 1897. Though not carried out, these threats may have had some effect, for overtime was said to constitute '30 per cent. on the day's ordinary work' at the Central Telegraph Office.[3]

The postal unions grew continuously throughout the decade. By 1900 the Postal Telegraph Clerks had 5,000 members; the provincial Postal Clerks and the Fawcett Association more than 3,000 each; and the Postmen's Federation over 23,000. Among minor organizations the most important was the Engineering and Stores Association. Altogether there were over 35,000 trade unionists among rather more than 167,000 postal workers, of whom 76,000 were unestablished.[4] Because of the relative security of their employment, the postal unions continued to grow between 1893 and 1896 when others were declining. Then, after the appearance of the disappointing Tweedmouth report, the rate of growth fell off just as unions in private industry began to gather strength with economic recovery.

Outside the Post Office, government manual employees were poorly

---

[1] Swift, op. cit., p. 261.   [2] Ibid., p. 298.
[3] Ibid., p. 224.   [4] *Annual Report of the Postmaster General*, Cd. 333, 1900, p. 18.

organized. The shipbuilding and engineering unions had some members in the dockyards and ordnance factories, and there were many small local dockyard unions; but they did not achieve official recognition, still less any form of collective bargaining. They did, however, help to win increases in pay and reductions in working hours by political action. In 1890, as part of the general campaign for the eight-hour day,[1] dockyard workers at Plymouth formed a Government Employees Eight Hours Committee, and similar bodies were set up in other centres. Heads of departments received identical petitions; mass meetings were held throughout the country on the same day; and resolutions were sent to Members of Parliament and the government. The agitation was directed by the Plymouth committee, in which members of the Amalgamated Society of Engineers took a leading part, while their national headquarters organized deputations to the House of Commons.[2]

Wider backing was secured in 1892 when the Trades Union Congress passed a resolution demanding union rates for employees of the government or government contractors, and an eight-hour day for all 'Government and municipal workpeople'.[3] Even more important, however, was support from outside the trade union movement. The grievances of government employees were publicized in the press and before the Royal Commission on Labour, for example, by Sidney Webb;[4] and they found an effective parliamentary champion in the leading Conservative spokesman on industrial relations, Sir John Gorst,[5] who was one of the most active members of the Royal Commission and had previously represented the dockyard town of Chatham.

On 6 March 1893 Gorst moved that 'no person should, in Her Majesty's Naval establishments, be engaged at wages insufficient for a proper maintenance, and that the conditions of labour as regards hours, wages, insurance against accident, provision for old age, etc. should be such as to afford an example to private employers throughout the country'.[6] This resolution was carried with the full approval of the government; the Secretary for War, Campbell-Bannerman, agreeing that they 'should show themselves to be amongst the best employers'. Much had been made

---

[1] See p. 292.

[2] *Workman's Times*, 22 July 1893, 26 Aug. 1893, and 27 Jan. 1894; and Amalgamated Society of Engineers, *Quarterly Report*, June 1893.

[3] The resolution specifically condemned 'Government officials at Woolwich Arsenal and elsewhere in employing workpeople at less than the current rate for the district'.

[4] *Royal Commission on Labour*, C–7063–1, 1893, Qs. 3779–81.

[5] J. E. Gorst (1835–1916) had served most effectively as agent for the Conservative Party in 1870–7 and 1880–2, before quarrelling with the leadership. Both as agent and as a member of the Fourth Party, Gorst showed the usual Tory Democrat concern for the working classes, together with an unusual knowledge of their problems. He was also an excellent debater, and just the man to embarrass the Liberals over their record on labour questions.

[6] *Hansard*, cols. 1109–80.

of the need to set such an example to private industry at the 1892 election, and the Liberals could not afford to be outflanked by the Conservatives now that Gorst had taken the initiative.

By the autumn of 1893 the Fabians, who along with other Radicals regarded this issue as a test of the Liberals' good faith towards the working classes, had lost patience. The famous article by Sidney Webb and Bernard Shaw, 'To your tents, O Israel!', justified their proposal for an independent party based on the unions by a detailed indictment of the government's failure to meet the grievances of its employees. But this verdict, published in November, was perhaps too hasty. Dockyard and ordnance factory workers, who generally earned less than those in comparable jobs in private industry, had already received wage increases during the year. Preparations to introduce the eight-hour day at Woolwich Arsenal were begun only a few weeks after Gorst's motion in the Commons, and the reduction took effect early in 1894. Over the next two years it was extended to the remaining ordnance factories, the dockyards, and two Post Office telegraph factories.

In addition to his concern for 'the public sentiment', Campbell-Bannerman hoped that better conditions would lead to better value for public money. Woodall, the Financial Secretary to the War Office, assured his constituents that 'as a man of business . . . he had not recommended these important changes until he had satisfied himself that they could be carried out not only with benefit to the workmen, but with advantage and even perhaps some saving to the nation'.[1] Nor need this be dismissed as an empty assurance. Successive Factory Acts had shown that reductions in the working day were rarely as costly as expected, and Joseph Chamberlain asserted that in his own experience, 'with such periods of labour as twelve hours, ten hours, and even nine hours . . . very considerable reductions may be made without any insuperable reduction in production'.[2]

The nineties also saw the first permanent organizations among clerical and professional civil servants. A Second Division Clerks' Association, set up in 1890, was 'blocked within the departments from appealing directly to the Treasury or Parliament'.[3] Separate approaches had to be made to each department, but no individual department was competent to take action on grades employed by more than one department. The union therefore 'fell into disuse', although some branches survived. In January 1891 over 200 second division clerks in the Post Office Savings Bank tried to draw attention to their grievances by refusing to work overtime; but their organization was smashed by dismissals, transfers, and compulsory retirements.[4] For the most part, less militant tactics were adopted. The

---

[1] Quoted in Rae, op. cit., p. 67.
[2] Speaking on the miners' Eight Hours Bill (*Hansard*, 23 Mar. 1892, col. 1587).
[3] R. V. Humphreys, *Clerical Unions in the Civil Service*, 1958, p. 42.   [4] Ibid., pp. 44–45.

Tax Clerks' Association, formed in 1892, found two Members of Parliament to take up their case, and in 1900 secured increased pay and the withdrawal of the surveyor's power to dismiss clerks.[1] Other associations were set up for customs watchers, customs officers, and even for surveyors themselves.

Teachers and Other White-collar Workers

Unions for clerical workers in private employment were even weaker and more ineffective than those of government employees. The National Union of Clerks, later to become the Clerical and Administrative Workers' Union, had a mere 82 members in 1900, though life assurance agents, with nearly 4,000 in five societies, had done better. This weakness has been explained by the 'counting-house' environment of nineteenth-century clerks, which was 'conducive to their estrangement from the mass of working men and to their identification with the entrepreneurial and professional classes'. Their dress and manners aped those of the 'master class, with whom they worked in a close and personal relationship . . . often . . . entrusted with confidential matters and delegated authority over other employees'. In addition they were 'socially isolated from one another and dependent on the goodwill of particular employers'.[2]

Trade unionism had, however, made greater headway among other groups of white-collar workers, especially the teachers, whose National Union of Elementary Teachers was already a powerful organization.[3] The annual review of the conditions governing grants to schools conducted by the Education Committee of the Privy Council gave the union ample opportunity for consultation with the Secretary of the Committee and his staff, and for pressure on Members of Parliament. In 1884 consultation had received a set-back when Sandford's successor as Secretary, Patric Cumin,[4] decided to ignore the union. But its officers still had access to the Vice-president of the Council, who acted as the parliamentary spokesman, and in 1890 Cumin was succeeded by Sir George Kekewich, who later wrote that 'the first thing to be done was to enter into direct relations with the teachers by recognising their Union and its officers. ... From that day until I finally left office, my relations with the teachers constantly grew more cordial and intimate.'[5]

From its foundation the union had paid much attention to political action. In 1891 the Teachers pursued an old objective by supporting a

---

[1] Ibid., p. 39.   [2] David Lockwood, *The Blackcoated Worker*, 1958, pp. 34–35.

[3] The title was changed to National Union of Teachers in 1889 because 'elementary' appeared too restrictive.

[4] The responsibility for Cumin's appointment lay with a man who was normally a good friend to trade unionism, A. J. Mundella, Vice-president of the Council from 1880 to 1885 (W. H. G. Armytage, *A. J. Mundella*, 1951, pp. 222–3).

[5] *The Education Department and After*, 1920, pp. 62–66, quoted in Tropp, op. cit., p. 138.

bill for a contributory pension scheme promoted by the London School Board, and a year later a Select Committee reported in favour of a general scheme. 'After a monster campaign by the N.U.T.',[1] this was approved without a division in February 1893, though legislation did not follow until 1898. By this time the union had its own representatives in the House. Previous attempts had failed through lack of funds and because of controversy between Liberals and Conservatives within the union. In 1888, however, 1s. was added to the annual subscription to finance representation, and James Yoxall[2] was an unsuccessful candidate at the general election of 1892, the year in which he became secretary. In 1895 Yoxall was returned as a Liberal for Nottingham North, and Ernest Gray, a vice-president, as a Conservative for West Ham North. In 1900 they were joined by T. J. Macnamara,[3] editor of the *Schoolmaster*, and practically a Lib-Lab.

Many of the Teachers' aims were shared by all supporters of educational reform, a cause which received powerful encouragement in 1888 from the publication of both the Majority and Minority Reports of the Royal Commission presided over by Viscount Cross. In addition, two powerful and progressive Vice-presidents were in charge of the department from 1892 onwards. The Liberal A. H. D. Acland was a member of the Cabinet from 1892 to 1895. Held in high regard by both Gladstone and Rosebery, he was thought to deserve 'special credit for keeping in touch with the labour people and their mind'.[4] Acland was succeeded by Gorst, who held office under Salisbury until 1902. Though not in the Cabinet and often at odds with his colleagues, Gorst generally determined Conservative policy on education, and his cordial relations with the teachers led the *Cotton Factory Times* to describe him as the 'Travelling Tinker to the schoolmasters' union'.[5]

Thus circumstances in the nineties were unusually favourable for agitation by the Teachers. With their approval, both Acland in 1893 and Gorst in 1899 raised the school-leaving age. Two other reforms also gave special pleasure to the union: Acland's admission of certificated teachers to the inspectorate in 1893,[6] and his abolition in 1895 of the system of 'payment by results' which dated back to the unpopular Code of 1862. In 1898 Gorst earned the gratitude of certificated teachers by overcoming

[1] Tropp, op. cit., p. 125.

[2] Yoxall, Sir James (1857–1925). President, National Union of Teachers, 1891–2; general secretary, 1892–1924. Liberal M.P., 1895–1918.

[3] Macnamara, T. J., P.C. (1861–1931). President, National Union of Teachers, 1896–1907. Liberal M.P., 1900–24. Parliamentary Secretary to Local Government Board, 1907–8. Parliamentary and Financial Secretary to the Admiralty, 1908–20. Minister of Labour, 1920–2.

[4] John Morley, *Recollections*, vol. i, 1917, p. 324.   [5] 27 Apr. 1900.

[6] Teachers were already eligible for posts as assistant inspectors and sub-inspectors. In 1893 the first sub-inspector was promoted to the inspectorate, and by 1902 six ex-elementary teachers were H.M.I.s.

the difficulties which had delayed the introduction of a pension scheme. A year later he created the Board of Education, which took over all the government's responsibilities in this sphere, and before leaving office he had paved the way for the remodelling of secondary education in 1902.

By 1895, at 1·88 millions, the number of children in board schools was rapidly catching up with the total of 2·45 millions in voluntary schools, and the union had good reason to take a close interest in elections to school boards. After the decision in 1893 by a 'Moderate' (or Conservative) majority on the London School Board to impose religious tests for teachers, over 3,000 refused to comply, and the Moderate majority was reduced in the election of 1894. The union also gave support to teachers standing at school-board elections, and 'there were instances when the whole force of the union was concentrated on the "capture" of a school board', by the return of 'an unjustly dismissed teacher' and his, or her, supporters.[1]

In dealing with school managements, the Teachers used methods akin to the techniques of craft control. They tried to limit numbers by pressing the department to raise the standards of pupil teachers, of training colleges, and of the certificate itself. In 1884, moreover, the union had established a fund to supply legal defence, and to support members 'who may suffer injury through the legitimate defence of Teachers' interests'.[2] After 1890 they began to declare posts 'black' if the attached conditions were within the law but obnoxious, as in the case of unusual extraneous duties or an exceptionally low salary. Members dismissed for objecting to such conditions were granted assistance from the Sustentation Fund; a black list was provided by the union's Register of Schools; and warning notices were sometimes published in the educational papers.[3] This, of course, was the old 'strike in detail'.

These increasingly militant tactics were associated with a change in the leadership. In 1888 a group calling themselves the 'Indefatigables', led by Yoxall and Macnamara, had begun to campaign for new policies and new blood on the executive. Yoxall was elected to that body in 1889 and Macnamara followed a year later. In 1892 Yoxall became secretary in succession to T. E. Heller, and Macnamara was appointed editor of the *Schoolmaster*; by 1894 half the executive could be described as 'young bloods of the 1890s'.[4] This group does not seem, however, to have been associated with the 'new unionism' of those years. Both Yoxall and Macnamara were opposed to any formal relationship with the trade union movement.

The 'shilly-shally' which the Indefatigables attacked arose out of religious divisions which now led to the development of sectarian

[1] Tropp (op. cit., pp. 146–7) quotes four instances, three of them successful.
[2] Donna F. Thompson, op. cit., p. 189.   [3] Tropp, op. cit., p. 146.
[4] *Schoolmaster*, 31 Mar. 1894, quoted in Tropp, op. cit., p. 152.

organizations within the union. The appearance of the Metropolitan Board Teachers' Association, which opposed the religious tests of 1893, was followed by the formation of the Metropolitan Voluntary Teachers' Association, which favoured them. In 1895 the National Association of Voluntary Teachers was formed with the aim of capturing the executive. It did not succeed, but its campaign might have split the union. Appreciating the danger, the Radical Macnamara and the Conservative Gray made an alliance to defend the official policy, and loyalists among the voluntary school teachers established their own National Federation. Following these examples, the factions learned to live together within the union.[1]

These differences did not hinder the rapid growth of the National Union of Teachers, for its membership rose from 15,000 in 1889 to nearly 44,000 in 1900. The solid core of the union was composed of the certificated teachers; but it also accepted assistant and additional teachers from the elementary schools, and later organized teachers in the central and secondary schools. In 1895 there were 53,000 certificated teachers, nearly 32,000 of them women; 28,000 assistant teachers, of whom 23,000 were women; and nearly 12,000 additional teachers. In that year the union's membership of nearly 33,000 included 83 per cent. of certificated men but only 35 per cent. of certificated women.[2]

Though they lacked the organization and experience of the Teachers, another group of white-collar workers, the shop assistants, enjoyed rapidly growing union membership. The Amalgamated Union of Co-operative Employees (originally the Manchester and District Co-operative Employees' Association) and the National Amalgamated Union of Shop Assistants, Warehousemen and Clerks (originally the National Union of Shop Assistants) were both founded in 1891, and by 1900 they claimed 6,700 and 7,500 members respectively. Most of the Shop Assistants' branches 'had to reorganise themselves from the nominal subscription, philanthropic, Early Closing Associations state of existence',[3] but the two unions continued to share a lively interest in early closing, and this meant bringing pressure to bear both upon Parliament and the local authorities.

In 1886 Sir John Lubbock[4] had succeeded in carrying the first Shop Hours Act, which limited the hours of young persons to seventy-four a week. The Act was 'generally unenforced and even to a great extent unknown'[5]

[1] This agreement to differ was facilitated by the existence of other internal organizations—of Class Teachers, Head Teachers, Non-collegiate Certificated Teachers, Rural Teachers—all intended to protect special interests within the union.

[2] Donna F. Thompson, op. cit., appendix 5; Tropp, op. cit., pp. 114, 157, footnote 46.

[3] National Union of Shop Assistants, *Annual Report*, 1892.

[4] Sir John Lubbock, later Lord Avebury (1834–1913), banker, scientist, and philanthropist. Liberal Unionist Member of Parliament, 1886–1900. He always maintained his interest in the shop assistants, and kept in close touch with the unions; but he also appears to have supported Collison's 'free labour' movement (see p. 173).

[5] B. L. Hutchins and A. Harrison, *A History of Factory Legislation*, 1911, p. 221.

until 1892 when Lubbock managed to get responsibility for its enforcement transferred to the local authorities, with power to appoint inspectors. Thereafter the unions and their sympathizers[1] tried to persuade the authorities to exercise these powers, canvassing candidates in London County Council and other local elections. Meanwhile agitation continued for limiting the hours of all shop assistants, and in the last years of the century Dilke presented a bill on these lines, but without success. Other grievances on which similar action was required were fines and deductions, especially those under the 'living-in' system which the Shop Assistants opposed. The Truck Act of 1896 failed to provide a remedy, and in 1898 they gave support to Broadhurst's bill for the abolition of fines.

The unions did not confine themselves to political action. In 1891 the Shop Assistants, helped by the trades councils, had secured early closing in Cardiff and Swansea 'by perpetual agitation on the part of the assistants, by their paying a recognised weekly subscription which was used to advertise it, and the support of the working men'.[2] In 1895 the Manchester branch began to publish lists of 'fair shops', where conditions were regarded as acceptable; and in 1896 the union conference debated the question of a minimum wage, though a decision on the issue was postponed then and for several years thereafter.[3]

Three years later the Shop Assistants went so far as to contemplate an official strike[4] to enforce 7 p.m. closing on several recalcitrant employers in Cardiff. The union's district committee supported the branch decision to strike, but the Lord Mayor intervened to secure a compromise. 'The significance of the Cardiff agitation', wrote the *Shop Assistant*, 'lies in the fact that it is the first instance on record of a body of assistants definitely deciding to use the machinery of the Union in enforcing their legitimate demands; first, for a voice in the regulation of their hours of labour, and secondly, in the matter of collective bargaining'.[5] A 'forward movement' had begun the year before with the appointment of Margaret Bondfield[6] as assistant secretary and John Turner, at that time an anarchist, as organizer. It was rewarded by a jump in membership from under 3,000 in 1898 to 7,500 in 1900.

[1] Speaking in the House on 21 Mar. 1893, Lubbock quoted the support of Burt, Fenwick, Burns, Arch, and Mabon, many trades councils, and the Trades Union Congress.

[2] *Royal Commission on Labour*, C-6894–IX, 1893, Q. 30872.

[3] See p. 452.

[4] Previously the secretary had assured the Royal Commission on Labour that 'we do not favour strikes' (ibid., Q. 30889). There were one or two unofficial strikes in 1899 and 1900.

[5] July 1899.

[6] Bondfield, Margaret, P.C. (1873–1953). Assistant secretary, National Amalgamated Union of Shop Assistants, Warehousemen and Clerks, 1898–1908. Assistant secretary, National Federation of Women Workers, 1915–21. Chief Woman Officer, National Union of General Workers, later National Union of General and Municipal Workers, 1921–38. Parliamentary Committee, later General Council, Trades Union Congress, 1917–24, 1925–9. M.P. 1923–4, 1926–31. Parliamentary Secretary to Minister of Labour, 1924. Minister of Labour, 1929–31.

The Co-operative Employees took their share in the campaign for early closing, but they gave more attention to industrial action than the Shop Assistants. Many of the elected management committees of the co-operative societies included trade unionists, and were more willing than private retailers to deal with the unions. The Co-operative Employees were able to achieve considerable success in their campaign for a minimum wage in the northern societies where their members were concentrated. If the aim of a 30s. minimum adopted by a Northern Delegate Meeting in 1899 remained an aspiration, a number of societies conceded scales with starting rates of 24s. or 25s.

The Co-operative Employees could exert pressure through more than one channel. Though they were refused direct representation at the Co-operative Congress in 1898 on the ground that the union was already represented by the delegate from the Trades Union Congress, the president and secretary attended in 1900 as delegates for societies which had not taken up all the places to which they were entitled. On the other hand, co-operative societies were not always model employers. In addition to complaints of favouritism and victimization, there were cases of long hours and low wages; and in the early nineties the Women's Co-operative Guild began an agitation over poor conditions for women, including those in the co-operative wholesale factories.[1]

These factories, and some of the retail societies, also employed skilled workers and thus had dealings with their unions. In 1882 a Joint Committee of Trade Unionists and Co-operators had been established 'to promote mutual understanding and to further Co-operative production'.[2] Towards the end of the decade there was much criticism of the co-operatives as employers, and their fraternal delegates were given a rough reception at the Trades Union Congress of 1888. The joint committee was therefore given the task of mediating in disputes between unions and the societies. In 1899, after complaints by the Bakers, the committee proposed that trade union rates and hours should apply in each branch of co-operative employment, and both congresses agreed. At the Trades Union Congress of 1900, however, the Tailors were accusing the Oldham society of employing 'blacklegs'.

Musicians formed a third white-collar group to make some progress in organization. Under the stimulus of the 'new unionism', the Musicians' Union was founded in 1893 by J. B. Williams, a young Manchester 'cellist. There already existed several purely professional bodies,[3] but Williams was determined to establish a trade union which would protect the conditions

---

[1] G. D. H. Cole, *A Century of Co-operation*, 1944, pp. 338–9.

[2] Sidney and Beatrice Webb, *The Consumers' Co-operative Movement*, 1921, pp. 190–1.

[3] One of them, the London Orchestral Association, founded in 1891, amalgamated with the union thirty years later.

of its members. This he did by laying down standards and trying to enforce them on individual employers. His branches were encouraged to affiliate to local trades councils, and several received help from them in negotiations. The first branch was in Manchester, and Manchester provided the head office and the executive during the early years. Birmingham was soon organized, and the union spread throughout the North. At first there was opposition to 'an EC composed mostly of Music Hall and Theatre Musicians, plus what was considered to be a boy General Secretary in an inferior Orchestral position';[1] but Williams and his executive won a vote of confidence in 1895. Thereafter membership fluctuated between three and four thousand.

The major sociological study of British white-collar unionism concludes that the degree of organization 'has been very closely associated with what may be called "bureaucratisation"'—that is regulation 'by impersonal rules which strictly exclude all forms of personal consideration between employer and clerk', thus destroying the paternalistic atmosphere of the 'counting house'.[2] The process was clearly related to the increasing size of the working unit and was more likely to be found in public than in private employment, and in government departments or establishments rather than among the local authorities. This must be an important part of any explanation, but other factors must also be taken into account when explaining the successes and failures of the period up to 1900.

Government employment, at least in the Post Office, may have helped the unions. Teachers were not directly employed by the government, but their success seems to have owed something to their ability to play off the Education Committee against school managers and school boards. Professional solidarity probably assisted the organization of both teachers and musicians, and the Co-operative Employees had the advantage of relatively amenable employers. But no convincing explanation is at hand for the greater success of trade unionism among assistants in private shops than among clerks in private offices. It is important to remember that almost every group of white-collar employment was expanding rapidly. Over the whole field, according to Bowley, the number of 'intermediate incomes' increased by no less than 133 per cent. between 1880 and 1913, whereas the total number of wage earners increased by only 24 per cent.[3]

Railwaymen

One of the chief obstacles faced by unions of shop assistants or clerks was that most of their employers were too small and ill-organized to

---

[1] E. S. Teale, 'The Story of the Amalgamated Musicians' Union', *Musicians' Journal*, Apr. 1929.   [2] Lockwood, op. cit., p. 141.
[3] A. L. Bowley, *The Change in the Distribution of the National Income, 1880–1913*, 1920, p. 16. 'Intermediate incomes' were incomes other than wages below the exemption limit for income tax of £160 per annum.

practise collective bargaining successfully, even had they been prepared to accept it. By contrast the railway companies, who were determined to resist it, were so large and well-organized that they could hope to brush aside the claim of the unions to bargain with them. Accordingly the railwaymen looked to Parliament to redress this inequality of strength. Over the past half century the railways had been the most regulated industry in the country, and the large volume of legislation had long since accustomed Members to intervention in railway matters. The public was prepared to be sympathetic, and the frequent debates on railway bills gave spokesmen of the unions plenty of opportunity to air their grievances.

The railway unions had, of course, no objection to industrial action. In 1887 Edward Harford,[1] secretary of the Amalgamated Society of Railway Servants, proposed a national standard scale of wages and hours, based on those prevailing in the best companies; and in the following year the men of the North Eastern Railway began to agitate for their own Darlington Programme. The boom years quickened enthusiasm for direct pressure on the companies, and in 1889 a 'new union', the General Railway Workers' Union, was founded under the inspiration of a group of socialists including Champion, who had failed to persuade the Railway Servants to reduce their subscription in order to make the Society accessible to the lower-paid grades.[2]

The leaders of the General Railway Workers derided the Amalgamated Society and the Associated Society of Locomotive Engineers and Firemen as mere friendly societies, useless as trade unions,[3] and proclaimed that 'the Union shall remain a fighting one, and shall not be encumbered with any sick or accident fund'. The new organization originated in London, where the Champion group was specially active and the Railway Servants were unusually weak. The Railway Servants' greatest strength lay in the North of England and South Wales, in 'areas where old-fashioned craft unionism was strong, or where the miners had managed to maintain some form of local organisation in the face of depression. . . . Even in counties where the proportion of . . . membership was fairly high, the branches tended to concentrate along a narrow industrial belt.'[4]

There was enough competition between the old and new unions to drive the Amalgamated Society to set up a section with reduced contributions for lower-paid workers; but this competition was not the cause of the Railway Servants' new militancy, which had already been developing over the previous two years. Taking a lead from Harford's proposal of 1887, the annual conference of 1889 formulated a national programme

[1] Harford, Edward (1838–98). General secretary, Amalgamated Society of Railway Servants, 1883–97. Parliamentary Committee, Trades Union Congress, 1887–93, 1894–8.
[2] Pelling, *Origins*, pp. 87–88.
[3] G. W. Alcock, *Fifty Years of Railway Trade Unionism*, 1922, p. 236.
[4] Gupta, op. cit.

centred on the demand for a shorter working day,[1] and the Associated Society followed suit in 1890. Union strength proved too patchy to sustain a general movement, however, and the campaign became a series of sectional actions by such grades as felt strong enough to make representations to their own companies. Drivers, firemen, guards, and signalmen were the most active, and on many lines they were able, through respectful deputations, to gain increases in wages and reductions in the working day.

Two of these local campaigns provided the only important instances during the decade in which the unions secured something like recognition. In South Wales the Amalgamated Society alone was involved, and its success was purely temporary. Three small lines, the Barry, the Rhymney, and the Taff Vale, played a key role in the economic life of the region by connecting the coal-mines and ironworks of the valleys with the Bristol Channel ports. In 1890 the Railway Servants managed to arouse interest in their demands, and the Lord Mayor of Cardiff, together with a considerable section of the public, favoured recognition and the negotiation of concessions. The Cardiff Chamber of Commerce, on the other hand, was hostile, for many of its members feared that this would lead to demands from other workers, especially the dockers.

They were supported by Sir William Lewis,[2] coal-owner and ironmaster, chief agent for the Bute property on which the Cardiff docks were built, and the dominant figure in local industrial life; but on this occasion at least Lewis was overruled. Under pressure from a strike which lasted a week, Inskip, the chairman of the Taff Vale Company, met Harford and negotiated a settlement on behalf of all three lines.[3] A year later, however, Inskip retired from the board and the new post of general manager was created. Its first holder, Ammon Beasley, shared Lewis's extreme hostility to trade unionism, and from 1894 he refused to deal with the union committee set up on the Taff Vale line. Thereafter none of the companies in South Wales was prepared to meet the union.

The only company from which the railway unions secured a degree of permanent recognition was the North Eastern, where the Railway Servants were 'much stronger than on any other railway'.[4] The company had a monopoly in its area and was one of the richest in the country.[5] Its board of

---

[1] A sign of the times was the readiness of delegates to announce their names when they spoke. Previously fear of victimization by the companies had kept them anonymous.

[2] Lewis, Sir W. T., later Baron Merthyr (1837–1914). President, Mining Association of Great Britain. Member of Royal Commission on Labour, 1891–4, and of Royal Commission on Trade Combinations and Trade Disputes, 1903–6.

[3] Gupta, op. cit.

[4] *Royal Commission on the Working of the Railway Conciliation and Arbitration Scheme of 1907, Minutes of Evidence*, Cd. 6014, 1911, Q. 13474. Evidence of A. Kaye Butterworth, general manager.

[5] G. P. Jones and A. G. Pool, *A Hundred Years of Economic Development in Great Britain*, 1940, p. 228.

directors was dominated by prominent local industrialists whose chief economic interests lay elsewhere—mainly in coal and iron.[1] During the boom which began in 1888 they had every reason to avoid even a partial stoppage which would disrupt the transport of raw materials and finished products to and from the collieries and ironworks. Moreover, trade unionism was strong in the area served by the company, and 'very inflammable'.[2] The directors were therefore nervous that a strike among railwaymen might spread to their own works.[3]

The board of the North Eastern included several Quakers—David Dale, Lowthian Bell, and members of the Pease family—who had played a leading part in developing the machinery of conciliation and arbitration in the local iron and coal industries. 'We have our board largely chosen from the big traders of the district who from childhood are accustomed to deal with trade unions', said Kaye Butterworth, the general manager, in 1911. 'Sir David Dale's name is a household word in the North, because the conciliation boards in the big industries are largely the outcome of his personality . . . and therefore really it would have been peculiar if the North Eastern had gone on different lines from other industries in the district.'[4]

In 1889 pressure for the Darlington Programme, which demanded a ten-hour day, a guaranteed wage, and higher rates for overtime, was supplemented by an agitation for a nine-hour day among the goods staff in the Newcastle and Gateshead area. The company signed agreements covering some of the issues involved with representatives of the grades concerned, and consented to arbitration by Spence Watson on other claims.[5] By agreeing to meet a committee of their men 'either alone or associated with any advisers whom they may select to accompany them',[6] the directors conceded a measure of recognition; for the 'advisers' selected were the secretaries of the Amalgamated Society, the General Railway Workers' Union, and the Tyneside and National Labour Union. Since the other companies had 'implored' them not to take this step, the North Eastern affected still to be maintaining the general policy of not negotiating with any but their own employees, 'in common with the directors of other railway companies'.[7] But the concession was not withdrawn.

Meanwhile the separate union of Scottish Railway Servants was

[1] *Railway News*, 3 Apr. 1897; and W. M. Acworth, 'Professor Cohn and State Railway Ownership in England', *Economic Journal*, Mar. 1899.

[2] *Railway News*, 7 Feb. 1891.   [3] Ibid., 7 Aug. 1897.

[4] *Royal Commission on the Working of the Railway Conciliation and Arbitration Scheme of 1907, Minutes of Evidence*, Cd. 6014, 1911, Q. 13474.

[5] W. W. Tomlinson, *The North Eastern Railway, Its Rise and Development*, 1914, p. 744. Spence Watson's award in Jan. 1890 gave the nine-hour day to some goods grades at Newcastle and Gateshead.   [6] *Railway News*, 20 Dec. 1890.

[7] *Royal Commission on the Working of the Railway Conciliation and Arbitration Scheme of 1907, Minutes of Evidence*, Cd. 6014, 1911, Qs. 10217 and 13447.

destroyed by the defeat of a strike for recognition in 1890. Several thousand footplate staff, guards, and signalmen were out for six weeks against the advice of their leaders and that of the Amalgamated Society, but with encouragement from John Burns and other socialists. Resumption of work was finally arranged between the companies and deputations composed only of their own men, a mode of settlement which demonstrated the complete failure of the strike to achieve its chief objective.[1] Though the companies made some reductions in hours, the union was so weakened and demoralized that in 1892 the main remnant of about 1,000 members sought refuge in the Amalgamated Society. Another handful of survivors tried to maintain their independence under the name of the Scottish Railwaymen's Union, but in 1895, when their debts forced them to dissolve, they joined the General Railway Workers' Union.[2]

The disastrous and protracted Scottish strike publicized the grievances of railwaymen everywhere and drew attention to the harsh attitude of the companies, especially their insistence upon long hours of work. The opportunity thus presented was seized by F. A. Channing, Liberal Member for East Northamptonshire and by this time the Railway Servants' most effective spokesman in the House.[3] On 23 January 1891 he introduced a resolution proposing the control of hours by the Board of Trade, and emphasized 'the constant source of danger ... to ... the travelling public' arising from 'what I must call a form of white slavery'. Channing received wide support, particularly from Scottish Members, and the Conservative government's alternative motion for a Select Committee of investigation was carried by a very narrow margin.

The Select Committee on Railway Servants contained only two trade unionists—Ben Pickard and John Wilson, both miners from the territory of the North Eastern Railway—and there were complaints that the large group of railway directors was over-represented. Nevertheless, Channing and his allies dominated the Committee throughout its existence. The unions were able to provide ample evidence of long hours, whereas the defence of the companies was ineffectual and their behaviour often arrogant.[4]

---

[1] *Royal Commission on Labour*, C-6894-VIII, 1893, Qs. 25180–933.

[2] In Ireland the Amalgamated Society enjoyed a brief period of power. By 1891 they claimed 3,500 out of 8,000 employed in the traffic grades, and had won concessions, including a degree of recognition, from some of the companies (ibid., Q. 26225). When trade declined, membership slumped and the companies reasserted their authority.

[3] He kept in close touch with Harford, and was a friend of Broadhurst, who had often dealt with railway questions as secretary of the Parliamentary Committee of the Trades Union Congress. In their report to Congress in 1889 the Committee had stated that they were already 'much indebted' to Channing (Trades Union Congress, *Annual Report*, 1889).

[4] A stationmaster named Hood was dismissed by the Cambrian Company after giving evidence. The Amalgamated Society and its friends brought the case before the Committee as a breach of parliamentary privilege. The Company's general manager and other directors were called to the bar of the House, where they offered an apology. This was accepted after a long debate in which attempts to insist on Hood's reinstatement failed (Alcock, op. cit., pp. 250–1).

Channing failed to carry the bulk of the Committee with him in his more far-reaching proposals; but the Majority and Minority Reports published early in 1893 both agreed that the claims of public safety justified statutory regulation of the hours of railwaymen.

The reports, like the original resolution, came at an opportune moment. The Railway and Canal Traffic Act of 1888 had required the companies to submit revised schedules of maximum rates which came into force on 1 January 1893; when some of them took advantage of increased maxima to raise certain charges, there was widespread resentment.[1] This coincided with the introduction of a bill to regulate the hours of railwaymen by the President of the Board of Trade, A. J. Mundella, acting promptly on the Majority Report. In close consultation with Harford, and helped by Michael Davitt[2] and Charles Fenwick,[3] Channing 'was able to amend the Government Bill . . . especially giving the men power to initiate action' by complaint to the Board of Trade,[4] and bringing all railway workers within the scope of the Act. Despite the sympathy of Mundella, however, Channing could not secure explicit recognition for the unions, the most ambitious recommendation of the Minority Report.

The outcome was the Railway Servants (Hours of Labour) Act, 1893, which provided that the Board of Trade could require a company whose hours were 'excessive' to submit a new schedule which kept them within 'reasonable limits'. The Webbs' verdict that 'little use was made' of the Act[5] is unfair both to the Board and to the unions, who had worked hard to ensure its passage. The effects were inevitably slower and more piece-meal than those of a general statutory limitation; but another authority considers it 'unquestionable that the Act was instrumental in reducing the number of hours worked by railwaymen, for, at any rate, twenty years after its passage'.[6] Moreover, from the point of view of the union leaders, who brought a considerable number of cases before the Board, there was the advantage that each complaint had to be taken up separately, so that every revised schedule was a fresh victory for them.

The use that was made of the Act probably helps to explain the continued growth of the two older unions through the depression of 1892–5. The Railway Servants rose from about 20,000 members in 1889 to 38,000 in 1895, and the Engineers and Firemen from 3,600 to 8,000. The General Railway Workers' Union, however, dropped steadily from 14,000 in 1889

[1] Jones and Pool, op. cit., pp. 233–4.

[2] Davitt, Michael (1846–1906). Founder of Irish Land League, 1879. Irish Nationalist M.P., 1892–3, 1895–1900.

[3] Fenwick, Charles, P.C. (1850–1918). Member, Northumberland Miners' Association. Secretary, Parliamentary Committee, Trades Union Congress, 1890–4. Liberal M.P., 1885–1918.

[4] F. A. Channing, *Memories of Midland Politics, 1885–1910*, 1918, p. 142.

[5] Webbs, *History*, p. 525.

[6] C. E. R. Sherrington, *The Economics of Rail Transport in Great Britain*, vol. i, 1928, p. 241.

to 4,000 in 1895. The lower-paid railway workers were the first to suffer from short-time and unemployment, but even so the contrast is striking. The 'new union' was thus struggling for survival while the established societies were gaining strength for an attempt to secure by industrial action the recognition which Parliament would not grant them in 1893.

During 1895–6 they revived and elaborated their national programmes, which were now lengthy documents. That of the Amalgamated Society would have entailed extensive and costly re-organization of railway-working, for its demands covered wages, hours, a guaranteed week, grading and promotion, night and Sunday duty, rest intervals, and lodging allow-ances, as well as many minor issues. When the programmes were sent to all companies with requests that they should meet the union leaders, few even bothered to reply. The Associated Society then fell back on the traditional presentation of petitions by rank-and-file deputations; but the Railway Servants chose to press the campaign for recognition, which came nearer to a unified, national agitation than any previous movement. 'Differences of grade are forgotten in the common good', declared the *Railway Review*;[1] membership jumped to 45,000 in 1896 and 86,000 in 1897; and some leaders began to talk of a national strike.

The campaign for recognition did not preclude local action on other issues, and disagreement within the union over an offer from the North Eastern company led to an unofficial strike. The strikers were dismissed, and the company threatened actions for breach of contract. Eventually, in February 1897, about 5,000 of its 30,000 employees in the traffic grades came out in protest and to enforce their original demands.[2] A week later the stoppage was ended by an agreement to withdraw the disciplinary measures and to refer the claims to arbitration.[3] After prolonged hearings Lord James issued an elaborate award, fifty-eight pages long, which gave the men several improvements. These did not save Harford from charges that he had negotiated with the company behind the back of the North Eastern committee, and that he had been drunk during the proceedings. Consequently the annual conference in October removed him from office[4] and Richard Bell[5] was elected secretary.

[1] 3 Dec. 1897. The *Review* had been acquired by the union as its official journal.

[2] *Report on the Strikes and Lockouts of 1897*, C–9012, 1898, pp. lxi–lxii.

[3] This reference to arbitration was greeted by the *Railway News*, the organ of the companies, as a grave new departure 'which must have far-reaching consequences' (3 Apr. 1897). The board chairman, Sir Joseph Pease, coal-owner and ironmaster, justified it to shareholders as necessary to avert a strike which would involve 'a great disintegration of the trade of the district' and threaten the competitive position of the local coal and iron undertakings (ibid.).

[4] Harford did not deny the charges and asked for clemency. The union had grown from 5,000 to 86,000 members during his fourteen years of office and the delegates voted him a hundred guineas a year for life.

[5] Bell, Richard (1859–1930). Organizing secretary, Amalgamated Society of Railway Servants, 1891–7; general secretary, 1897–1910. Parliamentary Committee, Trades Union

Bell, who was to prove himself one of the outstanding leaders of the period, took over just as the movement for recognition was reaching its climax. The Railway Servants now decided to ask Ritchie, the Conservative President of the Board of Trade, to arrange a joint conference with representatives of the companies, but the moment was ill-chosen. The Engineers' lock-out was dragging on, occupying the time and trying the tempers of Ritchie's department; and the engineering employers and their allies continued to allege that the Engineers in particular and trade unionism in general had come under socialist domination. Though Bell himself was no extremist, there were now as many socialists as Lib-Labs on his executive,[1] and it could be argued that any recognition of the Amalgamated Society would be a surrender to them.

Recognition, moreover, was a very different matter from the regulation of hours. It was one thing to appeal to Parliament or the Board of Trade when consciences could be stirred by evidence of overwork in what was in effect a public service. As the Board made plain, it was quite another to seek their help in order to secure rights which the government was reluctant to concede to unions of its own employees.

Railwaymen have onerous and responsible duties to perform, and they have deserved well of the State [said Ritchie in his reply]. They stand in an exceptional position among workmen, and Parliament has recognised this fact by passing legislation dealing with their hours of labour. . . . The Board have no reason to doubt that the several companies will listen to and discuss with the men *in their employment* . . . matters affecting the interests of the latter, but . . . the opposite policy, namely, that of endeavouring to deal with the companies as a body, presents no prospect of success.[2]

This insistence upon the 'exceptional position' of railwaymen was also an important part of the companies' case against recognition. The railways, they maintained, were different from other privately owned businesses because they offered a public service. Thus they were answerable, in a sense in which other businesses were not, for failures to achieve efficiency or safety, which could only be assured by imposing a high standard of discipline upon all their men. Where labour questions were concerned, it would be subversive of the discipline required for the companies to deal with outsiders. No 'intermediary', such as a union officer or an independent arbitrator, could therefore be allowed to come between a company and its own employees.[3]

Congress, 1899–1900, 1902–10. Executive Committee, Labour Party, 1900–3. M.P., 1900–10. Superintendent of Employment Exchanges, 1910–24.

[1] See p. 296.

[2] Quoted in Alcock, op. cit., p. 294, our italics. Ritchie concluded by asserting that a strike would be inconsistent with the special position occupied by railwaymen.

[3] *Royal Commission on Labour*, C–6894–VIII, 1893, Qs. 25949, 27950–1; also *Railway News*, 23 Apr. 1892.

It may be doubted, however, whether these arguments reveal the main reason for the bitter resistance to trade unionism on the railways. There was evidence enough in other industries that recognition did not necessarily lead to a breakdown of discipline. And spokesmen of the companies chose to ignore the experience of the prosperous North Eastern, which had dealt with union officers since 1889 without any loss of efficiency or increase in accidents, and was now prepared to accept arbitration. A more convincing explanation of the general attitude can be found in the tighter statutory control over railway rates which was established by a series of measures between 1888 and 1894. Together with a steady rise in working expenses, this control soon caused serious difficulties for many of the companies.

The ratio of working expenses to gross receipts, usually regarded by shareholders as the best test of managerial efficiency,[1] had remained stable during the eighties, but began to rise in the early nineties.[2] The increasing price of materials, the growing burden of local and national taxation, and the mounting cost of labour could not easily be covered by raising rates, for these were now subject to the approval of the Railway and Canal Commission, itself under constant pressure from traders and their organizations to keep charges down.[3] Fearing that before long dividends would be affected, most railway directors became convinced that it was vital to retain their relative freedom of manœuvre over wages, hours of work, and the general disposition of labour, unrestricted by collective bargaining with the unions.

With no help from the government, the Railway Servants could do little in face of the combined resistance of the companies. At a conference at the end of November 1897 delegates had to choose between a national strike and a return to local sectional movements relying on deputations. They were much exercised as to the volume of support needed to justify such a strike, and eventually set themselves the difficult task of collecting

[1] *Railway News*, 7 Oct. 1905. It was one of the standard measurements used by the Board of Trade in their annual reports on railway statistics and finances. W. M. Acworth, the railway economist, strongly criticized the 'working ratio' as a criterion of efficiency, but admitted that it was often thus used ('English Railway Statistics', *Journal of the Royal Statistical Society*, vol. lxv, Dec. 1902; and R. Price-Williams, 'Notes on Mr. Acworth's Paper', vol. lxvi, Mar. 1903).

[2] Between 1879 and 1889 the ratio had hovered around 52 per cent. (*Returns of the Capital, Traffic, Receipts and Working Expenditure of the Railway Companies of the United Kingdom for 1904*, Cd. 2623, 1905, p. xxiii). By 1893 it had risen to nearly 58 per cent. in England and Wales (*General Report on the Capital, Traffic, Working Expenditure and Profits of the Railway Companies etc., for 1900*, Cd. 749, 1901, p. 20).

[3] The outcry against the new rates of Jan. 1893 had led to the Railway and Canal Traffic Act of 1894, which laid on companies the onus of proving to the Commission the reasonableness of any increase imposed on or after 1 Jan. 1893 and complained of by a trader (Jones and Pool, op. cit., p. 234). Experience soon taught them that to raise their rates was 'a difficult thing to do' (*Railway News*, 29 Dec. 1906).

'75 per cent of the whole of the men's notices'. On 3 December, however, the *Railway Review* prejudged the issue in an outspoken article which asserted that 'it is all a question of the size of the battalions. Are they at present large enough? Candidly, we think not. And this is why we favour a further period of strengthening our forces before the final encounter.'

The Lib-Lab editor of the *Review*, Fred Maddison, a former compositor, had recently won the by-election at Sheffield caused by the death of A. J. Mundella. Censured by the executive and forced to resign from the paper, he was succeeded early in 1898 by the socialist, G. J. Wardle.[1] But the alacrity with which a militant executive accepted the fact that his article had caused 'a collapse' shows that Maddison's judgement was right. There was no more talk of a national strike; membership fell sharply; and the agitation broke up into purely sectional movements which enjoyed varying degrees of success locally through deputations or unofficial strikes.

Nevertheless, the Amalgamated Society could look back on the decade with some pride. In 1892 George Howell, an experienced observer, had noted that 'by its quiet persistent action, it has done much to better the condition of railway employés all over the kingdom ... and its influence is extending'.[2] Soon afterwards Charles Booth's *Life and Labour of the People in London* recorded that the union 'exercises considerable influence, particularly in educating public opinion regarding the disabilities of railway men, and in promoting legislative action on their behalf'.[3] By 1897 the very vehemence of the companies' resistance was a measure of the threat which they now felt themselves to be facing, and the *Railway News* declared that 'it is difficult to ignore the pretensions of the society. The time has now come for railway companies to combine, and act in concert.'[4]

Thus the largest private concentrations of economic power in the country were driven to find safety in numbers by what had looked like becoming a genuine 'all-grades' movement. Thereafter the companies remained together to continue their propaganda against the demand for recognition;[5] but by 1900 the unions could claim a membership of 78,000 of their 250,000 employees in the traffic grades. Despite the débâcle of 1897, the great majority of these, about 62,000, were members of the Amalgamated Society of Railway Servants, which had already recovered many of its heavy losses. The comparative caution of the engineers and firemen of the Associated Society had been rewarded by a modest expansion to 10,000; the General Railway Workers still numbered less than 5,000; and the

---

[1] Wardle, G. J., P.C. (1865–1947). Member, Amalgamated Society of Railway Servants. Editor, *Railway Review*, 1898–1919. Executive Committee, Labour Party, 1913–19. M.P., 1906–20. Parliamentary Secretary to Board of Trade, 1917–18. Parliamentary Secretary to Ministry of Labour, 1919–20.

[2] Howell, *Trade Unionism, New and Old*, p. 138.

[3] Booth, op. cit., vol. vii, 1896, pp. 344–5.

[4] *Railway News*, 9 Oct. 1897.   [5] Ibid., 4 Dec. 1897 and 28 July 1900.

United Pointsmen now stood at nearly 1,500. In addition, the Railway Clerks' Association, established in 1897, had a membership of 1,500.

Coal and Cotton

Whereas parliamentary methods were the main weapon of public servants, and were at least as important as industrial action for the railwaymen, many other unions adopted them as a supplementary means of attaining their objectives. Among them was another organization of transport workers, the Seamen, who shared some of the special opportunities for attracting public sympathy open to railwaymen. Assisted by the legal advice of George Howell, their secretary Havelock Wilson used his membership of the House from 1892 to 1900 to further the work of Samuel Plimsoll by promoting or amending a series of Merchant Shipping Acts, notably the consolidating Act of 1894.[1] During the Hull dispute of 1893 he was able to bring out the issues of principle involved—'free labour', union recognition, and the use of troops—and to win support for his demand that the employers should negotiate.[2] But these activities proved no substitute for industrial success and could not save his union from disintegration.

The use of parliamentary methods was not confined to any particular type of union. Most craft societies gave relatively little attention to them, but this was not a matter of settled policy. In the words of the Webbs, 'some powerful unions' were 'comparatively indifferent to the law as an instrument for obtaining the conditions of labour that they desire', so long as satisfactory results could be secured by other means.[3] Where craft methods were successful, as they generally had been in the control of wages and hours, the societies feared that statutory intervention might undermine their position. Where such methods were unsuccessful or inappropriate, however, they were ready to turn to Parliament. The Shipwrights, for example, did so when they sought to help their members in the Admiralty dockyards,[4] and the printing unions showed similar energy in pursuing a 'fair wages' clause to protect men working on government contracts.[5]

Among the unions which used parliamentary action as a second string to their bow, those of the miners and the cotton operatives were preeminent. This was not because their industrial methods were unsuccessful. On the contrary, the development of collective bargaining brought substantial advances to both groups during the decade after 1889. It was rather because their leaders recognized from experience that legislation provided the best form of control in certain fields, and even more because

---

[1] This Act, allegedly the largest to reach the statute book during the nineteenth century, confirmed the gains of twenty years of agitation, but still imposed a harsh disciplinary code on seamen.   [2] See p. 81.

[3] *Industrial Democracy*, p. 263.   [4] See p. 152.   [5] See p. 255.

each of them, with their large forces concentrated into a relatively small number of constituencies, disposed of a direct electoral strength that no other body of organized workers could equal.[1]

At first sight, the miners might appear to have had a clear advantage over the cotton operatives. After 1889 their unions forged ahead in total membership, while a majority of the members of the weavers' and card-room amalgamations were women and therefore without votes; coal dominated some constituencies to a degree that cotton could not emulate; and even the powerful Spinners were unable to send a representative to join the group of miners' leaders in the Commons. During the nineties, however, the Miners' Federation failed to attain the most cherished of its parliamentary aims, whereas the cotton unions scored a series of substantial successes. Within a limited sphere, persistent lobbying by the miners achieved something, for the Mines Regulation Act of 1887 was improved by amendments in 1894 and 1896. But these gains were entirely over-shadowed for most of them by the failure to carry an Eight Hours Bill.

The eight-hour day had been among the Federation's original 'objects of association', and the leaders were at first prepared to consider both political and industrial methods of pursuing it. They supported Cunning-hame Graham's abortive bill in 1889, and persuaded the Trades Union Congress of that year to make an exception to its reaffirmed objection to the control of working hours by legislation. The Parliamentary Committee was duly instructed to draw up a bill for men working underground; but within a few weeks a 'general conference' of the mining unions decided to take a ballot on the possibility of strike action for the eight-hour day, and the returns showed a considerable majority in almost all the central coalfields in favour of striking. When the matter was debated at the in-augural meeting of the Federation at Newport in November, both methods had their adherents and a choice between them was left open.

In the end the Federation decided in favour of legislation, and there seems little doubt that its leaders always preferred this course. The strength of trade unionism in the different districts varied considerably, and in any case they were not unanimous. The hewers of the North-east were bitterly opposed to all attempts to legislate for an eight-hour day;[2] the 'company unions' of South Wales, though sympathetic to the cause, refused to contemplate a strike because of their sliding-scale agreements. Yet if the eight-hour day was to be applied at all, it must be applied every-where. Moreover, as Pickard indicated some years later,[3] there was another

---

[1] See p. 271.

[2] See p. 104. George Jacques, a well-known Durham miner and member of the Independent Labour Party, conducted a campaign for the eight-hour day in the early nineties but with no success (*Workman's Times*, 9 June 1894).

[3] Miners' Federation of Great Britain, *Minutes of Special Conference on Eight Hours*, July 1902.

reason for rejecting industrial action. By such means, 'he had always held, and held today, in good trade they could get it; in bad trade they would lose it'. Only parliamentary success could guarantee 'permanence and universality'.[1]

The Federation leaders realized, however, that public opinion might turn against a demand for legislation from the unions if the question had not even been discussed with the coal-owners. They therefore met the employers in January and February 1891. On the union side the conferences were attended by representatives of the Federated area, South Wales, and Scotland, but Northumberland and Durham were absent. Pickard asked for an agreement upon the eight-hour day to be followed by joint application for a special rule under the Act of 1887 which would give it general and lasting effect. After an adjournment the owners rejected this proposal, thus leaving the miners free, in Pickard's words, 'to take such action as may be deemed necessary'. Since he had explained at the outset that they had approached the employers 'to meet an apparent public desire and sentiment', the whole proceedings had the air of a formality.[2]

When the Federation returned to lobbying for a bill of their own, they found that disunity among the mining districts could be as damaging politically as it was industrially. The leaders of the North-east could not prevent the Trades Union Congress from giving overwhelming votes for supporting the bill; but so long as they and not the Federation represented the miners on the Parliamentary Committee, the Committee usually failed to carry out its instructions from Congress. The Federation leaders therefore set out to oust their rivals. Though the campaign began early in 1891, it was not until 1893 that Ned Cowey of Yorkshire was able to drive John Wilson from the Parliamentary Committee for the last time,[3] and only in the following year that his Lancashire colleague, Sam Woods, replaced Charles Fenwick.

It was not possible, however, to dislodge the North-east from its dominant position among the miners' representatives in the House of Commons. Burt and Wilson continued to be determined opponents of the eight-hour day, and Wilson attacked successive bills, usually in close collaboration with Sir James Joicey, chief of the Durham coal-owners. Even as the paid servant of Congress Fenwick had remained loyal to his Northumbrian constituents, speaking and voting consistently against the measure. The only leader of the Federation with a seat in the House throughout the nineties was Pickard, though he was joined by Woods from 1892 to 1895

---

[1] The phrase is the Webbs' (*Industrial Democracy*, p. 255).

[2] *Proceedings at a Joint Conference of Representative Coalowners and the Miners' Federation*, 21 Jan. and 11 Feb. 1891.

[3] Pickard had beaten Wilson in 1890, but next year Wilson regained the seat (see p. 225).

and again from 1897 to 1900; while for much of the period Mabon was not a reliable ally. Consequently those hostile to an Eight Hours Bill could always point to the failure of the miners to get a majority of their own Members to endorse it.

In 1892, when the Bill first came up for a second reading, Lord Randolph Churchill and Joseph Chamberlain both supported it; but the Conservative Home Secretary, Matthews, argued against anticipating the Royal Commission on Labour which was examining the whole question. The government, however, had already indicated its attitude by appointing Burt and Mabon as Commissioners but no representative of the Federation, which thereupon boycotted the Commission. Only fifteen Conservatives and ten Liberal Unionists voted for the second reading, compared with ninety-nine Liberals and thirty-eight Irish Members, and the motion was heavily defeated.

Nevertheless, with only thirty-eight Liberals voting against them, the Federation had reason to hope, despite Gladstone's own prevarications, that the Liberal victory in the general election of 1892 might promise success. They did, indeed, secure a second reading in 1893; but the new government was not prepared to declare itself officially, Gladstone maintaining his equivocal position by 'speaking against the Bill and voting for it'.[1] In 1894 they got as far as the committee stage, where an amendment granting local option was carried by five votes, one of them Fenwick's. The Federation had always insisted that the eight-hour day must be universal, otherwise the districts exempt would enjoy a competitive advantage. The mutilated Bill was therefore withdrawn.[2]

After the return of the Conservatives in 1895, the Federation brought forward its original Bill every year but with even less success, though the second reading was defeated by only twenty-four votes in 1900 and was actually carried in 1901. The government gave them little encouragement. Since the miners showed few signs of wavering in their allegiance to the beaten and demoralized Liberals, the Conservatives with their comfortable majority had nothing to gain from attempting to meet the wishes of the Federation. Despite the vacillations of their leaders, most Liberals still gave consistent support in the House; but this was bound to be ineffective so long as the party was both weak and divided. Together with the miners' Members from the North-east, a substantial group of coal-owners and other Liberal employers remained determined and vociferous opponents of the Bill.

The cotton operatives also failed to win a statutory eight-hour day. During 1889 and 1890 the demand of the 'new unionists' for a general

[1] Page Arnot, op. cit., vol. i, p. 196.
[2] The Federation's manifesto for the general election of 1895 demanded: 'No local option! No district to be exempt from the Bill! No Handicapping!' (ibid., p. 269).

enactment had aroused a good deal of rank-and-file support in Lancashire. The weavers' amalgamation decided to give the campaign official backing, and their president, David Holmes,[1] spoke alongside Tom Mann and Ben Tillett at meetings held in 1891. In fact, however, neither Holmes and his colleagues nor the leaders of the spinners' and cardroom amalgamations really wanted a bill. In 1890 and 1891 they voted against resolutions in its favour at the Trades Union Congress;[2] when they appeared before the Royal Commission on Labour in June 1891 they opposed the legislative enforcement of an eight-hour day and insisted that their members were equally hostile. They maintained that any limitation of hours would mean reduced earnings, and that to force employers to compensate by raising piece rates would prejudice Lancashire's competitive position in the export trade.[3]

By the summer of 1892 slackening demand began to suggest that there might after all be advantages in a shorter working day. When the employers sought wage reductions,[4] allegedly in the hope of provoking a stoppage which would clear the accumulated stocks,[5] union leaders could hardly reject the case for an eight hours Bill, 'to do away with the necessity for lock-outs, which are brought about under the cloak of wages reductions'.[6] In September 1892 the Weavers instructed their delegates to Congress to vote in its favour, and by October the Legislative Council of the United Textile Factory Workers' Association had been told to draft a bill specifically for cotton.

After some persuasion, a group of Lancashire Members of both parties finally agreed in March 1894 to handle the bill in the House. But scarcely had these arrangements been made when the impetus began to falter. Exports of piece goods, which had been falling between 1890 and 1893, now started to rise.[7] As opportunities for earning expanded, feeling among the operatives turned against a limitation of hours,[8] and it was decided to hold a ballot of the Association late in 1894. Out of about 105,000 possible voters, 44,683 voted for the eight-hour day but no less than 42,512 against.

[1] Holmes, David (1843–1906). President, Amalgamated Weavers' Association, 1884–1906. Parliamentary Committee, Trades Union Congress, 1892–1901, 1902–4.

[2] In Sept. 1890 Thomas Birtwistle, secretary of the Accrington Weavers and the Weavers' representative on the Parliamentary Committee, refused to remain on the Committee 'because he could not accept the instructions of Congress to sponsor an Eight Hours Bill' (Roberts, op. cit., p. 127). A month later James Mawdsley of the spinners' amalgamation resigned for the same reason. They returned to the Committee in 1891 (see p. 254).

[3] C-6708-VI, 1892, Qs. 391–405, 732–4, 1072–4. Holmes later argued that 'it was very easy for trades who worked purely for home consumption . . . to agitate for this concession. But those engaged in the cotton trade . . . had to compete with Germany, where they worked between 60 and 70 hours [per week]' (Trades Union Congress, *Annual Report*, 1900.)

[4] See p. 115.   [5] *Cotton Factory Times*, 5 Aug. 1892.   [6] Ibid., 9 Dec. 1892.

[7] S. J. Chapman, *The Cotton Industry and Trade*, 1905, chart at p. 100.

[8] The *Cotton Factory Times* of 27 July 1894 reported a meeting at Accrington to protest against the bill.

This effectively killed the bill, and all that was needed was a decent disposal of the corpse. In 1895 the *Cotton Factory Times* noted that the campaign had been given up until 'the general surroundings' were 'more favourable', and by 1897 was even asserting that a limitation to eight hours would be 'suicidal'.[1]

In other directions, however, parliamentary action brought the cotton unions a series of victories. The first came in 1889 with the Cotton Cloth Factories Act, which controlled 'steaming' in the weaving sheds by laying down maximum humidities.[2] In 1882, when Birtwistle was chairman, the Parliamentary Committee had taken up the question, and the Weavers made it a major concern from 1884 onwards, the agitation reaching a peak in 1889 when a petition attracted 220,000 signatures. With Lord Cranborne, son of the Conservative Prime Minister, in the chair, union representatives met thirty Lancashire Members of Parliament and set up a joint committee to draft a bill. After failing to reply to several protests from the employers' association, the President of the Board of Trade, Hicks Beach, eventually agreed to hear their plea for a Royal Commission; but it was now too late for such delaying tactics and the bill went through.[3]

Meanwhile the Weavers had begun another agitation under Birtwistle's leadership. Their aim was the insertion into the Factory Bill promised by the Conservatives of a clause requiring weaving employers to furnish written particulars of the rate of wages to each worker, so that any mistake or fraud could be detected. Birtwistle secured the assistance of both Lancashire and Lib-Lab Members and reached a considerable measure of agreement with the employers, though negotiations on a joint bill broke down.[4] He then persuaded Sir Henry James, at that time Liberal Unionist Member for Bury, to take charge of the amalgamation's own bill, which ultimately formed the basis of the 'particulars clause' in the Factory Act of 1891.[5]

In 1895 the Liberals introduced an amending bill which applied the particulars clause to other textile trades besides weaving, and the Home Secretary was given power to extend it by order to industries outside textiles. On this occasion the spinners' amalgamation was the main force behind the campaign, which Mawdsley directed along the lines pioneered by Birtwistle. He encountered few serious obstacles. In the honeymoon period after the Brooklands Agreement the master spinners showed

[1] *Cotton Factory Times*, 30 Aug. 1895 and 17 Sept. 1897.

[2] Steaming was used to avoid breakages when weaving inferior cloths; windows were shut, floors kept wet, and the atmosphere made damp by injecting steam.

[3] During the passage of the Act union officials were attacked by the rank and file for not insisting upon the total abolition of steaming. Criticism died down once the new regulations came into force.

[4] *Cotton Factory Times*, 12 Dec. 1890.

[5] Birtwistle was appointed to the factory inspectorate to administer the clause, as the only man who could fully understand it.

themselves even more co-operative than the weaving employers had been in 1890–1,[1] while Asquith proved more sympathetic and businesslike than Matthews, his Conservative predecessor.

In spinning both sides of the industry were already working closely together on two other issues, bimetallism and the Indian import duties. As a device for increasing trade and employment, bimetallism had been much discussed during the Great Depression, and in 1892 the question was taken up by Mawdsley. Since silver was the currency of the East, which imported so many of Lancashire's cotton goods, employers and operatives alike looked to bimetallism to increase and stabilize the purchasingpower of India and other Eastern customers. Their reaction was thus all the more hostile when the Indian government imposed a duty on imported cotton late in 1894. Other trade unionists regarded the duties primarily as a problem for Lancashire, but Mawdsley and his colleagues were able to win widespread support for bimetallism, especially in the North of England. Among the officers of the Trade Union Monetary Reform Association, for example, were Drew, Gee, and Turner of Yorkshire's General Textile Workers, Kelley of the Lithographic Printers, who had their headquarters in Manchester, and Clynes, Lancashire district secretary of the Gasworkers.[2]

Early in 1895, however, the cotton lobby was rebuffed on both issues by the Rosebery government, which took its stand on Liberal principles of an orthodox currency and the freedom of dependencies to control their own fiscal policy. Even after the Conservative victory, Salisbury would offer no concession on bimetallism, but in 1896 he produced an acceptable compromise on the Indian duties. As a Tory stronghold Lancashire was important to the new government, and its attitude towards the cotton unions continued to be benevolent. When steaming again became a problem, a bill drafted with the agreement of all those concerned soon emerged as the Cotton Cloth Factories Act of 1897. By the end of the century, therefore, the cotton unions, unlike the Miners' Federation, could look back over the past decade with some satisfaction.

In explaining this contrast, the Webbs gave pride of place to the United Textile Factory Workers' Association, 'a political machine of remarkable efficiency', and 'better than the material out of which it is made',[3] for they saw in the cotton operatives when compared to the miners all the vices of the *petite bourgeoisie*. Indeed, the Webbs' description of the ideal federation for political purposes[4] is manifestly based on their account of the working of the Association.[5] This was certainly a useful device, yet by

---

[1] *Cotton Factory Times*, 26 Apr. 1895.
[2] Leslie Bather, *A History of the Manchester and Salford Trades Council*, Ph.D. thesis, Manchester, 1956.   [3] *Industrial Democracy*, p. 260.
[4] Ibid., pp. 270–6.   [5] Ibid., pp. 258–60.

their own admission its campaigns were not managed by the General Council of 'nearly 200 delegates from a hundred local branches', but by the Legislative Council, a body of full-time union officers who met 'in the parlor of a Manchester public-house' and assessed 'the complaints of the constituents . . . with cynical shrewdness'. Since the same men met frequently in any case, they could work together without a formal organization, and in practice the leadership of each campaign was left largely to the officers of the amalgamation most concerned.

Thus successful lobbying by the cotton operatives owed more to the talents of their leaders and the electoral influence of the unions themselves than to the Association. In 1896 its meetings were in fact suspended, ostensibly on the ground that 'the time was inopportune for any further extension of factory legislation',[1] though this consideration did not deter the Weavers from carrying through their agitation on steaming. The Association was most valuable as an outward and visible sign of cotton's strength and solidarity on matters of common interest such as the Indian import duties. It was revived in 1899, partly as a counter to the formation of the Cotton Employers' Parliamentary Committee,[2] but more specifically to promote twelve o'clock closing on Saturdays and to resist the raising of the minimum age for half-time work in the factories.[3] These were aims shared by all the unions, not the concern of a single amalgamation as had been the case with steaming.

In coal as in cotton there were Conservatives as well as Liberals among both leaders and rank and file. Thomas Ashton, secretary of the Lancashire Miners and of the Miners' Federation, was a Conservative, and conferences of the Federation were frequently reminded that the sentiments of such men should not be flouted.[4] Nevertheless, they were undoubtedly a minority. The miners' Members of Parliament all sat as

---

[1] Webbs, *Industrial Democracy*, p. 260, footnote. The fact that a scheme for bipartisan parliamentary representation had recently gone awry may have contributed to this decision (see p. 299).   [2] *Cotton Factory Times*, 28 Apr. 1899.

[3] Cotton operatives gave a variety of reasons for their attitude towards half-time. Sufficient juvenile labour was essential to the organization of the work; 'it teaches them to be more skilful with their fingers . . . and . . . also takes them out of the street' (*Royal Commission on Labour*, C–6708–VI, 1892, Qs. 350–1); raising the age would mean 'misery and suffering to the widow and orphans, and money only in the pockets of schoolmasters' (*Cotton Factory Times*, 26 May 1899); and 'if, as is the case, the children are willing and even anxious to go to work, and the parents are agreeable, whilst employers accept them, what has anyone else got to do with it?' (ibid., 5 June 1891). The leaders of the Yorkshire Textile Workers' Federation generally supported their Lancashire colleagues; but they worked as strenuously for the abolition of half-time as the cotton leaders for its continuance, the two groups clashing sharply at an International Textile Workers Congress in 1900. The National Union of Teachers thanked Turner and Gee for their co-operation in attacking the system (Turner, *Short History*, p. 82).

[4] At Leicester in 1894 delegates were invited to become members of the local Liberal club during their visit. Cowey announced that the invitation had been declined because 'the Miners' Federation was not a political society. It included men who represented all phases of political thought.'

Liberals, and there was hardly a mining constituency in the country outside Lancashire that the Conservatives could hope to win. The cotton unions, however, were more evenly divided between the two parties, and a majority of their members may have been Conservatives.[1] As a result there were many seats in Lancashire which either party could hope to win or fear to lose.

This contrast between the two groups of unions helps to explain their differing degrees of success in securing concessions from the Conservatives, who were in power for eight of the eleven years between 1889 and 1900. The Miners' Federation did indeed succeed in winning the support of an influential minority of Conservative Members for their Eight Hours Bill; but up to the end of the century this never took them as far as the second reading they had twice obtained from the Liberals. On the other hand, all the major victories of the cotton operatives occurred under Tory rule. Even the extension of the particulars clause in 1895 only reached the safety of the statute book after the fall of the Liberal government which had drafted it.

It can also be argued that the leaders of the Federation lacked the political realism of Mawdsley and his colleagues, though the latter's judgement seems to have deserted them when they adopted bimetallism. The miners' Eight Hours Bill was certainly a bolder and more far-reaching measure than any which was actually brought before the House on behalf of the cotton unions, and it bore the taint of socialism. Moreover, the Bill would have meant the direct regulation of the hours of adult males, without the railwaymen's excuse that public safety was involved. By comparison, the statutory control of hours in the cotton industry applied directly only to women and young persons. Even if the convention that Parliament must not restrict the freedom of grown men was wearing thin, *laissez-faire* susceptibilities still had to be respected.

Skilful political organization and tactics on the part of the cotton operatives or any other union could not by themselves account for the spate of both legislative and administrative improvements in the early nineties. One essential condition was the growth of public interest and sympathy which began with the investigations of the eighties into the condition of the poor and the causes of depression. This philanthropic sentiment, however, can hardly be disentangled from the mounting realization among politicians of both parties that concessions to labour were a means to electoral success. In this respect the creation by 1885 of a more democratic electorate was at least as important as the impact of trade union agitation in and after 1889.

[1] See p. 275. One foreign observer believed that 'the reason for this remarkable fact is that the Lancashire operatives, under the influence of their leader, Mr. Mawdsley, have espoused the cause of bimetallism, and expect to carry it through with the help of the Conservative party. They also think it will be the same party . . . that will extend the Factory Acts to India' (Schulze-Gaevernitz, *Social Peace*, 1893, p. 168).

Philanthropy and the extension of the county franchise clearly go far to explain parliamentary concern for the agricultural workers. After a brief flicker in 1889–92 their unions were virtually dead. Joseph Arch, a loyal Liberal satellite, sat in the House from 1892 to 1900, drinking his bottle of whisky a day but hardly opening his mouth for any other purpose. On the Conservative side Jesse Collings, a Radical fish out of water, plugged away feebly at the old cause. Industrial workers were better organized and had many more skilful advocates; yet the demands of the agricultural labourers for political rights or material betterment attracted as much attention as those of any other group. Neither party felt able to ignore their grievances. Between the Conservative county councils of 1888 and the Liberal parish councils of 1894 the structure of local government in the countryside was revolutionized. After the Conservatives passed the first Smallholdings Act in 1892, the Liberals tried to improve on it in 1894.

As the decade progressed, the pace of concessions to labour declined. After 1895 Salisbury's position appeared to be unassailable, and the government's benevolence towards the cotton operatives rarely extended to other organizations, although the Teachers were a notable exception. For other public employees, however, the Conservatives did very little, even though a readiness to improve the conditions of government workers had served as the test of Liberal sincerity for Tories like Gorst as well as for the Fabians. The Conservatives, moreover, had been the first to 'set an example to private industry' when they accepted the fair wages resolution, moved on 13 February 1891 by Sydney Buxton,[1] which had laid down that it was 'the duty of the Government, in all government contracts . . . to make every effort to secure the payment of such wages as are generally accepted as current in each trade for competent workmen'.

The resolution had been badly drafted,[2] and even when construed as prescribing wages 'generally accepted as current in each trade for competent workmen in the district where the work is carried out', its meaning left plenty of room for controversy. Grievances over its application mounted as the years passed,[3] and in March 1896 Buxton succeeded in persuading the government to appoint a Select Committee. The report in July 1897 concluded that 'the Departments, as a whole, have loyally

[1] Buxton, Sydney, P.C., later Earl Buxton (1853–1934). Liberal M.P., 1883–1914. Under-Secretary of State for Colonies, 1892–5. Postmaster General, 1905–10. President of Board of Trade, 1910–14. Governor-General of South Africa, 1914–20.

[2] Buxton's original wording was based on a resolution passed by the Trades Union Congress in 1890 which asked for the prohibition of 'sub-letting' and 'the recognised Trade Union rates of wages in the respective localities where any work may be done', but he toned it down under government pressure.

[3] At Congress in 1896 Havelock Wilson moved that 'this Congress condemns the Government for persistently refusing to carry out the fair wages resolution . . . and specially condemns them for retaining upon their list of contractors . . . certain notorious blackleg firms'.

endeavoured to interpret and carry out its provisions', but added important qualifications. The Irish departments had been particularly remiss; there was no uniformity in administration or in the terms of tenders and contracts; penalties were insufficient; subcontracting permitted evasion; and both Parliament and the unions lacked information.

Virtually nothing was done to meet these criticisms or the complaints which the unions voiced annually at the Trades Union Congress. Admittedly the reforming zeal of the early nineties was now largely spent; but there was also another consideration. While the employers' counter-attack at the end of the decade did the unions as a whole little direct damage, it nevertheless influenced Parliament and public opinion, and aroused doubts even among 'the friends of labour'. This probably affected the prospects of all proposals for improving working-class conditions; it certainly made less acceptable measures which might directly strengthen the unions, such as intervention to secure their recognition by the railway companies. It was now the government's turn to follow the example set by private industry in standing firm against any encroachment upon the prerogative of employers.

The Trades Union Congress

Though many unions took action on their own account, the movement's main political instrument was the Trades Union Congress and its Parliamentary Committee. Consisting 'only of Delegates representing bona fide Trades Societies, and Trades Councils',[1] Congress met annually, usually during the first week of September, at some regional centre selected by the previous Congress.[2] Until 1901 its president was always a local man, often the chairman of the trades council acting as host. Few presidents could resist the temptation to air their opinions in a lengthy address, and some lacked the ability to handle a large and frequently unruly gathering. Such guidance as Congress received came mainly from the Parliamentary Committee, whose report on the past year stood at the head of the agenda. The bulk of the programme consisted of resolutions on a wide range of topics sent in to the Committee by affiliated organizations and laid before Congress in no particular order. In addition, a few motions on matters of common concern, like employers' liability or the law on picketing, were presented by members of the Committee or other well-known leaders, generally at an early stage when the attention of delegates was easier to obtain.

'From the outset the proceedings are unbusiness-like', complained the

---

[1] Trades Union Congress Standing Orders, 1873, quoted in Roberts, op. cit., p. 74.

[2] Competition for the honour was often intense, and an industrial city or major port was usually successful. The most salubrious choices during the nineties were Norwich and Edinburgh. Apart from a visit to Southport in 1885, the first seaside resort chosen was Blackpool in 1917.

Webbs, who saw Congress as 'rather a parade of the Trade Union forces than a genuine Parliament of Labour'; but they were ready to admit its usefulness. 'An outward and visible sign of that persistent sentiment of solidarity which has . . . distinguished the working class', and 'a unique opportunity for friendly intercourse between the representatives of the different trades', Congress by its discussions revealed 'both to the Trade Union Civil Service and to party politicians, the movement of opinion among all sections of Trade Unionists, and, through them, of the great body of the wage-earners'.

While critical of the failure of the 'Front Bench' to take Congress in hand, the Webbs nevertheless realized that 'what more than anything else makes the Congress a holiday demonstration instead of a responsible deliberative assembly is its total lack of legislative power', for the resolutions passed could have 'no binding effect upon [its] constituents'. 'As a business meeting', therefore, once the views of delegates on the current agenda had been expressed, 'the whole function of the Congress is discharged in the election of the Parliamentary Committee, to which the representation of the Trade Union world for the ensuing year is entrusted.'[1]

Obsessed by their false analogy with cabinet government, and by over-enthusiastic impressions of the United Textile Factory Workers' Association, the Webbs were often contemptuous of the Parliamentary Committee, and chose to ignore many of the limits within which it was forced to work. Elected annually, the Committee in 1889 consisted of ten members—the total was increased to twelve in 1894—and a secretary who had no vote. Their duties had been laid down by Congress in 1873: 'to watch all legislative measures directly affecting the question of labour'; and 'to initiate whenever necessary such legislative action as Congress may direct or as the exigencies of the time and circumstances may demand'.

Not surprisingly, in view of its dependence upon a composite body which could not be driven without the risk of disruption, the Committee tended to behave as the unadventurous servant of Congress; but it was never subservient. Instructions thought to be impracticable or unwelcome might be disregarded or evaded;[2] and a cautious lead might be given, especially on matters of common interest like the legal status of the unions. Moreover, the older generation of leaders, once provoked, did not hesitate

---

[1] *History*, pp. 563–66. See also *Industrial Democracy*, pp. 265–78.

[2] On 6 Nov. 1889, after the Dundee Congress, the following entry was made in the Committee's *Minutes*: 'The General Resolutions. These were read and carefully considered, but it was agreed that they could not be deemed to be matter for executive consideration.' The same Committee, hostile to the eight hours movement, resolved on 19 Feb. 1890 that 'having found that that portion of the miners who are interested in' the miners' Eight Hours Bill 'have in public conference decided to adopt and back a Bill already before Parliament, this Committee considers itself relieved from any further responsibility in the matter for the present year'.

to use their power on the Committee to obstruct new movements which they considered obnoxious, such as that for a general Eight Hours Bill, and to strike at their enemies by a reform of Congress itself.

Even in quiet years, competition for election to the Committee was keen. There were perennial complaints of the bargaining for votes and, according to the Webbs, 'experienced officials of the old-established Unions' were 'busily engaged, both in and out of Congress hours, in arranging for the election of themselves or their friends'.[1] Since the Committee was the central lobby of the movement and its only nucleus of permanent organization, membership was not merely a personal honour but could also be directly useful to the union concerned. Consequently the Committee always included 'some of the ablest salaried officers of the movement'.[2] Much of their time and energy, however, was necessarily 'absorbed in the multifarious details of their own societies', and not in the business of Congress.[3] The Committee's minutes provide ample evidence for the Webbs' assertion that the agenda was 'habitually reduced to the barest minimum', while 'between the meetings the Secretary struggles with the business as best he can'.[4]

Occasionally, as in 1894–5,[5] the post of chairman was important, but normally the key figure on the Committee was the secretary. This was partly the result of Broadhurst's forceful reign between 1875 and 1890; yet even if his successors were lesser men the office carried its own authority, and the one real centre of the trade union world was to be found in a set of poky rooms in Buckingham Street, south of the Strand.[6] Here, as the Webbs commented in 1894, Congress expected 'the Parliamentary affairs of a million and a half members to be transacted by a staff inferior to that of a third-rate Trade Union'.[7] With a total income which, in the decade after 1889, rose from a mere £900 to just over £2,000 a year, the Committee could certainly not finance an elaborate headquarters or any lavish development of its activities.

Paid only for 'the leavings of his time and attention', the secretary was

---

[1] *History*, p. 566. On 6 Oct. 1894 the *Workman's Times* complained that Holmes of the Weavers had told a meeting of cotton delegates over their beer that 'some arrangements had been made for exchanging votes' and issued the necessary instructions. Holmes was elected chairman of the new Committee. Much the same point was made by delegates of the Boot and Shoe Operatives in 1900 (National Union of Boot and Shoe Operatives, *Biennial Conference Report*, 1900).

This, however, was a game that two could play. ' "Dirty work", said [John] Burnett, with a look of unutterable contempt in his clear grey eyes, "the sailor [Havelock Wilson] brought twenty votes, practically exchanging them for a seat on the committee. Too much of that sort of thing!"' (Beatrice Webb's diary, Sept. 1889, *Our Partnership*, p. 23). And in the *Labour Leader* on 8 Sept. 1894 Keir Hardie admitted that 'canvassing is doubtless bad in theory, but . . . the ILPers must be less guileless in future'.   [2] *Industrial Democracy*, p. 265.

[3] *History*, p. 567.   [4] Ibid., p. 568.   [5] See p. 259.

[6] It is clear from the *Minutes* of the Parliamentary Committee (19 Feb. 1890) that the tenure of the office was in Broadhurst's name and the furniture his own.   [7] *History*, p. 569.

Congress's one salaried official.[1] During the nineties he was always either a Member of Parliament or an officer of his society, and usually both. With a single clerk at his disposal, he had the assistance only of such experts as could be persuaded to help him, so that whenever possible the unions themselves were expected to draft bills or resolutions and to do their own lobbying, while the Committee gave them general support. Liaison was provided by the secretary, who also did his best to find parliamentary spokesmen when they were needed. It is hardly surprising that he was either grossly overworked or regarded as negligent.

Each year a number of resolutions passed by Congress demanded new legislation or administrative action by ministers. During October and November the Parliamentary Committee met to decide what steps should be taken. Much of the detailed work was done by 'the London committee', or 'sub-committee', which consisted of the chairman, vice-chairman, and secretary, together with such other members as were available in London. Once a bill or resolution had been drafted it was placed in the hands of one of the labour Members or those of a sympathizer like Buxton or Channing. But an opportunity of bringing the matter before the House had also to be found. With a bill this meant engaging the interest of as many Members as possible, in the hope that one of them would be successful in the ballot for private members' bills.

Deputations to ministers were timed to begin with the parliamentary session, which normally opened early in February. The first type, designed to put a particular case, was generally organized by the society concerned but given support by the Parliamentary Committee; the second, led by the Committee and 'commonly called the "omnibus deputation"', dealt with 'other questions of great importance affecting the workers which could not be very well put in the form of a Bill',[2] and might tramp round from minister to minister. Both types were often large in order to impress. In 1893, for example, the deputation to Gladstone on the miners' Eight Hours Bill consisted of sixty-two representatives of the Miners' Federation, nineteen Members of Parliament, and three of the Parliamentary Committee.[3] In the same year 200 assorted trade unionists waited upon Asquith as Home Secretary, and in 1895 his Conservative successor was approached on a wide variety of topics by a deputation of 250. Both groups were headed by members of the Parliamentary Committee.[4]

[1] Until 1896 the salary was £200 a year. On 11 Oct. 1892 the Committee agreed to recommend an increase to £300; but nothing was done, presumably because of hostility to Fenwick in Congress for his behaviour on the eight hours question. The secretary's clerical assistance had to be paid for out of his salary: the cost of this apparently averaged £40 a year during the early nineties (Parliamentary Committee, *Minutes*, 4 June 1896.)

[2] Trades Union Congress, *Annual Report*, 1896, Parliamentary Committee Report.

[3] Page Arnot, op. cit., vol. i, pp. 190–1.

[4] Trades Union Congress, *Annual Reports*, 1893 and 1896, Parliamentary Committee Reports.

If a deputation was rebuffed or a bill failed to reach the order paper, the Committee was usually resigned to reporting the fact to Congress before trying again next year. In March 1894, however, in conjunction with the London Trades Council, they organized a demonstration in Hyde Park against the Liberal government's decision to abandon its Employers' Liability Bill. This was an exceptional issue calling for exceptional treatment. Ever since 1880 the amendment of the Act of that year had been one of Congress's major aims, and the Committee were particularly anxious to put an end to the system of 'contracting-out' under which employers could get out of the obligations imposed by the Act. They had been led to believe that the Bill would satisfy all their requirements. When it was abandoned entirely they were understandably incensed.[1]

In the ordinary course of events the Committee would by this time have settled down to supervising the conduct of parliamentary business, seeing that promises were kept, bills presented, and speeches made. With the help of the London committee, the secretary did his best to deal with requests and complaints which flowed in from the unions. From time to time, to draw attention to its energy, the Committee passed resolutions for release to the press; circulars were sent out, exhorting the unions to action on matters of general interest, or in the hope of securing their aid in implementing Congress decisions. By the time of the Whitsun recess, as the end of the session in August came into sight, the Committee began to turn their attention to the next Congress, drafting their Report and asking for resolutions to build up the programme for the September meeting.

The Webbs criticized this whole procedure as inefficient and even ridiculous. 'The work annually accomplished by the Committee . . . has, in fact, been limited to a few deputations to the Government, two or three circulars to the Unions, a little consultation with friendly politicians, and the drafting of an elaborate report to Congress, describing, not their doings, but the legislation and other Parliamentary proceedings of the session'.[2] The deputations were 'futile', and the resolutions of Congress they presented were 'crude'.[3] The Committee was unable to give either practical or intellectual leadership to the movement.[4] Its ineffectiveness and unimportance were reflected in the fact that the 'central executives of the [major] unions seldom dream of communicating their desires to

---

[1] At an earlier stage, the Committee had been prepared to compromise over contracting-out if that would save the rest of their proposals. On 13 Feb. 1894 'it was resolved to accept an amendment limiting contracting out to . . . three years rather than to imperil the passing of the Bill'. Once the Bill had been abandoned in the face of strong opposition, the Committee denounced 'the action of these irresponsible legislators', but did not report the suggested compromise to Congress (Trades Union Congress, *Annual Report*, 1894.)

[2] *History*, p. 568.   [3] Ibid., p. 570.

[4] Ibid., pp. 571–2; *Industrial Democracy*, pp. 267–8. V. L. Allen has echoed these views in *Trade Unions and the Government*, 1960, pp. 8–9, 13, 16.

the Parliamentary Committee',[1] and conducted their own campaigns without reference to it.

Many of the deputations may have been futile, but the major unions, notably coal and cotton, certainly did not ignore the Committee. On the contrary, they were eager to be represented on it. The cotton leaders, for example, took great pains to maintain their two seats on the Committee, except in 1890, when Birtwistle withdrew at Congress because he refused to promote the general Eight Hours Bill and Mawdsley resigned on the same grounds a month later. But by the following year they had thought better of it, for their influence on the Committee was too useful to be abandoned. Despite their formidable political power, they were careful to keep the Parliamentary Committee fully informed and to solicit their aid at every turn.[2]

When the Weavers prepared to act against steaming in 1888, they added Broadhurst to the committee entrusted with the conduct of their bill.[3] On 2 November the Parliamentary Committee in turn instructed its sub-committee to support any deputation or other move arranged by the cotton operatives. At the same meeting the Committee asked Birtwistle, who was already in charge of the steaming agitation, to draft a new Factory and Workshops Bill. There was similar co-operation over the campaigns of 1894–5 and 1899–1901[4] for the amendment of the Factory Acts, and on a broader front the cotton leaders had been able to win the support of the Parliamentary Committee for bimetallism in 1892,[5] but in 1898 Congress rejected 'protection for silver'.[6] Even then Mawdsley led a deputation to the Committee and persuaded them to circularize the unions asking them to reconsider the matter[7], but he was again defeated at Congress in 1899.

The Miners' Federation were equally anxious to obtain the backing of the Parliamentary Committee. Indeed, lacking the contacts of the cotton operatives in the House and without direct representation there comparable

[1] *Industrial Democracy*, p. 266.

[2] Although convention forbade more than one representative for each trade, cotton was allowed two on the grounds that spinning and weaving were separate trades. In 1896 Allen Gee of the General Union of Textile Workers was elected to a place on the Committee, but was not allowed to take it up because Holmes of the weavers' amalgamation had received a higher poll and weaving was therefore already represented. Apart from 1890 to 1891 the cotton unions held two seats throughout the period, Mawdsley giving way to Mullin of the cardroom amalgamation in 1897. Coal held one place, in addition to the secretaryship, and the railwaymen (except for 1893–4) and the boot and shoe operatives one each. From 1894 Thorne represented the general labourers, and Havelock Wilson kept a place up to 1898. Apart from the special case of Burns, the engineers were not represented except in 1897–8.   [3] See p. 244.

[4] The majority of Congress was against the cotton operatives on the half-time question, first condemning it in 1896. The Parliamentary Committee, however, seems to have done nothing to implement this and subsequent resolutions.

[5] Parliamentary Committee, *Minutes*, 9 Feb. 1892; *Cotton Factory Times*, 1 July 1892.

[6] This is the title given to the debate by that staunch free-trader, W. J. Davis (op. cit., vol. ii, p. 169).   [7] Parliamentary Committee, *Minutes*, 12 Oct. 1898.

to that of the miners of the North-east, they at first depended heavily on the Committee's readiness to handle their Eight Hours Bill. This measure won the support of Congress in 1889, but the Parliamentary Committee, still dominated by opponents of the legislative control of working hours, evaded its instructions. Next year the Federation failed to persuade Congress to censure them for this, but an uneasy alliance with the 'new unionists' procured Pickard's election to the Committee. John Wilson won back his seat in 1891, however, and the Federation failed to find an opponent for Fenwick as secretary.

In 1892, therefore, they condemned the Parliamentary Committee's record as 'unsatisfactory and inconsistent' with the reiterated resolution of Congress, and tried in vain to depose Fenwick for 'both speaking and voting' against the Bill. By now the Federation had been able to make their own parliamentary arrangements, but this in no way diminished the struggle for power on the Committee. The influence of the North-east was eliminated only in 1894 when Woods ousted Fenwick, whose credit with Congress had finally been exhausted by his most recent vote against eight hours.[1] Thereafter Woods and Cowey, who had displaced Wilson in 1893, regularly brought the Committee into all the Federation's activities.

Coal and cotton were not alone in their anxiety to obtain the support of the Parliamentary Committee. In 1884 the London Society of Compositors had secured the backing of the Committee in their attempt to induce the Stationery Office to make trade union rates the basis for all its contracts, and had obtained 'fair wages' from the London School Board and the London County Council in 1889. Meanwhile Congress took up the general issue of fair wages,[2] and Broadhurst prepared to take the lead in consultation with the printers and the London Building Trades Committee. Hampered by illness and other troubles, however, he finally arranged for Buxton to move the resolution of 13 February 1891.

The importance of both Congress and the Parliamentary Committee in the eyes of trade unionists was further demonstrated by the battle to control them waged between the 'old guard' and the 'new unionists'. The latter had formidable obstacles to overcome. Up to 1889 Broadhurst had had no difficulty in repelling Keir Hardie's attacks,[3] and in that year John Wilson's motion of confidence in him was carried by an overwhelming majority. Even when Broadhurst had gone, his successor, Fenwick, was protected from censure, and thrice comfortably re-elected by a Congress hostile to his views on the eight-hour day. Such loyalty was a brake on change, especially when new blood could be absorbed without transforming the Committee's outlook. From his first election in 1889 Havelock Wilson

---

[1] See p. 242.
[2] A vaguely worded motion was passed in 1888, and a more precise resolution the following year.   [3] Roberts, op. cit., pp. 118–20, 124.

easily adapted himself, whatever attitude he struck in public. Later both Tillett and Thorne also fitted in, though neither shared Wilson's smooth opportunism.

In 1890 the 'new unionists' made important gains. Not only was the series of 'socialist' resolutions—headed by the demand for a statutory eight-hour day—more imposing than ever before, but there were also substantial changes in personnel. Broadhurst's resignation has indeed been taken as the end of an era, even though his enemies could hope for no support from his successor.[1] More promising, it seemed, were the changes in the composition of the Parliamentary Committee. One hero of the 'new union-ists', Havelock Wilson, jumped from bottom place among the successful candidates in 1889 to first in 1890, while another, John Burns, made his début. Yet too much could be made of the failure of all but three of the previous Committee to hold their seats. William Crawford was dead and George Shipton[2] had withdrawn to run for the secretaryship. Birtwistle and later Mawdsley refused the places to which they had been elected, as did Henry Slatter, the runner-up. Only then did one of these places pass to Burns, who came next, while Alexander Wilkie was co-opted into the other. But Wilkie, like Pickard, was no firebrand, and the other new men— G. D. Kelley of the Lithographic Printers, who had been co-opted to take Crawford's place; J. M. Jack, the Scottish Ironmoulders' secretary, who had already served from 1884 to 1889; Stuart Uttley, secretary of the Sheffield Filecutters and the Sheffield Trades Council; and William Matkin, secretary of the General Union of Carpenters and Joiners—were all Lib-Labs, though most of them had been helped by left-wing votes.[3]

The victories of the 'new unionists', however, did not give them control of Congress, where their weakness was revealed even in 1890. Previously, voting had been by show of hands, and each 'trades society' and trades council had sent as many delegates as it wished; but now the Miners' Federation asserted that they represented 'one-eighth of Congress, and they considered it was time the constitution of the Congress was altered' to suit. They easily carried a resolution that votes should be in proportion to the number of members for whom affiliation fees were paid, at the rate

---

[1] Nevertheless, Fenwick's defeat of Shipton, the epitome of 'old unionism' (see below), gave much pleasure, for example, to John Burns (Burgess, op. cit., p. 121).

[2] Shipton, George (1839–1911). General secretary, London Amalgamated House Painters, later London Amalgamated House Decorators and Painters, 1866–89. Parliamentary Committee, Trades Union Congress, 1875–82, 1883–4, 1885–90; secretary, 1886. Secretary, London Trades Council, 1872–96.

[3] After Congress the new Committee's *Minutes* showed some signs of flurry. On 2 Oct. it was decided 'after a lengthy discussion . . . that this committee use its best efforts to carry into effect the resolution bearing upon the Miners' Eight Hours Bill; and further, that with regard to the general Eight Hour Day, the Secretary and Sub-Committee be instructed to get drafted a Bill dealing with all Trades of the country, and submit the same to the next meeting of the Parliamentary Committee'.

of £1 per 1,000 members, which was bound to increase the weight of the larger associations, few of them friends of the 'new unionism'.

Thus at the time of their greatest strength in Congress, which they claimed had been won for socialism, the 'new unionists' could not prevent its machinery from being changed to their disadvantage. The Parliamentary Committee seized its opportunity. On the ground that 'the mandatory character of the amendment left no other course open to us', they revised standing orders so that the new system would operate from the beginning of the 1891 Congress, and proposed that the Committee's chairman should in future preside over Congress. But they had overreached themselves. After much confusion Congress decided, by a card vote taken under the new system, to return for the moment to the old standing orders, and then referred the whole problem back to the Parliamentary Committee.[1] Apparently chastened, the Committee evolved a 'compromise' which Congress accepted in 1892.[2]

Affiliation fees would be those suggested by the miners, but voting was to be by show of hands; each society was entitled to one representative for every 2,000 members; and trades councils were to send delegates only for those not directly represented through affiliated unions. Even so, the payment of £1 per 1,000 members was beyond the means of many trades councils. Between 1888 and 1892 the number affiliated had risen from 46 to about 130, claiming to represent half a million trade unionists. In 1893 the members represented fell sharply to 150,000 and sank to 66,000 in 1894. In their hey-day the councils had contributed many votes to the 'new unionists', and the loss was all the more damaging now that the membership of the new unions themselves was dwindling away in the trade depression. The total number of delegates, which had climbed from 165 in 1888 to 552 in the unruly Congress of 1891, fell to 495 in 1892 and 378 in 1894.

Expressing the general opinion, Joseph Burgess said that 'the smaller the Congress the better it is for the old school'.[3] The new regulations,

---

[1] Roberts, op. cit., pp. 143–4.

[2] The Committee had another reason for appearing chastened. On paper at least, its freedom of manœuvre was now restricted. On 26 Jan. 1893 Fenwick, allegedly quoting standing orders, told the Royal Commission on Labour that 'the duties of the parliamentary committee shall be to watch all legislative measures directly affecting the question of labour, to initiate *whenever necessary* such legislative action as congress may direct *or as the exigencies of the time and circumstances may demand*' (*Royal Commission on Labour*, C–7063–I, 1893, Q. 7179). This was the old version, but in 1892 'by a large majority' Congress had struck out the words italicized (Trades Union Congress, *Annual Report*, 1892). Fenwick's keeping of the minutes had already been attacked over the eight hours question (Roberts, op. cit., pp. 138–9); but he does not seem to have mended his ways.

[3] *Workman's Times*, 15 Sept. 1894. Burgess went on to say that 'new unions' always had a lower proportion of 'financial members' than established unions, so that payment of affiliation fees on their full strength penalized them. The Webbs found that 'in many cases' about half of the delegates to trades councils were sent by labourers' unions, while some craft societies

therefore, might have been expected to give them complete control of Congress, but in fact the socialists could still find a majority of delegates to support them. In 1893, when a scheme for supporting labour candidates was under discussion, James Macdonald, the socialist tailor, carried by 137 votes to 97 an amendment requiring the candidates to pledge themselves 'to support the principle of collective ownership and control of all the means of production and distribution'. At the Norwich Congress of 1894 socialist initiative was even more in evidence. By 219 votes to 61 Keir Hardie carried an amendment calling for the nationalization of the means of production, distribution, and exchange, and Congress also resolved that affiliated unions should ballot their members on the provision of government work at trade union rates for the unemployed.

Robert Knight's opening speech at Norwich typified the attitude of the more intransigent of the 'old school'.

The Trades Union Congress [he said] had become a gathering ground of advanced Socialists whose dreamy ideas find vent in strongly worded resolutions. We differ fundamentally and utterly in all such proposals as these, as they would curse labour with restricted freedom, with diminished resources, with arrested progress, with abject dependence and the demoralisation that all these things bring. If our friends who shout so loud at Congresses would depend more on individual effort and work a little more for their societies, and less for passing wild resolutions, it would be much better for those they are supposed to represent.

On the other hand, Havelock Wilson struck a lighter note that was to become more and more familiar. Styling himself 'one of the old reactionary gang', he supported Hardie's amendment but told Congress that 'it must not be supposed that it would be put in force twenty-four hours later on. . . . He did not believe he should live to see it carried into effect.'

As Tom Mann feared, 'many amongst the older trade unionists' now felt able to treat a 'Collectivist Resolution . . . as the mere expression of a pious opinion'[1] with which they might concur. This may account for the spectacle at Norwich of 'Henry Broadhurst and practically the whole of the Miners' Federation and the textile delegates voting with the majority'.[2] Nevertheless, whatever the attitude of such delegates to socialist resolutions, they steered clear of socialist candidates. In 1893 Hardie had secured only 25 per cent. of the votes for the secretaryship in a straight fight with Fenwick; in 1894 Mann, with 29 per cent., was third in a three-cornered contest.

The Norwich Congress evoked ridicule from *The Times*, and Geoffrey Drage, who had been secretary to the Royal Commission on Labour,

forbade their branches to affiliate to the councils (Webb Trade Union Collection E, Section A, vol. iv, quoted by Crowley, op. cit.).

[1] *Labour Leader*, 18 Aug. 1894.   [2] Ibid., 15 Sept. 1894.

urged 'the old school', 'the backbone of trade unionism', to combine against the socialists in order to prevent a repetition of these proceedings.[1] This was just what the Parliamentary Committee was doing. Under cover of a resolution carried by W. J. Davis in 1894, which was apparently designed only to improve the conduct of business, and of other motions remitted to its consideration for lack of time at Congress, a subcommittee reconstructed standing orders. Trades councils were to be excluded; votes were to be proportionate to affiliated membership; and in future a delegate would have to be either a full-time union officer or still working at his trade. This meant the exclusion of Hardie and two members of the Committee itself, Broadhurst, who had returned in 1893, and Burns, who won a place in his own right at the same time.

After a bitter and protracted struggle the Parliamentary Committee divided evenly over the proposals, which were carried by the casting vote of Holmes, the chairman. Broadhurst persistently and adroitly opposed them, supported by the three 'new unionists', Thorne, Tillett, and Havelock Wilson, and by Jack and the Irish representative, Sheldon. With Holmes were Mawdsley, Cowey, Harford, and William Inskip of the National Union of Boot and Shoe Operatives, all opponents of the 'new unionism', and Burns, who had served on the drafting sub-committee together with Holmes, Mawdsley, and Woods, the secretary.

Burns was moved by a growing antipathy to his old associates, and particularly towards Hardie; his socialism was increasingly suspect; and he was ready to sacrifice his own seat on the Committee because he saw his future as a politician. But he 'allowed himself to be used as the tool' of the leaders of coal and cotton, and it is clear that Mawdsley was the real 'hero of the *coup d'état*'.[2] When Tillett revealed something of the truth at Congress in 1895, he declared that the changes meant that 'Trafalgar Square methods had given way to Brummagem methods', an apt comment on Burns's political evolution and on Mawdsley's qualities as a manipulator.

Even before Congress met, Mawdsley was sufficiently confident to speak freely. 'We saw that Congress was losing whatever influence it had, and we were determined to pull it back again into the old paths.'[3] The victorious alliance certainly left little to chance. At Congress the new procedure of block voting prescribed by the new standing orders was used to carry them. In contrast to what had happened in 1891, and despite the many protests, they were accepted by 604,000 votes to 357,000. Moreover, in the election for the new Parliamentary Committee, Cowey, Mawdsley, Harford, Holmes, and Inskip filled the first five places. Thorne, Jack, and

---

[1] *Workman's Times*, 29 Sept. 1894.   [2] Beatrice Webb, op. cit., p. 48.
[3] Trades Union Congress, *Annual Report*, 1895. Mawdsley's remarks, made in an interview with the *Daily Chronicle* on 31 Aug., nearly a month earlier, were quoted in the debate.

Havelock Wilson came in ninth, tenth, and eleventh out of twelve, and Tillett was defeated.

At this time the Webbs were dismissing Congress as 'an unorganized public meeting, utterly unable to formulate any consistent or practical policy' instead of 'a deliberative assembly checking and ratifying a programme prepared, after careful investigation, by a responsible Cabinet'.[1] They delivered a powerful attack on the new standing orders, which would 'destroy the value of the Trades Union Congress as a deliberative assembly' and might lead to the defection of the smaller unions.[2] Events proved them wrong. They had also laid down that 'the paramount condition of stable federation . . . is that the constituent bodies should be united only in so far as they possess interests in common, and that in respect of all other matters they should retain their independence. The Trades Union Congress is a federation for obtaining, by Parliamentary action, not social reform generally, but the particular measures desired by its constituent Trade Unions.'[3] Now the Parliamentary Committee used its new authority, as 'a responsible Cabinet', to concentrate on this very aim.

Some attempt was made to rationalize the agenda. In 1894 Davis, as chairman of the Standing Orders Committee, had introduced the device of the 'composite resolution', with, in his opinion, 'good effect';[4] from 1895 the Parliamentary Committee took over the task.[5] Increased time and effort went into preparing Congress's programme, but something of the traditional disorder remained and was exacerbated by the growth of business. In 1898, in a moment of irritation, a lively Congress complained that 'the agenda is overcrowded', and resolved that 'in order to give opportunity of discussion the practice of the Parliamentary Committee in placing resolutions of their own on the agenda be discontinued'. The Committee paid no attention, and in 1900 standing orders were again revised. The Committee's chairman was given the task of presiding at Congress, while the Committee was to prepare the programme 'from resolutions forwarded by the respective societies, and be empowered to rearrange and place only such propositions which are generally accepted as coming within the objects and aims of Trade Unionism'. There was considerable opposition, especially to the change in the presidency;[6] but the block vote came to the Committee's aid.

---

[1] *Industrial Democracy*, p. 269. The first edition was published in 1897, with comments on the developments of 1895 added as a postscript to chapter iv.   [2] Ibid., pp. 276–8.

[3] Ibid., pp. 270–1.   [4] Davis, op. cit., vol. ii, p. 93.

[5] Standing Order 11, paragraph 5 now read: 'The Parliamentary Committee shall meet at least seven days before the meeting of Congress for the purpose of classifying resolutions and amendments. . . .'

[6] This was so despite the fact that the presidential address which the delegates had just heard was the longest ever delivered, and ranged from Darwin's theory of natural selection and quotations from Tennyson to details of ant communities and the religious beliefs of the Fiji Islanders.

Having reformed Congress, the Parliamentary Committee turned in the autumn of 1895 to tightening up its own methods of doing business. Members were to be fined if they failed to attend, and to forfeit their allowances if they came late or left early without the chairman's permission. A member who had not been present at a previous meeting could not raise questions on the minutes.[1] With the growth of business, meetings became much more frequent and less was left to the London committee. But this did not mean that the officers became less important. Indeed, it is clear that the duties of the chairman grew more onerous and responsible. In 1900, when it was decided that in future he should also be president of Congress, the Committee unanimously resolved that the chairman 'should be elected on his merits', and not by rotation as before.[2]

As secretary, Woods was at first more efficient than his predecessor. Fenwick had performed his parliamentary duties well enough, except on the eight hours issue; but his standard of office work was low and his minutes are thin and poorly kept. Woods was much more the Committee's servant than either Broadhurst or Fenwick. He bustled about his parliamentary duties, took trouble with reports and minutes, and made himself agreeable to the members. From 1896 the office was opened daily 'as a convenience to the Trades', and the secretary was given a full-time clerk.[3] But the volume of business became too much for Woods, especially when his health began to fail in 1900. In January of that year Davis resigned from the Committee in protest against the secretary's 'alleged neglect in connexion with the office work', withdrawing his charge a month later when Woods made 'an explanation'. Worse was to follow, and after his retirement in 1904 there was a good deal of embarrassed tidying up.

The new standing orders had facilitated control of Congress. Up to 1895 James Macdonald, Hardie, and Burns were the leading spokesmen of the socialists. Tillett and Thorne had supported them, but from 1894 Thorne was a loyal member of the Parliamentary Committee, and Tillett, though he did not regain the seat he lost in 1895, was too erratic to establish a following, even if he frequently caused a stir. Despite the loss of their leaders, however, the younger socialist delegates soon re-established

---

[1] Standing orders adopted by the Parliamentary Committee, 12 Feb. 1896. The *Minutes* show that these rules were not rigidly applied, but meetings appear to have become more orderly and business-like. On 8 June 1898 the Committee passed a firm resolution deploring Havelock Wilson's poor record of attendance. He was not re-elected at the subsequent Congress.

[2] This was announced to Congress by Davis, who had been an unusually competent chairman during 1898–9. For some time thereafter strict seniority ceased to determine the Committee's choice.

[3] 'In view of the recent great increase in the clerical work attached to the Parliamentary Secretary's duties', the Committee recommended Congress to increase the secretary's salary by £100 (Parliamentary Committee, *Minutes*, 4 June 1896) and this was done (Trades Union Congress, *Annual Report*, 1896). Previously, on 12 Feb. 1896, on Thorne's motion, the Committee had granted Woods £60 for 1895 and 1896 'for extra services and assistance'.

an 'opposition' whose most consistent spokesman of any stature was Pete Curran, a national organizer of the Gasworkers' union, a founder member of the Independent Labour Party, and the last of the Championites.

As late as 1896 there was an attempt at Congress to water down Hardie's famous motion of 1894, but in 1897 the 'opposition' won a large majority for a resolution to 'socialise the land and the whole of the means of production, distribution and exchange'. No doubt many leaders agreed with Pickard that this was 'a matter of pious opinion', but the miners did not vote against it. Hardie probably exaggerated when he claimed that the majority of delegates to Congress in 1898 had socialist sympathies, and that three-fifths of these were members of the Independent Labour Party;[1] but Tom Mann's prophecy that it was a mistake 'to suppose that by narrowing the basis of representation at the Congress . . . either Socialism or Socialists will be kept out'[2] had been amply fulfilled.

Equally important were the changes in the composition and opinions of the Parliamentary Committee. The victors of the *coup d'état* of 1895 were not the 'old guard' of 1889; and if the individualistic Liberalism of Gladstone had ever been dominant among Lib-Labs, it was so no longer. Inskip and Harford had little sympathy with new ideas, but Wilkie favoured common action with the socialists as practised by London Progressives such as C. W. Bowerman and W. C. Steadman, soon to be his colleagues on the Committee. Thorne, though a pillar of the trade union establishment, remained a loyal member of the Social Democratic Federation, and in 1897 a seat went to a member of the Independent Labour Party, Isaac Mitchell[3] of the Engineers. The Toryism of Mawdsley, the Committee's solitary Conservative, had room for a large element of collectivism, and even Cowey claimed to be 'a Socialist to a certain extent'.[4]

Opinions both in Congress and the Parliamentary Committee were also developing under the pressure of outside events. Long before the Taff Vale case, for example, the Committee was alive to the implications of the major decisions of the courts in trade union cases. In 1896 they responded at once to a suggestion made by the London Trades Council that they should promote an appeal for funds to carry *Lyons* v. *Wilkins* to a higher court.[5] For four years they tried to overcome union apathy in order that 'the law in regard to Picketing should be more clearly defined'.[6] In 1898 they reported to Congress their gratitude to Edmond Browne, a barrister,

[1] *Labour Leader*, 10 Sept. 1898, quoted in Philip P. Poirier, *The Advent of the Labour Party*, 1958, p. 72.

[2] *Labour Leader*, 20 Sept. 1895, quoted in Roberts, op. cit., p. 155. See also p. 294.

[3] Mitchell, Isaac (1867–1952). Secretary, Glasgow District, Amalgamated Society of Engineers, 1898–9. Parliamentary Committee, Trades Union Congress, 1897–8. Secretary, General Federation of Trade Unions, 1899–1907. Labour Department of the Board of Trade, 1907. Principal Conciliation Officer, Ministry of Labour, 1927–32.

[4] See p. 300, footnote 7. Hardie called him 'a Socialist at heart'.

[5] Parliamentary Committee, *Minutes*, 8 Apr. 1896.   [6] Ibid., 6 June 1898.

for help over workmen's compensation and 'for many other acts of kindness . . . rendered them in the past'. When the *Lyons* v. *Wilkins* appeal collapsed in 1900 they immediately accepted his 'offer to become Standing Counsel and legal adviser to the Parliamentary Committee',[1] hoping thus to offset 'the uninstructed henchmen of capital who are always to be found in the legal profession'.[2] In so doing they followed for once the Webbs' advice that they should employ professional experts.

Almost from the outset the Committee showed marked hostility to the Conservative administration of 1895. Their report to Congress in 1896 was sharply critical of the lack of 'any one really tangible and beneficial measure passed in the interests of labour', and went on to say that 'the working-class community need hold out [no] very high hopes of anything being done for them during the lifetime of the present Parliament'.[3] Two years later it seemed 'useless to expect any active measures of industrial reform'.[4] As a result, when the Salisbury government, largely under the influence of Joseph Chamberlain, did enter the field of labour legislation, the union leaders gave it little credit.

In 1894 the Royal Commission on Labour had reported in favour of 'some more rational and less barbarous method of settling industrial disputes than strikes and lockouts'. There followed the Conciliation Act of 1896, which empowered the Board of Trade to appoint arbitrators at the request of both sides, and conciliators at the request of either side, and to inquire into disputes. Even if this amounted to little more than what the Board's Labour Department was already doing, the Act established its authority beyond doubt. The Liberal James Bryce, in supporting the measure, said that he had hesitated over intervention, when President of the Board of Trade, 'feeling, as there was no statutory authority behind him, that he could only do so in a semi-official sort of way'.[5] Sir Charles Dilke,[6] however, described it as merely 'a good sort of shop front Bill'.[7] Some Lib-Labs, suspicious of the government's intentions, tried to suggest that there was some threat of compulsion, Pickard being particularly violent and confused. But in the end every union leader gave the Act qualified approval.

In 1897 the Lib-Labs were caught napping by the Workmen's Compensation Act. Chamberlain had based the measure on his long-standing conviction 'that no amendment of the Law relating to Employers' Liability will be final or satisfactory which does not provide compensation to workmen for all injuries sustained in the ordinary course of their

---

[1] Ibid., 2 Mar. 1900.
[2] Trades Union Congress, *Annual Report*, 1898, Parliamentary Committee Report.
[3] Ibid., 1896.   [4] Ibid., 1898.   [5] *Hansard*, 30 June 1896, col. 428.
[6] Dilke, Sir Charles (1843–1911). Liberal M.P., 1868–86, 1892–1911. Under-Secretary of State for Foreign Affairs, 1880–2. President of Local Government Board, 1882–5.
[7] *Hansard*, 30 June 1896, col. 421.

employment, and not caused by their own acts or default'.[1] Deep in the throes of the inquiry into the Jameson Raid, he nevertheless maintained control throughout the debates, and his opening speech on 3 May caught the opposition on the wrong foot. Both Asquith, the chief Liberal spokesman, and the Lib-Labs were made to look outmoded and petty, still hankering after the abandoned Bill of 1893 in the face of what the Webbs described as a 'revolutionary' measure.[2]

Some never recovered from the initial shock, but Asquith and Broadhurst soon swung round to critical support, pointing out the Bill's limitations and the danger of excessive litigation. Both were much impressed by the socialistic tendency of Chamberlain's proposals: Asquith compared it to the Elizabethan Poor Law as a device which would permit the continuous expansion of state regulation, while Broadhurst proclaimed that 'they had decided once for all a great principle from which Parliament could never go back . . . they had established the birthright of labour'.[3]

The only persistent opposition came from Tory back-benchers and from special interests, notably the exporting coalfields, always sensitive to increased costs. It was Joicey, the Durham coal-owner, who said that 'there was more socialism pure and simple in the Bill than in any Bill . . . submitted during the last half-century, and many of the arguments used in favour of it could be equally well applied to any Measure brought in to provide food, clothing and medical attendance for the working classes'.[4] He was supported by his faithful ally, John Wilson, still loyal to old-fashioned Liberalism, and typical of the miners' leaders from the North-east in sharing the owners' anxieties on the subject of costs.

The grudging comment of the Parliamentary Committee was that the Act 'scarcely touches the question of employer's liability in the sense in which it has always been understood in the past by the working classes'.[5] For the next two years Chamberlain confirmed their prejudices by giving very little consideration to the working man, despite his promises during the general election of 1895. Even when in 1899 the Chaplin Committee, urged on by Chamberlain, recommended a scheme for old-age pensions comparable to that advocated by Congress,[6] the outbreak of the South African War allowed the matter to be shelved, much to the somewhat sanctimonious disgust of the Parliamentary Committee.

It was not only the government's legislative record which gave offence. The Committee was also incensed by the cavalier attitude of some Conservative ministers to its traditional deputations. The trouble had begun

---

[1] *Hansard*, 20 Feb. 1893, col. 1961. [2] *Industrial Democracy*, p. 387.
[3] *Hansard*, 15 July 1897, col. 230. [4] Ibid., 18 May 1897, col. 767.
[5] Trades Union Congress, *Annual Report*, 1897.
[6] Steadman had first raised the question at Congress in 1897, and it was Steadman again who in 1901 demanded, on behalf of the Parliamentary Committee, that Chamberlain should redeem the pledges given in 1895.

as early as 1896. Goschen at the Admiralty was the chief culprit, and three years later he was still refusing to meet them. The Parliamentary Committee therefore reported to Congress that his conduct 'is unworthy of a British Minister, is discourteous to the working classes of this country, and contrary to the treatment which the Parliamentary Committee invariably receives at the hands of Cabinet Ministers'.

By this time, however, the employers' counter-attack had added to the forces driving Congress and the Parliamentary Committee to accept new ideas. In 1898, with the engineering lock-out in mind, Wilkie, the retiring chairman of the Committee, suggested that more state intervention was needed to settle disputes. 'Considering . . . the position taken up by some employers with regard to the Conciliation Act of 1896, it had become a question of serious importance to all trade unionists whether or not the provisions of the Act should not be considerably strengthened.' The Conservatives were willing to listen. In 1895 Chamberlain himself had asked for 'a Board of Arbitration, so influential, so authoritative, so dignified, that no body of employers or workmen would dare to refuse to submit their case to it'.[1] Now Ritchie, in 1898, proposed a National Conciliation Board of employers and workmen, 'who should act in the capacity of an appeal court' on issues not settled by local boards which could be set up in every 'large centre of industry'.

In reply the Parliamentary Committee resolved 'to request the President of the Board of Trade to inaugurate a Conference between Employers and Workmen to consider the best means of decreasing trade conflicts',[2] and later referred to his proposal as 'strong and statesmanlike'.[3] The next year, however, they reported to Congress—not without some unction— that the scheme had been killed by the refusal of the Employers' Parliamentary Council to have anything to do with it. In fact most unions were traditionally opposed to compulsory arbitration, and the experience of the decade had not changed their minds; but the opposition of the employers should be emphasized. Had the organization of British employers been less developed, and collective bargaining therefore rudimentary or absent, the pressure to imitate the colonial schemes of state intervention might have been far more difficult to resist.[4]

Meanwhile there had been an important change in the attitude of the

[1] *Hansard*, 5 Mar. 1895, col. 406.
[2] Parliamentary Committee, *Minutes*, 15 Dec. 1898; and Trades Union Congress, *Annual Report*, 1899.   [3] Ibid., 15 May 1899.
[4] At the Congress of 1899 Ben Tillett, who had been impressed by colonial arbitration schemes during his visit to Australasia in 1893–4, began his prolonged campaign for compulsory arbitration. In a thin vote he was defeated by two to one. Two years later, however, he was supported by Richard Bell, and greater interest was aroused. The poll was exceptionally high but, with coal and cotton opposed, the margin of defeat was only slightly narrowed. Thomas Ashton of the Spinners asserted that 'the best arbitrator in a trade dispute was a strong banking account'. Tillett continued to bring up the resolution, but it never did so well again.

Parliamentary Committee towards providing support for affiliated unions involved in disputes. In 1893 they had refused to take a hand in raising funds for the seamen and dockers on strike at Hull. 'While the Committee deeply sympathise with the men on strike yet having regard to the fact that the policy of the Parliamentary Committee has always been one of strict neutrality in Labour disputes the Committee are of the opinion that they would be forming a dangerous precedent if they were to depart from that policy in this case by issuing an appeal for funds.'[1] In 1897, however, Congress recorded its 'entire sympathy' with the engineers, and the Committee decided on its own authority to help in raising funds, eventually handling £23,500 of the total of £116,000 subscribed.

The next step was to provide a permanent system of strike insurance. In 1890 Congress had instructed the Parliamentary Committee to draw up a scheme for 'industrial federation', and had narrowly rejected another in 1895.[2] In 1897 Congress resolved to 'form one federation to render mutual assistance in disputes, strikes and lockouts affecting any Trade Unions affiliated to the federation', and a special committee was appointed to devise a scheme with the assistance of the Parliamentary Committee. The lead was taken by Robert Knight, the architect of the Federation of Engineering and Shipbuilding Trades, Alexander Wilkie, and Pete Curran, representing an alliance between the 'old' unionism and the 'new'. They proposed that Congress should take the initiative in forming a separate federation to which unions should be free to affiliate or not. A special Congress in January 1899 blessed the scheme, and later that year the Parliamentary Committee handed it over to an executive chosen by the first forty-four unions to join the new General Federation of Trade Unions.[3]

The new organization was conscious of its origins and the limits within which it was expected to work. Its secretary, Isaac Mitchell, as fraternal delegate to Congress in 1900, explained that 'the Federation had decided to confine themselves entirely to trade matters. The Trades Union Congress was a political body, as they dealt essentially with political questions. They were perfectly willing in the Federation to allow the Congress to look after the political interests of the workers, and had decided not to interfere with any political question of any description.'

The political methods of Congress were, however, not free from criticism. In 1897 the Parliamentary Committee itself informed Congress that 'the existing methods are not only expensive, cumbrous, and generally unsatisfactory, yet they have not been able to devise any better process of

---

[1] Parliamentary Committee, *Minutes*, 3 May 1893.

[2] Phelps Brown, op. cit., p. 249.

[3] The Federation's first report claimed 344,000 members compared with the 1,184,000 affiliated to Congress.

bringing their labour grievances before the Government',[1] and they emphasized the need to return more sympathetic, and preferably labour, Members, a theme that was thereafter reiterated annually with growing force. One sympathizer upon whom the Committee could immediately rely was Dilke, and from the end of 1897 his relationship with them became closer than before.

Early in 1898 Dilke arranged through Davis to revive his old custom of entertaining the Parliamentary Committee at the beginning of the session to discuss proposals for legislation on labour questions.[2] During the following spring he suggested to them the formation of 'a non-political party to deal with all labour questions of importance', promising 'valuable assistance from members on both sides of the House'.[3] This was a plan for an all-party group upon whom the Committee could call for assistance both in the House and on deputations to ministers. It prospered, first demonstrating its value during the agitation which led up to the Factory Act of 1901.[4] Dilke also helped the Parliamentary Committee with their attempts to galvanize the existing labour Members into greater unity and activity. Woods had already attempted this in 1897 during the debates on the Workmen's Compensation Act, apparently with some success,[5] but more formal steps were now needed. On 23 March 1899, therefore, a meeting of labour Members elected Burns and Woods as a subcommittee, with Fenwick as whip, 'to watch closely the order papers of the House of Commons, so as to be prepared when Labour questions were likely to be under discussion'.[6] Some progress along traditional lines was thus achieved, and by 1900 the Committee was laying great emphasis upon 'meeting the Labour and other M.P.s' to arrange for the handling of Congress resolutions.[7]

There were also moves towards co-operation with the socialists. As early as June 1896 the Parliamentary Committee had returned a civil reply to the request of the Independent Labour Party for a tripartite conference with the Fabians to secure 'greater unanimity amongst the Workers at Election times'.[8] Three months later the president of Congress, J. Mallinson, a moderate from the Edinburgh Cordwainers, referred to 'our friends the Socialists'. 'By all means let us have a workers' political party', he added, 'only let it be kept outside trade-unionism. There is plenty of work for such a party, and though it could render valuable assistance to trade-unionism, it could not take the place of the latter.' In 1898 the socialist

---

[1] Trades Union Congress, *Annual Report*, 1897, quoted in Allen, op. cit., p. 8.
[2] Davis, op. cit., vol. ii, p. 144.
[3] Parliamentary Committee, *Minutes*, 10 May 1899.
[4] See p. 365. [5] Parliamentary Committee, *Minutes*, 11, 24, 25 May 1897.
[6] Trades Union Congress, *Annual Report*, 1899, summarized in Davis, op. cit., vol. ii, pp. 160–1. [7] Parliamentary Committee, *Minutes*, 4 Dec. 1900.
[8] Ibid., 3 June 1896.

James O'Grady of the Alliance Cabinet Makers delivered the presidential address. After a favourable reference to the proposals for federation he went on to say that 'another committee should be appointed to draft a scheme of political organization, so that this may become a burning question at future Congresses on the ground that just as trades federation is a matter of vital necessity to our industrial organizations, so also will a scheme of political action be a vital necessity if we wish Parliament to faithfully register the effect of the industrial revolution on our social life.'

At this point the device of 'hiving-off', already applied to industrial federation, was used to allow Congress to make its boldest venture into new forms of organization, while still obeying the Webbs' injunction to confine itself to matters in which its members possessed 'interests in common'. On the motion of James Holmes of the Railway Servants, the Congress of 1899 had instructed the Parliamentary Committee to call a conference 'of all the co-operative, socialistic, trade unions, and other working organizations . . . to devise ways and means for securing the return of an increased number of labour members to the next Parliament'. The Committee joined with the Fabians, the Independent Labour Party, and the Social Democratic Federation to convene a conference in February 1900. Since few unions were represented except those prepared for joint action with the socialists, Hardie was able to carry his proposal for 'a distinct Labour Group in Parliament, who shall have their own Whips, and agree upon their policy'. The conference then proceeded to set up a permanent organization which was to endorse candidates, administer funds, and call future conferences.

In the atmosphere of 1895 neither industrial federation nor independent political organization would have appealed to the leaders who seemed to have established their domination over Congress that year. But within five years changes in their own number and opinions, and in the views of delegates, aided by the political and industrial events of the period, had led them to a compromise on both issues. Moreover, by 'setting its own survival above the scope of its activity, with an unconscious astuteness Congress had preserved its unity by establishing a separate channel to carry each of these disturbing currents away'.[1]

[1] Phelps Brown, op. cit., p. 248.

7

Parliamentary Representation and Socialism

Parliamentary Representation

PARLIAMENTARY action was clearly important to many individual unions and to the movement as a whole. Even when most of the working class were still without a vote they had benefited from efforts on their behalf by those whom the Webbs called 'willing politicians' and 'sympathetic philanthropists'. But consistent attention to their grievances in the House depended upon a substantial section of the workers acquiring the vote—and upon their using it to help well-disposed Members at the polls. At the same time the extension of the franchise meant that in some areas trade unionists could think of returning their own representatives, though if they attempted to do so this might conflict with the maintenance of good relations with their allies.

Since 1867 the working class had formed a majority of the borough electorate, and this was also the case in the counties after 1884. Nevertheless, the suffrage remained far from universal, for until 1918 the vote was confined very largely to male householders. In 1891 there were 7·36 million men of voting age and 4·81 million registered electors in England and Wales; in 1901 the comparable figures were 8·55 millions and 5·39 millions, and in 1911 9·95 millions and 6·41 millions. At first sight it would appear that in these years the electorate included 65 per cent., 63 per cent., and 64 per cent. of the adult male population;[1] but many men of property were qualified for more than one vote, and the registers recorded votes rather than voters, thus exaggerating the total of those enfranchised. If allowance is made for this factor,[2] these percentages fall to 60, 58, and 59 respectively. So 60 per cent. may therefore be taken as a reasonable estimate of the national average, and one which remains more or less constant between 1889 and 1910.[3]

[1] The proportions for Scotland were slightly lower, and for Ireland considerably lower. These and subsequent calculations are based upon the Census returns and the official returns of Parliamentary Constituencies (Electors, &c.).

[2] Precise calculations are impossible, but by 1910 the generally accepted figure for plural voters was about half a million; the previous twenty years had seen a gradual increase to this level. The most elaborate analysis is that by S. Rosenbaum (*Journal of the Royal Statistical Society*, May 1910). His original estimate was 450,000; but when Dilke argued that 'it was nearer double', Rosenbaum conceded that a total of 550,000 was possible (ibid., 'Discussion on Mr. Rosenbaum's Paper'). We have taken plural voters to be 400,000 in 1891; 450,000 in 1901; and 550,000 in 1911.

[3] An acute observer estimated the corrected proportion for 1914 at just over 61 per cent. (L. G. Chiozza Money, *Things that Matter*, 1914, p. 189).

This proportion was not uniform from constituency to constituency, and it was generally lower in working-class districts, especially in the big cities. In many of these, high mobility among potential electors added to the existing difficulties of getting on the register;[1] and in some there were considerable concentrations of aliens and of paupers, neither of whom were entitled to vote. Sidney Webb's calculations for London suggest that fewer than 44 per cent. of all adult males had the vote in 1889;[2] twenty years later the average for the sixty metropolitan boroughs barely reached 50 per cent. Throughout this period the seven Members for Tower Hamlets, the heart of the East End, were returned by an electorate consisting of some 35 per cent. of the adult males, and in the Whitechapel division the proportion sank to little more than 20 per cent.

If London was the extreme case, other large towns were not much better. Up to the end of the century Liverpool did not rise above 50 per cent., while as late as 1910 its Scotland division showed the same percentage as Tower Hamlets. Both Manchester and Bristol remained in the region of 55 per cent., with their poorer districts falling below this level. Elsewhere the situation was often more favourable. But even in cities which reached the national average, such as Leeds and Birmingham, the working class was still at a disadvantage, and the same was true of most of the smaller boroughs and virtually all the counties. Since the industrial areas were also increasingly under-represented as their population grew,[3] trade unionists were at a disadvantage in bringing pressure to bear upon Parliament, even though new opportunities had been created by the coming of the single-member constituency in 1885 and the subsequent tendency for boundaries between constituencies to follow class lines.[4]

Though no precise estimate is possible, it seems likely that the proportion of working men on the register was usually between 50 and 55 per cent., or in other words that roughly every other potential male trade unionist had the vote.[5] The percentage may have been higher among

[1] These were well described by Henry Schloesser, later Sir Henry Slesser, who complained of 'a cumbrous and iniquitous system of registration, with a long term of qualification, and an intentionally complex arrangement of claim, objection and revision' before the right to vote could be established (Fabian Tract No. 153, 1911, p. 3). In 1895 the Liberals claimed that 30 per cent. of London's potential working-class electors were disfranchised by this procedure (quoted by S. Maccoby, *English Radicalism, 1853–1886*, 1938, p. 313).

[2] Fabian Tract No. 8, 1889, p. 5.

[3] Charles Seymour, *Electoral Reform in England and Wales, 1832–1885*, 1915, pp. 516–17.

[4] During the nineties and later, the Trades Union Congress repeatedly echoed a widespread discontent with the electoral laws. In 1897 and again in 1898 it was unanimously resolved that 'the time has arrived when there should be a thorough reform . . . which should provide (1) for the reduction of the period of qualification for voters to the lowest possible point; (2) remove the cost of registration on to the public funds; (3) that the acceptance of parochial relief should not involve disfranchisement; (4) the abolition of plural voting' (Trades Union Congress, *Annual Reports*, 1897 and 1898).

[5] Overall estimates by contemporaries are rare, though assertions about specific constituencies, sometimes very implausible, are common enough. In 1901, however, James Sexton

unionists than among non-unionists, for union membership was commoner in the better-paid and more stable groups, the 'heads of families, or work-men earning a proper wage' regarded by Dilke as probable householders.[1] At no time, however, can the majority of working-class electors have been trade unionists, even if this was the case in some constituencies by 1910. Nevertheless, the proportion of adult males of 'the manual labour class' who were members of a union rose from one in nine at the beginning of 1889 to one in four in 1901 and to nearly one in three in 1910.[2] Thus it is clear that their electoral importance increased markedly during the period.

Because the degree of organization varied widely, trade unionists were not equally distributed even between predominantly working-class consti-tuencies. Even where they formed a significant part of the electorate, effective action might be hampered by their division among a number of unions. Decisive use of the trade union vote was therefore most likely in an area where a single union or federation of unions included a substantial proportion of the workers in some dominant industry. In this respect, according to the Webbs, 'exceptional political opportunities' were enjoyed by coal and cotton. In both, the bulk of the labour force was heavily concentrated in certain constituencies; within each area the workers were organized in a single union or federation; and by the end of the century union membership among adult males was unusually high.[3] Nowhere else was there a comparable coincidence of electoral power with industrial strength and solidarity.

Up to 1906 this power was used most effectively by Northumberland and Durham. With less than 20 per cent. of the industry's labour force, the North-east provided three of the five seats held by miners in 1889 and added a fourth in 1904, the most effective group of trade unionists in the House. In Northumberland a clear majority of the county's mineworkers lived in the Wansbeck division, whose Member, Charles Fenwick, was regularly returned by an electorate of which over 60 per cent. were miners.[4] At Morpeth, on the other hand, the proportion was probably no more than 40 per cent., but the seat had been held by Thomas Burt since 1874. More could hardly have been expected of Northumberland, though there was also a sizeable group of miners with the vote on Tyneside.

In Durham the miners did not make the same use of their opportunities. Mid-Durham, with an electorate of which over 60 per cent. were miners,

told the Trades Union Congress that 'there were 8,000,000 adult workers in the kingdom, of whom quite 3,000,000 must have votes' (Trades Union Congress, *Annual Report*, 1901). The modesty of this claim may be explained by his experience of Liverpool.

[1] Loc. cit.   [2] See p. 467.   [3] See p. 468.
[4] This and subsequent estimates of the strength of the miners' vote are based on the calcula-tions of R. G. Gregory in his Oxford D. Phil. thesis, *The Miners and Politics in England and Wales, 1906–1914*, to which we are much indebted. It should be noted that they relate mainly to 1906, and exaggerate the position during the early nineties in some of the faster-growing coalfields.

was represented by John Wilson, who had succeeded William Crawford in 1890. Four other divisions—North-west Durham (60 per cent.), Houghton-le-Spring (55 per cent.), Chester-le-Street (over 50 per cent.), and Bishop Auckland (45 per cent.)—all contained a larger proportion of miners than Morpeth. With about 35 per cent., both Barnard Castle—won by Arthur Henderson[1] of the Ironfounders in 1903—and South-east Durham were not far behind. Yet after 1886 none of these seats was contested by a miners' candidate until J. W. Taylor, secretary of the Durham Colliery Mechanics, won Chester-le-Street in 1906;[2] and when John Johnson[3] joined the other leaders in the House in 1904 he was elected for Gateshead, a working-class constituency but one with relatively few miners.[4]

Elsewhere the mining vote was most heavily concentrated in South Wales. Mabon's grip on the Rhondda was so complete that he was opposed only twice between 1885 and 1910. Until the end of the nineties there was no powerful bona fide union behind him; but in this exceptional constituency nearly 80 per cent. of the electorate were miners and whether they were trade unionists or not Mabon was their man. West Monmouth came next with some 65 per cent., and the seat was won by Thomas Richards[5] at a by-election in 1904. But Mid-Glamorgan and Glamorgan East, each with about 55 per cent., were not contested until 1910, and then unsuccessfully. On the other hand, Merthyr Tydfil, with 40 per cent., fell to Keir Hardie in 1900,[6] and in 1906 John Williams and William Brace won Gower and Glamorgan South, both with only 20 per cent.

Within the Federated area, Pickard and his successors, William Parrott and Fred Hall, held Normanton in Yorkshire with 40 per cent. The Yorkshire Miners' Association was almost as powerful in four other constituencies, but no further gains were made until John Wadsworth captured

---

[1] Henderson, Arthur, P.C. (1863–1935). District organizer, Friendly Society of Ironfounders, 1892–1902; general organizer, later honorary president, 1902–35 (union becoming National Union of Foundry Workers in 1920). Executive Committee, Labour Party, 1904–35; secretary 1911–35. M.P., 1903–18, 1919–22, 1923, 1924–31, 1933–35. President of Board of Education, 1915–16. Paymaster-General, 1916. Minister without Portfolio, War Cabinet, 1916–17. Home Secretary, 1924. Foreign Secretary, 1929–31.

[2] From 1885 to 1906 Chester-le-Street had been represented by Sir James Joicey, doyen of the North-eastern coal-owners. In North-west Durham the Member was the son of Ernest Jones the Chartist, L. Atherley-Jones, who managed to be legal adviser to the Miners' Federation and the Durham Miners at the same time.

[3] Johnson, John (1850–1910). Treasurer, Durham Miners' Association, 1890–6; financial secretary, 1896–1910. M.P., 1904–10.

[4] On 16 Jan. 1904 the *Labour Leader* asserted that 'eighty per cent of the electors of Gateshead are wage earners', but did not mention the miners specifically.

[5] Richards, Thomas, P.C. (1859–1931). General secretary, South Wales Miners' Federation, 1898–1931. Vice-president, Miners' Federation of Great Britain, 1924–30; president 1930–1. Executive Committee, Labour Party, 1918–20. M.P., 1904–20.

[6] This was due to unusually favourable circumstances (Frank Bealey and Henry Pelling, *Labour and Politics, 1900–1906*, 1958, pp. 46–49); but Hardie retained the seat thereafter.

Hallamshire in 1906. In Lancashire Sam Woods narrowly defeated a Conservative at Ince in 1892. The seat was lost in 1895 but recovered by Stephen Walsh in 1906, when Thomas Glover was also successful at St. Helens. In both, the proportion of miners was little more than 20 per cent., whereas at Newton it reached 45 per cent. and at Leigh and Wigan 50 per cent. Of these only Wigan was contested during this period, the local miners' agent, Thomas Aspinwall, failing to unseat a Conservative in 1892 and 1895.

The Midlands were later off the mark. Though the mining vote was limited at Hanley (15 per cent.) and at Nuneaton (25 per cent.), Enoch Edwards[1] and William Johnson[2] both made promising starts in 1900, the prelude to victory six years later. In North-west Staffordshire the proportion reached 30 per cent., but Cannock Chase had to wait for a representative until the election in 1907 of Albert Stanley, secretary of the Midland Federation. In several Derbyshire constituencies the electoral resources of the miners were greater than in either Staffordshire or Warwickshire. Yet only in 1906 with the success of their secretary, James Haslam, at Chesterfield (40 per cent.) did they begin to make use of them.[3]

Thus for fifteen years after 1889 the miners failed to increase their parliamentary representation, and it was not until 1909 that every major coalfield in England and Wales had at least one parliamentary spokesman.[4] Whether they favoured an Eight Hours Bill or not, most of the leaders pinned their hopes to the Liberal alliance in the House, and continued to acquiesce in local arrangements which merely protected that minimum of direct representation which the Liberals had been prepared to concede during the eighties. Even where it was arguable, as the Webbs insisted,[5] that 'elections in mining constituencies may be said to be entirely controlled by the miners' organizations', this 'control' was often exercised on behalf of their friends, and the discipline of the unions was for long used less to return their own nominees than to preserve the alliance.[6]

[1] Edwards, Enoch (1852–1912). General secretary, North Staffordshire Miners' Association, 1877–1912. President, Midland Miners' Federation, 1886–1912. Treasurer, Miners' Federation of Great Britain, 1889–1904; president, 1904–12. M.P., 1906–12.

[2] Johnson, William (1849–1919). General secretary, Warwickshire Miners' Association, 1885–1919. Treasurer, Midland Miners' Federation, 1886–1919. M.P., 1906–19.

[3] The addition of W. E. Harvey (North-east Derbyshire: 35 per cent.) in 1907 and of J. G. Hancock (Mid-Derbyshire: 40 per cent.) in 1909 gave Derbyshire a total of three Members. Only Durham, with three times Derbyshire's union membership, returned as many miners to the 1906 parliament. Northumberland, Yorkshire, Lancashire, and—after 1907—Staffordshire all sent two, and Warwickshire one. Nottingham, with a membership comparable to Derbyshire and at least one strong constituency (Mansfield: 45 per cent.), could only claim its secretary, Hancock, who was returned by a Derbyshire constituency.

[4] Scotland had to wait until 1910, when William Adamson was returned for West Fife.

[5] *Industrial Democracy*, p. 262.

[6] On 1 Nov. 1902 the Durham colliery unions resolved that 'the time has fully arrived when we ought to have increased Labour representation'. According to John Wilson, it was decided that 'there should be an increase of two. This was not done because they believed it to be a mathematically fair proportion of the county, but because it was best to move safely' (*History of*

Cotton had no Rhondda, Mid-Durham, or Wansbeck, and the cotton operatives could not hope to equal the electoral power of the miners. The Webbs 'calculated that of the 132,000 members of the United Textile Factory Workers' Association in 1895, no fewer than 102,000 lived in ten constituencies—nine in Lancashire and one in Cheshire'.[1] But about half the membership of the affiliated unions consisted of voteless women, and eight of these constituencies were mainly concerned with weaving, in which women predominated. The Webbs' detailed figures show clearly that no more than 50,000 of the men covered by the Association can have lived in the area. If some allowance is made for the piecers,[2] the total of adult males could increase to about 60,000, of whom 50–55 per cent. may have had the vote. Since the ten constituencies had nearly 160,000 registered electors in 1895, it seems possible that 20 per cent. of these were cotton unionists. Not all the adult male operatives were organized, however, so that the proportion of the electorate employed in the industry must have risen to about 30 per cent.

This was well below the average for the miners' strongholds, yet cotton also had its 'exceptional opportunities'. The Webbs claimed that 'the adult male Cotton Operatives of Oldham practically dominate the local electorate',[3] and the hard-headed James Mawdsley was prepared to fight a by-election there in 1899. Bealey and Pelling suggest that the constituency contained 'about 20,000 adult male textile unionists', but this is an exaggeration and it is most unlikely that the whole body of adult male cotton operatives amounted to much more than 20,000.[4] If the usual proportion had the vote, the percentage of Oldham's 29,000 electors who were cotton workers may have risen above 40 but can hardly have reached 50. Even though something approaching one-third of the members of the powerful spinners' amalgamation lived in the division, Mawdsley found the task too much for him.

the *Durham Miners' Association, 1870–1904*, 1907, pp. 327–8). The immediate response of the Northern Liberal Federation was to offer Johnson South-east Durham, the one Liberal loss in Durham in 1900.

After 1902 the policy in South Wales was to contest mining constituencies as they fell vacant, but not to disturb sympathetic Liberal Members so long as they wished to continue. Yorkshire was equally cautious.

[1] Bealey and Pelling, op. cit., pp. 16–17, quoting figures taken from a memorandum in the Webb Trade Union Collection E, Section A, vol. ix. The Webbs themselves referred less precisely to 'three-fourths of [the] 132,000 members' (*Industrial Democracy*, p. 258).

[2] The piecers' sections of the local spinners' unions were not included in the Association's affiliation figures. No very reliable statistics are available but probably 15,000–20,000 piecers were organized in 1895 (see p. 120). We assume that rather less than half were juveniles.

[3] *Industrial Democracy*, p. 264.

[4] Op. cit., pp. 17–18. The Webbs' memorandum lists 19,483 members of the Association in the Oldham division, 5,639 of them Spinners, but their detailed analysis suggests that less than 10,000 were adult males. Allowing for the piecers, the total of adult male cotton operatives who were trade unionists may conceivably have reached 15,000. On the other hand, the density of union membership was unusually high in Oldham.

Until 1906, when he was joined by A. H. Gill, secretary of the Bolton Spinners,[1] the cotton unions' only spokesman in the House was David Shackleton,[2] who had been returned at the Clitheroe by-election of 1902. Shackleton was unopposed, and at the time much was made of the constituency's '18,000 trade unionists';[3] but this was a weaving district with little other industry, and probably between 16,000 and 17,000 were members of the weavers' amalgamation in which women outnumbered men by three to two.[4] As a result, the total of cotton unionists with the vote may have been as low as 3,500. Nevertheless, when allowance is made for the density of union membership among the weavers it seems possible that some 40 per cent. of Clitheroe's 19,000 electors were cotton workers—not far short of the same proportion as at Oldham three years before.

United on their industrial objectives and ably led, the cotton operatives had hitherto been more successful lobbyists than the miners. That they were less successful in securing direct representation was due not only to their comparative weakness electorally but also to greater political disunity. Indeed, Lancashire, with its tradition of working-class Conservatism in coal as well as cotton, demonstrated that the trade union vote could never be completely disciplined. Not all workers in Lancashire, nor even necessarily a majority of them, voted Tory;[5] but their loyalties were more divided than those of trade unionists in most other areas, where the Liberals got the lion's share. Thus at Wigan, where the miners came to 'dominate the local electorate', their agent, the Liberal Aspinwall, twice failed to break a Conservative hold on the seat which survived the 1906 landslide. At Oldham, where widespread support for Conservatism coincided with the greatest concentration of cotton unionists with the vote, the Tory Mawdsley would not have been defeated if the trade union vote had been unanimous—or if Lancashire workers had shown an invariable preference for the Conservatives.[6]

---

[1] Gill was returned for Bolton which in 1895, according to the Webbs, had less than half as many members of the Spinners as Oldham, and in 1906 the proportion of its electors who were cotton operatives may not have exceeded 30–35 per cent.

[2] Shackleton, Sir David, P.C. (1863–1938). General secretary, Darwen Weavers' Association, 1894–1907. President, Amalgamated Weavers' Association, 1906–10. Parliamentary Committee, Trades Union Congress, 1904–10. Executive Committee, Labour Party, 1903–5. M.P., 1902–10. Labour Adviser to Home Office, 1910–11. National Insurance Commissioner, 1911–16. Permanent Secretary, Ministry of Labour, 1916–21. Chief Labour Adviser, 1921–5.

[3] Bealey and Pelling, op. cit., p. 109. Neither the contemporary orators nor the authors refer to the sex of these trade unionists.　　　　　　　　　　　　[4] *Cotton Factory Times*, 11 July 1902.

[5] The *Cotton Factory Times* always referred to political divisions among the cotton operatives, never to Conservative predominance, and for long exhorted its readers 'to place their own personal interests in front of the more or less imaginary interests that are supposed to constitute politics', and 'to let their candidates have whatever politics they choose so long as on labour questions they keep on the right side' (8 Feb. 1895).

[6] In fact Mawdsley was later blamed for standing 'distinctly as a party man' (*Cotton Factory Times*, 6 Feb. 1903). As a result, according to Hardie, the Liberals were able to divide the Spinners (*Labour Leader*, 15 July 1899).

Working-class Conservatism was not confined to Lancashire, however, and showed itself even among the miners of the North-east. At Bishop Auckland in 1892, a year of Liberal victory, a Tory working man, Eli Waddington, reduced his opponent's majority by polling 2,607 to the Liberal's 5,784. In 1895 at Wansbeck another Tory working man, J. J. Harris, polled 2,422 to Fenwick's 5,629, while in 1900 the Conservative vote rose to 4,283 against 5,474 for the Lib-Lab. At Morpeth, Maltman Barry, a journalist once associated with Champion and the Social Democratic Federation but now a Tory agent, polled 1,235 to Burt's 3,404 in 1895, and as many as 2,707 against 3,177 in 1900. In each case working-class support for Conservatism need not have been large, but it was there.

Quite apart from the special difficulties of Lancashire, the same general problem faced the leaders of the Miners' Federation. In 1894 Ned Cowey declared that the Federation 'was not a political society' but 'included men who represented all phases of political thought', and Pickard had to call John Wilson to order for 'comparing the merits of two political parties' after Wilson had been denounced as a 'special pleader' for Liberalism.[1] Most striking of all, when Salisbury referred publicly to trade unions as 'those cruel associations', the Federation's secretary, Thomas Ashton, himself a Conservative, was instructed to inform the Tory leader that 'a good number of the members of those "cruel associations" are strong supporters of his own party'.[2]

Nevertheless, the miners were the only group of trade unionists before 1902 to secure direct representation primarily through their own strength.[3] There were others, however—and not only the cotton operatives—who showed promise of being able to meet Bernard Shaw's 'indispensable requirements' of 'a compact industrial constituency, with its trades well organized, and working-class opinion ripe for independent action'.[4] In 1895 Northampton's boot and shoe workers almost succeeded in returning Edward Harford of the Railway Servants after their own secretary, William Inskip, had withdrawn.[5] Crewe apparently offered the best opportunity to the railwaymen, but it was Derby, one of several lesser concentrations, that Harford's successor, Richard Bell, fought and won in 1900. In the same year Alexander Wilkie of the Shipwrights was narrowly beaten at Sunderland, while John Hodge of the Steel Smelters also did well at Gower in the South Wales tinplate area after failing to find a constituency in Glasgow, his union's headquarters.[6]

[1] Miners' Federation of Great Britain, *Annual Conference Report*, 1894.
[2] Executive Committee, *Minutes*, 15 Feb. 1894.
[3] It might appear that the agricultural workers also achieved this result, since Joseph Arch was Member for North-west Norfolk from 1886 until his retirement in 1900. This was not due, however, to the strength of his union, which maintained at best a shadowy existence until its dissolution in 1895.
[4] Fabian Tract No. 49, 1894, p. 32.
[5] Fox, *Boot and Shoe Operatives*, pp. 198–9.
[6] Bealey and Pelling, op. cit., p. 44.

When trade unionists were successful in constituencies which had no great concentration of union members with the vote, or in which such voters were divided among a number of unions, the explanation was usually that they were standing in Radical strongholds where the working class had traditionally taken an active and sometimes independent part in politics. Thus in 1886 Henry Broadhurst was returned for Nottingham, where Feargus O'Connor had won Chartism's only electoral victory forty years before; while in 1894, 1895, 1900, and 1906 he was one of the Members for 'Radical Leicester'. Similarly, the prominent Lib-Lab, Fred Maddison, editor of the Railway Servants' *Railway Review*, succeeded the old Chartist, A. J. Mundella, at Sheffield in 1897, and restored Burnley to its customary left-wing allegiance in 1906. Since they and others like them were invaluable to the Liberals in the few constituencies of this type, both men continued to enjoy the party's full support.

In most areas, however, the middle-class managers of local Liberal associations refused to accept trade unionists as candidates. Even where the unions were weak, this difficulty could sometimes be overcome by the determined organization of a discontented rank and file. At Middlesbrough in 1892 Havelock Wilson created his own electoral machine[1] with no help from his disintegrating union. Having captured the seat in a three-cornered fight, he had only a Conservative to beat in 1895, 1900, and 1906, and failed to do so only in 1900. Initial opposition from the Liberals was also brushed aside at Battersea, where John Burns gained control in 1892 'through the voluntary efforts of a large number of engineers and workers' mobilized by the Battersea Labour League.[2] At Bradford, where trade unionism remained backward, Ben Tillett had the help of the Labour Union in 1892 and the Independent Labour Party in 1895. In 1900 his successor, Fred Jowett, was given a clear run by the Liberals and came within forty-one votes of the victory he was to win in 1906.

In London there were special difficulties. Except among the printers, the density of union membership was low, while the proportion of working men without a vote was generally high. Trade unionists were spread over a large number of organizations, and there were very few local concentrations of any size. In West Ham South the Gasworkers may have contributed something to Hardie's election in 1892 but could not save him three years later. They certainly helped their secretary, Will Thorne, when he tried to regain the seat in 1900, though it is doubtful whether more than one-tenth of Thorne's 4,439 votes came from his members.[3] At Battersea, on the other hand, there is no evidence that the Engineers

[1] J. H. Wilson, op. cit., pp. 246–50, 255–60.   [2] Jefferys, op. cit., pp. 137–8.
[3] The union is said to have had 1,700 members in West Ham in 1900 (Bealey and Pelling, op. cit., p. 45), but the town was divided into two constituencies. In 1895 and 1900 West Ham North was won by Gray of the Teachers, whose strength in London may also have helped Macnamara at Camberwell in 1900 and 1906.

dominated either the Labour League or the local electorate. Burns's control was maintained by the efficiency of a personal machine open to all.

Nevertheless, London was second only to the coalfields in returning trade unionists, and several 'friends of labour', such as Sydney Buxton and James Rowlands, sat for metropolitan constituencies. In addition to the successes of Hardie and Burns, W. R. Cremer won Shoreditch in 1886, 1892, and 1900, and George Howell Bethnal Green in 1886 and 1892. In 1897 Sam Woods was returned for Walthamstow, and W. C. Steadman for Stepney in 1898. Each of these victories owed something to a continuing tradition of working-class protest that was strongest in the East End; but they were also due to the conviction of the Liberal leadership that it was crucial to win seats in London,[1] and to the strength of the Radicalism and even collectivism which showed itself in the Progressive party on the London County Council.[2] London Liberals were now apparently prepared to encourage even a nominally independent candidate of 'advanced' views if he was likely to keep out a Conservative, and for the trade unionist a suitable arrangement with an existing party was quite as important as a strong and disciplined union vote.

In 1898 this was recognized by the London District Council of the Railway Servants when they decided to approach both party headquarters on the grounds that 'it will be a long time before we get a direct representative in the House of Commons without being first selected for a constituency, and one or other of the two principal parties declining to oppose him'.[3] The Conservative whips told the deputation that unless Bell, the prospective candidate, was a Conservative and had been adopted by a local association, they could do nothing. The Liberal whips, on the other hand, said that though the final decision must lie with the local association, they would help to find a constituency. Bell would not have to pledge support for the party, and if adopted would be 'supported by the entire Liberal Party machinery'.

These responses reflected the attitude of the party leaders. The Conservatives saw no need for separate labour representation. Balfour was typical in his insistence that existing Members of all parties could adequately represent the workers' interests, though he flattered Fenwick

---

[1] In 1886 the Conservatives and their allies won fifty of London's sixty-one seats. In 1892 the Liberals raised their share to twenty-five, but fell back to eight in 1895 and 1900. With forty-one Liberal seats, 1906 was to show what could be achieved.

[2] The extent of collectivism in the Progressive party can, however, be exaggerated. The real basis of this alliance between the Liberals and the Left was the opportunity which London offered—for example, through attacks on the City and on incompetent and corrupt oligopolists like the water companies—for political as much as social radicalism. Despite the poor record of the Liberals in parliamentary elections, the Progressives controlled the London County Council from 1889 to 1907, even though the alliance was showing signs of stress as early as 1895 (*London Trades Council*, p. 83; and Beatrice Webb, op. cit., pp. 70–72).

[3] *Railway Review*, 16 Dec. 1898, quoted in Gupta, op. cit.

by suggesting that there should be more men like him in the House.[1] Chamberlain, however, was less polite. In 1894 he referred to the trade union Members as 'mere fetchers and carriers for the Gladstonian party', and in 1900 declared that 'when they come into Parliament they are like fish out of water; their only use is as an item in the voting machine . . . not one of those gentlemen had ever initiated or carried through legislation for the benefit of the working classes, though occasionally they had hindered such legislation'.[2]

The Liberal leaders took a different view. Though they both had reservations, Gladstone and Rosebery were well disposed towards labour representatives and regarded some increase as desirable.[3] Speaking on behalf of the party shortly before the election of 1892, Sir George Trevelyan even suggested that 'if we had 40 or 50 working-men Members . . . we should say that they were not too many'.[4] This may have been an exaggeration, but there can be no doubt of the good intentions of Francis Schnadhorst as party agent and secretary of the National Liberal Federation or of Herbert Gladstone as chief whip from 1899. Schnadhorst was spurred on by his eagerness to cultivate the agricultural labourers' vote and to capture more of the London constituencies. On 27 May 1890 he told 'those who were anxious for labour representation . . . that there is only one means of getting it, and that is co-operation with the Liberal party'. At the same time he appealed 'to Liberals everywhere to give the most generous consideration to the claims of the working men. . . . I myself am very anxious to see a larger number of working men in the House of Commons.'[5]

Schnadhorst tried to live up to his words. If he sought to buy Hardie out of the Mid-Lanark by-election in 1888, it was with the offer of official support in another constituency.[6] In 1892 he extended his benevolence to both Hardie and Burns, though they claimed to run as independents. But there were close limits to what he could achieve. Early in 1891 the Metropolitan Radical Federation had suggested to the National Liberal Federation that fifty seats should be put at the disposal of 'direct representatives of Trade Unions and the Labour Party', meaning the Lib-Lab group in the House.[7] Schnadhorst was forced to reply that the local Liberal associations' choice of candidates could not be determined from the centre.

[1] *Hansard*, 25 Mar. 1892, cols. 1920–1.
[2] *The Times*, 1 Oct. 1900. He had in mind his Workmen's Compensation Act (see p. 263).
[3] Alexander Murray, later Master of Elibank and Liberal chief whip, defended his support for Robert Smillie in the Lanarkshire by-election of 1901 by saying that in his old age Gladstone had stressed the need for Liberal encouragement of labour candidates in working-class constituencies, 'lest the cleavage between Capital and Labour should become too conspicuous and engulf the traditional party system' (*The Times*, 7 Oct. 1901).
[4] *Hansard*, 25 Mar. 1892, col. 1927.
[5] *Western Daily Mercury*, 28 May 1890.   [6] Pelling, *Origins*, p. 68.
[7] R. Spence Watson, *The National Liberal Federation*, 1907, pp. 123–4.

'The difficulties attending the Labour representation question were very grave; but they did not arise from the leaders of the party. Wherever the demand for a Labour candidate exists, and a suitable man is within reach, the [Federation's] committee earnestly bespeak for him the generous support of the Liberal association.'[1]

The local organizations in both London and Lancashire showed some readiness to make concessions in order to weaken Conservative dominance; but in general the response from the constituencies was poor, even in the coalfields. Here, indeed, the Liberals had always been hard bargainers. In 1885 the Durham miners were granted a clear run in three seats, 'providing their candidature is endorsed by the Liberals in each division'.[2] In Bishop Auckland there was 'strong opposition', so that only two candidates stood—and were elected. In 1886, however, John Wilson was heavily defeated by a Conservative at Houghton-le-Spring, a result that can only be explained by a major withdrawal of Liberal support, and until 1902 the miners were allowed only one seat. In Yorkshire Pickard's right to Normanton was protected by an agreement, also of 1885, which gave the Liberals the mining vote throughout the rest of the West Riding.[3] There was no indication that they might become more generous. In South Wales, where Mabon had driven a Liberal from the Rhondda in 1885, no concessions could be expected.

Until after the end of the century there was no real improvement, and the extent of Schnadhorst's failure can be seen from the complaint of T. R. Threlfall, the secretary of the Labour Electoral Association, that in 1892 of 'thirteen Labour members . . . four ran in opposition to or without recognising the existence of the caucus, five represent constituencies where the miners absolutely dominate the position . . . and only four either captured the caucus or out-generalled it'.[4] Threlfall regarded the average Liberal association as 'a middle-class machine . . . hampered with class prejudice', and it was becoming clear that trade unionists could not rely on the exhortations of party managers to place their candidates. The occasional *coup* might still be possible—as in the case of Havelock Wilson's capture of Middlesbrough in 1892—but more prolonged and careful preparation was required in most constituencies,[5] as the Labour Electoral Association itself had already discovered.

[1] *Workman's Times*, 27 Mar. 1891. In the close paraphrase of Schnadhorst's letter given in Spence Watson, op. cit., p. 124, the wording is 'the generous *consideration* of the Liberal Association'. We have not seen the original, but this is the more plausible reading.

[2] John Wilson, op. cit., p. 195.   [3] Gregory, op. cit.

[4] *Nineteenth Century*, Feb. 1894, quoted in Pelling, *Origins*, p. 236. It was, of course, easier for working men to secure selection in constituencies which the Liberals were unlikely to win. Threlfall himself was defeated in Sheffield (Hallam) in 1886 and in Liverpool (Kirkdale) in 1892.

[5] This was emphasized by the Fabians in their election manifesto for 1892, which was written by Shaw (Fabian Tract No. 40, 1892, p. 6).

Founded by the Trades Union Congress in 1886 as the Labour Electoral Committee, the Association served a purpose for a time by setting up local associations for the promotion of labour candidates.[1] These helped to elect 'a considerable number of Trade Unionists' to town councils and other public bodies,[2] but the organization counted for little in parliamentary contests. After a short-lived attempt by the Championites to take it over, the Association turned its face firmly against socialism and the idea of an independent political party. Even as a possible Lib-Lab headquarters, it held no attractions for the Liberals and was therefore unable to find promising constituencies.[3] The Association also lacked funds,[4] and in 1890 its claim to represent 750,000 members[5] probably meant only that those attending its Congress came from organizations whose membership added up to that figure. By 1895 it was doubtful whether the eighty-nine delegates to the final Congress 'represented much more than themselves'.[6] Later in the same year the Association disappeared so quietly that nobody noticed.

In 1897 Cowey told the Trades Union Congress that 'money was still the golden key that opened the door to a seat in the House of Commons'. Money was certainly important, but it was not so important as trade union votes and Liberal support. His statement that 'only large and powerful societies could have their own members in the House of Commons, for only such societies could afford to keep their representatives in such a responsible position' was even further from the truth. With or without his union, Havelock Wilson continued to sit in the House, and Steadman of the 400-strong Thames Barge Builders was to join him in 1898. Moreover, Cremer, Howell, and Hardie, who were not official representatives of any union, had all managed to support themselves, as had Broadhurst after his retirement in 1890, while the Engineers gave Burns only a grant towards his 'wages fund'.[7]

---

[1] Cole, *British Working Class Politics*, pp. 102–4. Cole's account follows closely that of A. W. Humphrey, *A History of Labour Representation*, 1912, chapter vii.

[2] Ibid., p. 113.

[3] 'Ostensibly a Labour organisation, during the whole course of its existence it has never shown a spark of independence, being content with the humble role of Lazarus under Schnadhorst's table, happy at the throwing of a few crumbs of recognition in the shape of constituencies impossible for a capitalist liberal to successfully contest' (*Workman's Times*, 25 Nov. 1893).

[4] Though it gave Keir Hardie £400 for the Mid-Lanark by-election in 1888 and the promise of more if needed (W. Stewart, *Keir Hardie*, 1921, p. 39). This money may, however, have come from Champion, in his bid to capture the Association (Pelling, *Origins*, pp. 68–73).

[5] Humphrey, op. cit., p. 99.　　　　　　　　　　　　　[6] Cole, op. cit., p. 113.

[7] Contrary to a decision by the 1892 delegate meeting, 'no attempt was made to test the opinion of members on Parliamentary representation, although it was agreed that £100 a year should be granted to John Burns' (Jefferys, op. cit., p. 137). The Engineers continued their contribution until 1902, when the union affiliated to the Labour Representation Committee (Amalgamated Society of Engineers, *Journal*, Mar. 1905, quoted by Crowley, op. cit.).

Other unions also contributed to the John Burns Wages Fund, including Tillett's Dockers. At first they gave £52 a year, but in 1895 the grant was cut to £20 and discontinued in 1896.

This is the more surprising when the costs are considered. Threlfall told the Trades Union Congress in 1894 that 'a man could not run as a Labour candidate unless he has £200 or £300 or more to assist him'. These were minimum figures, barely enough to cover the returning officer's expenses, yet Harford is alleged to have spent only £300 at Northampton in 1895[1] and Hardie the same at Merthyr in 1900.[2] On the other hand, Bell's election in 1900 cost £900 and Hodge's perhaps £1,200.[3] Though the miners were looked after by their unions, some of the Lib-Labs may have received the grant which Liberal headquarters allowed for an election in a needy constituency,[4] while Burns and possibly Have-lock Wilson could rely on their own machines. There were also instances of Conservative help for a trade union or labour candidate designed to split the progressive vote. 'Tory gold' was supplied through Champion to Hardie, Burns, and two others in 1892,[5] and in 1895 Sexton received a subsidy at Ashton-under-Lyne through Mawdsley, who was a member of the local Conservative club.[6]

The second need was for a regular income. The Miners' Federation followed the practice of the North-east in laying down a standard rate of £350, together with 'a First-Class Railway Pass'.[7] Since they continued to receive their union salaries, Burt, Crawford, and Pickard drew £500 a year or more.[8] If he had been elected, Harford would have drawn his salary from the Railway Servants and been relieved of routine work.[9] In 1894 the Boot and Shoe Operatives proposed to pay £300 a year to their 'Parliamentary agent'.[10] Whether any Lib-Labs received salaries from the party is not known, though Schnadhorst's offer of £300 to Hardie in 1888 suggests that it was possible, and there is evidence that Broadhurst was paid piecework as a Liberal propagandist.[11] A public subscription was

---

'He had been asked to speak from time to time on behalf of the union, which was declined, and in fact not even undertaken to reply in a number of instances' (Annual Delegate Meeting, *Report*, 1896).   [1] Gupta, op. cit.   [2] Bealey and Pelling, op. cit., p. 50.
[3] The average expenditure of all candidates in 1900 was £705 (*Reformers' Year Book*, 1906, p. 79).
[4] Broadhurst, for example, was helped by a grant of £500 at Stoke in 1880 (H. J. Hanham, *Elections and Party Management*, 1959, p. 380).   [5] Pelling, *Origins*, p. 111.
[6] Sexton, op. cit., pp. 146-7.   [7] Page Arnot, op. cit., pp. 291, 361.
[8] Ibid., p. 291; Trades Union Congress, *Annual Report*, 1889; Leeds Independent Labour Party, *Forward*, June 1898. Woods and Wilson probably had the same. Fenwick was paid by his constituency—in effect, by the union (Gregory, op. cit.).
[9] Gupta, op. cit.   [10] Fox, op. cit., p. 194.
[11] When Sir George Trevelyan made the offer on Schnadhorst's behalf he indicated that they would do for Hardie 'as they were doing for others (he gave me names)' (Stewart, op. cit., p. 42, quoting Hardie's article in *Labour Leader*, 12 Mar. 1914).
In an interview in 1958 Schnadhorst's son, Mr. E. E. Schnadhorst, recalled that his father had employed Broadhurst as an itinerant lecturer for the Liberal Party. When Hardie alleged at the 1889 Trades Union Congress that 'being Secretary to the Trades Congress, and being regarded as their mouthpiece, he [Broadhurst] was considered worth £20 a week to go out and speak at meetings', Broadhurst did not deny it.

raised for Howell when he retired, but before that he must have lived on his journalistic and literary earnings. Hardie also relied on journalism, which was still needed when his friends paid him £160 a year after 1900.[1] Cremer was employed by the International Arbitration League, which he himself had promoted. Burns had his 'wages fund', and Havelock Wilson was adept at coping with creditors.[2]

Despite the difficulties faced by many of them, it does not seem likely that a shortage of funds kept down the total number of labour representatives in the House. Where the unions were involved, however, the costs were high in relation to their resources, and if numbers had risen considerably the increased expense would have become a serious consideration. The unions therefore had good reason to support the recurrent proposals that Members should be paid and that returning officers' expenses should be met out of the rates. During the nineties there was some hope that the Liberals would act on the second though not on the first of these suggestions, but nothing was done.

In estimating the number of labour representatives several classifications are possible. Cole lists 'Radical' and 'Labour' Members together,[3] so that his successful candidates in 1886 include Charles Bradlaugh, who can hardly be regarded as a systematic spokesman of labour, and two London doctors who had been returned as a result of the unrest among Scottish crofters. The first of these, Dr. R. Macdonald, was without trade union connexions of any kind. The second, Dr. G. B. Clark, was certainly a champion of many left-wing causes, but most of his speeches in the House were on topics like the defects of the Caithness railway service.[4] Also on Cole's list are James Rowlands, a small self-made businessman and London Progressive who was often helpful to the unions, and Cunninghame Graham, who had contacts with Hardie and Burns as well as the Miners' Federation,[5] but whose concern with labour was highly selective and sometimes unwelcome.[6]

---

[1] W. B. Gwyn, *Democracy and the Cost of Politics*, 1962, p. 160.

[2] J. H. Wilson, op. cit., pp. 279–82. Trade union leaders also had their sidelines. Mabon was 'a director of the London, Edinburgh and Glasgow Assurance Company, and also of the Calais Tramways' according to the *Pall Mall Gazette's The New House of Commons*, 1900, p. 70. Broadhurst had been a shareholder in Brunner Mond & Co. (Trades Union Congress, *Annual Reports*, 1888 and 1889; Hardie's allegations being confirmed in the *Minutes* of the Parliamentary Committee, 20 June 1889). Mawdsley left £4,190 gross (*Cotton Factory Times*, 18 Apr. 1902) and W. E. Harvey over £5,000 (*Derbyshire Times*, 11 July 1914, quoted in Gregory, op. cit.). [3] *British Working Class Politics*, appendix i.

[4] Nevertheless, Clark's record is remarkable. He was a member of the First International, the Scottish Home Rule Association, and the Fabian Society; he took part in Champion's attempt to capture the Labour Electoral Association (Labour Electoral Association, *Annual Report*, 1887); helped to found the Scottish Labour Party; and signed Hardie's Bill for nationalizing the mines in 1893. He also found time to edit a temperance journal, *The Good Templar*, and to act as Agent-General (unpaid) for the Transvaal—the one thing which led to an attempt to unseat him. [5] See p. 240.

[6] He was no friend of the orthodox labour representatives. In replying to one of his speeches,

With the doubtful exception of Rowlands, none gave the same degree of useful attention to labour legislation and working-class grievances as a dozen other 'friends of labour' such as Channing, Sir Henry James, Atherley-Jones or Gorst. The trade union vote in the constituencies of nearly all these men counted for something at least, but none of them was ever considered a labour representative. On the other hand, it would be possible to lean too far in the opposite direction. If the category were to be limited to the salaried 'parliamentary agents' of trade unions, the only labour representatives until Steadman entered the House in 1898 would have been the miners, with the possible addition of Broadhurst as secretary of the Parliamentary Committee up to 1890.

A labour representative may perhaps be taken to be a working-class Member with trade union connexions who concentrated on labour questions. Cremer would come under this heading: a founder-member of the Carpenters and Joiners, he seconded the fair wages resolution in 1891 and took a regular interest in civil service problems. Howell, who remained in close touch with the movement until his defeat in 1895, was always willing and diligent in his support for the measures of the Parliamentary Committee and the cotton unions, and for Havelock Wilson's shipping legislation. Because of his experience as a lobbyist and his legal expertize, both Broadhurst and Fenwick leaned heavily upon him. When Woods succeeded Fenwick as secretary of the Parliamentary Committee there came a break, probably because of differences over the eight hours question. Nevertheless, Howell remained respected and the Parliamentary Committee supported his public subscription in 1897. There can be no doubt, however, that much the most substantial of the labour Members was Broadhurst, despite his absence from the House between 1892 and 1894. Always accorded serious attention, he was often impressive, and, so long as he was fit, invariably active. His superiority was clearly manifest in his performance over workmen's compensation in 1897 when the rest of them were floundering.

Hardie was certainly a working man and a representative of labour, though he no longer had any direct connexion with the unions. But he was not accepted by the others, who distrusted him, as they had distrusted Cunninghame Graham, as a rootless, unreliable left-winger and a bad parliamentarian as well.[1] Arch did nothing whatsoever except symbolize Liberal exploitation of the growing discontent of agricultural labour. The Irish were separated from their English colleagues because for them Home

Broadhurst thanked God that 'the average British working man is wiser than some of the would-be friends who advocate his cause' (*Hansard*, 22 Apr. 1890, col. 1167).

[1] When Colonel Vincent, the Tory protectionist, seconded Hardie's amendment to the Address on unemployment on 7 Feb. 1893, Cremer accused Hardie of 'playing the game—consciously or unconsciously—of the Tory party on the other side. The hon. Member was being made a cat's-paw of' (*Hansard*, col. 765).

Rule came first. Davitt was of some importance: he helped the railwaymen over their Hours of Labour Bill in 1893, and was one of Schnadhorst's advisers on labour matters. Unlike Davitt, Austin and Crean were trade unionists, but apart from Austin's occasional questions they confined themselves to Home Rule.

In 1889, therefore, there was a distinct and recognizable parliamentary group of eight trade union representatives: the five miners—Burt, Crawford, Fenwick, Mabon, and Pickard— along with Broadhurst, Howell, and Cremer. Broadhurst was its leader, with Howell as his right-hand man. Of the others Burt and Fenwick were already respected figures. Burt was the man for general reflections, an eloquent protagonist of class-collaboration. Fenwick became secretary of the Parliamentary Committee in 1890 and was the group's specialist on problems like payment of Members and registration law. After 1890 John Wilson made his mark as an active committee man and a ready speaker. His predecessor Crawford, however, is alleged never to have opened his mouth in the House, and Mabon's oratory was designed for the Welsh valleys. Pickard, for all his force and shrewdness as leader of the Federation, was a failure as a parliamentarian. His interests were narrow; his speeches rare, bad, and sometimes muddled. Personal relations within the group seem to have been excellent, despite Pickard's isolation on the eight hours question.

In 1892 Broadhurst was defeated, but Woods joined the group, thus maintaining its size. He succeeded Fenwick in the secretaryship of the Parliamentary Committee in 1894, and soon proved himself a busier lobbyist. By this time Havelock Wilson had been accepted, having demonstrated both his 'respectability' and his parliamentary skill. Burns's acceptance took a little longer, but he was a member of the inner circle during the manœuvres of 1894–5 over the standing orders of the Trades Union Congress and continued to work with them thereafter. When Broadhurst came back in 1894 he brought the number up to eleven. In 1895 Cremer, Howell, and Woods were defeated, but Woods returned in 1897, when Fred Maddison joined the group. With Steadman's appearance in 1898 the total stood at eleven once more.

The verdict on this record cannot be favourable. Trade unions had made a considerable stir in the political world during the decade. They had attracted the attention of politicians, particularly on the left wing of the Liberal Party, and had gained a number of legislative concessions. Yet in a period in which their membership rose from three-quarters of a million to just over two millions, they had only been able to increase their parliamentary representation from eight to eleven. Moreover, the group in the House had lost some of its force and homogeneity, and in 1900 four of its members were defeated. Here were arguments to support those who believed in trying new methods of political action.

Local Representation and Trades Councils

The progress of local labour representation had been more rapid. According to the Labour Electoral Association, 'the number of representatives on local bodies increased from twelve to two hundred' between 1882 and 1892, and 'in 1895 there were six hundred Labour representatives on Borough Councils alone'.[1] These totals continued to rise thereafter, leading to a steady increase in union influence. The record of the 'new unionism' in this respect was perhaps the most impressive.[2] In most areas, there was no question of gaining power, but in 1898 the Gasworkers contributed to the result in West Ham when the local branches of the Independent Labour Party and the Social Democratic Federation, with Irish and Radical support, won control of the borough council— 'the first municipality in Britain to come under the control of "Labour"'.[3] The advance in London generally had been swift, and on the London County Council the labour representatives formed part of the successful Progressive Party, which allowed them nine seats.[4]

In 1891 G. D. Kelley was elected to the Manchester city council as a Liberal, and in 1895 was joined by Matthew Arrandale of the United Machine Workers. Both were prominent members of the Manchester Trades Council.[5] Birmingham got its first labour councillor, W. J. Davis, in 1880, Sheffield in 1886; by 1890 both had three or four.[6] 'Even a place like Southport is equal to . . . returning one or two working men. And Nottingham and Hull have each their working man members.'[7] On the other hand, neither Leeds nor Bradford was off the mark in 1890—'a curious circumstance [since Bradford] was one of the first places in the country to fall in line with the Labour Electoral Movement'. In the following year, however, the Bradford Trades Council got the Lib-Lab Sam Shaftoe on the town council, and Jowett of the Independent Labour Party was successful in 1892.[8] In Halifax, too, 1892 saw no less than four Independent Labour Party candidates 'swept on to the town council'. But in Leeds, 'a remarkable example of arrested development . . . the first authentic I.L.P. councillor . . . was not elected until 1906'.[9]

---

[1] Quoted from *Annual Reports* of 1892 and 1895 by Humphrey, op. cit., p. 97. By 1900 the Independent Labour Party claimed '63 Town Councillors, 4 County Councillors, 36 Urban and 3 Rural District Councillors . . . 51 members of Boards of Guardians and 66 members of School Boards' (Cole, op. cit., pp. 150–1).   [2] See p. 88.

[3] Bealey and Pelling, op. cit., p. 45.   [4] Ibid., p. 249.   [5] Bather, op. cit.

[6] *Workman's Times*, 11 July 1890. By 1897 the Sheffield Trades Council had five of its members, all Lib-Labs, on the council (Mendelson, Owen, Pollard, Thornes, *Sheffield Trades and Labour Council, 1858 to 1958*, n.d., pp. 41, 45).

[7] *Workman's Times*, 11 July 1890.

[8] E. P. Thompson, loc. cit., pp. 302, 308. The party paid Jowett £2 a week for his work on the council (Fenner Brockway, *Socialism over Sixty Years*, 1946, p. 44). The Battersea Labour League had paid John Burns two guineas a week after his election to the London County Council in 1889.   [9] E. P. Thompson, loc. cit., p. 302.

In the provinces the mechanism by which these victories were achieved varied from place to place and from time to time. According to Cole, the local Labour Electoral Associations were

instrumental in securing the election of a considerable number of Trade Unionists to serve on Town Councils and other public bodies. . . . But, as the Socialists began to capture the Trades Councils, especially after 1889, the strength of the L. E. A. was steadily undermined. One after another the local L.E.A.s broke away from the effective control of the central body, and followed an independent policy of their own; and in other cases there was a split, and a rival 'Labour Representation League' or 'Council' was set up.[1]

This account probably exaggerates the importance of the socialists, for the decline of the Labour Electoral Association was well advanced before they had captured many of the important councils. Manchester and Salford Trades and Labour Council, for instance, affiliated to its local association in 1890, but the association achieved little and had disappeared by 1894. In that year the trades council conducted its own negotiations for support in the school board elections. With the local Building Trades Federation, the Engineers, and the Independent Labour Party, it drew up a programme and sponsored three 'independent' candidates for Manchester and two for Salford. Four were members of the trades council, one of whom won a seat.[2] This alliance with the Independent Labour Party was no doubt fostered by Leonard Hall, the secretary of the Manchester Independent Labour Party, who was on the trades council, but the socialists had not at this stage secured control. By 1898, however, they had won five places on the executive of the trades council. Already in the previous year the council had refused to co-operate with the Liberals in the school board election, and had instead convened a conference at which a United Trades and Labour Party was established. This included, besides the trades council and individual unions, the Manchester branches of the Independent Labour Party and the Social Democratic Federation. One candidate was successful in Manchester, and another in Salford.

In Birmingham, 'several years of steady permeation'[3] by the Independent Labour Party on the trades council had begun by 1893 to undermine the concordat between the local Liberal and labour associations. In that year the trades council resolved to set up a fund and a committee to promote independent labour representation, 'as the interests of labour are apart and opposed to the interests of class monopoly'.[4] Of the ten committee members subsequently elected, five were members of the

[1] Cole, op. cit., p. 113. His account again follows Humphrey closely.
[2] The fifth was the suffragette, Mrs. Pankhurst, a member of the Independent Labour Party.
[3] *Workman's Times*, 23 Sept. 1893. Letter from David Miller, Birmingham Trades Council.
[4] Ibid.

Independent Labour Party. The committee's first recommendation to the trades council was that 'no candidate be accepted who retains his connexion with any political party'. Despite bitter opposition from Conservatives and Lib-Labs, this was carried by a two to one majority.[1]

In Liverpool, the trades council ran its first candidate for the city council in 1889: Matkin, secretary of the General Union of Carpenters and Joiners and of the local Labour Electoral Association. Over the next few years the council sponsored several other Lib-Labs, but by 1892 the socialists were gaining influence. A joint committee of the trades council, the Fabians and the Independent Labour Party was formed, and in December 1893 a permanent Labour Representation Committee was set up to promote united action for municipal elections, though the Lib-Labs were able to insist that candidates should run on strict 'trade union' lines. The well-organized Liverpool socialists seem to have overreached themselves, however, for in 1896 the trades council withdrew from the Committee, the majority of the affiliated trades refusing to sanction further action with outside bodies.[2]

At the beginning of the decade the interest of the trades councils in local elections was quickened by widespread attempts to secure fair wages clauses in local contracts, following the lead of the London County Council and the London School Board in 1889. Manchester Trades Council began its campaign in 1890, and in 1891 Manchester, Salford and Liverpool adopted the clause, as did the Manchester School Board. By 1894 fourteen of the largest towns in Lancashire had followed, but the county council still held out.[3] In Sheffield the school board had agreed in 1890 and the city council in 1891.[4]

This was the most important contribution which the councils made to the 'industrial' work of the unions during this period, for their industrial functions were disappearing as a result of changes in union structure and the development of collective bargaining. As the national unions absorbed local societies and increased their control over their branches, the scope for trades council initiative necessarily decreased. Previously trades councils had often intervened in local disputes, and even now they took part in setting up local systems of conciliation.[5] These had no place,

---

[1] *Workman's Times*, 14 Oct. 1893.

[2] W. Hamling, *A Short History of the Liverpool Trades Council, 1848–1948*, 1948, pp. 27–28.

[3] Bather, op. cit.

[4] Mendelson, Owen, Pollard, and Thornes, op. cit., pp. 45–46. By 1894 150 local authorities had adopted some kind of fair wages resolution (Webbs, *History*, p. 399).

[5] During the nineties, trades councils in London and other major centres co-operated with local chambers of commerce to set up general boards of conciliation which they hoped would be able to mediate, conciliate, and, if permitted, arbitrate in local disputes (*Royal Commission on Labour*, C–7421, 1894, p. 52). These boards had a few successes in minor trades, but were 'seldom called upon to settle cases' (*Report on the Strikes and Lockouts of 1910*, Cd. 5850, 1911, p. 111).

however, in the new types of negotiating procedure now being developed in the principal industries which provided for the reference of local disputes to central bodies within each industry. The funds of the national unions were replacing local collections and subscription lists as the main source of strike pay; where collections were needed to finance major disputes, such as those of the miners in 1893 and the engineers in 1897, the amounts were too large to be handled locally.

These changes were reflected in the composition of the major trades councils. London and Manchester were the most popular centres for the headquarters of national unions, and in the sixties and early seventies their secretaries played a big part in these two trades councils. It was through the London Trades Council that the Junta first tried to exercise its authority over the trade union movement as a whole.[1] Its members, however, transferred their interests to the Parliamentary Committee of the Trades Union Congress when this was firmly established in 1871. George Shipton, secretary of the London Amalgamated House Decorators and Painters, took over the secretaryship of the London Trades Council from George Odger in the same year. Though his union numbered only a few hundred, Shipton was the most considerable figure on the council in the eighties, and the only other union secretaries mentioned by the historians of the council as playing a part in its affairs at this time, Ben Cooper of the Cigar Makers and Steadman of the Barge Builders, came from unions even smaller than Shipton's. In Manchester the leaders of the major unions took longer to depart. During the eighties Mawdsley of the Spinners, Henry Slatter of the Typographical Association, Peter Shorrocks of the Tailors, and Kelley of the Lithographic Printers still found it worthwhile to attend the council, but by the end of the decade things were changing. Mawdsley ceased to be a delegate in 1890, and thereafter only Kelley remained, as secretary.

The departure of the union secretaries preceded the influx of the socialists into the trades councils and made their victory easier. In London the 'new unionists' swamped the council. 'In two years, its affiliated membership had been nearly trebled, the largest body of newcomers being the dockers, who, with Tom Mann as president of their society, affiliated to the Council in thirty-two branches, representing nearly fifteen thousand members.'[3] Mann was elected to the executive in 1889, and three more socialists in 1891. The shift of influence towards the socialists in Manchester and Birmingham has already been noted. The Oldham Trades Council in 1893 unseated J. R. Clynes from the presidency—by a margin of one vote—as too 'advanced', replacing him with the local

[1] See p. 40.
[2] *London Trades Council*, chapters 5 and 6.
[3] Ibid., p. 70.

secretary of the Engineers, said to be 'a believer in no politics in trade unions'; but the following year, when Thomas Ashton of the Spinners resigned the secretaryship, Clynes took his place.[1]

In the West Riding of Yorkshire many trades councils had been formed or re-formed by socialists and 'new unionists' between 1889 and 1893. Among them were Halifax, Huddersfield, Keighley, Brighouse, Spen Valley, Dewsbury and Batley, and the Yorkshire Federation of Trades Councils. 'In some cases, the Trades Council formed the local I.L.P. as its political arm'[2]; but all set about promoting independent political action. The Bradford Trades Council minutes reveal a gap between July 1889 and January 1893.

As the former minute-book closes, the . . . secretary, Sam Shaftoe, is a prominent unionist of the old Lib-Lab school, and the Council is still negotiating humbly with the Liberal Association for a member on their School Board Eight. When the latter minute-book commences . . . Shaftoe has disappeared, Cowgill —an I.L.P.er from the A.S.E.—is secretary, and the Council is functioning in close alliance with the I.L.P.[3]

But the socialists did not have it all their own way. On the London Trades Council George Shipton retained the secretaryship in 1890 against Fred Hammill, a socialist member of the Engineers, though the old dominant group had to acquiesce in some of the policies of the 'new unionists'. When Shipton retired in 1896, however, he was replaced by James Macdonald, a prominent member of the Social Democratic Federation. Perhaps the Lib-Labs would have fought harder to maintain their influence but for the fact that they were not dependent on the trades council for winning seats on the London County Council—their connexions with the Progressive party provided more effective machinery for that.

Elsewhere the Lib-Labs defended themselves more strenuously. In Liverpool in 1896 they managed to dissociate the trades council from the socialists. In December 1893 the Hull Trades Council, dominated by Lib-Labs, refused to back Tom McCarthy, the Dockers' organizer and Independent Labour Party member, when he proposed to stand as parliamentary candidate against C. H. Wilson, the Liberal shipowner and a leading figure in the 1893 dock stoppage.[4] Leeds Trades Council, 'a stronghold of the Liberal skilled unionists',[5] pursued a course similar to that of Liverpool. In 1891 Lib-Labs and socialists seemed to be drawing together, and 'a Labour Electoral Union was sponsored by the Council, on independent lines. But the Trades Council insisted on maintaining the right of veto over the Labour Union, and the old guard sought

[1] *Workman's Times*, 2 Dec. 1893; 26 May 1894.
[2] E. P. Thompson, loc. cit., p. 309.   [3] Ibid., p. 305.
[4] *Workman's Times*, 23 Dec. 1893.   [5] E. P. Thompson, loc. cit., p. 295.

to exercise this in the Liberal interest; finally, in 1892, it severed its connection with the Union.'[1]

In Accrington in 1893 five of the trades council delegates were on the
local Liberal Party executive committee, and the council was still refusing
to co-operate with the local Independent Labour Party.[2] In Dundee in
the same year 'the respectables of the Trades Council' refused even to
appear on the same platform as the socialist Enid Stacey when she was
helping to organize the local mill girls.[3] Sheffield Trades Council remained under the control of local Lib-Lab leaders drawn mainly from
the local cutlery and other metal-working societies even after the foundation of the Labour Representation Committee.[4] Indeed, they maintained
their independence until 1920.[5]

Socialist Infiltration in the Unions

In 1889 the socialists in the unions had included members of the Social
Democratic Federation and of the Socialist League, a few Fabians, and
members of several offshoots of the Federation and the League, such as
the Championites in London and the Bradford Labour Union. After the
foundation of the Independent Labour Party in 1893 the pattern soon
changed. The League was gone, and despite the incursion of some prominent figures in the Social Democratic Federation into union affairs
during the upsurge of 1889, the Federation as a whole and in particular its
leader, Hyndman, remained uninterested. Only in 1897 did the Federation
begin to encourage its members to belong to the appropriate unions.
Most of its best-known trade unionists—Burns, Mann, and Tillett, for
instance—had long since left. Thorne and James Macdonald remained,
but they were exceptional even in their own unions. In the Gasworkers,
Clynes, the Lancashire district secretary and a member of the Independent
Labour Party, was becoming second in importance to Thorne in the
conduct of union business, and both he and Curran were more representative of the union's political outlook than Thorne.

The 'independents' of the smaller groups were almost all absorbed into
the Independent Labour Party. The Fabians continued to go their own
way, but nearly all their provincial branches joined the new party, and
outside London's Progressive Party their direct influence in the unions
was small. There, however, they maintained close contacts with the
trade union members of the London County Council, who included
C. W. Bowerman of the London Society of Compositors, Steadman, and
Tillett.

[1] Ibid., p. 303.   [2] *Workman's Times*, 28 Oct. 1893.   [3] Ibid., 17 June 1893.
[4] Mendelson, Owen, Pollard, and Thornes, op. cit., pp. 46–47.
[5] Ibid. In 1904 a Sheffield Trades Council and Labour Representation Committee was
established in addition to the Lib-Lab Sheffield Federated Trades Council (pp. 49–50), and
the two were united only in 1920 (pp. 80–81).

Consequently, from 1893 'the socialists' normally meant 'the members of the Independent Labour Party'. From the first the leaders of the new party were determined to appeal to the unions and defeated an attempt at the second annual conference in 1894 to bind all members 'to support and vote only for candidates at any election who have adopted the objects, policy and programme of the Independent Labour Party, and who are not members or . . . nominees of the Liberal, Radical, Conservative, Unionist or Irish Nationalist Parties'.[1] After this and other initial difficulties were settled, the party gave something of a unified lead to socialists within the unions through its branches and the *Labour Leader*, and it did so tolerably realistically and not too tactlessly.

It was, however, the Social Democratic Federation which originally fostered the most popular rallying cry of the 'new unionist' period by reviving the demand for a statutory eight-hour day. In 1884 the Federation advocated a restriction of the working day of public servants to eight hours. By 1886 a general Eight Hours Bill had become part of its programme of immediate 'palliatives', and Tom Mann published a pamphlet which did much to arouse working-class opinion, then ripe for any proposal which promised to mitigate unemployment by sharing work. In 1887 the Trades Union Congress instructed the Parliamentary Committee to conduct a plebiscite on the issue, but the results declared in 1888 were so indecisive and ambiguous that Congress called for another. Once more the wording was confused and the results inconclusive, and after a full debate Congress in 1889 rejected the whole return.[2]

The movement rapidly gathered popularity. In January 1889 Burns had been elected to the London County Council on a programme which included an eight-hour day for public servants, and in the same year the Council of London Liberal and Radical Clubs, representing all the London constituencies, resolved in favour of limiting the hours of government and municipal servants to eight a day.[3] The initiative remained with the socialists, whose next move was a campaign which launched the annual May Day demonstrations, first held in 1890 in London and many provincial towns. These passed resolutions demanding not only the statutory eight-hour day but also nationalization of the means of production, distribution, and exchange, adult suffrage, payment of members, abolition of the House of Lords, and other socialist and radical reforms.[4]

---

[1] *Workman's Times*, 3 Feb. 1894. This proposal, known as 'clause 4', was supported not only by purists but also from practical considerations urged especially by Lancashire members. With cotton workers divided between the Conservatives and the Liberals, the Independent Labour Party in Lancashire feared that the party's appeal might be prejudiced if members were allowed to back their fancy when no party candidate was standing (ibid., 30 Dec. 1893; 3 Feb. 1894).

[2] The whole affair was handled by Mawdsley and Thomas Birtwistle for the Parliamentary Committee. Both were strongly opposed to the Eight Hours Bill.

[3] S. Webb and H. Cox, *The Eight Hours Day*, 1891, p. 31.

[4] These May Day demonstrations were lively and colourful. Describing the London

By 1890 both the composition and the opinions of Congress had undergone considerable changes. The 'new unions', with their temporarily inflated voting strength, were there in force; the rapidly growing Miners' Federation was prepared to support a resolution for a general Eight Hours Bill;[1] and several craft societies had been persuaded by their more advanced members to change their minds.[2] Thus Congress resolved by 193 votes to 155 that 'the time had arrived when steps should be taken to reduce the working hours in all trades to eight per day . . . and while recognising the power and need of trade organisation, the Congress is of opinion that the speediest and best method of obtaining this reduction for the workers generally is by Parliamentary enactments'.

The Scottish railway strike of 1890 for a ten-hour day and union recognition aroused public feeling[3] and Channing's narrowly defeated motion in January 1891 for statutory control of railway working hours won the support of many Conservatives as well as of the Liberal Party generally. It became increasingly common for parliamentary candidates of both parties to express themselves guardedly in favour of legal limitation of the working hours of railwaymen and of an Eight Hours Bill for miners.[4] Sidney Webb and Harold Cox were able to write that '. . . every politician knows in his heart of hearts that a reasonable Eight Hours Act will probably be one of the earliest fruits of the next general election'.[5] But this forecast proved too optimistic, for the campaign had already passed its peak.

After a confused debate, Congress in 1891 approved legislative enforcement only with the proviso that it should not apply 'where a majority of the organised members of any trade or occupation protest by ballot voting against the same'. Two years later trade option was dropped and Congress returned to the principle of universal application, but this now became a 'hardy annual' repeated almost every year up to 1910, usually without

demonstration of 1894 the *Workman's Times* of 12 May 1894 wrote: 'Right across the greensward to the Marble Arch, so far as the eye could see, the black masses of the demonstrators stretched, broken here and there by the fluttering colours of the banners and the scarlet uniforms of the bandsmen. There were nearly 60 bands present, from the full military band of the Gasworkers to the pipers of the South Side Labour Protection League. Round all the twelve platforms the people clustered in thousands.'

[1] The Federation leaders were really concerned only with the miners' bill, but procedural requirements made it impossible for them to advance their own cause except by supporting the general resolution (Page Arnot, op. cit., pp. 146–8).

[2] The traditional craft society argument against a statutory eight hours was that government intervention would weaken craft controls. On the other hand, crafts suffering from unemployment could claim that a statutory eight-hour day would increase the demand for skilled workers and thus reinforce craft privileges. Moreover, some craftsmen had never been completely dogmatic in their opposition to legislation. As early as 1887 Robert Austin wrote in the *Annual Report* of the Amalgamated Society of Engineers that industrial action was preferable, but 'if we fail, we can, as a last resource, seek the aid of Parliament to enact a law of eight hours' (quoted in Crowley, op. cit.). [3] See p. 232.

[4] Webb and Cox, op. cit., p. 36. [5] Ibid., p. 241.

serious debate. The Parliamentary Committee sometimes went through the motions of introducing a bill, only to see it disappear into limbo.

What force remained in the movement passed into campaigns for the legal limitation of hours in individual industries. The railwaymen got their Act of 1893; the miners persisted with their own bill; and for a time the cotton unions also ran an eight hours agitation. In other industries the idea of enactment was accepted as an article of faith, but few trade unionists continued to believe that there was any foreseeable prospect of getting it. Success needed not only organized pressure by the active minority of the movement but also the support of the rank and file. The weakness of the eight hours campaign was that in most trade unions by the middle nineties it could not call upon either.[1]

By this time, however, the 'old guard' at Congress were no longer concerned with the defeat of the socialist campaign on the eight hours issue. They were hoping for the elimination of socialist influence through the new standing orders of 1895,[2] a manœuvre often credited with dramatic success. With the exclusion of the trades councils, wrote Cole, 'the Socialist cause at the Trades Union Congress had suffered a very serious reverse'.[3] This opinion is supported neither by the record of subsequent resolutions passed at Congress,[4] nor by the position of the trades councils even before the new rule. Trades council affiliations had sunk drastically by 1894; the importance of the councils themselves was on the decline; and even in 1895 many of them were still under Lib-Lab control.

Moreover, continuing socialist infiltration in the unions themselves helped to compensate for the loss of socialist delegates from the trades councils. Tom Mann's contemporary comment was nearer the mark than Cole's later judgement. He predicted that the socialist

cause and men will continue to make themselves felt. It is amusing to those who know the facts of the situation to find friends discussing the subject as though the . . . 'New Unions' were essentially Socialistic, and the older unions were not so. There is as large a proportion of carpenters, masons, engineers and cotton operatives avowed Socialists, as is to be found amongst the gas workers, dockers, chemical workers and general labourers.[5]

There is no doubt, however, that the leaders of the 'new unionism', both national and local, were among socialism's firmest allies in the trade union movement. The Gasworkers and Tillett's Dockers had been led by socialists from the start. From 1893 the secretary of the National Union

---

[1] 'We are all eight-hour men now . . .' observed William Mosses of the Patternmakers to the 1906 Trades Union Congress, 'but . . . it has reached the academic stage. How is it we have lost so much interest . . .? I believe it is because . . . our members are not with us . . . . When our members are working so much systematic overtime it is sheer hypocrisy to ask for an eight-hour day.'   [2] See p. 259.   [3] Op. cit., p. 112.   [4] See p. 262.
[5] *Labour Leader*, 28 Sept. 1895, quoted in Roberts, op. cit., p. 155.

of Dock Labourers was Sexton, a foundation member of the Independent Labour Party, and in the National Amalgamated Union of Labour both A. T. Dipper and J. N. Bell, who succeeded him as secretary in 1898, were also members. All four unions could be relied upon to support their leaders in political matters, and many of the smaller unions of general labourers and transport workers voted with them at the Trades Union Congress.

Elsewhere it was only in the West Riding, among the woollen workers led by Ben Turner, Allen Gee, and W. H. Drew, that the socialists found an equally dependable foothold, though they had considerable influence also among the Boot and Shoe Operatives. In London, unofficial socialist leaders had put themselves at the head of a bitter agitation over outwork among boot and shoe workers, leading them to reject conciliation and come out on strike, and by October 1891 'had virtually captured effective power over the Metro branch.'[1] In the largest provincial centres, where new machinery and productive methods were provoking controversy, the socialists championed restriction of output and opposition to change. They won considerable influence in Northampton and captured effective control of the Leicester branch, one of the most prominent local leaders being T. F. Richards, a member of the Independent Labour Party.[2]

Their influence was also felt in the union's debates in 1894 concerning the proposed parliamentary candidature of the Lib-Lab Inskip. The 'nationalisation of the land, and the implements of production and distribution' was unanimously included among the objects of the union, and an even stronger phrase—'all means of production and distribution'—was written into Inskip's election programme. This proved too much for him and he withdrew.[3] Their victory did not mean that the socialists had taken control of the union, for the resolutions were carried only with the support of a group of 'middle-of-the-road' men; but it did mean that henceforth the union would be committed to support socialist proposals at the Trades Union Congress.

Among the Railway Servants the first signs of serious socialist influence appeared in the debate at the conference of 1894 over the projected parliamentary candidature of Harford, the secretary. The members of the Independent Labour Party joined with the Conservatives in ruling that Harford could only be allowed to stand if he remained independent of the two political parties.[4] Their next move came in 1895 as an immediate response to the decision of the union's executive to support the revised standing orders of the Trades Union Congress. They proposed that the

[1] Fox, op. cit., pp. 111–17.

[2] Ibid., pp. 207–8. In 1899 Richards provided further evidence of socialist influence in the union by winning 3,139 votes against 4,501 for W. B. Hornidge, the Lib-Lab candidate, in the final round of the elections for the secretaryship after Inskip's death.

[3] Ibid., pp. 196–9.

[4] Gupta, op. cit.

union should fill all the places to which it was entitled at Congress with delegates chosen by ballot of the membership, hoping to be able to return socialists.

The proposal failed both in 1895 and in 1896, but from 1897 onwards the socialists were able to exploit the growing feeling among railwaymen which expressed itself in rising membership and the all-grades movement. The executive elected for 1897 'was almost evenly divided between Socialists and Lib-Labs, as was shown from a very significant vote, taken in June 1897, as to whether Tom Mann or Sam Woods should be nominated for the secretaryship of the Parliamentary Committee of the T.U.C.'[1] The executive itself decided that there should be one Congress delegate for every 10,000 members, and the 1897 conference established selection by ballot.

In 1898 the executive installed G. J. Wardle, a member of the Independent Labour Party, as editor of the *Railway Review*; and in the following year condemned the decision of the Lib-Lab London Council to secure Liberal support for the projected candidature of Bell, the new secretary.[2] The leader of these moves had been T. R. Steels of Doncaster. In March 1899 he was off the executive, having served the two consecutive years allowed by the rules, but he persuaded his branch to send the new executive, for forwarding to the Trades Union Congress, the famous resolution which led to the establishment of the Labour Representation Committee. Only one member of the executive, a Lib-Lab, opposed it.[3]

In addition, the socialists had won support in some craft societies. On 11 August 1894 the *Labour Leader* claimed that the Carpenters and Joiners were 'rapidly advancing ILPwards'. Up to 1895 the Society had been represented at the Trades Union Congress by one delegate, usually the secretary. With socialist influence spreading in the branches, this method ceased to 'appeal to the democratic instincts of the younger members who were taking part in the forward social movements of their localities, and were chafing because the A.S.C. & J. seemed inactive when these movements were discussed at Congress'.[4] Accordingly, after a ballot, the delegation was increased to seventeen, fifteen elected by the members and two by the executive. This proved too radical, however, and two years later another change was made to twelve delegates, six chosen by the members and six by the executive.

The Friendly Society of Ironfounders had decided as early as 1890 to

---

[1] Gupta, op. cit.   [2] See p. 278.

[3] The other Lib-Labs on the executive supported it. Of the resolution itself Philip Snowden wrote that 'it is no secret now that [it] was drafted by Keir Hardie' (*An Autobiography*, vol. 1, 1934, p. 88). Crowley (op. cit.) asserts that 'between them Hardie and Ramsay Macdonald had drawn up a shrewdly devised resolution'. This is the view expressed in Godfrey Elton, *The Life of James Ramsay Macdonald, 1866–1919*, 1939, p. 99. Gupta (op. cit.) considers that Hardie's role 'remains obscure'.   [4] Higenbottam, op. cit., p. 143.

elect their Congress delegates by a general vote,[1] but in the Boilermakers' Society it was not so easy. Indeed, in 1894, with the approval of Knight and the executive, the Society voted to disaffiliate from Congress on the grounds that because of its 'altered composition and aims' during the past few years 'it no longer represents our views'. Some members objected that the vote was an outcome of hostile reports of Congress activities from delegates not chosen by the members, and next year the decision was reversed and a new rule introduced that henceforth Congress delegates must be elected.[2] By 1897 the *Labour Leader* claimed that 'some of the paid officials are avowed socialists',[3] and when Knight retired in 1900 he was succeeded by D. C. Cummings,[4] a member of the Independent Labour Party.

Among the Engineers, as among the Boot and Shoe Operatives, the socialists had increased their influence by putting themselves in the forefront of an aggressive industrial movement to resist technical and organizational change. Thus socialists intent on pursuing the class war to end all privilege allied themselves with members anxious to preserve their ancient privileges against the inroads of machines, piecework, and unskilled workers. The socialists were strongest in the London district, where George Barnes of the Independent Labour Party was active, often with the support of Burns, Mann, and Hammill. In 1891 Barnes was secretary of the London committee which supported Tom Mann for the secretaryship in opposition to John Anderson. Four years later he fought Anderson himself, and in 1896 defeated him.[5]

Whereas Anderson's supporters hoped that 'politics will never be allowed to dominate our great organisation', Barnes stood for 'a policy of direct Parliamentary representation for the Society, increased militancy in trade policy, [and] federation of all kindred societies'.[6] But two factors limited the extent of this socialist victory. Barnes's socialism was always restrained, and he became increasingly moderate as time passed. Secondly, he was always liable to be blocked by the executive, or both he and they by the Final Appeals Committee, while the districts followed their own inclination regardless of all national authority. He was unable to reform this cumbersome machinery, and eventually it drove him to resignation.[7]

---

[1] Fyrth and Collins, op. cit., p. 99.　　[2] Cummings, op. cit., p. 134.　　[3] 28 Mar. 1897.

[4] Cummings, D. C. (1861–1942). Yorkshire district officer, United Society of Boilermakers and Iron and Steel Shipbuilders', 1895–1900; general secretary, 1900–8. Parliamentary Committee, Trades Union Congress, 1901–8. Joined Labour Department of Board of Trade, 1908; Ministry of Labour, 1916. Member of the Industrial Court, 1919–40.

[5] See p. 162. Besides London, there was also a good deal of socialist activity in the provinces, for instance in Manchester, Hull, and Belfast (see p. 143). At Barrow, when Curran proposed to stand for Parliament as an Independent Labour Party candidate in 1894, he was supported by a committee of which the majority were members of the Engineers (*Workman's Times*, 7 Apr. 1894).　　[6] Jefferys, op. cit., p. 141.

[7] See p. 434. Among the other craft societies, the London Compositors had their socialist

There remain coal and cotton, the two greatest citadels of trade union power. Socialist infiltration had been able to make little headway in their governing bodies because of the low turnover among the existing Lib-Lab leadership. Members of the executive of the Railway Servants held office for only two years and were ineligible for immediate re-election, thus providing opportunities for socialist intervention. By contrast, the governing bodies of the cotton amalgamations were composed of the full-time officers of the local associations, among whom turnover was low, twenty or thirty years being required for a complete change-over. Similarly, the executive of the Miners' Federation consisted for the most part of the full-time officers of the constituent associations.

There were signs of change, however, in some of the local associations in both coal and cotton. Burgess claimed that the great coal and cotton conflicts of 1892-3 'have set a leaven to work',[1] and the growth of socialist influence in Lancashire, dominated by the coal and cotton industries, suggests that there may have been some truth in what he said. In 1894 Tom Mann, now secretary of the Independent Labour Party, described Lancashire and Yorkshire as 'the stronghold of the movement',[2] and Lancashire was the main source of the Social Democratic Federation's strength outside London. Of the Federation's eighty-two branches in February 1894, twenty-seven were in Lancashire and thirty in London.[3] By the end of 1893 the Burnley membership had risen to 1,100 and the branch had appointed a full-time secretary.[4]

This conjunction of socialist influence and union strength in Lancashire has not received the same emphasis as the contrast between socialist strength and union weakness in the West Riding of Yorkshire. Its effect was felt in a number of the local associations of the cotton unions. In 1895 a member of the Social Democratic Federation was elected vice-president of the Burnley Weavers' Association;[5] and the Federation's members had infiltrated into the Nelson Weavers' Association so successfully by 1893 that, according to a letter in the *Workman's Times*, the leaders were forced to rally their own supporters to maintain control of the quarterly meetings, raising the average attendance from 40 to over 400.[6] Even Mawdsley, while still disclaiming imputations of socialism, could look forward 'to a time when there would be no owners of capital, and the present possessors . . . would be simply managers', and went on to declare 'unequivocally for the independent representation of Labour

'ginger' group in the early nineties, and the London tailors provided in James Macdonald one of the most vociferous advocates of socialism.   [1] *Workman's Times*, 19 Aug. 1893.

[2] Monthly Report of the National Administrative Council of the Independent Labour Party, reproduced ibid., 7 Apr. 1894.

[3] *Justice*, 3 Feb. 1894, quoted in Pelling, *Origins*, p. 179.

[4] Tsuzuki, op. cit., pp. 96-97.

[5] Ibid., p. 99.   [6] 12 and 19 Aug. 1893.

in Parliament'.[1] The working man 'had been too long humbugged by aspiring politicians'.[2]

Though the cotton operatives had 'done a great deal by judiciously squeezing the present M.P.s representing the manufacturing districts . . . it could have been done better had there been one of their own men on the floor of the House'[3] and they envied the miners their parliamentary representatives. Their main ally in the House, Sir Henry James, also stressed the need for direct representation, since he had been 'much handicapped by not having the assistance of a practical man' to help him with the Factory Act of 1891.[4] In 1891 the *Cotton Factory Times* suggested that the United Textile Factory Workers' Association should establish its own parliamentary fund,[5] but it was not until 1894 that the Association held a ballot on the question of representation. Although the majority in favour was only 3,000 in a poll of almost 80,000, the leaders decided to go ahead with a bi-partisan scheme under which Mawdsley would stand as a Conservative and David Holmes of the Weavers as a Liberal. But 'strong party feeling' among their members caused the Spinners to withdraw,[6] and this killed the scheme.[7]

Two contemporary events probably influenced the attitude of the Spinners. The first was that by the end of 1894 the Independent Labour Party had won 'a good socialist majority' on the Oldham Trades Council.[8] This led the local Spinners to withdraw from the council, though not until after the demise of the bi-partisan scheme.[9] The second was the success of their traditional lobbying tactics in the passage of the 1895 Factory Act,[10] which caused them a good deal of satisfaction. When speaking in support of the bi-partisan scheme, Mawdsley had to admit that the cotton operatives had won from Parliament by existing methods 'better laws and administration than any other section of workers'.[11] There the matter was left until Mawdsley's candidature at the Oldham by-election in 1899. His defeat could be taken as an argument in favour of independent

[1] Ibid., 19 Aug. 1893. [2] Ibid., 3 Mar. 1894.

[3] *Cotton Factory Times*, 27 June 1890.

[4] Ibid., 8 Feb. 1895. James had originally made his complaint in a letter to the United Textile Factory Workers' Association (ibid., 31 July 1891).

[5] 31 July 1891. [6] Ibid., 29 Mar. 1895.

[7] The *Cotton Factory Times*, referring presumably to the socialists, blamed the 'independent-minded section of the delegates [who] would not listen to any overtures to secure representation by arrangement with parties . . . and so demonstrative have been their protestations against forming an alliance that the failure . . . may be traced to their conduct' (19 Apr. 1895).

[8] *Labour Leader*, 1 Dec. 1894. Clynes of the Gasworkers was appointed secretary to the trades council (see p. 290).

[9] The reasons they gave were that the council was 'dealing with political questions in addition to trade matters', and had imposed a levy 'for the purpose of local labour representation' (ibid., 3 Aug. 1895). [10] *Cotton Factory Times*, 26 Apr. 1895.

[11] Crowley, op. cit., quoting from the reports and circulars of the United Textile Factory Workers' Association in the Webb Collection.

representation,[1] but it was not enough to win the support of the cotton unions for the Railway Servants' resolution at the 1899 Trades Union Congress.

The Lancashire miners also showed signs of socialist influence. In 1893 the Social Democratic Federation won a seat on Burnley council. 'Thanks to the miners' lockout for such a result', wrote the local correspondent of the *Workman's Times*, 'Comrade A. G. Wolfe permeated socialism among the miners. They not only voted for us, but worked with an enthusiasm and determination never excelled.'[2] In the other federated coalfields of England and Wales, however, there was little evidence of socialism. The Independent Labour Party made an effort to exploit the 1898 stoppage in South Wales and established thirty branches;[3] but most of them fell away, and socialism had little to do with Hardie's return for Merthyr in 1900.[4]

Scotland was the one constituent association of the Miners' Federation in which the socialists had won a clear victory before 1900.[5] Keir Hardie had been the pioneer of trade unionism in Ayrshire, and the local associations in Lanarkshire had been built up by a group of socialists, including William Small, who became secretary of the Lanarkshire Federation in 1893. When the Scottish Miners' Federation was formed in 1894 another Lanarkshire member of the Independent Labour Party, Robert Smillie, became president, and the secretary, Chisholm Robertson, was also a socialist.[6] The Scottish delegation therefore became the spearhead of socialism at the conferences of the national Federation. In 1897, for instance, Smillie moved a resolution in favour of complete public ownership. In this he was supported only by his own delegation, but when a proposal for the nationalization of the land, the mines, and the railways was moved by Lancashire, it won an overwhelming majority.[7]

Outside the Federation the Independent Labour Party was able to achieve lasting successes in Durham, where it made a considerable effort from 1894 onwards.[8] Here its members enjoyed an advantage as the champions of a militant industrial policy which socialists in other coalfields

---

[1] Keir Hardie read it in this way (*Labour Leader*, 15 July 1899).

[2] 11 Nov. 1893.   [3] Pelling, *Origins*, pp. 191–2.

[4] Bealey and Pelling, op. cit., pp. 46–49.

[5] The strength of socialism among Scottish miners goes some way to explain the 'pronounced' socialist feeling in the separate Scottish Trades Union Congress, eight of whose ten members belonged to the Independent Labour Party in 1898 (*Labour Leader*, 3 Apr. 1898). In Mar. 1899 the Scottish Trades Union Congress foreshadowed the decision of the British Congress later in the same year by passing a resolution asking for a special Congress of 'working-class organisations . . . to decide on united working-class action at the next general election' (ibid., 6 May 1899).

[6] Page Arnot, *Scottish Miners*, pp. 73–74, 92.

[7] Even Yorkshire abstained, and only 6,000 votes were recorded against the resolution. During the debate Cowey expressed some of the sentiments which prevailed among 'middle-of-the-road' leaders. 'I am a Socialist to a certain extent, but I am a "possibilist" ' (ibid., p. 94).

[8] Welbourne, op. cit., p. 294; Pelling, op. cit., p. 190.

were unable to exploit. In the Federated area the objectives of a floor to wages and a statutory eight-hour day were the official aims of the union, fully supported by the Lib-Lab leaders. In the North-east, however, the leaders rejected both these aims, and also opposed affiliation to the Federation, thus allowing the local socialists to appear as the champions of national unity as well. By January 1898 there were two socialists on the executive of the Durham Miners' Association, and Tom Mann was invited to speak at the miners' gala that year.[1]

In both coal and cotton the union leaders were also exposed to socialist influences as a result of their international contacts. For cotton these began in 1894, when the first International Textile Workers' Congress was held in Manchester, with the woollen union leaders also there. But despite some of his collectivist utterances at this time, Mawdsley and his colleagues showed no more sign of absorbing continental socialism from such contacts than did the Miners' Federation leaders from the Miners' International Federation established in 1890. This held annual conferences at which the main business was the legislative enforcement of the eight-hour day. The British delegation, with Burt and Pickard as chairman and secretary of the conference, and Cowey as the main spokesman, thought it useful that 'we've come to know their theories', but clearly considered it more important to 'have taught them some real trade union principles'.[2] Pickard remained bitterly hostile to any manifestation of socialism in the ranks of the Federation. To him the socialists were 'the men who were trying to pull their Societies to pieces. The sooner they killed those men the better.'[3]

The two dockers' unions were brought in touch with their continental counterparts during a strike in Stockholm, and in 1896 Tillett's executive was instructed by the annual delegate meeting to open negotiations 'with a view to concerted action'. An international transport federation was established, and Tom Mann told the delegate conference in 1899 that 'very great advantage was immediately felt as a result of its formation both here and on the continent'. The dockers had little need, however, to import their socialism from abroad and this was also the case with some of the union representatives who came into contact with the continental socialists at the congresses of the Second International. At Zürich in 1893 there were sixty-four British delegates, including thirty-seven trade union and trades council representatives; and in London in 1896 there were 190 out of 476.[4] A number of them, however, were by no means

---

[1] Welbourne, op. cit., p. 301.

[2] Page Arnot, *The Miners*, vol. i, chapter 5; Miners' Federation of Great Britain, *Annual Conference Report*, Jan. 1894.

[3] Leeds Independent Labour Party, *Forward*, July 1898.

[4] Cole gives a full account of the 1896 Congress in *A History of Socialist Thought*, vol. iii, 1956, pp. 27–35.

usual representatives of the unions. At Brussels in 1892 the Gasworkers' delegation included, along with Thorne, Edward Aveling, representing the moribund Dublin and Belfast districts, and his wife, Eleanor Marx. Cole records that in 1896 'one or two anarchists got in as Trade Union delegates'.[1] Most of the British contribution to the debates came from socialist members of the delegations. In 1896 Hyndman, Lansbury, Sidney Webb, Hardie, Dr. and Mrs. Pankhurst, Belfort Bax, Aveling—now representing Australia—and Bruce Glasier all spoke.

The attitude of most trade unionists was summed up by the secretary of the United Builders' Labourers, who 'protested that the Trade Unions had been brought to the Congress on false pretences, outvoted in the British delegation, and made to listen to a lot of "disquisitions on an ideal society which is as far off as the millennium"'.[2] The Parliamentary Committee, in its report to the Trades Union Congress in 1896, noted the 'linguistic, racial, and other complications' of the international Congress, and, 'having regard to all that took place' there, questioned 'whether it would be a wise and prudent policy for the Trades Union Congress in the future to identify itself with Congresses of this character'.

This survey of socialist activity in the unions reveals no marked impact on growth or industrial policy. The socialists helped some of the 'new unions' to organize, but the major increases in membership during the period occurred in unions where their influence was small. The great advances in collective bargaining owed little to them. Indeed, in many unions they joined with the old-fashioned champions of local autonomy in resisting procedures for the collective settlement of disputes; and where they were able to put themselves at the head of industrial movements, as among the Boot and Shoe Operatives and the Engineers, it was by taking the lead in agitations against technical change which were doomed to failure.

Politically, however, they were more successful. Socialist influence goes a long way to explain the votes of the seven major unions—the Boot and Shoe Operatives, the Carpenters and Joiners, the Railway Servants, the two dockers' unions, the Gasworkers, and the National Amalgamated Union of Labour[3]—which must have supported the resolution on independent labour representation at the 1899 Congress. Even so, their votes totalled only 229,597, and the resolution was passed by 546,000 to 434,000. Since coal and cotton, with a combined strength of 351,140,[4] both voted

---

[1] Cole, op. cit., p. 27.

[2] Ibid., p. 34. Some were less restrained. The Boot and Shoe delegates, for example, reported the 1896 Congress as 'a fiasco ending in a farce', and the 1897 Congress as a scene of 'great confusion' in which Hyndman 'had to be protected by a bodyguard against the anarchists' (*Fifty Years, The History of the National Union of Boot and Shoe Operatives, 1874–1924*, 1924, pp. 45–46). [3] The Engineers had disaffiliated from Congress in 1898.

[4] Of the 233,000 votes cast by the miners, 213,000 were from the Federation and the rest from

against, most of the smaller unions must also have supported it. Some of them may have been dominated by socialists or by alliances between socialists and those who advocated militant industrial policies on other grounds. But these considerations cannot explain all the support for the resolution and other factors were at work.

The leaders of the cotton operatives and the miners did not put up their major spokesmen, or marshal an imposing array of arguments, or attempt to isolate the socialists. W. E. Harvey of Derbyshire, speaking for the miners, doubted if many unions genuinely wanted representation in this way, and thought those that did should be prepared to pay for it themselves, like the miners. Thomas Ashton of the Spinners spoke only briefly, and the attitude of the cotton unions was set out more fully by the *Cotton Factory Times*. It was based entirely on practical considerations.

No doubt, if some schemes of labour representation in Parliament could be agreed upon by the organised workers of the country, and such representation to be free from party politics and solely in the interest of the labouring classes by securing reasonable legislation for wage earners, the spinners and twiners of Lancashire and the adjoining counties would be strongly in favour of supporting such a policy both by money and influence.[1]

As it was, however, 'among the trade unions most of the largest may not even send representatives',[2] and the groups which should form 'a united labour party' were 'too much split up into factions'.[3]

The decision which led to the formation of the Labour Representation Committee must therefore be attributed as much to the fact that the Lib-Labs did not organize its defeat as to the drive and political skills of the socialists. In this the debate exemplifies the relationship between the two groups throughout the decade. The Lib-Labs had the controlling positions and the numbers, but after the revision of Congress's standing orders they were not united in opposition to the socialists nor, despite the lead given by Pickard, to the growth of socialist influence within their own unions. This growth continued in spite of the decline in the overall numbers of the Independent Labour Party after 1895,[4] from which it was saved only by the formation of the Labour Representation Committee.

The socialists, of course, had the advantage of youth. The Lib-Lab leaders in Parliament and at Congress—Pickard, Burt, Wilson, Holmes, and Knight—together with the Conservative Mawdsley, were a group of old or ageing men; but

Northumberland. Previously both Durham and Northumberland had been affiliated to Congress through the Miners' National Union. In 1898 Durham withdrew from this shadowy organization which was then dissolved. Northumberland immediately reaffiliated to Congress on its own, but Durham did not return until 1905. This must have cost the opposition some 70,000 votes.   [1] 9 Feb. 1900.

[2] Ibid., 12 Jan. 1900.
[3] Ibid., 9 Feb. 1900.   [4] Pelling, *Origins*, appendix A.

though the older Trade Union officials [wrote Snowden] were as bitterly opposed to the new Party as the Liberals, there were many of the younger officials of the unions who were ardent supporters of the I.L.P. These men did great service to the party in these early years. They not only worked for the Party inside the Trade Unions, but gave their week-ends generously to speaking from the Socialist platform.[1]

In time these men would come to be the leaders of the trade union movement, but by 1899 the process was not yet far advanced.

Moreover, while some Lib-Labs, such as Pickard, remained sworn enemies of socialism, others were increasingly prepared to accept parts of the socialist case, as were Cowey and even Fenwick.[2] They were disappointed with the legislative results of the later years of the decade. They were dissatisfied with their failure to add significantly to trade union representation in Parliament. They were alarmed by the engineering lockout and the employers' counter-attack on both the industrial and the political fronts. Indeed, they had already applied one of the lessons which the socialists drew from the lock-out by seeking closer industrial unity through the General Federation of Trade Unions. During the dispute Inskip, the staunchest of Lib-Labs, drew attention to the 'steady fusion between what is known as the old and new unionism . . .' and went on to say that 'the introduction of some of the questions by the newer party were, and will be, calculated, eventually, to be for the good of the whole'.[3] In 1899 socialist preaching found many of his colleagues well on the way to conversion.

[1] Op. cit., vol. i, pp. 71–72.

[2] At the Trades Union Congress of 1896 Fenwick asked to be told 'plainly and honestly what was meant by the nationalisation of the means of production and exchange; give them some tangible scheme, and they would go with them as far as it was possible for honest and moral-minded men to go'.

[3] National Union of Boot and Shoe Operatives, *Monthly Report*, Sept. 1897.

8

The Law and the Taff Vale Judgement

The Courts and the Unions, 1890–1900

BRITISH trade union law has always been a mystery to laymen, to trade unionists, and probably to most lawyers as well. Many of the crucial decisions of the judges have been based on common law as much as upon varying interpretations of the statutes themselves. In most fields of the common law there exist slowly evolving doctrines which inform and explain such decisions; but the doctrines applicable to cases concerning trade unions or trade unionists have from time to time been subject to sudden and far-reaching change. Consequently there have been periods when it has been impossible to foretell what the courts would decide in almost any issue that might be brought before them.

In these circumstances the historian is well advised to attempt no more than to record the major decisions and to set out what seem to have been the main reasons for them in terms which may appear crude and over-simplified to the specialist in trade union law. For trade union history, however, the significance of these decisions lies in their effect on the minds of the trade unionists and employers who had to cope with their consequences, and on the minds of the legislators who from time to time were compelled to intervene with a new statute. Few of these understood the niceties of the law, and most had to act without comprehending its subtleties.

In the seventies and eighties the balance of opinion had come to favour the freedom of workers to combine in order to match the bargaining strength of their employers. But at the same time society as a whole still attached the highest value to the rights of the individual and of property. In such a context, the Acts of 1871–6 appeared at first to provide an acceptable legal framework within which the unions could carry out their functions without unreasonable damage to others.[1] This was not because of the skill of those who drafted them, however, for in places they were defective and obscure. It was rather because the period which followed was one of trade union weakness marked by a series of major defeats in the industrial field. Employers therefore had little incentive either to seek help from the courts or to agitate for a revision of the Acts.

---

[1] See pp. 45–48.

Both these processes began as soon as the unions regained their strength from 1889 onwards. In the course of the legal probings which followed as employers tested the law in the courts, the shortcomings of the statutes were gradually exposed. Questions concerning the authority of trade unions over their members had been expressly excluded from the courts by the 1871 Act; their power over other workers was defined only in the clauses of the 1875 Act concerning picketing;[1] and the Acts said nothing, except in relation to gas and water supply, about the possibility that strikes might inflict hardship upon the public. Now, with the unions in the ascendant, there was a danger, apparent not only to employers but also to less partisan observers, that they might tyrannize over members and coerce non-members, and that their bargaining power might not merely match but actually exceed that of the employers.

Since the Acts were either silent or inconclusive on these issues, the courts turned for guidance to the common law, and above all to one of its central doctrines, the sanctity of contract. In a society which permits combination, however, there can be no absolute freedom of contract for the individual, since combinations cannot be effective without limiting the individual's freedom to contract. Trade unions, for example, necessarily limit the freedom of their own members to make contracts with employers. In addition, their activities usually circumscribe the freedom of non-members to contract with employers and of employers to contract with them. Sometimes unions also interfere with the freedom of employers to contract with their customers.

Faced with these difficulties, the courts resorted to the assessment of motive. Combinations could be permitted to interfere with the contractual freedom of others so long as their aim was the genuine protection of their own interests, and the harm done was the unavoidable consequence of this protection; but 'malicious' interference with the rights of others could not be allowed. Since human motives are always mixed, this distinction drove the courts to attempt to determine which motive predominated in each case.[2] The new doctrine could easily be used to restrict combinations thought to be too powerful, and this was now the attitude of the courts towards the unions.

---

[1] These, while laying down penalties for various types of intimidation, including watching or besetting 'with a view to compel', declared that 'attending at or near' a man's house or place of work 'merely to obtain or communicate information shall not be deemed a watching or besetting'.

[2] The doctrine of predominant motive was developed in a decision of the House of Lords in *Mogul Steamship Co.* v. *McGregor, Gow and Co.* (1892). The defendants were a combination of employers who brought pressure to bear on a business rival. It was held that they had committed no actionable wrong in conspiring to drive their rival out of business, because their predominant motive had not been malice but the lawful aim of promoting their own trade. The immediate effect of the decision was to emphasize and support the rights of combination and therefore, by implication, those of the trade unions.

Even if malice was held to have predominated, however, the courts were precluded by the Conspiracy and Protection of Property Act of 1875 from finding a criminal conspiracy in any act done 'in contemplation or further-ance of a trade dispute', except where the act would have been criminal even if committed by only one person. It was therefore necessary to develop the doctrine of civil conspiracy, outlined by the decision of the Court of Appeal in *Temperton* v. *Russell* in 1893. If those who had suffered from a malicious interference with their freedom of contract chose to bring an action, the courts could award damages—not, it was held at this time, against the unions themselves, since they were not corporate bodies with a legal personality, but against the officers and members concerned.

Meanwhile, the outcome of the conflicts with the 'new unions' during 1889-91 had turned very largely on the ability of the employers to find substitute labour to replace strikers, and they were therefore vitally interested in the law relating to picketing. What they wanted most of all was adequate police protection for their 'free labour',[1] and they were still trying to attack picketing through the criminal law. The courts were often willing to circumvent the prohibition on criminal conspiracy in trade disputes by reading criminal intimidation into threats of any kind, and the 'new unionists' gave many hostages to fortune—in the Leeds gas strike, for example.[2] Initially, the employers met with some success, notably in the conviction of Havelock Wilson;[3] but in 1891, in the case of *Curran* v. *Treleaven*, which arose from the Plymouth dock strike of the previous year,[4] the Queen's Bench decided that a charge of intimidation could only succeed if the action threatened would, if executed, have been a criminal offence.

Thus the most important judicial decision of these years was a victory for the unions' though it came too late to be of much service to the 'new unions' and left union leaders uneasy over the obscurities which had been revealed in the picketing section of the Act of 1875. 'None of them desired to act contrary to the law of the land', said William Inskip, 'but the Conspiracy Act of 1875 was so lax that it was construed in almost every case according to the wish, whim or desire of the judge, who might be interested or prejudiced.'[5] For very different reasons their experience turned the minds of employers also towards reform of the law. The Cham-ber of Shipping of the United Kingdom, for example, urged that 'in consequence of the hindrance to men willing to labour caused by the obstruction of organised pickets, it is desirable . . . to render illegal the practice of picketing in force during strikes and labour disputes'.[6]

---

[1] See pp. 68, 72, 75, 94. [2] See p. 69.
[3] See p. 76. [4] See p. 72.
[5] Trades Union Congress, *Annual Report*, 1894. The series of annual resolutions at the Trades Union Congress demanding the amendment of the Act began in 1891.
[6] Shaxby, op. cit., p. 8.

Employers were soon to discover, however, that civil actions offered them their best chance of help from the law, and the lesson was learned not in the great stoppages in coal and cotton in 1892–4 but in disputes with individual employers mainly in the craft trades. When the whole of a major industry was closed down, an employer had little to gain by going to the courts, even when the opportunity arose. But the traditional craft method of gradually extending union strength through piecemeal attacks provided circumstances in which he could expect more help from the law.

In *Temperton* v. *Russell* the Court of Appeal had before it a case of boycott. In order to bring pressure to bear on a Hull building employer whose men were on strike, a local committee of building unions tried to dissuade another employer, Temperton, from supplying him with materials. When Temperton refused, the unions imposed a boycott upon him also. Temperton thereupon brought a civil action for damages. It was not alleged that the union officers had coerced or intimidated the workers, who were certainly within their rights, and it would have been lawful for an individual to persuade them to do what they did. Because they had combined together, however, the union officers and the committee were guilty of 'maliciously procuring and coercing others to break contracts with the plaintiff' and of forming a 'conspiracy to injure' him. They were held liable for damages.

In 1895, in *Trollope* v. *London Building Trades Federation*, it was held actionable for union officers to publish 'black lists' of non-union firms and of free labourers, on the argument that this amounted to a conspiracy to injure. The next round, however, went to the craftsmen, in *Allen* v. *Flood*, which ended its long journey through the courts in 1898. Flood and Taylor were shipwrights in a London firm who were alleged to have done work which the boilermakers regarded as their own. In 1894 T. F. Allen, London district officer of the Boilermakers, informed the firm's managing director that unless Flood and Taylor were discharged the boilermakers would strike. The two men were thereupon discharged and subsequently brought an action against Allen for malicious damage. No question of intimidation or coercion under the 1875 Act was involved; no loss or breach of contract was suggested; and no charge of conspiracy made.

The Lords held that Allen had violated no legal right of the plaintiffs, since he had done no unlawful act and used no unlawful means. Where neither the act nor the means of 'trade interference' employed by an *individual* was unlawful, his motive, malicious or not, was immaterial. Allen's triumph was believed by the unions at the time to have established 'the right of workmen to decide with whom they should work',[1] and the right to threaten employers with a stoppage unless men obnoxious to them were discharged, 'provided that the threat was an individual one'.[2] The

---

[1] Trades Union Congress, *Annual Report*, 1898.   [2] Cummings, op. cit., p. 151.

Parliamentary Committee's Report to the 1898 Congress was exultant. 'It is impossible to over-estimate the value of this . . . decision to trade unions, and it marks an important turning point in a great industrial controversy.'

Their jubilation was short-lived. In the following year the Court of Appeal turned its attention once more to picketing in the case of *Lyons* v. *Wilkins*. Wilkins was the secretary of the Amalgamated Society of Fancy Leather Workers which in 1896 sought to strengthen a strike against Lyons, a leather goods manufacturer, by striking also against a firm which worked for him on subcontract, and picketed both firms. Lyons was granted an injunction restraining the unionists from 'maliciously inducing, or conspiring to induce, persons not to enter the employment of plaintiffs', though it was agreed that there had been no violence or threats. The Court of Appeal upheld the injunction in March 1896, certain of its dicta illustrating 'the way in which the political arguments for free labour were now finding legal justification'.[1]

Lyons then prosecuted Wilkins, the case being heard in 1897. Mr. Justice Byrne's judgement in February 1898 largely supported the 1896 dicta, his main point being that picketing was lawful only if confined to 'communicating information', and that picketing to 'persuade', for example, to strike, not being the communication of information, was an actionable offence. The Court of Appeal again upheld the decision in 1899. It was during this case that Lindley, one of the judges, declared that 'You cannot make a strike effective without doing more than what is lawful'.[2] It is therefore not surprising that the Parliamentary Committee's Report to the 1899 Congress stressed that the case was 'a very important one, and its far-reaching consequences affect the position of every trade union', and that Congress resolved to appeal to the movement for funds to take the case to the House of Lords.

In the same year the verdict in *Charnock* v. *Court* illustrated the extreme lengths to which judicial hostility to picketing could be taken. During a strike, a firm of Halifax master joiners brought workmen over from Ireland. The union sent two men to the port of Fleetwood, fifty miles away, to persuade the Irish not to break the strike and to offer them their fare back. The men were found guilty of watching and besetting. The effect was to render actionable any communication even of the most peaceable kind, except by letter, between strikers and men whom the employer was seeking to engage.[3]

Next came the *Quinn* v. *Leathem* judgement by the House of Lords in 1901. This decision gave supreme judicial sanction to the principle laid

---

[1] Saville, loc. cit., p. 347.

[2] Citrine, op. cit., p. 15.

[3] W. M. Geldart, 'Report of the Royal Commission on Trade Disputes', *Economic Journal*, June 1906.

down by the Court of Appeal in *Temperton* v. *Russell* that 'conspiracy to injure' gave cause for action. The plaintiff, Leathem, was a Belfast butcher with some non-unionists on his staff. When the defendants, officers of a local butchers' assistants' union, asked him to discharge them, he refused. They then persuaded one of the butchers who was accustomed, though not contractually bound, to deal with Leathem to stop doing so. Leathem sued for conspiracy to injure and won his case at every level. As in *Temperton* v. *Russell*, the case turned on whether the defendants' motive had been to injure Leathem or to defend their own legitimate interests. The decision was that they had acted maliciously, though no unlawful act had been committed by any of the defendants individually. Thus the advantages gained in *Allen* v. *Flood* were destroyed, for whatever the exact line of distinction drawn between the two verdicts it was now clear that any attempt to enforce a closed shop might well lead to an action for damages.

The cumulative effect of this series of decisions was most confusing. 'Speaking for myself', wrote R. B. Haldane in 1903, 'I should be very sorry to be called on to tell a Trade Union Secretary how he could conduct a strike lawfully. The only answer I could give would be that, having regard to the diverging opinion of the Judges, I did not know.'[1] If so eminent a lawyer could not say what actions were going to be lawful or not, the layman could be excused confusion, and it is understandable that trade unionists should suppose that the courts could choose to grant damages against them for almost any action they chose to pick on, by finding their motives to be malicious and their action a conspiracy to injure.

Even so, the unions as such were apparently still protected. Though in *Trollope* v. *London Building Trades Federation* and in *Pink* v. *Federation of Trade and Labour Unions* in 1892, 'civil proceedings were successfully taken by employers against combinations of workmen', these cases were 'not seriously defended, not fully argued, and not carried to the highest tribunal'.[2] Consequently it was still the prevailing view, in the absence of a decision to the contrary by the House of Lords, that the 1871 Act precluded the possibility of suing a trade union, and certainly of recovering damages from its collective funds.[3]

This view had been positively affirmed in *Temperton* v. *Russell*. The plaintiff sued union officers and a joint union committee not only as individuals but in their 'representative character' on behalf of all the

---

[1] 'The Labourer and the Law', *Century Review*, Mar. 1903, quoted in Halévy, op. cit., vol. v, p. 273, footnote.

[2] Webbs, *Industrial Democracy*, Introduction to the 1902 edition, p. xxv, footnote.

[3] In *Warnham* v. *Stone* (1896), 'a judge of the High Court was capable . . . of making a Trade Union a party to a suit, and attaching its corporate funds for damages'; but his decision was reversed by the Court of Appeal (ibid., p. 858, footnote).

members of the unions concerned. This was an early example of a legal form, the 'representative action', which developed outside the field of industrial relations during the succeeding years to facilitate actions by and against an unincorporated aggregate of people in cases where the persons represented had a 'common interest'. Success in *Temperton* v. *Russell* would have meant that the collective union funds, as well as the individual officers, would have become vulnerable to attack through representative actions. The Court of Appeal held, however, that the representative action could not be used in the case of trade unions, and that the plaintiff was not entitled to sue the officers in their representative character but only as individuals.

The Majority Report of the Royal Commission on Labour[1] indicated some dissatisfaction with this position. They noted that *Temperton* v. *Russell* showed how 'persons injured by the action of trade unions and their agents can only proceed against the agents personally, and, whilst they may obtain verdicts against them . . . be unable to recover adequate damages'. This, they thought, illustrated 'the inconvenience which may be caused by the existence of associations having . . . very real corporate existence and modes of action, but no legal personality corresponding thereto'.[2] The Report also noted the implications of this situation for collective bargaining. Since it was conducted between organizations which had no legal personality and which could not, therefore, sue or be sued for damages 'occasioned by the breach of such agreements by sections of their members', there was as a result 'collective action without legal collective responsibility'.[3]

The Majority Report itself made no recommendations on these points, but the chairman, the Duke of Devonshire, together with David Dale, Sir Michael Hicks Beach, Leonard Courtney, Sir Frederick Pollock, Thomas Ismay, George Livesey, and William Tunstill, appended *Observations* which took up the question of legal incorporation. Incorporation is the customary means by which an association of persons can acquire legal personality, including the right to sue and be sued, and there had long been a school of thought which held that the unions ought to be granted the full rights and obligations of corporate bodies. Now this 'small though influential section'[4] of the Commission suggested that trade unions and employers' organizations should both be free, if they chose, to acquire full corporate personality.

This would enable them to enter into legally binding collective agreements

---

[1] The signatories of the Majority Report included two of the trade union members, Thomas Burt and Edward Trow. The other four—Tom Mann, James Mawdsley, William Abraham, and Michael Austin—signed a Minority Report for which, according to Beatrice Webb (op. cit., pp. 41–42), Sidney Webb was largely responsible, especially in the legal aspects.

[2] C-7421, 1894, p. 41. [3] Ibid., p. 54.

[4] Trades Union Congress, *Annual Report*, 1894, Parliamentary Committee Report.

with the consequence that in cases of breach of contract they would be liable to be sued for damages payable out of their collective funds. Such a change 'would also afford a better basis for arbitration in industrial disputes than any which has yet been suggested',[1] since it would provide the means by which the respective bodies could discipline any recalcitrant members into accepting the award. Admittedly there was no evidence that public opinion was 'as yet ripe for the changes . . . which we have suggested', but they might nevertheless ultimately prove to be 'the most natural and reasonable solution'.[2]

The signatories made no reference to the fact that the acquisition of corporate personality would also render trade union funds vulnerable in civil actions for wrongs other than breach of contract, but the dissenting trade unionists among the Commissioners were alert to this danger. Their Minority Report insisted that 'to expose the large amalgamated societies . . . to be sued for damages by any employer . . . or by any discontented member or non-unionist, for the action of some branch secretary or delegate, would be a great injustice'.[3] Taking its cue from the minority, the Parliamentary Committee's Report to Congress in 1894, while admitting that 'in its optional form' the proposal for incorporation was 'perhaps not dangerous', declared that it would 'require to be carefully watched'.[4]

The case of *Bailey* v. *Pye*, which ended in January 1897, provided more ammunition for the campaign for incorporation by showing the difficulty of recovering damages without it. Bailey, a firm of glass merchants and bevellers, claimed damages for injury to business alleged to have been inflicted by members of the National Plate Glass Bevellers' Union. The firm was awarded damages against the members to a total of £1,217; by September 1897 only £5 had been recovered.[5]

So long as it is a question of formulating trade demands, of . . . delivering ultimatums, of setting in motion . . . strikes, and directing the system of pickets . . . the 'organisers' and 'secretaries' [of trade unions] are invested with a representative character. . . . But when it comes to the question of framing a writ against them, these officers of a well-drilled army, acting on a common plan and disposing of a common purse, sink at once into individual artisans with no greater and no less responsibilities than any other private citizens.[6]

[1] C–7421, 1894, p. 116.   [2] Ibid., p. 119.
  [3] Ibid., p. 146. Mantoux and Alfassa noted that the minority, while insisting upon the danger to the unions of unlimited financial liability, did not directly contest the arguments advanced in the *Observations* (op. cit., pp. 11–12).
  [4] This section of the Report was prepared by Henry Broadhurst and John Jack of the Scottish Ironmoulders, both members of 'the old guard' (Parliamentary Committee, *Minutes*, 28 Aug. 1894). The Report was adopted unanimously by Congress.
  [5] Shaxby, op. cit., pp. 34–36.
  [6] *The Times*, 15 Jan. 1897. In the late nineties there was a move by some employers to promote legislation imposing full legal liability upon the unions. Shaxby, in his book published by Lord Wemyss's Liberty Review Publishing Company (see p. 173), referred to 'the elaborate

The Taff Vale Judgement and its Effects

In July 1901 the courts delivered their final assault on the unions by destroying this privilege. The House of Lords decided, in the Taff Vale case, that the Amalgamated Society of Railway Servants, though not a corporate body, could be sued in a corporate capacity for damages alleged to have been caused by the action of its officers, and that an injunction could be issued restraining it not merely from criminal but also from other unlawful acts.

The case had its origins in the preceding year. With the South African War approaching its climax, coal prices were running high and demand was still increasing. The railwaymen of South Wales, encouraged by James Holmes, West of England organizer of the Amalgamated Society and a militant socialist, decided to seize the moment both to improve their position and to win recognition for the union. The Society was strong locally, and its bargaining position had been strengthened by the calling up of reservists.[1] The agitation eventually concentrated upon the Taff Vale line, which was the essential link between the ports and the steam-coal collieries on which the fleet, foreign coaling stations, and the mercantile marine mainly depended.[2] Holmes, moreover, was spoiling for a fight with the general manager, Ammon Beasley,[3] their tempers having been roused by an acrimonious exchange over the alleged victimization of a signalman named Ewington. With his approval, a number of the Company's employees handed in their notices to expire on 20 August 1900.

Up to this point the campaign in South Wales had been unofficial, Holmes having, not for the first time, taken the initiative without seeking the sanction of the Society's executive. Richard Bell, the secretary, had tried on previous occasions to persuade them to curb Holmes;[4] but the

proposals . . . advanced in some quarters to give trade associations a corporate standing' (op. cit., p. 77). Mantoux and Alfassa (op. cit., p. 31) refer to 'the Bill to that effect drafted by the Employers' Parliamentary Council', of which Wemyss and the engineering employers were the leading spirits (see p. 174). Halévy points out that Mantoux and Alfassa date the Bill 1897, but that the Council was not formed until 1898 (Halévy, op. cit., vol. v, p. 270, footnote).

[1] In the Oct. 1899 issue of the *Railway Review* there had appeared an article urging railwaymen to take advantage of the labour scarcity produced by the calling up of reservists. The agitation began in South Wales, 'the men there making no secret of the fact that that district was chosen . . . because of the abnormally high price of coal then prevailing, and the consequent pressure which . . . would be put upon the railway companies by the colliery proprietors to prevent a strike' (*Railway News*, 25 Aug. 1900).

[2] This point was made by Sir Edward Clarke, counsel for the Taff Vale Railway. The continuous running of the line was a matter of the 'highest national importance', especially at times when naval efficiency was vital (*Transcript* of shorthand notes of the case, 3 Dec. 1902, published by the union).

[3] Holmes wrote in a report for the *Railway Review* for 13 July 1900: 'There is nothing I would like better than to measure swords with this Taff Vale Railway dictator' (quoted in Osborne, op. cit., p. 178). The remark was deleted by the editor, the socialist G. J. Wardle.

[4] Osborne, op. cit., pp. 176–7.

executive included a strong section of militants,[1] and Bell could not rely on its support. When he opposed official recognition of the Taff Vale strike he was once again overruled. Though the executive condemned the irregular manner in which the strike had been called, it resolved to give financial support, and Bell was sent to take charge.

Beasley refused to meet the union and prepared for battle. He advertised for substitute labour, even in the *Railway Review*, and called in Collison's Free Labour Association. Determined to make full use of the law, he offered a reward of £100 for information against anyone damaging railway property and secured the imprisonment of two men for this offence; 400 summonses were issued against those who had come out without giving proper notice, sixty of whom were dealt with before the strike ended, each being fined £4. Beasley was also well aware of the dangers involved in picketing since *Lyons* v. *Wilkins*.[2] At the first opportunity he therefore applied for an injunction, not only against Bell and Holmes as individuals but also against the union itself, to restrain unlawful picketing.[3]

Attempts at mediation were made by the Cardiff Chamber of Commerce, by the Board of Trade, and eventually by Sir William Lewis.[4] With his assistance, a settlement was reached before the end of August under which the men returned on the terms and conditions existing before the strike. The Ewington case was referred to arbitration by the President of the Board, and the Company agreed to examine the 'possibility' of a conciliation board that did not involve recognition of the union. While the strikers had gained none of their original demands, Beasley had 'earned the gratitude not only of the shareholders of the Taff Vale Company, but of British railway shareholders at large'.[5]

The heaviest blow was still to fall, however. Mr. Justice Farwell had already granted the Company's application for an injunction against Bell and Holmes as individuals. On 5 September 1900, when the strike was over, he also granted the injunction against the union, declaring that 'the Legislature, in giving a trade union the capacity to own property and the capacity to act by agents has, without incorporating it, given it two of the essential qualities of a corporation; essential, I mean, in respect of liability for tort. . . . For . . . wrongs arising . . . from the wrongful conduct of the agents of the society . . . the defendant society is, in my opinion, liable'.

[1] See p. 296.

[2] In March Beasley had even circulated a leaflet on the subject to the Company's employees. The leaflet was based upon material supplied by the Employers' Parliamentary Council (Bealey and Pelling, op. cit., p. 58).

[3] Beasley 'had a passion for litigation. . . . He . . . loved litigation for its own sake' (Lord Askwith, *Industrial Problems and Disputes*, 1920, p. 91). His application for an injunction against the union was in defiance of legal advice (Phelps Brown, op. cit., p. 194).

[4] See p. 231.

[5] *Railway News*, 8 Sept. 1900.

This view was described by the Liberal *Daily News* as 'contrary to the opinion held by all lawyers who had professionally considered the subject'.[1] When the Court of Appeal reversed Farwell's decision two months later *The Times* declared this 'not altogether unexpected', and suggested that the House of Lords, to which Beasley now intended to appeal, would have difficulty in disposing of their arguments. Such a situation made even more urgent the need for legislation making trade unions 'responsible to the law for their action'.[2] Contrary to this forecast, however, the Lords restored Farwell's original judgement in July 1901.

Has the Legislature [asked Lord Macnaghten] authorised the creation of numerous bodies of men, capable of owning great wealth and of acting by agents, with absolutely no responsibility for the wrongs they may do to other persons by the use of that wealth and the employment of those agents? In my opinion Parliament has done nothing of the kind. I can find nothing in the Acts of 1871 and 1875 . . . from beginning to end, to warrant such a notion.

The Lords' decision[3] to uphold the injunction against the Amalgamated Society made it possible for Beasley to proceed with an action for damages against the union itself, 'for having conspired to induce the workmen of [the] company to break their contracts, and also for having conspired to interfere with the traffic of the company by picketing and other unlawful means'. The case was heard in December 1902 and resulted in the Company's favour, the two sides agreeing to settle for a payment by the union of £23,000 to cover both damages and the Company's costs. The expenses of the earlier stages of the case brought its total cost to the Railway Servants to £42,000.[4]

So far the adverse decisions of the courts, irritating and threatening though they were, had not greatly influenced the course of trade union development. They had had no discernible effect on the engineering lockout of 1897–8. Unions in coal, cotton, printing, steel, and dozens of lesser industries had continued on their way with little thought of what the courts might, or might not, say. Now it seemed that a case could be brought on the grounds of almost anything that might be done in a trade

---

[1] 22 Nov. 1900, quoted in *A Report of the Picketing Cases on the Taff Vale Railway*, Parliamentary Committee, Trades Union Congress, December 1900. [2] Ibid.

[3] The decision applied only to unions registered under the procedure provided for by the 1871 Act. But *obiter dicta* by Lords Macnaghten and Lindley during the Taff Vale hearing declared that even an unregistered union could be sued in a representative action, 'and an injunction and judgment for damages could be obtained in a proper case in an action so framed'. This ran directly counter to the Court of Appeal's judgement in *Temperton* v. *Russell*, and a modern authority on trade union law considers it 'extremely doubtful . . . whether . . . a representative action in tort could ever have been brought against a trade union' (Citrine, op. cit., p. 456).

[4] This was less than two-thirds of a year's income at this time. The union's steady accumulation of funds was momentarily halted in 1903 at £279,000, but by 1904 was climbing again and had reached £305,000 (*Report on Trade Unions in 1902–1904*, Cd. 2838, 1906, p. 155).

dispute, not only against the members and officers but against the union itself; and there was no clear limit, short of an empty treasury, to the damages which could be awarded against a union's funds. Had the unions been disposed to make light of Taff Vale a series of subsequent decisions in which heavy damages were awarded against them pressed home the lesson.[1]

It would be a mistake, however, to see the Taff Vale decision as part of a gigantic plot to destroy the unions in which free labourers and the Law Lords were but two groups of conspirators.[2] True, Beasley was their sworn enemy, and he had used free labourers as well as the courts. But the question at issue was whether a union should be legally responsible for the actions of its officers, and behind this question lay problems of the relationship between trade unions, the state, and society about which opinion was honestly divided. Few believed that Taff Vale could be taken as the last word on the subject. The courts had been searching for the limits of trade union action in uninformative statutes and in common law doctrines designed for an earlier society. Naturally enough, their discoveries did not constitute a consistent code. The House of Lords had decided that the unions must be legally responsible, but neither lawyers, employers, nor trade unions could be sure for what they would be held responsible unless the decisions of the past ten years were clarified and rationalized.

All these considerations were reflected in the trade union reaction to the Taff Vale case. The unions appreciated its importance at once. News of the granting of the injunction against the Amalgamated Society of Railway Servants in September 1900 came to the Trades Union Congress while it was still in session, and standing orders were suspended to allow a special debate. Richard Bell pointed out all the implications and declared that the effect would be to render trade unions 'practically useless', while Edmond Browne, standing counsel to the Parliamentary Committee, thought the injunction 'one of the most dangerous things ever done against Trade Unions'. There was unanimous support for a motion proposed by G. D. Kelley which instructed the Committee 'to call the attention of the trade societies of the country to the [Taff Vale] judgement, pointing out the absolute and urgent necessity of the case being fought right through the House of Lords . . . and . . . obtain from each society their consent to a contribution, *pro rata*, for the purpose of prosecuting the appeal'.

While the battle proceeded in the courts, Edmond Browne advised the unions to revise their rules in order to minimize the danger of actions

[1] See p. 326.

[2] While they described the cumulative effect of decisions hostile to the unions as 'a kind of judicial *coup d'état*', Mantoux and Alfassa concluded that there was no evidence of a concerted plan behind them (op. cit., p. 82). During 1902 they had interviewed, among others, George Barnes and Francis Chandler, both of whom dismissed any such suggestion (ibid., pp. 265-75).

being brought against them—an ill-drafted expulsion rule, for example, might allow an expelled member to bring a case against his union. Browne also pointed out that what made the unions specially vulnerable was the combination of Taff Vale and the existing state of the law on picketing, as defined by the Court of Appeal in *Lyons* v. *Wilkins*; and he recommended that Congress should as soon as possible secure a decision by the House of Lords on this question.[1] Meanwhile, the implications of Taff Vale were not, he thought, all bad—for example, a union could now sue a vindictive employer who tried to break up or injure the union.[2]

It was not enough to appreciate the importance of the Taff Vale case, however; the unions had to decide what was to be done about it. The widespread opinion of the rank and file was that the legal position had been satisfactory before Taff Vale and the related decisions of the Lords, and that there should be a return to the position which had previously existed under the Acts of 1871–6. But to many of the union leaders the problem did not seem as simple as that. These Acts made no direct reference to the general liability of trade unions. The 1871 Act, it is true, had prohibited the courts from entertaining legal proceedings concerning breaches of agreement in a specific range of internal trade union affairs, but these were not in question at the moment. The general liability of the unions remained where it had been before 1871, and if the House of Lords now held that unions had always been liable, little remained of the *status quo* to which rank and file members wanted to return.[3]

The unions could certainly ask Parliament for new legislation to give them the immunity which they thought they had once possessed. But it was extremely unlikely that Parliament would agree. The leading lawyers in both parties were opposed to such a step. The Conservative Attorney-General, Sir Robert Finlay, expressed the strongest possible objection to complete immunity. 'It would be a marvellous thing', he told the Commons, 'if an association of individuals were to be at liberty to employ servants and officials for the purpose of doing a certain class of acts relating to trade disputes, and yet not be liable in the case of injury being done by those acts.'[4] In the Liberal Party both Asquith and Haldane saw the need for clarifying legislation and were willing to help the unions with

[1] An appeal to the Lords on the *Lyons* v. *Wilkins* case had originally been intended. Funds collected by the Parliamentary Committee had been handed over to the union. But a technical slip—called a 'blundering mistake' by the Parliamentary Committee—on the part of the solicitors resulted in the petition for appeal being lodged a month too late and therefore being refused. Dilke's version that the appeal was withdrawn on legal advice (see Saville, loc. cit., p. 348, footnote) is clearly based upon a misreading of the correspondence between the parties printed in the Trades Union Congress, *Annual Report*, 1900, pp. 33–36.

[2] Letter from Browne to the Parliamentary Committee, quoted in the Trades Union Congress, *Annual Report*, 1901.

[3] For the legal arguments see Webbs, *History*, pp. 601–2, footnote.

[4] *Hansard*, 14 May 1902, col. 311.

drafting; but they accepted the essential legality of the Taff Vale decision and believed that the unions could not claim privileged immunity.[1] Some trade unionists, indeed, concluded that 'to put the whole Trade Union position in the melting-pot of Parliament as at present constituted involves the danger of coming out rather worse than better'.[2]

Many of their middle-class sympathizers shared the views of the parliamentary lawyers. Sidney Webb, convinced that collective bargaining was played out and that statutory regulation of wages and conditions could both avoid the suffering and losses caused by strikes and protect those too weak to organize, saw Taff Vale as a step towards full corporate status, legally enforceable agreements, and compulsory arbitration.[3] J. M. Ludlow, who had given so much help in the legal battles of thirty years before, advised them to meet the consequences of the judgement 'by increased prudence and straightforwardness in their proceedings, and greater care in the selection of their members and officers. . . . Any attempt to overrule the judgement would be simply futile and wholly injudicious. . . . The time will come when that judgement will be felt to have been a blessing in disguise, by forcing Trade Unions to rise to the full height of their responsibilities.'[4]

Ernest Aves,[5] who believed that the proper course was to press for legislation ensuring that no action could be maintained against a union unless it was proved that its governing body had expressly authorized or been privy to the acts complained of,[6] was convinced that there now existed 'widespread acceptance . . . of the new legal position. . . . The most responsible leaders and advisers of the trade unionists no longer expect a reversal to the earlier state of things.' They recognized, in his opinion,

that . . . the old rude weapon of the strike is lost, and it is one of the most satisfactory features of the situation that this loss is by no means generally regretted. . . . Internally, they perceive the necessity for stricter discipline, and for more centralised executive authority, both as regards administration and the control of the funds: the powers of branch officials and of 'organisers' will, it is seen, have to be much more strictly defined than in the past. In another direction, the more extended formation of Joint Conciliation Boards is almost certain to follow.[7]

[1] See pp. 369, 393.

[2] Amalgamated Society of Engineers, *Annual Report*, 1902. The same point was made in the *Journal* of the Amalgamated Society of Tailors and Tailoresses, Oct. 1903.

[3] *Industrial Democracy*, Introduction to the 1902 edition; *Report of the Royal Commission on Trade Disputes and Trade Combinations*, Cd. 2825, 1906: *Recommendations*, and *Memorandum* by Sidney Webb.   [4] 'Labour Notes', *Economic Journal*, Dec. 1901.

[5] Aves, Sir Ernest (1857–1917). Social investigator and writer. Co-operated with Charles Booth in his inquiry into London life and labour. Appointed Commissioner by the Home Office to investigate Australian and New Zealand wage boards, 1907–1908. Chairman of first Trade Board set up under the 1909 Trade Boards Act.

[6] 'Labour Notes', *Economic Journal*, Mar. 1902.   [7] Ibid., Mar. 1903.

Aves correctly represented the views held by many trade union leaders at this stage. While all of them would have been ready to accept Frederic Harrison's dictum that 'the social and political tone of the time invariably colours the bias of all courts of law',[1] they were willing to consider whether the Taff Vale decision might not yield some advantages. Already in August 1901, for example, James Sexton had written that 'there are those in the labour movement sanguine enough to think that the decision in the Taff Vale case will be a blessing in disguise, and will tend to strengthen executive control and minimise, if not entirely kill, irresponsible action in localities. It may be so. Time will tell.' Sexton went on to argue that if unions were to be put on the same legal footing as limited companies, they must demand the powers as well as the responsibilities of such organizations.[2]

By this time Richard Bell had had second thoughts, and was also prepared to accept legal liability. 'I have all along held views', he wrote in the *Railway Review*, 'which did not gain much popularity . . . as to the conduct and actions of some of the rank and file and the younger bloods of our trade unions. . . . Rules, executive committees and responsible officials have been ignored.'[3] The Taff Vale judgement could almost be welcomed as 'a useful influence in solidifying the forces of trade unionism and in subjecting them to wholesome discipline'.[4] He also seems to have believed that the Lords, by investing unions with the liability of being sued in a corporate capacity, had conferred upon them the power of concluding legally enforceable agreements, thus furthering the cause of compulsory arbitration,[5] which he had very much at heart as a means of overcoming the railway companies' resistance to recognition.

Bell's view was shared both by the miners' leaders of the North-east and by Pickard. George Barnes thought that the real danger lay 'in the uncertainty of the law and the large discretion left to judges'. Trade unionists should demand guaranteed picketing rights, and also 'that the liability of a union should be strictly limited to acts expressly authorised by the central authority of the unions acting within the scope of their authority by rule'.[6] The *Cotton Factory Times* went further. 'We have not been much surprised', was the paper's comment on the appeal for assistance to the Railway Servants, 'at some of the appeals which have been made for help by societies whose members are fonder of breaking the law than of putting their hands in their pockets to pay for it.'[7] The remedy

---

[1] Writing in Sept. 1901, quoted by Halévy, op. cit., vol. v, p. 273, footnote.
[2] Amalgamated Union of Clothiers' Operatives, *Monthly Gazette*, Aug. 1901.
[3] 2 Aug. 1901, quoted in Bealey and Pelling, op. cit., p. 75.
[4] *Clarion*, 27 July 1901, quoted ibid., p. 75.
[5] Ibid., p. 81.
[6] Amalgamated Society of Engineers, *Annual Report*, 1902.
[7] 7 Sept. 1900.

was for the unions to accept the decision, to abandon picketing, which was an outworn device, and to appoint more intelligent officials.[1]

Bell and like-minded union leaders were encouraged in these views by their antipathy towards the militant socialists who were so ready to promote unofficial strikes, and who called most loudly for a return to the legal *status quo*. W. E. Harvey, the Derbyshire Miners' agent, declared that the Taff Vale decision 'would never have been given but for the harum scarum action on the part of the I.L.P. and socialistic men'.[2] If the decision could be used to restrain these militants who, they thought, fomented dissension and wasted the resources of the unions upon alien objectives, there was a great deal to be said for it, always provided the unions could secure satisfaction on the issue of picketing.

In these circumstances, the movement's leaders approached the question of new legislation with considerable hesitation. The Parliamentary Committee had no immediate proposals for political action to put before Congress in September 1901. In his presidential address C. W. Bowerman confessed that 'numerous and varied opinions' had been expressed and advised Congress 'to make haste slowly', especially as picketing, 'the most vital question, has not yet been decided'.[3] The Committee believed that with 'a judicious amendment of the rules . . . it will be possible to avert many of the difficulties created by the decision of the House of Lords, especially in the direction of protecting the funds of the unions'. While he insisted that the moral to be drawn was 'the imperative and absolute necessity of securing increased representation in the House of Commons', he also believed that 'opinions will necessarily differ as to the wisdom of taking political action with the view to restoring the unions to their former position—the present balance of parties offering little encouragement to workmen to enter upon such a course of action'.

The resolution of Congress that all unions should 'use their best endeavour to bring about such an alteration of the law as will meet with the approval of this Congress' may have represented a concession to the rank-and-file feeling that something must be done; but its passing committed the leaders to no specific line of action, and Bell himself seconded the motion. In December, however, the Parliamentary Committee had consultations with Dilke and three leading Liberal lawyers—Asquith, Haldane, and Sir Robert Reid. Browne was then instructed both to draw up a bill 'in regard to picketing', and to discuss with Francis Palmer, an authority on company law, the possibility of some scheme 'for the protection of Trade Union Funds'.[4]

---

[1] 16 Nov. 1900 and 13 Sept. 1901.   [2] J. E. Williams, op. cit., p. 389.

[3] In 1901 Browne reiterated his view on the vital importance of the picketing question, both in person at Congress and in his formal opinion in the Parliamentary Committee's Report. Until it was settled, it was 'of no use whatever for them to be doing anything in connection with the Taff Vale decision' (Trades Union Congress, *Annual Report*, 1901).

[4] Parliamentary Committee, *Minutes*, 4 Dec. 1901 and 4 Feb. 1902. Palmer suggested what

After a Parliamentary Committee deputation to Ritchie, the Home Secretary, and Lord James of Hereford, Chancellor of the Duchy of Lancaster, which fully confirmed union fears about the dangerous state of the law on picketing, Richard Bell introduced in May 1902 a bill designed to protect peaceful picketing, but in the face of government hostility it made no progress. Meanwhile the Parliamentary Committee had enlisted the help of Campbell-Bannerman, the Liberal leader, and his whips in their attempts to bring the question before the House. Under the Committee's leadership, the movement staged one of its most impressive demonstrations of lobbying[1] in support of a motion put forward by Wentworth Beaumont, the Liberal Member for Hexham, on 14 May 1902, demanding 'legislation . . . to prevent workmen being placed by judge-made law in a position inferior to that intended by Parliament in 1875'—an ambiguous wording which left open what it was that Parliament had intended. The motion was only defeated by 203 votes to 174, a highly satisfactory result, especially in view of the fact that the Irish party, usually a good friend to the unions, had abstained on this occasion.

Thus encouraged, the Parliamentary Committee next sought to secure approval from the 1902 Congress for more concrete proposals. They were instructed to demand legislation which would:

1. Clearly confer upon the unions the right of voluntary association enjoyed under the Trade Union Act, 1871. . . . 2. Legalise peaceful picketing and persuading. 3. Make it perfectly legal for men to withdraw their labour other than in breach of contract, and also for unions to sanction such withdrawal, and for officials to advise or convey the decision to withdraw under all circumstances where men are pursuing the objects of Trade Unions. 4. To clearly define the law of conspiracy so that what is legal for one man to do shall not be either a criminal offence or an actionable wrong if done by many in combination. 5. To generally define and codify the laws of Trade Unions and Industrial Disputes.

In its Report to Congress the Parliamentary Committee had declared that 'no permanent remedy will be devised, and . . . there will be no real security to the Trade Union funds until the law is again reversed to its former position, as it stood prior to the Taff Vale case definitions'. These were bold words, designed to placate the more militant delegates; but the protection of funds was specifically mentioned only in the preamble to the resolution placed before Congress, and this was moved by Bell. Thus on the most difficult question the Committee still retained full freedom of action.

In November 1902 the Parliamentary Committee met representatives

---

became known as the 'subsidiary companies scheme' as a way of protecting union funds from legal attack, each union setting up a subsidiary company to which it would transfer its funds. This cumbrous solution met with such an unenthusiastic reception from the unions that the Parliamentary Committee was glad to disown it.   [1] Bealey and Pelling, op. cit., p. 92.

of the General Federation of Trade Unions and the Labour Representation Committee, and a joint subcommittee was set up to draft a bill along with Edmond Browne. After approval by the three bodies it was submitted to Reid, and it appears that Haldane and Asquith were also consulted. The result of these discussions was a bill of three clauses. The first followed Bell's bill of the previous year in providing protection for pickets; the second abolished the doctrine of civil conspiracy so far as trade disputes were concerned; and the third ruled out actions for damages against a union 'unless it be proved that [the] member or members . . . acted with the directly expressed sanction and authority of the rules'. The Congress resolution provided no express authority for this third clause, but it represented the views of the Liberal lawyers; a Conservative-dominated Parliament would certainly yield no more; and at this stage it was acceptable to the union leaders.

The draft bill was eventually approved by a conference of delegates summoned by the three national organizations in March 1903. Just before David Shackleton introduced the second reading, the Speaker detected an inconsistency between the title of 'Trade Disputes Bill' and the third clause, which therefore had to be dropped. The truncated bill was defeated by 258 votes to 228 on 2 May, but the government had shifted its ground a little since the previous year. The Conservative Prime Minister, Balfour, now took the view, not that legislation was unnecessary, but that nothing could be completed in the present session and that there must first be an inquiry. Accordingly a Royal Commission was appointed 'to inquire into the subject of disputes and Trade Combinations, and as to the law affecting them, and to report on the law applicable to the same, and the effect of any modifications thereof'.[1]

By this time, however, there were indications of a hardening of attitude among trade unionists in favour of a more far-reaching reform. The delegates of the Labour Representation Committee, which on the whole represented the more radical unions, had pressed for complete immunity at the joint conference of the three labour organizations in March 1903, and there had been many protests when Shackleton pressed on with the mutilated bill. The controversy was renewed at Congress in September. Ben Cooper, secretary of the Cigar Makers, moved the resolution which, as a delegate of the Labour Representation Committee, he had moved at the joint conference in March, instructing the Committee 'to draft Bills to be submitted to Parliament which will definitely secure the immunity of Trade Union funds against being sued for damages, and thus obtain

---

[1] For the Liberals Haldane had already suggested that the government should 'ask one of our great Judges to preside over a small Commission to report upon the whole matter' (*Hansard*, 14 May 1902, col. 323); and in 1903 he seconded a motion for a Select Committee 'to inquire into the existing law as it affects Trade Unions' (ibid., 4 Mar. 1903, cols. 1439–40).

for Trade Unions that protection which Members of Parliament, legal authorities and Trade Unionists believed existed prior to the Taff Vale judgment'.

The debate once more revealed that many leaders were still unsympathetic towards such a proposal.[1] The president, William Hornidge of the Boot and Shoe Operatives, told Congress that 'there is divided thought amongst Labour leaders as to what should be the spirit as well as the literal wording of' the bill, and the debate on Cooper's motion proved his point. When Tillett's Dockers moved an amendment in favour of clause 3,[2] Bell, Sexton, and John Ward of the Navvies all supported the amendment. Shackleton told Congress that he could now support neither the resolution nor the amendment. In order to get 'something practical . . . done during the next year or so', he proposed a return to a bill of only two clauses to deal with conspiracy and picketing 'without mixing them up with any question of liability'. With this division among the leaders the amendment was lost by 276 votes to 28 on a show of hands, and Cooper's motion became the policy of Congress, henceforth accepted both by the leaders and the rank and file.

What explains this radical and rapid change of approach? And why should the leaders be so ready to acquiesce in the defeat of a course which they had strongly advocated and skilfully advanced over the last two years?

The answer to the first question seems to lie in the effect of the costs in the case for damages which followed on the original Taff Vale decision. Only when this was settled in January 1903, bringing the total cost of the case to the Railway Servants to £42,000, did the unions fully realize the dangers of their situation. In 1901, for instance, the *Cotton Factory Times*, reflecting the feeling of many union leaders on the whole question, showed a relaxed attitude. The employers were not going 'to wage war on labour . . . and mulct trade unions in damages for the fun of the thing':[3] in any case, picketing did more harm than good;[4] and its columnist had asked whether it would 'not be better to accept the Taff Vale decision in its entirety, and so conduct matters in future as to prevent the unions from becoming involved in legal proceedings?'[5]

Before the end of the year, however, the paper had to take into account the injunction obtained by the employers against the Blackburn Weavers in a picketing case. The weavers' amalgamation appealed to the

---

[1] The Management Committee of the General Federation of Trade Unions was still recommending the course which it had urged all along: 'that the unions accept responsibility for acts committed by their agents, if such acts are sanctioned by the rules of the union' (General Federation of Trade Unions, *Annual Report*, 1903).

[2] In the course of the debate, Tillett said that 'if Mr. Bell and his colleague James Holmes had done six months in prison it would have been better for them all. Mr. Bell's liberty was not worth £40,000'.   [3] *Cotton Factory Times*, 6 Sept. 1901.

[4] Ibid., 13 Sept. 1901.   [5] Ibid., 20 Sept. 1901.

Parliamentary Committee for support in taking the case to the Lords, and in January 1902 representatives of the Lancashire Federation of Trades Councils agreed to ask the Parliamentary Committee to seek amendments to the 1875 Conspiracy and Protection of Property Act and the Trade Union Acts.[1] In March, however, on legal advice, the Blackburn case had to be settled out of court, and the attitude of the *Cotton Factory Times* began to harden. By December 1902 'Taff Vale Number Two' was seen as 'a bit of comic opera' and 'a flagrant wrong'. Together with the original judgement, it had 'placed the rights of workmen in serious jeopardy, and we are tempted to wonder if justice is slumbering'.[2] In January 1903 the paper was demanding 'a stern fight . . . to bring about by legislation at least the *status quo* of ten years ago'.[3]

A clue to the answer to the second question—why the leaders acquiesced in their defeat—is contained in Shackleton's speech to Congress in 1903 concerning the feasibility of legislation. Besides promising support for internal trade union discipline, clause 3 had seemed to offer, because of its restraint, a chance of immediate action. Admitting that the bill was 'very moderate', the *Journal* of the Amalgamated Society of Engineers for April 1903 stated that its justification rested upon 'the prospects of early success'.[4] With the announcement of the Royal Commission these prospects had gone. If the government had desired to obtain a moderate bill with the consent of the unions, they could almost certainly have had it in 1903. Since the government chose to reject the overtures of the union leaders, however, the latter had very little incentive to oppose the clamour of their followers for complete immunity, the 'permanent remedy'.

Any chance of success for those leaders who still hoped to win their members back to a moderate policy was killed by the choice of Commissioners, which caused an uproar in the unions. The inclusion of Sir William Lewis, who had a fair claim to be considered the leading industrial opponent of trade unionism,[5] was provocative, and the chairman, Graham Murray, later Lord Dunedin, Lord Advocate for Scotland, had recorded his vote against the motions in the House in May 1902 and again in May 1903. The balance might have been redressed by the fact that two of the three remaining members were Sidney Webb and Sir Godfrey Lushington, neither of whom was hostile to the unions. But Webb had made public his view that the unions would not be justified in claiming the restoration of complete immunity from legal proceedings,[6] while

---

[1] *Cotton Factory Times*, 31 Jan. 1902.   [2] Ibid., 26 Jan. 1902.   [3] Ibid., 2 Jan. 1903.

[4] '. . . It had been expected that such a conciliatory measure as the one put forward by Mr. Shackleton would have received no bitter opposition from its opponents. The bill—too mild as some of us thought it—simply asked for that *modicum* of justice which we considered to be equitable. . . .' (National Union of Boot and Shoe Operatives, *Monthly Report*, May 1903).

[5] See p. 231, and footnote 2.

[6] For example, in the Introduction to the 1902 edition of *Industrial Democracy*, p. xxxiii.

Lushington had called Taff Vale 'just and salutary law'.[1] The fifth member was Arthur Cohen, K.C., a lawyer of similarly conventional views.

'We would have raised no objection', declared the Management Committee of the General Federation of Trade Unions, 'if the Commission had been balanced by the inclusion of two direct representatives of labour.'[2] As it was, the refusal of the unions to co-operate was a foregone conclusion. Balfour defended his choice of 'a small Commission', which could act 'with relative rapidity' but which 'could not profess to represent every interest', as made 'simply in order that the question might not be indefinitely shelved'.[3] Nevertheless, delay was the inevitable and obvious consequence.

[1] *Natioual Review*, Dec. 1901, quoted in the *Annual Report* of the General Federation of Trade Unions, 1903.

[2] General Federation of Trade Unions, *Annual Report*, 1903.

[3] *Hansard*, 22 Apr. 1904, col. 975.

9

Collective Bargaining under Taff Vale

The Effect of the Taff Vale Judgement on Strikes

FROM 1899 to 1907 there was a period of industrial peace unparalleled between 1891, when adequate strike statistics start, and 1933, when a comparable period began. The annual average of working days lost through disputes was less than three millions, and in no year was the total as large as five millions. By contrast, the average for the years between 1891 and 1898 was over twelve millions and in only one year was the total less than five millions. And from 1908 to 1932 there were only six years, scattered over the whole period, showing a figure less than five millions, and the annual average (excluding 1926) was fourteen millions. A similar variation, of smaller amplitude, is to be found in the number of stoppages reported in each year. Between 1891 and 1898 the annual average was 743; between 1899 and 1907 the average was 505; and from 1908 to 1932 it was 712.[1]

The accepted explanation for this unwonted peace is the deterrent effect on the unions of the Taff Vale judgement. A strike, so the argument runs, might lead to legal action on a number of counts, and union funds were now liable to suffer; consequently, trade union officers and committees avoided strikes whenever they could. 'Trade Unionism had to a great extent lost its sting', wrote the Webbs;[2] and Cole and Postgate were even more emphatic that 'the Taff Vale Judgment of 1901 had so paralysed Trade Union action that, despite the high profits which were being made, they were powerless to strike for higher wages'.[3] More recent historians have offered the same explanation.[4]

There is evidence to support them. The courts continued to remind the unions of the penalties which striking might entail, and the Blackburn picketing case,[5] the Glamorgan Coal Company case,[6] the Denaby Main case,[7] and the first decision in the Ward, Lock & Co. case,[8] all served as

---

[1] *Report on the Strikes and Lockouts of 1895*, C–8231, 1896, p. 55; *Twenty-First Abstract of Labour Statistics*, Cmd. 4625, 1934, p. 125; *Twenty-Second Abstract of Labour Statistics*, Cmd. 5556, 1937, p. 127.   [2] *History*, p. 603.

[3] *The Common People*, 1946, p. 458.

[4] For example, Phelps Brown, op. cit., pp. 194–5.

[5] See p. 323.   [6] See p. 338.

[7] In this case an injunction to prevent the union disbursing strike benefit was upheld by the House of Lords, although the company concerned failed in its claim for damages, which was also carried to the Lords.   [8] See p. 347.

additional deterrents. Union records abound with instructions such as those issued after Taff Vale by Francis Chandler,[1] secretary of the Carpenters and Joiners, warning all

> Managing Committees and Officers generally . . . to carefully guard against affording any employer or individual the opportunity of taking advantage of this latest innovation against trade unions . . . it is impossible to do anything of an active character during a strike without running immense risks of either actions for damages against the society or prosecutions of members for conspiracy or intimidation, therefore the most sensible plan . . . is to avoid strikes as far as possible. . . .[2]

Union leaders frequently warn their members, however, against striking, and it cannot be assumed that the possession of a new argument suddenly made their exhortations effective. In 1903, for example, the Gasworkers' executive notified its districts that because of the law 'as defined by judges', they must order back to work all strikers coming out without the executive's authority. Nevertheless, Will Thorne had to report to the union conference of 1904 that 'members have threatened to leave the union if the E.C. did not allow them to come out on strike. The District E.C. have pleaded to the [national] E.C., the men have been allowed to come out, and they have been kept out. Thus, hundreds of pounds have been paid away, with the result that the men were beaten, and then . . . left the union.'

To assess the impact of the Taff Vale judgement it is necessary to determine the precise period during which the deterrent effects of Taff Vale were felt. The Lords did not deliver their decision until July 1901 and the full implications were not appreciated until the financial settlement of January 1903. The statutory reversal of the judgement became a real possibility when the Liberals took office in December 1905; highly probable after the election of January 1906; and almost certain once Campbell-Bannerman had committed himself to it in March.[3] Although the details were not settled until the autumn, fears of legal action must have been greatly diminished from the beginning of the year. Consequently the period during which the Taff Vale judgement exerted its full effect on annual strike statistics consisted at most only of the four years from 1902 to 1905. Measured in terms of the size of stoppages, however, the period of industrial peace lasted nine years, for the annual number of working days lost was below five millions in every year from 1899 to 1907.

This is the first reason for scepticism over the accepted explanation.

---

[1] Chandler, Francis (1849–1937). Secretary, London district, Amalgamated Society of Carpenters and Joiners, 1876–88; general secretary, 1888–1919. Parliamentary Committee, Trades Union Congress, 1895–1900, 1901–4, 1905–11, 1916–17. Member of Royal Commission on Poor Law, 1906–9.

[2] Issued in Oct. 1901, and quoted in Higenbottam, op. cit., pp. 162–3.

[3] See p. 394.

The second concerns the number of stoppages. Table 3 shows that these four years were unquestionably the most modest in this respect during the nine-year period. But there is nothing surprising in this, for they were years of depression. Unemployment rose from 2·5 per cent. in 1900 to 4·0 per cent. in 1902, 4·7 per cent. in 1903, and 6·0 per cent. in 1904. In 1905 came a recovery to 5·0 per cent. which continued into the two following years.[1] This tallies with the general tendency revealed in British strike statistics for the number of stoppages to fall off in years of bad trade. What was exceptional during 1902–5 was the small number of working days lost; for, in contrast to the number of stoppages, their size and duration tends to rise during years of bad trade.[2] A striking example of this general tendency came immediately at the end of the period in 1908. Unemployment rose rapidly; the number of working days lost jumped to nearly eleven millions compared with two millions in 1907; and the number of stoppages fell from 585 to 389, hardly more than the average of 377 for the four Taff Vale years.

Thus the unusual feature of 1902–5 was not the decline in the number of stoppages, but the low rate of working days lost in a period of depression when unions might have been expected to be forced into large-scale lock-outs to fight wage cuts. This feature was more marked in some industries, however, than in others. Whether we take working days lost, numbers of stoppages, or numbers of workers involved (Table 4), the experience of 1902–5 shows marked variations from industry to industry compared with the four previous years and the four subsequent years.

These variations do not, of course, show that Taff Vale had no effect, but they do suggest that additional influences were at work. There is, moreover, another impressive contrast between industries to be drawn. From 1893 to 1898 the annual average number of working days lost in mining and quarrying, in metals, engineering and shipbuilding, and in textiles was over eleven millions. For 1899–1907 their combined average is just over two millions. The corresponding total for the remaining industries reveals a far less marked drop, from an average loss of 1,272,000 working days in the first period to 727,000 in the second. Whatever the causes of the difference between the two periods, therefore, they operated primarily on coal, cotton, engineering and shipbuilding, and not equally over all industries. The problem cannot therefore be analysed further without exploring the experience of individual industries during the years under discussion.

---

[1] *Fifteenth Abstract of Labour Statistics*, Cd. 6228, 1912, p. 6.

[2] 'In the eighteen years of falling prices which Britain has experienced since 1890 a total of nearly 390 million working days have been lost in strikes, giving an average of nearly 22 million a year. Over the same years the average number of strikes works out at about 530. On the other hand, in the 48 years of rising prices the average of working days lost is under 6 million, and the average number of strikes almost 1,130' (H. A. Clegg and Rex Adams, *The Employers' Challenge*, 1957, p. 2).

Decline and Stagnation

The first years of the century saw, in general, a slackening in the pace of development in industrial relations after the rapid and far-reaching changes of the previous decade, and in some instances the unions lost

TABLE 3

Number of disputes, 1899–1907

YEAR	DISPUTES
1899	710
1900	633
1901	631
1902	432
1903	380
1904	346
1905	349
1906	479
1907	585

TABLE 4

Strike statistics, 1898–1909

Period	Building	Mining and quarrying	Metals, engineering, shipbuilding	Textiles	Clothing	Transport	Miscellaneous	Total
			Number of stoppages					
1898–1901	613	584	506	415	167	139	296	2,720
1902–5	151	512	303	256	103	50	167	1,542
1906–9	75	560	383	402	167	88	247	1,922
			Number of workers involved (ooo's.)					
1898–1901	76	411	85	127	12	42	49	802
1902–5	24	363	73	55	10	8	21	554
1906–9	7	496	130	262	28	20	18	962
			Number of working days lost (ooo's.)					
1898–1901	2,535	16,020	2,742	1,514	260	451	1,579	25,101
1902–5	988	5,861	1,554	603	275	146	344	9,772
1906–9	173	5,072	5,601	6,948	459	242	304	18,799

SOURCE: *Sixteenth Abstract of Labour Statistics,* Cd. 7131, 1913, pp. 160–1.

ground. This was true of the two major general unions. Both had experienced some expansion in 1900. The Gasworkers recruited sett-makers in the Midlands, laundryworkers in Scotland, electric power-station operatives in Aberdeen, quarrymen and limestone workers in Buxton, and telephone operators in Hull, Leeds, and Middlesbrough, bringing membership to 48,000, the highest figure since 1891. The expansion of the National

Amalgamated Union of Labour continued into 1901, when it claimed over 22,000 members. For both unions, however, there followed a decline until 1905. By the end of that year the Gasworkers had slumped to 28,000, and the National Union had slid slowly down to 17,000.

The Gasworkers' major loss was in its London district, which fell from almost 15,000 members in 1900 to under 6,000 in 1905. In 1900 the building labourers, the largest section in London, had voted overwhelmingly in support of a strike to enforce a wage claim. The other building labourers' unions refused to ballot, and Thorne commented that 'there never was, and never will be, a better chance for the London builders to get an advance than there was this summer. That chance is now lost.' The story was repeated in 1901. The Gasworkers felt that they could bring out their London building members and rely on the rest of the union to support them, but lacking comparable resources the other unions would risk only a deputation to the London Master Builders, which was rebuffed. In Birmingham membership slumped with the collapse of the Alliances in the metal trades,[1] and Thorne commented after the event that the union had 'never been favourable to the formation of an alliance with the employers . . . as the interests of employers and workmen are in opposite camps'.[2] The Scottish district had to be written off altogether during 1901.

Scotland also proved troublesome for the National Amalgamated Union of Labour, but it was the persistent erosion of membership at the centre, on the Tyne, Wear, and Tees, that caused the union its most pressing problems. The shipyards were especially weak and this was blamed on a failure at Armstrong Whitworth's Elswick Works. Here the union had ordered a strike for an advance, but changed its mind before the notices expired, and the membership had melted away, spreading disaffection along the Tyne. An amalgamation of the smaller North-east districts in 1902 failed to arrest the decline, and other methods had to be relied upon. The union's leaders appreciated that regular card inspection by the shop stewards was one of the secrets of strong and stable membership,[3] and in 1904 they prescribed monthly returns by shop stewards to the branches in all the central districts together with quarterly visits of full-time officers to each shop steward. Meanwhile losses at the centre were to some extent offset by continued growth in two outposts of the union—on the Medway and the Mersey.[4]

---

[1] See p. 195.

[2] National Union of Gasworkers and General Labourers, *Quarterly Report*, June 1902.

[3] Best of all, of course, was an understanding with the employers. 'In Palmer's Shipyard [at Jarrow] every man who is not a member of our union, and refuses to do so [*sic*], will be sacked' (National Amalgamated Union of Labour, *Conference of Executive Council and District Delegates*, 23 Mar. 1901).

[4] London was granted a full-time officer in 1901 and the Mersey in 1902.

The first requirement of stable membership was recognition by the employer. 'What is the use', asked Clynes of the Gasworkers, 'of men being in a union if they [the employers] are to act as though no union was in existence?'[1] But recognition by itself was not enough. To maintain its hold on the militants, who in turn held the rank-and-file members, the union had also to produce results. Failure to win concessions would eventually lead to apathy against which only the strictest of closed shop agreements could stand firm. An unsuccessful strike, or failure to take advantage of a moment which seemed ripe for a claim, were both likely to destroy the members' confidence.

Both points are emphasized by the experience of Tillett's Dockers. After they failed to regain a foothold in London by a strike in 1900,[2] they were forced back on their stronghold of Swansea. The district secretary told the conference of 1902, when the total membership was 12,000,[3] that

they numbered five to six thousand members in the Swansea District. . . . The relations between the employers and themselves had been of the most cordial nature. They might say there was no office door in the whole of the district that was not readily opened to any official of the Dockers' Union when he had business with the employers. During the last four years in particular, the greatest feature of their work had been the formation of the Conciliation Board for tinplate workers.

At this time, moreover, the prosperity of the tinplate trade favoured the unions. 'From 1899 until 1913 the tinplate industry experienced a period of almost continuous prosperity which enabled the new union organisation and the Conciliation Board to become established and the habit of negotiation about wages and other matters to become accepted.'[4] The Gasworkers also had a foothold in the trade, and their South Wales district was alone among their districts in maintaining its membership between 1900 and 1905.

The provincial Tramwaymen, re-named in 1901 the Amalgamated Association of Tramway and Vehicle Workers, managed to maintain their membership at just over 10,000, but not their share of a rapidly expanding labour force.[5] In that year their agreements in Manchester and Salford were consolidated and improved; and in 1902 a new agreement was signed with the Potteries Electric Traction Company and a conciliation board

---

[1] National Union of Gasworkers and General Labourers, *Quarterly Report*, March 1900.

[2] They demanded a conciliation board, and a return to the practice of engaging labour outside the gate in order to assist union recruitment. They were defeated, as were the lightermen when they struck for fifteen weeks that winter for an advance and over the interpretation of their overtime agreement.

[3] Between 1900 and 1905 the union's membership fluctuated between 12,000 and 14,000.

[4] Minchinton, op. cit., p. 137.

[5] Between 1902 and 1903 alone the mileage of tramway lines in England and Wales increased from 1,187 to 1,455, an increase of 23 per cent. (Amalgamated Association of Tramway and Vehicle Workers, *Annual Report*, 1904).

established at Bradford. In the following year the union successfully resisted a lock-out by the Edinburgh company to break the union and to convert the fifty-four hour week into an average of fifty-four hours over a period.[1] On the other hand, a venture into London through the absorption of a London tramway workers' union added more anxiety than strength, and in April 1905 a strike at St. Helens brought the union its 'first defeat . . . during the whole of the seventeen years that it has been in existence'.

While the Tramwaymen had to deal with conversion from steam, which had largely replaced horses by the turn of the century, to electricity, which had won the day by 1905, the London Cab Drivers faced an even more serious development. Already in 1900 the growth of underground railways, the transfer of omnibus traffic to new routes, and 'the increasing congestion of traffic in the London streets'[2] were causing the leaders of the cabmen to 'recognise it as a dying trade; we stand in the position of a physician anxious to sustain life in a valuable patient; nothing could be worse than a strike and if the masters force it upon us it will mean throwing a bucket of water over our patient and killing him'.[3] For all this, however, it took a five-day strike in July 1904 to persuade the proprietors' association to meet them in full negotiation—the first time for several years—and to concede a reduction in the daily charge for hiring the cabs. The agreement pulled their numbers up from 3,000 to 6,000, but the total was back to 3,000 within the year.

Next year an even more potent danger had appeared: the motor-cab. There were only twenty on the London streets at the end of 1905, but a far larger number were on order. The union had to resolve the same sort of question as a craft society faced with technical change: should its members refuse to have anything to do with motor-cabs, or should they accept the new work at a high rate of pay? Eventually the union came down in favour of the second course on the ground that, since the cars would certainly come, they should be driven by union members. It even offered cheap courses of driving instruction, and proposed a motor-cab co-operative in which drivers would be proprietors.

As their membership was spread more widely and thinly over the country the 'new unions' became involved in more inter-union conflicts. Unlike the craftsmen, their members could not claim a prescriptive right by training to a particular type of work, so they quarrelled over members instead of over jobs, laying claim to organize workers in a particular firm or on a particular site. On the Tyne, trouble often flared up between branches of the National Amalgamated Union of Labour and of the Gasworkers, though the leaders were always prepared to meet each

---

[1] *Annual Report*, 1903.   [2] *The Cab Trade Record*, Jan. 1901.
[3] Ibid., Nov. 1903.

other, and the National Amalgamated Union also fought the local brick-layers' labourers' union. The worst offence was for a union to close a job to outsiders and then refuse to accept transfers from other unions, so that workers belonging to other unions must join as new members and lose their accrued benefits. When a paid-up member of the Gasworkers at Neath Galvanizing Works refused to join Tillett's Dockers except by transfer, 'a deputation of the Dockers' Union went to the manager and insisted that the man be dismissed. . . . They talk about the tyranny of employers, and of judge-made laws!', commented the Gasworkers' district secretary.[1]

The Tramwaymen and Cab Drivers had offered a range of benefits since they were founded. Depression turned the general unions further in the same direction. In 1904 Thorne explained to his members that contributions would have to be increased to cover disablement benefits of £25 and £50 because of the competition 'of several labourers' unions offering many benefits. . . . I am convinced that these unions cannot pay the benefits if they are to do any real fighting. . . . This union has always been recognised as a fighting union, as we believe in getting more material advantages than merely being a rate saving institution, but I cannot close my eyes to . . . this keen competition.'[2] Benefits were no novelty to Thorne, and to call any of the general unions 'fighting unions' by this time was to make a bold claim. But probably none of their secretaries would have been prepared to go so far in the other direction as Charles Duncan of the Workers' Union who, with his membership down from 3,000 in 1900 to just over 1,000, wrote in his *Annual Report* for 1905 that 'it is becoming increasingly evident that the wide range of Benefits which constitutes the dominant feature of this Union is appealing to the steady and thoughtful workmen to make some provision against the day of misfortune'.

Although the cotton operatives and the miners were in a far stronger position than the general unions, and weathered the bad years with com-parative ease, they were unable to make any important new advances. Union membership in cotton rose slightly, and in coal there was a small decline; but both changes were negligible compared with the total member-ship of about half a million in coal and a quarter of a million in cotton.

Lancashire continued to grumble about a number of old problems. The suicide of a female weaver at Darwen in June 1901 brought up the old complaint of 'driving'. After long negotiations the local employers were willing to abolish 'slating', but not to withdraw the overlookers' right to dismiss. Bad material was still the chief complaint of the Spinners, who also asserted that the Brooklands disputes procedure gave employers too many opportunities for delay and evasion. In 1900 they promoted an

[1] National Union of Gasworkers and General Labourers, *Quarterly Report*, Mar. 1903.
[2] Ibid., June 1904.

amendment to achieve quicker settlements, but soon they were looking for another;[1] and each successive year brought a new crop of disputes.

The cardroom amalgamation also accused the employers of bad faith in their use of the Brooklands procedure. In a prolonged strike which ran from 1902 through 1903 and most of 1904 at the Curzon Mill in Ashton—in its early stages leading to talk of a general lock-out—the original cause of the dispute was lost in a difference over the interpretation of the agreement. Behind this lay a more general complaint by the amalgamation that, in the absence of a uniform list for cardroom operatives, there was no standard by which to settle local wage disputes. Though agreement was reached in 1903 on a 'flat cards' list which covered about 4,000 workers,[2] negotiations on a general list ended in deadlock and the dispute was complicated by redundancy caused by new machinery.

Despite these disputes the Labour Correspondent's *Report on the Strikes and Lockouts of 1903* noted a steady decline in textile stoppages over recent years, and the same 'very low level' of disputes was also recorded for 1904. The *Cotton Factory Times* considered that in view of the difficulties of the trade its 'freedom from serious disputes' was 're-markable'.[3] These difficulties were not sufficient, however, to drive the cotton employers to seek general wage reductions, and recovery came early to their industry. All went smoothly when the weavers' amalgamation decided as early as January 1905 that it was time to press for an advance of $7\frac{1}{2}$ per cent. The employers asked for a month's grace and then conceded 5 per cent. in March, promising further consideration of the balance during the following January.

In spinning there was rather more friction.[4] In May 1905, after the cardroom operatives had secured several local increases, notably in Wigan, the two amalgamations agreed on a joint application. In July the employers replied by asking for a three months deferment, and thereby nearly provoked a strike. Ballots in both unions showed overwhelming majorities in favour of immediate action. When the Bolton employers replied with notice of a reduction it seemed that the peace was about to be broken. Before the end of the month, however, an eighteen hours conference—even longer than the famous Brooklands meeting—produced a novel

----

[1] In 1905 the spinners' amalgamation put forward the proposal that whenever there was a bad-spinning complaint in a mill within three months of the reference back of a similar complaint to a joint committee, the operatives should be free to strike without further negotiations. 'It would, at any rate, compel some of the notorious bad spinning firms to provide reasonable work sometimes, if only for three months at a stretch . . .' (*Cotton Factory Times*, 9 June 1905).

[2] *Report on Collective Agreements*, Cd. 5366, 1910, pp. 164–6.

[3] 5 Feb. 1904.

[4] There had been some closing of the ranks in spinning in 1904 when the Bolton Employers' Association joined the Federation of Master Cotton Spinners, thus bringing the fine- and coarse-spinning sections into a single organization; and when the two operatives' amalgamations agreed on joint action on all individual mill disputes.

settlement. The Bolton proposal was withdrawn and a six months peace was arranged with an advance of 5 per cent. for the first three months which was then to be withdrawn. Meanwhile the proposal abandoned five years earlier—to establish a sliding scale—was to be explored once again.

Unlike cotton, the coal industry could not avoid wage reductions since the fall in prices was too great; but for the first time the reductions took place all over the country through agreed procedures. The Federated area looked like running into trouble, however, even before the end of the 1899–1901 boom. In February 1901, with wages already at the agreed maximum of 60 per cent. above 'standard', coal prices were still rising. Debarred from seeking a general advance, the miners began to force up colliery piece rates in several districts.[1] The owners sought a board ruling that a change in the 'local conditions' prevailing in 1888 was a violation of agreement, but Pickard insisted that such matters lay outside the scope of the board.

Within a few months, however, prices were falling, and by the end of 1903 wages had been reduced to 45 per cent. above standard, though this was still well over the agreed minimum of 30 per cent., which the miners managed to raise to 35 per cent. in the new agreement of February 1904, the maximum remaining at 60 per cent. At the same time the principles of wage determination were set out in greater detail.

The Board shall agree upon a selling price of coal being proportionate to a certain rate of wages. Alterations in the selling price . . . shall not be the sole factor for the decision of the Board, but one factor only; and either side shall be entitled to bring forward any reasons why, notwithstanding an alteration in the selling price, there should be no alteration made in the rate of wages.[2]

No alteration exceeding 5 per cent. was to be made at any one time.

The only serious protest against the reductions of 1902 and 1903 came from the pit lads. Lord James had given his casting vote in favour of a general 10 per cent. reduction in May 1902, and beginning in Yorkshire in July the pit lads ceased work in colliery after colliery. Their action was unofficial and not concerted, but it spread through the central coalfields until nearly 17,000 lads were out and 86,000 men laid off in consequence. Each colliery made its own settlement, and in some the cut was modified or withdrawn. In all 872,000 days were lost in the year's most serious dispute. A similar outburst on a smaller scale followed the 5 per cent. cut of 1903.

[1] Page Arnot, op. cit., vol. i, pp. 310–11.

[2] *Report on Collective Agreements*, Cd. 5366, 1910, p. 27. At the beginning of these negotiations the owners had put forward only the first sentence of this passage as a proposed principle. The Miners' Federation opposed it strongly as smacking too much of a sliding scale, and insisted on the qualifying sentences (Miners' Federation of Great Britain, *Minutes of Conferences of the Federated Area Conciliation Board*, Nov. 1903–Jan. 1904). The *Report on Collective Agreements* noted, moreover, in 1910, that the agreement referred to in the first sentence had 'not yet been carried into effect' (p. 27).

As usual the exporting coalfields suffered bigger price reductions and larger wage cuts. Between 1900 and 1904 the miners' wage in the West of Scotland fell from 100 per cent. above standard to the minimum of $37\frac{1}{2}$ per cent. At this point the owners asked for a reduction in the minimum. Since successive agreements under the recently established board had already made the relationship between prices and wages almost mechanically precise, the minimum (and the maximum) was the only distinction from the old sliding-scale agreement, and the owners' demand 'cut right across the established policy on which the M.F.G.B. had been built up'.[1]

The Scottish miners therefore appealed to the Federation in July 1904 to operate Rule 20. A delegate conference was very loath to do so, but the question was put to a vote of the lodges and the emotional appeal of solidarity carried the day. When Enoch Edwards[2] and other leaders told the Scottish owners of the Federation's decision, negotiations took a different turn. The minimum remained at $37\frac{1}{2}$ per cent., but it was related to a higher coal price than before. Consequently the Scottish miners suffered no immediate loss, but at the cost of forgoing some of the advantage they would otherwise have received when prices began to rise again.

In Northumberland and Durham wages were settled 'not quite automatically',[3] but nevertheless in fairly close correspondence with movements of prices. Over this period the fluctuations were smaller than in Scotland, though neither county had a minimum. Durham fell from 65 per cent. above standard in 1900 to $27\frac{1}{2}$ per cent. above in 1905, and Northumberland from $61\frac{1}{4}$ per cent. to 15 per cent. In 1905 the Durham Miners tried to negotiate a minimum of 30 per cent., but as current wages were below this level they not unnaturally failed to convince the owners.

South Wales was the one coalfield in which there was major progress in collective bargaining. In 1902 the South Wales miners gave six months notice to terminate the sliding-scale agreement of 1898, and after protracted negotiations a conciliation board took its place in January 1903. The agreement introduced a minimum of 30 per cent. and a maximum of 60 per cent. above the standard of 1879, and in South Wales, like the Federated area but unlike Scotland, the selling price of coal was not to be the sole determinant of wage rates. Even at this stage, however, the owners tried to avoid strengthening the union by giving it formal recognition, and the signatories for the miners were recorded not as union officers but as 'representatives of the workmen'.[4]

---

[1] Page Arnot, *Scottish Miners*, p. 102.

[2] On the death of Pickard in 1904, Edwards, formerly the treasurer, had been elected president. Sam Woods was too infirm for the post, and remained a nominal vice-president. William Abraham (Mabon) became treasurer.

[3] Industrial Council, *Inquiry into Industrial Agreements*, Cd. 6953, 1913, Q. 13318.

[4] 'The employers have abstained from entering into any bargain with the union as a union' (statement of Sir William Lewis to the *Royal Commission on Trade Disputes and Trade*

But the union was already too strong to be affected by tactics of this kind. Even in 1905, when the rates had fallen from 73¾ per cent. above standard in 1900 to the minimum of 30 per cent., the membership was 111,000 in a labour force of 166,000. 'The old antagonism between neighbouring towns and valleys began to disappear. The free fights between the county men and the Irish gave way to trade union solidarity, and the new trade union instincts were in process of creation.'[1] A militant policy of refusing to work with non-unionists cemented this new solidarity and led to a rising number of strikes.

South Wales was also the centre of a growing agitation concerning 'abnormal places', or positions at the coal face in which a hewer was unable to achieve his usual level of output because of particularly difficult working conditions. The custom was for management to meet the consequent short-fall in earnings by granting an allowance. Some allowances were included in pit price lists, but many were arranged through bargaining on the spot between the hewer and the overman or the undermanager. Soon after the turn of the century, however, colliery managements became generally less amenable in granting allowances, for they had to meet increases in costs due to statutory burdens recently imposed on the industry—the Coal Mines Act of 1896, the Workmen's Compensation Act of 1897, the export tax on coal of 1901, and the new safety regulations issued in 1902—and 'naturally cast about them for sources of economy'.[2]

The strength of the unions prevented economies through general wage reductions apart from those agreed by the conciliation boards, and the growing confidence of the men in their own power may have added to the persistence with which they pressed their claims for allowances in the pits. Certainly the depression aggravated the problem, and from 1904 onwards disputes over abnormal places took either first or second place among the causes of working days lost through strikes in coal-mining. In the last quarter of the nineteenth century, the exceptionally rapid rate of expansion in South Wales and the urgent need to attract labour had led to a relatively generous grant of allowances;[3] and the tightening up was more universally and vigorously applied there than in any other coalfield. Moreover, geological conditions were more difficult in the Welsh valleys than in England, and the need for allowances arose more frequently.

Another reaction of the owners to the growing power of the South

Combinations, Cd. 2826, 1906, Q. 1427). They conceded, however, the right of miners' agents to deal with pit disputes. Unsettled disputes were referred to the conciliation board or to a joint subcommittee. The Scottish coal-owners also had set up their conciliation board in 1900 with 'miners or miners' representatives', but the agreement of 1904 renewing it was with the Scottish Miners' Federation (*Report on the Rules of Voluntary Conciliation and Arbitration Boards*, Cd. 3788, 1908, pp. 81–84).

[1] Ness Edwards, *History of the South Wales Miners' Federation*, 1938, p. 22.
[2] H. S. Jevons, *The Coal Trade*, 1915, p. 527.
[3] Ibid., pp. 120–1, 526.

Wales Miners' Federation was a direct consequence of the Taff Vale decision. The 'stop-day', a device to restrict output and stiffen selling prices, had been fairly common in the South Wales coalfield. In 1903, however, seventy-one colliery companies sued the Federation for damages for 'wrongfully and maliciously procuring and inducing workmen to break their contracts'. At its first hearing the action failed on the grounds that malice had not been proved; but the Court of Appeal reversed this decision and granted damages, its judgement being sustained by the House of Lords in 1905.

The leaders of the Miners' Federation felt it to be a weakness that the Federated area, Scotland, and South Wales were working under separate agreements. In 1902 Pickard urged that if 'they intended to work together they could not have three separate schemes, they must try to have one scheme. . . . What they wanted was the whole of the men in that Federation bound together fighting with one object in view.' The Southport resolution of that year laid down 'that no section of this Federation enter into any wages agreement . . . beyond the end of 1903 . . . [so as] to permit of a general movement being taken to secure a minimum wage for all the districts, and to raise said minimum to a higher standard'.[1] Since the Scots miners could, under their agreement, give notice of termination at any time, it fell to the Federated area and South Wales to synchronize. But the owners in both areas showed strong hostility to this strategy, and for the time being the miners had to accept the statement of the chairman of the Federated owners that he would 'never be a party to any arrangement that will give an opportunity to the whole [of the] miners to terminate at one time'.[2]

For the Amalgamated Society of Railway Servants also the period was one of decline. The Taff Vale agitation had been only one of almost sixty local movements between 1899 and 1903 and the majority were unsuccessful. The resistance of the railway companies was encouraged by the outcome of the Taff Vale dispute and stiffened by rising costs. The sharp increase in coal prices during the South African war had threatened railway dividends. In England and Wales the ratio of working expenses rose to a peak of 64 per cent. in 1901,[3] and company chairmen lamented the statutory obstacles to raising their charges.[4] Their economies—larger locomotives with longer trains, power-signalling, reduced staffs, and a general speeding-up—meant increased work or responsibilities for their employees with no corresponding increases in pay. At the same time they

---

[1] Miners' Federation of Great Britain, *Minutes of Annual Conference*, Oct. 1902.

[2] Miners' Federation, *Minutes of Special Conference*, Feb. 1904.

[3] It had been 55·7 per cent. ten years earlier (*General Report on the Capital, Traffic, Working Expenditure and Profits of the Railway Companies of the United Kingdom for 1900*, Cd. 749, 1901, p. 20; *Returns of the Capital, etc., of the Railway Companies, etc., for 1904*, Cd. 2623, 1905, p. xxxvi). See also p. 237.   [4] *Railway News*, 18 Aug. 1900.

strengthened the Railway Association by appointing the first full-time
secretary, W. (later Sir) Guy Granet.[1] Links were established with Collison's National Free Labour Association, and a scheme was set afoot for
the registration of a mobile reserve force of railwaymen for breaking
strikes wherever they might occur.[2]

Railwaymen have never been as strike-prone as miners or dockers, and
stoppages on the railways are rare, though they are generally large when
they do occur. These years, however, were remarkably free from stoppages.
This may have been partly due to the Taff Vale decision, for of all unions
the Railway Servants had most cause to mark its lessons. On the other
hand, the *Railway Review* was anxious that the consequences should not
be exaggerated, and argued in 1902 that 'the full effective power of trade
unionism is still with us, so long as the men are organised and undertake
to conduct their affairs in a thoroughly courageous and straightforward
manner. Those who have thought the days of action by the A.S.R.S. are
over should take new grace, and try to preach and practice a more solid
and perfect organisation'.[3]

Membership in the Amalgamated Society fell, however, from 62,000
in 1900 to 53,000 in 1904. The General Railway Workers' Union also
declined, and had less than 4,000 members in 1904. The Associated
Society of Locomotive Engineers and Firemen showed greater resistance.
Having opened its ranks to electric trainmen and to the engine cleaners,
the starting grade for footplate staff, the union rose from 10,000 in 1900
to 12,000 in 1904. The United Pointsmen and Signalmen advanced even
more rapidly from 1,500 in 1900 to 2,500 in 1904.

In 1901 Albert Fox[4] replaced T. G. Sunter as secretary of the footplate
men. Sunter had been a 'quiet and unobtrusive pilot',[5] whereas Fox was
a 'gaunt Calvinistically minded'[6] martinet, who found it difficult to maintain good relations with the autocratic and impatient Bell. There were
plenty of grounds for mutual suspicion. Bell feared that joint advance
movements for footplate men would strengthen Fox's union rather than
his own, while Fox suspected that Bell was out to make the Amalgamated
Society the sole bargaining agent for railwaymen.[7] Moreover, while the
Railway Servants were fundamentally in favour of amalgamation, the
Engineers and Firemen were always disposed to see an advantage in going
ahead alone, unencumbered by weaker groups—an attitude which seemed
justified by their relative success in the sectional movements of previous
years.

[1] Ibid., 27 Oct. 1900. [2] Ibid., 22 Sept. 1900; 5 Jan. 1901.
[3] Quoted in the *Cab Trade Record*, Nov. 1902.
[4] Fox, Albert (1857–1914). Vice-chairman, Associated Society of Locomotive Engineers and
Firemen, 1896–9; chairman 1900–1; general secretary, 1901–14.
[5] Raynes, op. cit., p. 115.
[6] N. McKillop, *The Lighted Flame*, 1949, p. 75. [7] Gupta, op. cit.

The most impressive advance over these years, however, was achieved by the Railway Clerks' Association, which rose from 1,500 in 1900 to nearly 5,000 in 1904. Previously the Amalgamated Society had tried without much success to organize clerks, but it readily agreed to withdraw.[1] The companies provided an incentive to organize by reducing salaries,[2] but quite apart from this there was much work for a clerical union. Some companies had no salary scales; a standard working week existed only in the major offices; and clerks were often expected to act as strike-breakers. As it grew the Association began to imitate the manual workers' unions in the use of petition and deputation, and also to show a peculiar aptitude for parliamentary work which was to prove its value in subsequent years.

Progress in Collective Bargaining

Most of the major developments in industrial relations during this period occurred in the craft trades, and were associated with the growth of employers' organizations. The societies still faced threats from new machinery and from the introduction of less skilled labour. The employers regarded many of their cherished rules as drags on enterprise, to be broken if the opportunity offered. As always, their leaders hesitated between a blind resistance to change and an attempt to make the best of it. In the years of depression from 1902 to 1905, however, the societies were cautious in pressing new demands, but at the same time they were not weakened sufficiently to tempt the employers to a frontal attack. This was especially true in the engineering industry, in which the combatants were licking their wounds after the great conflict of 1897–8.

Leaders on both sides punctiliously observed the new agreement. After general wage increases in the years 1896–8, engineering and shipbuilding employers in the major centres refused further concessions;[3] but during 1899 and 1900 claims were pressed in many of the smaller districts, and in some instances where they were rejected by the local employers increases were recommended by a Central Conference. Such decisions, the Amalgamated Society of Engineers told its members, 'had always been loyally given effect to by the local employers concerned'.[4]

District bargaining was meanwhile expanding its scope to cover more

---

[1] *Royal Commission on the Working of the Railway Conciliation and Arbitration Scheme of 1907, Minutes of Evidence*, Cd. 6014, 1911, Q. 6610.

[2] G. D. H. Cole and R. Page Arnot, *Trade Unionism on the Railways*, 1917, p. 93.

[3] The Boilermakers' report for 1900 tried to make a virtue of the fact that 'no demands [have] been made for advanced wages in any of the large shipbuilding districts, although trade has been . . . very prosperous' by claiming that 'the policy of squeezing when the opportunity occurs, to be squeezed in return when a change takes place, is not a good policy for either ourselves or the employers, and as we . . . have agreed to forbear, so we in our turn trust that such forbearance will be returned' (United Society of Boilermakers and Iron Shipbuilders, *Annual Report*, 1900). In the event they were disappointed (see p. 349).

[4] Amalgamated Society of Engineers, *Journal and Monthly Record*, June 1903.

than changes in wage rates. The Engineers' district by-laws and port rules, hitherto drawn up unilaterally by district committees to cover such matters as piece-work, overtime, 'dirty' money, travelling allowances, night work, and trial trips, were increasingly becoming the subject of negotiation and district agreements with employers' associations. This was encouraged by the Engineers' executive and implicitly sanctioned by the Engineering Employers' Federation in 1905,[1] the latter usually being consulted by the local employers before an agreement was signed. Some of these agreements covered considerable areas. In 1902, for example, the Amalgamated Society and the Bristol Channel Employers' Federation assimilated conditions of labour and working rules in all the Bristol Channel ports into one uniform code.[2] On one issue the coverage had already become industry-wide, thus constituting another step forward in national bargaining. In 1901 all the local agreements on conditions for sea-going engineers on trial trips of warships were superseded by a national agreement between the Society and the Employers' Federation.[3]

As regards shop disputes about the operation of the new machinery, bargaining brought the Society no gains. During the war-time boom a few employers bowed to branch pressure for the operation of new machinery by skilled men alone, but most of them held the Society rigorously to the 1898 settlement and referred such issues to the disputes procedure. Local employers' associations then invariably passed them on to the Central Conference, where Federation representatives remained adamant that employers' freedom of action in this field must be preserved.[4] As a result feeling sometimes ran high, especially in the North-east.

In all kinds of shop disputes, Society members now found that in federated firms their position had been 'drastically changed' by the combined effect of the disputes procedure and the greatly increased unity among employers, now 'a compact body welded together by class interests'. 'Previous to the 1897 lockout', declared a statement by the Engineers' executive in 1914, '. . . the state of disorganisation amongst the employers enabled us to secure our demands [in shop disputes] with little or no previous negotiation. . . . Individual firms could easily be approached. . . .'[5] Under the agreement, however, the individual employer could refer a shop dispute to a local conference and thus confront the Society with the weight of his association—which could if necessary make it 'a Federation question'.

---

[1] Amalgamated Society of Engineers, *Monthly Report*, Oct. 1905.

[2] These negotiations can be followed in the *Journal and Monthly Record* during 1901–2.

[3] The union *Journal and Monthly Record* for Feb. 1901 commented that the agreement would 'substitute for constant higgling with unwilling employers and local associations the guarantee which experience has proved attaches to an arrangement with the Employers' Federation executive'.

[4] *Decisions of Central Conference, 1898–1925*, 1926, Engineering and Allied Employers' National Federation.

[5] Amalgamated Society of Engineers, *Monthly Journal and Report*, June 1914.

The frustration and delays resulting from this procedure were permanent irritants to craftsmen who had so long enjoyed a position of strength, and it was mainly for this reason that the members of the Amalgamated Society voted in 1901 to reject a revised version of the 1898 settlement which had recently been negotiated. It contained a few minor improvements, particularly a recommendation that 'consideration' should be given to craftsmen displaced by machinery by finding other work for them. But the essential clauses remained. Other reasons for its rejection were 'the absence of provision for the payment of the day-work rate of wages [as a minimum] to those asked to work piece-work, and . . . the irritating references to non-society men'.[1]

Rank-and-file feeling on the machine question revealed itself in another way. By a small majority, the conference of 1901 created a Machinists' Section open to semi-skilled men who had been in the trade for two years and who received not less than 75 per cent. of the craft rate. As soon as the decision was known 156 resolutions poured in from the branches, four-fifths of them condemning it.[2] Many branches continued their opposition and by 1904, when the Society's membership was 94,000, only 4,000 members had been recruited to the new section.

The return of depression in 1902 brought wage reductions throughout the industry and with them severe unrest on Clydeside and the North-east coast. In the North-east, employers had not only been applying the 1898 settlement in its full rigour, but in certain cases, according to the Amalgamated Society's district officer, had also been making 'a dead-set . . . against working conditions and customs that have existed in the trade for many long years'.[3] Moreover, they had rejected all wage claims during the boom years on the grounds that trade was not yet good enough, and the employers at Central Conference had supported them. Thus the Society's members were understandably hostile to the employers' suggestion of a reduction in December 1902 and, when a Central Conference recommended a smaller reduction, they rejected this also in two successive ballots and came out on unofficial strike. A majority of the Newcastle District Committee put their names to a circular prepared by a local ginger group in support of the strike. Ordered back by their executive, the strikers stayed out, whereupon the executive instructed the local officers to stop payment of benefits and the men returned to work.

On the Clyde a similar series of events beginning in January 1903 led to a strike supported by the Glasgow District Committee, which decided to pay strike benefit. The executive suspended the Committee and

---

[1] Amalgamated Society of Engineers, *Journal and Monthly Record*, Feb. 1902.

[2] Jefferys, op. cit., p. 166. 'A very general fear exists', wrote one member in the union's *Journal and Monthly Record* for June 1902, 'that the inclusion of machinists under the new rule will level down the wages. . . .'

[3] Amalgamated Society of Engineers, *Journal and Monthly Record*, Apr. 1900.

demanded that the benefits paid be refunded. Barnes notified local officials that they would be held personally responsible for 'any further moneys illegally paid'.[1] These measures put an end to the strike. One aftermath was the defeat of the four full-time executive councilmen who came up for re-election shortly afterwards. There were strong indications of local manipulation of the votes, but when they appealed nothing could be proved.[2] The executive suffered a further humiliation when the Final Appeals Committee ordered them to pay the strike benefit withheld from the Glasgow strikers. Among the many reasons by which the executive justified its actions on these two strikes—that the employers had been loyal to the disputes procedure; that the members of the other unions, which had accepted the reduction, were 'indifferent if not hostile'; that trade was bad and public opinion antagonistic—the Taff Vale decision was not included.[3]

At this time the employers were beginning to introduce a new method of payment by results, the 'premium bonus' system. In contrast to 'straight piecework', under which earnings increased in direct proportion to output, the premium bonus system paid the worker for the 'time saved' if he did a piece of work in less than a standard time. There were several formulas for relating earnings to time saved, but under most schemes the worker could earn no more than double his time rate, however much he produced. Thus his earnings rose less than proportionately with output, thereby reducing wage costs per unit of output to the employer.

The system was highly unpopular with most engineering unions, but in 1902 the executive of the Amalgamated Society and the Employers' Federation signed the Carlisle Memorandum, which removed all union restrictions on the system in return for several concessions. Each piece-worker was to be guaranteed his time rate, regardless of output; overtime and nightshift rates were to be paid to piece-workers on the same basis as to other workers in the same shop; and the time allowance was to be revised only if the methods or means of manufacture were changed.[4]

Members of the Engineers were asked to give the system a 'fair and honest' trial, but the branches sent in so many protests that the executive, influenced also no doubt by the members' rejection of the revised procedure agreement the previous year, decided not to submit the Memorandum to a vote. The basis of the Memorandum remained no more than

[1] Barnes, op. cit., p. 61.

[2] *Journal and Monthly Record*, Oct. 1903. Meetings addressed by Barnes as labour candidate for a Glasgow division were disrupted by angry members of his own union (Barnes, op. cit., pp. 61–62).

[3] Amalgamated Society of Engineers, *Executive Council Statement*, 21 May 1903, reproduced in *Journal and Monthly Record*, June 1903.

[4] Engineering and Allied Employers' National Federation, *Thirty Years of Industrial Conciliation*, 1927, p. 33.

a statement by the executive that they would have to yield if the employers brought a case under the agreement before a Central Conference.[1] Most of the smaller craft societies, who had not signed the 1898 settlement and were not bound by these decisions, maintained a rigid opposition to the system. The Patternmakers warded off most of the attempts to introduce it in their work,[2] and the National Amalgamated Tin-Plate Society was 'fairly successful' in its policy of local resistance.[3]

A notable feature of the period, however, was the growing desire of employers to limit the freedom of manœuvre possessed by these sectional societies. In 1898 the employers at Sunderland and Middlesbrough tried to apply the new disputes procedure to the Patternmakers over some disagreements about overtime and piece-work, but were rebuffed.[4] A more ambitious attempt by the Employers' Federation in the following year to bring the Patternmakers into a national conciliation board based on the disputes procedure also failed, the scheme—arrived at through 'discreet negotiations'—being favoured by the union's secretary but rejected by the members.[5]

Nevertheless, local employers' associations seeking uniformity in wage movements in their district succeded in using the disputes procedure as a lever for bringing all the sectional societies into line with whatever agreement they negotiated with the 'signatory' unions. Soon after the 1898 settlement a joint committee of engineering societies in Sheffield submitted a claim for higher wages and a shorter working week. The employers rejected both claims, thus causing them to be submitted to a Central Conference from which, of course, the 'non-signatory' unions were excluded. The claim for a reduction in working hours was withdrawn, and a wage offer accepted by the Engineers and 'perforce concurred in by the other societies'. The 'mistake we made', declared the Pattern-makers, 'was in associating with trades whose free movement was restricted by their agreements with the employers . . .'.[6] Events in Bradford and mid-Lancashire in 1899, and in Barrow in 1900 and 1905, similarly revealed a growing tendency for collective bargaining to be dominated by the Engineers, working with the employers through the disputes procedure.[7]

Occasionally a strong sectional society could resist the general trend. In 1903 the Belfast employers agreed on a wage reduction with the Amalgamated Society of Engineers and applied it without even notifying

---

[1] From the point of view of the executive and the officers, the premium bonus system had the advantage of reducing the cost of errors in rate-fixing and therefore the likelihood of disputes arising out of the alteration of piece rates. George Barnes, the secretary, was on record in favour of the system in 1902 (*The Premium System of Paying Wages*, 5th edition, 1917).

[2] Mosses, op. cit., pp. 151, 164, 165–6, 194.   [3] Kidd, op. cit., p. 209.
[4] Mosses, op. cit., p. 145.   [5] Ibid., pp. 151–2.
[6] Ibid., p. 144.   [7] Ibid., pp. 149, 150, 155, 173.

the Patternmakers. The Patternmakers thereupon came out on an official strike, the Amalgamated Society's patternmakers remaining at work. After some weeks the employers withdrew the reduction.[1]

Clydeside witnessed in 1905 the last serious bid for independence by any of the sectional societies. Nearly 800 members of the Patternmakers, 13 per cent. of their total strength, struck in April for a $\frac{1}{2}d.$ an hour advance. The signatory societies then submitted a similar claim, which was rejected at Central Conference. The Patternmakers stayed out until, in September, when trade had improved, the employers offered $\frac{1}{4}d.$ an hour to the signatory societies at another Central Conference, and subsequently also to the Patternmakers. This settled a strike which had cost the Patternmakers £16,000. Their secretary commented in 1922 that

it will always be a debatable point whether our strike or the general improvement in trade was the cause of the advance to the engineers, which was the prelude to the settlement. . . . Certain it is that we gained considerable wisdom and not a little discretion as one of the results. . . . We have not had a strike of anything like the same magnitude . . . anywhere . . . since that memorable struggle.[2]

In addition to these growing wage links between unions there were also growing links between districts, both in engineering and shipbuilding.

At Barrow the engineers' wages change one month later than those for similar occupations on the Clyde, and the shipbuilders follow the Tyne. The Clyde is also followed, both by engineers and shipbuilders, at Belfast and the East Coast of Scotland. The ironmoulders' wages all over Scotland have recently risen and fallen together.[3] Wages of engineers at Arbroath and Montieth change with those at Dundee. The platers' and rivetters' lists for iron shipbuilding at Southampton provide that their rates shall be 5 per cent below those on the North-east Coast, and follow their changes after a month's interval.[4]

In the printing industry, local employers' associations were growing in numbers and strength, and with the turn of the century came four new national organizations. The Linotype Users' Association, representing the chief provincial newspaper proprietors, was now augmented by the Federation of Northern Newspaper Owners, the Federation of Southern Newspaper Owners, and the Irish Newspaper Society. In the book and general printing trade the British Federation of Master Printers was set up in 1901[5] with the object, among other things, of showing a united front

---

[1] Ibid., pp. 161–2.   [2] Ibid., pp. 171–2.

[3] District negotiations in the Scottish ironmoulding industry had given place to central conferences when the Scottish Employers' Federation of Iron and Steel Founders was formed in 1898. From 1899 'demands from either side were first exchanged' between Jack, the Scottish Ironmoulders' secretary, and Morrison, the employers' secretary, and 'were usually followed by a conference . . .' (Fyrth and Collins, op. cit., p. 106).

[4] A. L. Bowley and G. H. Wood, 'Statistics of Wages in the United Kingdom during the last hundred years', *Journal of the Royal Statistical Society*, Sept. 1905.

[5] E. Howe, *The British Federation of Master Printers*, 1950, *passim*.

to the societies. One of its rules laid down that 'no step of general importance to the printing trade as a whole shall be taken by any federated association or individual member, without previous consultation with the council'.[1] The Federation also turned its face against the recognition of 'working rules' unless drawn up with its agreement,[2] thus setting out to strike a blow at the method of unilateral regulation and extend the scope of collective bargaining. The Linotype Users' Association took the same attitude.

Officials of all these national organizations 'took a prominent part' in the settlement of local disputes,[3] and in 1904 representatives of the Master Printers' Federation met the Typographical Association in national conference for the first time to discuss apprenticeship and the operation of monotype machines.[4] Although the employers supported their plea for an increase in the number of apprentices by the argument that the trade was forced to recruit its craftsmen from the 'rat' offices and unorganized country districts instead of the large organized offices where systematic training could be given, no agreement could be reached on apprenticeship either at this or at a subsequent conference in 1905. The 1905 conference did, however, agree on a wage scale and a $52\frac{1}{2}$ hour week (48 for night work) for monotype keyboard operators.

Meanwhile the Linotype Users' Association had approached the society for a national agreement on piece rates, which had been left to local bargaining in the 1898 settlement; and in 1903 a set of *Rules for Piecework on Linotype Machines* was drawn up. Both these national agreements were triumphs for the society. The linotype rates were set so high that most employers reverted to 'stab' or time rates, hoping to cut costs by pressing operators into a higher output, and by 1907 the new scale had been completely abandoned.[5] The society was also largely successful in resisting the employers' attempts to get higher output by introducing devices such as bonuses and mechanical indicators for measuring individual performance.

This sharpened the employers' complaint against restriction of output. They asserted that the societies, in their desire to spread work and maintain employment, were conspiring to make the machines economically unattractive, a charge repeated by Pratt in his anti-union diatribe.[6] G. B. Dibblee, a Fellow of All Souls College and manager of the *Manchester Guardian*, offered a more sober appraisal which discounted the idea of a conspiracy, but registered 'just objection' to the union policy of obstructing the introduction of composing machines and hampering their use.[7]

In 1900 the hand compositors in London had decided to strike for the

---

[1] Musson, op. cit., p. 162.   [2] Ibid., pp. 163–4.   [3] Ibid., p. 163.
[4] Ibid., pp. 162–3.   [5] Ibid., p. 241.   [6] See p. 475.
[7] 'The Printing Trades and the Crisis in British Industry', *Economic Journal*, Mar. 1902.

forty-eight-hour week already enjoyed by linotype operators and for an increase of 2s. in their stab rates to bring them to 40s. The Board of Trade intervened and eventually the parties agreed to accept arbitration by G. R. Askwith,[1] who awarded an increase of 1s. and a reduction of hours from 54 to 52½. Fifteen employers rejected the award and closed their doors to members of the society.[2] Over the next few years the reduction in hours to fifty-two or thereabouts was gradually extended to many other London operatives and to some provincial centres, where linotype operators had enjoyed a forty-eight-hour week since 1898. Scottish workers did better still; half the membership of the Scottish Typographical Association gaining the fifty-hour week in this period.

The London advance movement also enabled the Operative Printers' Assistants to consolidate their position in 1901–2 with collective agreements laying down minima for flat machine workers and for rotary press assistants on both news and general work. From this firm base of recognition by the employers the union launched out in 1903 into the provinces, becoming, in 1904, the National Society of Operative Printers' Assistants. A certain amount of somewhat fluctuating growth followed, together with some important agreements such as that with the Lancashire Newspaper Society in 1905.[3]

In 1901 the London bookbinders began a forward movement controlled by a joint committee of the several societies. A strike in 1902 was followed by arbitration which increased their minimum from 32s. to 35s. for forty-eight hours, with payment of overtime after 52½ hours instead of after fifty-four. In addition there was to be a conciliation board for drawing up price lists and settling disputes. Despite some disappointment with the rates settled by the boards, the societies regarded 'the establishment of a comprehensive price list as an important prerequisite to future advance . . .'.[4]

The London printing trade was also notable for two law cases in which the employers tried unsuccessfully to exploit the Taff Vale decision. In 1904 members of the Operative Printers' Assistants employed by Ward, Lock & Co. were discharged and subsequently picketed the works. The firm then brought an action for damages against the union and its secretary, which was tried in the King's Bench Division and resulted in an award of damages. The Court of Appeal, however, reversed the decision on every point.[5] Meanwhile a firm named Straker had begun a similar action against the London Society of Compositors. When the firm introduced

---

[1] Askwith, Sir George, later Baron Askwith (1861–1942). Assistant Secretary of Railway Branch of Board of Trade, 1907–9. Controller-General, Commercial, Labour and Statistical Department of Board of Trade, 1909–11. Chief Industrial Commissioner, 1911–19.

[2] Howe, op. cit., p. 21.

[3] Child, op. cit.; R. B. Suthers, *The Story of NATSOPA*, 1929, p. 26.

[4] Howe and Child, op. cit., p. 230. [5] Suthers, op. cit., p. 25.

female operators on monotype machines the Compositors struck, and the London Printing and Kindred Trades Federation recommended all affiliated societies to withdraw their members in support, which they did. The firm first sought an injunction restraining the unions from picketing, but were unsuccessful. They then brought an action for conspiracy against the London Society of Compositors and its secretary together with the secretaries of the other societies which had joined the dispute, claiming £10,000 damages. The decision in the Ward, Lock case seems, however, to have deterred the firm from pressing its suit, and probably the London Master Printers' Association from supporting it.[1]

In Scottish tailoring the early years of the new century witnessed the same kind of conflict over craft regulations as the English trade had seen in the early nineties. In April 1902 the Glasgow tailors won an advance of $\frac{1}{2}d$. per hour.[2] The Edinburgh employers, faced with the same demand in 1903, persuaded the Glasgow employers to withdraw their concession and join them in an attack upon the craft regulations of the Scottish National Operative Tailors. They wanted freedom to employ outworkers, non-unionists, day-wage men, and apprentices to any number they desired. No society official was to enter their workshops; craft rules must be agreed by the employers; and there was to be a uniform time 'log'. The Aberdeen employers joined the movement in June.

In September 1903 a settlement was agreed between the union and the Scottish section of the National Federation of Merchant Tailors. There was to be no wage increase in Edinburgh and the withdrawal of Glasgow's increase was confirmed. The masters were granted most of the liberties they wanted except that the apprenticeship rules were to remain. The uniform time log was to be drawn up by a joint committee, and each town was to form its own committee for settling disputes.[3]

In furniture neither the formation of the National Amalgamated Furniture Trades Association in 1902 by a fusion of the Alliance and Scottish Cabinet Makers, nor the accession of the socialist, A. G. Gossip, to the secretaryship in 1905, caused any move away from craft policies and attitudes. But the number of employers' associations more than doubled between 1900 and 1902, and there was a growth in the number of local agreements, though most of them were confined to a single craft.[4]

The one major craft industry which experienced no development in collective bargaining was shipbuilding. The Boilermakers' national agreement on apprentices came up for renewal in 1900, and the consequent negotiations removed the limitation on numbers. This, together with the

[1] Bundock, op. cit., pp. 143–4.
[2] *Report on the Strikes and Lockouts of 1903*, Cd. 2112, 1904, pp. 34–35.
[3] Amalgamated Society of Tailors and Tailoresses, *Journal*, Oct. 1903.
[4] Robertson, op. cit.

interpretation placed on the agreement by the Shipbuilding Employers' Federation, 'now a much more strongly organised body', rendered it practically worthless to the union.[1]

Outside the Federated area[2] the Society retained some favourable agreements which laid down apprenticeship ratios,[3] but within the area it attempted to revert to unilateral regulation. Under a new rule of 1901, branches where apprentices exceeded 'the number allowed in rule' could be called upon by the district committee to take steps to restore the proper ratio of one to every five journeymen. Another new rule prohibited overtime, unless sanctioned by the district committee and the executive, whenever the proportion of members signing the 'donation and vacant book' rose above 10 per cent.[4] On this point also the Society managed to obtain some settlements in the non-federated ports.[5]

In 1903, with unemployment rising in the shipbuilding trades to 12 per cent.,[6] there came wage reductions. Most districts were affected by cuts in both 1902 and 1903, and on both occasions a minority of the crafts on the North-east coast resisted the change. In 1902 there was a strike of ship joiners and plumbers, except those affiliated to the Wear Conciliation Board, where the employers secured their reduction through arbitration. Despite several joint conferences there was no settlement until February 1903, when the plumbers agreed to arbitration. The joiners held out until March, and then accepted a modified reduction. Next year two societies of shipsmiths, along with their strikers, held out from November 1904 to June 1905 before they accepted a reduction. Collison was brought in and supplied smiths recently discharged from Portsmouth and Devonport dockyards.[7]

Outside the craft trades, the iron and steel industry recorded two important developments in collective bargaining, one in heavy steel and the other in tinplate. In March 1905, 'shortly after the employers had formed themselves into the Steel Ingot Makers' Association . . . especially to deal with labour questions', Hodge negotiated a full sliding-scale agreement with them, in addition to the existing tonnage rate agreement.[8] At first it applied only to the melting departments, but it was gradually

---

[1] Cummings, op. cit., p. 128.

[2] The area included Scotland and the North of England down to the Mersey and the Humber.

[3] *Report on Collective Agreements*, Cd. 5366, 1910, p. xxxi.

[4] E. A. Pratt, *Trade Unionism and British Industry*, 1904, pp. 55–56.

[5] *Report on Collective Agreements*, 1910, pp. xxiv–xxv.

[6] *Fifteenth Abstract of Labour Statistics*, Cd. 6228, 1912, p. 8.

[7] According to Collison, his men were kept out of the yard belonging to Sir Christopher Furness, Member for West Hartlepool, who hoped to stand for Parliament again and did not want to prejudice his electoral chances. Sir Theodore Doxford, Member for Sunderland, who did not intend to stand again, invited them in (op. cit., pp. 227–8).

[8] Carr and Taplin, op. cit., pp. 277–8. Earnings therefore varied both with changes in output and with changes in selling prices.

extended to all production workers. Hodge did not record the reasons for his change of mind. Perhaps the most important was the willingness of the employers to drop their insistence on negotiating not with the unions as such, but with 'representatives of the workmen employed' at the works covered by the agreement. They still insisted, however, on the branches countersigning agreements reached with the union. Another reason may have been the 1904 agreement to bring the Scottish and North-east masters into one price-regulating combine. Hodge believed this to have been effective in holding up prices,[1] and it would have been a characteristic calculation on his part to see this as the occasion for a link between prices and wages.[2]

Not all Hodge's members shared his views, and some branch secretaries thought it best to sign the agreement without consulting their members.[3] A few refused to sign at all and, since the employers would not accept Hodge's signature on their behalf, the executive had to exert pressure to bring them to heel.[4] Rumblings of discontent continued for some years.

In the currently prosperous tinplate industry,[5] Hodge and Tillett concentrated on extending the authority of the conciliation board. The unions put pressure on employers to join the Welsh Plate and Sheet Manufacturers' Association; the members of the Association in return co-operated in maintaining union membership in their works.[6] The coverage of the board increased from 50 per cent. of the industry's output in 1899 to 80 per cent. in 1912.[7] The union leaders were most solicitous for the welfare of the trade. In 1901 Hodge unsuccessfully urged the appointment of experts to explore the opening up of new markets, offering £1,000 from union funds towards the cost;[8] in the following year production was suspended for a week by joint agreement in order to strengthen the markets;[9] and in 1903 Tillett tried to promote a joint conference on new uses for tinplate.[10]

---

[1] British Steel Smelters' Association, *Monthly Report*, May 1905.

[2] The relevant price was to be the average net selling price actually realized for steel plates. Hitherto, where wages had been related to trade conditions, the criterion had been 'quoted' prices. Adjustments were to be automatic at intervals of three months.

It was also laid down that changes in tonnage rates were to be allowed only if conditions of production changed. This was now a fairly common event with the introduction of mechanical charging, the 'hot metal' process, and increases in furnace capacity and the size of ingot moulds. Most of the issues raised were 'settled without undue friction' (Pugh, op. cit., pp. 147–8).

[3] British Steel Smelters' Association, *Monthly Report*, Oct. 1905.

[4] Ibid., Aug. 1905.   [5] See p. 209.

[6] Industrial Council, *Inquiry into Industrial Agreements*, Cd. 6953, 1913, Qs. 1281–5. The report also quotes a striking instance of Hodge's disciplinary methods. When in 1910 his members in one tinplate works came out on unofficial strike, each received a telegram fining him £2 and enjoining him to return to work or suffer expulsion (Q. 1204).

[7] Ibid., Qs. 1179–80.   [8] Pugh, op. cit., p. 121.

[9] British Steel Smelters' Association, *Monthly Report*, Feb. 1903. 'Being afraid of the Taff Vale nightmare', however, the board did not ask the unions to stop the non-federated works.

[10] Ibid., Mar. 1903.

The picture was not wholly idyllic, however, for there was a good deal of bickering between the unions. In 1901 they had set up a Wages and Disputes Board to concert policy among themselves, but it broke up three years later when the tinhousemen out-voted the millmen on a mill question. For a year the parties met the employers separately in what were, in effect, two conciliation boards, and when they were formally reunited in 1905 it was only on condition that they took no part in each other's affairs.

The Building Industry

The most striking developments in collective bargaining occurred in the building industry, in sharp contrast with the conflict of the previous decade. The change from conflict to peace coincided with the change from ten years of boom to ten years of depression. One gauge of the building cycle, the unemployment percentage amongst carpenters and plumbers, rose steadily from 1·3 per cent. in 1898 to 8·3 per cent. in 1905.[1] General improvement elsewhere had a negligible effect in building, and the figure for 1907 was 7·3 per cent., rising to 11·7 per cent. in 1909.[2]

With falling employment all the unions lost members, though the three which paid unemployment benefit held up relatively well. Thus the Plumbers remained steady over the decade at 11,000; the National Amalgamated House and Ship Painters, having absorbed most of the smaller painters' societies in 1904, retained 15,000 members in 1910, as many as all the amalgamating unions between them had possessed in 1900; and the Amalgamated Society of Carpenters and Joiners fell only from 65,000 to 56,000.

The other societies showed far worse results and between 1901 and 1909 the combined funds of the twelve principal building unions fell from £457,000 to £262,000.[3] The membership of the Operative Bricklayers fell from 39,000 to 23,000; the Stonemasons from 19,000 to 7,000. The Scottish Masons fought an exhausting and unsuccessful struggle against a reduction in 1904 and were virtually extinct by 1907.[4] Among the minor organizations, the General Union of Carpenters and Joiners fell only from 8,000 to 6,000, but the Associated Carpenters and Joiners and the Manchester Order of Bricklayers both lost over half their members. The four major labourers' unions fell from a total of 24,000 to a total of 8,000, and dozens of minor ones disappeared.

To some extent the cyclical changes were reinforced by developments in building methods. Several innovations were spreading during the

---

[1] *Twelfth Abstract of Labour Statistics*, Cd. 4413, 1908, p. 3.
[2] *Fourteenth Abstract*, &c., Cd. 5458, 1911, p. 7.
[3] *Fifteenth Abstract*, &c., Cd. 6228, 1912, p. 204.
[4] By comparison the diminutive Operative Masons and Stonecutters of Aberdeen, with their highly favourable agreements (see p. 155), held their membership throughout.

period, including ferro-concreting, the substitution for joinery of wood-work prefabricated on machines, and the substitution of asphalt concrete for lead on roofs. By these means work was transferred to new groups of specialist workers whose narrow range of competence made them in-eligible for membership of the craft societies.

These circumstances presented the employers with a favourable opportunity for a counter-attack. Encouraged by the Taff Vale decision, they might have been expected to seek revenge for their defeats of the previous decade, but they did nothing of the kind. Instead the Council of the National Federation of Building Trade Employers, as the old National Association of Master Builders was now renamed, urged caution upon its members in 1901.

> The National Council . . . having observed that several Local Associations . . . have given notice to their workmen for a reduction of wages, hereby suggests . . . that it would be much better policy to aim at freeing the trade from such restrictions as paying incompetent men full wages, limitation of apprentices, and interference with business management, than attempting to lower wages. This Council strongly urges all Local Associations to aim at attaining these objects rather than attempting to lower wages.[1]

The first part of the Council's advice was certainly followed. Only in four years of the decade, 1904–6 and 1909, did the number of building workers whose wages were reduced exceed the number receiving increases. Even in these years the reductions never affected more than 1 per cent. a year,[2] whereas between 1896 and 1900 no year had brought increases to less than 6 per cent.[3] It is equally remarkable that in every year between 1900 and 1909 a larger proportion of building workers gained a reduction in working hours than suffered a cut in wages. This is true even if we exclude the rearrangement of winter hours in London which brought a reduction of about half-an-hour a week to 70,000 London workers in 1905.

The positive recommendation of the Council, that the local associations should try to throw off craft restrictions, was largely ignored. In 1902 the Lancashire and Cheshire Federation promoted an attempt to fix a single terminal date for all agreements, so that the employers could show a united nation-wide front to the societies. There was little enthusiasm. London employers considered their best interest lay in separate nego-tiation.[4] The president of the National Federation feared the attempt would cause 'great disruption' and 'do great damage'. Eventually the

---

[1] National Federation of Building Trade Employers, *Minutes*, 2 July 1901.

[2] Half the total number affected over the four years were in Scotland: in 1904 the masons and bricklayers of Glasgow and Edinburgh; in 1905 the Glasgow carpenters and joiners; and in 1909 the Glasgow joiners, masons, and bricklayers again.

[3] *Report on Changes in Rates of Wages and Hours of Labour in 1905*, Cd. 3172, 1906, p. 13.

[4] National Federation of Building Trade Employers, *Minutes*, 28 Jan. 1902.

Council recommended that agreements should terminate on either 1 May or 1 November.[1]

In the absence of a concerted national challenge, an attack by employers on craft rules would have had to take the form of local skirmishes. There is, however, no evidence of this. There was on the contrary a remarkable decline in the annual number of stoppages. Between 1893 and 1901 this annual figure was always between 100 and 200; between 1902 and 1910 it was never higher than forty-four and for the closing five years was around a score. The notes on the workings of conciliation and arbitration machinery contained in the Labour Department's annual *Report on Strikes and Lockouts* suggest a generally restrained and peaceful relationship. The 1908 *Report*, referring to 'a number of Local Boards and Committees', recorded that 'owing to the continued depression . . . the number of cases brought before [them] has been comparatively small, both sides apparently being content to allow matters to remain *in status quo* and not to press for alteration of rules'.[2] In 1912 the vice-president of the employers' federation declared: 'Between 1901 and 1911 we have had really a lovely time; it has been very quiet.'[3]

Moreover, had the employers decided to counter-attack, they might have been expected to concentrate on the Plasterers, who had been the spearhead of militancy during the nineties.[4] There were, indeed, complaints that its branches were not abiding by the 1899 agreement. In 1902 the master plasterers of the North declared that they could not enforce it, and conferences with Michael Deller, the secretary, offered no assurances. Further complaints brought an amendment to the agreement in 1904, permitting an employer to pay the rates of his own district even when working in a higher-rated district.[5] By 1908 another series of grievances centred on the pressure by society members to make foremen take their side. Despite all this, however, the employers stood by the 1899 agreement, and at a joint meeting of the Emergency Committee of the Federation with the National Association of Master Plasterers in 1902 no seconder could be found for a motion to abrogate the agreement.

Unemployment may, of course, have led to a good deal of covert evasion of craft regulations by workers as well as by employers. Where competition between workers for jobs led to their compromising their own craft principles, no dispute would arise. Plastering, for instance, saw an increase in 'labour-only sub-contracting'; machine-joinery brought unskilled low-paid workers into direct competition with craftsmen; and some employers paid bonuses to foremen to speed up the rate of work. Such practices were

[1] Ibid., 22 July 1902.
[2] Cd. 4680, 1909, p. 130.
[3] Industrial Council, *Inquiry into Industrial Agreements*, Cd. 6953, 1913, Q. 10130.
[4] See p. 157.
[5] National Federation of Building Trade Employers, *Minutes*, 12 Apr. 1904.

more prevalent in the South, where the unions and conciliation were relatively weak, than in the North.[1]

The organized employers showed a persistent attachment to the methods of collective bargaining. Now that unemployment had curbed the indiscipline of the union branches, the employers' Yorkshire Federation revived the proposal for a national conciliation board.[2] In 1904 the matter was discussed at a conference between the northern Federations and the major crafts—the three carpenters' societies; both orders of bricklayers, the masons, plumbers, plasterers, and painters—and eventually a complicated procedure was drawn up. In the first instance disputes were to be handled by local joint standing committees in the craft concerned. If unresolved they were to be considered by a local joint board of all the crafts. The next stage was a Centre Board, there Being one board for each of the Federation centres. And, finally, the matter could be referred to a national board.[3]

The Plasterers and Plumbers, who had their own separate national procedures, held aloof, as did the Painters. So, in the first instance, did the Amalgamated Society of Carpenters and Joiners, but it soon reversed its decision. 'As a means of securing privileges . . . or preserving those we enjoy, strikes have lost their ancient power', declared a statement to the members, 'no doubt largely due to the formation of powerful employers' associations and federations throughout the country . . . coupled with . . . the law throwing its protective wing over the "blackleg workman" . . .'.[4]

The first meeting of the national board was held in October 1905, and in the course of the next two years the system was gradually filled in, taking root most rapidly in the Midlands and the North. Scotland, London, and a number of southern towns held aloof, retaining such local boards as already existed, and there still remained a number of centres with no joint arrangements. By 1910 the boards and committees in the building industry known to the Labour Department numbered 111 and covered about 125,000 workers out of close on a million. But this is not a reliable index of the limits of joint regulation, for there were numerous local codes of working rules and conciliation procedures which did not provide for standing committees and boards.

In his *Builders' History* Postgate describes the societies' 'utter inability to protect their members' standard of life'[5] in this period. The development of conciliation procedures was the result of the leaders' desire for

---

[1] In his novel *The Ragged-Trousered Philanthropists*, Robert Tressell paints a vivid picture of the harsh conditions of building workers and of union weaknesses during this period of depression. It must be noted, however, that he worked as a painter in Hastings, and his novel describes the industry on the South Coast.   [2] See p. 159.

[3] *Second Report on the Rules of Voluntary Conciliation and Arbitration Boards*, Cd. 5346, 1910, pp. xvi–xvii.   [4] Higenbottam, op. cit., p. 147.

[5] p. 371. The chapter is entitled 'The Dead Hand'.

'peace at all costs with the employers', who were 'inclined to agree, now that the first shock of the trade collapse was over, and the unions had accepted the longer hours, lower wages and worse conditions demanded'.[1] This is a closely packed portmanteau of mis-statements. Hours in some places had been shortened; wage reductions had affected no more than 1 per cent. of the labour force in any one year; worse conditions had not been accepted by the unions. It was the employers who, in their desire for peace, if not 'peace at all costs', had made the advances, and the societies, or some of them, who were 'inclined to agree'. The organized building employers had shown a stronger and more persistent interest in the joint regulation of their industry than other craft employers, and they took the opportunity which the building depression offered them to strengthen joint regulation by means of a national procedure for settling local disputes.

The General Federation of Trade Unions

A new factor in collective bargaining was the General Federation of Trade Unions, established in 1899. The Federation had got off to a fair start, with unions totalling 343,000 members affiliated by the end of 1899.[2] Thereafter, in a period when total trade union membership stagnated, it maintained a steady rate of growth to 424,000 by 1904, by which time it had accumulated a fund of over £100,000.

A system of strike insurance might have been expected to encourage the more strike-prone unions in their militancy. On the other hand, the need to accumulate funds was the major consideration for the Management Committee. The Federation offered unions 'a scheme of mutual insurance against being involved in a dispute too protracted for their own funds, but it could survive only if it could ensure that such disputes were rare'.[3] Moreover, like other union leaders, its Committee preferred peaceful settlements where they could be had. 'Generally speaking we have followed the policy', declared the *Annual Report* of 1902, 'which was laid down last year, . . . of narrowing down disputes to their smallest possible limits, and . . . seeking to effect settlements where possible.'

Rules were drawn up to this end, and the Federation was soon intervening in negotiations to discourage strikes.[4] Heavy expenditure in the early years, including £9,000 on the Penrhyn dispute, led them to suggest a strengthening of the 1896 Conciliation Act by establishing a national conciliation board which could inquire into any stoppage and, if necessary,

---

[1] Ibid., p. 380.

[2] According to the Federation's *Annual Report*, 1911. The Board of Trade's *Reports on Trade Unions* give somewhat different figures—373,000 in 1899 and 396,000 in 1904. The general trend, however, is the same.

[3] Phelps Brown, op. cit., p. 249. Pp. 257–63 of this book offer the only serious assessment of the Federation's work yet published.   [4] Ibid., p. 260.

issue recommendations.[1] In 1903 the Federation's activities in 'establishing permanent boards at which future differences may be discussed in a business-like way' were being described in its *Annual Report* as 'much better work' than providing strike benefit.

In 1905–6 the officers of the Federation took a prominent part, together with the Federation of Engineering and Shipbuilding Trades, in negotiating weekly (as against fortnightly) payment of wages for shipbuilding and engineering workers on the Clyde;[2] and in this instance they showed themselves willing to fight. The two federations held a joint conference in Glasgow on 22 December 1905 at which it was unanimously resolved 'that the societies affiliated to both organisations take a ballot of their members as to whether they shall enforce the payment of weekly wages by a stoppage of work if necessary'.[3] In March 1906 the ballot showed a big majority for a strike and when a Central Conference failed to resolve the issue strike notices were served for June; but on 21 May the local associations of shipbuilding and engineering employers agreed to the change.

Apart from this episode, however, caution was the characteristic of the Federation. Because of it, and because of the insignificance of those strikes which were supported, Phelps Brown suggests that 'the word must soon have got around that there was nothing to be got out of the Federation except chickenfeed'.[4] Consequently, he says, 'too many strong unions had refused to come in at the start, and none had been persuaded to join since'.[5] Nevertheless, it would be wrong to conclude that the Federation was a collection of weak and unimportant organizations, condemned to impotence from the start. Sixty per cent. of its original membership was in five unions: the Engineers (85,000), the Gasworkers (48,000), the Boot and Shoe Operatives (28,000), the cardroom amalgamation (22,000), and the National Amalgamated Union of Labour (22,000). These five were among the fifteen largest in the country, though the Federation included only 18 per cent. of total trade union membership. Moreover, the Federation continued to attract large unions. The Boilermakers brought in 52,000 members in 1906, and the weavers' amalgamation 100,000 members in 1907. There were, of course, big unions outside: the Miners, the Railway Servants, and the Carpenters and Joiners among them; but then the Federation did not include the great majority of small unions either.

[1] A resolution on these lines was moved by a member of the Federation's Management Committee, James Holmes of the Hosiery Workers' Federation, at the 1903 Trades Union Congress and carried. A bill was introduced into the House, but made no progress.

[2] Phelps Brown, op. cit., p. 260.

[3] Amalgamated Society of Engineers, *Monthly Report*, Jan. 1906. This large and diverse group of unions was considering strike action during the Taff Vale period and before the reversal of the decision by Parliament was assured.   [4] Op. cit., p. 259.

[5] Ibid., p. 263. On p. 249 Phelps Brown states categorically that 'the big unions did not come in'.

Phelps Brown's verdict that 'an enterprise which could grow only by calculated audacity was stunted by prudence and parsimony'[1] is equally unacceptable. A lavish expenditure of other people's money would have killed the Federation quicker than anything else. The success of the Federation would depend, declared the *Journal and Monthly Record* of the Amalgamated Society of Engineers in September 1900, upon 'wise, sagacious management. . . . There should be no endorsement of wild cat strikes nor pandering to mere abstractions, but . . . a determined effort . . . to build up . . . the confidence of fair and level-headed trade unionists.' The Federation could be congratulated that 'caution' had been the 'distinguishing feature' of the successful annual meeting just held.

It was this caution and its discriminating scrutiny of claims which recommended the Federation to the unions and enabled it to grow until it was in a position to play a large part in the trade union world. Up to 1905, however, it had not played such a part because it was not called upon to do so. There were few major disputes which the Federation might have been called upon to finance, and in which it could therefore intervene. Accordingly 'as a practical force in industrial relations it was negligible'.[2]

White-collar Unions and Public Employees

Whereas for most manual workers' unions the period of Taff Vale was in terms of membership one of decline, stagnation or hesitant advance, the major unions of white-collar workers and public employees grew steadily and confidently. The National Union of Teachers rose from 44,000 members in 1900 to 58,000 in 1905; the five major unions of postal employees from 36,000 to 51,000; and the two main shop assistants' unions from 14,000 to 29,000. Meanwhile the Municipal Employees' Association leaped from 1,500 to 11,000.

The principal event for the Teachers was the Education Act of 1902. This embodied major reforms of the educational system which the union had long supported, providing for a comprehensive scheme of elementary and secondary education administered by the central government and the major local authorities and giving additional financial assistance to the denominational schools. The union would have preferred *ad hoc* authorities to the county and county borough councils, but in their eyes this was a minor matter.[3] Moreover, both board school and voluntary school

---

[1] Ibid., p. 263.

[2] Ibid., p. 250. 'The annual meeting', wrote a delegate of the Amalgamated Society of Engineers in 1905, 'is . . . a very decent picnic, involving change of air for a few days. One sees the same old faces, the ample waistcoats and gold watch chains, accompanied by fat cigars, which are to be seen at the Trades Union Congress and other meetings. . . . Business is not taken as seriously as it might be, lasting on the first day for about 90 minutes and on the second something like 4¼ hours' (*Monthly Report*, Aug. 1905).

[3] It was, however, taken seriously by many other trade unionists and by the Trades Union Congress itself. See p. 367.

teachers united in welcoming the assistance granted to denominational schools.

All sections of the union had previously condemned the Church of England for opposing reform except on its own terms. Now they rejected the complaints of the Nonconformists on the grounds that 'the vital interests of the children should not be sacrificed to the "theologians".'[1] The union played a prominent part in the passage of the Act, lobbying successfully not only for narrow professional objectives, such as the requirement that no teacher should be dismissed without the consent of the local authority, but also for wider aims, notably the principle that a majority of the members of each education committee should be elected councillors.[2]

One of the immediate effects of the Act was a rapid extension of collective bargaining. Previously only the larger school boards had dealt with the unions, but now many of the new authorities wanted to draw up comprehensive salary scales, and the union 'did a great deal of work in preparing and circulating information on existing scales of salaries for the guidance of L.E.A.s and in advising on the principles upon which scales should be constructed'. Soon it 'formulated a standard scale of salaries for certificated teachers in primary schools'.[3]

Another important development was an alliance with the associations of secondary school headmasters and teachers over the issue of registration. The union was in favour of a single register of all teachers, and had successfully campaigned against an order by the Teachers' Registration Council set up under an Act of 1899 requiring the separate registration of elementary school and secondary school teachers.[4] In 1908 there began a prolonged series of negotiations by the various teachers' organizations to establish a satisfactory registration council.

Post Office workers, disappointed with the results of the Tweedmouth Committee and the Norfolk–Hanbury conference, continued to campaign through Parliament for another inquiry into their wages and salaries, and for a satisfactory pension scheme. So persistent was their lobbying that on 30 April 1903 the Postmaster General, Austen Chamberlain, told the House that Members had applied to him for protection from the attentions of the unions. Later in the year, however, Chamberlain appointed a 'business committee' to decide on their claims,[5] and its report was so favourable to postal employees that the government tried to suppress it.

The Bradford proposals included a radically simplified system of classification in nearly all branches of the department which would have resulted

---

[1] Tropp, op. cit., p. 180.　　　　　[2] Donna F. Thompson, op. cit., appendix iv.
[3] Tropp, op. cit., pp. 203–4.　　　　　[4] Ibid., pp. 195–7.
[5] Along with Charles Booth, and directors of the Co-operative Wholesale Society and of Harrods, it included Sir Edward Bradford, chief of the Metropolitan Police, as chairman, and Samuel Fay of the Great Central Railway.

in a large number of wage increases. They also introduced the principle of the 'marriageable wage' at the age of twenty-six, when a man should be earning enough to afford to marry in reasonable comfort, and suggested substantial increases to achieve this aim.[1] After much agitation, the government published the report, but the unions made the mistake of adding new claims of their own to the demand for the Bradford proposals, which alone, according to the new Postmaster General, Lord Stanley, would have cost more than £1 million.[2]

In 1905 Stanley announced his counter-proposals.[3] The principle of the marriageable wage was accepted, but the total cost of the new scheme was cut down by 75 per cent. Stanley rejected the other recommendations on the grounds that they 'were not supported by a comparison of Post Office wages with those current in other occupations. . . . The true standard of wages in the Post Office service is that obtained by a comparison with the rates of wages current in similar occupations outside.'[4] In the House he launched an attack on union methods. Quoting a union circular, he described it as '. . . nothing more nor less than blackmail. It was nothing more nor less than asking Members to purchase votes for themselves at the general election at the expense of the public Exchequer. Both sides would have to make up their minds that some means should be devised by which there should not be this continual blood-sucking on the part of the public servants.'[5]

An earlier Postmaster General had said much the same in 1892,[6] as indeed had Stanley's predecessor Austen Chamberlain only two years before, but in neither case had their remarks attracted much attention. It was a sign of the times, therefore, that these words should win notoriety as 'Stanley's blazer', and Stanley was to regret them when he was challenged and beaten by a labour candidate at Westhoughton in Lancashire at the next election. This election presented a new opportunity to the postal unions and more than half the members returned in 1906 were pledged to support their demand for yet another committee.

Meanwhile a Royal Commission under Lord Courtney had reported in 1903 on the question of civil service superannuation. The official attitude was that pensions were paid *ex gratia*, whereas the unions argued that they were 'deferred pay' which belonged as of right to an employee or, if he died, to his dependants. The Majority Report of the Commission recommended some provision for the dependants of a civil servant who died before reaching pensionable age, but nothing was done until 1909

---

[1] *Report of the Committee on Post Office Wages*, Cd. 2170, 1904.
[2] *Hansard*, 9 Aug. 1904, col. 1636.
[3] Ibid., 6 July 1905, cols. 1354–64.
[4] These words are quoted from the *Report of the Postmaster General* for 1905, Cd. 2634, pp. 24–25.
[5] *Hansard*, 6 July 1905, col. 1365.   [6] See p. 217.

when an Act provided for a lump sum payment on death or retirement in return for a reduction in the rate of pension itself.

Thus the postal workers did not achieve much progress towards their aims in this period, but they enjoyed some parliamentary success and the constant agitation which they kept up provided an activity round which to build their organization. They maintained their national joint committee for common action, though there were frequent differences between its constituents. 'The postmen and the sorters were constantly at each other's throats, as were the P.T.C.A. and U.K.P.C.A.,[1] which organised virtually the same grades in the provinces. The only time that the four principal unions in the Department were in harmony was when they ganged up on the engineering grades and maintained that the latter were not postal servants at all.'[2]

The Co-operative Employees maintained their pressure on local societies for improved salaries and reductions in hours. The period was relatively uneventful for them. 'Our aims are "conciliatory not bellicose". The constant records of our successes in improving conditions for our members . . . show that a conciliatory policy is quite as effective as a fighting one could ever be, in the Co-operative movement at any rate. . . .'[3] One reason for timidity was noted by a visitor to the union conference of 1903, who emphasized 'the extent to which the purely provident benefits of the A.U.C.E. overshadow the trade benefits in the minds of many delegates'.[4]

The major problem agitating the union was their relationship with the more militant Shop Assistants, who by this time had organized a large number of co-operative workers. The Shop Assistants took the view that all distributive employees were eligible for membership, but they made no 'special efforts' to organize co-operative workers. Relationships between the two ranged from proposals for amalgamations and joint working to recriminations and poaching.

Meanwhile the agitation for more effective early closing legislation went on. Following the report of a Select Committee of the Lords in 1901 which had been set up on his initiative, Lord Avebury[5] persuaded Parliament to pass a new Shop Hours Act in 1904. This empowered local authorities to fix hours at which shops should be closed (including a half day) but through a cumbersome procedure and only with the agreement of two-thirds of the shops affected. Both unions rejected this as useless, and the Shop Assistants mounted a considerable campaign against his bill, and in favour of their own demand for uniform and compulsory

---

[1] Postal Telegraph Clerks' Association and United Kingdom Postal Clerks' Association.

[2] Leo Martinuzzi, *The History of Employment in the British Post Office*, B.Litt. thesis, Oxford, 1952.

[3] *Gleanings*, journal of the Amalgamated Union of Co-operative Employees, Sept. 1905.

[4] Ibid., Nov. 1903.

[5] See p. 226, and footnote 4.

closing of all shops. Dilke, who sponsored a measure on these lines, was now regarded as their main parliamentary champion.

The Municipal Employees' Association grew by opening new branches and by absorbing local unions of corporation manual workers such as cleaners, sweepers, sanitary workers, bath attendants, roadworkers, park-keepers, and even tramwaymen and gasworkers. In 1902 its part-time secretary, Albin Taylor, became a full-time officer, and by 1905 his energetic tactics had brought a rapid increase in membership. His dictatorial temperament caused trouble, however, and in November 1904 a London branch went so far as to send a deputation to the executive complaining about his behaviour.

Although in 1905 a coherent programme began to emerge when a conference approved the objective of a standard wage of 30s. in London and 28s. in the provinces, nevertheless the bulk of the union's work still consisted of deputations to the committees of local authorities or to their chief officers to remedy grievances. From the first it took an active interest in council elections, and in the promotion of a bill to enable local authorities 'to establish Superannuation and Provident Schemes' for their employees.

The Causes of Industrial Peace

It is now possible to return to the question posed at the beginning of this chapter: can the deterrent effect of the Taff Vale judgement explain the unwonted industrial peace of the first few years of the twentieth century?

In building, the previous decade had been a period of continuous high employment and industrial strife, and this was followed by ten years of depression and industrial peace. During the depression, however, there were remarkably few attempts to cut wages or increase hours. The tranquillity of this second period can be explained largely as the result of two circumstances: unemployment, which rendered the unions and their members less aggressive; and the unwillingness of the employers to counter-attack, which allowed the unions to avoid defensive battles. There is evidence that some of the union leaders thought the Taff Vale decision made it essential to avoid strikes,[1] but they were enabled to do so by these two other circumstances, which persisted, as did industrial peace, after Taff Vale was reversed.

A similar explanation covers those industries where the general depression of 1902–5 did not lead to widespread attempts to cut wages and increase hours. Printing and textiles, particularly cotton, fall into this category, as does transport.[2] There is also another factor affecting transport.

---

[1] See p. 327.
[2] The largest single group of transport workers affected by a wage reduction during the period were the coal-trimmers in the South Wales ports in 1902.

Unorganized or weakly organized workers frequently strike in years of good trade, but they lack the resources to sustain a defensive struggle during depression. Outside the Bristol Channel, Liverpool, and Belfast, dockers were virtually unorganized at this time, and the railwaymen, who had not felt themselves strong enough to fight the companies for recognition in 1897, were hardly likely to stand up to them now. A combination of these explanations can be advanced to cover two other relatively badly organized groups, the clothing and 'miscellaneous' industries.

There remain two major groups with strong unions which did suffer wage cuts: mining and quarrying, and metals, engineering, and ship-building. Along with cotton, these industries must provide the test of any analysis, for the three together account for the lion's share of the decline in working days lost which made this such a remarkable period of industrial peace.[1]

The round of wage cuts in engineering and shipbuilding did meet with opposition when members of some unions on the North-east coast and on the Clyde came out on strike. Their national leaders, however, used every effort first to prevent, and then to contain and settle the stoppages, for both sides in engineering were still recovering from their exhausting battle of 1897–8 and were anxious that the new procedure for dealing with disputes should be made effective.

Following the great disputes of the nineties in the Federated area, in Scotland, and in South Wales, every coalfield in the country now had an established method of negotiating changes in miners' wages. Moreover, wages did not fall below the minimum rates which were now written into most of the agreements outside Northumberland and Durham, though in Scotland the minimum was preserved only by mortgaging future increases. Had the employers been driven to launch a direct attack on these minimum rates, it is likely that Rule 20 would have been called into operation and the whole Federation would have come out in a bigger strike than the country had yet seen.

If this reasoning is valid for engineering and coal-mining, it has a parallel in cotton, for the spinning lock-outs of the early nineties had led up to the Brooklands Agreement. Thus the most satisfactory answer to the question is that the stoppages of the nineties had led to the establishment of systematic collective bargaining in these three major industries; that both sides were anxious for the new methods to work; and that their efforts, aided by the relative mildness of the depression, were by and large successful.

Had British employers wished to be rid of trade unions, the depression years of 1902–5, with the Taff Vale precedent valid in every court, were as favourable an opportunity as ever presented itself. There are, however,

[1] See p. 328.

relatively few instances of organized employers taking advantage of it to attempt to weaken or destroy the unions. This was not because employers were inactive. Important new employers' organizations, such as the British Federation of Master Printers, were founded, and several existing organizations were reorganized and strengthened. Moreover, in some industries the employers were willing to take the initiative, and where they did so, as in building and printing, it was to strengthen and extend systems of collective bargaining and to enlarge the scope of joint regulation.

This can be taken as evidence that most employers were not 'anti-union'. Some of the leaders of the employers' counter-attacks in the previous decade had proclaimed their intention to be rid of the unions, who had naturally seized upon such statements. The Shipping Federation had suited action to the word, and it seemed in 1897 that the engineering employers would prove apt pupils. But the experience of the first five years of the twentieth century suggests that, despite Taff Vale, the majority of organized employers preferred to make a serious attempt to work with the unions.

10

Politics, 1900–10

Parliamentary Activities, 1900–5

AT the general election of 1900 the trade union group in Parliament lost four of its eleven members: Sam Woods, W. C. Steadman, Havelock Wilson, and Fred Maddison. On the other hand, the Labour Representation Committee could claim to have gained its first two seats: Keir Hardie's at Merthyr Tydfil and Richard Bell's at Derby. The group had already lost some of its original homogeneity, and these changes did little to alter its character. Henry Broadhurst was rejoined by another elder statesman, W. R. Cremer; the old guard of the miners still held five seats; and John Burns survived at Battersea. Bell had received Liberal backing, and his views hardly differed from those of Wilson or Maddison, while Hardie, the sole representative of the Independent Labour Party, also owed much to Liberal support and was anxious to consolidate the new alliance between socialism and the unions.

Over the next five years a series of by-elections increased the size of the group from ten to fifteen, but again its character was little affected. In 1904 the purely Lib-Lab element was strengthened by the return of two more miners—Thomas Richards for West Monmouth and John Johnson for Gateshead.[1] In addition the Labour Representation Committee endorsed three successful candidates: David Shackleton of the Weavers at Clitheroe in 1902, and in 1903 Will Crooks of the Coopers at Woolwich and Arthur Henderson of the Ironfounders at Barnard Castle. Had there been no Labour Representation Committee, both Shackleton and Henderson might well have stood simply as Lib-Labs, while Crooks had received the blessing of the National Liberal Federation and remained a loyal member of the Progressive party on the London County Council.

At first the group behaved much as before, and there was little to show for the attempts to encourage greater cohesion made by Woods at the end of the nineties. Burns claimed that in the previous Parliament 'they had not called themselves independent, they had not worn the trilby hats and red ties, but they had done the work'.[2] From 1900 to 1902, however, none of the labour Members sat on the Parliamentary Committee, and the

---

[1] On Ben Pickard's death, also in 1904, William Parrott, the new secretary of the Yorkshire Miners, succeeded him at Normanton.

[2] *Labour Representation Conference Report*, Mar. 1900.

decline in the health and efficiency of its secretary, Woods, as well as his disappearance from the House, further reduced the possibilities of effective co-ordination. Burns himself was taking the place of the ageing Broad-hurst as the most prominent of working-class representatives, but not even three years of flattery from his old enemy Hardie could persuade him to give the group the leadership it lacked. Finding that Burns could not be relied upon, the Committee preferred to put its business in other hands, though they continued to respect him and he was to prove useful in 1905.

In these circumstances the Parliamentary Committee were understand-ably eager to take advantage of Sir Charles Dilke's desire 'to aid the main aspirations of the Trades Union Congress', which had led to his re-establishment of close contact with them in 1898.[1] From 1900 to 1902 Dilke was the Committee's main link with Parliament, and their reports to Congress are fulsome in his praise. Moreover, in March 1900 he had already gone some way towards making good his offer of the previous year to form a 'non-political party' on their behalf. By bringing together Members of both major parties to work with the labour representatives, the Parliamentary Committee, and 'the trades very closely affected', Dilke was able 'to influence the Government in dropping the most retrograde measure of modern times', the abortive Factory and Workshops Amendment Bill.[2]

The Act of 1901 was much more satisfactory, and Dilke was again thanked by the Committee for his help in securing 'the only redeeming feature of the session'. For the first time his *ad hoc* organization had attracted the valuable support of the Irish party under John Redmond.[3] Like its predecessors, the measure was regarded within the movement primarily as the concern of the cotton unions, whose agitation had reopened the question in 1899. Factory legislation had become a highly technical matter in which the expertize of their officials was unrivalled, and the new Act embodied a reduction of hours which affected their members more than anyone else. They did not always see eye to eye with Dilke,[4] however,

---

[1] See p. 267. The description of Dilke's aims is that of W. J. Davis, with whom Dilke had arranged in 1898 to revive his 'elaborate system of feasting' trade union leaders, as Ramsay MacDonald called it (Bealey and Pelling, op. cit., p. 184). According to Davis, 'from 1901 to 1906 the luncheons were followed by a conference of Labour and Radical members . . . where arrangements were made to support Labour Bills or to oppose reactionary proposals' (S. Gwynn and G. M. Tuckwell, *The Life of Sir Charles W. Dilke*, vol. ii, 1917, p. 356, footnote).

[2] Trades Union Congress, *Annual Report*, 1900, Parliamentary Committee Report.

[3] James Sexton declared that 'the only Labour Party they had today was the Irish Party . . . but for the assistance received from the Irish Members they would never have got the Factory Bill' (Trades Union Congress, *Annual Report*, 1901). In fact, however, Redmond's support caused some uneasiness because of the explosive nature of the Irish issue in Lancashire politics. The cotton leaders claimed that 'there was no bargain whatever over the matter', since 'the Irishmen had good reasons for the course they pursued from their own point of view. They are no friends of the Government, and if a vote of theirs will help to embarrass it so much the better' (*Cotton Factory Times*, 25 Oct. 1901).

[4] Ibid., 26 July; 2 Aug. 1901. They believed that Dilke and the Yorkshire textile

and the *Cotton Factory Times* once more deplored the absence of 'direct representatives of their own' from the floor of the House.[1]

Most of the other measures sponsored by Dilke and his associates at this time also served the interests of particular unions. With their assistance, the Miners' Federation plodded on with the Eight Hours Bill, which received a second reading in 1901 but not in 1902. A week after this set-back the Federation tried a new approach. Pickard's Coal Mines Employment Bill, which proposed to limit the hours of boys under sixteen, would have been almost as effective in restricting the hours of adult males as the limitation of the hours of women and young persons in cotton, and in addition would have controlled entry by excluding from underground work all who had not been so employed before the age of eighteen. This novel suggestion, the result of growing depression, was heavily attacked and Pickard could not save his bill by withdrawing its second clause. In 1903 the Federation had no better luck with a further bill introduced by Dilke himself.

Similarly, the railwaymen were always anxious to extend statutory regulation of their conditions, and in 1900 their lobbying had won widespread support for a useful measure tightening up safety precautions.[2] Thereafter the attention of the unions, led by the Railway Servants, was concentrated on the working of the 1893 Act. Despite his preoccupation with Taff Vale, Bell found time during the winter of 1901–2 to bombard ministers with forty-one complaints about excessive hours of work,[3] and in February 1902 he seconded a resolution calling for closer control moved by Captain Norton, a friend and colleague of Dilke's who frequently worked with the trade union group in the House.

Like the Parliamentary Committee and Congress itself, the group and its allies did not confine their activities to promoting the narrower interests of the unions. In 1900, for example, the growing problem of working-class housing had been raised by Steadman with the backing of other London Progressives, including T. J. Macnamara of the Teachers. Under the Housing Act of 1890 local authorities already had power to clear slums. Following a resolution moved by Ben Tillett and accepted by Congress in 1899, Steadman proposed that the authorities should also be empowered to build cheap houses in new areas. The Progressives continued their

workers were endangering '12 o'clock stoppage' on Saturdays by asking the government to limit the hours of adult males.

[1] 'It is somewhat humiliating for officials to have to go begging "cap in hand" to capitalistic members when by organizing their forces they could do the work themselves' (*Cotton Factory Times*, 9 Aug. 1901). See also p. 299.

[2] Despite the deterioration in his relations with the Railway Servants after his dismissal as editor of the *Railway Review*, Fred Maddison was one of their most effective spokesmen on this question. Until his defeat at the general election of 1900 he was an active member of Dilke's 'party' (Trades Union Congress, *Annual Report*, 1900, Parliamentary Committee Report).

[3] Bealey and Pelling, op. cit., p. 201.

campaign after the passage of the Conservative government's inadequate measure in 1900, and the demand still featured prominently in the Parliamentary Committee's election programme five years later.

In 1902, as the questions of free trade, education, and old-age pensions came to the fore, wider issues began to occupy more of the time and energy of Congress and its spokesmen than for many years past. Free traders almost to a man, they were incensed by the revival of an import duty on corn to help finance the South African War. So far the war had tended to divide the unions rather than to unite them. At Congress John Ward of the Navvies was refused a hearing for his anti-war resolution in 1901, and even in 1902 the majority which condemned the war as 'unjust' was only two to one.[1] In 1901 another of Hicks Beach's expedients, the export duty on coal, had been treated as a matter for the miners, who were left to call a national miners' conference which sent their five Members to protest to the Chancellor.[2] Now, however, Congress unanimously declared that the corn tax was 'destructive of good sound fiscal policy, contrary to the principles of free trade, and a determined attempt to drive in the thin end of the wedge of the old protective laws which deprived the working-classes of cheap bread'.

The unions also shared many of the Liberal, and more particularly the Nonconformist, objections to Balfour's Education Act of 1902, but their special concern was to restore separately elected school boards. By now many trade unionists had served on these bodies, and their disappearance appeared likely to reduce the opportunities for effective labour representation. The new education committees were no substitute, and 'without popular control there would not be efficiency; all sorts of things would be done in a hole-and-corner fashion if the representatives of the public possessed no adequate supervision'.[3] With W. J. Davis taking the lead in the agitation, as he had on free trade, the Parliamentary Committee continued to work on sympathetic Members and tried to arouse local feeling through the trades councils.

Besides using their normal methods of lobbying, the Committee organized 'demonstrations of the trades' in London on both free trade and education during 1902. On Steadman's initiative a similar broad appeal had already been launched earlier in the year on old-age pensions when the Parliamentary Committee had arranged a conference with the Co-operative Congress, which apparently also collaborated on the other two

---

[1] The voting was 591,000 to 314,000.

[2] When they returned unsuccessful the conference even debated a strike; but only the exporting districts favoured this course. In its final resolution, the conference felt the need to 'repudiate the statement made that the miners and owners are acting in collusion to bring about a general stoppage of the collieries as being malicious and untrue' (Page Arnot, op. cit., vol. i, pp. 336–8).

[3] Trades Union Congress, *Annual Report*, 1903.

occasions.[1] The meeting arose out of a resolution of Congress in 1901 which insisted that pensions should be 'a civil right which may be claimed by any citizen', and reminded the government of 'the pledges given by its supporters at the General Election of 1895, which, up to the present time, have been ignored'[2]—not least by Chamberlain, whose lavish promises they had most in mind, and who declared only a week before the demonstration that the moment for action had still not arrived.[3]

In 1903 Chamberlain again incurred the wrath of Congress when he opened his campaign for tariff reform. This major 'departure from the principles of free trade' was denounced as 'most mischievous and dangerous', and trade unionists were further angered by what James Sexton called Chamberlain's 'carrot': his suggestion that the proposed duties on imports might pay for old-age pensions.[4] They were equally scornful of the claim that tariff reform could provide a cure for unemployment, a problem which came to occupy the unions more and more from 1903 onwards. As depression deepened, the threat to many of their members grew increasingly serious; but even greater priority had to be given to a question which affected all of them—the reform of trade union law.

In January 1903 a settlement was reached in the second Taff Vale case, the Company's successful suit for heavy damages against the Railway Servants. The first case had already produced three abortive responses during 1902: Palmer's 'subsidiary companies' scheme, Bell's bill to protect picketing, and Beaumont's ambiguous motion on the subject. The second case added to the urgency of the bill which the three national organizations had drawn up on the instructions of Congress in September 1902, and which Shackleton presented to the House in May 1903. It also encouraged the growing demand within the movement for complete legal immunity, which carried the Congress of September 1903.[5]

The Parliamentary Committee obediently took up its new charge. The subcommittee interviewed Dilke, who agreed to drop his own bill in favour of theirs; Edmond Browne worked on the draft with Dilke and Sir Robert Reid; and Bell consulted the Speaker about a title. On 16 December 1903 the Committee approved a new version of clause 3 which was later accepted by the other national organizations: 'an action should not be brought against a trade union or other association aforesaid for the recovery of damages sustained by any person or persons by reason of the

[1] Parliamentary Committee, *Minutes*, 1901–2, *passim*.

[2] Trades Union Congress, *Annual Report*, 1901.

[3] Speaking at Birmingham on 6 Jan. 1902. The conference favoured non-contributory pensions of 5s. a week at 60; and the Parliamentary Committees of the Trades Union Congress and the Co-operative Congress arranged to lobby the government jointly (Parliamentary Committee, *Minutes*, 15 Jan. 1902).

[4] Trades Union Congress, *Annual Report*, 1903.

[5] See p. 322.

action of a member or members of such trade union.'[1] As before, Bell and Shackleton handled the parliamentary preparations and persuaded a Durham Liberal, J. M. Paulton, to introduce the Trade Disputes Bill in April 1904, when it got a second reading but went no further.

The main reason for this advance was the continued loyalty of the Liberals, but the majority of thirty-nine was provided by fifty Irish Members who fulfilled an agreement between Redmond and the Parliamentary Committee by catching the night ferry from Dublin to record their votes.[2] In return for future support, Redmond now asked that the Bill's definition of conspiracy in clause 2 should be widened to protect agitation by the United Irish League. Eventually he agreed not to press his demand if the Committee would ask the next Congress to approve a suitable revision of the clause. When Shackleton reported the discussions, he merely suggested that the matter be left with the Parliamentary Committee, and assured Congress that they would 'certainly be careful not to prejudice their own Bill'.[3]

Meanwhile, in March 1905, another Liberal, T. P. Whittaker, had reintroduced the Bill,[4] and the second reading was carried by 122 votes, including those of the Irish. Some Liberal speeches, however, foreshadowed damaging amendments. Rejecting legal immunity, Asquith held that the dangers of Taff Vale would 'almost entirely disappear' provided 'they could once get such a limitation of the law of agency as would protect the union and . . . its funds from the acts of those who were not definitely authorised to bind it'.[5] Atherley-Jones was more specific: the Bill 'could be limited . . . so that trade unions should be liable for wrongful acts when they expressly authorised these wrongful acts'.[6] Opponents of the measure, inspired by the Employers' Parliamentary Council, could

---

[1] The Parliamentary Committee was anxious to control the drafting, and reproved Browne for bringing the General Federation of Trade Unions and the Labour Representation Committee into contact with Reid; but 'to obviate any friction with the two other bodies . . . these should be invited to render all help to the Bill after completion' (Parliamentary Committee, *Minutes*, 20 Jan. 1904).

[2] *Hansard*, 22 Apr. 1904, col. 997. This further evidence of the Irish party's readiness to assist trade unionists reflects not only Redmond's tactical calculations but also a revived connexion between the Irish Left, led by Davitt, and the labour movement (T. W. Moody, 'Michael Davitt and the British Labour Movement, 1882–1906', *Transactions of the Royal Historical Society*, 1953, pp. 73–76). A parliamentary link was provided by Eugene Crean, an associate of Davitt's and 'the secretary of one of the Irish Trades Associations' (*Pall Mall Gazette*, loc. cit., p. 53).

[3] Trades Union Congress, *Annual Report*, 1905. Referring to Redmond's modified suggestion, the Parliamentary Committee said 'we thought it advisable to agree to the proposition' (ibid.). A copy of the *Annual Report* was sent to Redmond, who was asked to draft a clause; there is no record of any reply.

[4] The Parliamentary Committee had asked the Miners' Federation whether, in view of its general importance, they could give the Bill precedence over their Eight Hours Bill if they were lucky in the ballot. With typical singlemindedness the miners said that they could not 'see [their] way clear to give first place' (Miners' Federation, *Report of Special Conference*, 13 Feb. 1905).

[5] *Hansard*, 10 Mar. 1905, col. 1097. [6] Ibid., col. 1087.

B b

not be expected to neglect such openings. In committee they forced its promoters to submit to a wider definition of 'molestation' in picketing, but when the Solicitor-General refused to accept the conspiracy clause as a basis for discussion the labour Members walked out.[1]

Over their other major problem the unions found the government more amenable. During 1904 the Labour Department's index of unemployment among trade unionists had risen from 6·1 per cent. in January to 7·1 per cent. in December.[2] In September a worried Congress instructed the Parliamentary Committee to obtain 'such legislation as would empower both local and central authorities to deal adequately with the problem'; but Balfour refused to summon an autumn session. In October, however, Walter Long, President of the Local Government Board, proposed a scheme of relief for the London unemployed which went beyond the ordinary scope of the Poor Law.[3] The Committee at once followed what had now become its established procedure[4] and called a conference along with the General Federation of Trade Unions and the Labour Representation Committee, the first of a series on the whole question.

In February 1905 an elaborate report was presented to Balfour by a deputation led by the Parliamentary Committee. The government was contemplating legislation modelled on Long's plan for London, to which the report gave qualified approval. The bill was largely permissive, enabling local authorities and charitable organizations to set up Distress Committees in the larger towns, and extending existing powers to grant relief from the rates. In March, however, a further conference of the three organizations demanded more, including a national scheme with Treasury finance, and joint demonstrations were organized throughout the country.

The labour Members, on the other hand, soon had to concentrate upon bolstering up the Conservatives' faith in their own bill, as this came under attack from both sides in the House. In the end, drastically amended, it became the Unemployed Workmen Act of 1905. As Lloyd George remarked, the measure contained 'the germs of a revolution', yet could 'do very little good, except that it recognised a very important principle . . . the right of a man to call upon the State to provide him with work. The

---

[1] Burns was praised by Sexton as chairman of the Parliamentary Committee for his 'able leadership' at this stage (Trades Union Congress, *Annual Report*, 1905).

[2] *Fifteenth Abstract of Labour Statistics*, Cd. 6228, 1912, p. 7.

[3] W. H. Beveridge, *Unemployment: A Problem of Industry*, 1930 edition, pp. 160–1.

[4] Following the precedents of 1902, 'national conferences' had been held in 1903 on Taff Vale and housing, both 'on the initiation and under the auspices of the Parliamentary Committee' but also 'with the co-operation of the . . . General Federation of Trade Unions and the Labour Representation Committee' (Trades Union Congress, *Annual Report*, 1903, Parliamentary Committee Report). Together with Davis, Bell was the prime mover in this development. As chairman of the Parliamentary Committee, Bell also organized a widely supported conference in Mar. 1904 to protest against the introduction of indentured Chinese labour into South Africa (Trades Union Congress, *Annual Report*, 1904; Parliamentary Committee, *Minutes*, 1904, *passim*).

State replied by recognising the right but would not provide the work.'[1]
Even so, administrative machinery of a sort had been made available,
and the movement was encouraged to assert 'the right to work' more
strongly than before.

The session had revealed some improvement in the performance of the
trade union group, and after Congress the Parliamentary Committee
launched its most impressive campaign so far. The help of trades councils
and individual unions was enlisted for work in the constituencies, while
meetings in the major cities were addressed by members of the Committee.
Meetings of this type had first taken place during the winter of 1904–5,
when the immediate aim was to win support for the principles of the Trade
Disputes Bill. Now the prime objective was to commit the Liberals to an
unequivocal acceptance of the Parliamentary Committee's detailed proposals. With an eye on the approaching election, the campaign was therefore broadened to include not only further provision for unemployment
and an extension of the Workmen's Compensation Act, but also wider
issues on which the party and the unions were already in agreement,
notably free trade, education, and Chinese labour.

On this last question the attitude of the unions was forthright. During
the nineties Congress had protested against the immigration of 'foreign
pauper labour', and in the South African war, it seemed, money and lives
had been 'sacrificed in order that white labour in the Transvaal should be
ousted and replaced by yellow slave labour. . . . One of the chief reasons for
employing Chinese labour was the dislike of the mineowners for the British
working man, with his Trade Unions and his determination to see things
fairly adjusted.'[2] Nevertheless, the government largely failed to win union
support for their Aliens Act of 1905, which sought to keep cheap foreign
labour out of Britain. The bill met only 'half-hearted resistance by the
Liberal party';[3] but after the defeat of Hardie's amendment excluding 'men
brought into this country under contract, or to take the place of workmen
during a trade dispute', the labour Members denounced the measure as
'fraudulent' and joined Dilke and sixty other Liberals in opposing it.

Thus the Conservatives failed to upset the growing *rapprochement*
between the unions and the Liberals which had been evident since 1902.
The predominant tone during these years both on the Parliamentary
Committee and in the House was strongly Lib-Lab. The Committee was
swayed by Davis and Alexander Wilkie of the older generation and Bell
and Shackleton of the new. Though they differed in their attitude to the
Labour Representation Committee, they were all, with the intermittent

[1] *Hansard*, 7 Aug. 1905, cols. 432–3.
[2] Trades Union Congress, *Annual Report*, 1904, Parliamentary Committee Report.
[3] *Reformers' Year Book*, 1906, p. 63. Halévy recorded that 'an entire group of Liberal members who represented working-class constituencies, particularly in the east of London, voted for
the Bill' (op. cit., vol. v, p. 375).

exception of Bell, 'middle-of-the-road' men, and agreed on the need for new techniques and greater efficiency. Once Congress had been persuaded to increase affiliation fees by 50 per cent. in 1902 the subsequent rise in income was put to good use, despite Woods's incapacity as secretary.[1] As a result of their activities the Parliamentary Committee's reputation stood higher in 1905 than in 1900.

The trade union group in Parliament, on the other hand, remained amorphous and unorganized until the belated improvements of 1905. After 1902 Dilke's importance declined,[2] partly because Taff Vale had led him to bring his clients into touch with Liberals who could be even more useful to them—the party's leader, Campbell-Bannerman, the chief whip, Herbert Gladstone, and its leading lawyers, Asquith, Haldane, and Reid— and partly because first Bell and then Shackleton came to the fore. Moreover, in 1902 Bell was re-elected to the Parliamentary Committee, thus restoring a direct link between the Committee and the group. Soon Shackleton was also working with them regularly, though he did not become a member of the Parliamentary Committee until 1904.

From 1902 a new vigour was thus apparent, but the group was slow to change its ways. Divided among themselves, the miners were rarely of much use to others. Broadhurst and Cremer were ageing, and Burns seldom made his services available. Often absent through illness, Hardie remained isolated. Both he and Crooks were clumsy tacticians, useful mainly when forceful appeals to sentiment were needed. By contrast, Bell, for all the enemies he made, was an energetic and effective parliamentarian, if increasingly erratic in his attendance. In 1905, however, the careful argument, the crucial lobbying, and the beginnings of genuine organization were provided by Shackleton, assisted by Henderson. Behind the temporary façade of Burns,[3] their efforts at last gave the group something of the force and cohesion it had so far lacked.

[1] Steadman succeeded Woods after Congress had met in 1904, his appointment being confirmed in 1905 to last 'so long as his work and conduct gave satisfaction' in place of the old system of annual election (Trades Union Congress, *Annual Report*, 1905). In future the post was to be full-time, though the new standing order expressly laid down that this was not to exclude 'parliamentary duties'. As late as 1902, when complaints in the Parliamentary Committee about his incompetence were at their height, Woods had told Congress he could manage on a part-time basis. After some opposition the secretary's salary was then fixed at £250 per annum, tax free; a further £150 was to be paid for clerical assistance (Trades Union Congress, *Annual Report*, 1902).

[2] There is some evidence that by 1902 the Parliamentary Committee was becoming uneasy that its reliance on Dilke was tending to exclude the labour Members. On 30 Apr. the secretary was instructed to 'arrange for a meeting of Labour M.P.s *alone* to confer with the Committee at least once a year on Labour legislation' (Parliamentary Committee, *Minutes*); and on 28 May plans were made for closer liaison with the trade union group—through Burns and Fenwick as whips—similar to the arrangements of 1899 (Trades Union Congress, *Annual Report*, 1902, Parliamentary Committee Report). But the Committee continued to maintain good relations with Dilke and thanked him for his services (Parliamentary Committee, *Minutes*, 8 July 1902).

[3] In yet another attempt to provide a formal constitution for the group Burns had been

The Labour Representation Committee

Though Hardie had failed to realize his ambition of turning the nominees of the Labour Representation Committee into 'a distinct Labour Group' in the House, the Committee's strength in the country was growing, and its importance was demonstrated by the battle between the socialists and the Lib-Labs for control. This clash did not occur immediately. Whatever their views on collaboration with the socialists, most of the Lib-Labs had not striven to prevent the creation of the Committee. Equally, most of them did little to encourage its early growth, and for a time failed to make up their minds whether to ignore the Committee entirely or to try to ensure that it was controlled by Congress.

Many important Lib-Labs were not present at the founding conference in February 1900. Wilkie and Davis, who did attend, wanted to make the Committee a department of the Parliamentary Committee;[1] at the other extreme, the Social Democratic Federation demanded a separate socialist party. The leaders of the Independent Labour Party were thus able to steer a middle course between the representatives of the Parliamentary Committee and the Federation by proposing to combine organizational independence with doctrinal tolerance. They also succeeded in electing to the secretaryship Ramsay MacDonald, a member of the party but acceptable as a moderate; and despite Wilkie's protests the socialist societies were allotted five of the twelve seats on the executive, a proportion quite unjustified by their numbers.[2]

In these delicate circumstances MacDonald had to concentrate on winning over the unions, whose leaders he treated with deferential caution. In July 1900 he sought the permission of the Parliamentary Committee to address Congress on 'the aims and objects of his Committee'. This was refused, but the Parliamentary Committee offered to incorporate a brief statement in their own report. MacDonald supplied them with a carefully worded document. His Committee felt that 'its first important task' was 'to get at the Trade Unions'. 'Unwilling to come to any hasty decision' on the important question of candidatures, they trusted that their eventual decision would be 'acceptable to all the sections represented on the Committee'.[3]

elected chairman, with Bell and Fenwick as whips, on 15 Feb. 1905; but it is clear that these elections were engineered by Shackleton, who stage-managed the group's activities during the session on behalf of the Parliamentary Committee (Parliamentary Committee, *Minutes*, 1905, *passim*).

[1] When Hardie asked Wilkie to suggest a name for the new organization, he chose 'The Industrial Representation League' (*Labour Leader*, 31 Mar. 1900). During most of 1900 Hardie used the title suggested by Bell—'The United Labour Party'.

[2] The Independent Labour Party's anxiety to compromise is to be explained by the importance to its survival of a prominent position within the Committee. The decline in party strength was continuing. As late as 27 June 1900 the usually sanguine Hardie referred to 'the parlous state of our movement', and the party was on the verge of bankruptcy (Poirier, op. cit., p. 94).

[3] Trades Union Congress, *Annual Report*, 1900, Parliamentary Committee Report.

While he wooed the unions, avoided conflict with the Parliamentary Committee, and tried to establish the independence of his organization, MacDonald had also to keep the lines open for electoral arrangements with the Liberals if his Committee was to fulfil its primary purpose of improving labour representation.[1] He had, therefore, every reason to avoid making enemies, especially among the Lib-Labs. Yet if growth was to continue this would not be easy. Within the unions, propaganda on behalf of the Committee was conducted largely by members of the Independent Labour Party, who were often at loggerheads with their Lib-Lab leaders on industrial as well as political issues.

For twelve months after the election of 1900, affiliations to the Committee in fact rose hardly at all, and 'it looked as if this new effort was going to share the fate of previous attempts to secure the direct representation of Labour'.[2] In September 1901 Congress set up a committee, which included Wilkie and another prominent Lib-Lab, W. B. Cheesman of the Fawcett Association, to consider the future of labour representation, a decision difficult to reconcile with its approval of a resolution expressing 'gratification with the success of the Labour Representation Committee' and appealing to all unions to join. The House of Lords, however, had just announced its decision in the first Taff Vale case, and this was to prove a far more effective recruiting agent than any resolution of Congress.

As Table 5 shows, there were two major waves of affiliation to the Committee—in 1900–1 and again in 1902–3. Virtually all the unions listed in the first wave had affiliated before the general election of October 1900; and the majority of those in the second joined within twelve months of the delivery of the Lords' judgement.

Most of the important unions which came in during 1900 had special reasons for doing so. Bell, John Hodge, Sexton, and Tillett had already shown their parliamentary ambitions, and the early affiliation of their unions might increase their chances of winning a seat. Thorne was about to stand at West Ham for the first time, and the Boot and Shoe Operatives had long since decided to seek a 'parliamentary agent'. The secretaries of the Shipwrights and the Brassworkers, Wilkie and Davis, were leading Lib-Lab supporters of direct representation; Davis had been a candidate in 1892, and Wilkie fought Sunderland in 1900. Moreover, apart from the ambitions and interests of their chief officers, three of the unions, the Gasworkers and the two dockers' organizations, were socialist-dominated survivors of the 'new unionism'. There were also powerful socialist factions

---

[1] Bealey and Pelling, op. cit., pp. 126–9. As early as 14 Mar. 1900 Woods as secretary of the Parliamentary Committee had urged MacDonald to approach Herbert Gladstone 'with a view of adopting a larger number of Labour candidates' (ibid., p. 34).

[2] Snowden, op. cit., vol. i, p. 94. He also refers to 'the feeling of despondency' at the Committee's conference in 1901.

TABLE 5

Trade union affiliations to the Labour Representation Committee, 1900–6

	Number of unions	Affiliated union membership	Unions affiliating on more than 10,000 members	L.R.C. union membership as a proportion of T.U.C. membership *	Number of affiliated trades councils
February 1900–1	41	353,070	Blastfurnacemen (10,000) Boot and Shoe Operatives (32,084) Brassworkers (10,000) Compositors, London Society of (11,415) Dock Labourers (12,000) Dock, Wharf, Riverside and General Labourers (13,829) Gasworkers and General Labourers (48,038) Ironfounders (18,357) Railway Servants (60,000) Shipwrights (18,000) Steel Smelters (10,509) Typographical Association (16,000)	29%	7
February 1901–2	65	455,450	Builders' Labourers, United (12,000) Labour, National Amalgamated Union of (23,000) Plasterers (11,000) Postmen's Federation (24,000) Shop Assistants (11,000) Stonemasons (20,000)	32%	21
February 1902–3	127	847,315	Bleachers, Dyers and Kindred Trades (10,000) Boilermakers (49,000) Carpenters and Joiners, Amalgamated Society of (62,000) Engineers (84,000) Locomotive Engineers and Firemen (10,000) Textile Factory Workers' Association, United (103,000)	56%	49
February 1903–4	165	956,025	Bricklayers (37,500) Miners' Federation, Lancashire and Cheshire (37,000) Plumbers (11,500)	67%†	76
February 1904–5	158	855,270‡	Painters and Decorators (10,966)	56%§	73
February 1905–6	158	904,496		58%	73

* Trades Union Congress membership is that for the following September in each case.
† The rise in this percentage is partly explained by a fall in the total affiliated to the Trades Union Congress between 1903 and 1904.
‡ The decline was due to the compulsory levy introduced at the beginning of 1904. This reduced the number of small unions affiliating, and caused others to affiliate on a smaller membership (Labour Representation Committee, *Annual Report*, 1905).
§ An additional cause of the fall in this percentage was the reaffiliation of the Engineers and the Durham Miners to the Trades Union Congress in 1905.

among the Railway Servants and the Boot and Shoe Operatives, and socialists were active in the two printing unions.[1]

The Taff Vale judgement of July 1901 took some time to affect the decisions of union executives, who had first to arrange for ballots of their

[1] C. W. Bowerman, secretary of the London Society of Compositors, was a Fabian and a strong supporter of labour representation; and in 1900 the Typographical Association elected as its secretary a member of the Independent Labour Party, A. W. Jones.

members and then act on the results. The great majority of the recruits of 1902–3 affiliated during the first six months of 1902, and there can be little doubt that the judgement provided a powerful incentive. The chief exception, the United Textile Factory Workers' Association, was held up by a constitutional provision which required the assent of all its affiliates to the proposal. The matter had been raised in January 1902, when the weavers' amalgamation decided to recommend affiliation; but the Association itself was unable to approach the Labour Representation Committee until February 1903.

Thereafter the Committee rounded up the remainder of the building trades, and in May 1903 brought in the first of the miners' unions, the Lancashire and Cheshire Miners' Federation. The rest of the miners now formed the one important omission from its lists. By 1905 the difference between the membership of the Committee and of Congress was 600,000. Part of this can be explained by many unions affiliating only a proportion of their membership to the former, whereas this was not the normal practice with Congress affiliations; but just under 400,000 is accounted for by the absence of the Northumberland and Durham Miners' Associations, and, apart from Lancashire, of the Miners' Federation.[1]

Pickard had been bitterly hostile to the original proposals for the Labour Representation Committee,[2] and its formation prompted him to tighten up his own arrangements. Introduced in 1901, his Labour Fund Scheme was accepted by the Federation in 1902.[3] With membership obligatory and a levy of 1s. a year, the scheme was allegedly 'not established for the purpose of wrecking any political party', for it did 'not in any way prevent any member running as a candidate under any name he may assume if this Board adopt him'. From 1903 the scheme was to remain unaltered until it had been tested in a general election; but by 1905 both Scotland and South Wales favoured affiliation to the Labour Representation Committee, though neither followed Lancashire in joining on its own. If the Committee's advance and its ability to enforce a modest levy had already weakened Pickard's case, the election of 1906 was to destroy it.[4]

---

[1] As early as 28 Feb. 1903 the *Labour Leader* had described the Committee's Newcastle conference as 'the trades congress without the miners'.

[2] 'I should like to ask why we as a Federation should be called upon to join an Association to find money, time, or intellect to focus the weaknesses of other Trade Unionists to do what you are doing for yourselves' (Miners' Federation of Great Britain, *Annual Report*, 1899, quoted in Page Arnot, op. cit., vol. i, p. 353).   [3] Ibid., pp. 358–62.

[4] The cotton leaders had long accepted most of Pickard's arguments for 'sectional representation', and the reasons given for their change of mind are instructive. While the predominant trade should provide the candidate, 'no single branch of Labour in any constituency is numerically strong enough of itself to elect a member of Parliament. The aim of the National Committee is to combine the whole of the Labour forces. This will add strength to candidates brought out under its auspices. It will also minimise the possibility of two Labour candidates opposing each other. . . . The National Committee . . . does away with the idea of sectional representation' (*Cotton Factory Times*, 6 Feb. 1903).

Long before this, however, the second wave of affiliations in 1902 had made it clear to other Lib-Lab leaders that the Labour Representation Committee had come to stay, and the Clitheroe by-election later in the year further emphasized the point. They therefore decided that the Committee must be brought under proper control. Their plans were to counter the influence of the socialists within the organization by bringing the National Democratic League into affiliation;[1] to revive the proposal for subordinating the Committee to the Parliamentary Committee; and to bind more closely to the latter the trade union group in the House.

Within the Parliamentary Committee the preparatory moves were initiated by Davis with Wilkie's backing, and there can be little doubt that Steadman as chairman and Woods as secretary were willing allies. It was a propitious moment for the Lib-Labs to reassert themselves. Since 1900 there had been talk of the possibility of some new link between labour and the Liberals, and after Taff Vale union leaders were driven into a closer association first with the party's left wing, including Dilke and his friends, and then with some of its front bench. Now, in the early months of 1902, agreement on broader issues such as education seemed likely to strengthen the connexion still further.

During the annual conference in February, Davis attacked 'professional men, journalists and adventurers' who tried 'to creep into the movement' in terms reminiscent of the Parliamentary Committee's anti-socialist tirades in 1894–5. But the most prominent role in the campaign was played by the new chairman of the Labour Representation Committee, Bell, who launched the detailed programme in the *Railway Review* on 23 May. Declaring that 'through having three separate organisations our power and influence are far less than they ought to be', he proposed centralization as the remedy. 'The Trades Union Congress should be the main body, with a decent office in a prominent place, at which the work of the Parliamentary Committee, the [General] Federation [of Trade Unions] and the Labour Representation Committee' could be co-ordinated. The Parliamentary Committee should be increased to twenty-one members, and three subcommittees should deal with the three separate aspects of the single movement's work.

Plans were soon made to strengthen the Parliamentary Committee's links with the trade union group in the House,[2] and in July Bell and

---

[1] Founded in Oct. 1900, the League was an alliance of progressive groups with a radical programme of constitutional reform. Tom Mann was its full-time organizer until 1901, and built up a membership mainly in London and South Wales. Primarily a Lib-Lab organization, the League's vice-presidents in 1902 included Bell and Steadman, and Woods was also associated with it. The League co-operated with the London Trades Council, and had the backing of *Reynold's Newspaper*, whose editor W. M. Thompson was its founder.

[2] Trades Union Congress, *Annual Report*, 1902, Parliamentary Committee Report. See p. 372, footnote 2.

Steadman, representing their respective committees, met Dilke's Liberals and the new chairman of the National Democratic League, John Ward. 'Several Labour M.P.s were present and Labour matters were discussed', particularly the possible allocation of 'an agreed number of constituencies to Labour nominees'.[1] The next step was to approach Congress. As spokesman of its committee on labour representation,[2] Sexton moved that 'Congress, while hailing with satisfaction the vigorous efforts of individual trades on the question . . . is of the opinion that the most successful method to utilise the forces of Labour in Parliament would be by concentrated effort from an organised centre'. The Parliamentary Committee, therefore, should 'be instructed to call and take part in a conference of all bona-fide Labour organisations already actively engaged in the question . . . on the basis of common action'.

The socialist James O'Grady at once put an amendment substituting 'Labour Representation Committee' for 'Parliamentary Committee' and 'requested' for 'instructed'. When Wilkie failed to have the amendment ruled out of order, Sexton accepted it and the amended resolution was carried by 'a large majority'.[3] This was a serious set-back, but the Lib-Labs were encouraged to continue with their scheme when Congress approved part of Bell's programme by accepting a subsequent resolution which suggested that 'the various Labour bodies . . . all offsprings of previous Congresses, should have their offices in the one building'.

In February 1903, Wilkie, as fraternal delegate from the Parliamentary Committee, told the Labour Representation Committee at Newcastle that it was 'one special stream . . . of the general movement', and hoped that it would 'bear onwards to fruition their objects as Trade Unionists, as well as Labour representatives'. In order to provide the stream with a Lib-Lab tributary, Ward moved to admit 'any other organisation which is prepared to adhere to the objects of the Committee', and his seconder, W. E. Clery, made plain that 'this vote was being taken specially on the question of the affiliation of the National Democratic League'. When they were defeated by 118 votes to 48,[4] it was clear that the Lib-Labs had provoked uncommitted delegates into siding with the socialists, who now intensified their efforts to secure the Committee's independence.

Pete Curran was able to carry a resolution obliging the executive to 'abstain from identifying themselves with or promoting the interests of any section of the Liberal or Conservative parties'. Though he had to accept an amendment excluding 'officials of affiliated organisations', the

---

[1] Parliamentary Committee, *Minutes*, 8 July 1902. See also Bealey and Pelling, op. cit., pp. 135–6.   [2] See p. 374.

[3] It is not easy to understand the part played in this manœuvre by Sexton. He had been a member of the Parliamentary Committee since 1900, and his speech showed he was profoundly dissatisfied with the situation as it was. But he was also a member of the Independent Labour Party.   [4] On this occasion Sexton spoke for the socialists.

ban was then extended without further discussion to Members of Parliament and candidates. But even more important was the acceptance of the executive's proposal for a Parliamentary Fund. Based on a voluntary levy of 1*d*. a member and designed to cover 25 per cent. of the electoral expenses of approved candidates as well as a grant of £200 a year to those who were successful, the fund was essential if the Committee was to do more than endorse candidates financed by its affiliates.

The secretary of the Independent Labour Party, John Penny, had repudiated Henderson's suggestion of a 4*d*. levy as an 'extravagant proposal', which might be thought to have 'come from the Socialist benches in some way or other'. Since the fund would enable the executive both to promote candidates who were not 'merely trade representatives', and to 'have some amount of control over the members of Parliament who would be elected', the socialists were anxious not to risk its defeat by asking for too much. Once the danger was past, however, Philip Snowden forced through a resolution pressing the Committee's nominees in the House to form a 'distinct' group in accordance with the constitution.[1] And Jack Jones of the Gasworkers, speaking for West Ham Trades Council, only narrowly failed with his annual motion in favour of 'Public Ownership of the means of production, distribution, and exchange'.

In 1904 the socialists consolidated some of their gains. Since societies covering more than half the affiliated membership had sent in contributions to the Parliamentary Fund,[2] the executive detected 'a willingness . . . to regard payments to this fund as a compulsory duty'. As 'those who have subscribed would have a just ground for complaint' if the others did not follow their example, they had contributions made compulsory and retrospective. In the same spirit, Bell, who even as chairman had supported Liberals whenever he could, was found guilty of 'a breach of the provisions of the constitution safeguarding the independence of the Labour Party'. His action in congratulating the Liberal victor at the Norwich by-election, where G. H. Roberts[3] stood for the Committee, had been 'a serious departure from the principles upon which this movement is founded'.

Some delegates wanted Bell's name removed from the list of candidates until he pledged himself to uphold the constitution, but the chairman, Hodge, persuaded them that 'it was the duty of the body which paid Mr. Bell to deal with him'. If he was upheld by the Railway Servants' executive,

[1] Hardie disposed of a suggestion that other labour Members should be asked to join the group by pointing out that this might mean that the Committee's nominees would be outvoted.

[2] These included the United Textile Factory Workers' Association, the Boot and Shoe Operatives, the Engineers, and the Gasworkers, but not the Railway Servants, the Carpenters and Joiners, or the Bricklayers.

[3] Roberts, G. H., P.C. (1869–1928). National organizer, Typographical Association, 1904–6. Executive Committee, Labour Party, 1910–18. M.P., 1906–23. Lord Commissioner of Treasury, 1915–16. Parliamentary Secretary to Board of Trade, 1916–17. Minister of Labour, 1917–19. Food Controller, 1919–20. Resigned from government 1920. Joined Conservative Party 1923.

'then the L.R.C. Executive would have to act'.[1] During the debate a similar attitude was displayed by MacDonald. Revealing that, like Bell, neither Wilkie nor Isaac Mitchell had signed the constitution at all, and that Crooks, Steadman, and Ward had not signed the amended version of 1903, he added that 'each case was being dealt with . . . in order that all might be brought into line'.

Nevertheless, the socialists did not have things all their own way. The majority voting against Jones's annual motion was larger than in 1903, and the Lib-Labs showed that they, too, could amend the constitution to suit themselves. D. C. Cummings of the Boilermakers[2] proposed that power should be taken to sanction exceptions to the ban on co-operation with the Liberals and Conservatives, and that the pledge should no longer be enforced by the alternative of resignation. He was supported by Havelock Wilson, who claimed to have 'broken no pledges, because he had absolutely and emphatically refused to sign any', and by Sexton, but they were defeated by 533 to 422. Next day, however, Shackleton put the case for the second amendment alone. When he explained that the executive thought the words 'or resign' were 'a hindrance to their success and unnecessary, illogical and could not be applied', he was seconded by Hardie, and the revived amendment was carried by 'a large majority'.

This move towards mutual toleration reflected a new approach by the Lib-Lab leadership. Once the Labour Representation Committee could finance itself, there was little chance of turning it into an appendage of the Parliamentary Committee. Since their plans had failed, the Lib-Labs now decided to accept, even to support, the independence of the Labour Representation Committee, but to draw it into an alliance to pursue a series of objectives on most of which it was possible, and indeed necessary, to work also with the Liberals. With the Parliamentary Committee as senior partner, and the General Federation of Trade Unions thrown in as a makeweight, the alliance was to be based on a recognition that both committees had the right to undertake all kinds of political activity.

The new approach became evident at Congress in 1904, in the presence of the first fraternal delegates from the Labour Representation Committee, MacDonald and Henderson.[3] With the Committee in mind, it was agreed that 'any resolution to endorse or amend the constitution of an independent

[1] On the other hand, Havelock Wilson was applauded for suggesting that 'to call a man a traitor and to use other hard names would not help their cause forward'. This was all the more remarkable when it is remembered that Wilson's union had only just affiliated, and that he had fought the Labour Representation Committee ever since its foundation (Bealey and Pelling, op. cit., pp. 134, 152).

[2] Cummings had been a member of the Independent Labour Party, but his views had apparently mellowed.

[3] MacDonald's greetings were appropriate to the occasion. 'The Labour Representation Committee is neither sister nor brother to Congress, but its child. We come therefore to offer our filial respects.'

and outside body is not in order'. As chairman, Bell said that this decision embodied his own view and that 'of the majority, if not the whole, of the Parliamentary Committee'. At the same time Davis secured Congress's agreement that the Parliamentary Committee should be given authority to endorse candidates, provided they were 'in favour of the reforms that may be advocated by the Trades Union Congress', and already endorsed by a 'bona-fide Trade Union, the General Federation of Trade Unions or the Labour Representation Committee'.

Guided by Davis, Bell took the lead in the Parliamentary Committee at Congress, in the parliamentary group, and in a series of conferences between the national organizations. But a capacity for conciliation was not his most obvious accomplishment, and by 1905 he was at a disadvantage in having ceased to be a candidate approved by the Labour Representation Committee. The change of course therefore helped to bring forward Shackleton, a man of greater stature and a better conciliator, who had become chairman of the Labour Representation Committee in 1904. In his presidential address in 1905,[1] Shackleton repeatedly emphasized that 'independence does not mean isolation', and advocated co-operation not only with other labour Members but also with the two major parties whenever one of them acted in the direct interests of labour.[2]

This proposal recalled almost exactly the terms of Hardie's definitive amendment of 1900 in favour of a 'distinct Labour Group . . . which must embrace a readiness to co-operate with any party . . . promoting legislation in the direct interest of labour'. Nevertheless, Bell's resolution sanctioning alliances with other parties was heavily defeated. Now that the Committee had come to stay and its independence was assured, many delegates shared Snowden's desire for 'a party of their own', not 'a sort of influence upon other political parties'.[3] But the Labour Representation Committee was still far from being the movement's sole political arm. Its future might well depend upon a greater willingness to share the political representation of labour with the Lib-Labs of the Parliamentary Committee, whose job it was to influence 'other parties'.

Though by-election victories had added to its strength, they did not offer conclusive proof that the Labour Representation Committee had a decisive advantage in winning seats. Shackleton's unopposed return for Clitheroe certainly showed that the major parties could be outmanœuvred by speed and determination, but Henderson's success in a three-cornered contest at Barnard Castle was less remarkable. Henderson had been agent for the retiring Liberal Member, and a substantial minority of the local

[1] Following the precedent set by Congress in 1901, the Committee had replaced a local conference chairman by its own outgoing chairman.

[2] In constituencies with no labour candidates, he wanted discretion for the executive 'to take such action as the circumstances call for'.

[3] Labour Representation Committee, *Annual Conference Report*, 1905.

caucus would have been happy to see him as their official candidate. The eventual choice, Hubert Beaumont, was dominated by Sam Storey, chairman of the Northern Liberal Federation and an active opponent of the Labour Representation Committee. Moreover, he aped his master's 'favourable attitude to Protection'.[1] Similarly, Crooks's personal triumph at Woolwich had owed as much to his associates, the London Progressives, as to the Labour Representation Committee.[2]

The Committee still faced two major questions: how should it behave towards Lib-Lab candidates? and to what extent would its own candidates be opposed by the Liberals? Since 1903 MacDonald's secret negotiations with Herbert Gladstone had sought for a solution to the second problem,[3] and a move towards settling the first came in November 1904. When the Lib-Lab Thomas Richards stood for West Monmouth, the South Wales Miners' Federation was not affiliated to the Labour Representation Committee. The question of endorsement did not arise; but as Richards alleged he was not running as a Liberal, and as he was not opposed by a candidate sponsored by the Committee, the question of support did. After Richards's telegram 'stating that he was the Labour Candidate only, and that, if returned to the House of Commons, he would work with the Labour Group', the executive decided that the constitution did not preclude support, and 'several went to West Monmouth and gave assistance'.[4]

Together with the acceptance by Congress in 1904 of Davis's resolution giving the Parliamentary Committee power to endorse candidates, this decision formed the background to the Caxton Hall conference on 16 February 1905. Here representatives of the three national organizations came to an electoral agreement. Their 'concordat' laid down that candidates of the Labour Representation Committee were to receive 'the loyal and hearty support of all sections' of the movement. In return the Committee was to follow the precedent of West Monmouth and support 'all Labour and Trade Union candidates approved by the Parliamentary Committee . . . in so far as its constitution allows'—a signal recognition of its rise to independence. 'In constituencies where no Labour candidate is running', however, they were to make it clear that 'their national constitution does not require abstention on the part of electors', thus keeping the way open for arrangements with the Liberals.

The agreement was followed by plans for closer co-operation in other

[1] Bealey and Pelling, op. cit., pp. 152–4.

[2] After the election Crooks's assiduous support of the Liberals was a bitter disappointment to Hardie (ibid., pp. 191–2).   [3] See p. 385.

[4] Labour Representation Committee, *Annual Conference Report*, 1905, Report of the Executive. Richards's telegram was disingenuous. He had previously been adopted as the Liberal candidate; he received Liberal support during the election; and when he entered the House he joined the other miners (Bealey and Pelling, op. cit., p. 231).

spheres. A further meeting at the House of Commons on 5 May, which included many labour Members, decided that the three secretaries should confer regularly on all political matters, and that every effort should be made to avoid 'overlapping' between their organizations. Reverting to the old proposal that 'when practicable . . . the offices of the three organisations should be in the same building',[1] the meeting also echoed another and more important part of the Lib-Lab scheme of 1902 when it recommended 'the formation of a National Labour Advisory Board to consist of three members from each of the three National Organisations together with their Secretaries'.[2]

This time, however, the immediate impetus towards centralization came from the Labour Representation Committee. Despite pressure from MacDonald, the Parliamentary Committee decided in July to leave the proposal to the new Committee elected by Congress in September.[3] Meanwhile, the officers of the three bodies met frequently and from the start dealt with issues outside the Caxton Hall 'concordat', notably the campaign on the Unemployed Workmen Bill. In November the Joint Board was formally constituted, and held its inaugural meeting on 29 November 1905 at the Parliamentary Committee's new headquarters. Its first action was to protest at the absence of a representative of 'the organized Labour movement' from the Royal Commission on the Poor Law whose appointment was one of Balfour's last acts as Prime Minister.[4]

Thus both the socialists and the Lib-Labs had achieved considerable successes. The Labour Representation Committee had secured the affiliation of a clear majority of all trade unionists, and now enjoyed the financial and organizational independence for which the socialists had worked so assiduously. On the other hand, Lib-Labs formed the great majority of the largest labour group the House had yet seen; they had initiated and led a series of impressive campaigns in the country, in which the Labour Representation Committee had co-operated as junior partner to the Parliamentary Committee; and they had signed a reciprocal pact with the new organization on electoral arrangements. Unable to defeat one another, the two groups faced the coming election as allies.

[1] In 1903 the Parliamentary Committee's office had been moved from Buckingham Street to larger premises in Victoria Street. On 18 May 1905 the Committee decided to return to the Strand by renting still larger offices in Effingham House, Arundel Street (Parliamentary Committee, *Minutes*). This remained their headquarters until 1911.

[2] Labour Party, *Annual Conference Report*, 1906, Report of the Executive.

[3] Parliamentary Committee, *Minutes*, 27 July 1905. At Congress the project was given a cautious airing by Sexton in his address as chairman. A later resolution demanding the merger of the three organizations into 'one representative body' was defeated by 'a large majority' (Trades Union Congress, *Annual Report*, 1905).

[4] Parliamentary Committee, *Minutes*, 29 Nov. 1905. See also Roberts, op. cit., p. 191. A member of the Parliamentary Committee, Francis Chandler of the Carpenters and Joiners, was appointed to the Commission soon afterwards.

The Election of 1906

Since 1900 the Labour Representation Committee had regarded fifty candidates at the next election as its proper aim. This figure was reached by the end of 1905, and the final list included thirty-five candidates sponsored by affiliated unions as well as three other active trade unionists. Up to the beginning of 1903 endorsement was slow: only eight candidates had been formally approved, though eleven more names came before the annual conference in February. Twelve months later the total had risen to thirty-eight, and in addition there were five existing Members of Parliament.[1] Some of this rapid increase may be explained by the Committee's development into a viable organization during 1903; but it was primarily due to the widespread desire for direct representation stimulated by the Taff Vale judgement, the full effects of which were not apparent in the Committee's list until 1904.[2]

At first, arrangements between a candidate and his constituency usually preceded endorsement by the Committee, which was careful to point out that it could not 'itself promote or put forward candidates . . . its proper work is to "recognise" and assist candidates put forward by affiliated organisations who signify their acceptance of our constitution'.[3] As the Committee's authority increased, however, MacDonald and his assistant, James Middleton, accumulated a mass of information about the opportunities available. Before long affiliated societies and their nominees began to approach the Committee in the first place and came to rely on MacDonald's assistance in finding constituencies.[4]

This change of emphasis was important if the Committee was to take advantage of the electoral understanding with Liberal headquarters, and may have enabled MacDonald to help the Independent Labour Party, which provided as many as ten of the fifty candidates endorsed.[5] Central

[1] Labour Representation Committee, *Annual Conference Reports*, 1903 and 1904, Reports of the Executive.

[2] The Engineers, for example, decided to affiliate in Feb. 1902, and nominated five candidates whose names came before the Committee in Feb. 1903. They were not included in the *Annual Conference Report* as formally approved until twelve months later, two years after the Society's affiliation.

[3] Labour Representation Committee, *Annual Conference Report*, 1903, Report of the Executive.

[4] The executive first found it necessary to deny undue interference in 1904: 'we have acted only after a representative local conference of labour and socialist organisations has requested us' (Labour Representation Committee, *Annual Conference Report*, 1904, Report of the Executive). Such conferences were arranged, and action taken, either through the trades councils or local labour representation committees. There were seventy-three of the former affiliated to the Committee by the end of 1905, and two local labour representation committees had applied for membership—as they were enabled to do by the amended constitution of 1905 (ibid., 1905 and 1906).

[5] The party realized, however, that it could not afford to give the unions cause to think that it was exploiting the alliance. Five of its candidates fought the same constituency in 1906 as in 1900, and were either national leaders or prominent local men. Two others, Clynes and Summerbell,

control was further strengthened by the amendments of 1903–5, especially the establishment of the Parliamentary Fund and the continued insistence on candidates signing the party pledge. Most of the laggards, including Mitchell and Wilkie, eventually toed the line, leaving only Steadman and Ward to be excluded from the list along with the unrepentant Bell.[1]

The Parliamentary Committee apparently made no use of its power of endorsement until just before the election. The task was entrusted to its secretary, Steadman, who took the line of accepting any reputable candidate who applied.[2] Fifty-one candidates were endorsed, fifteen of whom, mostly miners, were not on the Labour Representation Committee's list, and thirty-one were successful. It is impossible, however, to deduce that these fifty-one were the 'trade union' candidates, for there were some curious anomalies. In South Wales Mabon and William Brace were endorsed, but the other Lib-Lab miners, Richards and John Williams, were not. In the North-east Thomas Burt and Charles Fenwick did not bother to apply, whereas an Independent Labour Party candidate, Thomas Summerbell, received endorsement, as did another member of the party, J. W. Taylor, secretary of the Durham Colliery Mechanics, at Chester-le-Street.

There was nothing haphazard about the electoral preparations of the Labour Representation Committee, the most important of which was the alliance concluded between MacDonald and Herbert Gladstone. In return for 'friendliness', the Liberals granted the Committee a clear run in some thirty seats, twenty-five of which were listed in the initial agreement of 1903. The story of this alliance has already been told,[3] though the means by which Gladstone persuaded his constituency associations to fall into line are not yet wholly clear. This is an important exception, for the constituencies had been the trouble in previous elections, despite goodwill towards labour at Liberal headquarters. Few concessions were made in South Wales, Yorkshire, and the North-east, where Liberalism remained strong and under the control of business men, and in Scotland none at all. Significantly, it was in Lancashire, an area of long-standing Liberal weakness, that co-operation with the Committee was most complete.

were also well known and had strong local backing. Of the remaining three, who were unsuccessful, one at least, Bruce Glasier, was a carpet-bagger, and may have been placed at Bordesley by MacDonald. But he was also editor of the *Labour Leader* and a leader of the party.

[1] Bell continued to enjoy the support of his union, but neither the Barge Builders nor the Navvies could afford to finance representatives of their own. Steadman was secretary of the Parliamentary Committee, and in addition had Liberal backing (Bealey and Pelling, op. cit., p. 252). Ward, however, was 'greatly concerned' at the omission of any mention of payment of Members from the King's Speech in 1906, for he was then 'in receipt of only 50s. a week' for all purposes (Clynes, op. cit., vol. i, p. 114).

[2] Parliamentary Committee, *Minutes*, 20 Dec. 1905. Candidates were required to give a suitable answer to the question: 'Are you in general agreement with the reforms endorsed by the Trades Union Congress?'

[3] Poirier, op. cit., chapter x; Bealey and Pelling, op. cit., chapter vi.

Liberal prospects, which were poor when the negotiations began, had greatly improved by 1905, and the difficulties of maintaining the alliance were increased by the need for secrecy. Local arrangements became clearer as the election drew near, but obstinate militants on both sides could not be brought into line by being told that they must respect a national agreement. MacDonald, for example, was horrified by a proposal that Gladstone himself should be opposed at West Leeds; but in killing it he was able to secure the help of O'Grady, the Committee's nominee in East Leeds, who argued that such a step would compel the Liberals to retaliate by opposing him. In some instances MacDonald was unsuccessful. Barrow was not on the agreed list, but Charles Duncan, secretary of the Workers' Union, insisted upon standing with the endorsement of his old union, the Engineers. Luckily for MacDonald, the Liberals accepted the situation.

In these circumstances it is not surprising that his Committee's election manifesto reproduced the demands of the Radical wing of the Liberal Party.[1] Free trade, Chinese labour, and the taxation of land values were common to both. The issue of unemployment had recently been canvassed by Campbell-Bannerman as much as by Keir Hardie. There was only an oblique reference to Taff Vale, but the Trade Disputes Bill was now virtually Liberal policy, even if some leaders had reservations.[2] Possibly there was more emphasis on social problems than was usual among Liberals. The 'aged poor' and 'underfed schoolchildren' were mentioned, as were the slums. But differences, even of emphasis, were insignificant compared with the common ground. In both parties, first place was given to the slogans of political Radicalism and the defence of traditional Liberal dogmas like free trade and Home Rule for Ireland.[3]

The programme of the Parliamentary Committee showed more concern for social problems, and was much more specific. The Committee asked all Trade Unionists and wage-earners to vote . . . only for candidates who were pledged to

The principles embodied in the Trade Disputes Bill;

The amendment of the [Workmen's] Compensation Act, so as to give compensation to all workers in every trade from the date of the accident;

The amendment of the Truck Act, to prevent stoppages of any description from wages;

The amendment of the Unemployed Act, so that employment can be found, at Trade Union rates, for those unable to obtain work;

[1] Poirier, op. cit., pp. 245–6; Bealey and Pelling, op. cit., pp. 264–5.

[2] On taking office shortly before the election, Campbell-Bannerman promised a measure 'on the general lines of the Parliamentary Committee's . . . at an early date and without unnecessary delay' (Parliamentary Committee, *Minutes*, 21 Dec. 1905). This undertaking was given wide publicity and echoed by a majority of Liberal candidates. But see p. 394 and footnote 3.

[3] Despite Redmond's alliance with the Parliamentary Committee, Irish voters in Great Britain were instructed to vote Liberal, and to vote labour only where the labour candidate was not opposing a Liberal pledged to Home Rule.

The abolition of enforced Chinese labour in South Africa;
The establishment of a State Pension Fund at 60 years of age;
An extension of the Housing of the Working Classes Act;
The Returning Officers' Fees to be a charge upon the National Exchequer;
Adult Suffrage; and
The establishment of an Eight-hour Working Day.[1]

These demands were all based on resolutions accepted by Congress in recent years, and the only omission of importance, at first sight surprising, was free trade. But there could be no doubt of the views of the great majority of trade unionists on this question, which had loomed large in the Parliamentary Committee's autumn campaign, and was the main election issue. Indeed, there was much justice in Burns's summary of the results: 'the new Labour Party' and their trade union colleagues 'were floated into Parliament on the river of free trade'. Where would they have been, he asked, 'but for free trade, education, and the Chinese labour question?' As it was, 'many of them were elected by Radical enthusiasm, Liberal votes, and trade union funds'.[2]

These results must be compared with the situation at the dissolution when there were fifteen labour Members—the seven miners together with Broadhurst, Burns, Cremer, Bell, Hardie, Shackleton, Henderson, and Crooks. Though they had usually formed a 'trade union group', only ten of the fifteen ranked as trade union representatives in the narrower sense. Hardie never had been, while Broadhurst, Burns, and Cremer were no longer. Crooks's only connexion was his membership of a coopers' union. Finally, now that Bell had refused to sign the pledge, only four of the fifteen were endorsed by the Labour Representation Committee.

Twenty-nine of the Committee's candidates were successful in the election of 1906. Twenty-one of them, including two miners, were also trade union nominees, and seven were sponsored only by the Independent Labour Party. But one of the latter, J. R. Clynes, was a full-time officer of the Gasworkers, who after the election received a grant from the union towards his political expenses in addition to his union salary. It is probably best, therefore, to classify him as a trade union Member. The twenty-ninth Member was Crooks. In addition Taylor accepted the whip immediately the session had begun. Thus the new House contained thirty Labour Representation Committee Members, twenty-three of them also active trade unionists.

The total of trade union Members is forty if Clynes is included. Sixteen were miners, and of the remaining twenty-four, three came from the

[1] Trades Union Congress, *Annual Report*, 1906, Parliamentary Committee Report.

[2] *The Times*, 10 Dec. 1907. We owe this quotation to Dr. A. K. Russell. Burns was addressing the Leeds Liberal Federation. At the meeting the other main speaker was Herbert Gladstone, whose private opinion coincided with that publicly expressed by Burns (Bealey and Pelling, op. cit., p. 280).

printing unions, three from the Railway Servants, and two each from the Engineers, the Steel Smelters, the Shipwrights, the cotton unions, and the Gasworkers. Eight other unions had a single Member. After Taylor had accepted the whip, thirteen of the miners' Members were outside the Labour Representation Committee, and four from other unions—Bell, Steadman, Ward, and Havelock Wilson.[1] This leaves three doubtfuls: Broadhurst, Burns, and Cremer. Burns, however, entered the Cabinet; Broadhurst retired a few weeks after the election; Cremer had ceased to pay close attention to labour questions and died in 1908. It therefore seems reasonable to neglect them.

Thus in 1906 there were thirty Labour Representation Committee Members, twenty-three of them also trade union Members. In addition there were seventeen other trade union Members, thirteen of them miners. In all forty-seven Members had a clear organizational link with the labour movement.

Parliamentary Work, 1906–10

On 12 February 1906, three days before the annual conference accepted the executive's recommendation that 'in future the title "The Labour Party" should be adopted instead of "The Labour Representation Committee" ', the Parliamentary Labour Party held its first meeting. Many of its thirty members had socialist affiliations, and when Hardie insisted upon standing for chairman he was elected by a majority of one over Shackleton, who was appointed vice-chairman.[2] Macdonald became secretary of the parliamentary party as well as the party in the country, and Henderson chief whip. Though it was repeated unanimously in 1907, Hardie's election was primarily a sentimental gesture. As might have been expected, he was 'not a success as chairman', and the 'humdrum everyday work' in the House fell to Henderson, whose patient service paved the way for his succession to Hardie in 1908. For the next two years, with Roberts as chief whip, Henderson 'without being brilliant . . . discharged his difficult task with efficiency' before handing over to his vice-chairman, Barnes, in 1910.[3]

---

[1] The number would be increased to five if the president of the Agricultural Workers, George Nichols, were included; and the total of trade union Members would then become forty-one. Nichols, however, was a politician rather than a genuine trade unionist. Similarly, Fred Maddison and Clem Edwards no longer had any direct trade union connexions. The Conservative Sir Fortescue Flannery, a member of the Engineers and endorsed by its executive, had lost his seat at Cardiff in 1906 (Bealey and Pelling, op. cit., pp. 274–5).

[2] Ibid., pp. 278–9. In Apr. 1906 Hardie claimed that eighteen of the Parliamentary Labour Party were also members of the Independent Labour Party, but gave no names (Independent Labour Party, *Annual Conference Report*, 1906).

[3] Snowden, op. cit., vol. i, pp. 125–6, 175–6. Snowden's is the best account of the organization of the parliamentary party by one of its members, and is confirmed by the less comprehensive commentary in Elton, op. cit., chapter vi, and Clynes, op. cit., vol. i. Much of the relevant information is assembled in Robert McKenzie, *British Political Parties*, 1955, chapters vi and vii.

In the event, some of the trade union Members paid tribute to Hardie's record; but it had been generally assumed that they would make Shackleton first chairman of the parliamentary party. Already a respected figure in the House, Shackleton stood out among the trade unionists of 1906, who 'felt that the selection of a purely trade union member was justified by the numerical strength of the trade unions in the party, and . . . would prevent any suspicion . . . that the Socialist section was using the movement for its own purposes'.[1] When Hardie fell ill early in 1907 Shackleton took over, much to his colleagues' satisfaction. Of the two members of the Independent Labour Party who might have competed with him, Snowden was a lone wolf who concentrated upon fiscal questions in the House, while MacDonald had still to acquire a parliamentary reputation in keeping with his standing in the movement. Besides, both agreed that it would be 'a little awkward at present to put a "mere" Socialist in the chair because it might hinder the process of consolidation'.[2]

Shackleton's refusal to accept nomination as chairman in 1908 was therefore a major embarrassment. Henderson was the best available substitute, acceptable both to the trade unionists and to those of the Independent Labour Party who believed it 'better to give an old gang leader a chance after Hardie and get a Socialist in two years from now (if we could)'.[3] Shackleton had been angered by criticism of his leadership during 1907 by the *Labour Leader*,[4] and confirmed in his refusal by the passage of a resolution early in 1908 that tried to make socialism 'a definite object' of the Labour Party, which he denounced as 'breaking away from the federal understanding'.[5] But with Henderson, his old assistant, as chairman, with the leaders of the Independent Labour Party anxious to preserve the alliance, and with his standing in the House and among trade unionists secure, Shackleton could wield great power. Before and after 1908 he usually took the lead on important issues, both in Parliament and outside, and was always in charge of any direct dealings with the Liberal government.

[1] Snowden, 24 Feb. 1906, quoted by Bealey and Pelling, op. cit., p. 278.
[2] MacDonald to Glasier, late in 1907, quoted by Elton, op. cit., pp. 159–61. From 1906 to 1909 MacDonald was chairman of the Independent Labour Party as well as secretary of both the Labour Party and the Parliamentary Labour Party. [3] Elton, loc. cit.
[4] Ibid. The reference is probably to the *Labour Leader* of 6 Sept. 1907. In a review of the session, Shackleton's leadership was given much praise, and compared favourably with Hardie's. However, the final comment was that 'if he failed . . . to show the highest qualities of leadership, that is because no man who is not a Socialist can be an ideal leader for a party which in the main consists of Socialists'.
[5] Labour Party, *Annual Conference Report*, 1908. The resolution was not treated as a formal amendment to the constitution, and the party's 'object' continued to be 'to secure the election of Candidates' to parliament and to 'organise and maintain a Parliamentary Labour Party, with its own whips and policy'. Early at the same conference, indeed, an amendment to the constitution in similar terms was overwhelmingly rejected with the support of the Independent Labour Party leaders.

The ascendancy of Shackleton probably contributed to a more informal organization of the parliamentary party after 1908. Originally it had been decided that during the session the officers should meet daily and the whole party once a week, 'to discuss plans of campaign, select speakers for Parliamentary debates and set up committees to deal with outstanding questions'.[1] During 1906 and 1907 an elaborate system of standing and special committees was employed, and their doings were carefully reported to the annual conference. In 1908, however, Henderson merely referred to 'much unseen work' accomplished by these committees, and thereafter they cease to be mentioned. Similarly, attendance at the House was excellent in 1906, but during the following year it began to fall away, causing a good deal of anxiety to the whips. Part of the decline was certainly due to the pressure of 'Trade Union duties . . . always a weak spot in the Labour Party' as the enthusiasm of the first year waned. Thereafter the leaders concentrated on turning out the vote on big occasions only, and here they were usually successful. At other times erratic attendance was accepted as normal.[2]

In 1906 there had been much feeling that the parliamentary party should be firmly disciplined by majority rule. The problem arose not over socialism, as some trade unionists had predicted, but on education. Both the Labour Party and Congress were committed to secular education, but inevitably some of their members took a different line, especially the Catholics, whose chief spokesman, Sexton, insisted that education 'was not a matter for the Labour Party at all' since it would 'produce internecine strife'. Thorne, on the other hand, said that 'there was going to be a tightening up of the Party claims, and the man in the minority who would not stand by the views of the majority should have his "screw" stopped'.[3]

Though the party's constitution provided that Members must 'agree to abide by the decisions of the Parliamentary Party in carrying out the aims of this Constitution', the latter met the immediate difficulty facing several representatives of Lancashire constituencies by a conscience clause which permitted its members to abstain, or even to vote against the majority.[4] This was hardly a final solution and the problem remained, as the growth of indiscipline in and after 1910 was to demonstrate. Meanwhile, once education disappeared from the parliamentary agenda during 1907, the new ruling matched the lenient attitude of the party's leaders in the House.

[1] Clynes, op. cit., vol. i, pp. 111–12.

[2] Snowden, op. cit., vol. i, pp. 161–2 and *passim*. Clynes, when first elected, discovered that 'in common with a number of other new Labour members, I now found my Trade Union work rather a handicap' (op. cit., vol. i, p. 112).

[3] Labour Party, *Annual Conference Report*, 1907. Sexton's position was explained later in the same year: 'the union he represented was composed of men of deep religious feeling, who subscribed to the Parliamentary fund, but would not subscribe to a fund for the abolishing of religious teaching from the day schools' (Trades Union Congress, *Annual Report*, 1907).

[4] Snowden, op. cit., vol. i, pp. 134–5 and *passim*.

The trade union group, or 'Trade Union Labour Party' as it originally aspired to be called, was never tightly organized. Its members apparently resisted an attempt early in 1906 to establish a formal 'Labour Party within the Liberal Party',[1] and it remained a loose association of Lib-Labs, of whom there were initially twenty-one. Thirteen of the seventeen active trade unionists were miners, who thus dominated the group numerically. Enoch Edwards was elected chairman, with Bell as vice-chairman, and Fenwick acted as secretary until 1908, when he was succeeded by Ward. In general, the older miners played little part and the lead was taken by officials of the Federation, notably Edwards and Brace, along with Ward. Despite his office, Bell took little interest in the group and sometimes struck out on his own, even on railway questions.[2] Wilson and Steadman held aloof, while the membership of Cremer and Nichols was purely honorary. Two of the most prominent members, notorious for their anti-socialist activities, now had no trade union connexions at all—Fred Maddison and Henry Vivian, the champion of co-partnership.

In spite of its two trouble-makers, the group's relations with the Parliamentary Labour Party were friendly from the start.[3] This was not because of any formal connexion in the House, for an attempt to create one soon revealed a divergence. In 1906 Sexton carried a resolution at Congress which reverted to Bell's old suggestion that the three national organizations should be concentrated in one building, and proposed that the two parliamentary groups should confer to secure 'perfect political unity of action . . . on strict independent lines'. It was agreed that the two groups should meet once a month, with special meetings at the request of either. When the trade union group demanded, however, that the meetings should be attended only by '*bona fide* members of a Trade Union', the Labour Party replied that 'our Socialist colleagues . . . were members of our party by virtue of' Congress's decision in 1899 to promote the formation of such a party, and complained that Maddison and Vivian had been allowed to attend despite their opposition to candidates approved by both the party and Congress.[4]

On the initiative of the Parliamentary Committee negotiations were resumed, and in June 1908 agreement was reached on the basis of a new condition: that the members of both groups should 'in no way oppose sitting members of the Labour Party or Trade Union Group or candidates endorsed by the Parliamentary Committee . . . and . . . the Labour Party'— though a minority of the trade union group would have liked to persist in

[1] Humphrey, op. cit., p. 169.   [2] Gupta, op. cit.

[3] Questions of status arose, however. Fenwick and Brace opposed the claim of Hardie and Shackleton that the Labour Party should be represented on all important committees of the House, especially those 'directly affecting the working class' (*Hansard*, 8 May 1906, cols. 1275–81).

[4] Trades Union Congress, *Annual Report*, 1907, Parliamentary Committee Report.

the group's claim to be a third endorsing body.[1] Just before the terms were agreed, however, the miners had voted to join the Labour Party, a decision which, when it was implemented six months later, reduced the trade union group to an almost negligible rump.[2]

In practice the work of the two groups was already co-ordinated by other means. Of the Parliamentary Committee elected in 1905, Bell and Shackleton were also Members of Parliament, and after the election they were joined in the House by A. H. Gill of the Spinners, Wilkie, James Haslam of the Derbyshire Miners, and Thorne, as well as the secretary, Steadman. Thus three of the Committee's thirteen members, Bell, Steadman, and Haslam were in the trade union group and five in the Labour Party, with little difference of outlook between them. United on questions directly affecting the unions, all were Lib-Labs in spirit.

Though Thorne was still a member of the Social Democratic Federation, he was no doctrinal purist and found little difficulty in working with his colleagues on the Parliamentary Committee both before and after he entered the House. Similarly, when Barnes, a member of the Independent Labour Party, joined the Committee in 1906, bringing its parliamentary representation up to nine out of thirteen members (including the secretary),[3] he was able to agree with the others on most issues. Service as secretary of one of the major unions had mellowed his socialist convictions, as his behaviour in the Parliamentary Labour Party was to demonstrate.[4]

The lead which the Parliamentary Committee was thus able to give to both groups was further emphasized by the position of Shackleton. Besides being vice-chairman of the parliamentary party for the sessions of 1906 and 1907, and acting-chairman in Hardie's absence, he was elected chairman of the Parliamentary Committee for two successive terms from 1907 to 1909, a most exceptional honour.[5] During the following year he

---

[1] Trades Union Congress, *Annual Report*, 1908, Parliamentary Committee Report.

[2] By 1908 the group included fifteen miners among its twenty-three members. According to one account, there were sixteen votes for the agreement, while Maddison and Vivian formed the vociferous core of the minority (*Labour Leader*, 19 June 1908). Except for Burt, Fenwick, and John Wilson, all the miners accepted the Labour Party whip early in 1909. Steadman—when his salary was increased from £250 to £300 by Congress—had exclaimed that he was 'just as keen and enthusiastic a supporter of the Labour Party . . . as any man in that party' (Trades Union Congress, *Annual Report*, 1907). The same Congress bound all future secretaries to become members of the Labour Party when candidates for Parliament. Steadman, however, never applied for the whip.

[3] In 1907 the nine Members of Parliament were re-elected to the Parliamentary Committee, but its numbers had now been increased to seventeen including the secretary.

[4] He had already argued that 'the Socialists were a danger in that they were inexperienced in Trade Union construction and in the internal management of Trade Union affairs' (Trades Union Congress, *Annual Report*, 1905).

[5] The last case was that of J. D. Prior in 1876–7. At the height of Bell's influence the possibility of renewing his chairmanship had been considered but rejected as 'a bad precedent' (Parliamentary Committee, *Minutes*, 10 Sept. 1904).

continued to direct the work of the Committee as vice-chairman under the nominal authority of Haslam, just as he continued to exert great influence on the parliamentary party during Henderson's leadership.

Shackleton's personal ascendancy had been confirmed by his successful conduct of the Trade Disputes Bill, which throughout 1906 occupied the centre of the stage for all trade unionists. Before the election Campbell-Bannerman had met the Parliamentary Committee and promised an early measure on 'the general lines' of the Committee's own Bill.[1] Afterwards, however, the continuing doubts of the lawyers in the Cabinet were strengthened by the long-delayed Report of the Royal Commission.[2] The Majority Report, signed by Dunedin, Cohen, and Webb, declared that the Taff Vale judgement 'involved no new principle and was not inconsistent with the legislation of 1871'. It recommended further legislation which would expressly legalize strikes, and the act of persuading to strike, unless this involved inducing men to break their contracts. No individual should be held liable for any act merely on the ground that it constituted an interference with another person's trade, business or employment, and the unions should be protected against actions for civil conspiracy in trade disputes.

On picketing, the clauses on violence and intimidation and watching and besetting were to be replaced by a prohibition of acts which caused 'a reasonable apprehension in the mind of any person that violence will be used to him or his family, or damage be done to his property'. Unions were not to be freed from liability for wrongful acts, but it should be made possible for the 'central authorities of a union [to] protect themselves against the unauthorised and immediately disavowed acts of branch agents'. Benefit funds were to be separated from trade funds and made immune from liability. Finally, the unions should be allowed to enter into legally enforceable agreements both with employers and with their members.[3]

Fortified with the arguments of the Commission, Haldane and Asquith, supported by the law officers, Sir John Walton and Sir William Robson, argued that clause 3 of the Committee's Bill giving complete immunity from actions for damages was a legal monstrosity. Rumours of dissension within the Cabinet soon reached the Parliamentary Committee, who

[1] See pp. 322, 368.
[2] The publication of the Report had been delayed not only by the Balfour government but also, apparently, by the Liberals, in case it might 'prove inconvenient' during the election (Poirier, op. cit., pp. 246–7).
[3] *Report of the Royal Commission on Trade Disputes and Trade Combinations*, Cd. 2825, 1906. Webb added a rider in favour of compulsory arbitration in the belief that industrial conflict of the old type was outmoded. He later described the Commission as 'a fiasco', but regarded the Act of 1906 as ' a too sweeping legalisation which led, in after years, to an inconvenient reaction' (Beatrice Webb, op. cit., p. 267, footnote). The minority of Lewis and Lushington regarded their colleagues as over-generous to the unions.

decided to accept no compromise and to proceed with their own Bill 'in exactly the same shape as it was before'.[1] They began to whip up support generally, but especially within the Liberal Party, many of whose members had given pledges during the election. Appropriately enough, it was Walter Hudson of the Railway Servants who reintroduced the Bill on 22 February.

On 28 March Sir John Walton brought in the government's measure which adopted Asquith's approach of 1905 and proposed 'so to define the law of agency . . . that no act can be made the foundation of a claim for redress from union funds unless it is perfectly clear that that act was authorised by the governing body of the union'. He attacked the trade union proposal for immunity as 'class privileges. . . . Do not let us create a privilege for the proletariat and give a sort of benefit of clergy to trade unions.'[2] For the moment, Shackleton contented himself with asserting that candidates had not been asked 'whether they were in favour of a Bill to deal with this subject, but . . . whether they were in favour of the Bill introduced by himself and others. So far as they could ascertain, an overwhelming majority had supported them at the general election.'[3]

The following evening forty-four Members drawn from both groups met the Parliamentary Committee at the House to consider tactics. 'In consequence of the unsatisfactory nature of the Government Bill', they decided to go ahead with their own and Shackleton was deputed to see Campbell-Bannerman, from whom he managed to obtain an assurance 'to support our Bill when brought forward for discussion'.[4] As a result, the Bill received its second reading the next day by 416 votes to 66. Hardie displayed a photograph of one of Walton's election posters carrying an explicit pledge to support the Committee's Bill, and shortly afterwards the Prime Minister intervened to advise the House to pass the second reading, insisting that 'on the third point there is a difference—not a difference of object, but of method' which could be disposed of in committee. Meanwhile, the principle of the Bill would be embodied in the government's own measure.[5]

On 24 April the amended Bill was submitted by Walton's deputy, Robson, who conceded that the government could hardly proceed 'without first considering or consulting' the opinions of the trade unions.[6]

---

[1] The decision was publicized at once. The Committee also agreed that 'immediate steps should be taken with the object of securing unity of action between all Labour M.P.'s' (Parliamentary Committee, *Minutes*, 1 Feb. 1906).

[2] *Hansard*, 28 Mar. 1906, cols. 1304, 1307.

[3] Ibid., col. 1312. In fact only some 60 per cent. of Liberal candidates appear to have given pledges, not all of them in favour of the Committee's Bill, and the proportion among Conservatives was considerably lower (A. K. Russell, *The General Election of 1906*, D.Phil. thesis, Oxford, 1962).   [4] Parliamentary Committee, *Minutes*, 29 Mar. 1906.

[5] *Hansard*, 30 Mar. 1906, cols. 48, 53–54.

[6] Ibid., 25 Apr. 1906, col. 1495. Like Walton, Robson may have been embarrassed by his

Thereafter, the vote against the Bill rarely approached fifty and only twice exceeded this figure during its concluding stages. The struggle was not yet over, however. At the head of the united groups in the House, Shackleton had to conduct a lengthy and watchful campaign in close touch with Edmond Browne, and with Dilke and Clem Edwards, the best informed of their Liberal sympathizers.[1] During the committee stage in July and August Shackleton himself concentrated on the vital immunity clause, leaving picketing, conspiracy, and inducement to breach of contract largely to Dilke. The government still wanted to include several qualifications but these were left over to the report stage for final settlement.

Between 22 and 24 October further meetings of Members from both groups with the Parliamentary Committee, the Labour Party, and the General Federation appointed a subcommittee under Shackleton to arrange the final details with Walton. Eventually minor modifications in the picketing clause were traded for satisfactory concessions on immunity.[2] The Conservatives had throughout shown little anxiety to oppose the measure, and Balfour did not force a division on the third reading. The Employers' Parliamentary Council attempted to strike a last blow for 'the interests of trade and the freedom of labour' by persuading receptive peers to amend the Bill;[3] but the Lords' amendments were swiftly and firmly rejected, and the measure received the royal assent on 20 December. The previous evening the Parliamentary Committee, the Labour Party, and the General Federation of Trade Unions had given Shackleton a 'complimentary banquet' in recognition of his 'tact, judgement, and ability' in promoting the Act.[4]

The only other important measure of 1906 was the Workmen's Compensation Act, the second of Campbell-Bannerman's two 'sops to Labour'. For years the shortcomings of Chamberlain's Act of 1897 had been debated by the unions, and Congress had evolved detailed proposals to close a number of loopholes in administrative procedure, to improve scales of compensation, and to extend the coverage to all workers.[5] In 1906 Herbert Gladstone as Home Secretary seems to have surprised the labour Members by bringing in a government Bill very much on the lines of the Congress proposals.[6] Under the 1897 Act the only workers covered were

---

past, for when consulted on the bill of 1904 he had pronounced it 'excellent' (Parliamentary Committee, *Minutes*, 18 Feb. 1904).

[1] Dilke and Edwards were first called into conference as early as May (Parliamentary Committee, *Minutes*, 16 May 1906).

[2] Parliamentary Committee, *Minutes*, 22 and 24 Oct., 21 Nov. 1906. The whole development of the measure is summarized at length in the Parliamentary Committee's Reports to Congress in 1906 and 1907.

[3] Trades Union Congress, *Annual Report*, 1907, Parliamentary Committee Report.

[4] Ibid.   [5] Trades Union Congress, *Annual Report*, 1903.

[6] Even socialists were impressed: the bill was 'about as bold a one as a British capitalist administration could be expected to bring forth' (*Labour Leader*, 30 Mar. 1906).

those expressly included; now only those expressly excluded were not covered. Barnes, the spokesman of the parliamentary party on this issue, could only welcome the bill and suggest minor changes.[1] The one significant concession secured by the unions was a consultative committee to advise the minister on the schedule of industrial diseases recognized as warranting compensation. As a result the schedule was radically enlarged in 1907. On the other hand, the government was not yet prepared to insist upon compulsory state insurance, though it was ready to institute departmental inquiries into the problem. These were to have far-reaching consequences.

In addition to these major measures, 1906 saw the Liberals accept a permissive Act enabling local authorities to provide school meals, and allow O'Grady's amendment to the Aliens Act prohibiting the importation of aliens 'during times of labour disputes' to pass the Commons without opposition, though it was rejected by the Lords—'a deliberate insult to the industrial classes'.[2] Burns, as President of the Local Government Board, was responsible for dealing with unemployment, and current prosperity made it easy for both groups to give him a fair start. They welcomed the Treasury grant of £200,000 to the Distress Committees, MacDonald promising 'the wholehearted assistance of the Labour Members'. He added, however, that they hoped to see 'a new organization' to deal with unemployment before the Royal Commission on the Poor Law published its report,[3] whereas Burns had insisted that the report must precede action both on unemployment and on old-age pensions.[4] Similarly, the response of the Parliamentary Committee was friendly but reserved. 'We frankly admit that this sum is totally inadequate from the point of view of the magnitude of the problem, but we must not forget that this is the first time a Government has realised its responsibility towards the unemployed problem by a grant from national funds.'[5]

If 1906 was both productive and promising, 1907 gave 'grave dissatisfaction to the Labour Party' in and out of parliament.[6] The Independent Labour Party took the lead on unemployment. For the government Burns merely repeated that the annual grant must suffice for the 'two or three

[1] *Hansard*, 20 Feb. 1906, cols. 259–65.
[2] Trades Union Congress, *Annual Report*, 1906, Parliamentary Committee Report.
[3] *Hansard*, 19 July 1906, col. 433.
[4] Ibid., 26 Feb. 1906, col. 894; 14 Mar. 1906, cols. 1356–7.
[5] Trades Union Congress, *Annual Report*, 1906, Parliamentary Committee Report.
[6] Snowden, op. cit., vol. i, p. 159. The 'relative success' of the Labour Party in 1906 earned the recognition of the socialists (*Labour Leader*, 28 Dec. 1906), and they realized one important reason for this. Campbell-Bannerman had 'displayed an honourable . . . regard for the obligations of his party towards Labour measures and . . . held his reactionary followers in rein'. Parliament, therefore, had 'shown a more favourable, or at least a more amenable, mood towards Labour and social reform than was generally expected'. By contrast, 1907 was 'a wasted session' (ibid., 30 Aug. 1907).

years until the Commission had reported'. The issue was 'one of the most delicate, difficult and serious with which we have to deal', directly affecting half the departments.[1] Asquith stressed that whatever was done about old-age pensions could only be financed 'by economies in other branches of public expenditure' or by 'considerable readjustment both of the methods and of the objects of our taxation'.[2] He showed no sign of accelerating his own gradual fiscal reforms, though he undertook to find the means for an unspecified scheme for old-age pensions to be considered twelve months later.

In July MacDonald introduced for the first time the Labour Party's solution to the unemployment problem: the 'right to work' bill.[3] Based on the inquiries of the Joint Board, and supported by the trade union group, this proposed to make it the duty of the local authorities to compile registers of the unemployed and to 'prepare schemes for providing work' or, failing work, 'maintenance should necessity exist for the necessaries of life'. A new national committee would itself initiate schemes, and would 'co-ordinate the work of local authorities and advise the Local Government Board'. The cost was to fall mainly on the rates, supplemented 'when there was . . . exceptional distress' by a government grant; and the rights and interests of the unions were to be carefully safeguarded.

This far-reaching extension of the Act of 1905, introducing 'the double principle of the right to live and the right to work',[4] did not reach a second reading; and the rest of the session was barren except for some minor amendments to the Factory Acts. Apart from routine lobbying,[5] much of the time and energy of the Parliamentary Committee and the labour Members was taken up by a series of select and departmental committees to which the government had referred almost all the other issues dear to labour, thus following the precedent which it had established by postponing action on unemployment until the Royal Commission reported. A select committee was appointed on Post Office wages, and departmental committees inquired into evasions of the fair wages clause and 'the probable economic effects of a limit of eight hours to the working day of coal miners'. A third departmental committee looked into the operation of the Truck Acts, while a select committee on home work was set up in 1907.

These last two committees were both concerned with 'sweating', which was more a preoccupation of radicals and philanthropists than of the trade

---

[1] *Hansard*, 20 Feb. 1907, col. 960. The mildness of the labour reaction led the Conservative Walter Long to wonder how he would have been treated had he made such a speech when President of the Local Government Board (ibid., cols. 962–3).

[2] Ibid., 13 Feb. 1907, col. 224.

[3] Ibid., 9 July 1907, cols. 1446–8. Its parliamentary title was 'The Unemployed Workmen Bill'. [4] Halévy, op. cit., vol. vi, p. 256.

[5] Relations between the unions and the administration at the departmental level had already improved considerably, especially with Haldane at the War Office, Tweedmouth at the Admiralty, and Buxton at the Post Office.

unions. A desultory campaign of many years standing was enlivened in 1906 by a Sweated Industries Exhibition organized by the *Daily News*. The philanthropists won the support of all the national labour organizations as well as many individual unions and trades councils for a National Anti-Sweating League, though they feared that their campaign might be prejudiced by the attempt of trade unionists to use the agitation as a lever to eliminate all forms of outwork.[1] For some years Dilke had been proposing a bill to secure joint boards with statutory wage-fixing powers. In April 1907 the bill was introduced by Henderson, followed by the appointment of the Select Committee on Home Work.[2]

The first of the committee reports was a big disappointment. Though Buxton had readily agreed to receive representations from the officers of the postal unions, whether or not they were postal employees, the Select Committee on Post Office Servants (or Hobhouse Committee) gave little satisfaction. It recommended increases for most grades, but they were tiny compared with those claimed by the unions, to whom the figures came as a shock. Buxton, however, took the view that both he and the Post Office staff had intended 'to accept the Committee's findings whatever those findings might be'. The committee had shown where the standards of the Post Office 'fell short of the standard of a good employer . . .'. He could not withhold improvements 'recommended by the . . . Committee for attaining that object'. Equally he could not 'retry the case', and go beyond the committee's recommendations.[3]

In 1908, as other committee reports became available, the legislative pace began to quicken once more, producing some return for much patient work by the unions and their representatives. The committee on the miners' eight-hour day havered over the crucial question of costs. There would be offsetting factors but its enforcement must lead to 'a temporary contraction in output' and a consequent loss to the country 'whose gravity would be determined by the extent to which the parties would co-operate to minimise its effects'.[4]

The committee's main contribution was to show the hours currently worked, though its findings would have been even more valuable had there not been confusion over the phrase 'bank to bank'. To most witnesses it meant the time between winding the first cage down the shaft and when the last cage reached the surface at the end of the shift. The committee, however, interpreted it as the time between winding the first cage down and the first cage up. On this basis they discovered that underground

[1] National Anti-Sweating League, *Report of a Conference on a Minimum Wage*, 1907; Trades Union Congress, *Annual Report*, 1907, Parliamentary Committee Report.
[2] Labour Party, *Annual Conference Report*, 1908, Parliamentary Report.
[3] *Hansard*, 20 Feb. 1908, cols. 1059–60.
[4] *Departmental Committee on the Probable Economic Effects of a Limit of Eight Hours to the Working Day of Coal Miners, Final Report, Part 1*, Cd. 3505, 1907, p. 36.

workers in general averaged nine hours and three minutes, but with substantial variations between different categories of workers and between regions.

These variations explain not only the long-standing opposition of the North-east to a statutory eight-hour day[1] but also the tactics of Lancashire, which were to affect the form of the 1908 Act. Over the years uneasiness had been growing among Lancashire miners—who worked the longest underground shift of nearly ten hours—that to reduce hours to eight at one stroke would result in a sharp fall in piece-work earnings. Yet Lancashire was only the extreme case, and in most other coalfields there were groups of faceworkers who, fearing that an eight-hour day would bring a substantial decline in earnings, were not enthusiastic for its immediate introduction.

By 1906 the Federation had decided, against the opposition of Yorkshire and Scotland, to base its Bill on the principle of introducing the eight hours gradually in order to give the industry time for adjustment. The Bill as amended proposed to spread the adjustment over a period of four years, and this precedent was followed by Herbert Gladstone in the government's bill, which was tabled late in 1907 and provided for eight hours, exclusive of one winding time, to be introduced over three years. Subsequently, under pressures and counter-pressures from the Mining Association, other commercial and industrial interests,[2] and the Federation, he substituted eight hours excluding *both* winding times, for an intermediate period of five years, to be followed by eight hours excluding one winding time.

The House of Lords cut out the second part of these proposals, so that the final version became an eight-hour day permanently excluding both winding times. With much grumbling from Scotland and Yorkshire, the Federation, with Durham and Northumberland now in the fold, accepted this as the best that they could get. Outside Lancashire and South Wales it meant relatively little to many of the hewers, whose current national average was eight hours and thirty-six minutes including one winding time. 'What the Act . . . calls an eight-hours day is, in fact, on an average nearly a nine-hours day, and in not a few cases appreciably more than a ten-hours day.'[3]

In January 1907 the Parliamentary Committee, conscious that many

---

[1] This opposition continued to embarrass the Federation's political campaign and goaded Pickard into suggesting a direct attack on the North-east unions by sending in a Federation organizer 'with a hard face and . . . a heart strong enough for anything' to capture their members (Miners' Federation, *Annual Conference*, Oct. 1902). Nobody followed this lead.

In 1902 their long series of failures with the Eight Hours Bill turned their minds once more to negotiations with the owners. They were met with a flat refusal but even so they shied away from proposals for a strike.

[2] A Coal Consumers' Defence League, formed in 1907, comprised shipping interests, railway companies, gas companies, and large corporations of every kind.

[3] *First Report of the Royal Commission on the Coal Industry*, Cmd. 359, 1919, p. xv.

Members of Parliament 'had definitely pledged themselves to support a pension scheme', and encouraged by their recent success over the Trade Disputes Act, had launched a campaign to induce the government to honour its own half-promises. Barnes acted as spokesman in the House, and later moved the resolution at Congress which reiterated the demand for pensions 'of not less than 5*s*. per week to *all* persons 'of 60 years of age and upwards'.[1] During the following winter the Committee and the party organized a national agitation, and Asquith decided he could anticipate the findings of the Royal Commission on the Poor Law sufficiently to provide for old-age pensions in his 1908 budget. On 7 May he outlined the scheme which was pushed through during June and July by Lloyd George, his successor as Chancellor of the Exchequer.

When Asquith had taken Campbell-Bannerman's place as Prime Minister in April, the change was 'viewed with some disquietude by the Labour Party'.[2] His behaviour since 1906 had done little to remove the widespread impression that, though he had some sympathy for working-class demands, he was slow and ungenerous in making concessions. His pensions scheme matched this reputation only too closely. Pensions at the rate of 5*s*. a week were not to start until the age of seventy, and then only for those with incomes of less than 10*s*. Even Henry Chaplin's select committee in 1899 had recommended 5*s*. at sixty-five, and no one had yet suggested that pensions should be paid merely to those who had lived out their three score years and ten in penury. In addition, payment was to start only in 1909 and the budget made no provision to cover the cost beyond the current financial year. The Parliamentary Committee had to take what comfort they could from the reflection that 'although far from satisfactory, the measure is at least the most important attempt to grapple with the problem of old age that has hitherto been made', and determined to seek 'the earliest opportunity to amend the Bill'.[3]

Unemployment was rising sharply by the beginning of 1908, and Henderson led an attack on Burns's policy during the debate on the King's speech. After a special joint conference of the national organizations, the 'right to work' bill was reintroduced in March, and MacDonald stressed that it was a product of the Joint Board, backed by all the forces of labour.[4] Though Burns, helped by Maddison and Vivian, counter-

[1] Trades Union Congress, *Annual Report*, 1907.

[2] Snowden, op. cit., vol. i, p. 177. On the formation of Campbell-Bannerman's government, Hardie had called Asquith and Haldane 'cold-blooded reactionaries of the most dangerous type' (*Labour Leader*, 22 Dec. 1905). By 1908, however, Snowden held that Asquith might 'go far in the way of social reform . . . if he were sure of success in his attempts' (op. cit., pp. 178–9).

[3] Trades Union Congress, *Annual Report*, 1908, Parliamentary Committee Report.

[4] *Hansard*, 13 Mar. 1908, cols. 19–20. Victor Grayson, fresh from his by-election victory at Colne Valley, attacked the bill as insufficient. It would not touch 'the present chaotic disorganisation of their system of industry' (ibid., col. 63). His later conduct on the issue led to his suspension from the House in October.

attacked vigorously,[1] the bill secured 116 votes at its second reading. In October Asquith promised legislation for the next session, and meanwhile increased the grant available for the Distress Committees to £400,000. Keir Hardie insisted that this would be 'quite inadequate to meet the pressing demands of the unemployed this winter', and MacDonald launched a damning indictment of the Local Government Board and its President. 'The cause and origin of all their complaints was the slowness, the want of sympathy, the sort of *non possumus* attitude that had characterised the administration of this Act [the Act of 1905] by the Local Government Board.'[2]

If Burns was exhausting his credit with the working class, the Liberals badly needed to revive their reputation as social reformers. Just such a revival was already being planned by the formidable combination of Lloyd George and Winston Churchill, fresh from their recent interventions in industrial relations[3] and confident of developing the alliance with labour. The first requirement was adequate finance, which the budget of 1909 was designed to secure. Thereafter it would be possible to embark upon major reforms, among them a solution to the problem of unemployment. During the winter of 1908–9 the two men launched their campaign in terms still vague but already attractive.

Early in 1909 the long-awaited publication of the Reports of the Royal Commission on the Poor Law provided, especially in the Minority Report, a mine of suggestions upon which Churchill—like so many others—was prepared to draw. One of the first to respond was Shackleton. Though the Parliamentary Committee stood aloof, he was soon associated with the Webbs' agitation for the enactment of the minority's proposals; and in his presidential address to Congress in September 1909 he praised Churchill's work at the Board of Trade and eulogized Lloyd George's budget as 'the greatest financial reform of modern times', in which 'we see great possibilities . . . we see for the first time the opportunity of finding the money without unduly taxing the poor to keep the poor' during old age and unemployment.

The main objective was announced by Lloyd George in his budget speech. Treating labour exchanges as the essential preliminary but no more, 'the Board of Trade have been . . . endeavouring to frame . . . a scheme which, while encouraging the voluntary efforts now being made by trade unions to provide unemployment benefit for their members, will extend the advantage of insurance to a very much larger circle of

---

[1] The 'opinions and sentiments' of Burns, Maddison, and Vivian on this occasion were repudiated by Congress by the surprisingly narrow vote of 826,000–801,000 (Trades Union Congress, *Annual Report*, 1908). The special joint conference in March had firmly rejected, under Independent Labour Party leadership, an attempt to insert a socialist amendment into its main resolution in support of the bill (Labour Party, *Annual Conference Report*, 1908).

[2] *Hansard*, 26 Oct. 1908, cols. 1646, 1705.   [3] See pp. 424, 433, 436, 459, 460.

workmen, including unskilled labourers'.[1] After this appetizer, the bill
for the establishment of labour exchanges, which fulfilled Asquith's
promise of legislation in 1909, was introduced by Churchill.

He related the proposed exchanges to two defects singled out by the
Royal Commission: lack of mobility and lack of information; and emphasized his desire 'to co-operate in every way in the closest and frankest
terms' with the unions, who would be encouraged to rent rooms at the
exchanges and thus 'avoid the necessity . . . of conducting their meetings
in licensed premises'. Moreover, if it was not to degenerate into mere
'distress machinery', the scheme would have to be associated with a system
of unemployment insurance, and this in turn could only work if made
compulsory, with contributions from the state as well as from the workers
and the employers. In the first instance it would have to be applied to
selected trades. 'The relation of the insurance scheme towards the unions
must be most carefully considered'; they must be safeguarded 'from anything like the unfair competition of a national insurance fund'.[2] In July,
therefore, the Parliamentary Committee agreed to appoint a subcommittee
to advise him on 'matters connected with the scheme affecting the Trade
Unionists of the country'.[3]

Though Henderson had described the plan for labour exchanges as 'the
Right to Work Bill in penny numbers',[4] Churchill's reception was cordial.
The Parliamentary Committee had been warned of both parts of the
scheme by the previous autumn, and had sent a deputation led by Shackleton to study the German system of exchanges and 'the working of their
compulsory insurance scheme for sickness and invalidity'.[5] They returned
with considerable admiration for German achievements, and concluded
that they had no need to fear 'a tendency to weaken or even supplant trade
organisations'.[6] Meanwhile, the Committee accepted that 'the Government are pledged to introduce next year a limited scheme of national
insurance against unemployment', and approved of contributions being
made compulsory and divided between workers, employers, and the state.

Some of this goodwill, however, was dissipated as the year passed. One
of the safeguards for the unions was that they should be represented on
the local advisory committees to be established in connexion with the
exchanges. But suspicion among the militants that the labour exchanges
might turn out to be uncomfortably like the 'free labour exchanges' of the
Free Labour Associations and the Shipping Federation was deepened by
the delay in the appointment of these committees. They had still not been

[1] *Hansard*, 29 Apr. 1909, cols. 488–9. [2] Ibid., 19 May 1909, cols. 505–9.
[3] Trades Union Congress, *Annual Report*, 1909, Parliamentary Committee Report.
[4] *Hansard*, 19 May 1909, col. 519.
[5] Parliamentary Committee, *Minutes*, 29 Oct. 1908.
[6] Trades Union Congress, *Annual Report*, 1909, Parliamentary Committee Report. See also
Hansard, 19 May 1909, col. 524.

appointed when Congress met in September 1910, though the first exchanges were opened on 31 January, with Richard Bell as their superintendent.

Moreover, the unions realized that the exchanges would not provide work. Only legislation on the lines of the 'right to work' bill could do that,[1] and when Congress assembled to find little sign that the pledges of Lloyd George and Churchill were being redeemed, it unanimously demanded that the government should support the bill.[2] In addition, during the debates on Churchill's measure Barnes had voiced the first opposition to the contributory principle in national insurance, an opposition that was later to grow dramatically both in the party and in the unions.[3]

The committees on the Truck Acts and on home work had reported in 1908. The first, despite its perceptive analysis of the problem and a number of useful detailed recommendations,[4] was completely ignored.[5] The second set out an unambiguous demand for an immediate and major reform, by finding in favour of the principle of the minimum 'living wage'. Earnings of a very large number of people—mainly women home workers —were so small as to be barely sufficient to sustain life, even with very long hours, and conditions were often crowded, insanitary, 'altogether pitiable and distressing'. The evidence showed 'that sweating still exists in such a degree as to call urgently for the interference of Parliament'. Statutory wages boards were needed to lay down legally enforceable minimum rates.[6]

During the debate on Henderson's bill in 1907, Herbert Gladstone had already declared that the government could not promise any new legislation or accept the principle of a legal minimum wage, but strong pressure was brought to bear when the committee's report appeared. Most of it came from Dilke and his friends, although MacDonald and his wife, with other members of the Independent Labour Party, also took their share in the campaign. The Parliamentary Committee was well disposed but played little part in inducing the government to change its mind.[7]

The Trade Boards Bill which Churchill introduced in March 1909 provided for boards comprising representatives of the employers and

---

[1] The bill was reintroduced by Hodge on 6 Apr. 1909 and secured 115 votes on the second reading.

[2] Lloyd George had recently made it clear that nothing could be done about national insurance until 1911 at the earliest. It should then be possible to start with a 'liberal State subsidy' (*Hansard*, 30 June 1910, col. 1142).

[3] Ibid., 3 May 1909, col. 798.

[4] Cd. 4442, 1908.

[5] Sir Frank Tillyard, *The Worker and the State*, 3rd edition, 1948, p. 102.

[6] *Report of the Select Committee on Home Work*, H.C. 246, 1908.

[7] One special case, however, took up much of its time from 1907 to 1910. O'Grady brought forward charges of sweating by the Salvation Army which greatly excited Congress. The Parliamentary Committee found General Booth a tough and evasive negotiator, but secured some satisfaction, though delegates in 1910 were still inclined to remain suspicious.

workpeople of the trade concerned, together with independent members nominated by the minister, to be set up in the ready-made tailoring, cardboard box-making, machine-made lace finishing, and chain-making trades. The boards were empowered to fix minimum wage rates which became legally enforceable when confirmed by the minister. The Act laid down that the criterion for the establishment of a board was the prevalence of exceptionally low wages, and powers were given to the minister to extend the system to other trades where this situation was deemed to exist.

Thus the scheme 'did not involve Parliament, Cabinet or any Central Department in the responsibility of actually fixing a rate'.[1] Essentially the system was one of compulsory collective bargaining applied to trades in which collective bargaining had not arisen spontaneously or was ineffective. 'The principles on which we are proceeding', said Churchill, 'are to endeavour to foster organisation in trades in which, by reason of the prevalence of exceptionally evil conditions, no organisation has yet taken root, and in which, in consequence, no parity of bargaining power can be said to exist.'[2]

To some extent the principle of state interference in the wages and conditions of private industry had already been sanctioned by the various fair wages resolutions, which the Commons amended in the same month. Continued complaints by the unions[3] had led to the appointment of yet another departmental committee in 1907, and their report of the following year was a useful compilation of current practices and union grievances.[4] The basic difficulty, however, was the selection of rates for comparison. The existing resolution referred to wages 'generally accepted as current in each trade for competent workmen in the district where the work is carried out'. The Parliamentary Committee took the view that current rates were only 'fair' rates if they were the rates agreed by the unions;[5] but the report suggested no change whatever in the wording of the resolution, and for the rest made only minor recommendations.

On 10 March 1909 Hodge moved a modification of the resolution which would have given the unions what they wanted. Roberts, in seconding, said that 'no clause will ever be perfectly satisfactory unless it is based upon

---

[1] Henry Clay, *The Problem of Industrial Relations*, 1929, p. 243.

[2] *Hansard*, 24 Mar. 1909, cols. 1791–2. Previously the point had been well put by Toulmin, the Liberal Member for Bury: 'we must as far as possible follow the natural growth of labour in this country, the orderly development of trade unionism. Where this natural evolution stops or lags the State must step in' (ibid., 21 Feb. 1908, col. 1198).

[3] One had already been dealt with. In 1906 the Parliamentary Committee got the Admiralty to supply them with copies of tender forms and the names of firms invited to tender, so that objections could be lodged against any particular firm.

[4] *Departmental Committee on the Working of the Fair Wages Resolution*, Cd. 4422 *(Report)* and Cd. 4423 *(Minutes of Evidence)* 1908.

[5] Of 169 boroughs in England and Wales which had approved fair wages clauses, ninety-six enforced 'current', 'prevailing' or 'recognized' rates; forty demanded 'jointly agreed' rates; and twenty-nine mentioned trade union rates specifically (Cd. 4422, p. 51).

strict trade union principles'.[1] At this point the government put up Buxton[2] to move an amendment in which the essential words were: 'not less favourable than those commonly recognised by employers and trade societies (or, in the absence of such recognised wages and hours, those which in practice prevail amongst good employers) . . .'; and Hodge withdrew his motion. Nevertheless, the unions continued to criticize the administration of the resolution, and in 1909 and 1910 Congress instructed the Parliamentary Committee to seek a resolution in favour of a 30s. minimum for adult government workers in London, and a bill compelling employers and employed to fix district minima in all industries.

In the 1910 debate at Congress one delegate complained that 'if you wait until your Shackletons, Ramsay MacDonalds and Hendersons get you a 30s. minimum, you will have to wait another 16 years'. Even the Parliamentary Committee reported that 'from the legislative point of view Labour has so far gained little' from the government in 1910—a sharp contrast with the 'sincere satisfaction' of 1906, when the Committee looked forward to a 'bright, happy and comfortable future' with labour representatives who had shown themselves able 'to amend bad laws and bring in good ones'.

Certainly there was no recurrence of the situation in which the labour Members had forced the Liberals to retreat on the Trade Disputes Bill. On this issue they had probably commanded more ministerial votes than the government, for many of Campbell-Bannerman's followers shared his sense of accumulated obligation to the working class. Thereafter the labour Members had to wait for the reports of committees appointed by the government, and accept government bills introduced at the government's pleasure. Asquith showed himself less generous than Campbell-Bannerman, and by 1910 his colleagues seemed preoccupied with other questions despite the hopes held out by Lloyd George and Churchill in 1908–9.

On the other hand, 1906–10 was a period rich in achievement compared with the previous ten years of Conservative rule. A series of acts had embodied substantial social reforms; perhaps the government had been pushed sooner and further than they intended over pensions and unemployment; and Lloyd George and Churchill had depended heavily on the union leaders for the drafting and administration of their measures. Thus it came about that while many of the rank and file became critical of the limited attainments of their parliamentary representatives, the latter, though they wanted more and complained of the government's tardiness and parsimony, were conscious of much solid achievement. Shackleton summed up their approach when he said 'the Labour Party is essentially

---

[1] *Hansard*, 10 Mar. 1909, col. 421.
[2] Buxton had introduced the first fair wages resolution into the House in 1891. See p. 248.

a practical party. It contains within it men who have had large experience in dealing with the every-day affairs of life, and who have learnt how to make use of their opportunities', however meagre.[1] Thus they got from the government what they could. They might have chosen to kick against the pricks, but this would have brought nothing but the momentary satisfaction of their left-wing critics.

Politics Outside Parliament

The 1906 election was followed by a honeymoon period throughout the movement almost as amicable and conciliatory as in the House of Commons. Admittedly Tillett tried to make trouble by moving a resolution at the 1907 Labour Party conference demanding that 'every Labour Party Member of Parliament, candidate, and delegate shall be a member of a bona fide Trade Union', and was only narrowly defeated.[2] On the other hand, he failed to prevent the Parliamentary Labour Party, in conjunction with the executive, being given the right to select 'the time and method of giving effect' to instructions of the annual conference. For 'a composite Party . . . composed of the Socialist movement and of the Trade Union movement', insisted Hardie, 'there must be some freedom of action'.[3]

In the same spirit, the conference, on the initiative of the leaders of the Independent Labour Party, overwhelmingly rejected an attempt to amend the party constitution to make 'the overthrow of the present competitive system of capitalism and the institution of a system of public ownership' a definite objective, despite the fact that a very similar resolution had slipped through without debate two years before. 'Was it desirable', Hardie asked, 'that those Members in the House of Commons who were not Socialists should be cleared out? . . . their Trade Union allies had been as honourable, as loyal, and as faithful as men could be.'

Such handsome sentiments were handsomely reciprocated when later in 1907 Congress censured the two marginal members of the trade union group, Maddison and Vivian, for opposing the successful Labour Party candidate, Pete Curran, at the Jarrow by-election in July. Both on behalf of the group and of the miners, Brace and Enoch Edwards rose to condemn the two miscreants, and even Bell emphasized the virtues of solidarity. Moreover, Edwards went on to say that he hoped they would face the next general election as a united party, for 'before we are much older we shall not have two parties, but one'.[4]

Edwards had reason to be conciliatory, for in the previous year a Federation ballot had only narrowly defeated a proposal to affiliate to the Labour

[1] Presidential address to the Trades Union Congress of 1909 (*Annual Report*, 1909).
[2] Labour Party, *Annual Conference Report*, 1907.
[3] Ibid.
[4] Trades Union Congress, *Annual Report*, 1907.

Party.[1] Small majorities in South Wales, Yorkshire, and Scotland favouring affiliation had been just outweighed by an almost complete rejection in the Midlands districts.[2] In 1908 another ballot approved affiliation by 213,137 votes to 168,446.[3] After several months of negotiation over details, the Federation was accepted into membership early in 1909, and all its representatives in Parliament except Burt, Fenwick, and Wilson took the Labour whip, thus halving the strength of the trade union group.

During 1906 much of the Joint Board's time was spent considering unemployment, especially as it affected the organized worker. Having reported that the Unemployed Workmen Act was almost worthless to trade unionists, MacDonald and Mitchell were then asked to draw up a more satisfactory measure, which eventually emerged as the 'right to work' bill, first introduced in 1907. In addition, the Board circularized the unions suggesting the abolition, or at least reduction, of overtime and the working of short time 'so that a shortage of employment might be met collectively'.[4]

This work was entrusted to the Joint Board by the Parliamentary Committee, which still regarded itself as senior partner but was content for Steadman to hand over some of his tasks to the other two secretaries. Mitchell of the General Federation had more time to spare than MacDonald, and he was also well-adapted to serve as a builder of bridges between the different sections of the movement, with his long service as a 'fraternal delegate' from one body to another.[5] On the other hand, the Parliamentary Committee was, as ever, wary of anything which threatened to increase expense, for this could not easily be shared. When the Board discussed the issues raised by Sexton's resolution in favour of closer unity at the 1906 Congress,[6] the Parliamentary Committee dragged its feet on the concentration of all the head offices into a single building and the foundation of a labour newspaper, largely because the unions would have been expected to find the money.

The prevention of 'overlapping' between the work of the three bodies was a persistent problem facing the Board, and here the initiative usually came from the Labour Party. The Parliamentary Committee was once

[1] Besides other arguments in favour of affiliation, its protagonists could now point out 'what a huge saving could be made by smashing up the M.F.G.B. Scheme of mongrel politicians', with its high rate of contributions (Secretary, Mexborough Trades Council, to MacDonald, 27 June 1906, *Labour Party Letter Files*). We owe this reference to Mr. R. G. Gregory.

[2] Page Arnot, op. cit., vol. i, pp. 364–5.

[3] Ibid., pp. 365–6. Northumberland joined the Federation in 1907 and Durham in Jan. 1908. Durham, however, did not take part in the 1908 ballot, for its legal advisers took the view that its rules precluded participation. Though the Durham membership of 98,510 was larger than the majority for affiliation, it can hardly be suggested that Durham's vote would have swung the balance the other way; for by now at least a sizeable minority in Durham would have voted for the party. [4] *Report of Joint Board*, 4 June 1907.

[5] Late in 1907, however, he joined the Labour Department of the Board of Trade and was succeeded by W. A. Appleton of the Lacemakers. [6] See p. 391.

more against change, and especially distrustful of attempts at 'strict definition' which threatened to limit its own scope or that of Congress. When
this was suggested by MacDonald on behalf of the party at a special
meeting, held without the General Federation, Shackleton, as chairman
of the Committee, explained that 'the Labour Party is naturally antagonistic to any government; the Parliamentary Committee are in a somewhat
different position, and are of opinion that it would weaken the power of
Labour generally to give up their right to approach Ministers year by year
with the different resolutions passed at Congress'.[1]

Despite these failures the Labour Party forced the discussion of a formal
constitution for the Board, and in March 1908 a draft was accepted by the
Parliamentary Committee. This ruled that the Board must 'consider and
decide' references from any one of its constituents on 'questions affecting
them jointly' or those not clearly within the province of one of them.
Otherwise it empowered the Board to do what it was already doing: to
undertake political activities on which the constituents were agreed;
to determine the bona fides of trade unions affiliating to all three; and to
consider whether or not to encourage new unions in occupations where
unions already existed. Finally, there was a new power to intervene in
trade disputes, but only with the explicit approval of the unions concerned.[2]

The Joint Board, in fact, could only do whatever its constituents were
agreed that it could do. The effective veto rested with the Parliamentary
Committee, though the clause on overlapping meant that its junior partners
now had formal cause for complaint if consultation were withheld.
Originally the Board had served as a centre for co-ordinating labour's
political campaigns at a time when the Parliamentary Committee was
as interested in the next election as the party itself. After the election,
interest switched to legislation and lobbying, mostly handled by the two
parliamentary groups. Once the 'right to work' bill had been drafted
there was little for the Joint Board to do, and a constitution could not
find work for it.

It could not make much of its new role in inter-union disputes. The
Parliamentary Committee had already been moving cautiously in this field
for some years under a rule empowering it to intervene in an inter-union
dispute if definite charges of 'blacklegging' were made. An amendment to
standing orders in 1907 enabled the Committee to arbitrate whether
blacklegging was involved or not. But experience showed that the

---

[1] Parliamentary Committee, *Minutes*, 19 Dec. 1907. By contrast, the 1907 conference of the
Engineers, ever ready to disparage Congress, found a new excuse for disaffiliating in that 'the
old-time functions of the Congress have become obsolete. . . . This cap in hand business gives
way to the Labour Party in the House of Commons itself, respectfully demanding what is wanted,
and endeavouring, with some success already, to see that they get it' (*Monthly Journal*, July
1907).   [2] Parliamentary Committee, *Minutes*, 19 and 25 Feb.; 18 Mar. 1908.

Committee lacked the moral authority for this enlarged role and in 1908 it reverted to the more limited function. Meanwhile, the Joint Board had been asked to intervene in the relations between the labourers' unions, and in particular to resolve their dispute with the Municipal Employees' Association,[1] but the Board had no more authority than the Parliamentary Committee to enforce its recommendations.

Soon afterwards the Board was snubbed by Shackleton. At its meeting of 11 July 1909, Henderson, as chairman of the party, complained that he had not been notified when the Parliamentary Committee met Churchill three days before to discuss the details of the labour exchanges, and that the Board was being by-passed. Shackleton, who was well satisfied with the outcome of the discussions, held at Churchill's request, explained that the difficulty was simply in finding dates for urgent meetings. In October he stonewalled again when Henderson complained that the Parliamentary Committee had been meeting Churchill to discuss the proposals for a national insurance scheme; and in November, when the Royal Commission on the Poor Law was about to report, the Labour Party, foreseeing further trouble, demanded 'some understanding in accordance with the terms of the constitution'[2] and prepared to raise the whole question at the next conference.

On 23 February 1910 the Parliamentary Committee revealed the reasons for its attitude. It would 'agree to see the Board of Trade if requested by them on the subject of Insurance against unemployment, and if the question should thereafter arise of the intervention of the Joint Board in the matter, they be informed that the Board of Trade are unwilling to deal with the Joint Board as this latter body has affiliated to it an independent and possibly opposing political party'. All 'necessary information' on the negotiation over any 'subsequent legislation' would of course be given to the Joint Board, which was to be informed that, in meeting the Board of Trade, the Parliamentary Committee was only fulfilling the instructions of Congress.[3] If Churchill had intended to sow a little mischief his efforts were well rewarded, for friction and distrust continued to mar the relations of the Committee and the party through the Joint Board during the rest of 1910.

By now, many militants had become discontented with the Independent Labour Party leaders, who were so outnumbered by trade union Members that they could not help but appear to be following the trade union lead unless they gave manifest signs of independence. Since this might well have split the Labour Party and destroyed everything that had been achieved for the socialists as well as for the unions by 'the federal understanding' since

---

[1] See p. 449.
[2] Parliamentary Committee, *Minutes*, 11 July; 6 Oct.; 4 Nov. 1909.
[3] Ibid., 23 Feb. 1910.

1900, they chose instead to show an extremely conciliatory spirit, however irksome men like Hardie might find it on occasion. But this meant following Shackleton and his colleagues in a course which could well be represented as using electoral 'independence' merely for the more successful pursuit of Lib-Lab objectives by Lib-Lab tactics in the House.

There was also trouble over Lib-Lab alliances in the constituencies, especially in miners' seats—quite apart from the 'old gang' of North-east representatives who refused the Labour whip. Despite the progress of socialist influence among the miners, especially in Durham and Scotland,[1] the Yorkshire Miners' Association was still predominantly Liberal in its sympathies,[2] while in South Wales the Lib-Lab leaders were largely successful in their struggle to preserve their existing alliances with the local Liberals. In Derbyshire, where Liberalism was still virtually unchallenged, J. G. Hancock of the Nottinghamshire Miners won a third seat for the miners in 1909; like Haslam in 1906 and Harvey in 1907, before the days of affiliation, he accepted Liberal endorsement and used the Liberal Party machine in his campaign. Despite the embarrassment they caused the executive of the Labour Party, all three signed the constitution and accepted the whip. Their readiness to do so was the only political difference between them and Burt, Fenwick, and Wilson. Nevertheless, Enoch Edwards refused to consider the suggestion that the three veterans be allowed to run as official Federation candidates in 1910, insisting that no exceptions be allowed now that the other miners' representatives had swallowed the pill.[3]

The first result of the miners' affiliation was thus to reinforce the Lib-Lab tendencies of the bulk of the party leadership, and to enhance the discontent of socialists, for whom it raised the spectre of the old obstructive alliance between coal and cotton. Writing to Glasier on 27 December 1908, Hardie gloomily assumed that 'we are in for another year of Henderson's chairmanship, which means that reaction and timidity will be in the ascendancy with disastrous effects on our side of the movement in the country. . . . Then when the miners come in the Annual Conferences will be controlled by Coal and Cotton, and . . . that means more reaction.'[4]

Many of Shackleton's Lancashire colleagues still thought that 'trade unionists are paying the piper while outside influences call the tune'.[5] In 1907, despite protests at this 'distinct breach' of the 'foundation

---

[1] See p. 300.

[2] *Labour Leader*, 4 Feb. 1910.

[3] Gregory, op. cit.

[4] Quoted in Pelling, *A Short History of the Labour Party*, 1961, p. 21. Hardie continued: 'I confess to feeling sore at seeing the fruits of our years of toil being garnered by men who were never of us, and who even now would trick us out'.

[5] *Cotton Factory Times*, 3 Feb. 1905.

agreement',[1] the United Textile Factory Workers' Association led the move to reduce the representation of socialist societies on the party's executive, a move which achieved some success in 1908 at the very conference where Shackleton defended 'the federal understanding' against the socialists.[2] It was hardly surprising, therefore, that after a survey of Lancashire, on the eve of the miners' affiliation to the Labour Party, Frank Rose of the Independent Labour Party concluded that 'in no great section of the industrial class is the progress towards truer social ideals less pronounced'. The cotton operatives in the main were not even inspired by 'the primary idea of the community of working-class interests', and for all its limited success in the area in the past, revolutionary socialist propaganda was now merely a waste of time and effort.[3]

Nevertheless, it was from the borders of Lancashire that there came the first dramatic evidence of the revolt of the socialists. Campaigning within a few miles of Oldham, Victor Grayson, a young member of the Independent Labour Party, scraped home at Colne Valley in July 1907 as a 'Labour and Socialist' candidate without the endorsement of the party and with only the local support of the Independent Labour Party. He refused to sign the Labour Party constitution and sat in the House as an 'Independent Socialist', though the Independent Labour Party leaders, gravely embarrassed, subsequently agreed to give him a parliamentary allowance.

The electoral success of 1906 had given a powerful impetus to the hopes, as well as the membership, of all the socialist societies. The revival of the Social Democratic Federation,[4] which had withdrawn from the Labour Representation Committee in 1901, helped to put the rank and file of the Independent Labour Party on the alert for any undue readiness of its leaders to compromise. Even before Grayson's election the *Labour Leader*, responding to a flood of critical letters, had begun a series of articles justifying compromise. In one of them, Barnes explained that in present circumstances the Labour Party must not try to force the pace by obstruction, like the old Irish party, once so much admired; but should 'support and strengthen' social legislation proposed by a basically friendly government, which might, of course, require some stimulation.[5]

This did little to restrain those whose doubts were symbolized by Grayson. The triumph at Colne Valley led during the next two years to a succession of disastrous by-elections with candidates promoted locally against the advice of the leaders. And at the conference of the Independent

[1] *Labour Leader*, 25 Jan. 1907.   [2] Labour Party, *Annual Conference Report*, 1908.
[3] *Labour Leader*, 22 Jan. 1909. Rose had been elected to the Parliamentary Committee in 1905, but was later debarred from membership because his trade union status was merely that of a parliamentary candidate endorsed by the Amalgamated Society of Engineers (Trades Union Congress, *Annual Report*, 1906, Parliamentary Committee Report).
[4] Its name was changed to the Social Democratic Party in 1908.
[5] *Labour Leader*, 21 June 1907 and *passim*.

Labour Party in 1909 Grayson had enough support to carry the reference back of the National Administrative Council's criticism of his conduct. Only the resignation *en masse* of the respected 'old guard' of Hardie, MacDonald, Snowden, and Glasier brought the conference to heel.

Meanwhile, Grayson had been suspended from the House for making scenes in protest against the unemployment policies of both the government and the Labour Party. Campaigning as a 'clean Socialist'—despite his growing addiction to the bottle—he found many sympathizers among the Independent Labour and Social Democratic Parties for his demand for an end to the 'labour alliance'. This was to lead to the foundation in 1911 of the British Socialist Party; but already in 1910 four members of the National Administrative Council of the Independent Labour party, led by Leonard Hall, afterwards one of the founders of the new party, were ready to echo Grayson in a new statement of policy known as the 'Green Manifesto'.[1]

From within the unions Tillett, perpetually seeking influence with the rank and file and perhaps the most dependable weathercock of the period, produced a pamphlet, *Is the Parliamentary Labour Party a Failure?*, which denounced the party's leaders as 'toadies', 'sheer hypocrites', and 'Press flunkeys to Asquith', 'softly feline in their purring to Ministers and their patronage', whose attitude to unemployment betrayed their neglect of socialism as well as the temptations of the Liberal alliance. At the Labour Party conference in 1909 Henderson and Shackleton once more joined with the leaders of the Independent Labour Party to defend the freedom of the Parliamentary Labour Party against the dictates of the annual conference, and were able to emphasize their arguments by angrily ridiculing Tillett's attack.[2]

In 1910 came signs of a more searching criticism, belittling not merely the record of the Labour Party, but also parliamentary action itself. In 1903 the Socialist Labour Party had been established on Clydeside under the inspiration of the American Daniel De Leon, and it followed him in the development of his industrial unionist doctrines. One of its founders, James Connolly, the Irish nationalist and socialist, subsequently spent several years in America working for De Leon's Socialist Labour Party and for the Industrial Workers of the World, the trade union organization which De Leon helped to found. When James Larkin established the Irish Transport and General Workers' Union, Connolly hailed it as Ireland's first industrial union,[3] and he joined forces with Larkin on his return to Ireland in July 1910.

---

[1] Tsuzuki, op. cit., pp. 167 ff., for both developments. The Manifesto declared that 'Labour must fight for Socialism and its own hand against BOTH the Capitalist parties IMPARTIALLY' (quoted in Pelling, *Short History*, p. 25).

[2] Labour Party, *Annual Conference Report*, 1909.

[3] C. Desmond Greaves, *The Life and Times of James Connolly*, 1961, p. 187.

At much the same time Tom Mann returned to England from Australia, where he had also acquired the anti-political doctrines of the majority of the Industrial Workers of the World which, along with Connolly, had split from De Leon in 1908.[1] In addition to playing his part in the foundation of the Transport Workers' Federation,[2] Mann had set up the Industrial Syndicalist Education League by the end of 1910. At the preliminary conference in November Larkin was present, and Tillett sent a letter of support.[3]

Tillett, swinging with the wind once more, moved a resolution at Congress in September 1910 in favour of the 'confederation of all Trade Unions' to arrange for all collective agreements to be terminable at the same date. This was passed by an overwhelming majority, and an even greater majority voted for a more extreme resolution in favour of 'one big union'. Mosses criticized both proposals as silly, but the Parliamentary Committee held its hand. Its tactical wisdom was demonstrated by the inquiry subsequently undertaken to discover from affiliated unions what they thought should be done to implement the two resolutions. There was no enthusiasm; indeed, there was hardly any response. The Parliamentary Committee did not have to fear that either Congress or the major unions were about to become syndicalist. But this did not mean the Committee had nothing to fear from the syndicalists, any more than the leadership of the Labour Party could ignore the evidence of mounting discontent.

The Osborne Judgement and the 1910 Elections

The very right of unions to undertake political action was threatened by the decision of the House of Lords in December 1909 to uphold an injunction taken out by a member of the Railway Servants, W. V. Osborne, restraining the union from spending its funds for political purposes. The injunction was given on five distinct grounds during its passage through the Court of Appeal and the Lords, but not one of them was relied upon by all members of the three courts.[4]

The main ground was that though trade unions had never been incorporated, they had many of the characteristics of corporate bodies and were

---

[1] De Leonite influence also had an effect upon a new venture in working-class adult education at Oxford actively supported by Congress and a number of individual unions. Ruskin Hall, later Ruskin College, was founded in 1899 by two Americans to provide university-type education for working men. Some of its students, impatient for more rapid social change, felt that the College teaching, instead of pursuing the traditional university 'liberal' education favoured by the governing council with its official trade union representatives, should present a revolutionary 'class-conscious' philosophy. Dennis Hird, the College principal, was in sympathy with this view, and his efforts to press it resulted in his dismissal in 1909. He then led a breakaway of students from the College and set up what afterwards became the Central Labour College, supported by the South Wales Miners' Federation and the Railway Servants (Roberts, op. cit., p. 236). [2] See p. 452.

[3] Roberts, op. cit., pp. 237–8. It may be noted that Tillett, before writing the 1908 pamphlet referred to above, had recently visited Australasia and seen Mann.

[4] There is an interesting analysis in Humphrey, op. cit., appendix vii.

formed under statute. Consequently they must, like statutory corporations, be forbidden to perform any act not authorized by statute. The purposes of a trade union were set out in clause 16 of the Trade Union Amendment Act of 1876, which gave a definition of the term for the purposes of the Act. They did not include political action, which must therefore be *ultra vires*.[1] The Act had also been silent on the payment of benefits, but these were held to be incidental to the regulation of conditions of employment, which political activities were not. Among the subsidiary grounds given, considerable play was made with the pledge required of members of the parliamentary party to support the party constitution.[2] Lord James, who took the common-sense view that the definition of 1876 was not intended to be exhaustive, gave this as his main reason for concurring with the decision.

The Webbs used these complex and sometimes conflicting arguments to support their view that the decision was a 'grave miscarriage of justice' in which the Lords showed both prejudice and ignorance. The 'animus behind their extraordinary judgement', they wrote, was 'the deepest resentment of the lawyers', excited by the Act of 1906, and 'a quite exaggerated alarm among members of the governing class' caused by 'the progress of the Labour Party'.[3] Of Osborne they said that he was 'liberally financed from capitalist sources'; and the effect of the judgement was that 'up and down the country discontented or venal Trade Unionists were sought out by solicitors and others acting for the employers; and were induced to lend their names to proceedings for injunctions against their own Unions'.[4]

[1] The Osborne judgement had been foreshadowed by a decision of the Registrar of Friendly Societies in 1905 when he refused to register the rules of the Railway Clerks' Association on the grounds that they included in their statement of objects a provision for parliamentary representation, and that this was not among the statement of objects for which unions had been legalized by the Acts of 1871–6. The same Registrar, however, both before and after this, registered rules which, though not including parliamentary representation among the objects, nevertheless provided for it by authorizing governing bodies to levy for the purpose with the members' consent. The matter caused much concern among trade unionists, and the Parliamentary Committee drew up a model rule (Trades Union Congress, *Annual Report*, 1906, Parliamentary Committee Report).

[2] The Webbs wrote that Lord James 'objected to Trade Unions paying a Member of Parliament who was (as was quite incorrectly assumed) bound by a rule of the paying body requiring him to vote in a particular way, not on labour questions only, but on all issues that might come before Parliament' (*History*, p. 626). The pledge required candidates and members to 'accept this Constitution' and to 'agree to abide by the decisions of the Parliamentary Party in carrying out the aims of this Constitution'. In 1904 (p. 380) the enforcement of the pledge by resignation had been omitted, and in 1906 (p. 390) some latitude for conscience had been agreed within the parliamentary party.

The extent to which Members were bound by the pledge is thus arguable, but the 'quite incorrectly assumed' of the Webbs cannot be justified. Certainly many believed at the time that a pledge existed (*Labour Leader*, 31 Dec. 1909 and *passim*).

[3] Webbs, *History*, p. 626.

[4] Ibid., pp. 608, 631.

There can be no doubt that the privileges given to the trade unions by the 1906 Act had appeared to virtually the whole legal profession as legally improper.[1] It might be possible to tolerate such privileges so long as they were assumed to exist, and allowed to go unchallenged, as they were for nearly twenty years after 1876; but to grant them positively and expressly by statute was too much. If the legal status of the unions was to be redefined it should be by extending to them the rights and obligations of incorporation. This was a view shared by many trade union leaders, at least during their initial reaction to Taff Vale; by most of their legal advisers; and at all times by Sidney Webb himself. It is therefore understandable that the judges sought for some statutory authority for imposing a quasi-corporate status upon the unions—even if they stretched the law in doing so.

The result was to threaten with destruction the existing pattern of trade union political activity and thus to please all the enemies of the Labour Party.[2] In assessing the force of class prejudice, however, two factors must be considered. The first is that up to 1909, despite Conservative fears of the 'revolutionary' implications of the election of 1906, class feeling rose nowhere near the pitch to which it had been aroused by the 'new unionism' and the engineers' lock-out in the nineties, or to which it was again aroused after 1909, especially during the labour unrest of 1911 and 1912. There had been a decade of relative industrial peace, and the Labour Party in Parliament had shown itself to be far from revolutionary. The second reason for caution is that Osborne's support came from within the unions as well as from without. The judgement of the Lords was as much in favour of old-fashioned Lib-Labs and Conservative working men as of the ruling class and its alleged agents.

Osborne himself was no renegade. The official historian of the Railway Servants, who knew him personally, described him as an upright man who made a fetish of conscience and personal liberty.[3] He refused to assist others in conflict with the union on industrial affairs;[4] he was elected secretary to some of the conciliation boards established under the 1907 scheme; and he retained these positions after leaving railway service, doing 'good work on them'.[5] Osborne's own version of the affair was given in a book which is a panegyric of old-fashioned trade unionism.[6] And after his triumph he

[1] G. R. Askwith, *Lord James of Hereford*, 1930, pp. 294–5.
[2] Among them was the Anti-Socialist Union, with the Duke of Devonshire as president and Walter Long as vice-president, and with the sole object of 'opposing and defeating the forces and organisations operating for Socialism in this country'. One of its pamphlets, published in 1910, warned that the socialists' purpose was to secure control of union funds for use to further revolutionary ends (J. B. Wilson, *The Socialist Plot to Capture the Trade Unions*, Anti-Socialist Union Pamphlet No. 12, 1910). [3] Alcock, op. cit., pp. 338, 340.
[4] Ibid., p. 408. The executive of the union expelled Osborne, but was forced to readmit him as a result of an action which was settled out of court.
[5] Ibid., p. 379. [6] *Sane Trade Unionism*, 1913.

wrote to the Parliamentary Committee stating that his 'Trade Union Political Freedom League did not desire to hinder the Trades Congress in their work so long as it was not subservient to a particular political section'.[1]

Osborne asserted that the funds for his action were subscribed by individual workmen and trade unions. According to Alcock, full accounts were shown to Osborne's branch, and Alcock himself saw 'some of' the subscription lists. Osborne certainly invited the Parliamentary Committee 'to have the bona-fides of his action . . . investigated by an impartial person', but the offer was not taken up. His claim becomes credible in view of the fact that the costs of the case were small, especially by comparison with those for Taff Vale.[2] Shackleton's account to Congress in 1910 shows that the total costs amounted to a little over £7,000. The Railway Servants had to pay £2,600 for the two hearings, just over £1,000 going to cover Osborne's costs before the Court of Appeal. Before the Lords, costs were nearly £4,500,[3] just over £500 being for Osborne. Even if Osborne's costs at the first hearing, which were not recovered from the other side, were heavier than at the later stages, it was not impossible for him to have collected these sums from individual working men and trade union branches.

The origins of the case go back to the quarrels between Bell and the socialists. In 1904, when MacDonald and Shackleton urged the Railway Servants' executive to press Bell to sign the constitution of the Labour Representation Committee, the Liberals and Conservatives in the union rallied to Bell's support. Some branches refused to pay a political levy imposed in 1903, and at the union conference of 1904 their representatives were strong enough to defeat an attempt by the socialists to compel the union's parliamentary representatives to sign the constitution. Among these recalcitrant branches was Walthamstow where Osborne was secretary. Legal advice suggested that the rules had not been properly followed in 1903, so in 1905 the relevant resolution was re-drafted and re-imposed.

Osborne objected on the ground that the union's political activities were at the 'dictation' of the Labour Party. 'Let them have Parliamentary representation as much as they liked', he told the conference of 1905, 'but let it be by and under the control of their own people.'[4] The quarrel reached its climax at the conference of 1906, where the socialists at last succeeded in carrying a rule binding future union parliamentary representatives and candidates to accept Labour Party discipline. Osborne then applied for an injunction which was refused at the first hearing in July 1908; granted by the Court of Appeal in November of the same year;[5] and upheld by the Lords in December 1909.

---

[1] Parliamentary Committee, *Minutes*, 14 Sept. 1910.   [2] See p. 315.
[3] At this stage the Joint Board took over responsibility on behalf of the whole movement.
[4] Quoted in Alcock, op. cit., p. 336.
[5] Among the members of the Court of Appeal was Farwell, L.J., who, as Justice Farwell, had given the initial judgement in the first Taff Vale case.

Osborne's decision to go to court came just before the final debates in the House on the Trade Disputes Bill. According to Osborne, one of the labour Members confided to a friend that section 4, subsection 1 of the Bill,[1] if enacted, would exclude an action such as he proposed. On this reaching Osborne, 'the Attorney-General was approached indirectly on the subject. He promised that in any event he would guard the right of members to prevent the illegal use of their funds.'[2] The addition of subsection 2, maintaining the liability of the trustees of a trade union to be sued, except over trade disputes, had the desired effect, although the labour Members apparently did not appreciate its significance.[3]

Osborne's aim was not to prevent political action as such, but to contest the union's right to enforce its political levy and subscribe to the funds of the Labour Party. Here he was in agreement with the Railway Servants' own chief officer, Bell, who wrote in 1907 that thousands of trade unionists 'who have been and are loyal to the first and main objects of Trade Unionism, namely, "to improve the conditions and protect the interests of the members", object to it being extended outside these objects. . . . While . . . the members in most Unions approve of someone representing the interests of their Unions in Parliament, they by no means approve of their money going to pay Socialist representatives.'[4]

The extent of trade union support for this point of view did not become evident until the movement set about the task of remedying the situation in 1910. The Joint Board had already begun to discuss the problems raised by the Osborne case in the summer of 1909. As soon as the Lords announced their verdict in December a special joint conference was arranged for February 1910, which agreed to uphold the right of trade unions to engage in political activities, 'provided that their members agree', and asked for immediate action 'to secure the amendment of the law'.[5] At

---

[1] The amended version of clause 3, conferring legal immunity.   [2] Osborne, op. cit., p. 131.

[3] Ibid., pp. 131–2. The insertion of subsection 2 was indeed a last-minute adjustment to the Act. Walton, the Attorney-General, insisted upon some such proviso if the phrase 'or officials' was to appear in the crucial subsection 1. The wording was worked out in conjunction with Asquith and Rufus Isaacs, and accepted by Shackleton as 'the best way out of the difficulty' (Parliamentary Committee, *Minutes*, 21 Nov. 1906).   [4] Op. cit., pp. 88–89.

[5] Labour Party, *Annual Conference Report*, 1910, Special Conference Report. B. C. Roberts suggests that 'the decision of the House of Lords took the trade unions by surprise. It was only after a number of injunctions had been granted . . . that the seriousness of the situation dawned upon the unions. . . . It was not until Aug. 1910 that the three organizations clearly stated their attitude to the decision' (op. cit., p. 225).

There seems little evidence for any of these statements. It is true that the Labour Party's *Annual Conference Report* of Feb. 1911 declared that the party 'had to wait until injunction after injunction had been granted so as to enlighten the Unions as to what had happened'; but the Joint Board could not have got off the mark more quickly than it did. A month after the Lords' decision the General Federation of Trade Unions wrote in its *Quarterly Report* that trade unions had been anticipating the decision for months. '. . . The verdict caused little surprise. . . . One thing is certain, and that is the impossibility of accepting the fiat of the House of Lords. . . . The law must be amended.'

this point the miners asked for an amendment making clear that the qualification was to be: 'provided that a *majority* of their members agree'. Smillie pointed out that 'some of them had to go back to their districts and face a very considerable opposing minority which wanted to prevent them getting the rights they were present at the Conference to claim'.

On 13 April 1910 Taylor brought a resolution before the House to the effect that 'the right to send representatives to Parliament and to municipal administrative bodies, and to make financial provision for their election and maintenance, enjoyed by Trade Unions for over forty years and taken from them . . . should be restored'. The debate showed that several Liberal Members took the strongest objection to the compulsion of 'a member of a trade union . . . to subscribe to the support of opinions of which he does not approve'.[1] Robson, now Attorney-General, suggested that the remedy lay in the payment of salaries to Members of Parliament.[2]

This was quite unacceptable, and the Joint Board pressed on with a bill which in effect restored the pre-Osborne position. Duly introduced, it was met by a government statement that no facilities could be granted for its consideration. A special conference of the Miners' Federation in August 1910 showed the rising temper of the unions. By this time injunctions had been obtained in South Wales, Lancashire, Nottingham, and Derby. Several delegates suggested defiance of the law, but in the end the conference contented itself with a strongly worded resolution in favour of overturning the decision, which was 'unfair, undemocratic, and opposed to Government by majorities'.[3]

Armed with this resolution, the miners set out to persuade Congress in September to send the Parliamentary Committee back to redraft its own resolution in stronger terms. Two delegates spoke in favour of the Osborne decision, however, and Shackleton urged restraint. He argued that any legislation could only come through a government bill, and that there was little hope of repeating the *coup* of 1906; moreover, in negotiating with the Prime Minister it was embarrassing to be unable to deny the charge that the unions were not speaking with one voice on the issue.[4]

The miners, nevertheless, carried Congress, making clear beyond doubt that the movement favoured a return to the position in which union rules and majority decisions committed all members, and in which unions had free disposal of all funds collected for whatever purpose. However, when Asquith announced the government's intentions in November 1910, the

---

[1] *Hansard*, 13 Apr. 1910, col. 1330. [2] Ibid., col. 1354.

[3] Page Arnot, op. cit., vol. i, pp. 349–51.

[4] Under the Trade Union Act of 1913, which was the eventual outcome of the Osborne controversy, any union wanting to undertake political activity had to secure a majority in a ballot of the membership. These ballots yield the best evidence of the extent of opposition to the socialists. Among the miners, for example, 194,800 voted against a political fund compared with 261,643 for; among the weavers 75,893 voted against, and 98,158 for.

unions found they were to have only half the loaf. In addition to a promise of payment of Members and official election expenses, the provision of funds 'for Parliamentary and municipal action and representation and kindred objects' was to be included among the purposes of trade unions, 'provided that the opinion of the union is effectively ascertained, and that there shall be no compulsion upon any member to contribute to the fund'. In answer to questions he made plain that there would be a special levy for a separate fund, and no member was to be 'injuriously affected if he refuses to pay'.[1]

Because of the rejection of the 1909 budget by the Lords, and the subsequent Liberal proposals for curbing their powers, the Labour Party had to face two elections, in January and December 1910. The Osborne judgement had virtually no effect on the finances of the party in the first election because the only injunction in force was that against the Railway Servants. The precedent was quickly seized upon, however, and other trade unionists, some of them prompted and backed from outside,[2] hurried to seek injunctions to stop the political activities of their unions. In January 1911 the Labour Party reported that it had been 'severely handicapped by the old register and the financial impediment which the Osborne Judgment placed in our way'.

Its financial statement showed that the immediate financial difficulties could be exaggerated. In January 1909 the party had reported that subscriptions to the Parliamentary Fund totalled £8,348 for the previous year. The adherence of the miners sent subscriptions for the following year up to £13,622, and the balance to £14,755. Between February 1910 and February 1911 the injunctions began to affect subscriptions; but they fell only to £10,014, with a further £1,738 raised by a special appeal. Thus, even though the costs of maintenance rose to £8,730 during the year, and £7,290 was spent in meeting election expenses, the party could still report a balance of £8,411 in February 1911, about £1,300 lower than that of 1909.[3] Some unions, however, must have run into trouble over expenditure in the constituencies in December 1910, for of the twenty-two unions which had been restrained by injunctions up to February 1911, twenty had Members in the House. Nevertheless, the main effect was sharply to reduce the opportunities open to the party of backing candidates in seats it could not hope to win for propaganda purposes.

[1] *Hansard*, 22 Nov. 1910, cols. 275–6.

[2] The methods by which this was done were exposed in *Parr* v. *Lancashire and Cheshire Miners' Federation*. The shorthand notes of the case are included in the executive minutes of the Miners' Federation of Great Britain, 14–17 Aug. 1912, and reproduced in part in Page Arnot, op. cit., pp. 136–8.

[3] Labour party, *Annual Conference Reports*, 1909–11. This increase in maintenance payments followed on the decision of the Party in Sept. 1910 to pay maintenance 'to all Members of the Parliamentary Party', and these grants were continued into 1911 until the payment of Members relieved them of the burden.

In both elections the alliance with the Liberals remained in force: in January only one of the forty successful candidates was opposed by a Liberal—who lacked official support—and only two of the forty-two in December.[1] In declared policy also there was no more to distinguish the Labour Party from the Liberals than in 1906. The programmes of the party and the Parliamentary Committee were compounded of what was left over from 1906: measures foreshadowed by the government but not yet fully defined, such as national insurance and the reform of the House of Lords, together with two measures of their own—the 'right to work' bill and the complete reversal of the Osborne judgement, both of them already rejected by the government.

Indeed, in the eyes of many, especially after the parliamentary performance of their representatives since 1906, identification with Liberalism was closer than ever. The leaders of the movement agreed with their Liberal allies quite as completely as in 1906 in condemning the Conservative policies, which were based on tariff reform and a Chamberlainite adumbration of social betterment, and designed to distract attention from the central problem of the Lords. Even the defence of free trade in 1906 could not compare with the overriding importance of reforming the powers of the Lords in 1910, since 'socialism presupposes democratic government'.[2] With pardonable exaggeration, Hardie declared that 'the Labour Party had ceased to count'.[3]

The record of the party in the two elections must be set against its position before the dissolution. As a result of by-election victories, the total of active trade unionists in the House had risen from forty in 1906 to forty-five. Largely because of the affiliation of the miners, thirty-eight of these were now members of the Parliamentary Labour Party. Including the six Independent Labour Party Members and Crooks, this made the party forty-five strong, as compared with the total of thirty in 1906. There was also Grayson, a member of the Independent Labour Party but not a trade union Member. Of the new trade union Members three were miners—Harvey, Hancock, and W. E. Stanley of the Midland Miners'

[1] The Parliamentary Committee seems to have ceased to attach much importance to sponsoring candidates on its own. There is no record in its *Minutes* nor in its Report to Congress of endorsements in January. On 17 Nov. 1910, however, the Committee empowered its acting secretary, Bowerman, 'to use his discretion as to endorsing' candidates for December.

[2] *Labour Leader*, 24 Dec. 1909, putting the arguments for 'a policy of moderation . . . especially in the matter of candidatures'. On 18 Nov. 1909 the Parliamentary Committee had publicly denounced 'the autocratic actions of an unrepresentative House of Lords, which has always proved itself hostile and obstructive to measures of social reform and progress', and welcomed the election turning on this issue as 'the long desired opportunity' to remove such an obstacle. Its election manifesto for Dec. 1910 was entitled: 'Commons v. Lords: Which Shall Prevail?'

[3] Independent Labour Party, *Annual Conference Report*, 1910. There was perhaps more force in his observation that 'the Movement seems to be drifting without any settled policy' (*Labour Leader*, 11 Mar. 1910).

Federation, who brought the miners' strength up from sixteen to nineteen. In addition, Pete Curran of the Gasworkers had won Jarrow in 1907, and Joseph Pointer, parliamentary representative of the Patternmakers, was elected for the Attercliffe division of Sheffield in 1908. Burt, Fenwick, and John Wilson of the miners, together with Bell, Steadman, Ward, and Havelock Wilson, formed the rump of the trade union group.

In January 1910 the Labour Party put up seventy-eight candidates, of whom forty were successful. Crooks and Summerbell, one of the six original Independent Labour Party Members, both lost their seats, along with five Labour Party trade unionists outside the miners' group. There was also one gain in this category—J. H. Thomas[1] of the Railway Servants, who won Bell's old seat at Derby. So far this gives a net loss of six seats, but the miners, with one net gain, reduced the overall loss to five. The three old miners' leaders from the North-east were also returned, making twenty miners in all, but Ward was the only other member of the trade union group to survive. Bell, whose quarrel with socialism had finally led to his resignation as secretary of the Railway Servants in 1909,[2] did not stand; nor did Havelock Wilson. Steadman was defeated, temporizing to the end. In all, the number of trade union Members fell from forty-five to thirty-nine.

During the year only two by-elections were fought, both unsuccessfully. The general election in December, however, brought a net gain of two, though the number of candidates fell from seventy-eight to fifty-six. The miners lost two seats in Lancashire but gained one in Cumberland, and Willie Adamson, secretary of the Fife Miners, won their first Scottish seat in West Fife. With the defeat of J. A. Seddon of the Shop Assistants there was one less trade union Member, but this loss was offset when Summerbell's old seat at Sunderland was regained by F. W. Goldstone, a member and later an officer of the National Union of Teachers. The remainder of the Labour Party showed two gains: Crooks was back, and George Lansbury won Bow for the Independent Labour Party. Burt, Fenwick, Wilson, and Ward all survived, so that, counting Goldstone, the total of trade union Members remained at thirty-nine, just over half of them miners.

The final outcome of the two elections was therefore a reduction in the

---

[1] Thomas, J. H., P.C. (1874–1950). President, Amalgamated Society of Railway Servants, 1905–6; organizing secretary, 1906–10; assistant general secretary, 1910–17 (National Union of Railwaymen after 1913); general secretary, 1917–19; parliamentary general secretary, 1919–31, except for nine months in 1924. Parliamentary Committee, later General Council, Trades Union Congress, 1917–24; 1925–9. Executive Committee, Labour Party, 1929–30. M.P., 1910–36. Colonial Secretary, 1924. Lord Privy Seal, 1929–30. Secretary of State for Dominion Affairs, 1930–5. Colonial Secretary, 1935–6.

[2] Relations between Bell and the other two parliamentary representatives of the Railway Servants had become bitter. Bell crossed them in many ways, including a speech in the House against railway nationalization. The union conference of 1909 debated a resolution calling for his resignation, but finally passed a less damaging amendment.

Labour Party from forty-five to forty-two and of trade union Members from forty-five to thirty-nine. The Independent Labour Party had one less direct nominee than in 1906. There was nothing here to quieten the mounting criticism of the militants within the party and the unions, and nothing to rekindle the movement's waning political enthusiasm and purpose.

In these circumstances it was ill-prepared to sustain a loss of a different kind. In December 1910 Albert Smith, secretary of the Nelson Overlookers, was returned for Clitheroe in place of Shackleton, who had just accepted a government appointment with a view to becoming National Insurance Commissioner in the following year. His part in the preparation of the Labour Exchanges Act and the government's insurance scheme added to his obvious qualifications for the post. In addition, he had shown signs of irritation with his colleagues behind the scenes and publicly with the delegates at the 1910 Trades Union Congress. Many more years of service might have been expected of him had he remained, for he was only forty-seven and had a distinguished civil service career before him.

11

Mounting Industrial Discontent, 1906–10

The Railway Conciliation Scheme

THE economic improvement of 1905, which had already encouraged the cotton unions to take the offensive, continued through 1906 and into 1907. It brought a rapid increase in the membership of the railway unions—from 77,000 in 1904 to 139,000 in 1907—and allowed them to launch their first important assault on the companies since 1897. Co-operation between the major unions was ruled out, however, by the animosity between their secretaries, Bell and Fox, and by different policies over recognition.

In April 1905 the Associated Society of Locomotive Engineers and Firemen appealed to all footplate men to support a national programme, addressing a special message to footplate members of the executive of the Amalgamated Society of Railway Servants.[1] Their main aims were the eight-hour day and a guaranteed week, along with concessions on wages and lodging allowances, and promotion by seniority. The Amalgamated Society was slow in countering this bid: its executive sanctioned a number of sectional claims in January 1906, but not until the following November was an all-grades programme formulated. The central demands were an eight-hour day for traffic grades and a ten-hour day for the rest—claims which had the attraction of simplicity compared with a complicated set of different wage demands for the many grades. Together with the proposal for time and a quarter for overtime, and time and a half on Sundays, their acceptance would have led to a considerable increase in earnings. There were also claims for a guaranteed week and for an increase of 2s. per week for 'all grades . . . who do not receive the eight-hour day'.[2]

Bell considered recognition to be vital. He regarded an all-grades movement as the best means to exact it from the companies, and specifically asked each company to allow him to accompany a deputation to its board. Fox, however, maintained 'that recognition of itself was not worth fighting about, for it was only a means to an end, and not an end in itself'.[3] He also

---

[1] Raynes, op. cit., p. 130.

[2] *Report on the Strikes and Lockouts of 1907*, Cd. 4254, 1908, p. 49. One feature of the subsequent campaign was a census of existing rates compiled with the assistance of W. T. (later Sir Walter) Layton, which showed that 38 per cent. of railwaymen received 20s. a week or less, and another 50 per cent. between 21s. and 30s. The companies attacked the census, but its accuracy was confirmed by the Board of Trade wage census for 1907, finally published in 1912. See p. 479 and footnote 3. [3] Raynes, op. cit., p. 138.

suspected that for Bell it meant recognition of the Railway Servants as the organization representative of all railwaymen. These suspicions had been sharpened by Bell's willingness in 1905 to accept the principle of an unaccompanied motorman when the London Metropolitan District Railway became electrified.[1] The Associated Society, which stood firm for two men in a cab, regarded the incident as evidence that Bell was willing to undercut their conditions in his eagerness to win recognition for his own union.

When the programme was presented in January 1907, all the companies except the North Eastern[2] refused to meet Bell, and they refused again in February and July. Their spokesman Lord Claud Hamilton, chairman of the Great Eastern, insisted that both they and their employees must remain 'untrammelled by the coercion and tyranny of an outside, irresponsible body'.[3] This intransigence was widely resented, however, and there was much public sympathy with the railwaymen, especially over their claims for shorter hours. On 6 March the House of Commons accepted a resolution moved by the Lib-Lab W. E. Harvey, which declared that hours of work on the railways were excessive and demanded fresh legislation should the existing Act prove inadequate. The Board of Trade became 'increasingly active in examining complaints',[4] and in May its President, Lloyd George, indicated to the companies that the situation was being carefully watched.

These warnings went unheeded and in September, with membership rising rapidly, the Amalgamated Society announced its intention of conducting a strike ballot on the question of 'representations by the society's officials to negotiate the National Programme'. Faced by this threat, the companies on 12 October showed no signs of weakening and a clash seemed imminent. 'Should the refusal of the Directors to meet the railwaymen's officials lead to a paralysis of trade and danger to the travelling public, the responsibility will . . . rest entirely on the shoulders of the Railway Directors', declared the Parliamentary Committee of the Trades Union Congress.[5] Most observers agreed with this verdict, and the results of the ballot, announced by Bell on 3 November, were unambiguous. Of some 98,000 ballot papers issued just over 88,000 were returned, with nearly 77,000 in favour of a strike.

But the government had intervened, and separate meetings with representatives of both sides began at the Board of Trade on 25 October. 'In view of the distress and . . . serious dislocation to trade which would have been

---

[1] Raynes, op. cit., pp. 130–1. By 1906, however, the Railway Servants' programme included the demand that 'the system of working with only one man in motor cab be abolished on electric railways'.   [2] See p. 231.   [3] Quoted in Phelps Brown, op. cit., p. 301.
[4] *The Reformer's Year Book*, 1908, p. 180.
[5] Parliamentary Committee, *Minutes*, 16 Oct. 1907. The Committee, 'representing the whole Trade Union movement', also expressed 'their hearty and active sympathy with the railwaymen in their efforts to obtain recognition'.

caused by a general railway strike', Lloyd George was determined 'to take measures to bring the parties to an agreement'.[1] The companies must therefore be forced to accept his intervention. 'The Conciliation Act [of 1896] itself is a poor thing', he told Campbell-Bannerman. 'It is only the knowledge that there is something behind it that will induce the Directors to pay any attention.' Consequently, 'if the Directors refuse conciliation ... we must ... at once introduce a measure making Arbitration in railway disputes compulsory in all cases where the Board of Trade considers ... the dispute warrants such a course being adopted'. Armed with this threat, Lloyd George had little difficulty in getting the companies to talk, and he did not hesitate to use it during the negotiations which followed.[2]

When the meetings began, it quickly emerged that the crucial issue was the demand for recognition, and this was the only topic discussed.[3] After much debate the Board of Trade suggested that each company should have a system of conciliation boards and that the members need not be its own employees. This scheme would have enabled union officers to be elected to the boards, and was rejected by the companies. Lloyd George thereupon put forward a number of variations on the plan while continuing to urge the central principle of 'outside' representation. Eventually, in place of union recognition, the companies offered to include independent arbitration as the final stage in the conciliation system. Lloyd George agreed, and 'then there was the question of getting the unions to accept it'.[4]

According to J. H. Thomas, who had become the union's organizing secretary in 1906, the scheme was submitted to the companies and then to the unions all within 'a few hours'. The union representatives had no chance of discussing it except for a brief period during the evening on which it was adopted, and did not meet the company representatives at all.[5] G. R. Askwith believed that Bell had made Lloyd George's task easier by conceding that he was 'not going to press for recognition if he obtained a satisfactory method of dealing with grievances, consideration of the programme, and more opportunity for the men to deal with the conditions of their lives'.[6] Since the scheme appeared to satisfy these requirements, 'after a good deal of consideration and a good deal of reluctance, it was accepted by the unions'.[7]

In settling how long the agreement should run, the companies pressed hard for ten years, the unions for three, and compromise was reached on

[1] *Report on the Strikes and Lockouts of 1907*, Cd. 4254, 1908, p. 50.

[2] Frank Owen, *Tempestuous Journey*, 1954, p. 155; and William George, *My Brother and I*, 1958, p. 212. See also Phelps Brown, op. cit., p. 301.

[3] *Royal Commission on the Working of the Railway Conciliation and Arbitration Scheme of 1907, Minutes of Evidence*, Cd. 6014, 1911, Q. 12912, evidence of Sir Guy Granet, now general manager of Midland Railway, and secretary of the Committee of Company Chairmen which negotiated with Lloyd George.

[4] Cd. 6014, Q. 12912.
[6] Askwith, op. cit., p. 121.

[5] Ibid., Q. 1935.
[7] Cd. 6014, Q. 12912.

seven. The companies were consistent to the end: the agreement they signed was not with the unions but with Board of Trade representatives, including Lloyd George, who in turn signed separate agreements with the Amalgamated Society, the Associated Society, and the General Railway Workers' Union.[1] Whether the union leaders came to an understanding with Lloyd George not to raise the issue of recognition again during the term of the agreement remains unclear. Company spokesmen later asserted that they had signed the agreement at Lloyd George's 'urgent request' and under 'great pressure', on the understanding—'a solemn bargain'[2]—that the agreement 'provided an alternative to the recognition of the trade unions'[3] for the whole of its term—an understanding 'clearly laid down in the minutes of the meetings between the President of the Board of Trade and the directors'.[4] They also declared that the union leaders were parties to this understanding, but the Royal Commission of 1911 found no evidence that this was so.[5]

The scheme was complex. Within each company, the men were to be grouped into sections for which there were to be separate sectional boards. Their representatives on the boards had to be company employees elected under Board of Trade supervision by the workers of each section. Any question which a sectional board could not settle was to be referred to a central board whose workers' representatives were chosen from the employees' side of the sectional boards. If the central board failed to agree, or if either the directors or the men refused to accept the board's settlement, the matter could be referred to an independent arbitrator.[6] There were important provisos. Only questions concerning wages and hours could be dealt with, and in the first instance all claims had to be put through 'the usual channels'. This meant application to the departmental officers by the old method of petition and deputation. If the company rejected the claims or failed to reply within two months, the conciliation process could then begin at the sectional board level.

Eleven major companies signed the initial agreement on 6 November 1907, and thirty-five others signed Notices of Adhesion later. The North Eastern Railway, which recognized the unions, set up a conciliation scheme of its own,[7] and a few small lines also held aloof. But there was virtually industry-wide coverage: by 1909 the companies with conciliation

---

[1] *Report of the Board of Trade on the Railway Conciliation Boards*, Cd. 4534, 1909, appendix A.

[2] Cd. 6014, Q. 12912.   [3] Ibid., Q. 9067.

[4] Ibid., Q. 9068.   [5] *Report*, Cd. 5922, 1911, p. 10.

[6] Before whom a union officer was allowed to act as advocate.

[7] The scheme provided for one board with subcommittees handling the specialized interests. The men's secretary was a union officer—Bell himself in the first instance—and the board handled 'conditions of service' as well as wages and hours. But for all that, the agreement setting it up was not an agreement with the union, and there was no automatic provision for arbitration (Cd. 6014, Qs. 117, 129, 13452, 13472).

schemes[1] employed between them over 97 per cent. of the relevant grades of railway servants in the United Kingdom.

The year 1908 was largely occupied in setting up the boards and conducting the elections. According to Thomas, this gave some companies scope for delaying tactics, for interfering in elections with a view to securing the return of non-unionists, and for victimizing those elected as secretaries to the boards.[2] Over the railways as a whole, 808 out of a total of 890 workers' representatives were trade unionists, 720 of them members of the Amalgamated Society; but there was at least one sectional board, on the Great Eastern Railway, in which non-unionists were in a majority.[3] Once the boards were established, the submission of claims gave the companies further opportunities for obstruction. Some not only insisted on the men going through the full forms of the 'usual channels', but also made those forms as rigid and as time-consuming as possible.[4]

The working of the system produced further disappointments. The years 1908–9 were years of depression and 'a very severe reduction' in railway revenues. 'There is no doubt', said one general manager in 1911, 'that the settlements which were arrived at . . . in 1909 were to some extent tinged by the pessimism which existed at that time in the railway world.'[5] Besides this, overtime was cut down;[6] there were regradings and reclassifications of staff which the unions suspected were intended to minimize the financial burden of wage increases;[7] certain companies insisted that the right to interpret awards was a managerial prerogative; and the unions alleged preferential treatment of non-unionists.

The railway clerks and the footplate men had additional grievances. The clerks had been excluded from the scheme and at conferences in May 1908 and May 1909 affirmed their wish to be included,[8] believing that this would enable their union to enlarge its foothold. The strongly organized footplate men of the Associated Society, on the other hand, felt that inclusion limited their powers. They were covered by the same machinery as the weaker grades, and were inevitably in a minority on the central boards. Moreover, the limitation of negotiation to wages and hours was a retrograde step for them. Previously, 'whatever subject we wanted to discuss we were always able to discuss directly if necessary with the directors of the company'.[9] Such issues as fines, suspensions, medical

---

[1] *Report on the Strikes and Lockouts of 1908*, Cd. 4680, 1909, p. 139. Of these, two, in addition to the North Eastern Railway, recognized the Amalgamated Society—the North Staffordshire and the Barry lines, both small. The Barry company conceded recognition in 1908 after a dispute in which 95 per cent. of all grades handed in strike notices (Cd. 6014, Qs. 1997–8).

[2] Industrial Council, *Inquiry into Industrial Agreements*, Cd. 6953, 1913, Q. 13540.

[3] Cd. 6014, Q. 7599.   [4] Ibid., Qs. 29–32.

[5] Sam Fay of the Great Central (Ibid., Q. 11813).

[6] Partly a result of Board of Trade pressure on companies to reduce the hours worked.

[7] Industrial Council, *Inquiry into Industrial Agreements*, Cd. 6953, 1913, Q. 13540.

[8] Cd. 6014, Q. 6643.   [9] Ibid., Q. 3885.

examinations, eyesight tests, and promotion were vital to footplate staff, but some companies were using the letter of the agreement to exclude them from discussion.[1]

In 1908 their *Annual Report* stated that '. . . we believe that the locomotive men's salvation lies in minding their own business and dealing with employers direct, and that a wide berth for the Conciliation Scheme is the best advice we can give'.[2] Here and there the footplate men followed this advice successfully; but in other companies their efforts were rebuffed and they were held to the strict terms of the agreement.[3] Their membership, however, held up remarkably well during these years of unemployment and disappointment, whereas the Railway Servants fell from 98,000 in 1907 to 74,000 two years later, and the General Railway Workers also suffered losses.

By bold tactics Lloyd George had forced the companies to take their first reluctant steps towards collective bargaining with the unions, but the conciliation scheme itself could only be a temporary expedient. Lloyd George hoped that experience of the scheme would encourage the companies to take further steps later, but if it did not then trouble was bound to recur. The unions were still unrecognized, and the deputation system still exposed the active spirits to the danger of victimization. To them the scheme could not appear as more than a concession which would prepare the ground for advance to full recognition.

The Craft Societies in the Doldrums

The years of prosperity brought few great changes to the craft societies. At one extreme, the building workers remained in the downswing of their building cycle, which was little affected by the general economic revival. At the other, the printing craftsmen maintained a firm grip on the industry, extending their system of controls to cover new technical developments.

The difficulties of the craft societies are best illustrated by one of the few victories of the period—the revision of the national engineering agreement in 1907, when the signatory unions won some valuable modifications in the procedure for dealing with disputes. Previously the first stage had been for the workmen directly affected to organize a deputation to their employer, which clearly identified the active union members. Now alternative procedures allowed a local union officer to take up an issue direct with the secretary of the local employers' association, or either party to apply for a local conference. The procedure was speeded up by a ruling that a local conference must be held within twelve days of the application, and that a Central Conference must convene at the 'earliest date which can be conveniently arranged' to consider issues left unsettled by local conference. A further gain was a safeguard against victimization by the employers,

[1] Cd. 6014, Q. 459.   [2] Raynes, op. cit., p. 141.   [3] Cd. 6014, Q. 3922.

who guaranteed that 'no workman shall be required, as a condition of employment, to make a declaration as to whether he belongs to a trade union or not'.[1]

Apart from these changes, the agreement touched on every important craft issue without resolving any one of them. The 'machine question' was becoming even more acute with the emergence of a recognized class of 'semi-skilled' workers—'an intermediate class between the unskilled worker and the skilled mechanic'.[2] Since the Amalgamated Society of Engineers would take no effective steps to recruit this new class,[3] they could only repeat the old arguments for the payment of the skilled rate on all new machines. At the same time their executive, faced with the threat of retaliation by the employers, curbed union branches which tried to impose this policy by coercion. The Manchester District Committee, suspended in 1906 for defying the executive on this issue, asked 'how long this peace-at-any-price policy is to continue? . . . How long are the results of the debacle in 1898 to be with us? . . . The time has arrived when the engineering industry shall cease to be the happy hunting grounds of the handyman. . . .'[4] The most the Federation would grant in the 1907 revision was that 'consideration . . . be given to the case of workmen who may be displaced, with a view, if possible, of retaining their services on the work affected or finding other employment for them'.

The amount of permitted overtime was reduced from forty hours a month to thirty-two, but all the escape clauses remained, as did the ban on a general limitation of the number of apprentices, though the unions could now 'bring forward for discussion the proportion of apprentices generally employed in the whole federated area'. More adequate attention was paid to systems of payment by results, which were spreading rapidly[5] without protection for the workers under them except for those paid on the unpopular premium bonus system which was covered by the Carlisle Memorandum.[6] Now a further agreement extended the guaranteed time rate and the other safeguards contained in the Memorandum to all forms of piecework.

The continued support by the Engineers' leaders for the premium bonus system was strongly resented by many members. Other unions had already

---

[1] Engineering and Allied Employers' National Federation, *Thirty Years of Industrial Conciliation*, 1927, pp. 15, 70–71.

[2] *Select Committee on Fair Wages, Minutes of Evidence*, Cd. 4423, 1908, Q. 4188.

[3] 'The average A.S.E. member has indicated in the most unmistakable manner that the A.S.E. shall remain an organisation of fully-skilled and trained men. I believe he is wrong, but he . . . gives no indication of altering. . . .' (George Barnes, Amalgamated Society of Engineers, *Annual Report*, 1908).

[4] Amalgamated Society of Engineers, *Monthly Report*, Nov. 1906.

[5] In 1886 between 6 and 7 per cent. of fitters and turners, and 11 per cent. of machinemen, were paid by results; by 1906 the figures were 33 per cent. and 47 per cent. (Jefferys, op. cit., p. 129).   [6] See p. 343.

shown their hostility towards it.[1] The Trades Union Congress condemned the system in 1907, and in 1909 two conferences of the affected societies considered how to abolish it. A committee of inquiry collected evidence in a number of industrial centres and reported that the system was spreading from the ordnance, motor-car, locomotive, and electrical sections to marine and general engineering establishments, and from fitting and machining metals to moulding and woodwork.[2] It recommended joint action for total abolition.

This was heroic but unrealistic. A further conference in April 1910 agreed on joint action, but another in August showed signs of disunity and uncertainty and decided only that 'steps should be taken to ascertain the opinion of the workers as to the course to be adopted in an effort to deal with the question'.[3] A ballot returned 95,738 votes to 9,965 in favour of total abolition, by strike action if necessary; but the majority in the Amalgamated Society of Engineers was only three to one, and the executive declared that it was 'not going to lead on the matter'.

The Engineers also rejected a national settlement on hours. The general practice was a fifty-three or fifty-four-hour week with two breaks a day for meals. Some firms, however, worked fifty, forty-nine, or even forty-eight hours on a one-break system. The 1907 proposal for fifty-one hours with one break would seem to have offered a big improvement to most engineers, and the executive of the Amalgamated Society appealed to the members for support on the grounds that they were already morally committed to acceptance; but it was turned down. Nevertheless, despite this further evidence of craft traditionalism, the one-break system gradually spread as individual firms adopted it.

The employers considered that the 1898 agreement had helped, along with the decisions of the House of Lords in the *Taff Vale* and *Quinn* v. *Leathem* cases, to bring them industrial peace. Sir Andrew Noble, senior partner in Armstrong Whitworths, told the Royal Commission on Trade Disputes and Trade Combinations of 1903 that there was greater security in the industry, and that the procedure worked well. 'In very few cases have disputed questions run the whole course of this procedure without some way having been found out of the difficulty.'[4] The record of Central Conferences from 1905 onwards,[5] however, shows that issues which did reach the national level were not easily resolved. In 1905 there was no agreement on thirteen out of sixteen items discussed; in 1906 on ten out of twenty-seven; and in 1907 on twenty-three out of thirty-five.

[1] See p. 344.
[2] The 1906 Board of Trade earnings inquiry showed between 4 and 5 per cent. of male engineering and boilermaking workers on premium bonus. In 1909 the Amalgamated Society carried out their own census which showed 9 per cent. of its members working on the system.
[3] Trades Union Congress, *Annual Report*, 1910, Parliamentary Committee Report.
[4] *Minutes of Evidence*, Cd. 2826, 1906, Q. 2410.
[5] *Report on the Strikes and Lockouts of 1905*, and subsequent *Reports*.

The failure of the national negotiators to settle so many issues, either by revision of the agreement or by dealing with individual disputes, gave encouragement to local action particularly over payment by results. The district committees of the Amalgamated Society varied in their attitude to piece-work. In some Lancashire towns, where 80 per cent. of the men in the textile machine shops were paid by results, the earnings of piece-workers were protected by a percentage increase in piece rates wherever time rates were raised. Elsewhere only their nominal time rate was raised with the timeworkers' wages, and the piece rates which determined their actual earnings were unchanged. Some branches still resisted the extension of piece-work or even opposed it entirely. There were also local variations in the method of settling piece rates. Only in a very few places were there formal procedures for collective bargaining in the workshop over matters such as this. Often rates were settled by the 'principle of mutuality', which allowed individual bargaining on this issue between the worker and his foreman or rate-fixer.[1] But in other instances employers fixed the prices at will, and workers complained if they did not yield adequate weekly earnings.

Changes in products, in tools and machines, and in workshop practice and organization added further complexities. To cope with them district committees were revising their by-laws and port rules, either unilaterally or by agreements with local employers' associations—some of which were reached after reference to Central Conference. But they could not cover the finer points of machine-manning and piece rates, or the growing number of disputes over discipline, clocking in and out, and job cards. On these matters the decision depended on the strength and quality of union leadership in the shop, where the shop steward had already made his appearance.

The 1892 conference of the Engineers had given district committees the power to appoint shop stewards, and to define and direct their activities. They were already an established institution in a few districts such as Tyneside, where in 1890 it was 'the custom amongst the larger trades in the factories and shipyards' to depute shop stewards, 'and in some cases vigilance committees', to see that members remained in benefit and to tell newcomers that 'they will have to join or they can't work there'.[2] In some places their functions were expanding. The Manchester District Committee allowed shop committees to negotiate piece rates with foremen, and by 1897 Manchester employers were complaining of 'forms of interference . . . surreptitiously and continuously exercised by shop stewards'.[3] In 1896

---

[1] The 'principle of mutuality' was embodied in the 1898 settlement. The local officers of the union could, of course, attempt to guide the members in these individual negotiations.

[2] *Workman's Times*, 28 Nov. 1890.

[3] Federated Engineering and Shipbuilding Employers, *Second Series of Examples of Restriction and Interference*, 16 Nov. 1897, Glasgow.

the Glasgow Employers' Association, referring to 'members of the newly formed Vigilance Committee of the A.S.E. known as Shop Stewards', complained of cases 'where individual men were quite satisfied with the pay and the increases they had received but yet were practically driven out of the shop' by shop stewards.[1] In the following year a Clyde firm reported how shop stewards 'repeatedly checked one of the turners for turning out too much work'.[2] Glasgow and London shop stewards were also said to be vigilant over the observance of craft rules. Here and there union works committees were set up to discuss factory rules and other matters with management.[3] By 1909 stewards were being elected, at least in some shops, in most of the major centres, and their number and functions continued to grow.

Some of the societies which were not parties to the 1898 agreement were able to extract advantages from their position. The Friendly Society of Ironfounders, for example, continued to press for a ratio of one apprentice to three journeymen, and in Sheffield, where the ratio had been exceeded, the union conducted a successful campaign to restore it.[4] On the other hand, a number of weaker societies decided they were better off under the disputes procedure. The Electrical Trades Union signed in 1906; the Amalgamated Toolmakers and the National Society of Smiths and Hammermen in 1908; and the National Society of Amalgamated Brassworkers in 1909. The stronger sectional societies still remained aloof, and firmly rebuffed the Leeds employers when in 1907 they refused to negotiate with the sectional societies unless they came under the procedure agreement.

Even for them, however, the advantages of independence were dwindling. William Mosses, secretary of the Patternmakers, wrote that he knew of no instance of a sectional society obtaining any advantage through separate negotiations in 1909, and that by 1910 'it was evident that however a conference varied in numbers and personnel the pace was set by the big battalions, and their settlement of general questions applied to all'.[5] To some extent these powerful independent societies were being brought under their own separate conciliation procedures. In the North-east patternmakers were regulated by a board, and another covering ironfounders, which had broken up in 1903, was re-established in 1907.[6] In 1909, at the instigation of the employers, a board was set up to cover ironfounding in Lancashire,[7] thereby bringing the proportion of the

---

[1] Scottish Engineering Employers' Association, *Diamond Jubilee Handbook*, 1953, p. 2.

[2] Federated Engineering and Shipbuilding Employers, *First Series*, &c., 4 Nov. 1897.

[3] *Works Committees* (*Industrial Reports No. 2.*), Report of an Inquiry made by the Ministry of Labour, 1918, pp. 71–72, 93–95.

[4] S. Pollard, *The History of Labour in Sheffield*, 1959, p. 241.

[5] Mosses, op. cit., pp. 208–9.

[6] *Report on the Strikes and Lockouts of 1907*, Cd. 4254, 1908, p. 133.

[7] Fyrth and Collins, op. cit., p. 121.

Friendly Ironfounders' membership covered by this mode of regulation to nearly half.

While the Engineers set the pace in district wage bargaining, its members would permit no central co-ordination of these movements, even by their own executive.[1] In February 1908 a serious stoppage began on the North-east coast, where the members of the three signatory societies rejected reductions which had been accepted by the conciliation boards of the Patternmakers and Ironfounders, and by the twenty-two other unions affected. At a Central Conference in January the leaders of the signatory unions had 'declined to accept any reduction on their own responsibility, but undertook to submit the employers' proposals to a ballot of the men'.[2]

At the subsequent district ballot the vote went in favour of a strike, which began on 20 February. Lloyd George intervened and secured an offer by the employers to maintain the existing skilled rate of 36s. until Easter, when the issue would be decided by a referee. These terms, recommended by the national leaders, were likewise voted down. By this time a local unofficial movement within the union was circulating leaflets demanding that 36s. should be recognized as a guaranteed minimum. This demand for a minimum 'living wage' was seen by the employers as the effect of socialist agitation and 'the transformation of commercial problems into class problems'.[3] They had 'specially guarded', said Sir Andrew Noble, 'against a minimum rate in [the] agreement with the Societies . . ., for the reason . . . that there are very different degrees of skill'.[4]

After further talks between Lloyd George and national and local representatives, it was decided to hold yet another ballot. Barnes toured the affected centres, explaining the new proposals in more detail, and met with a rough reception.[5] In Glasgow he spoke of an 'undemocratic feeling' among the rank and file which expressed itself in mistrust of officials and the transfer of power into the hands of unofficial movements.[6] Soon after this speech the executive expelled four Tyneside members for issuing 'inflammatory' leaflets, an act promptly followed by a protest meeting.

Barnes was now openly criticizing the Society's constitution which, he said, put the control of a strike into the hands of the locality concerned. The only circumstances in which a general ballot of the whole membership could be taken on whether to close a strike was when all local means of

[1] See p. 342.
[2] *Report on the Strikes and Lockouts of 1908*, Cd. 4680, 1909, p. 49.
[3] *Newcastle Weekly Journal*, 6 June 1908.
[4] *Select Committee on Fair Wages, Minutes of Evidence*, Cd. 4423, 1908, Q. 5452. In the 1907 revision the employers had conceded that in fixing the rates of skilled workmen 'the Employer shall have regard to the rates prevailing in the district . . .'. But the operative clause was still that 'employers have the right to employ workmen at rates of wages mutually satisfactory . . .'.
[5] *Newcastle Weekly Chronicle*, 14 Mar. 1908.
[6] Ibid., 25 Apr. 1908.

settling it had failed—a clause open to wide variations in interpretation—
or when the executive and the district committee had a difference of
opinion. Barnes demanded a general ballot on the latter grounds, and
resigned when the executive declared this 'premature in the light of the
district ballot taken so recently'.[1]

After the men had rejected further offers, the employers announced in
July 1908 that the dispute had been referred to their Federation executive,
who now threatened a general lock-out of all three societies if work was not
resumed. Another ballot in August gave plenary powers to the union
executives who thereupon accepted the reduction along with a guarantee
of no further wage alterations for six months. They were also to co-operate
with the employers in considering 'in what respect the present procedure
for dealing with wages questions shall be amended in order to avoid stoppages of work'. The terms were submitted to the membership under a
renewed threat of lock-out and accepted by 4,609 votes to 3,739.[2] A Central
Conference then discussed the employers' desire for 'a Wages Board, so as
to avoid stoppages of work in future . . . applicable to any . . . part of the
country'. But the discussions made no progress and in December 1908 the
matter was 'adjourned *sine die*'.[3]

The one clear consequence of the dispute was the loss of 'one of the
most efficient and able secretaries since William Allan'.[4] Barnes's resignation was an escape from an almost intolerable situation, for opposition to
central authority within the Society had become so strong that the Final
Appeals Committee was reversing more executive decisions than at any
other period in the Society's history, at some meetings as many as half of
those referred to it. Rejection by the membership of agreements negotiated
with the employers was a common enough occurrence, but when Barnes
found that not even his executive dared to support him[5] he decided it was
time to go.

Though the employers' proposal for a wages board had come to nothing,
a different technique for regulating general wage movements began to win
acceptance. In February 1909 a local conference on a dispute in Hull
decided that, in return for the employers withdrawing a demand for a
reduction, the standard rate of Amalgamated Society members in federated shops in Hull would remain unchanged for five years. This innovation
spread rapidly during succeeding months. London, Sheffield, Barnsley,

---

[1] *Newcastle Weekly Journal*, 4 Apr. 1908.

[2] *Report on the Strikes and Lockouts of 1908*, Cd. 4680, 1909, p. 54. The total of working days
lost by the dispute was 1,700,000.

[3] Amalgamated Society of Engineers, *Monthly Report*, Nov. and Dec. 1908.

[4] Jefferys, op. cit., p. 168.

[5] When the executive had crushed the unofficial stoppage on Clydeside five years earlier, it
was subsequently ordered by the Appeals Committee to pay the strike benefits which it had
withheld, and all four of its members who stood for re-election shortly after were unseated.
See p. 342.

and Barrow signed five-year agreements; Manchester and Newton three-year agreements.[1] The new secretary of the Amalgamated Society, Jenkin Jones, conceded that 'chaining up . . . both sides for five years . . . in some districts no doubt will absorb attention and possible criticism', but 'we have every reason to believe this will be a great advantage to our members and the society seeing that the present rate is the highest obtained . . . in the shipbuilding and engineering trade'.[2]

In shipbuilding the Boilermakers had run into bad times. Their last sustained period of high employment had been that of 1897–9. Having risen from 2·1 per cent. in 1899 to 11·7 per cent. in 1903, unemployment dropped only to 7·0 per cent. in 1906, rose again to 22·7 per cent. in 1908, and was still 21·4 per cent. in 1909.[3] During the good years the Society had made over-generous revisions in benefits, with the result that the heavy burden of payments had produced financial weakness and a decline of rank-and-file confidence in the leadership. A specially elected finance committee had to impose sharp cuts in benefits and an increase in contributions in January 1909.

Meanwhile the old weakness on Clydeside had reappeared. 'Some disaffected members . . . have formed themselves into a "Vigilance Committee", but instead of vigilantly assisting in setting their house in order, they are very assiduously disintegrating it further'.[4] In 1906 the members had embarked on an unauthorized strike to secure a wage increase already granted in the North-east and elsewhere,[5] and were only forced back by the threat of a general lock-out of all boilermakers in the North-west. During this stoppage the employers on the North-east coast gave notice to terminate their 1894 procedure agreement with the Boilermakers, 'with a view to securing a more effective Agreement on a national basis'.[6] Negotiations followed with the Shipbuilding Employers' Federation and produced the Edinburgh Agreement of 1907, a temporary settlement which the Boilermakers declared later was 'forced upon us at the point of the bayonet'.

The Agreement pledged the Society 'not to interfere with the alterations of yard customs, although these . . . meant the withdrawal of previous privileges and the reduction of wages, . . . to admit to our membership, without penalty, apprentices who had gone from yard to yard during trade disputes, blacklegging our members . . . and to work unlimited overtime,

[1] Amalgamated Society of Engineers, *Monthly Report*, Mar. 1909 to Sept. 1909.
[2] Ibid., Apr. 1909.
[3] *Fifteenth Abstract of Labour Statistics*, Cd. 6228, 1912, p. 3.
[4] Amalgamated Society of Engineers, *Monthly Journal*, Dec. 1907 and Mar. 1909; United Society of Boilermakers and Iron and Steel Shipbuilders, *Monthly Report*, Jan. and Apr. 1909.
[5] Almost 600,000 working days were lost.
[6] *Report on the Rules of Voluntary Conciliation and Arbitration Boards*, Cd. 3788, 1907, p. 144.

at the discretion of the employers'.[1] Further negotiations were to seek a permanent agreement to rule out 'extreme measures' by either side until full discussions had been held; but these were interrupted by an even larger stoppage.

In December 1907, with trade once more depressed, the employers in all shipbuilding areas demanded wage reductions and met no resistance except, as in engineering, on the North-east coast. During renewed negotiations the North-east employers modified their demands, which were then accepted by societies representing about three-fourths of the men concerned, but rejected by 5,000 members of the Shipwrights and other woodworking unions, who came out in January 1908. Lesser threats having failed to intimidate the strikers, the Shipbuilding Employers' Federation proposed a general lock-out of the unions involved.[2] When the local men voted to continue the stoppage, the unions held a national ballot which came down strongly in favour of arbitration. This, however, was refused by the employers, who in April locked out 13,000 members in Scotland and the North of England, putting 22,000 other workers out of work as a consequence. The unions not directly involved were naturally anxious to achieve a settlement, and the Boilermakers were particularly incensed at their impotence. Their *Monthly Report* for April argued that recent experience in engineering and shipbuilding must hasten the coming of compulsory arbitration. With that, they could reasonably demand the closed shop, and then the loss of the right to strike would only remove a costly and almost ineffective weapon.[3]

Meetings between the President of the Board of Trade and the contesting parties finally secured a settlement under which the North-east strikers were to accept the reduction and a conference was to be held between the Employers' Federation and all the shipbuilding societies to consider setting up a permanent disputes procedure. These terms were accepted by a tiny majority—24,145 to 22,110—which it was said was contributed by the men outside the strike area.[4] The stoppage had cost 1,700,000 working days—exactly the same loss as in the parallel engineering stoppage.

Negotiations subsequently held between the Federation and all the

[1] United Society of Boilermakers and Iron and Steel Shipbuilders, *Monthly Report*, Apr. 1909.

[2] The employers' side of the Wear Conciliation Board had already given notice to terminate the Board 'in order that the questions in dispute should be dealt with on a national basis' (*Report on the Strikes and Lockouts of 1908*, Cd. 4680, 1909, p. 42).

[3] Quoted in the *Sunderland Weekly Echo*, 17 Apr. 1908. At the Trades Union Congress of 1908 their secretary, Cummings, proposed a motion, which Wilkie of the Shipwrights seconded, that the Board of Trade be given powers to inquire into, and report on, any dispute if requested to do so by either side. 'Pending such . . . report no strike or lockout shall take place.' It was defeated by 978,000 votes to 616,000, and a similar attempt in 1909 also failed.

[4] *Newcastle Weekly Chronicle*, 30 May 1908.

shipbuilding unions except those of the labourers produced an agreement which was provisionally signed in December and ratified by membership vote in March 1909. General wage movements were to be negotiated nationally by the Federation and the unions;[1] and were to apply to all the crafts covered by the agreement and to every federated firm. A minimum period of six months must elapse between general movements, which were to be standardized at 5 per cent. for piece-work rates and 1*s.* per week for time rates. An application for a general wage change must be preceded by a preliminary conference between the Federation and the unions 'to discuss the position generally'.

The branches and districts did not welcome national regulation of wages. 'While they say it might be quite easy', said Cummings, 'to get a national reduction, it would be exceedingly difficult to organise a national advance.' The Federation chairman assured him that one of the employers' main aims was uniformity in advances as well as in reductions. 'One of the gravest causes of warfare . . . has been sectional disputes, has been trades asking for different rates and advances at different times in different districts. . . . This clause must be passed if we are to arrive at a satisfactory conclusion.'[2]

For 'questions other than general fluctuations in wages' there was a procedure essentially similar to the engineering agreement, though rather more elaborate, leading up to a Central Conference. If all this failed, 'either party desirous to have such question further considered, shall, prior to any stoppage of work, refer same for final settlement to a Grand Conference to be held between the Federation and all the Unions parties to this agreement'. Existing machinery for dealing with piece-prices and demarcation was to be built into this scheme. There were to be no stoppages until the procedure had been exhausted, and the agreement was to run for at least three years, thereafter subject to six months' notice on either side.[3] The unions pressed for a final court of arbitration or a neutral chairman, but the employers refused.

[1] 'Our strong desire', the Federation chairman told the union representatives, 'is that you gentlemen should have greater powers . . . I don't think . . . that we will really have industrial peace until the delegates have greater powers' (*Notes of Conference between the Executive Board of the Shipbuilding Employers' Federation and representatives of the various Shipyard Trades.* Edinburgh, 11 June 1908).

[2] *Notes of Conference*, &c., 28 Oct. 1908. Helpers, other labourers, enginemen and cranemen were excluded from the agreement, largely because the treatment of these groups varied so widely between districts. In the North-east there was now an employers' board which arbitrated on differences between platers and helpers, whereas Clydeside employers had no dealings whatever with the helpers, there being only an informal understanding that when the platers received an advance they paid a proportionate increase to their helpers.

[3] *Report on the Strikes and Lockouts of 1908*, Cd. 4680, 1909, pp. 41–47. One consolation of the new agreement for the Boilermakers was that it put an end to the concessions on craft rules which the Federation had forced them to yield in 1907 pending a national system of dispute settlement (*Monthly Report*, Apr. 1909).

Since the Boilermakers and the employers in the North-east had already reached preliminary agreement on provisions of this kind before the strike began, it seems probable that, but for the woodworking societies' resistance to the 1908 wage reduction, a situation similar to that in engineering would have developed, with some societies committed to a national disputes procedure and others outside it. The strike, however, created a situation in which the Shipbuilding Employers' Federation was able to sweep them all in. The Federation kept up its drive to contain the unions. The discharge note system was introduced throughout the whole Federated area, and when the unions challenged it at Central Conference the employers declared their action a matter of yard administration which the new disputes procedure was never intended to cover.[1] Disaffection among the Boilermakers now spread to Liverpool, where a group of members calling themselves the Mersey District Aggregate Committee circularized the district committees of the Society attacking the new agreement.[2]

For both engineering and shipbuilding the North-east coast continued to be the main trouble spot, as it had been in the first five years of the century. Throughout this complicated series of disputes and negotiations, as in the equally involved dealings of the depression of 1903–4, it was the men of the North-east who refused to compromise. Elsewhere reductions were accepted, but here they were rejected by a strong unofficial movement basing itself on the principles of 'the living wage' and local union autonomy.[3]

Like the shipbuilding employers, the Federation of Master Printers sought to contain the craft societies within a complete national system of collective bargaining. In 1907 they resolved that 'the time has arrived when a definite effort should be made to establish a permanent joint board . . . to which . . . all disputes may be referred for solution or arbitration . . .'.[4] The Printing and Kindred Trades Federation was approached and a board eventually established in 1909. The Typographical Association, the Bookbinders, and a number of minor societies agreed to participate, but the London Society of Compositors was among those which remained outside, one of their members saying that 'if we accepted it, our chief weapon would be gone'.[5] The societies which joined the board, however, differed from the Compositors only over the question of tactics, for they refused to submit cases to it. Although representatives continued to be elected for several years, it was ultimately allowed to lapse.[6]

---

[1] *Minutes of Meetings of Standing Committee under the Shipbuilding Trades Agreement*, July 1909.

[2] United Society of Boilermakers and Iron and Steel Shipbuilders, *Monthly Report*, June 1909.

[3] 'In recent years there has been growing a desire for what is termed "local rule", and to be . . . "masters of their own destiny". . . . No true advance or good can come without true and complete executive control' (Boilermakers' *Monthly Report*, May 1908).

[4] Child, op. cit.

[5] Howe, op. cit., p. 22.   [6] Musson, op. cit., p. 295.

The Federation were no more successful in their attempts to secure national agreements on craft issues. In 1907 they asked the Bookbinders and Machine Rulers to negotiate an agreement 'clearly defining on national lines the . . . work to be done by members of the Union, and . . . the . . . work which might be performed by female labour'. A conference was held during the following year, but no agreement could be reached, and no headway was made by subsequent correspondence.[1]

An approach to the Typographical Association proved equally abortive. When a conference of the Association in 1908 introduced 'a whole series' of new and revised rules which 'were to be enforced upon employers' without consultation,[2] the Federation and the Linotype Users' Association protested at once, demanding a conference to negotiate any changes which might be required. The society's executive conceded that it was 'better to get this matter of the new rules settled between the national bodies rather than to cause . . . a hundred little difficulties' by negotiating at branch level,[3] but protracted negotiations in 1909 led nowhere. The employers brought up their grievances about all the old unresolved craft issues; the Master Printers concentrating on apprenticeship rules and the Linotype Users on overtime, the output of linotype machines and the society's claim to control the rotary machine department. When the conference finally broke down the branches demanded local enforcement, and the executive had no choice but to agree. During 1910 the branches began to serve notice of the new rules up and down the country, and it was a reasonable expectation that trouble lay ahead.[4]

The Federation's attempts to foster collective regulation did not extend to the National Society of Operative Printers' Assistants, which was still weak compared with the craft societies. In 1907, after securing improved agreements in London,[5] the union sought a comprehensive agreement covering the whole of the provinces but was rebuffed by the Federation, who went on to check it at local level. In 1908 the Leeds branch struck for recognition from their employers' association, which was one of those which still hoped to maintain its freedom concerning the operation of rotary machines. When the strike threatened to involve the whole of the Leeds printing trade the Federation advised all those associations which had not yet conceded recognition to refrain from giving it.[6] Soon afterwards the discovery of financial irregularities caused wholesale losses of

---

[1] Bundock, op. cit., pp. 75–76.

[2] One of them, for example, was designed to enforce the society's authority over rotary minders and other machine operators.

[3] Musson, op. cit., p. 164.

[4] Ibid., p. 166.

[5] The agreements came into effect in 1908, and union membership doubled by the end of the year to 7,100, 1,600 of them women.

[6] Child, op. cit.

membership. In 1909 George Isaacs[1] took over the secretaryship of a union virtually bankrupt, and began the task of reconstruction.[2]

There were, however, important developments in collective bargaining in one section of the industry. In 1906 the London Society of Compositors threatened to strike the whole of London when a firm of general printers with whom they were in dispute began recruiting non-union labour. The newspaper proprietors, realizing that the stoppage would cause far greater damage to them than to the rest of the trade, withdrew from the London Master Printers' Association, set up the Newspaper Proprietors' Association, and signed separate agreements with the Compositors and the other London unions.[3]

The National Printers' Warehousemen and Cutters, which had expanded into the provinces and had begun to admit women in 1904, secured from this new employers' association an agreement on 30s. for a forty-two-hour week consisting of six seven-hour night shifts. They also negotiated an agreement with the newly formed Federation of Wholesale Agents which improved the long hours and low wages of the London wholesale publishing trade; but almost at once the Federation circularized the men offering them holidays and sickness benefit in addition to the new rate if they would abandon the union. Many did so, and thereafter conditions reverted to pre-agreement levels.[4]

The skilled Tailors persisted in their ambivalent attitudes to new methods and to less skilled workers. In 1899, when the Society decided to break with tradition by opening a Female Section—duly formed the following year—[5] the editorial of its *Journal* reiterated the old demand that the employers should 'work with us to put a ring fence round the order trade, and send the sweater to the factory; that is the primal change we have been waiting for these thirty years. . . . All things else will drop into their appointed place.'[6] On the other hand, societies of Jewish tailors were approached to join the Amalgamated, and by 1905 there was a small nucleus of Jewish membership in London. In the early years of the new century the *Journal* began a campaign to educate the members in the need to work 'in the interest of the whole industry rather than in the interest of a small and narrowing section . . .'.[7] The Society must accept machinery and subdivision of labour in the organized shops, and go outside the craft trade to organize the factory worker. The factory could not be ignored or destroyed, and the only hope of the Society was to regulate factory conditions, thereby protecting the skilled worker also.

Many leading craft employers had long been ready to endorse this

---

[1] Isaacs, George (b. 1883). General secretary, National Society of Operative Printers and Assistants, 1909–47. M.P., 1923–4, 1929–31, 1939–59. Minister of Labour, 1945–50.
[2] Suthers, op. cit., p. 32. [3] Howe, op. cit., p. 15.
[4] Bundock, op. cit., pp. 139–41, 147–8. [5] See p. 138.
[6] May 1899. [7] Dec. 1901.

attitude, for it promised a more effective regulation of competition. The Federation president told the Fair Wages Committee in 1908 that 'what is wanted is . . . more and better organisation to unite those who are doing an inferior class of work'. He had told the Society's leaders: 'You must get your sub-stratum right before you can build a decent social fabric for yourselves.'[1]

Even so, it was an uphill battle. The *Journal* admitted that 'it is not easy for men who, even forty years ago, were in complete control of an industry, to take up a rear-rank position, especially if the front rank is a petticoat one. Bitter antagonism has been shown, and harsh language used.'[2] When the Oldham branch president asked if the Society's policy on Jewish tailors meant that 'men that work for the sweater are entitled to come to our Club House and claim to be received by us as members?', the *Journal* commented that 'these questions are being asked in many branches. They have blocked the way of every E.C. elected.'[3] The process of educating the members had at least begun to have some effect, however, for the 1908 conference endorsed by a large majority an executive proposal that the Society should regulate work done on the subdivisional system.

Nevertheless, the organizing secretary held that the members would view the new policy 'with considerable disfavour',[4] and the executive proceeded with great caution. At a conference with the National Federation of Merchant Tailors in August 1909, when the employers urged the executive formally to accept outwork and the day-wage system, they fell back on the craft argument that both tended to undermine union conditions, and no agreement was reached.[5]

Recent experience in London had not strengthened the expansionists' case. With the prosperity of 1906 had come an agitation among the East End Jews for the abolition of outwork. Their resentment was concentrated on the 'domestic middlemen', the smaller contractors who took work out from some tailors and wholesalers and pressed their employees hard in the search for cost reductions. When the master tailors resisted their workers' demand for the abolition of outwork, a large-scale strike followed, with 5,000 workers remaining out for about eleven days, 650 establishments being affected.[6] The leaders of the Amalgamated Society soon took over and the strikers joined in their thousands, maintaining a remarkable discipline.

The stoppage ended when an important wholesale employer came forward with a proposal which he asserted would abolish sweating by attacking the 'irresponsible competition' which lay at the root of it.[7] The consequent agreement negotiated with the London Master Tailors'

[1] *Select Committee on Fair Wages, Minutes of Evidence*, Cd. 4423, 1908, Q. 4952.
[2] May 1905. [3] Ibid., Dec. 1906.
[4] Ibid., June 1908. [5] Ibid., Sept. 1909.
[6] *Report on the Strikes and Lockouts of 1906*, Cd. 3711, 1907, p. 96.
[7] Amalgamated Society of Tailors and Tailoresses, *Journal*, July 1906.

Improvement Association reduced the working day from thirteen hours to twelve; substituted day-work for piece-work; and provided for a conciliation board. It also laid down that all workers in federated firms must be members of the union, and that no member must work for a non-federated firm.[1] This, it was hoped, would be the means through which competition would be controlled.

There followed an astonishing influx of Jewish workers into the Society; for a short period the nominal London membership stood at something like 10,000.[2] Union and trade papers alike rhapsodized over this 'astonishing transformation in the whole conditions of a great industry . . . on lines which yield every hope of permanence, and the complete fusion of the interests of employer and employed'.[3] The 'entire industrial and economic position of some twenty thousand people had at one blow . . . been entirely revolutionised. . . . Nothing like it . . . has ever been effected by any trade union in the same space of time.'[4]

A warning note, however, came from the *Outfitter*. The London trade was being undercut by Leeds and Bristol, and the master tailors' organization must be extended to all centres, with the defaulting minority who refused to toe the line being dealt with by Parliament. In London, meanwhile, employers who could not accept the terms must leave the trade; or their men must be encouraged to strike until they came into line.[5] But this implied a strength of which the East End tailors were not yet capable. Depression brought back all the old weaknesses: the struggle for work, the undercutting, the mutual mistrust. Despite the setting-up of the conciliation board 'to put a stop to . . . illegal and unfair competition', with a fund jointly subscribed to finance strikes upon defaulting employers, the rot soon set in. By 1908 the board had collapsed, the membership had disappeared, and the fruits of victory had become, in the words of the *Journal*, 'as ashes in the mouth'.[6]

Meanwhile the West End branch, the largest in the Society, had seceded. Its members, with their high wage rates and special craft regulations, had long seen themselves as a superior class. For some years they had been manœuvring to absorb the other London branches and operate as an independent unit which was merely federated with the provincial branches. These attempts failed and in 1905 about 900 of the West End craftsmen broke away to become the London Tailors and Tailoresses, led by James Macdonald, secretary of the London Trades Council. They decided 'that never again would a provincial organisation be allowed to interfere with London trade regulations and London ambitions'.[7]

[1] Amalgamated Society of Tailors and Tailoresses, *Journal*, July 1906.
[2] Ibid., Aug. 1906.   [3] Ibid., July 1906, quoting from *Men's Wear*.
[4] Ibid., July 1906.   [5] Quoted ibid., July 1906.   [6] Ibid., Oct. 1908.
[7] Ibid., Sept. 1908. See also issues of July and Aug. 1905.

The Amalgamated Union of Clothiers' Operatives, centred on Leeds, more than doubled its membership over the decade from 1,400 in 1900 to 3,300 in 1910. The majority of the new recruits were women factory workers of the wholesale trade, who appear to have been influenced both by the anti-sweating agitation which began in 1906 and by the establishment of the first Trade Board in 1909. The union complained that the Amalgamated Society of Tailors was cutting in to organize the factory workers, including women and girls, and was using its entrenched position on local trades councils to hamper the organizing efforts of the Clothiers' Operatives in new areas. One member commented in 1910 that 'the excessive zeal, enthusiastic interest, and overflowing sympathy displayed by the A.S.T. for the Jewish workers in East London savours very much of the solicitude of the cannibal for the newly arrived missionary'.[1]

For all that, the long-term decline in the membership of the Amalgamated Tailors continued, and from 18,000 in 1891 it was down to 12,000 by 1910. One sign of the limited success of the new policies was the female membership, which fluctuated between 300 and 400 until the coming of the Trade Board, when it rose to 700. But there was not much here to show that it paid to keep up with the times, and the evidence could equally well support the argument that craftsmen should continue to fight for their own hand so long as they could.

Similarly, for most of the societies in the minor craft trades, including furniture, coachmaking, cutlery, leather, glass-making, and cigar-making, it was a period of decline or at best stagnation. The Journeyman Silk Hatters also suffered losses, but the Felt Hatters grew substantially after a compromise settlement of a strike at Denton to limit the operation of certain machines by youths, in which the Stockport employers had locked out their workers in support of their Denton colleagues. Otherwise only the two bakers' unions showed significant gains.

Inter-union Conflict

Between 1900 and 1910 there was no repetition of the great demarcation battles over shipyard jobs of the previous decade. The Shipwrights, for example, were allowed to proceed undisturbed with the absorption of local societies in Newport, Gloucester, and on the Wear, and of several small national societies, including the Ship Constructive Association, which organized Admiralty shipwrights, the United Drillers, hitherto under the Boilermakers' 'protection', and the Amalgamated Drillers.[2] Among the engineering societies, 'there was scarcely a trade against whom charges were not made by the Society [of Engineers] and counter-charges were as frequent',[3] but few of them reached the stage of a serious stoppage.

[1] Amalgamated Union of Clothiers' Operatives, *Monthly Gazette*, Mar. 1910.
[2] During this process of absorption the Society was re-named the Ship Constructive and Shipwrights' Association.   [3] Jefferys, op. cit., p. 158.

Other industries, however, provided abundant evidence of continuing inter-union conflict, whether over jobs or over members. The dispute between the Typographical Association and the London Societies had been exacerbated in 1902 when the Compositors proposed to extend their radius from fifteen to thirty miles from the centre of London. Since this would have involved the absorption of twelve branches of the Typographical Association, war would have been declared; but the proposal was dropped, as was a similar plan in 1904.[1] On their side, the Typographical Association alleged that members who moved to London met with refusal to recognize their cards and obstruction in securing jobs. Reciprocity agreements, which also included the Scottish Typographical Association and the Dublin Typographical Society, were drawn up, but no serious attempt was made to operate them.[2]

In 1907 matters were brought to a head by a complex quarrel over the situation at a Reading branch of a large London firm. The Compositors and the Printing Machine Managers set up branches in towns around London and the Typographical Association set up a branch in London. The Compositors changed their name to the London and Provincial Society of Compositors, and the Machine Managers deleted 'London' from their title and claimed to be a national society.[3] The Parliamentary Committee of the Trades Union Congress recommended amalgamation, and during 1908–10 several conferences were held to discuss various schemes. The principle was unanimously accepted; a constitutional framework was provisionally agreed on; and for a time enthusiasm ran high. But the project foundered when the London Societies refused to surrender their individual autonomy, demanding control over their own funds, the admission of new members, the London agreements, and the calling of strikes.[4]

The most serious of these inter-union disputes arose from the widening craft interests of the Typographical Association. Whereas at one time its concern had been mainly with provincial compositors, the turn of the century had seen a growing interest in such previously neglected groups as readers and, more important, machinemen, including platen and rotary minders. The fact that London already had specialist societies for these groups resulted in clashes on such issues as geographical demarcation, recognition of cards, and transfer of members. Already in the nineties, some socialist members of the Typographical Association, like their counterparts among the Engineers, had started to demand more 'democratic' constitutional forms and a wider solidarity. Any proposal to admit

[1] Musson, op. cit., p. 274.	[2] Howe and Waite, op. cit., pp. 272–3.
[3] Similar trouble arose between the Typographical Association and the Operative Printers' Assistants, who had moved into the provinces and were refusing to give up their rotary assistant members to the Typographical Association when they were promoted to full rotary minders.
[4] The Scottish society, also party to the discussions, made similar demands.

semi-skilled or unskilled groups whose existence was to some extent a threat to the dominant craftsmen of the society would have met fierce resistance; but suggestions to bring in groups of allied craftsmen were more palatable, and the machinemen had now come to be highly skilled men occupying a key position in the trade.[1]

Conflict between unions was not universal, however, even in printing. During 1907–10 an amalgamation brought together the provincial Bookbinders and Machine Rulers and the three small London societies, which had fallen upon hard times, to form the National Union of Bookbinders and Machine Rulers. The provincial society had already negotiated a demarcation agreement with the National Printers' Warehousemen and Cutters during a series of conferences in 1907–8. In 1908 the Scottish Typographical Association absorbed the Edinburgh Press and Machinemen's Society and in 1910 won a victory there on its long-standing grievance over the employment of women, who now did most of the work on the monotype machine at a rate less than half that of the men.

The agreement, won by the threat of a general printing strike throughout the city, laid down that all new keyboards and 50 per cent. of making-up and correcting was to be reserved for male union labour. In return the Edinburgh branch was to keep the peace over wages and hours for the next three years. The society acknowledged the support of the women during the struggle by taking responsibility for their organization and re-forming the Edinburgh Female Compositors' Society. During the previous three years the question of female labour had also been settled to the society's satisfaction in Dundee and Perth, and in Aberdeen after a fifteen weeks' strike.[2]

As a result of these expansions and amalgamations the Typographical Association, the Scottish society, and the Bookbinders showed a more rapid rate of growth than most printing unions. The membership of the Typographical Association grew from 16,000 in 1900 to 21,000 in 1910, and both the Bookbinders and the Scottish society from 4,000 to 5,000. By contrast, the London Compositors—with less leeway to make up—moved only from 11,000 to 12,000. Most of the smaller societies showed some growth, and several new ones appeared, notably the National Union of Journalists, which was founded in Manchester in 1907 and had achieved national coverage and 1,900 members by 1910, virtually all men though women were admitted on equal terms. During its early years it concentrated on fighting legal cases on behalf of members and on developing means of protecting their professional 'rights'.

Though the Printing and Kindred Trades Federation failed to find any remedy for inter-union disputes, it added a little to its authority in other ways. Following the foundation of the national employers' organization,

[1] Musson, op. cit., p. 251.   [2] Gillespie, op. cit., pp. 204–6.

the powers of the Federation had been somewhat extended, and it now received a regular income which enabled it to pay strike benefit. Each union executive, however, determined the eligibility of its members for this benefit, which was paid out automatically by the Federation secretary. When the Federation tried to exert its authority by insisting on prior consultation it was firmly put in its place.[1]

There was a considerable growth of local federations from 1904, and after 1907 they began to play a part in initiating local movements, especially for reducing hours.[2] This opened up new possibilities for the national body, which approached the Federation of Master Printers in 1908 on the subject of a forty-eight-hour week, arguing that it would promote a better standard of work, and that new machinery had increased output and displaced labour. The employers gave no ground, but joint conferences were held, so that the Printing and Kindred Trades Federation achieved some status in the collective bargaining process, a precedent of considerable importance.

Conflict between unions was not confined to the craft trades. The Associated Iron and Steel Workers ran into trouble both with Tillett's Dockers and Hodge's Smelters. The Associated maintained control of its Midland and Northern boards, and in 1900 the Midland board extended its authority to cover the growing sheet trade of South Wales by means of the Welsh Sheet Trade Local Committee. It was here that trouble began. When the Lysaght Company opened sheet mills in Newport in 1898 they had abandoned the contract system and paid all production workers straight tonnage rates. After the establishment of the new Committee, however, they reverted to 'the general trade custom of the roller having full charge of his own mill and the employment of his own men'.[3] The Associated was jubilant, but the underhands, back on day rates, began to join Tillett's Dockers.

The Dockers obtained a settlement for them in Neath, and by 1902 the Welsh Committee was discussing a proposal to put all day workers on tonnage rates. The Associated managed to resist this, but were forced into one concession. Though the underhands continued to receive a day wage they were to have a bonus on output over a fixed amount. The Associated hit back, however, by insisting that the bonus was to be paid only to 'such daymen as are or agree to become members of, and subject to' the union and the Welsh Committee,[4] and that any contractor paying above the agreed rate 'shall be discharged'.[5]

Hodge was firmly set on recruiting the day-wage men employed by contractors in the English steel mills, with the aim of eventually smashing

---

[1] Musson, op. cit., pp. 293–4.   [2] Child, op. cit.   [3] Pugh, op. cit., p. 76.
[4] Even then they did not always get it (Pugh, op. cit., p. 158).
[5] *Report on Collective Agreements*, Cd. 5366, 1910, p. 76.

the whole contract system.[1] The logical end of such a campaign could only be to drive the Associated out of business unless they acquiesced in this revolution in their members' status and income. Frontier skirmishing finally exploded in 1909–10 in the Hawarden Bridge dispute, as grim an inter-union battle as any in British history.

The firm, John Summers & Sons, was one of the principal sheet-makers in the country. The part of their plant which worked on what was called the 'Staffordshire mill process' was organized by the Associated and regulated by the Midland Wages Board. When the firm laid down a steel-making plant to provide their own bars for steel sheet, this plant was organized by Hodge's union, which also controlled the millmen in what was called the 'Welsh mill process'.[2] About a hundred of the day-wage underhands employed by the Associated's contractor members had joined the Associated, but were refused admission to branch meetings and told that the tonnage men had no intention of being swamped by them. Early in 1909, therefore, the Steel Smelters began to admit them 'and soon a branch was formed which about eighty-five per cent of the men joined'.[3] The contractors met this move by 'a process of intimidation and coercion', the firm meanwhile maintaining a position of neutrality. This was soon abandoned, however, for one of active support of the contractors when, in November 1909, the Steel Smelters' executive demanded that the contract system be abolished and that all production workers be paid by the ton. The firm refused, and Hodge brought the day men out.

After the stoppage had lasted some time, Summers were ready to do a deal with Hodge. Under an arrangement reached in February 1910, Hodge was to be allowed virtually to drive the Associated out of the plant.[4] The contract system was to be abolished and the contractors locked out unless they agreed. The day men were to be put on tonnage rates which, while bringing them higher earnings than they had received as day men, fell below those previously paid by an amount necessary to cover the firm's costs in undertaking duties hitherto performed by the contractors. Hodge guaranteed to muster enough competent workers from other parts of the country to take the place of the contractors.[5]

The Associated lost no time in bringing its case before the Parliamentary Committee of the Trades Union Congress. Hodge had broken up the

---

[1] He was hampered by the fact that some of his own members in the melting shops employed day-wage helpers on certain ancillary tasks. With the turn of the century Hodge began urging these members to put their helpers on tonnage rates, but met with resistance (British Steel Smelters' Association, *Monthly Report*, Jan. 1902).

[2] Trades Union Congress, *Annual Report*, 1910, Parliamentary Committee Report.

[3] Pugh, op. cit., p. 158.

[4] British Steel Smelters' Association, *Monthly Reports;* the Associated Iron and Steel Workers, *Ironworkers' Journal* for 1909–10; and the Trades Union Congress, *Annual Report*, 1910.

[5] 'Serious local disturbances occurred when attempts were made to introduce steel-workers from other districts' (Board of Trade, *Labour Gazette*, Feb. 1911).

system of pay which 'has existed from time immemorial',[1] undercut the standard rates of the Associated, and agreed with management to fill the vacancies of the locked-out men. The subcommittee[2] which heard the case urged immediate reversion to the *status quo ante*. The Steel Smelters rejected this recommendation, and refused to appear before the renewed inquiry on the grounds that the subcommittee had already prejudged the issue. When the Parliamentary Committee found for the Associated, the Steel Smelters rejected the report, refused to pay the costs, and disaffiliated from Congress.

Meanwhile adequate skilled labour was proving difficult to find, and in the end Hodge had to admit his failure to carry through the arrangement as originally planned. Thereupon, after further stoppages, interventions by G. R. Askwith and the Steel Ingot Makers' Association, and protracted discussions, an agreement between all three parties, countersigned by the Board of Trade and the Association, was finally reached on 29 December 1910. The contract system was to be abolished, but the Associated was given exclusive jurisdiction over all the workers involved.[3] As time passed, the underhands in other sheet mills took advantage of the precedent thus established, until they had achieved the three essential conditions for which the Smelters had fought: a piece-work basis of wages; payment by the firm direct; and direct representation on all matters affecting terms and conditions of employment.

The contract system had also survived in the Sheffield steelworks,[4] where as late as 1908 it was described by the Labour Department of the Board of Trade as the typical form of engagement. Unionism was weak even among the contractors, and Associated membership had seldom risen above 200. Though Hodge's union grew rapidly there after the turn of the century Sheffield retained its reputation as a black spot, and in 1907 the union appointed a district organizer to 'crack' this 'hard nut'.[5] In that year, the union won recognition at the Grimesthorpe works after a strike against the intimidation of its members,[6] and this and other successful strikes at individual firms gave a considerable fillip to union growth in the district.

Several unions were competing for blastfurnacemen. The National Federation of Blastfurnacemen opened new district associations in the East Midlands and South Wales, and won a major victory in North Lincolnshire where the employers conceded recognition and a sliding scale after a five weeks' stoppage in 1909.[7] These advances did not, however,

---

[1] Trades Union Congress, *Annual Report*, 1910, Parliamentary Committee Report.

[2] Composed of David Shackleton (Weavers), J. H. Jenkins (Shipwrights), and W. Mosses (Patternmakers). [3] Pugh, op. cit., p. 162.

[4] Though the Sheffield wire-drawers had secured its abolition in 1897 (Pollard, op. cit., p. 231). [5] Ibid., p. 233.

[6] Pugh, op. cit., p. 144. [7] Owen, op. cit., p. 22.

prevent competition from the general unions. Tillett's Dockers were organizing blastfurnacemen in South Wales, and the Gasworkers obtained a sliding-scale agreement and a conciliation board covering some 600 in Nottinghamshire and Derbyshire. In Scotland they had been recruited by the Associated Society of Millmen in 1900 when it had become the Amalgamated Steel and Iron Workers. The employers, however, refused to expand the scope of the wages board for blastfurnacemen to include machinery for settling works disputes, and it remained limited to determining general wage movements by means of a sliding scale.[1] This, like the shortcomings of the union's boards in the manufactured iron and manufactured steel trades,[2] reflected the weakness of the Amalgamated compared with the Associated and Hodge's union.

In another field, the general unions and the Dockers had joined with other 'new unions' to do battle with the rapidly growing Municipal Employees' Association. Their real grievance was that the Municipal Employees were expanding while they were marking time, but they rationalized this into two more respectable complaints. It was a weakness 'to divide workmen employed by public authorities from their fellows in the same occupations employed by private firms',[3] for instance corporation tramwaymen and gasworkers from company tramwaymen and gasworkers. This argument would have carried more weight if all classes of workers covered by these unions were not already split up between a dozen organizations. Secondly, they argued that municipal employees were extremely unlikely to be called out on strike, whereas dockers, colliery surface workers, and engineering and shipbuilding labourers drew considerably on their unions' strike funds, often through disputes in which they had no direct part. Consequently it was possible for a union catering only for corporation workers to offer a 'cut-price' trade unionism.

The Municipal Employees' Association was not without problems of its own. Rapid growth from 1,500 in 1900 to nearly 16,000 by 1906 had necessitated the appointment of a number of officers to assist Albin Taylor, the secretary. One of them, Peter Tevenan, quickly fell foul of the imperious Taylor and the struggle between them was ended only when Taylor was suspended at a special meeting in March 1907 by eleven votes to ten. He then departed to found the National Union of Corporation Workers with a number of dissentient branches, taking about 5,000 members with him.[4] By 1910, however, under Taylor's successor, Richard Davies, the Municipal Employees had recovered to over 13,000 members, whereas the Corporation Workers were down to 3,500.

---

[1] Industrial Council, *Inquiry into Industrial Agreements*, Cd. 6953, 1913, Q. 2167.
[2] See p. 207.
[3] National Union of Gasworkers and General Labourers, *Quarterly Report*, Mar. 1907.
[4] Municipal Employees' Association, *Executive Council Minutes*, Jan.–June 1907.

Meanwhile, the other unions continued their complaints. At Huddersfield, the Municipal Employees were enrolling lamplighters who had been members of the Gasworkers; at Belfast and Gateshead they were 'filching' members of the National Amalgamated Union of Labour;[1] and they were taking in tramwaymen who should have joined the Amalgamated Tramway and Vehicle Workers. In 1907 the aggrieved unions took their case to the Trades Union Congress and to the Joint Board, who decided that no new union catering for general labourers would be affiliated, thereby ruling out Taylor's new union, and that unions catering exclusively for municipal employees should be assimilated into the 'national' unions by May 1910. The Municipal Employees stood firm, however, and were disaffiliated from both Congress and the Labour Party.

This controversy at least had the advantage that it brought the other unions together, and in 1908 the General Labourers' National Council came into being with ten affiliates, including the Gasworkers, the National Amalgamated Union of Labour, the Amalgamated Tramway Workers, Tillett's Dockers, and the Workers' Union. Apart from co-ordinating their attacks on the Municipal Employees, its main function was to minimize conflict between its constituents by providing for recognition of cards and a procedure for handling inter-union disputes.[2]

In the main, these were depressing years for the 'new unions'. Membership stagnated or sagged, especially with the heavy unemployment of 1908. By 1910 the National Amalgamated Union of Labour and the Gasworkers had both reached their lowest point since 1889, and had been giving a good deal of their attention to cutting organizational costs and curtailing benefits. The membership of the National Union of Dock Labourers rose to 22,000 in 1908 with an influx of Irish transport workers due to a fiery young orator, James Larkin, who had recently been appointed an organizer. Crossing to Belfast for the Labour Party conference in January 1907, he began a campaign among the dockers, and soon Sexton, the secretary, was claiming 1,200 members, 'some concessions, and almost complete recognition'.[3] Subsequently, however, the employers 'commenced to harass the men who had joined the union',[4] and in July the dockers struck to reaffirm their rights. At the same time the carters were locked out in retaliation for a strike against two firms.

The city of Belfast [was] held up by a state of civil turmoil, [with] guards at the railway-stations, double sentries with loaded rifles at alternate lamp-posts of the Royal Avenue . . . and ten thousand soldiers in and about the city. There

[1] National Union of Gasworkers and General Labourers, *Quarterly Report*, Dec. 1907; Amalgamated Association of Tramway and Vehicle Workers, *Annual Report* 1908; National Amalgamated Union of Labour, *Executive Council Minutes*, 1 June and 4 Aug. 1906.

[2] Amalgamated Association of Tramway and Vehicle Workers, *Annual Report*, 1908.

[3] National Union of Dock Labourers, *Annual Report*, 1906.

[4] Ibid., 1907.

had been fights in the streets, charges of cavalry, the Riot Act read, shooting to disperse wrecking mobs, a few men and women killed and scores wounded, and the whole business of the city at a standstill.[1]

In August, as a result of mediation by Askwith, and on the advice of Larkin, the carters settled for an increase in wages in return for an undertaking to work with non-unionists. It was Sexton, however, who negotiated the recognition of the dockers, also in return for an undertaking to work with non-unionists, but this time the terms were condemned by Larkin.[2]

By the end of the year, Sexton boasted that 'every man working in or about the docks was enrolled',[3] and that Larkin had now organized a branch of 2,000 in Dublin. But the strike had cost the union £7,000, the bulk of its reserves, and the Irish members were 'from a financial point of view far from satisfactory'.[4] An unofficial dispute in Dublin led to Larkin's suspension in December 1908 and his appointment next month as secretary of the newly founded Irish Transport and General Workers' Union. Proclaiming a revolutionary philosophy from the start, this organization managed to survive Larkin's imprisonment for embezzlement of strike funds, and an adverse verdict on a charge of libel brought against him by Sexton.[5] Although most of the Belfast men refused to join the 'breakaway', the membership of the parent National Union was almost halved by this setback.

In 1910, however, there were signs of renewed union vitality on the waterfront in England. The National Sailors' and Firemen's Union reappeared among the Labour Department's returns with a membership of 7,000 in 1906 and 12,000 in 1910. A new union of Ships' Stewards, Cooks, Butchers, and Bakers claimed nearly 4,000 members. Tillett's Dockers jumped from its customary 12,000–13,000 up to 18,000 by the end of the year. Some of the gains were in London, where a Port of London Organizing Committee covering all the unions was established in 1910. Prominent in these developments was Tom Mann, who returned that summer from his long stay in Australia. At the request of the union executive, he undertook an organizing campaign and with customary enthusiasm spoke at meetings in London, Sharpness, Port Talbot, Middlesbrough, Hull, Southampton, Cadishead, Avonmouth, and Bristol, finding time as well to launch a syndicalist movement and a new journal, the *Industrial Syndicalist*.[6]

Meanwhile, Ernest Bevin[7] had achieved a less spectacular but no less

[1] Askwith, op. cit., p. 109.
[2] R. M. Fox, *Jim Larkin, The Rise of the Underman*, 1957, pp. 60–61; Sexton, op. cit., p. 207.
[3] National Union of Dock Labourers, *Annual Report*, 1907.   [4] Ibid., 1908.
[5] R. M. Fox, op. cit., pp. 69–70; Sexton, op. cit., pp. 205–6.
[6] *Dockers' Record*, Sept. 1910.
[7] Bevin, Ernest, P.C. (1881–1951). District and later national organizer, Dock, Wharf, Riverside, and General Workers' Union, 1911–20; assistant general secretary, 1920–2. General

important increase in membership by organizing the Bristol carters. There were several strikes in the Bristol docks during 1910, and in September Tillett confided to the dockers that he thought 'the [Shipping] Federation had made up its mind to tackle the Bristol Channel Ports, which were the highest paid in the country, but the Bristol Channel Ports were prepared, and if the Federation did not recognise the strength of the unions they would have to fight a colossal organisation right through the country'.[1] The champion of conciliation and compulsory arbitration was reverting to the militant phrases of twenty years earlier. His 'colossal organization' began to take shape later in the same month, when a meeting of sixteen unions resolved in favour of a federation for all transport unions. In November a committee of five began to draft a constitution.

Growth, Especially in Coal and Cotton

Most white-collar and Post Office unions continued to grow. In the five years to 1910 the Amalgamated Union of Co-operative Employees doubled its membership to 30,000 and claimed to have organized 'nearly half those eligible'.[2] Moreover, on the North-east coast they had branched out from the retail field to organize workers in soap factories belonging to the Co-operative Wholesale Society, thus running into conflict with the National Amalgamated Union of Labour. The major internal issue in the union was whether to establish a strike fund. Its advocates did not 'desire a strike, or even anticipate the possibility of such an event', but suggested that 'if it were known to committees that it had been established, they might possibly lend a more ready ear to the pleas of the union'.[2] Its opponents, on the other hand, held that 'a strike was not essential to success, and a strike of shopworkers, or co-operative employees would be foredoomed to failure'.[3] In the end a cautious executive proposal was accepted which amplified the rules to provide support for members losing their jobs, whether through strikes, lock-outs or discharges resulting from union action.[4]

The Shop Assistants, who already provided strike benefit, grew but slowly. Their *Journal* recorded that the Co-operative Employees had 'for years been working amongst Co-operative Societies with considerable success to secure that all their members over 21 years of age . . . shall be paid a minimum of 24*s*.',[5] and a subcommittee was established to consider the adoption of a minimum wage for all shop assistants. The principle was accepted by the conference of 1910, but the decision meant little, partly because each district could fix its own minimum rate so long as it received

secretary, Transport and General Workers' Union, 1922-46. General Council, Trades Union Congress, 1925-40. M.P., 1940-51. Minister of Labour, 1940-5. Foreign Secretary, 1945-51. Lord Privy Seal, 1951.

[1] *Dockers' Record*, Sept. 1910.
[2] *Gleanings*, Nov. 1908.
[3] Ibid., May 1910.
[4] Ibid., July and Nov. 1910.
[5] *The Shop Assistant*, July 1909.

executive endorsement, but more because a union which covered only 21,000 shop assistants could not go far in enforcing a general standard by direct trade union action, which was the only method open to it.

In 1907 a militancy unusual among non-manual workers brought out on strike the London variety artistes, musicians, and music-hall employees, whose conditions of employment had hitherto been completely unregulated. The formation in 1906 of the Variety Artistes Federation, nearly 4,000 strong, was followed at once by a conflict over contracts which affected twenty-two London variety theatres, picketed by more than 2,500 strikers, and, according to Askwith, was 'followed by the whole of Great Britain with more interest than . . . an international football match. . . . After a few weeks of this excitement, which proved to be very expensive, a suggestion was made, I believe by Mr. Somerset Maugham . . . that a dull arbitration might be useful.'[1] Askwith himself was appointed, and the result, after twenty-three formal sittings and innumerable conferences, was a complete national code, a model contract, and a procedure for settling disputes.

The National Union of Boot and Shoe Operatives, unable to resist technical change and with its role in collective bargaining circumscribed by agreement, had been in decline since 1895. Its membership dwindled; local joint regulation of the industry fell into decay in several places; and during 1905–6 the union's largest branch, at Leicester, lost a further 3,000 members after scandals concerning embezzlement.[2]

Two important developments, however, came out of this period of decline. The union discovered a means of regulating the wages and work load of machine workers, most of whom were paid time rates and were apt to suffer from 'driving' by foremen to increase output. 'Quantity statements' were negotiated on the local boards which specified the amount of work to be done for an agreed wage. The branches could choose either to discourage additional output, so that the wage remained a fixed time wage, or to permit it at piece prices derived from the quantity statement.[3] The second development was that the union became firmly wedded to the principle of a minimum wage, and branches began establishing local minima wherever they could, strongly encouraged by the national leaders, who set a target of 30s. per week.

The union attracted much attention with the Raunds March in 1905. James Gribble, a militant socialist member, led a march of 115 picked volunteers to London as a protest against the low wages paid in the army and navy boot trade at Raunds in Northamptonshire. The Raunds March, among the first of its kind, was a great success. It achieved wide publicity

---

[1] Askwith, op. cit., pp. 103–4. The strikers hired the Scala Theatre and produced a show of their own to raise funds (ibid.).

[2] Alan Fox, op. cit., pp. 247–8.   [3] Ibid., pp. 264–9.

and led to an inquiry presided over by Askwith, which gave the workers a satisfactory statement of prices and a conciliation board.[1]

It was not, however, until 1907 that the union's fortunes began to show a steady improvement, for it was only then that economic recovery affected the boot and shoe industry, although, once begun, this improvement continued through the general depression of 1908. In 1907, therefore, the minimum wage campaign received a stimulus which enabled the president to claim in the following year that the 30*s.* target had been achieved in those places 'where the most of our members are employed'.[2] Besides this there was a resumption of national negotiations with the employers' federation which, after months of hard bargaining, resulted in a 52½-hour working week and a number of other concessions.

A revival of pottery unionism had begun in 1906 when its meagre forces were consolidated into the National Amalgamated Male and Female Pottery Workers, open to all the general run of factory operatives. The new union launched an agitation for a 15 per cent. wage increase which led to the conciliation board being revived in 1908, but its independent chairman rejected the claim. Moreover, two issues vital to the union were excluded entirely from the board's competence—limitation of apprentices and the practice known as 'good from oven' whereby operatives received no pay for faulty work.[3] Thereafter the inrush of members stimulated by the agitation ebbed rapidly away. By 1910 the number of women trade unionists was less than in 1890.

Among textile workers, the Scottish jute and linen unions continued to maintain an impressive female membership,[4] and won a wage increase for the spinners in 1906 after a strike involving 20,000, though the weavers were forced back at the old rates. In the dyeing and finishing trades the employers' combines, the Bradford Dyers' Association and the British Cotton and Wool Dyers' Association, had extended their control into Lancashire where the unions were weaker than in Yorkshire and conditions inferior, and then told their West Riding employees that further concessions would make it impossible to keep abreast of their Lancashire competitors. Consequently, having failed to persuade the Bolton Bleachers, Dyers, and Finishers to amalgamate with them, the Yorkshire unions—the Amalgamated Society of Dyers and the Huddersfield organization, renamed the National Dyers and Finishers in 1905—proceeded to try to organize the Lancashire workers for themselves.

So determined was the Bradford Dyers' Association to remain competitive in Lancashire markets that a claim by the Yorkshire unions in 1905 for

---

[1] Alan Fox, op. cit., pp. 285–9.   [2] Ibid., p. 316.
[3] *Second Report on Rules of Voluntary Conciliation and Arbitration Boards*, Cd. 5346, 1910, pp. 276–81.
[4] A new Dundee and District Jute and Flax Workers' Union, formed in 1906, had 5,000 members by 1910, 4,000 of them female.

a 10 per cent. wage increase was not settled until January 1907, the Association at first demanding a completely free hand in machine-manning and work-organization. Eventually, in return for conceding the increase, the Association was given the right to reduce its labour force by an agreed percentage, thus allowing reorganization of plant and machinery, on condition that the men displaced during 1907 should be compensated, the Association matching the benefit already paid to them by their union.[1] This agreement was renewed year by year, even in January 1909, when provision was made for reductions in wages. These reductions were arranged through a characteristically elaborate agreement, for their amount was to depend upon the extent of the fall in annual earnings of the combine in 1908, when these were revealed by the financial accounts.[2] Though this arrangement produced a 10 per cent. cut, it did not interrupt the growth of the unions. The Amalgamated Society rose from 5,000 members in 1905 to 11,000 in 1910, the National Society from 1,500 to 4,000. The Bolton union jumped from 5,000 in 1905 to 11,000 in 1907, and held its gains.

The puny woollen unions also showed signs of growth. In 1906 a strike of unorganized workers prompted the Colne Valley manufacturers 'to call the trade union officials in to get these men to agree to something'.[3] The General Union of Textile Workers was then able to sign an agreement with the newly formed Huddersfield and District Woollen Manufacturers' and Spinners' Association, giving the willeyers and fettlers of the Colne Valley a standard wage and working week, and overtime rates. In the same year it persuaded the Association to improve the terms on which weavers were to operate the faster looms now coming into the mills. Now that the General Union was making some small impact the employers agreed to a code of disciplinary Mill Rules in 1908, one clause of which gave the union the right to take the case of a summarily dismissed operative before a joint committee. In practice this procedure was soon accepted as a means of settlement of any issue in dispute, including wages.[4] By 1910 union membership had crept up to over 4,500, still a very low figure but the best for many years.

The National Union of Woolsorters continued a steady growth to almost 2,000. Though still without collective bargaining machinery, the union was building up reliable friendly benefits and in general adopting the attitudes and methods of the craft societies such as the Warp Dressers and Twisters. It was the Bradford Woolcombers who in 1907 secured the first substantial collective agreement in the industry by negotiating a

---

[1] *Report on the Strikes and Lockouts of 1907*, Cd. 4254, 1908, pp. 136–7.

[2] *Report on Collective Agreements*, Cd. 5366, 1910, p. 223. The Gasworkers were also a party to these as to all the previous agreements.

[3] Industrial Council, *Inquiry into Industrial Agreements*, Cd. 6953, 1913, Q. 5421.

[4] Ibid., Q. 5398, and appendix xi, p. 598.

general advance of 5 per cent. for nearly 4,000 workpeople. A further demand in 1909 for the abolition of weekend labour was largely successful and brought a sudden rise in membership to 6,500 in 1910, 2,000 of them women.

The only two substantial sections of textile trade unionism to show a decline were hosiery and lace. Both were hunted and harassed by employers in low-cost areas, while employers in high-cost areas sought concessions from them in order to meet competition. In Leicester hosiery the machinery of collective bargaining was still in abeyance.[1] The highly paid Nottingham lacemakers, having successfully warded off employers' attacks on their rates since 1889, lost some ground in 1905 through an arbitration award by Askwith which remodelled the old price lists. Although the men received some gains they considered on balance that the award was unfavourable, and adopted it only after three ballots.[2]

Even the agricultural labourers were not entirely quiescent. In 1906 George Edwards founded the Eastern Counties Agricultural Labourers' and Small Holders' Union in Norfolk. He had been associated with earlier farmworkers' unions and had been a Liberal Party speaker. Liberals helped him with funds and the union started off with Edwards as secretary, and George Nichols, a Liberal Member of Parliament, as president. The union thus began as a Liberal vehicle for organizing the rural vote, its objects being 'to enable the labourers to secure proper representation on all local bodies and Imperial Parliament, protection from political persecution and better conditions of living'.[3] Until 1909 it concerned itself with small individual disputes, accident and victimization cases, and provision of legal assistance.[4] At this point restlessness among the members forced the executive to finance several sporadic strikes for wage increases.[5] After violent fluctuations the union membership stood at 4,000 members in 1910.

All this progress, however, was insignificant compared with the advance of coal and cotton. Together they were responsible for half of the rise in total trade union membership from 1,997,000 in 1905 to 2,565,000 in 1910. The figure for coal rose from 480,000 to 708,000 and for cotton from 213,000 to 275,000.[6] By 1910 the two groups of unions had just short of a million members, and provided about 40 per cent. of the country's trade unionists. Moreover, union growth in coal was accompanied by consolidation, for Northumberland affiliated to the Federation in 1907 and Durham in 1908. The old controversy had lost its significance with the passage of the Eight Hours Act; and time had removed the personal obstacles to

---

[1] Industrial Council, *Inquiry etc.*, Q. 10795.   [2] Cuthbert, op. cit., p. 62.
[3] M. Madden, *The National Union of Agricultural Workers, 1906–1956*, B.Litt. thesis, Oxford, 1956.   [4] G. Edwards, op. cit., p. 111.   [5] Ibid., chapters xi–xiii.
[6] *Fifteenth Abstract of Labour Statistics*, Cd. 6228, 1912, pp. 194–5. The figure for total trade union membership given above differs from that given in the *Abstract*, being the final revised figure published in the *Ministry of Labour Gazette*, Oct. 1937.

unity. Pickard was dead; Burt was ageing;[1] and John Wilson's influence in Durham was on the decline.

In both industries the growth in membership was assisted by a determined effort to stamp out non-unionism. The campaign in the South Wales coalfield was the most violent. The Board of Trade reported that 'in the case of disputes arising out of refusals to work with non-union men . . . the figures for 1906 are the highest on record. Of the 50,750 workpeople affected by such disputes in 1906, no less than 45,995 were coal miners in South Wales and Monmouthshire, where a determined effort was made by members of the South Wales Miners' Federation to compel all non-unionists to join the Federation.'[2] In the same year 'a strong agitation' in Lancashire by the cotton unions was under way.[3] The Weavers proposed to boycott non-members, and learners were not to be accepted unless they undertook to join the union.[4] In May 1907 the Rochdale Trades Council proposed to revive a form of pressure customary in Lancashire. No delegate was to be eligible for any office unless his wife and working children were members of the appropriate union.[5]

For the Spinners the non-unionist problem applied chiefly to the piecers, who, they complained, were behaving 'very independently' and lapsing in considerable numbers. This may explain the decision of the Bolton Spinners in 1908 to make specific provision for the piecers in their agreement with the employers. The Oldham agreement already regulated the piecers' wages, but in the Bolton province they had varied from mill to mill. The new agreement gave 2,800 piecers an advance varying from 6*d*. to 2*s*. 6*d*. per week,[6] but disaffection persisted.

The cardroom amalgamation was vigorously organizing the growing number of female ring-spinners and pressing the Spinners to extend their 'mutual support' agreement on disputes at individual mills to cover disputes arising from the refusal to work with non-unionists. Hitherto, both had acted independently on the question. The Spinners agreed,[7] but the Board of Trade records no stoppages against non-unionists during these years. Threats may have been enough to bring the offenders into line. The Weavers were equally active. By 1907 some weaving districts claimed up to 95 per cent. membership,[8] and by May 1908 the *Cotton Factory Times* was boasting that 'non-members must be an insignificant minority'.[9]

[1] Ben Tillett was reported as saying 'Burt's a darling, but he doesn't understand things now' (Collison, op. cit., p. 40).
[2] *Report on the Strikes and Lockouts of 1906*, Cd. 3711, 1907, pp. 17–18.
[3] *Cotton Factory Times*, 12 Oct. 1906.   [4] Ibid., 4 Jan. 1907.
[5] The *Cotton Factory Times* wanted the rule to apply to all trades council delegates (17 May 1907).
[6] *Report on Collective Agreements*, Cd. 5366, 1910, p. 162.
[7] This, thought the *Cotton Factory Times*, should enable the Spinners to 'put the finishing touches to their almost perfect organisation, as far as numbers are concerned' (3 Jan. 1908).
[8] Ibid., 27 Dec. 1907.   [9] 29 May 1908.

In 1908 there was talk of closing the ranks in another sense besides that of eliminating non-unionists, when proposals were made for merging the three major amalgamations into one society under one executive. But the only consolidation achieved was on the manufacturing side, where in 1905 the weavers' and overlookers' amalgamations had formed what eventually became known as the Northern Counties Textile Trades Federation. Subsequently the other specialist groups such as twisters, warp dressers, tape sizers, cloth lookers, and warehousemen joined the Federation, and by 1909 its coverage was almost complete.[1]

With returning prosperity, the cotton industry had begun to suffer another bout of 'bad material' disputes. In 1906 the number of disputes of all kinds in the industry reached a total of eighty, the highest since 1896, and 60 per cent. of these concerned compensation for alleged bad material supplied to spinners and weavers. The following year saw a total of ninety-four disputes, fifty-seven of them on this issue. Despite the gains they had made, the unions remained dissatisfied with the machinery for handling these disputes, and in March 1906 the Spinners secured an amendment to the Brooklands Agreement intended to yield quicker decisions. If a complaint about bad spinning was renewed within three months of a previous settlement, representatives of the joint committee which dealt with the case were to inspect the spinning within three days. Failure to bring about a settlement would be followed within three days by a top-level meeting between employers and union. If this did not resolve the deadlock the operatives were free to strike.[2]

In practice, the amendment failed to satisfy the union, and feeling about the Brooklands Agreement became even more hostile later in the year, when a clash arose over the procedure to be followed in cases where a grievance on work or wages arose out of changes introduced by management. In March 1907 the Spinners gave notice to withdraw from the Agreement so far as bad spinning disputes were concerned, but the Master Spinners' Federation refused to accept a partial cancellation. Negotiations dragged on, but in 1908 the depression brought a marked slackening in the incidence of stoppages. In 1909 the industry was 'scarcely affected by disputes',[3] and the matter passed into the background. Dissatisfaction on the weaving side had been equally acute, and by early 1907 the weavers' amalgamation were asking to be released from their joint rules so far as bad material disputes were concerned. The negotiations which followed introduced a speedier procedure in May 1908.

[1] *Cotton Factory Times*, 2 Apr. 1909. In 1909 the Federation secured an agreement with the Cotton Spinners and Manufacturers' Association which provided all the unions with a conciliation procedure akin to that of the Weavers, and added a final stage of negotiation between the Federation and the employers' association before resort to a stoppage.

[2] *Report on Collective Agreements*, Cd. 5366, 1910, p. 138.

[3] *Report on the Strikes and Lockouts of 1909*, Cd. 5325, 1910, p. 10.

Meanwhile, general wage increases had been negotiated. In January 1906 the Weavers received $2\frac{1}{2}$ per cent., the balance of the $7\frac{1}{2}$ per cent. that they had claimed a year previously; and in April the Spinners and Cardroom Operatives won back the 5 per cent. advance that had been granted for only twelve weeks in 1905. In further claims in 1907 the Weavers were unsuccessful, but the other two groups, again acting together and threatening strike action, were granted a further 5 per cent.[1]

Two other disputes were also settled in favour of the spinning unions. In December 1907 intervention by Lloyd George himself secured a modification of the Brooklands Agreement to give an increase of 3s. a week to some 5,000 Oldham employees on 'fine' counts.[2] Next month a dispute in two Oldham ring-spinning mills was settled by an agreement providing for immediate negotiations on a uniform list for ring-spinners, and bringing them within the scope of the Brooklands Agreement.

By this time, however, the tide of prosperity had turned, and in July 1908 the Master Spinners' Federation decided to seek a 5 per cent. reduction. When the unions refused to recommend acceptance, the Federation gave a month's notice of a lock-out. At a joint conference on 10 September, ten days before the stoppage was due to start, the operatives admitted that trade was depressed but sought to postpone the cut as long as possible. The employers 'were perfectly ready to defer the reduction till January, but they were not prepared to defer the definite settlement of the question whether there should be a reduction or not'. The operatives 'offered to take a reduction in January *if the state of trade then warranted a reduction*, but these terms were refused by the employers. No doubt had they been accepted, disagreement would have arisen in January as to the state of trade.'[3] The Spinners' executive then recommended acceptance of the employers' offer, and, although it was rejected by 74 per cent. of their members voting, this fell short of the 80 per cent. required to sanction a strike. Consequently, when the employers refused their suggestion that the reduction should be considered again after a 'stop month', the Spinners accepted it as from the first pay day in January.[4] The cardroom amalgamation, though now isolated, held out and the stoppage began on 19 September, putting the spinners out of work and rendering idle a total of 120,000 workers.

---

[1] On this occasion the Bolton Spinners acted with the rest for the first time.

[2] 'Lloyd George made a personal visit to Manchester and, though he did not succeed in his apparent desire to be appointed umpire, he was at least successful in . . . persuading [the mill-owners] to agree to a joint meeting of owners and operatives' (Halévy, op. cit., vol. vi, p. 114). 'Such . . . concern for peace has created a new interest in the work of the Board of Trade, and has indicated the possibilities of greater usefulness of this department to the industries of the country. After all, one cannot overlook the fact that much depends on the policy of the man at the top' (*Cotton Factory Times*, 13 Dec. 1907).

[3] 'Current Topics', *Economic Journal*, Dec. 1908.

[4] *Report on the Strikes and Lockouts of 1908*, Cd. 4680, 1909, pp. 55–60.

When the Spinners as well as the cardroom amalgamation applied to the General Federation of Trade Unions for lock-out pay, the cardroom leaders argued that the Spinners were not eligible since they were no longer in dispute with the employers. The Federation managed to calm them, and paid benefit to both groups. For a brief period in mid-October it seemed as if the Federation might take over the negotiations, when it submitted a proposal for an immediate 5 per cent. reduction and reconsideration of the whole matter in three months' time. This was rejected, however, and the Federation leaders withdrew, 'the task', remarked the *Cotton Factory Times* patronizingly, having 'proved too big' for them.[1]

On 27 October a conference of mayors of the Lancashire cotton towns urged both sides to end the conflict. The Spinners, feeling that their position as signatory to a settlement was hampering them in taking a part in the negotiations to settle the dispute, persuaded the Master Spinners' Federation to release them from the agreement to accept a reduction in January. After further conferences, the Mayor of Salford proposed that the mills should be reopened and the 5 per cent. reduction be made from March 1909. This was accepted by both sides, and an agreement signed on 6 November ended a stoppage which had lasted seven weeks and cost nearly five million working days.

The *Cotton Factory Times* counted the cost. The employers had cleared their stocks at enhanced prices, whereas the operatives had lost wages, depleted their union funds, and suffered an internal rift. The only way to avoid a repetition was 'to arrive at some fair method of fixing wages automatically in accordance with the state of trade'.[2] Others had reached the same conclusion. Winston Churchill, now President of the Board of Trade, invited the parties to a joint conference 'to discuss the advisability of adopting some equitable scheme for the future automatic regulation of wages'.[3] Conferences followed in Manchester under the chairmanship of Sir Edward Clarke, K.C., but deadlock was reached in October 1909 over the standard from which advances or reductions were to be reckoned.

Among the miners, Yorkshire and Scotland had continued to urge that all Federated areas should arrange for their agreements to terminate at the same time, thus making possible a joint struggle to unify and raise the minimum. The objections of the Federated coal-owners to this arrangement were no longer strong enough to stop them accepting a conciliation board agreement terminating simultaneously with the South Wales agreement in March 1910. Since Scotland could give notice at any time, the union had achieved its objective.

Meanwhile, the industry had managed to avoid a major stoppage over wages, although not without difficulty. At first, negotiations for advances

[1] 23 Oct. 1908.   [2] 13 Nov. 1908.
[3] *Report on the Strikes and Lockouts of 1908*, Cd. 4680, 1909, p. 60.

and reductions proceeded smoothly enough in the English Federated area,[1] but the Federation was now to be tested in the exporting districts of Scotland and South Wales with their more widely fluctuating prices.

After the compromise of 1904 the Scottish miners began to lay claim to a minimum which would bring them nearer the general level of wage rates in the English Federated area, and fixed on 50 per cent. above standard, or roughly 6s. per day. Federation conferences during 1908 accepted this figure and pledged support on the basis of Rule 20. Accordingly, in May 1909, the Scottish miners rejected the owners' proposal for a reduction below 50 per cent., and refused arbitration. When the owners gave notice of a lock-out the Federation held a ballot of the lodges which went heavily in favour of applying Rule 20. Meanwhile, on 22 July 1909, Churchill called a joint meeting of the Scottish owners and miners and Federation representatives, and a subcommittee was appointed with Askwith in the chair which reached a settlement on 30 July 1909.[2]

This established a sliding scale even more mechanical in operation than before, and an arrangement, suggested by Askwith, whereby if ascertained prices, for a period of months, did not warrant the 50 per cent. minimum, then for the same number of months afterwards any increased percentage due as a result of a rise in prices was to be reduced by $6\frac{1}{4}$ per cent.[3] Thus a minimum was established, but only at the expense of permitting the owners to recoup the losses which they might sustain in supporting it. The same principle was now applied in the Federated area. In August 1909, with coal prices falling, the owners applied for a reduction within the limits laid down in the current agreement. Edwards argued, however, that the Scottish crisis had left the men exceptionally restless and unsettled, and the owners, too, were convinced that if the reduction was enforced there might well be a strike.[4] The 'recoupment' principle was therefore introduced.[5]

---

[1] It seems that the Federation had achieved its objective of having other factors besides price taken into account. Lord James, independent chairman of the Federated Board, said in his award of a 5 per cent. advance in Dec. 1907 that increased production in 1907 over that of 1906 was 'a very important factor—as well as the selling price of coal—in determining the question. . . .' (*Minutes of the Conciliation Board of the Federated Area*, 10 Dec. 1907).

[2] At a meeting on 16 July with the miners' leaders alone, Churchill had told them that if nothing else could be done the government would rush through legislation referring the dispute to compulsory arbitration. 'As he was leaving the room, Mabon . . . turned on him with the remark . . . "Mr. Churchill, you cannot put 600,000 men into prison" ' (Askwith, op. cit., p. 131).

[3] *Report on Collective Agreements*, Cd. 5366, 1910, p. 34. Robert Smillie, president of the Scottish Miners' Federation, refused to sign, but the agreement was ratified without him.

[4] *Minutes of the Conciliation Board of the Federated Area*, 12 Aug. 1909.

[5] No claim for a wage increase was to be made until the selling price exceeded 7s. 10·21d. by such an amount as would recoup the owners for the disadvantage incurred by the payment of the present wage rate during the period when the selling price was less than 7s. 10·21d. Notice to end the board was not to be given until the price had recovered to that level and remained there long enough for recoupment (*Report on the Strikes and Lockouts of 1909*, Cd. 5325, 1910, pp. 95–96).

These events showed that the wage pressures generated by price changes were too powerful to be contained within any simple framework of maximum and minimum rates. Just as attempts by owners to hold an agreed maximum in the face of rising prices were likely to produce unrest at the pit level, so attempts by miners to hold a minimum in the face of falling prices resulted at best in the postponement of their 'wage losses' to the future. Consequently, the principles on which the Federation was based could be maintained only by means of temporary expedients.

Wage fluctuations in South Wales, though much larger than in the Federated area, were yet smaller than in Scotland. The fall in percentage above standard between 1900 and 1905 was $43\frac{3}{4}$ compared with West Scotland's $62\frac{1}{2}$; between 1907 and 1909, $12\frac{1}{2}$ compared with Scotland's $37\frac{1}{2}$. The first downward phase, which brought the percentage from $73\frac{3}{4}$ in 1900 to 30 in 1905, was the nearest South Wales got to trouble in this connexion, for the agreement minimum was 30 per cent.[1] But prices began rising immediately after, and the percentage rose to 60 in 1907 and fell back only to $47\frac{1}{2}$ in 1909, well above the minimum. There were, however, other difficulties.

The conflict over 'abnormal places' became more acute in 1907, when a court case on the subject went against the miners. Previously they had often recovered allowances for working in abnormal places through a county court action, the judge giving many favourable decisions where it could be shown that the allowances had the sanction of long custom. This practice ended in 1907, when the county court, now under a different judge, decided in the *Walters* v. *Ocean Coal Company* case that allowances which were not specifically provided for in the price list were merely gratuities given *ex gratia* and not recoverable at law.[2] 'That decision', declared William Brace in 1913, 'was the means of upsetting everything . . . at . . . every . . . firm, broadly, in the coalfield. . . . Things went from bad to worse.'[3]

The general decline in output per head throughout the industry increased the urgency of the issue not only in South Wales but in all the coalfields. In 1889 the average annual tonnage of coal produced per person employed in the industry had been 314, whereas in 1908 it stood at 273; for underground workers alone the decline was from 393 tons to 339. Average pithead prices meanwhile had fluctuated, but the general trend had been downward, from a peak of 10s. 10d. in the 1900 boom to 9s. in the subsequent boom of 1907 and 8s. 1d. in 1909. In an industry in which wages were so large a part of total costs, declining output and declining prices meant falling piece-work earnings, and increased the bitterness of negotiations over new price lists.

---

[1] *Report on the Strikes and Lockouts of 1905*, Cd. 3065, 1906, p. 110.
[2] Jevons, op. cit., pp. 531–2.
[3] Industrial Council, *Inquiry into Industrial Agreements*, Cd. 6953, 1913, Qs. 15934–5.

The primary cause of falling productivity was, of course, worsened geological conditions, but the Eight Hours Act added to the problem. After 1909 there were places which might have yielded tolerable earnings in nine hours work, but did not do so in eight. There was also the problem of 'overcrowding'. Falling output led the owners to introduce more workers on to the face.[1] This helped to maintain the output of the colliery, but at the expense of adding to the difficulties of each faceworker in maintaining his individual earnings. At successive national conferences on the wages question in 1910 and 1911 spokesmen differed on the cause of falling earnings, some attributing it to the effect of shorter hours and fixed 'contract' prices,[2] and others to overcrowding;[3] but no one doubted that 'a great many men are going into the mines and not getting a wage'.[4]

The general understanding in the negotiations which followed the Eight Hours Act was that those piece-workers who would have a shorter time at the face would have to do their best to maintain their earnings. On the other hand, time-workers, whose hours were being generally reduced in most coalfields, were to have their rates increased in compensation. This, however, still left problems. Many of them had previously worked regular overtime. In South Wales, for example, many day-wage men 'were paid a half turn for working an hour at night, and thus they got a decent wage for the day. They have had that decent wage struck off because of the Eight Hours Act.'[5]

Initially, however, the most troublesome consequence of the Act was the introduction of new shift systems and, as might have been expected, the trouble came mainly in the North-east. When the arrangements under the Act were applied in the Federated coalfields in July 1909, there was a rash of strikes but settlements were reached fairly quickly. In Northumberland and Durham, by contrast, no agreement was reached on the method of application until December, and when it came into force in January 1910 the majority of the men in both coalfields stopped work, 85,000 in Durham and 30,000 in Northumberland. Settlements were made colliery by colliery and by the end of January the number of strikers was reduced to 12,000 in Durham and 11,000 in Northumberland, where the principal difficulty was the owners' proposal to introduce a three-shift system in a number of pits. These two groups then showed a fierce tenacity. The last

[1] 'Overcrowding' was also attributed to the employment of more men underground owing to the growing stringency of safety regulations.

[2] Enoch Edwards at the Special Conference of 9 Mar. 1909, and Carter (Nottingham) at the Special Conference of 24–26 Jan. 1911. Nottingham 'contractors' had a special problem since they had to pay out of their reduced contract earnings the unaltered daily wages of the day-wage men whom they employed.

[3] Herbert Smith (Yorkshire) and C. Walkden (Lancashire) at the Special Conference of 24–26 Jan. 1911.

[4] Swann (Durham) at the Special Conference of 28–29 July 1911.

[5] Vernon Hartshorn (South Wales) at the Special Conference of 28–29 July 1911.

8,000 Durham men did not give up the struggle until 8 April 1910, and in Northumberland it took all the wiles of the local leaders, the Federation, and the representatives of the Board of Trade, led by Askwith, to win a small majority for a return to work in a ballot of the remaining strikers on 15 April.[1] Altogether over two million working days were lost.

In South Wales negotiations began early in 1909, soon after the owners had received legal advice that the Act would automatically abrogate the current agreement.[2] They proposed to change from their traditional single shift to a double shift system, and to make full use of a clause in the Act allowing longer shifts to be worked provided the total hours in excess of eight per day did not exceed sixty over the year—although the Miners' Federation of Great Britain had decided that this clause must be disregarded. After difficult negotiations, in which the Federation promised the South Wales miners financial support but not a sympathetic strike, agreement was reached on 3 July. The question of double shifts was set aside, but the union agreed to accept such new methods of working as the owners might introduce, subject to an appeal to arbitration on issues of safety, and to allow the sixty hours clause to be settled by the courts, which could not help but find for the owners since it was permitted by the Act.

The new methods sanctioned by this agreement exacerbated the widespread ill-feeling over abnormal places, and unrest grew with a further fall in output per head of 7·6 per cent. in the fourth quarter of the year.[3] By the end of the year the South Wales Miners' Federation had drafted a thoroughgoing set of amendments to the agreement, including a minimum of 4s. for all men in abnormal places, and a minimum of 3s. 4d. a day for every worker in the coalfield. This notion of an overall minimum wage reflected the emergence of a new group of socialist contestants for power among the South Wales miners—Noah Ablett, George Barker, Vernon Hartshorn, C. B. Stanton, and James Winstone. Following the formation of the Plebs League by supporters of the new Central Labour College[4] to promote 'independent working-class education', they set up a South Wales Wing with Winstone as president, Barker as vice-president, and Ablett as chairman of the committee. The League preached Marxism and the class war through educational classes and the *Plebs Magazine*, which showed marked hostility towards the established leaders.[5]

Their influence led the men to refuse plenary powers to their official leaders in the negotiations to revise the agreement, but they could not persuade the Federation to call a national strike on their behalf. A national conference in March 1910 advised the Welshmen to come to terms, and

[1] *Report on the Strikes and Lockouts of 1910*, Cd. 5850, 1911, pp. 19–21.
[2] E. W. Evans, op. cit., p. 193.
[3] D. Evans, *Labour Strife in the South Wales Coalfield, 1910–1911*, 1911, p. 195.
[4] See p. 413, footnote 1.
[5] *Plebs Magazine*, Feb. and May 1909.

next month another compromise settlement was arranged. The owners dropped their proposal to use the sixty hours clause and agreed to raise the minimum percentage above standard from 30 to 35 per cent. For their part, the miners agreed to the introduction of 'afternoon' and 'overlapping' shifts and to working double shifts in special circumstances. Nothing, however, was done about a minimum wage, or about abnormal places, which continued to cause frequent local stoppages.

Thus by 1910 declining earnings were raising the temperature of industrial relations throughout the coalfields, with South Wales near to flashpoint on the abnormal place issue. In the cotton industry fifteen years of industrial peace had been broken by a county-wide spinning lock-out in 1908. The depression of 1908 had robbed the railwaymen of the benefits they had hoped to obtain under their new conciliation scheme. The printing industry was preparing for a battle on craft issues. And on the waterfront, labour was stirring after almost two decades of slumber.

12

Growth and Change, 1889–1910

Growth

FROM about 750,000 at the end of 1888, trade union membership rose to 2,025,000 in 1901. Growth had been spectacular up to 1892; from 1896 there was a further, steadier increase. After some years of stagnation, membership rose again between 1905 and 1907, climbing to 2,513,000. There followed a slight decline, but in 1910 a new peak of 2,565,000 was reached. The 'occupied population' of the United Kingdom also rose over this period. In the census years of 1891, 1901, and 1911, totals of 16·5, 18·3, and 20·2 millions were returned; but they included groups normally outside the scope of trade union organization, such as domestic servants, farmers and their families, the armed forces, and the professions.[1] Once these and similar groups have been excluded,[2] the totals fall to 12·1, 13·7, and 15·3 millions. If the revised figures are then compared with trade union membership in 1888, 1901, and 1910, it appears that in these years the proportion of workers organized was roughly 6 per cent., 15 per cent., and 17 per cent.

The Board of Trade's *Report on Trade Unions in 1896* offered an estimate of the total of adult males of the 'manual labour class' from which a more realistic calculation can be made, since trade unionism was rare among women, young persons, and non-manual workers. The Labour Department's tentative figure was 'about 7,000,000'.[3] The *Report* for 1897 gave the same estimate, declaring that it was not 'easy from the returns of the last census . . . to fix with certainty the number of persons engaged in various industrial occupations', and that 'no exact comparison can be made between the number of trade unionists and the total numbers employed in each trade'.[4] On the assumption that this group grew at the same rate as the occupied population—though its growth must have been somewhat slower, since the white-collar group was growing faster than the occupied population as a whole—then the figure for adult male manual workers in 1888 was about 6·5 millions, for 1901 about 7·25 millions, and for 1910 a little over 8 millions. If these totals are compared with those of

---

[1] The only important professional trade union was the National Union of Teachers, which was excluded from the Board of Trade's returns.

[2] 'Commercial occupations' are not excluded; unions in this category were covered by the Board's figures, and the shop assistants' unions were becoming important by the end of the period.　　　[3] C–8644, 1897, p. xvi.　　　[4] C–9013, 1898, pp. xxii–xxiii.

male trade unionists, the degree of organization seems to have been rather more than 10 per cent. in 1888, about 25 per cent. in 1901, and about 30 per cent. in 1910.[1]

Thus, excluding self-employed persons and those in the professions, probably about one 'occupied person' in sixteen was a trade unionist at the beginning of 1889, and about one in nine among adult male manual workers. In 1892 trade unionists were about one in eight of the occupied population and one in five of adult male manual workers. In 1901 the proportions were rather less than one in six and one in four, rising to rather more than one in six and almost one in three by 1910. But these are overall figures, and they conceal very different trends as between the various industrial groups. Some of these are revealed in Table 6, which sets out trade union membership and the total numbers employed for all those groups with more than a negligible degree of organization, except teachers.

Here again, precision is unattainable, and the figures of trade union 'density' are estimates. Trade union membership figures for 1888 are well supported for some groups, but for others they are little more than guesses. Moreover, none of the occupational groups is exactly co-terminous with the trade union group with which it is compared. Some reasons for this are given in footnotes to the table, and there are others, notably a tendency for many unions to disregard boundaries between industries. For instance, members of the general unions worked in textiles, in mines and quarries, in metals and engineering, in building, and in transport. Similarly, members of the transport unions worked in metals, as did some building craftsmen.

The table shows that an appreciable part of the trade union growth during this period can be explained by the rapid expansion of industries in which the unions were already strong. Mining and Quarrying, and Metals, Engineering, and Shipbuilding—the two groups with the highest trade union density in 1888—both expanded their labour force by about 60 per cent. between 1891 and 1911, compared with a growth of 22 per cent. in the occupied population as a whole. Even if each of these groups had only maintained its original density, the proportion of trade unionists in the occupied population would have risen. In fact, however, there was an increase in every group.

Mining and Quarrying led the field. Since organization among surface workers was poor, union membership among men working underground may have been 75 per cent. or more by 1910, and in many parts of the country probably reached 100 per cent. among faceworkers. The steadiest

[1] Among other factors for which allowance would have to be made to produce a more precise estimate are the inclusion of some young persons in the trade union figures and the rapid growth of organization among several white-collar groups during the period.

TABLE 6

Density of union organization, 1888–1910

Industrial Group	Sub-group	1888			1901			1910		
		Estimated trade union membership (000's)	Occupied persons 1891 Census* (000's)	Trade union density (%)	Trade union membership† (000's)	Occupied persons 1901 Census* (000's)	Trade union density (%)	Trade union membership† (000's)	Occupied persons 1911 Census* (000's)	Trade union density (%)
Metals, Engineering, and Shipbuilding		190	1,250	15	339	1,644	21	370	2,020	18
	Shipbuilding‡	35	97	36	78	128	60	75	164	46
Mining and Quarrying		150	761	19	531	944	56	731	1,214	60
Textiles§		120	1,520	8	246	1,462	17	380	1,614	24
	Cotton§	90	565	16	189	546	35	274	622	44
Building		90	956	10	250	1,336	19	157	1,213	13
	Carpenters and Joiners‖	35	276	13	84	338	25	65	269	24
Transport		60	1,195	5	180	1,498	12	245	1,698	14
Railways		20	223	9	76	322	24	116	378	31
Clothing		40	1,355	3	66	1,396	5	67	1,410	5
Printing and Paper		30	267	11	58	334	17	74	409	18
	Printing	24	114	21	47	139	34	63	176	36
Woodworking &c.		20	243	8	41	308	13	39	333	12
Other Trades		50	..	..	270	..	..	383	..	..
General Labour		..	..	..	112	..	..	119	..	..
Shop Assistants		..	..	..	19	..	..	56	..	..
National Government		..	101	..	45	146	31	86	202	43

* *Seventeenth Abstract of Labour Statistics*, Cd. 7733, 1915, pp. 296–303.

† Ibid., pp. 200–1. The figures for the trade union groups in this table do not add up to the totals of trade union membership quoted in the Appendix. See Appendix, note 2.

‡ The trade union figure for shipbuilding includes *all* boilermakers, a proportion of whom worked in the engineering industry. The density of organization in the shipyards may therefore be exaggerated, though a number of engineers and carpenters worked in the shipyards.

§ The trade union figures for textiles and for cotton in 1901 and 1910 include piecers. About 20,000 piecers were organized in 1900 and nearer 30,000 in 1910.

‖ The trade union figures for carpenters and joiners exclude labourers, who are included in the census returns. The degree of organization amongst craftsmen must therefore have been considerably higher than the figures suggest.

rate of increase was in Textiles. Cotton contributed most, though dyeing and finishing and linen and jute also made progress. By 1910 the degree of organization among adults in cotton probably exceeded 50 per cent., with the spinners close on 100 per cent. Clothing, on the other hand, was the one group which showed a drop in density between 1892 and 1901, largely because of the decline of the Boot and Shoe Operatives after 1895.

By 1910 big advances in Transport had been made by the railwaymen, who must be included among the well-organized industries after 1901. Outside the railways, however, the organization of transport workers was still thin. Among other industries the growing strength of Post Office trade unionism had brought employees in national government high on the list, well ahead of Printing and only just below Shipbuilding. If Shop Assistants were still far behind but pulling up rapidly, General Labour had stagnated after its impressive start twenty years before.

Compared with coal, cotton, and the railways, or even with government employees and shop assistants, the record of the craft trades was poor. Printing continued to advance slowly; but Shipbuilding, which led the field in 1888 and 1901, had fallen back sharply by 1910. The other craft trades all showed a drop in density after 1901. In Metals and Engineering the unions secured only a slight increase in membership in a fast-growing industry; in Furniture, where industrial growth was slow, the unions lost members. The slump in Building brought a decline in membership far exceeding the decline in the labour force. While the carpenters' unions grew most rapidly up to 1901 and subsequently held their gains fairly well, the others advanced only fractionally over the whole period.

The growth of white-collar unionism outstripped the rate of increase among manual workers, especially after 1901.[1] It was helped by the exceptionally rapid expansion of white-collar occupations,[2] and was impressive largely because organization, except in teaching, had been virtually non-existent at the beginning of the period. In 1910 the Teachers had a membership of 69,000, giving a density of 23 per cent. in the profession as a whole compared with 6 per cent. in 1888, and well over 50 per cent. among certificated teachers, with whom the union was primarily concerned. By this time there was also a high degree of organization in the Post Office, among co-operative shop assistants, and musicians. In private employment, something had been achieved among shop assistants but almost nothing among clerks.

There are no reliable figures for female trade union membership before 1896. In that year the total, excluding teachers, was 142,000, with 86,000 or 60 per cent., in cotton.[3] After 1896 the expansion of the cotton unions

---

[1] See pp. 357, 452.

[2] See p. 229.

[3] In cotton, women were almost as well organized as men. In 1910 the proportion was 39 per

was mainly responsible for totals of 152,000 (65 per cent. cotton) in 1901, and 278,000 (54 per cent. cotton) in 1910. Between 1901 and 1910, however, there was also a significant growth in female membership in linen and jute (17,000), silk (6,000), shop assistants (6,000), employees in national and local government (18,000), and general labour (7,000).[1] The figure for national and local government in 1901 is in some doubt, but for the other four groups the increase had been no less than 200 per cent.

Besides reflecting the general growth of white-collar unionism, these gains were a delayed tribute to the middle-class women who had fostered female trade unionism through the Women's Trade Union League, founded by Emma Paterson in 1874. The League promoted many local women's unions, the great majority of which foundered, and also offered help to other unions who opened their doors to women.[2] A considerable number of men's unions did alter their rules, especially during 1889–92, but with little effect. By 1901, when Lady Dilke had replaced Mrs. Paterson, women's trade unionism hardly existed outside cotton, linen, and jute. In 1903, however, an ex-shop assistant, Mary Macarthur,[3] was made secretary of the League,[4] and in 1906 she federated the tiny local bodies sponsored by the League into a general union for women, the National Federation of Women Workers. By 1910 the Federation, assisted by the Trade Boards Act, had 6,000 members.

From the foregoing figures, it is clear that the craft societies were less successful in recruiting members than those unions which attempted to organize all or most of the workers in a given establishment or industry, such as the miners' associations, the cotton amalgamations, the Railway Servants, and the Teachers. Secondly, there appear to have been special advantages in public employment, like the civil service or teaching, and in semi-public employment, such as that offered by the co-operatives. Both these trends were affected by the growth of collective bargaining. 'Industrial' unions benefited from agreements with an individual employer or an

---

cent. compared with 44 per cent. for the whole industry. In 1901 the proportions had been 29 per cent. and 35 per cent.

The figures of total female trade union membership are the final revised figures. For cotton there exist final revised figures for 1910, but not for the earlier years; but this probably has little effect on the comparisons. See Appendix, note 2.

[1] *Eighteenth Abstract of Labour Statistics*, Cmd. 2740, 1927, pp. 178–9.

[2] Drake, op. cit.; and Mary Agnes Hamilton, *Women at Work*, 1941, esp. chapters 4 and 5. In Manchester a Women's Trade Union Council was formed with the help of C. P. Scott and other sympathizers. In 1904 Christabel Pankhurst split the Council over female suffrage. By 1910 her section had 3,000 affiliated members, and the original Council 2,600. Many members of both organizations were in mixed unions (Bather, op. cit.).

[3] Macarthur, Mary (Mrs. W. C. Anderson) (1880–1921). General secretary, Women's Trade Union League, 1903–21. President, National Federation of Women Workers, 1906–8; general secretary, 1908–21. Executive Committee, Labour Party, 1919–21.

[4] She had been introduced to Lady Dilke by Margaret Bondfield, then women's officer of the Shop Assistants.

employers' association, for an agreement gave them authority to organize all or most of the employees in the firm or firms concerned. The craft societies, however, were designed for unilateral regulation on behalf of the skilled workers alone, and they found adaptation to the new situation difficult. As for public authorities, once they had recognized a union, they had to face the risk of political reprisals if they decided to retract, or even to put obstacles in the way of its organization.

Collective Bargaining and its Shortcomings

The development of collective bargaining was the outstanding feature of this period. In 1889 only cotton weaving had a national agreement. By 1910 national agreements had also been signed by the unions and the employers' federations in engineering, shipbuilding, cotton spinning, building, printing, iron and steel, and footwear. Moreover, almost every other well-organized industry, except the railways, had evolved its own system of collective bargaining, even if not yet on a fully national basis.[1] Coal was in an intermediate position. There was no national agreement, but that covering the Federated area applied to half the industry—to all the English coalfields except Northumberland and Durham—so that it cannot be classified merely as a 'local' or 'regional' agreement.

This transformation of industrial relations was the consequence not only of trade union growth but also of a rapid increase in organization among employers. In the craft industries, indeed, they had given the lead towards collective bargaining, and some of the national agreements represented a joint victory for employers and trade union leaders over the hostility of a rank and file which was still wedded to the traditions of unilateral regulation. Between 1899 and 1907 it might well have been argued that the conclusions of the Royal Commission on Labour were being proved correct.[2] Strong organization on both sides, together with provision for discussion, bargaining, and, if need be, outside conciliation or voluntary arbitration, seemed to be ushering in an era of industrial peace.

By 1910, however, the evidence was no longer so convincing. The depression year of 1908 had seen the outbreak of major disputes in cotton, shipbuilding, and engineering. In shipbuilding the clash led to a national agreement intended to avoid a repetition of conflict in the industry, but the engineering stoppage arose not from any fault in the procedure already established but from a refusal to use it, while in cotton well-tried negotiating machinery was used to the limit and failed to avert a strike. Thus it became apparent that collective bargaining was no panacea.

---

[1] This development has not been sufficiently recognized by historians of the period. For example, in his *Life and Times of Ernest Bevin*, Alan Bullock writes that in 1910 'as a consequence of [their] weakness and disunity, the status of trade unions was still only half-accepted either by employers or by the state. . . . The engineers alone were sufficiently well-organised to secure national, as distinct from limited local, agreements' (vol. i, 1960, p. 26).   [2] See p. 485.

More than anything else, the workers wanted the growing power of their unions to secure a steady wage for them, and an end to the cuts of the bad years. Their leaders sought to give them what they wanted by negotiation with the employers, backed up by threats and, if necessary, by strikes. But few employers could control the prices at which they sold, and therefore could not guarantee to maintain wages in a depression. Thus the cotton operatives, the shipbuilders, and the engineers stopped work rather than accept wage reductions, and the miners avoided a stoppage only by mortgaging the future. Afterwards the two sides of the shipbuilding industry tried to anticipate further trouble by completing their bargaining structure. In cotton, having done this already, they turned their attention to automatic formulas for wage fluctuations. In mining they hoped for the best.

Outside intervention had proved no remedy. Following the lead of Lloyd George at the Board of Trade, Churchill and Askwith put their energies into keeping the peace, but government intervention could neither prevent the stoppages nor bring them to a speedy conclusion once they had begun. The General Federation of Trade Unions was equally powerless, although the important unions in cotton, shipbuilding, and engineering were all affiliated. The Federation intervened in a major dispute for the first and only time when it burned its fingers in the cotton stoppage and withdrew[1], never again to take part in industrial negotiations of any importance.

Nor were stoppages over wage reductions the only failure of collective bargaining. It was also unable to resolve disputes over craft privileges. Admittedly the new machinery contained them better in the first ten years of the new century than in the last decade of the old. In building, largely due to its own cyclical depression, the contrast with the previous period was remarkable; but in engineering and shipbuilding, and above all in printing, differences over craft rules caused frequent trouble, and there was no guarantee that they would not lead again to large-scale strikes. Elsewhere, there were similar intractable problems. Collective bargaining had not ended the battle over non-unionism in coal and cotton; 'bad material' had come close to wrecking cotton's negotiating machinery; and 'abnormal places' were causing increasing difficulties in South Wales.

One consequence was a growing distrust of collective bargaining among the rank and file. For the union leaders, as joint authors of the new procedures, collective bargaining had come to stay. Despite its shortcomings, they saw in it the guarantee of union stability, one source of their own power, and the best means available for winning benefits for their

---

[1] See pp. 357, 460. Between Dec. 1907 and Dec. 1908 the reserve funds of the Federation fell from £162,210 to £74,729. £65,000 was spent on the cotton dispute and £34,000 on the North-east coast. By 1910 the reserves were back to £100,000.

members. The rank and file, anxious to protect their privileges and customs from encroachment by the employers, and responsive to the growing agitation for a 'living' minimum wage, did not see collective bargaining in the same light. It might have done much for their leaders, but what was it doing for them? By 1910 a rift between leaders and local militants was beginning to widen in a number of unions.

The situation was complicated by the peculiar behaviour of the economy during the ten years after 1900. The income of the British worker had suddenly ceased to grow. In 1910 the index of wage rates stood at about the same figure as in 1900, whereas prices had increased by almost 10 per cent. Wages had fallen in the depression of 1902–4 which followed the South African War, but prices had slowly risen. When prosperity returned between 1905 and 1907 wages rose as well as prices, but before the workers could make good their earlier losses the sharp depression of 1908–9 brought wages down again while prices continued to move upwards.[1]

These wage movements presented a marked contrast to the experience of the previous decade. There were no official wage indexes at this time and the estimates of different authors vary, but every index shows a considerable increase in real wages from 1889 to 1900 compared with a decline between 1900 and 1910.[1] The rise in money wages from 1889 to 1900 was about 15 per cent. Up to the outbreak of the South African War the trend in prices was downwards; a sharp increase then brought them back almost to the level of 1889. Thus there must have been a rise of well over 10 per cent. in real wages between 1889 and 1900, compared with a fall of nearly 10 per cent. between 1900 and 1910. Even if there were no statistics to guide them, the workers had become aware of this change in their fortunes by 1908–10.

The years 1900–10 are probably the only considerable period since the Napoleonic Wars in which real wages have not actually risen, and so unusual a deviation requires some explanation. One which no longer receives much support among economic historians is that the division of the national income became more unequal, for even though the proportion received by wage earners fell slightly between 1900 and 1910 the reason seems to be the continued rise in the numbers of those receiving 'intermediate incomes'.[2] Thus a fall in the share of the national income going to wages was matched by a decline in the proportion of wage-earners to the occupied population.

The check to real wages must therefore have been part of a general slackening in the growth of the national income, and recent estimates all show a marked decline in the rate of increase, from about 30 per cent.

[1] See Appendix.
[2] Between 1880 and 1913 this class more than doubled, whereas the increase in the occupied population as a whole was only about 40 per cent.

between 1889 and 1900 to about 10 per cent. from 1900 to 1910,[1] or only fractionally more than was necessary to keep pace with the rising population. With real wages falling, it would still appear that the experience of wage-earners was less favourable than that of other classes. Nevertheless, though many craftsmen feared the competition of the semi-skilled machine operator, the total number of high-paid jobs was growing faster than the number of low-paid. The relative decline of the agricultural labour force is only one example of the process. Thus a worker who stayed in the same job was probably worse off in 1910 than in 1900; but taking transfers into account, wage-earners were almost as well off at the end of the decade as at the beginning.[2]

This failure of the national income to do more than keep pace with population is associated with a decline in the rate of increase in production, and therefore, since the occupied population increased, a decline in the rate of increase in productivity, or output per worker. According to Hoffmann,[3] industrial output per employed person actually declined between 1901 and 1911, but although his is the only index available it has frequently been criticized. While experience varied considerably from industry to industry,[4] it is at least clear that overall output and productivity rose little, if at all, despite widespread complaints from the unions about mechanization and 'speeding-up'.

Some economic historians have sought an explanation for 'the climacteric of the nineties'[5] in wars, in increased lending abroad, in declining home investment, in the exhaustion of the innovations of the industrial revolution, and in union restrictions; others have argued that the turning-point can be found in the seventies, for whatever allowances are made for error in Hoffmann's index it shows that the rate of increase in productivity was falling continuously over the last quarter of the century.[6] If this is accepted, however, there still remains a puzzle. Falling productivity affected wages only after the turn of the century.

The solution lies in the changing terms of trade. Whichever index is used, it is clear that the terms of trade had been moving in Britain's favour over the last quarter of the nineteenth century, and thereafter ran against her

[1] A. R. Prest's series ('The National Income of the United Kingdom, 1870–1946', *Economic Journal*, Mar. 1948) gives increases of 29 per cent. from 1889 to 1900, and 11 per cent. from 1900 to 1910. C. H. Feinstein's revised index ('Income and Investment in the United Kingdom, 1856–1914', ibid., June 1961) makes them 30 per cent. and 13 per cent.

[2] Bowley, *Change in the Distribution of the National Income, 1880–1913*, pp. 13–14, 19–20.

[3] W. G. Hoffmann, *British Industry, 1700–1950*, translated by W. O. Henderson and W. H. Chaloner, 1955, p. 38, table 6.

[4] E. H. Phelps Brown and S. J. Handfield-Jones, 'The Climacteric of the 1890's: A Study in the Expanding Economy', *Oxford Economic Papers*, Oct. 1952.

[5] Ibid. See also A. C. Pigou, 'Prices and Wages from 1896–1914', *Economic Journal*, June 1923.

[6] D. J. Coppock, 'The Climacteric of the 1890's: A Critical Note', *Manchester School*, Jan. 1956.

for some twenty years. Up to 1900 this advantage masked falling productivity; thereafter it accentuated its effects. What remains in doubt is whether this reversal in the terms of trade is alone sufficient to account for the stagnation in national income, and if not, what other factors were at work. Until these questions are answered the course of real wages from 1889 to 1910 cannot be fully explained. In the meantime it is clear that the decline in the rate of growth of output and productivity continued after 1900. This might have been due to a slackening in the rate of growth in investment per worker, but estimates of the growth of capital suggest that there was no falling-off at during this period.

An explanation popular at the time was that productivity declined because of the restrictive practices of the trade unions. Edwin Pratt, correspondent of *The Times*, produced an alarmist account[1] of the evil effects of British trade unions on production, and his complaints were widely echoed.[2] Most economic historians have hesitated to attribute much importance to this factor, but recently E. J. Hobsbawm has suggested that 'from the 1890s on . . . it is at least possible that certain groups of workers now began systematically to allow their output to sink unless held up by incentives, or else that the weakening of older forms of labour discipline or tradition produced the same result'.[3]

As his evidence for union limitation of output Hobsbawm gives the mining industry, the London building trades, and Lancashire cotton spinning, in which he says that output per head remained roughly stable 'from the 1890s on'.[4] From 1900 to 1910 the building industry was depressed, employment was falling, and most of the unions suffered heavy losses in membership. The employers, moreover, seem to have felt no need to continue the battle against craft restrictions which had absorbed so much of their energy over the previous ten years.[5] It is unbelievable that under these conditions productivity was stable because union restrictions were off-setting the employers' attempts to cut costs.

[1] Pratt, op. cit.

[2] Pelling, *America and the British Left*, chapter v; and Halévy, op. cit. vol. v, pp. 214–18.

[3] 'Custom, Wages, and Work-Load in Nineteenth Century Industry', in *Essays in Labour History*, edited by Briggs and Saville, p. 122.

[4] Hobsbawm, loc. cit , p. 122. He quotes as his authorities G. T. Jones, *Increasing Return*, 1933, and Jewkes and Gray, op. cit. The latter argue (pp. 42 ff.) that costs of production in cotton spinning began to rise in the fourth quarter of the nineteenth century; and that the chief causes were that 'the trade unions in the mule spinning industry were extremely powerful', and that the industry was in a quasi-monopoly position.

Their cost tables would give the opposite result, however, if they began in the boom year of 1876 instead of the depression year 1886 (Roland Smith, op. cit.). In addition their cost figures include only labour costs, and these may have been balanced by increases in productivity which continued to the turn of the century. They admit that it does not 'appear that the trend of profits was downwards'. Finally, the rising wages of spinners may have been due to their strong union, but cardroom wages were rising faster, even during the eighties and nineties when their union was far weaker than the spinners' amalgamation.

[5] See pp. 157, 352.

Equally, the evidence seems to be that craft restrictions caused less trouble in shipbuilding and in engineering (where piece-work was extending rapidly) than in the nineties. Were the charge made against the printing unions it could be more easily sustained, but neither their members nor their employers seem to have suffered much as a result. There were good reasons, however, for a decline in the rate of progress in coal and cotton. By 1890 the British coalfields were already faced with the problems of narrowing seams and deepening mines, and thereafter productivity 'fell steadily downward'.[1] In cotton the mule spindle and the Lancashire loom had been developed almost to the peak of their achievement, and future increases in productivity were to come from ring-spinning and the automatic loom. There is accordingly no need to turn to trade union restrictions as a causal factor, and no evidence that they will serve as an explanation. The workers were not the authors of their own difficulties but the victims of economic circumstances outside their control.

Trade Union Government

Collective bargaining was largely responsible for the main development in trade union government during the period: the trend towards fully representative executives. Hitherto the craft societies, on grounds of economy, had managed with a 'local' executive drawn from the town in which the union's headquarters were situated. The powers of this body were usually limited in two ways. In the first place, it had to work with a general secretary elected by the union as a whole, and within rules laid down either by a meeting of delegates elected by the whole membership or by a ballot of the membership. Secondly, there was very little for it to do. The main function of headquarters was to administer funds according to the rules, and the most that was demanded from the executive was a decision in doubtful cases concerning the payment of contributions and benefits. It was not intended to be a policy-making body in the modern sense. The basic craft principles were unchanging and known throughout the trade, and it was left to the localities to enforce them.

The governing bodies of the cotton amalgamations and the Miners' Federation, on the other hand, consisted almost entirely of the full-time officers of the local associations or county unions, which had possessed representative executives from the start.[2] Consequently, whereas the executives of the craft societies were ill-adapted for the task of general negotiations with employers' associations because of their limited knowledge and responsibility, the machinery of union government in cotton and coal proved well suited to deal with the issues which arose as the area of collective bargaining expanded. Among other unions, the Railway Servants

---

[1] Arthur J. Taylor, 'Labour Productivity and Technological Innovation in the British Coal Industry, 1850–1914', *Economic History Review*, Aug. 1961.　　　　　[2] See p. 39.

had adopted a representative executive at an early stage, but others abandoned their local executives in order to meet the new problems now arising in their dealings with employers, as did the Boot and Shoe Operatives in 1888, the Steel Smelters in 1891,[1] and the Locomotive Engineers and Firemen in 1893.

In the craft societies it was above all the impact of technical change upon collective bargaining that revealed the weakness of the old structure and led to pressure for reform. The Engineers, for example, would permit a local executive to interpret the rules on superannuation benefit, but not to decide the union's policy on 'the machine question'. Their executive was made fully representative in 1892; the Boilermakers followed suit in 1895; and the Typographical Association in 1903. Many smaller societies also made the change, including the Electricians in 1907 and the Manchester Order of Bricklayers in 1908.[2] Some craft societies still retained the old methods, among them the Ironfounders and most of the building unions.[3] Even here there was some change, however. In 1898 the Carpenters and Joiners were sufficiently moved by the new spirit to extend the right to vote in executive elections to all branches within fifty instead of twenty miles of Manchester; and in 1904 they also extended the right to nominate candidates to the fifty-mile limit.

Some credit for the change must be accorded to the 'new unionists' and the socialists, particularly among the Engineers. They were in favour of democratic principles in union government, and they also appreciated that the larger the number of elective positions, the greater the opportunity for socialist infiltration.[4] This was particularly evident in the change to representative delegations to the Trades Union Congress.[5] But this connexion between socialism and pressure for democratic reform must not be exaggerated. Some of the 'new unions' themselves were slow to adopt representative institutions. The Gasworkers were content with a 'London weekly executive' until 1908, when they changed to an executive of two representatives from each district, one of whom was to be the full-time district secretary. The executive of the National Amalgamated Union of Labour became nationally representative only in 1923.

[1] In Hodge's union the alteration was made because of the danger that his members on the North-east coast would secede rather than let an executive of Glasgow members negotiate for them.

[2] The new executives of the Engineers and the Boilermakers were full-time; elsewhere they were composed of members still working at the trade.

[3] The Tailors' executive was already fully representative, but elected by the delegate conference.

[4] In 1898 the Leeds plumbers, prevented by the executive of the United Operative Plumbers from striking on a wage issue, were urged by the Leeds Independent Labour Party *Forward* to press for a more democratic constitution, with a representative executive 'so that all the country will not have to be bossed by any particular town' (July 1898).

[5] See pp. 295–7. Some craft societies, such as the Carpenters and Joiners and the Ironfounders, reformed their Trades Union Congress delegations but kept their local executives.

Useful as these changes were in improving communications between leaders and the rank and file, they do not seem generally to have diminished the authority of the full-time officers, and the latter did not obstruct reform. A pliable executive was not of much value to a secretary if it could not help him to persuade the members to follow its decisions, and Robert Knight seems to have been responsible for the new full-time representative executive of the Boilermakers.[1] The executive of the Engineers, on the other hand, could sometimes prove a thorn in the flesh of their secretary. Whether this made the union government more or less responsive to the members is hard to say; it certainly made government more difficult.

The number of full-time officers in the major craft societies in this period increased faster than the membership. Traditionally these unions had managed with very few. In the great reform of 1892, however, the Engineers jumped from four to seventeen. In the same year the Carpenters and Joiners appointed eight organizers and an assistant secretary, thus jumping from one to ten. The new executive of the Boilermakers in 1895 almost doubled the corps of full-time officers. There were wide variations in the ratio of members to officers in other unions. The miners relied heavily on the checkweighmen to look after branch organization, and had relatively few full-time 'agents'. In cotton, however, every local association appointed a full-time secretary if it could, and often a full-time 'collector' as well, so that the ratio of officers to members was high.

Some of the 'new unions', also, required heavy staffing. The Seamen needed a full-time officer in each major port, since 'lay' officers were normally at sea. Both of the dockers' unions needed a large number because of the difficulties of organizing casual workers. In 1910 Tillett's union had thirty-seven full-time officers for 15,000 members, while the Gasworkers had only fifteen for 32,000 members.[2] Any attempt to estimate totals would produce highly suspect figures, but it seems probable, with the coming of the 'new unions' and the changes in the craft societies, that the number of officials grew faster than total union membership.

The growth of collective bargaining may also help to explain the proliferation of trade union federations during this period. The Labour Department's *Report on Trade Unions in 1908–1910*[3] lists five pages of them. Most were local, but there were thirteen, besides the General Federation of Trade Unions, with more than 50,000 members. These were the Miners' Federation (597,000), the Durham Mining Federation (124,000), the

---

[1] Before the reform, an informal group of full-time district 'delegates' had assisted him to govern the union (see p. 13). Now the position was regularized, without inconvenience to Knight.

[2] Nevertheless, the Sheffield district secretary of the National Amalgamated Union of Labour complained to his executive of the difficulty of competing with the Gasworkers. 'Where we have one official, they had three or four, with as many clerks' (National Amalgamated Union of Labour, *Executive Council Minutes*, 7 Mar. 1906).   [3] Cd. 6109, 1912, pp. 116–20.

British Metal Trades Federation (204,000), the Federation of Engineering and Shipbuilding Trades (372,000), two of the three cotton amalgamations,[1] the Northern Counties Textile Trades Federation (128,000), the United Textile Factory Workers' Association (144,000), the Printing and Kindred Trades Federation (68,000), the Association of Woodworking Trade Unions (80,000), the National Federation of Shop Workers and Clerks (58,000), the General Labourers' National Council (89,000), and the National Joint Committee of Postal and Telegraph Associations (66,000).

The most important of these were federations properly so-called in that they had powers co-ordinate with those of their constituents, having taken over the task of dealing with the employers on a national scale. These were the Miners' Federation and the cotton amalgamations. The Printing and Kindred Trades Federation made gestures in this direction. Both the Durham Mining Federation and the Northern Counties Textile Trades Federation brought together a major union and its satellites to deal with the employers. The United Textile Factory Workers' Association dealt with politics, and the Federation of Engineering and Shipbuilding Trades and the General Labourers' Council were mainly concerned with inter-union disputes. Most of the remainder were organizations of negligible importance.

Comparative Wages and Earnings

The Board of Trade conducted wage censuses in 1886 and 1906. The first suffered from a number of shortcomings and is in many respects not comparable with the second, which was far more elaborate, though it excluded coal-mining.[2] The evidence assembled was analysed by Bowley,[3] and, with the addition of his estimates for mining, comparisons between 1886 and 1906 can be made for a few major industrial groups, as in Table 7.

Since wages in most industries rose by a few points between 1886 and 1888, and either rose or remained stable from 1906 to 1910,[4] these figures give a very rough guide to the movements of money earnings over the period 1889 to 1910. But they somewhat exaggerate the upward movement in all industries except mining, where average earnings rose by about 7 per

---

[1] The Labour Department always classified the spinners' amalgamation as a single union, and the cardroom and weavers' amalgamations as federated. There is no apparent reason for this distinction.

[2] *Enquiry into Earnings and Hours*: I. *Textile Trades in 1906*, Cd. 4545, 1909. II. *Clothing Trades in 1906*, Cd. 4844, 1909. III. *Building and Woodworking Trades in 1906*, Cd. 5086, 1910. IV. *Public Utility Services in 1906*, Cd. 5196, 1910. V. *Agriculture in 1907*, Cd. 5460, 1910. VI. *Metals, Engineering and Shipbuilding Trades in 1906*, Cd. 5814, 1911. VII. *Railway Service in 1907*, Cd. 6053, 1912. VIII. *Paper, Printing etc. Trades; Pottery, Brick, Glass and Chemical Trades; Food, Drink, and Tobacco Trades; and Miscellaneous Trades in 1906*, Cd. 6556, 1913.

[3] A. L. Bowley, *Wages and Incomes in the United Kingdom since 1860*, 1937, p. 50, table X.

[4] Ibid., p. 8, table II.

cent. between 1906 and 1910. In 1906 the average earnings for adult males were between 28s. 6d. and 29s. 6d.[1] In round terms, therefore, 30s. would then be regarded as a 'good average' adult male urban worker's wage—the equivalent of average earnings of £3. 10s. in 1930, £4. 10s. in 1940, £7. 10s. in 1950, or £15 in 1960.

TABLE 7

Earnings, 1886 and 1906*

Industry	Average earnings in a full week for males (men and boys) in shillings		Percentage Increase 1886–1906
	1886	*1906*	
Coal-mining	21·2	31·5	49
Wood-working	21·4	27·1	27
Metals, Engineering, and Shipbuilding	23·0	28·1	22
Textiles	19·4	22·9	18
Railways	22·0	25·3	15
Gas & Water	26·5	26·4	—
All groups for which comparison can be made	21·2	26·7	26
Agriculture	16·3	18·3	12

* For women the only available comparison is that female earnings in textiles rose from 11·2s. to 13·4s., an increase of 20 per cent.

Miners were excluded from the 1906 census, but if the relationship between the earnings of men and of boys remained roughly the same between 1886 and 1906 the average earnings of adult miners must have been about 33s. by 1906. Since surface workers have always earned considerably less than men working underground, and faceworkers have always earned more than other underground workers, the average for underground workers was probably over 35s. and the average for faceworkers as much as 40s.

The average for adult males was 32s. 5d. in engineering, 33s. in building and in furniture, and 35s. 11d. in the shipyards.[2] General labourers in engineering averaged only 21s. whereas builders' labourers varied, according to the craft trade with which they were associated, between 23s. 9d. and 26s. 4d. Building craftsmen ranged from 34s. 7d. to 38s. 4d. according to

[1] Bowley, op. cit., p. 49.

[2] These and subsequent figures are the averages for a full week, excluding overtime and short time. For most occupations the actual earnings did not differ greatly from full-time earnings, except for considerable overtime on the railways. For all male workers (men and boys) full-time earnings were 26s. 8d. in 1906 and actual earnings were 27s. (ibid., p. 51, table XI).

trade, and in engineering both fitters and turners took home just over 36*s*. In shipbuilding, however, the platers, riveters, and caulkers on piece-work—the 'large majority' in these trades—formed a labour aristocracy. Caulkers averaged 54*s*. 8*d*., riveters 55*s*. 7*d*., and platers 71*s*. 3*d*., rising to 82*s*. on the Tyne, Wear, and Tees. Nevertheless, one-fifth of the men in the shipyards received less than 25*s*.

The iron and steel industry provided further examples of high earnings. The average for men in tinplate was 42*s*., and for the rest of the industry, excluding pig-iron production, 39*s*. 1*d*. Piece-workers on the open-hearth process averaged 72*s*. 2*d*., 88*s*. 0*d*. in Scotland. Tinplate rollers averaged 62*s*. 10*d*.

Printing was another well-paid trade. Adult males averaged 36*s*. 10*d*. On the daily newspapers hand compositors averaged 62*s*. 7*d*. on piece-work and 50*s*. 4*d*. on time work, and machine compositors 69*s*. 7*d*. on piece-work; but these were the aristocrats. In the rest of the trade, hand compositors averaged 33*s*. 7*d*. on time work and 37*s*. 8*d*. on piece-work, although even here machine compositors on piece-work averaged 54*s*. 9*d*. Bookbinding craftsmen averaged between 33*s*. 0*d*. and 47*s*. 7*d*., according to their trade.

In the clothing industries men averaged 30*s*. 2*d*. The figure for bespoke tailoring was 33*s*. 6*d*., the cutters reaching 55*s*. 1*d*., and no less than 50*s*. 11*d*. in the dress and millinery workshops, where the fitters and cutters averaged 74*s*. 7*d*. The ready-made boot and shoe trade averaged 28*s*. 8*d*. The highest paid groups were piece-working finishers at Leicester, at 36*s*. 2*d*. In textiles men averaged 28*s*. 1*d*. For jute the figure was 21*s*. 7*d*.; for linen 22*s*. 4*d*.; for wool 26*s*. 10*d*.; for cotton 29*s*. 6*d*.; for hosiery 31*s*. 5*d*.; and for lace 39*s*. 6*d*. Cotton spinners averaged 41*s*. 2*d*., 45*s*. 9*d*. in Bolton, and 41*s*. 10*d*. in Oldham; adult 'big' piecers on time work 18*s*. 4*d*., and 'little' piecers 11*s*. 11*d*. In cotton weaving men averaged 25*s*. 3*d*., 27*s*. 7*d*. in Burnley.[1]

Gas supply (32*s*. 6*d*.), electricity supply (31*s*. 7*d*.), and trams and buses (30*s*. 6*d*.) were all reasonably well paid, but water supply (28*s*. 8*d*.) fell behind. In the county and rural district areas corporation workmen ('road, sanitary, &c.') averaged only 17*s*. 11*d*., but they earned 26*s*. 3*d*. in the boroughs and urban districts.

The railways were bad payers. The average for men was 24*s*. 4*d*. for a full week, though the inclusion of overtime and short-time working brought the average up to 26*s*. 8*d*. Only drivers (45*s*. 11*d*.), foremen (35*s*. 9*d*.), goods guards (31*s*. 2*d*.), and mechanics (31*s*. 8*d*.) came above 30*s*. Signalmen averaged 27*s*. 6*d*., porters 19*s*. 9*d*., and permanent-way labourers 21*s*. 8*d*. The lowest-paying occupation was agriculture. Inclusive

[1] High earnings for weavers in Burnley reflect the spread of the 'six-loom' system there. See p. 118.

of allowances in kind, earnings were 18s. 4d. in England, 18s. 0d. in Wales and Monmouthshire, 19s. 7d. in Scotland, and 11s. 3d. in Ireland. Food, drink, and tobacco averaged 26s. 4d., with 22s. 9d. in grain milling and 22s. 11d. in distilling. The pottery, brick, glass, and chemicals trades averaged 29s. 2d.

The overall average for women was between 13s. and 14s. In the clothing trades they averaged 13s. 6d. and in textiles 15s. 5d., but in the paper and printing trades only 12s. 2d. Though there were a few other occupations in which they could earn a good deal more than the average, such as fitting and cutting in dress and millinery workshops with as much as 33s. 5d., by far the best among the major occupations for women was cotton with an overall average of 18s. 8d., and 20s. 7d. in weaving (24s. 11d. in Burnley). In wool women averaged 13s. 10d., in jute 13s. 5d., and in linen only 10s. 9d.

To summarize: if a 'good average' wage-packet for a man was 30s. in 1910, craftsmen in most trades would expect something like 35s., though in the shipyards and on the daily newspapers they might earn as much as £3 or more. Workers in iron and steel and at the coalface—who did not serve an apprenticeship—averaged £2 a week and might earn much more. In the textile trades men earned less than 30s., with cotton spinners as the major exception. On the railways, earnings were below even textiles, though engine-drivers received almost twice the average. In most occupations labourers earned between 20s. and 25s., except on the land, where the average was about 18s. Women averaged between 13s. and 14s., but could expect nearly 40 per cent. more in cotton.

It is not difficult to establish an association between the development of collective bargaining and changes in the distribution of union membership, or in methods of union government; but the economic results of collective bargaining are not so evident, and these figures do little to elucidate them.

There is a clear association between high earnings and high trade union density. Coal-mining, shipbuilding, printing, cotton spinning, and tinplate manufacture all provide evidence of this, while among women workers cotton weaving was both the highest-paid and the best-organized occupation. But there are a few notable exceptions. Railwaymen were relatively ill paid and relatively well organized, though the higher paid grades— drivers, guards, and signalmen—also had the higher union density; boot and shoe operatives were probably above average for organization and below average for earnings. The association may, however, prove either that trade unionism provides high earnings or that high earnings encourage trade unionism, and this period offers little evidence to settle the question.

It is equally difficult to interpret the relationship between wage changes and union growth. Earnings rose far more rapidly in mining than in any other group, and the miners' unions had the fastest rate of growth. But which was cause and which was effect? Since the big increases in earnings and in organization came in three successive boom periods—1889–92, 1898–1900, and 1905–7—it would seem likely that the economic conditions created the opportunity for the wage increases, which in turn gave trade union organization its chance.[1] Among the rest, earnings rose faster than average in woodworking, though trade union membership increased far less than in some other industries. Textiles and railways improved their earnings less than most industries but their trade union membership more. Engineering and shipbuilding performed relatively ill on both counts. Finally, the public utilities improved not at all. Their workers were still relatively highly paid in 1906, and had had an even greater relative advantage in 1886. Among them the gasworkers were the best paid, and the largest grade, the gas-stokers, earned 41s. 11d. in London in 1906.

Public Standing

The main obstacle to presenting a clear estimate of the public standing of trade unions is the wide range of opinions which have been voiced at every period of their history. Thus some historians regard trade unions as having achieved acceptance in the legislative concessions of the seventies; others after the upsurge of 1889; others during the First World War; and still others would postpone the date until the Second World War. In each period there is plenty of evidence in the speeches of statesmen, the editorials of newspapers, and the actions of employers, that trade unions were welcome. In each period, at least until 1940, there is also evidence that trade unionism had many convinced opponents in public life and in industry.

One example will serve. In 1891 the engineering employers on Tyneside were seeking to persuade local branches of the Engineers to establish a procedure for conciliation.[2] In 1897, however, 'the real plans of the "autocrats of Elswick", the "Pseudo-Napoleons of Newcastle", to use the London employers as a catspaw with which to destroy the trade union movement were exposed. . . . Mr. Siemens . . . told the press that the object of the lockout was "to get rid of trade unionism altogether" '.[3] Yet in 1904 a prominent engineering and shipbuilding employer from Tyneside, Sir Benjamin Browne, could assert that

what we want is to negotiate with the workmen as much as possible on absolutely equal terms. . . . I am all for Unions, but my impression is that if Unions and

---

[1] Part of the growth in coal-mining unionism was due simply to the expansion of the industry's labour force (see p. 467). This in turn may have owed something to the rapid increase in miners' earnings. The increase of 125 per cent. in coal-mining employment between 1883 and 1913 'could not have taken place' but for 'a growth in wage-rates and earnings exceeding that in the national economy as a whole . . .' (Taylor, loc. cit.). But we are here concerned primarily with the relationship between rising earnings and rising union density.

[2] See p. 127, footnote 2.   [3] Jefferys, op. cit., p. 145.

employers were encouraged a little more, they would be able to do their work, so that stoppages would be the rarest thing in the world. . . . I have always advised employers myself that we get on far better when we go through the Unions than when we act independently of the Unions.[1]

Clearly any generalization based upon any one of these pieces of evidence would be misleading.

Trade unions were already accepted in 1889. The Liberal Party claimed to welcome, and the Conservative Party at least tolerated, trade unionists as Members of Parliament. Trade union deputations were received by ministers, and trade unionists could become ministers. Trade unions were recognized as important bodies by the press, and they could often obtain favourable publicity if they took care to do so. In nearly all the craft trades, in cotton, in iron and steel, and in some coalfields, many individual employers, and such employers' associations as there were, met the unions and did business with them. All this was still true at the end of the period, but there had been five important developments.

After a series of legal decisions, two Royal Commissions, and much parliamentary debate, the privileges of trade unions had been extended by statute and made far more precise. Only their power to finance political activities remained contested, and even here they had already been promised legislation which would remove most of the obstacles raised by the courts.

Secondly, the unions had ended their direct and almost exclusive dependence upon the Liberals by helping to form the Labour Party. By attracting both Liberals and Conservatives among working-class electors the Labour Party had sharply increased the number of trade union Members of Parliament and also of trade union representatives on local authorities. But the new party continued to draw protection from an electoral understanding with the Liberal leadership, and in most respects its parliamentary attitude remained that of a Lib-Lab pressure group. Since the Liberal ministries of 1905 to 1910 were ready to make considerable concessions to working-class demands, it was not yet possible to assess the effect of the party's emergence upon trade union standing with governments generally.

Thirdly, trade unions were now recognized by employers over a far wider range of industry than in 1889—in coal-mining, for example, and in public employment. They had even achieved some status, if not recognition, on the railways.

Fourthly, the quality of acceptance in industry had changed with developments in their functions. The status of unions rested increasingly on written agreements, rather than on custom and practice. Their central

[1] *Royal Commission on Trade Disputes and Trade Combinations*, Cd. 2826, 1906, Qs. 2782, 2828, 2927.

function was less to serve as a means by which workers could regulate their own affairs as they wished, and more to negotiate with employers in laying down the terms and conditions under which work should be performed.

This being so, the grounds for a defence of trade unionism had shifted. Previously the unions had been defended primarily on their right to freedom of association. If men wanted to combine they should be free to do so. Now it was increasingly argued that they were making a positive contribution to social welfare by joining with the employers in regulating industry so that order should prevail.

This change had been recognized by the Royal Commission on Labour and by the Conciliation Act of 1896. In their *Final Report* the Commissioners noted that

in some of the principal industries a steady extension has for many years past taken place in the scale and importance of trade unions and employers' associations. . . . When organisations on either side are so strong as fairly to balance each other, the result of the situation is a disposition, already realised in certain cases, to form a mixed board, meeting regularly to discuss and settle questions affecting their relations. . . . The most successful of these institutions are those which have been formed in the trades where organisations on either side are strongest and most complete. . . . We hope and believe that the present rapid extension of voluntary boards will continue.

The state, they concluded, should assist only by extending the information, statistical, and advisory services of the Labour Department, and by giving power 'to appoint, upon the receipt of a sufficient application from the parties interested . . . a suitable person to act as arbitrator', whose decision 'would not possess legally binding effect'.[1]

The Act of 1896 was designed to carry out these last two recommendations, but recognition of the virtues of collective bargaining led to the fifth and final change. In an age when *laissez-faire* was giving way to government intervention, the Royal Commission's philosophy proved in the last resort untenable. If collective bargaining was capable of bringing so many advantages, it was unreasonable to expect governments to stand aside. After 1906 Lloyd George and Winston Churchill, as Presidents of the Board of Trade, and their officials in the Labour Department, intervened in industrial relations to a degree far beyond the expectations of the majority of the Royal Commission or of the legislators of 1896.[2]

Thus, despite the difficulty of making a dependable estimate of their position in the public esteem, it is beyond doubt that by 1910 the unions had become more closely integrated into the fabric of society. The

[1] *Royal Commission on Labour*, C–7421, 1894, pp. 36, 97, 100, 101.
[2] 'By the force of his personality, Mr. Lloyd George has made his office . . . transcend the statutory duties imposed upon it' (*The Economist*, 29 Feb. 1908, quoted in Halévy, op. cit., vol. vi, p. 115).

proliferation of joint committees, conciliation boards, arbitration agreements, and procedures for avoiding disputes had brought their leaders
into more frequent and formal relationships with the employers than ever
before. And the state was taking an increasing interest in their affairs.

The 'Working-class Movement'

The years covered by this volume have been seen by many historians as
a period in which working-class organization grew from a narrow sec-
tionalism into a 'movement'. The Webbs, for instance, wrote that the
increase in trade union membership after 1889 'was of less importance than
what may, without exaggeration, be termed the spiritual rebirth of organizations which were showing signs of decrepitude. The selfish spirit of
exclusiveness which often marked the relatively well-paid engineer, carpenter, or boilermaker of 1880–85, gave place to a more generous recognition of the essential solidarity of the wage-earning class.'[1]

Sometimes the phrase 'labour movement' is used merely as a convenient
form of collective reference to the various labour organizations within a
country. In this sense Britain had a labour movement in 1889 as much as
in 1910, and a labour movement can be composed of entirely selfish sectional bodies. Such a movement, however, need have no 'essential solidarity'. To provide this, the separate organizations must find common
interests and aims which they are prepared to pursue together. In this
respect the formation and growth of the Labour Party was the most
obviously impressive development of the period, for by 1910 all the major
unions had come into this single political organization. Its success can be
measured by the comparison between Broadhurst's parliamentary group
of eight in 1889 and Shackleton's bloc of nearly fifty votes in the House
of Commons in 1910, and by the series of measures demanded by the
unions which became law between 1906 and 1910.[2] But even this need
have meant no more than the inclusion of separate sectional organizations
within a single inclusive interest group, which could not aptly be described
as a 'spiritual rebirth'.

There is, however, a usage of the word 'movement' which distinguishes
it sharply from a pressure group. In this sense a movement looks outside
itself—to the good of society as well as its own betterment, and to a
national following as well as its own membership.

In 1910 the unions and the Labour Party came nearer to constituting
a movement in this sense than had the unions by themselves in 1889. With

---

[1] *History*, p. 420. For similar expressions of opinion, see Halévy, op. cit., vol. v, pp. 219–20;
and Pelling, *Short History*, pp. 1–5.

[2] Since the Labour Party was not in a position to defeat the government, except possibly over
the Trade Disputes Bill of 1906, this legislation reveals not only the strength of the Labour
Party but also a genuine broadening of Liberal social policy since Gladstone's day, combined
with the desire of the Liberals to outmanœuvre the socialists by setting themselves up as the
true 'friends of labour'.

its demands for old-age pensions, school meals, fair wages, and 'the right to work', the programme which the Trades Union Congress and the Labour Party pursued after 1906 covered the badly organized and poorer sections of the working class quite as much as the organized and better paid. At the same time it could be presented as the beginnings of a reform of society as a whole. The programme possessed the qualities of both altruism and working-class solidarity far more than anything that the unions had claimed in 1889.

Thus far the fusion of interest groups into 'movement' may be established, but the nature and causes of the change deserve more careful scrutiny than they have usually received. In the first place it should be seen as a shift in emphasis rather than a transition from one category to another. Trade unions had already possessed something of the aura of a movement before 1889, and in 1910 they were interest groups no less than at any other time.[1] By the sixties, for example, the unions provided the basis of the working-class Radical movement which fought for the extension of the franchise; the right of working men to combine; the security of their organizations; safety regulations in mines and factories; and the liability of employers to compensate injured workmen.

Broadhurst, Howell, and Burt were among the younger leaders of this movement and, narrow though their outlook might appear by 1889, they still came forward from time to time as the champions of Radical 'progress' as well as the representatives of sectional unions whose aim was to protect the status of the better-paid worker. Indeed, much of the success of the Independent Labour Party in winning over the unions was due to the willingness of Keir Hardie and his colleagues to accommodate their theories and their programmes to this working-class Radicalism whose current still ran deep and strong at the end of the century.

Part of the explanation for the growth of a movement lies in alterations in the structure of the trade unions themselves. Some of the craft societies made attempts to broaden their scope, though the results were meagre. The greatest growth was achieved by unions such as those of the miners and the cotton weavers without craft exclusiveness, even if the miners especially could be as narrowly selfish as any. The attempt of the 'new unions' to bring trade unionism to all sections of the working class had largely failed; but some of them kept the aim alive as 'general' unions, and

---

[1] The Webbs made the point admirably. 'The sense of solidarity has . . . never been lacking among those active soldiers and non-commissioned officers who constitute the most vital element in the Trade Union army. The generous aid from trade to trade, the pathetic attempts to form General Unions, the constant aspiration after universal federation, all testify to the reality and force of this instinctive solidarity. The Collectivist faith of the "New Unionism" is only another manifestation of the same deep-rooted belief in the essential Brotherhood of Labour. But . . . the basis of the association of these million and a half wage-earners is, primarily, sectional in its nature . . . and not directly for the advancement of the whole working class' (*History*, 1920 edition, p. 678, quoting the first edition of 1894).

their affiliation to the Trades Union Congress gave it also a claim to represent the whole of the working class.

These structural alterations were the first response of the unions to new functional needs arising out of their changing circumstances, which were to lead to more thoroughgoing reorganization in later years. The advance of national collective bargaining was broadening the scope of union action; new methods of production were undermining craftsmen's skills and threatening their traditional privileges; and existing political methods were showing decreasing returns. The effect of these changing circumstances was reinforced by the reactions of the employers. Their developing organizations made large-scale collective bargaining possible; their counter-attack over craft rules drove the unions to set up the General Federation of Trade Unions in self-protection; and they applauded the attitude of the courts which led to the Taff Vale judgement and strengthened union readiness to accept independent political organization.

There were thus good reasons for the existence of a more clearly delineated working-class movement by 1910. But the change must not be exaggerated. In the House of Commons, the new Labour Party was more often the agent of a sectional interest than the herald of a new social order. The unions could still appear selfish and callous. Craftsmen still fought for their exclusive privileges, and such lip-service as they might pay to the ideal of universal organization had little effect on their action in the branch or the workshop. Every union, skilled and unskilled, fought for jobs and members, and little mercy was shown to the weaker party. Each group pursued its own industrial objectives without thought for the others and many political objectives were still narrow and sectional. Considerable sections of both Conservative and Liberal opinion within the unions resented the alliance with the socialists, and sometimes fought against it.

It is therefore misleading to speak of a 'labour movement' as a constant in the history of this period. The term describes an aspect revealed by the unions and their political arm from time to time. The quality showed more clearly in 1910 than in 1889. A sympathetic leader could sometimes call it out; an astute leader could sometimes use it for his own ends; and it might sometimes assert itself unbidden. But it was often apparent only to the discerning eye, rarely visible in day-to-day union business, and only very rarely powerful enough to override the self-interest of any individual union.

Appendix

Year	Total union membership (000's)	Number of stoppages beginning in year	Total working days lost by all stoppages in progress during year (000's)	Average retail prices[6] (1850 =100)	Average money wages[6] (1850 =100)	Percentage unemployed[7]
1889	679[1]	1,211[3]	3,730[4]	91	156	2·1
1890	871[1]	1,040[3]	7,473[4]	91	163	2·1
1891	1,109[1]	906[3]	6,809[4]	92	163	3·5
1892	1,576[2]	700[3]	17,248[4]	92	162	6·3
1893	1,559	599[5]	30,439[5]	89	162	7·5
1894	1,530	903	9,506	87	162	6·9
1895	1,504	728	5,701	84	162	5·8
1896	1,608	906	3,565	83	163	3·3
1897	1,731	848	10,327	86	166	3·3
1898	1,752	695	15,257	87	167	2·8
1899	1,911	710	2,503	86	172	2·0
1900	2,022	633	3,088	89	179	2·5
1901	2,025	631	4,130	90	179	3·3
1902	2,013	432	3,438	91	176	4·0
1903	1,994	380	2,320	92	174	4·7
1904	1,967	346	1,464	93	173	6·0
1905	1,997	349	2,368	92	174	5·0
1906	2,210	479	3,019	92	176	3·6
1907	2,513	585	2,148	95	182	3·7
1908	2,485	389	10,785	97	181	7·8
1909	2,477	422	2,687	97	179	7·7
1910	2,565	521	9,867	98	179½	4·7

[1] The first report on trade unions by the Labour Department of the Board Trade appeared in 1887 (*Statistical Tables and Report on Trade Unions*, C–5104). It covered only eighteen unions. Year by year the Department's coverage extended until by 1892 it had become very nearly complete.

[2] The figures for 1892–1910 are the final revisions published in the *Ministry of Labour Gazette* for Oct. 1937. Those issued in the Department's current reports contain traps for the unwary. At frequent intervals the Department discovered unions which had not previously sent in returns, and made a practice of asking such unions to return membership figures for the previous years of their existence. These were subsequently incorporated in revised figures, both for the overall totals and for the separate 'industry groups', which were published as 'comparative statistics' going back ten years. While the final revised figures for total membership are available, the Ministry cannot now trace the final revised figures for the separate industry groups for 1892–1910. So although the industry group figures currently published do not add up to the final revised totals they cannot now be corrected. The latest published industry group figures for 1892–4 can be found in the *Tenth Abstract of Labour Statistics*, Cd. 2491, 1905; for 1895–6 in the *Report on Trade Unions in 1902–4*, Cd. 2838, 1906; for 1897–8 in the *Sixteenth Abstract of Labour Statistics*, Cd. 7131, 1913; and for 1899–1910 in the *Seventeenth Abstract of Labour Statistics*, Cd. 7733, 1915. In the 1926 *Survey of Industrial Relations* (Balfour Committee on Industry and Trade) can be found still later figures for certain selected industry groups of

1897 only. These suggest that the earlier figures considerably understate union membership in national and local government, and among seamen.

³ *Second Abstract of Labour Statistics*, C–7900, 1895. The Department's system of enumerating stoppages changed between 1889 and 1892, and the first reliable figure is that of 1893.

⁴ To calculate 'working days lost' one must know the number of workers involved in each stoppage and its duration. The Department had this information about only 597 of the stoppages of 1889 (*Annual Report on the Strikes and Lockouts of 1889*), 652 of those in 1890 (*Annual Report* for 1890), 606 in 1891, and 503 in 1892 (*Annual Report* for 1895). It is probable, however, that the others were small and brief, and that the annual totals of working days lost would not be substantially affected by their inclusion. From 1893 the coverage was virtually complete.

⁵ The figures for 1893 to 1910 are the final revisions published in the *Twenty-first Abstract of Labour Statistics*, Cmd. 4625, 1934. 'Working days lost' include those lost by workpeople who, though not directly participating in the stoppage, were thrown out of work.

⁶ Sir Walter T. Layton and Geoffrey Crowther, *An Introduction to the Study of Prices*, 1938, appendix E, table 1. There were no comprehensive official indexes at this time for retail prices and wage rates. Layton and Crowther used information gathered by A. L. Bowley and G. H. Wood. Other indexes are available, but any differences between them and the Layton and Crowther sets are not significant for our purpose.

⁷ *Fifteenth Abstract of Labour Statistics*, Cd. 6228, 1912, p. 6. This index was based on returns made to the Department by those trade unions which paid unemployment benefit. 'They do not cover directly more than a small fraction of the industrial field' (W. H. Beveridge, *Unemployment: A Problem of Industry*, 1909, 1930 edition, p. 18). 'As a measure of the *volume* of unemployment the trade union returns must be disregarded. . . . As an indication of the *movements* of the labour market they retain their value . . . ' (ibid., p. 22). Our italics.

Index

Ablett, Noah, 464.
Abraham, William ('Mabon'), biog., 19 n., 19, 105–6, 124, 125, 242, 272, 280, 283 n., 285, 311 n., 385, 461 n.
Acland, A. H. D., 224.
Accrington Trades Council, 291.
Adamson, William, 273 n., 421.
Admiralty Dockyards, 349.
  eight-hour day, 152, 221, 222.
  trade union recognition, 152.
  wages and conditions, 152, 221, 222, 239.
Agricultural Labourers' and Small Holders' Union, Eastern Counties, 388 n., 456.
Agricultural Labourers' Union, National, 35, 36, 179, 180, 276 n.
Agriculture and Fishing:
  employment, 4, 35, 180, 181, 474.
  sociology of countryside, 35–36.
  trade union membership, 1, 4, 35, 179–81, 456.
  wages, 35, 480, 481–2.
Alcock, G. W., 415, 416.
Aliens Act, 1905, 371, 396.
Allan, William, 8 n., 40, 41, 434.
Allen v. *Flood*, 308–9, 310.
Amalgamated Societies, *see* Craft Societies, and Junta.
Amalgamated Trades, Conference of, 41.
Anderson, John, 142, 162, 297.
Andrew, John, 186.
Applegarth, Robert, 10, 40, 41, 44.
Appleton, W. A., 407 n.
Apprenticeship, 4–5, 7, 8, 15, 27.
  building, 13, 14, 156–9.
  clothing, 348.
  engineering, 140, 141, 167, 429, 432.
  furniture, 160, 348.
  glass, 5, 170.
  lace, 193.
  pottery, 197, 454.
  printing, 145–6, 346, 439.
  shipbuilding, 151–2, 169, 348–9, 435.
Arbitration, 9–10, 14, 86, 155 n., 263, 265, 436 n., 485.
  compulsory, 177, 265, 318, 319, 425, 436.
Arch, Joseph, biog., 35 n., 35, 36, 179, 181, 248, 276 n., 284.
Armed forces, use of in strikes, 69, 71, 72, 80–81, 82, 107–8, 450–1.
Armstrong-Whitworth, 161, 330, 430.
Arrandale, Matthew, 286.
Ashley, W. J., 203.
Ashton, Thomas (Miners), biog., 20 n., 20, 98, 102, 246, 276.
Ashton, Thomas (Spinners), 265 n., 290, 303.
Askwith, G. R., biog., 347 n., 347, 425, 448, 451, 453, 454, 456, 461, 464, 472.

Aspinwall, Thomas, 273, 275.
Asquith, H. H., 86, 108 n., 245, 252, 264, 317–18, 320, 322, 369, 372, 393, 394, 397, 400, 401, 402, 405, 412, 417 n., 418.
Atherley-Jones, L., 272 n., 284, 369.
Aucott, William, 204.
Austin, Michael, 285, 311 n.
Austin, Robert, 142, 285, 293 n.
Aveling, Edward, 92 n., 302.
Aves, Ernest, biog., 318 n., 318–19.

Bailey v. *Pye*, 312.
Baking industry, 127–8.
Bakers' and Confectioners' Union, Amalgamated Operative, 128, 228, 443.
Bakers' Union, Scottish Operative, 127, 443.
Balfour, A. J., 278–9, 322, 325, 370, 383.
Ball, Sydney, 166.
Barge Builders, River Thames, 281, 385 n.
Barker, George, 464.
Barnes, Alfred, 101–2.
Barnes, George, biog., 162 n., 142 n., 162, 164, 167, 175, 177, 297, 316 n., 319, 343, 388, 392, 396, 400, 403, 411, 429 n., 433–4.
Barry, Maltman, 276.
Bartley, James, 65.
Bass, Michael, 32.
Battersea Labour League, 277, 277–8, 286 n.
Bax, Belfort, 302.
Beach, Michael Hicks, 244, 311, 367.
Bealey, Frank, 274.
Bean, George, 176.
Beasley, Ammon, 231, 313, 314, 315, 316.
Beaumont, Hubert, 382.
Beaumont, Wentworth, 321, 368.
Bedstead Workmen's Association, 194.
Beehive, 41.
Bell, J. N., 295.
Bell, Lowthian, 232.
Bell, Richard, biog., 235 n., 176, 213 n., 235, 236, 265 n., 276, 278, 282, 296, 313–14, 316, 319, 320, 321, 323, 339, 364, 366, 368, 369, 370 n., 371–2, 373 n., 374, 377, 377–8, 379–80, 381, 385, 387, 388, 391, 392, 392 n., 403, 406, 416, 417, 421, 423, 424, 425, 426 n.
Besant, Annie, 61, 90.
Beston, W. F., 65.
Bevan, W., 54.
Bevin, Ernest, biog., 451 n., 451–2.
Bimetallism, 245, 247, 254.
Birmingham Alliances, 84–85, 155, 194–5, 197, 198, 210, 330.
Birmingham Trades Council, 287–8, 289.
Birt, G. R., 72.
Birtwistle, Thomas, 39, 243 n., 244, 244 n., 254, 256, 292 n.